Applications of Fuzzy Optimization and Fuzzy Decision Making

Applications of Fuzzy Optimization and Fuzzy Decision Making

Editor

Vassilis C. Gerogiannis

MDPI • Basel • Beijing • Wuhan • Barcelona • Belgrade • Manchester • Tokyo • Cluj • Tianjin

Editor
Vassilis C. Gerogiannis
University of Thessaly
Greece

Editorial Office
MDPI
St. Alban-Anlage 66
4052 Basel, Switzerland

This is a reprint of articles from the Special Issue published online in the open access journal *Mathematics* (ISSN 2227-7390) (available at: https://www.mdpi.com/journal/mathematics/special_issues/Fuzzy_Opti).

For citation purposes, cite each article independently as indicated on the article page online and as indicated below:

LastName, A.A.; LastName, B.B.; LastName, C.C. Article Title. *Journal Name* **Year**, *Volume Number*, Page Range.

ISBN 978-3-0365-2265-4 (Hbk)
ISBN 978-3-0365-2266-1 (PDF)

© 2021 by the authors. Articles in this book are Open Access and distributed under the Creative Commons Attribution (CC BY) license, which allows users to download, copy and build upon published articles, as long as the author and publisher are properly credited, which ensures maximum dissemination and a wider impact of our publications.

The book as a whole is distributed by MDPI under the terms and conditions of the Creative Commons license CC BY-NC-ND.

Contents

About the Editor vii

Preface to "Applications of Fuzzy Optimization and Fuzzy Decision Making" ix

Huirong Zhang, Zhenyu Zhang, Lixin Zhou and Shuangsheng Wu
Case-Based Reasoning for Hidden Property Analysis of Judgment Debtors
Reprinted from: *Mathematics* **2021**, *9*, 1559, doi:10.3390/math9131559 1

Hsin-Chieh Wu, Horng-Ren Tsai, Tin-Chih Toly Chen and Keng-Wei Hsu
Energy-Efficient Production Planning Using a Two-Stage Fuzzy Approach
Reprinted from: *Mathematics* **2021**, *9*, 1101, doi:10.3390/math9101101 19

Nickie Lefevr, Andreas Kanavos, Vassilis C. Gerogiannis, Lazaros Iliadis and
Panagiotis Pintelas
Employing Fuzzy Logic to Analyze the Structure of Complex Biological and Epidemic
Spreading Models
Reprinted from: *Mathematics* **2021**, *9*, 977, doi:10.3390/math9090977 37

Vecihi Yiğit, Nazlı Nisa Demir, Hisham Alidrisi and Mehmet Emin Aydin
Elicitation of the Factors Affecting Electricity Distribution Efficiency Using the Fuzzy
AHP Method
Reprinted from: *Mathematics* **2021**, *9*, 82, doi:10.3390/math9010082 61

Katarzyna Poczeta, Elpiniki I. Papageorgiou and Vassilis C. Gerogiannis
Fuzzy Cognitive Maps Optimization for Decision Making and Prediction
Reprinted from: *Mathematics* **2020**, *8*, 2059, doi:10.3390/math8112059 87

Georgios Drakopoulos, Andreas Kanavos, Phivos Mylonas, and Panagiotis Pintelas
Extending Fuzzy Cognitive Maps With Tensor-Based Distance Metrics
Reprinted from: *Mathematics* **2020**, *8*, 1898, doi:10.3390/math8111898 103

Hsin-Chieh Wu, Yu-Cheng Wang and Tin-Chih Toly Chen
Assessing and Comparing COVID-19 Intervention Strategies Using a Varying Partial Consensus
Fuzzy Collaborative Intelligence Approach
Reprinted from: *Mathematics* **2020**, *8*, 1725, doi:10.3390/math8101725 129

Hyoshin Kim and Hye-Young Jung
Ridge Fuzzy Regression Modelling for Solving Multicollinearity
Reprinted from: *Mathematics* **2020**, *8*, 1572, doi:10.3390/math8091572 153

Marjana Čubranić-Dobrodolac, Libor Švadlenka, Svetlana Čičević, Aleksandar Trifunović
and Momčilo Dobrodolac
Using the Interval Type-2 Fuzzy Inference Systems to Compare the Impact of Speed and Space
Perception on the Occurrence of Road Traffic Accidents
Reprinted from: *Mathematics* **2020**, *8*, 1548, doi:10.3390/math8091548 169

María Carmen Carnero
Waste Segregation FMEA Model Integrating Intuitionistic Fuzzy Set and the PAPRIKA Method
Reprinted from: *Mathematics* **2020**, *8*, 1375, doi:10.3390/math8081375 189

Hsin-Chieh Wu, Toly Chen and Chin-Hau Huang
A Piecewise Linear FGM Approach for Efficient and Accurate FAHP Analysis: Smart Backpack Design as an Example
Reprinted from: *Mathematics* 2020, *8*, 1319, doi:10.3390/math8081319 . . . . **219**

Konstantinos Kokkinos and Vayos Karayannis
Supportiveness of Low-Carbon Energy Technology Policy Using Fuzzy Multicriteria Decision-Making Methodologies
Reprinted from: *Mathematics* 2020, *8*, 1178, doi:10.3390/math8071178 . . . . **237**

Shougi S. Abosuliman, Saleem Abdullah and Muhammad Qiyas
Three-Way Decisions Making Using Covering Based Fractional Orthotriple Fuzzy Rough Set Model
Reprinted from: *Mathematics* 2020, *8*, 1121, doi:10.3390/math8071121 . . . . **263**

Min-Chi Chiu, Tin-Chih Toly Chen and Keng-Wei Hsu
Modeling an Uncertain Productivity Learning Process Using an Interval Fuzzy Methodology
Reprinted from: *Mathematics* 2020, *8*, 998, doi:10.3390/math8060998 . . . . **295**

C. J. Luis Pérez
Using a Fuzzy Inference System to Obtain Technological Tables for Electrical Discharge Machining Processes
Reprinted from: *Mathematics* 2020, *8*, 922, doi:10.3390/math8060922 . . . . **313**

Martin Gavalec, Ján Plavka and Daniela Ponce
EA/AE-Eigenvectors of Interval Max-Min Matrices
Reprinted from: *Mathematics* 2020, *8*, 882, doi:10.3390/math8060882 . . . . **339**

Tran Manh Tuan, Luong Thi Hong Lan, Shuo-Yan Chou, Tran Thi Ngan, Le Hoang Son, Nguyen Long Giang and Mumtaz Ali
M-CFIS-R: Mamdani Complex Fuzzy Inference System with Rule Reduction Using Complex Fuzzy Measures in Granular Computing
Reprinted from: *Mathematics* 2020, *8*, 707, doi:10.3390/math8050707 . . . . **359**

Sarbast Moslem, Muhammet Gul, Danish Farooq, Erkan Celik, Omid Ghorbanzadeh and Thomas Blaschke
An Integrated Approach of Best-Worst Method (BWM) and Triangular Fuzzy Sets for Evaluating Driver Behavior Factors Related to Road Safety
Reprinted from: *Mathematics* 2020, *8*, 414, doi:10.3390/math8030414 . . . . **383**

About the Editor

Vassilis C. Gerogiannis holds a Diploma in Computer/Software Engineering and a PhD in Software Engineering from the University of Patras, Greece. He is a full-time Professor and Chair in the Department of Digital Systems at the University of Thessaly, Greece. He is also an Adjunct Professor, teaching Software Engineering, at the Hellenic Open University. From 1992 to the present, he has participated as a software engineer, project manager and research director in several R&D projects funded by EU or national organizations. He has authored/co-authored more than 130 papers published in international journals/conference proceedings, which have been cited in a plethora of publications. He acts as a guest editor, member of editorial boards and reviewer for international journals. He serves as a general chair, program chair, member of the organization/technical committee and invited speaker for international conferences. He has received the "best paper award" in three international conferences. His research interests include software engineering, project management and fuzzy decision making.

Preface to "Applications of Fuzzy Optimization and Fuzzy Decision Making"

During the last decades, fuzzy optimization and fuzzy decision making have gained significant attention, with researchers aiming to provide robust solutions for complex optimization and decision problems characterized by non-probabilistic uncertainty, vagueness, ambiguity and hesitation. The aim of this Special Issue is to expand the applicability of fuzzy optimization and decision making by applying state-of-the art techniques based on fuzzy technology, computational intelligence and soft-computing methodologies for solving real-life problems. The response of the scientific community has been significant, as many papers have been submitted for consideration; finally, eighteen (18) papers were accepted, after a careful peer-review process based on quality and novelty criteria.

The paper by Zhang et al. [1] proposes a case-based reasoning method for the judgment of a debtor's hidden property analysis, which employs crisp and interval numbers as well as fuzzy linguistic variables and develops a hybrid similarity measure to improve the efficiency of handling law enforcement cases.

The paper authored by Wu et al. [2] studies the energy-saving effects brought about by yield improvement in a factory and proposes a two-stage fuzzy approach to estimate the energy savings. The actual case of a dynamic random-access memory factory was used to illustrate that product yield learning can greatly reduce electricity consumption.

The work by Lefevr et al. [3] studied HIV spread with fuzzy-based simulation scenarios by employing the observation and analysis of real-world networks and by introducing a fuzzy implementation of epidemic models. The simulation results demonstrate that the existence of fuzziness plays an important role in analyzing the effects of the disease spread.

In the paper by Yiğit et al. [4], the performance and efficiency of energy supply companies with respect to productivity is examined with reference to a case study of an electricity distribution company. The factors and their corresponding weights were determined using the analytical hierarchy process (AHP) and the fuzzy AHP methods.

In the paper authored by Poczeta et al. [5], the main idea was to systematically create a nested structure, based on a fuzzy cognitive map (FCM), in which each element/concept at a higher map level is decomposed into another FCM that provides a more detailed and precise representation of complex time series data.

Drakopoulos et al. [6] studied cognitive graphs, which are effective tools for simultaneous dimensionality reduction and visualization in deep learning. In this paper, fuzzy cognitive graphs are proposed for representing maps with incomplete knowledge or errors caused by noisy or insufficient observations. The study presents the construction of a cognitive map with a tensor distance metric, as well as a fuzzy variant of the map.

Wu et al. [7] propose a varying partial consensus fuzzy collaborative intelligence approach for assessing an intervention strategy for tackling the COVID-19 pandemic. In the varying partial consensus fuzzy collaborative intelligence approach, multiple decision makers express their judgments on the relative priorities of factors critical for an intervention strategy.

The paper authored by Kim and Jung [8] proposes an α-level estimation algorithm for ridge fuzzy regression modeling, addressing the multicollinearity phenomenon in the fuzzy linear regression setting. By incorporating α-levels in the estimation procedure, a fuzzy ridge estimator that does not depend on the distance between fuzzy numbers is constructed.

The paper authored by Čubranić-Dobrodolac et al. [9] aims to examine a relationship between the speed and space assessment capabilities of drivers associated with the occurrence of road traffic accidents. The method is based on the implementation of the interval type-2 fuzzy inference systems (T2FIS) and was tested on empirical data.

The work in the paper authored by Carnero [10] studied segregation in health care waste management and intended to produce a classification of failure modes. It applied failure mode and effects analysis (FMEA), by combining an intuitionistic fuzzy hybrid weighted Euclidean distance operator, and the multi-criteria method Potentially All Pairwise RanKings of all possible Alternatives (PAPRIKA).

Wu et al. [11] propose the piecewise linear fuzzy geometric mean (PLFGM) approach to improve the accuracy and efficiency of estimating the fuzzy priorities of criteria. The PLFGM approach was applied to the identification of critical features for a smart backpack design.

Kokkinos and Karayannis [12] performed a comparative analysis of low-carbon energy planning, evaluating different multicriteria decision-making methodologies. The methodologies were applied on a case study in Thessaly Region, Greece. The application of fuzzy goal programming (FGP) ranked four energy types in terms of feasibility, the stochastic fuzzy analytic hierarchical process (SF-AHP) evaluated the criteria, and the F-TOPSIS technique assessed these criteria.

The paper authored by Abosuliman et al. [13] examines decision-theoretical rough sets (DTRSs). The proposed model is based on the loss function of DTRSs. Based on the grade of positive, neutral and negative membership of fractional orthotriple fuzzy numbers (FOFNs), various methods are established for addressing the expected loss expressed in the form of FOFNs.

Chiu et al. [14] propose an interval fuzzy number (IFN)-based mixed binary quadratic programming–ordered weighted average (OWA) approach for forecasting the productivity of a factory. The methodology has been applied to a real case indicating that it was superior to several existing methods in terms of various metrics for evaluating the forecasting accuracy.

The paper authored by Pérez [15] examines technological tables in electrical discharge machining to determine optimal operating conditions for process variables. The study presents a methodology based on a fuzzy inference system aiming to assist in selecting the most appropriate manufacturing conditions in advance.

Gavalec et al. [16] aimed to investigate the eigenvectors for maximum and minimum matrices with interval coefficients. In this study, the properties of EA/AE-interval eigenvectors were examined and characterized by equivalent conditions. Numerical recognition algorithms working in polynomial time are described, and the results are illustrated by numerical examples.

Tuan et al. [17] propose a new Mamdani complex fuzzy inference system with rule reduction using complex fuzzy measures in granular computing (M-CFIS-R) along with fuzzy similarity measures, which are integrated in the form of granular computing. Experiments on various decision-making datasets demonstrate that the proposed M-CFIS-R performs better than M-CFIS.

The paper authored by Moslem et al. [18] aims to evaluate and prioritize the significant driver behavioral factors related to road safety. The suggested method integrates the best–worst method (BWM) with triangular fuzzy sets for optimizing the complex decision-making problem.

As the Guest Editor of this Special Issue, I am grateful to all the authors who contributed their articles. I would also like to express my gratitude to all the reviewers for their valuable comments for the improvement of the submitted papers. The goal of this Special Issue was to attract quality and novel papers in the field of "Fuzzy Optimization and Fuzzy Decision Making". It is hoped that these selected research papers will be found impactful by the international scientific community and that these papers will motivate further research on fuzzy techniques for solving complex problems in various disciplines and application fields.

References

1. Zhang, H.; Zhang, Z.; Zhou, L.; Wu, S. Case-Based Reasoning for Hidden Property Analysis of Judgment Debtors. *Mathematics* **2021**, *9*, 1559, doi:10.3390/math9131559.
2. Wu, H.-C.; Tsai, H.-R.; Chen, T.-C.T.; Hsu, K.-W. Energy-Efficient Production Planning Using a Two-Stage Fuzzy Approach. *Mathematics* **2021**, *9*, 1101, doi:10.3390/math9101101.
3. Lefevr, N.; Kanavos, A.; Gerogiannis, V.C.; Iliadis, L.; Pintelas, P. Employing Fuzzy Logic to Analyze the Structure of Complex Biological and Epidemic Spreading Models. *Mathematics* **2021**, *9*, 977, doi:10.3390/math9090977.
4. Yiğit, V.; Demir, N.N.; Alidrisi, H.; Aydin, M.E. Elicitation of the Factors Affecting Electricity Distribution Efficiency Using the Fuzzy AHP Method. *Mathematics* **2021**, *9*, 82, doi:10.3390/math9010082.
5. Poczeta, K.; Papageorgiou, E.I.; Gerogiannis, V.C. Fuzzy Cognitive Maps Optimization for Decision Making and Prediction. *Mathematics* **2020**, *8*, 2059, doi:10.3390/math8112059.
6. Drakopoulos, G.; Kanavos, A.; Mylonas, P.; Pintelas, P. Extending Fuzzy Cognitive Maps with Tensor-Based Distance Metrics. *Mathematics* **2020**, *8*, 1898, doi:10.3390/math8111898.
7. Wu, H. C.; Wang, Y.-C.; Chen, T.-C.T. Assessing and Comparing COVID-19 Intervention Strategies Using a Varying Partial Consensus Fuzzy Collaborative Intelligence Approach. *Mathematics* **2020**, *8*, 1725, doi:10.3390/math8101725.
8. Kim, H.; Jung, H.-Y. Ridge Fuzzy Regression Modelling for Solving Multicollinearity. *Mathematics* **2020**, *8*, 1572, doi:10.3390/math8091572.
9. Čubranić-Dobrodolac, M.; Švadlenka, L.; Čičević, S.; Trifunović, A.; Dobrodolac, M. Using the Interval Type-2 Fuzzy Inference Systems to Compare the Impact of Speed and Space Perception on the Occurrence of Road Traffic Accidents. *Mathematics* **2020**, *8*, 1548, doi:10.3390/math8091548.
10. Carnero, M.C. Waste Segregation FMEA Model Integrating Intuitionistic Fuzzy Set and the PAPRIKA Method. *Mathematics* **2020**, *8*, 1375, doi:10.3390/math8081375.
11. Wu, H.-C.; Chen, T.; Huang, C.-H. A Piecewise Linear FGM Approach for Efficient and Accurate FAHP Analysis: Smart Backpack Design as an Example. *Mathematics* **2020**, *8*, 1319, doi:10.3390/math8081319.
12. Kokkinos, K.; Karayannis, V. Supportiveness of Low-Carbon Energy Technology Policy Using Fuzzy Multicriteria Decision-Making Methodologies. *Mathematics* **2020**, *8*, 1178, doi:10.3390/math8071178.
13. Abosuliman, S.S.; Abdullah, S.; Qiyas, M. Three-Way Decisions Making Using Covering Based Fractional Orthotriple Fuzzy Rough Set Model. *Mathematics* **2020**, *8*, 1121, doi:10.3390/math8071121.
14. Chiu, M.-C.; Chen, T.-C.T.; Hsu, K.-W. Modeling an Uncertain Productivity Learning Process Using an Interval Fuzzy Methodology. *Mathematics* **2020**, *8*, 998, doi:10.3390/math8060998.
15. Pérez, C.J.L. Using a Fuzzy Inference System to Obtain Technological Tables for Electrical Discharge Machining Processes. Mathematics **2020**, *8*, 922, doi:10.3390/math8060922.
16. Gavalec, M.; Plavka, J.; Ponce, D. EA/AE-Eigenvectors of Interval Max-Min Matrices. *Mathematics* **2020**, *8*, 882, doi:10.3390/math8060882.

17. Tuan, T.M.; Lan, L.T.H.; Chou, S.Y.; Ngan, T.T.; Son, L.H.; Giang, N.L.; Ali, M. M-CFIS-R: Mamdani Complex Fuzzy Inference System with Rule Reduction Using Complex Fuzzy Measures in Granular Computing. *Mathematics* **2020**, *8*, 707, doi:10.3390/math8050707.
18. Moslem, S.; Gul, M.; Farooq, D.; Celik, E.; Ghorbanzadeh, O.; Blaschke, T. An Integrated Approach of Best-Worst Method (BWM) and Triangular Fuzzy Sets for Evaluating Driver Behavior Factors Related to Road Safety. *Mathematics* **2020**, *8*, 414, doi:10.3390/math8030414.

Vassilis C. Gerogiannis
Editor

Case-Based Reasoning for Hidden Property Analysis of Judgment Debtors

Huirong Zhang [1], Zhenyu Zhang [2], Lixin Zhou [3,*] and Shuangsheng Wu [4]

1 School of Labor Relationship, Shandong Management University, Jinan 250357, China; 14438120140358@sdmu.edu.cn
2 School of Automation, Nanjing University of Science and Technology, Nanjing 210094, China; zhangzhenyu@njust.edu.cn
3 Business School, University of Shanghai for Science and Technology, Shanghai 200093, China
4 School of Economics and Management, Tongji University, Shanghai 200092, China; wss0810@tongji.edu.cn
* Correspondence: zhoulixin1861@hotmail.com

Abstract: Many judgment debtors try to evade, confront, and delay law enforcement using concealing and transferring their property to resist law enforcement in China. The act of hiding property seriously affects people's legitimate rights and interests and China's legal authority. Therefore, it is essential to find an effective method of analyzing whether a judgment debtor hides property. Aiming at the hidden property analysis problem, we propose a case-based reasoning method for the judgment debtor's hidden property analysis. In the hidden property analysis process, we present the attributes of the enforcement case by crisp symbols, crisp numbers, interval numbers, and fuzzy linguistic variables and develop a hybrid similarity measure between the historical enforcement case and the target enforcement case. The results show that the recommendations obtained with the information and knowledge of similar historical cases are consistent with judicial practice, which can reduce the work pressure of law enforcement officers and improve the efficiency of handling enforcement cases.

Keywords: law enforcement; case-based reasoning (CBR); similarity measure; hidden property; judgment debtor

1. Introduction

Due to the influence of the whole society's low legal consciousness, lack of the social credit system, imperfections of the property supervision system, and other factors, a large number of judgment debtors try their best to evade, confront, and delay law enforcement by concealing and transferring their property and even resort to violent means to resist law enforcement. In China, valid legal instruments are difficult to implement, and we call it "difficulty in law enforcement." The problem of "difficulty in law enforcement" seriously affects the realization of people's legitimate rights and interests and promotes credibility and power of China's justice. Moreover, the Supreme People's Court's statistical data show that from 2016 to 2018, there were about six million enforcement cases per year on average, and every law enforcement officer needed to handle about 150 enforcement cases every year. The existing staffing is far from meeting the needs of judicial enforcement. Therefore, it is essential to study an effective method to analyze whether a judgment debtor hides property, which improves the efficiency of enforcement cases and reduces law enforcement costs.

The decision whether hidden property analysis of a judgment debtor is needed mainly relies on the law enforcement officers' own case handling experience to judge whether the judgment debtor has concealed property. Still, the process of handling cases is often restricted by subjective and objective factors such as information asymmetry and personal prejudice. Besides, hidden property analysis information comes from the Supreme People's

Court's inspection and control system. The system is connected with the Ministry of Public Security, the Ministry of Transport, the People's Bank of China, and banking financial institutions. It can include the real estate, deposits, ships, vehicles, and other judgment debtor information. It can cover the main property forms and relevant information on the judgment debtor. The existing inspection and control system involves various data forms, such as crisp symbols, crisp numbers, interval numbers, and fuzzy variables. For example, the gender of the judgment debtor is male or female, expressed as a crisp symbol, and the annual income is a crisp number. When describing the value of the attribute "frozen property," it is impossible to accurately estimate the exact amount of frozen property such as houses and vehicles according to the market value. Generally, an interval value is more reasonable than describing the attribute by a crisp number. Meanwhile, considering there are no unified quantitative methods to express attributes such as credibility, consumption level, and work, fuzzy linguistic variables provide a suitable tool for presenting the attribute values given by expert judges. Thus, fuzzy logic is implemented to express the imprecision and vagueness of the enforcement cases' attributes.

The existing method of hidden property analysis has four aspects of characteristics and is shown as follows. Firstly, there is no unified and feasible method to facilitate the operation in the decision-making process of enforcement cases; it mainly depends on the law enforcement officers' experience to deal with enforcement cases. Secondly, law enforcement officers are under high pressure and have to deal with many enforcement cases. Therefore, there is no effective analysis method to preliminarily judge the possibility of concealment of the judgment debtor's property. It is impossible to find out the hidden property of a judgment debtor. Thirdly, the existing inspection and control system involves various forms of data, such as text data, crisp symbols, crisp numbers, interval numbers, and fuzzy variables. Fourthly, it mainly depends on the law enforcement officers to screen the data, which need to be processed quantitatively.

We developed a case-based reasoning (CBR) approach to hidden property analysis of a judgment debtor through the above analysis. CBR is a methodology that imitates the reasoning and thinking process of human beings. It mainly uses specific knowledge of historical cases to solve new problems by searching for historical cases similar to new problems, which provides a useful technology for analyzing the possibility of property hidden by a judgment debtor. The main idea of the CBR approach to hidden property analysis is to extract the experience of historical enforcement cases to analyze whether the judgment debtor has concealed property or not. Specifically, the significant attributes of the historical enforcement case and the target enforcement case, such as credibility and consumption level, are presented. Then, the hybrid similarity between the historical enforcement case and the target enforcement case are calculated. Moreover, the hybrid similarity is used to extract several similar historical enforcement cases with reference significance for the target enforcement case. The historical case set's empirical knowledge helps to analyze and assess whether the judgment debtor conceals property in the target enforcement case. The case reasoning process is shown in Figure 1.

The contributions of our work are as follows. Firstly, we develop the framework of CBR-based hidden property analysis of a judgment debtor which provides a fast and useful tool to analyze the possibility of the property concealed by a judgment debtor. It solves the decision-making problem of the target enforcement case according to the experience of historical cases, assists law enforcement officers in finding out the hidden property of judgment debtors, and improves the accuracy and efficiency of the enforcement cases' judgments. Secondly, in the enforcement case presentation process, we use four types of data transformed from the Supreme People's Court's inspection and control system: crisp symbols, crisp numbers, interval numbers, and fuzzy linguistic variables. Thirdly, we propose a hybrid similarity measure method including the four types of data, which is simple and effective. Finally, we give the optimal recommendations for hidden property analysis, including the four types of data in CBR, not just case retrieval.

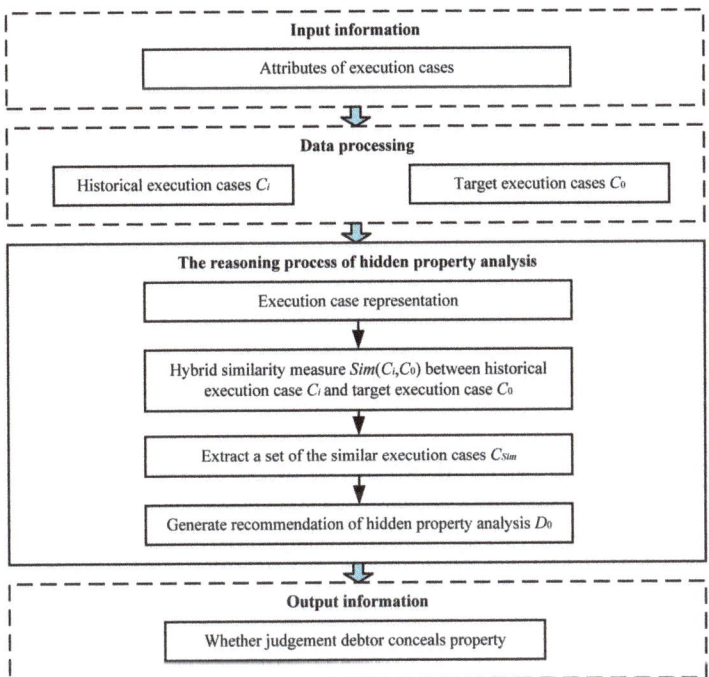

Figure 1. Flowchart of CBR for hidden property analysis of judgment debtors.

The rest of our work is constructed as follows. Section 2 reviews some related literature about hidden property analysis and CBR. Section 3 develops a CBR model for hidden property analysis of a judgment debtor. The framework of the CBR-based model for hidden property analysis, enforcement case presentation, a measure of hybrid similarity between a historical case and the target case, extraction of similar historical cases, and generation of recommendations are introduced. Section 4 provides a case study concerning hidden property analysis of a judgment debtor. Some conclusions are presented in Section 5.

2. Literature Review

At present, China is still in the primary stage of socialism. There are some problems, such as weak awareness of the rule of law, lack of social integrity, severe lag in the implementation of the legal system, laws and regulations, resulting in the phenomenon of "difficulty in law enforcement." The problem of "difficulty in law enforcement" seriously affects the social harmony and stability, the fairness and justice of the law, and the authority of justice, which the society is widely concerned about. Hidden property analysis of a judgment debtor acts as an essential link to solve the problem of "difficulty in law enforcement."

Scholars have been paying more attention to the use of computers and information technology to detect fraud and money laundering of criminal suspects. Bell [1] analyzed and summarized the cases of concealment or transfer of property in the United States. Meanwhile, billions of dollars of losses are caused by credit card transaction fraud every year in the United States; the key to reducing these losses is to study practical fraud detection algorithms. In the face of the characteristics of nonstationary distribution, high imbalance, and dispersion of data, Dal Pozzolo et al. [2] developed a credit fraud detection approach based on the machine learning technology to assist fraud investigators. However, there is still no public dataset on the credit card fraud that can be used to test the effectiveness of the algorithm. For online payment fraud, van Vlasselaer et al. [3] proposed an extended method for detecting fraudulent credit card transactions at online stores. The method mainly adopts the basic principle of RFM (recency, frequency, monetary), combines the characteristics of transaction behavior and the internal characteristics of historical customer transaction data, and verifies the algorithm through online transaction data. The results show that the algorithm considers transaction behavior characteristics and customer history and has a better prediction effect than other methods. Based on the financial transaction data, the Polish police identified the money laundering mode of a criminal suspect. Based on the case handling experience of the Polish police, Dreżewski et al. [4] developed a set of money laundering detection systems using the Apriori algorithm, the PrefixSpan algorithm, the FP growth algorithm, and the Eclat algorithm. They visualized the analysis results, which were used to detect the capital flow of criminal suspects to assist in polishing police investigations of money laundering crimes. Van Vlasselaer et al. [5] put forward a time-weighted network algorithm to identify enterprises that evade paying taxes and intentionally go bankrupt. The results show that the recognition accuracy of the algorithm is as high as 55%. Aiming at fraud in electronic payments, Carcillo et al. [6] proposed an extensible real-time fraud detection system which combines big data tools (Kafka, Spark, and Cassandra) with the machine learning method. The method can solve the problems of imbalance, instability, and feedback delay. The experimental results on a large number of original credit transaction datasets show that the framework can effectively detect fraud in a large number of credit card transactions. Recently, some researchers have focused on judgment debtors. Zhang et al. [7] analyzed the possibility of law enforcement on the basis of the judgment debtor's credibility and number of transferred assets and constructed a hybrid TODIM framework to assess which the judgment debtor is more likely to repay the debt. Wu et al. [8] used a hesitant fuzzy linguistic distance method to measure whether the judgment debtor conceals property. He et al. [9] developed a novel probabilistic linguistic three-way multi-attribute decision-making method to analyze whether the judgment debtor features a concealing property behavior and ways of concealing property.

From the above analysis, a set of feasible and practical models and methods have not been formed to solve the problem of hidden property analysis of a judgment debtor. The primary purpose of hidden property analysis of a judgment debtor is to quickly and effectively assess whether the judgment debtor is likely to conceal their property. It is more efficient to extract a set of similar historical enforcement cases using the CBR technology to decide whether the judgment debtor has hidden property. The CBR technology is a useful tool to solve such problems. The main idea of the model is to analyze and assess whether the judgment debtor is likely to conceal property by extracting similar case sets from the historical enforcement case database. For complex problems with characteristics that are challenging to express and inability of establishing mathematical models, the CBR method has a perfect effect on solving such problems by imitating the human reasoning and thinking process [10–14]. So far, the research on CBR has mainly focused on the research framework and the calculation method of the similarity measure.

In the research of the CBR research framework, Wei and Dai [15] expressed the uncertainty of emission characteristics of traffic pollution sources by interval-valued intuitionistic fuzzy sets. They put forward the framework of traffic emission prediction based on the CBR method. Facing case presentation with mixed multiformat attribute values, Zheng et al. [16] transformed crisp numbers, interval numbers, and multigranularity linguistic variables into intuitionistic fuzzy numbers to present the attributes of gas explosion accidents and developed a new hybrid multi-attribute case retrieval method to extract similar historical cases. Construction risk identification mostly depends on expert knowledge or prior knowledge of the project. Somi et al. [17] introduced a new risk identification framework for renewable energy projects based on CBR. In the CBR model, fuzzy logic is used to describe the uncertainty in the process of risk identification, and similar historical renewable energy projects are extracted, which is conducive to improving the level of risk management in the construction stage. Cai et al. [18] established a case base, extracted the features of EEG, and established a CBR method for depression recognition, and the accuracy rate of the developed CBR approach is 91.25%. Hu et al. [19] point out that CBR is widely used in engineering cost estimation, project bidding, bidding procurement, environment and sustainable management. Pla et al. [20] developed a distributed medical diagnosis decision support tool by using the CBR method, which significantly improved the efficiency of medical diagnosis under joint operation. El-fakdi et al. [21] used CBR to evaluate the case specificity in complex surgery or minimally invasive surgery and used 82 patients with aortic valve implantation in the Affiliated Hospital of Renne University as samples for demonstration. Ramos et al. [22] proposed a CBR framework based on gradient boosting feature selection and applied it to the differential diagnosis of squamous cell carcinoma and adenocarcinoma to improve the accuracy of diagnosis. The generalization ability of the method was verified by training and evaluating two independent datasets. To simulate the memory process of the human brain, Herrero [23] introduced a bottom-up CBR-learning framework and trained a group of cooperative/competitive reaction behaviors of the Aibo robot in the RoboCup environment to test the effectiveness of the proposed framework.

Similarity measure plays a significant role in CBR, which directly affects the accuracy of analysis results. In the research of similarity measure, Gilboa et al. [24–26] proposed that the similarity of cases mainly consists of average similarity and action similarity, considered the decision scheme by pairing the problem with the decision scheme, and introduced the weighted utility function to test the consistency of the preference order. Caramuta et al. [27] divided the complex decision-making problem into several nodes and obtained similarity of the decision-making problem using the graph theory method. To express the uncertainty of features in cases, Fan et al. [28,29] developed a comprehensive similarity measure to solve the problem of data diversification in the CBR method. The data types included crisp numbers, interval numbers, intuitionistic fuzzy numbers, hesitant fuzzy numbers, interval type-2 fuzzy numbers. Besides, Zhang et al. [30–34] introduced some similarity measures for the fuzzy environment. Chergui [35] studied the semantic similarity method in the community question-answering system and proposed a semantic Bayesian reasoning method for the semantic uncertainty implied in a natural language text, which had an excellent experimental effect in the community question-answering system.

Considering the advantages of the CBR method in solving complex decision-making problems, the CBR method has been extended to the legal field. Through the analysis and summary of users' transaction behavior, Adedoyin [36] proposed an improved CBR method for mobile remittance fraud detection, trying to detect abnormal patterns in transactions. The performance of this method is better than that of the single feature method. To solve the problem of employee information leakage, Boehmer [37] proposed a method of employee behavior identification based on the CBR technology, directed acyclic graphs, and the Hamming similarity measure. To crack down on illegal immigration, Chang [38] put forward a method combining CBR and expert systems to classify and analyze the patterns of illegal smuggling and restore the investigation system of cracking down on illegal smuggling. Han et al. [39] extracted the characteristics of network crime and used the CBR technology to identify hackers.

Although significant achievements have been reached in the existing research, there are still some areas to be improved.

(1) So far, there is no research on hidden property analysis of a judgment debtor. Considering the complex and changeable decision-making environment, the difficulty in feature extraction, and the difficulty in establishing a decision-making model, it is urgent to study a fast and effective method of analyzing the possibility of hidden property.

(2) In the process of case presentation, attribute values are mainly expressed by crisp numbers. With the diversification of data types, the existing case presentation in CBR cannot satisfy the needs of case presentation. It is necessary to fully consider various forms of data, such as crisp symbols, crisp numbers, interval numbers, and fuzzy linguistic variables.

(3) The similarity measure in CBR considers one data type or two and has no consideration on various types of data.

(4) The existing CBR research has focused on case retrieval and cannot provide recommendations.

3. CBR Approach to Hidden Property Analysis of a Judgment Debtor

3.1. The Framework of the CBR-Based Hidden Property Analysis of a Judgment Debtor

In this section, we introduce the research framework of hidden property analysis of a judgment debtor based on CBR, as shown in Figure 2. The research framework consists of two parts: the research content and the relevant theoretical methods, which are placed on the left and right sides of the frame diagram, respectively. The research content includes the preparation stage and the stage of hidden property analysis. In the preparation stage, we prepare the current hidden property analysis problem and regard it as the target case. Besides, we collect some similar enforcement cases and regard them as historical cases. The stage of hiding possibility analysis mainly includes four steps: (1) case presentation structurally presents the attributes of the target case and the historical case; (2) hybrid similarity measure calculation of the similarity measure under various attributes represented by different types of data between the target case and the historical case and aggregation thereof to form the hybrid similarity measure; (3) extraction of similar historical enforcement cases, ination of the similarity threshold, and selection of a historical enforcement case set with high similarity based on the threshold value; (4) generation of a recommendation regarding the hidden property analysis problem according to the extracted similar historical enforcement cases and decision whether the judgment debtor may be concealing their property.

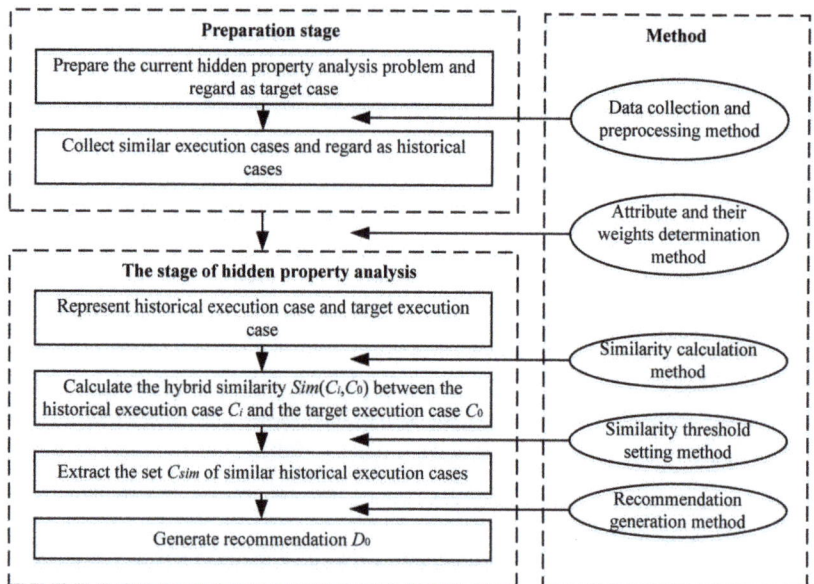

Figure 2. The framework of CBR for hidden property analysis of a judgment debtor.

3.2. Enforcement Case Presentation

In the process of hidden property analysis of a judgment debtor, case presentation mainly presents the historical enforcement cases and the target enforcement case according to a specific format, which provides the basis for the CBR process. Therefore, the appropriate and effective case presentation is essential for hidden property analysis. An appropriate case presentation method can improve the efficiency of extracting historical enforcement cases and enhance the accuracy of the results of hiding property analysis. The enforcement case presentation is as follows:

The CBR-based hidden property analysis approach includes historical enforcement cases and target cases. The case can be presented as "Case = {Enforcement case situation, hidden property analysis result}."

Case: $C = \{C_1, C_2, \ldots, C_n\}$ and C_0 represent the set of historical enforcement cases and the target enforcement case, respectively, where C_i represents the ith historical enforcement case, $i \in N = \{1, 2, \ldots, n\}$. In the target case C_0, the result of hidden property analysis is unknown, which needs to be solved by the proposed method.

Enforcement case situation: Let $Q = \{Q_1, Q_2, \ldots, Q_m\}$, $q_0 = \{q_{01}, q_{02}, \ldots, q_{0m}\}$, $q_i = \{q_{i1}, q_{i2}, \ldots, q_{im}\}$ be the collection of the attributes of enforcement cases, historical enforcement cases, and target enforcement cases, respectively, where Q_j, q_{ij}, q_{0j}, respectively, represent the jth attribute of enforcement cases, historical enforcement cases, and target enforcement cases, $j \in M = \{1, 2, \ldots, m\}$. Let $w^P = \{w_1^P, w_2^P, \ldots, w_m^P\}$ be the weight vector of the attributes of the enforcement case, where w_j^P is the weight of the jth attribute of the enforcement case.

Meanwhile, the attribute values of target enforcement cases q_{0j} and the attribute of historical enforcement cases q_{ij} can be expressed in the form of crisp symbols, crisp numbers, interval numbers, and fuzzy linguistic variables. For example, when the attribute is "gender", the value can be expressed as male or female. The value of the attribute "annual income" can be expressed as a crisp number. When describing the value of the attribute "frozen property," it is impossible to accurately estimate the exact amount of frozen property such as houses and vehicles. An interval value is more reasonable than describing the attribute by a crisp number. Meanwhile, considering there are no unified quantitative methods to express attributes such as credibility, consumption level, and work, fuzzy linguistic variables provide a suitable tool for presenting the attribute values given by the expert judges.

To distinguish between different data types, the attribute set of the enforcement case includes four subsets: crisp symbol attribute set Q^I, crisp number attribute set Q^{II}, interval number attribute set Q^{III}, and fuzzy linguistic variable attribute set Q^{IV}, satisfying $Q = Q^I \cup Q^{II} \cup Q^{III} \cup Q^{IV}$, where $Q^I = \{Q_1, Q_2, \ldots, Q_{m_1}\}$, $Q^{II} = \{Q_{m_1+1}, Q_{m_1+2}, \ldots, Q_{m_2}\}$, $Q^{III} = \{Q_{m_2+1}, Q_{m_2+2}, \ldots, Q_{m_3}\}$, $Q^{IV} = \{Q_{m_3+1}, Q_{m_3+2}, \ldots, Q_m\}$, and the corresponding subscript sets are $M^I = \{1, 2, \ldots, m_1\}$, $M^{II} = \{m_1 + 1, m_1 + 2, \ldots, m_2\}$, $M^{III} = \{m_2 + 1, m_2 + 2, \ldots, m_3\}$, $M^{IV} = \{m_3 + 1, m_3 + 2, \ldots, m\}$, satisfying $M^I \cup M^{II} \cup M^{III} \cup M^{IV} = M$.

Hidden property analysis result: Let $D = \{D_1, D_2, \ldots, D_h\}$ be the attribute set of the results of hidden property analysis, where D_l represents the lth attribute of the result, $l \in H = \{1, 2, \ldots, h\}$. Let $d_i = \{d_{i1}, d_{i2}, \ldots, d_{ih}\}$ and $d_0 = \{d_{0,1}, d_{0,2}, \ldots, d_{0,h}\}$ be the eigenvalue vectors of the judgment results of the hidden property of historical enforcement case C_i and target enforcement case C_0, then $d_0 = \{d_{0,1}, d_{0,2}, \ldots, d_{0,h}\}$ needs to be solved in the problem.

To sum up, the presentation of historical enforcement case C_i and target enforcement case C_0 is shown in Table 1, in which X represents the results of hidden property analysis in target enforcement case C_0.

Table 1. Presentation of historical enforcement cases C_i and target enforcement case C_0.

	Attributes of the Enforcement Case Situation								Attributes of the Results of Hidden Property Analysis			
	Q^I			...	Q^{IV}				D_1	D_2	...	D_h
	Q_1	Q_2	...	Q_{m_1}	...	Q_{m_3}	Q_{m_3+1}	...	Q_m				
C_1	q_{11}	q_{12}	...	q_{1m_1}	...	q_{1m_3}	q_{1m_3+1}	...	q_{1m}	d_{11}	d_{12}	...	d_{1h}
C_2	q_{21}	q_{22}	...	q_{2m_1}	...	q_{2m_3}	q_{2m_3+1}	...	q_{2m}	d_{21}	d_{22}	...	d_{2h}
...	...	...	...	...	...	...	...	...	...	...	...	...	...
C_n	q_{n1}	q_{n2}	...	q_{nm_1}	...	q_{nm_3}	q_{nm_3+1}	...	q_{nm}	d_{n1}	d_{n2}	...	d_{nh}
C_0	q_{01}	q_{02}	...	q_{0m_1}	...	q_{0m_3}	q_{0m_3+1}	...	q_{0m}		X		

3.3. Hybrid Similarity Measure between Historical Enforcement Cases and the Target Enforcement Case

In enforcement cases, the attribute values mainly include four data types: crisp symbols, crisp numbers, interval numbers, and fuzzy linguistic variables. The similarity measures of different data types are also different. Here, we introduce the similarity measures of attribute values of the four different data types.

(1) Crisp symbols

When the attribute value is a crisp symbol, that is, $Q_j \in Q^I$, all the possible values of the attribute can be provided by a simple enumeration method. For example, when the attribute is "gender," the value can be expressed as male or female. Let q_{ij}^I, q_{0j}^I be the attribute values of historical enforcement case C_i and target enforcement case C_0, respectively, represented by crisp symbols; then, similarity measure $sim(C_0, C_i)$ under attributes Q^I between historical enforcement case C_i and target enforcement case C_0 is defined as follows:

$$sim(C_0, C_i) = \begin{cases} 1, q_{ij}^I = q_{0j}^I, \\ 0, q_{ij}^I \neq q_{0j}^I, \end{cases} \quad i \in N, j \in M^I \quad (1)$$

(2) Crisp numbers

When the attribute value is a crisp number, that is, $Q_j \in Q^{II}$, if q_{ij}^{II}, q_{0j}^{II} are, respectively, the attribute values of historical enforcement case C_i and target enforcement case C_0 represented by the crisp number, the calculation formula of the different degree under attribute Q^{II} between historical enforcement case C_i and target enforcement case C_0 is as follows:

$$\delta\left(q_{ij}^{II}, q_{0j}^{II}\right) = \frac{1}{\Delta_j^{IImax}} \sqrt{\left(q_{ij}^{II} - q_{0j}^{II}\right)^2}, i \in N, j \in M^{II} \quad (2)$$

where $\Delta_j^{IImax} = \max\left\{\sqrt{\left(q_{ij}^{II} - q_{0j}^{II}\right)^2} | i \in N\right\}$, $\delta\left(q_{ij}^{II}, q_{0j}^{II}\right) \in [0, 1]$.

Under attribute Q^{II}, similarity measure $sim(C_0, C_i)$ between historical enforcement case C_i and target enforcement case C_0 is based on the distance measure considering the reflexivity, symmetry, and other properties of the similarity and constructed using the negative exponential function [40–42]. Therefore, the calculation formula is as follows:

$$sim(C_0, C_i) = \exp\left[-\delta\left(q_{ij}^{II}, q_{0j}^{II}\right)\right], i \in N, j \in M^{II} \quad (3)$$

(3) Interval numbers

When the attribute value is an interval number, that is, $Q_j \in Q^{III}$, the interval number has certain advantages in describing the uncertainty of the attribute value. For example, when representing the attribute value of "frozen property," the specific amount of frozen property, such as houses and vehicles, cannot be accurately estimated according to the market circulation value. Generally, the attribute value is expressed with an interval number, which is more reasonable than the crisp number. Suppose q_{ij}^{III} and q_{0j}^{III} are the attribute values of historical enforcement case C_i and target enforcement case C_0 expressed by interval numbers, where $q_{ij}^{III} = \left[\underline{q}_{ij}, \overline{q}_{ij}\right]$, $q_{0j}^{III} = \left[\underline{q}_{0j}, \overline{q}_{0j}\right]$; then, the calculation formula of the different degree between historical enforcement case C_i and target enforcement case C_0 is as follows:

$$\delta\left(q_{ij}^{III}, q_{0j}^{III}\right) = \frac{1}{\Delta_j^{IIImax}} \sqrt{\left(\underline{q}_{ij}^{III} - \underline{q}_{0j}^{III}\right)^2 + \left(\overline{q}_{ij}^{III} - \overline{q}_{0j}^{III}\right)^2}, i \in N, j \in M^{III} \quad (4)$$

where $\Delta_j^{III\max} = \max\left\{\sqrt{\left(q_{ij}^{III} - q_{0j}^{III}\right)^2 + \left(\overline{q}_{ij}^{III} - \overline{q}_{0j}^{III}\right)^2} | i \in N\right\}$, $\delta\left(q_{ij}^{III}, q_{0j}^{III}\right) \in [0,1]$.

Under attribute Q^{III}, similarity measure $sim(C_0, C_i)$ is as follows:

$$sim(C_0, C_i) = \exp\left[-\delta\left(q_{ij}^{III}, q_{0j}^{III}\right)\right], i \in N, j \in M^{III} \tag{5}$$

(4) Fuzzy linguistic variables

When the attribute values are fuzzy linguistic variables, that is, $Q_j \in Q^{IV}$, fuzzy linguistic variables have certain advantages in the expression of uncertainty and fuzziness of the attribute values. For example, there is no unified quantitative standard for the attribute "credibility," and fuzzy linguistic variables such as "poor," "medium," and "good" are usually used. Suppose that q_{ij}^{IV} and q_{0j}^{IV} are the attribute values of historical enforcement case C_i and target enforcement case C_0 represented by fuzzy triangular numbers, respectively, where $\tilde{q}_{ij}^{IV} = \left(d_{ij}^a, d_{ij}^b, d_{ij}^c\right)$, $\tilde{q}_{0j}^{IV} = \left(d_{0j}^a, d_{0j}^b, d_{0j}^c\right)$. Different degree $\delta\left(q_{ij}^{IV}, q_{0j}^{IV}\right)$ between historical enforcement case C_i and target enforcement case C_0 is as follows:

$$\delta\left(q_{ij}^{IV}, q_{0j}^{IV}\right) = \frac{1}{\tilde{\Delta}_j^{\max}}\sqrt{\left(q_{ij}^a - q_{0j}^a\right)^2 + \left(q_{ij}^b - q_{0j}^b\right)^2 + \left(q_{ij}^c - q_{0j}^c\right)^2}, i \in N, j \in M^{IV} \tag{6}$$

where $\tilde{\Delta}_j^{\max} = \max\left\{\sqrt{\left(q_{ij}^a - q_{0j}^a\right)^2 + \left(q_{ij}^b - q_{0j}^b\right)^2 + \left(q_{ij}^c - q_{0j}^c\right)^2} | i \in N\right\}$, $\delta\left(q_{ij}^{IV}, q_{0j}^{IV}\right) \in [0,1]$.

Under attribute Q^{IV}, similarity measure $sim(C_0, C_i)$ is

$$sim(C_0, C_i) = \exp\left[-\delta\left(q_{ij}^{IV}, q_{0j}^{IV}\right)\right], i \in N, j \in M^{IV} \tag{7}$$

(5) Calculate the hybrid similarity measure between historical enforcement cases and the target enforcement case

Using Equations (1)–(7), similarity measure $sim_j(C_0, C_i)$ of attribute Q_j between historical enforcement case C_i and target enforcement case C_0 can be obtained, and the hybrid similarity measure can be obtained by aggregating similarity measure $sim_j(C_0, C_i)$ of attribute Q_j.

Suppose that $Sim(C_0, C_i)$ is the hybrid similarity measure between historical enforcement case C_i and target enforcement case C_0; then, the calculation formula of the hybrid similarity measure is as follows:

$$Sim(C_0, C_i) = \frac{\sum\limits_{j=1}^{M} sim_j(C_0, C_i)w_j}{\sum\limits_{j=1}^{M} w_j} \tag{8}$$

Obviously, $Sim(C_0, C_i) \in [0,1]$ and the larger $Sim(C_0, C_i)$, the higher the similarity between historical case C_i and target case C_0.

3.4. Extraction of Similar Historical Enforcement Cases

Usually, similar historical enforcement cases are extracted by the hybrid similarity measure. The higher the hybrid similarity measure between a historical case and the target case, the more referential it is to the target case. Therefore, it is necessary to extract historical enforcement cases and construct a set of similar historical cases. To obtain a more reasonable similar historical case set, we need to set the hybrid similarity threshold.

Let τ be the similarity threshold, then the calculation formula of similarity threshold τ, according to the principle in [28], is defined as follows:

$$\tau = Sim^{(+)} - \frac{Sim^{(+)} - Sim^{(-)}}{3} \tag{9}$$

where $Sim^{(+)} = \max\{Sim(C_0, C_i) | i \in N\}$, $Sim^{(-)} = \min\{Sim(C_0, C_i) | i \in N\}$.

When $Sim(C_0, C_i) > \tau$, it means that the historical enforcement case has a high similarity with the target enforcement case and can be used for reference, so historical enforcement cases with high similarity are extracted. According to this principle (Equation (9)), all the historical enforcement cases greater than similarity threshold τ are extracted, and set C^{Sim} of similar historical enforcement cases is constructed as follows:

$$C^{Sim} = \{C_i | i \in N^{Sim}\} \tag{10}$$

where $N^{Sim} = \{i | Sim(C_0, C_i) > \tau, i \in N\}$, N^{Sim} being the subscript set of similar historical enforcement cases with vital reference significance. Obviously, $C^{Sim} \subset C$, $N^{Sim} \subset N$.

3.5. Generation of Recommendations for Hidden Property Analysis

As a result of hidden property analysis, the attribute value can be composed of crisp symbols, crisp numbers, interval numbers, or fuzzy linguistic variables. When the attribute value is a crisp symbol, the most frequent opinion is considered the recommendation opinion. For example, among the five similar enforcement cases extracted, in four of the extracted cases, the judgment debtors concealed property. In one of the extracted cases the judgment debtor had no hidden property. Therefore, we can judge that the judgment debtor in the target case also concealed their property. When the attribute value is a crisp number, an interval number, or a fuzzy linguistic variable, the attribute of the recommendation of hidden property analysis is aggregated with the attribute values from similar enforcement cases, and the weight of each similar historical case is converted using the hybrid similarity measure. The calculation method of the attribute value as a result of hidden property analysis in the target enforcement case is as follows:

(1) If attribute value d_{0l} of the result of hidden property analysis is a crisp symbol, attribute value d_{0l} is defined as follows

$$d_{0l} = \{d_{kl} | k = \{i | \max_i(Sim(C_i, C_0)), i \in N^{Sim}\}\} \tag{11}$$

(2) If attribute value d_{0l} of the results of the analysis of the possibility of hidden property is a crisp number, an interval number, or a fuzzy linguistic variable, attribute value d_{0l} is defined as follows:

$$d_{0l} = \frac{\sum_{1}^{i = N^{Sim}} d_{il} Sim(C_i, C_0)}{\sum_{i}^{i = N^{Sim}} Sim(C_i, C_0)} \tag{12}$$

To sum up, the steps of the CBR approach for hidden property analysis of a judgment debtor are as follows:

Step 1: calculate similarity measure $sim(C_i, C_0)$ of attribute Q_j between historical enforcement cases C_i and target enforcement case C_0 using Equations (1)–(7).

Step 2: give the weight vector W of the attributes of the enforcement case situation.

Step 3: calculate hybrid similarity measure $Sim(C_i, C_0)$ between historical enforcement cases C_i and target enforcement case C_0, using Equation (8).

Step 4: ensure similarity threshold τ with Equation (9).

Step 5: extract historical cases with vital reference significance according to the extraction rules of similar enforcement cases (Equation (10)) and construct set C^{Sim} of similar historical enforcement cases.

Step 6: using Equation (11) or (12), calculate attribute value d_{0l} of the results of hidden property analysis and give optimal recommendation.

4. Case Study

4.1. The Process of Hidden Property Analysis

The CBR-based approach is a useful tool to extract similar historical cases and use the information and knowledge of similar historical cases to generate the recommendation of the target enforcement case effectively. To improve the efficiency of handling enforcement cases, we took the decision-making of enforcement cases as an example to demonstrate effectiveness of the proposed method.

Considering that a judgment debtor is the subject of the enforcement case, we selected some features of the judgment debtor as the attributes of the enforcement case, including gender (Q_1), age (Q_2), annual income (Q_3, 10,000 yuan/year), frozen property/enforcement target amount (Q_4), educational background (Q_5), comprehensive family strength (Q_6), work nature (Q_7), transaction behavior (Q_8), consumption level (Q_9), and credibility (Q_{10}). The data types of each attribute are shown in Table 2. For fuzzy linguistic variables, the linguistic term set used is shown in Table 3. $W = (0.1, 0.1, 0.1, 0.1, 0.1, 0.1, 0.1, 0.1, 0.1, 0.1)^T$ is the weight of the attributes of enforcement cases given by the experts. We collected 15 historical cases ($C_1, C_2, \ldots, C_{15}$) shown in Table 4.

Table 2. The meanings of the attributes and their corresponding data types.

Attributes	Meanings of Attributes	Data Type of the Attributes
Q_1	Gender	Crisp symbol
Q_2	Age	Crisp number
Q_3	Annual income	Crisp number
Q_4	Frozen property/enforcement target	Interval number
Q_5	Educational background	Fuzzy linguistic variable
Q_6	Comprehensive family strength	Fuzzy linguistic variable
Q_7	Work	Fuzzy linguistic variable
Q_8	Trading behavior	Fuzzy linguistic variable
Q_9	Consumption level	Fuzzy linguistic variable
Q_{10}	Credibility	Fuzzy linguistic variable

Table 3. Linguistic terms of fuzzy linguistic variables and their corresponding triangular fuzzy numbers.

Linguistic Terms	Educational Background	Comprehensive Family Strength	Work	Trading Behavior	Consumption Level	Credibility	Corresponding Triangular Fuzzy Number
s_0	-	Extremely bad	Extremely unstable	Extremely risk preference	Extremely high	Extremely bad	(0, 0, 0.17)
s_1	Middle school degree	Very bad	Very unstable	Very high risk preference	Very high	Very bad	(0, 0.17, 0.33)
s_2	High school degree	Bad	Unstable	Risk preference	High	Bad	(0.17, 0.33, 0.5)
s_3	Senior college degree	Medium	Medium	Medium	Medium	Medium	(0.33, 0.5, 0.67)
s_4	Bachelor's degree	Good	Stable	Risk-averse	Low	Good	(0.5, 0.67, 0.83)
s_5	Master's degree	Very good	Very stable	Very risk-averse	Very low	Very good	(0.67, 0.83, 1)
s_6	Doctor's degree	Extremely good	Extremely stable	Extremely risk-averse	Extremely low	Extremely good	(0.83, 1, 1)

Table 4. Attribute value Q_j of historical enforcement cases C_i and target enforcement case C_0.

	Q_1	Q_2	Q_3	Q_4	Q_5	Q_6	Q_7	Q_8	Q_9	Q_{10}	Recommendation
C_1	M	52	15.6	[0.00, 0.00]	s_4	s_3	s_2	s_2	s_2	s_3	D_1
C_2	M	28	10.3	[0.05, 0.15]	s_2	s_3	s_2	s_3	s_2	s_2	D_1
C_3	M	32	12.1	[0.10, 0.14]	s_4	s_4	s_3	s_2	s_3	s_3	D_1
C_4	M	46	17.5	[0.00, 0.12]	s_5	s_4	s_4	s_4	s_4	s_4	D_3
C_5	M	57	7.6	[1.30, 1.40]	s_3	s_5	s_2	s_1	s_1	s_2	D_3
C_6	M	39	12.3	[0.00, 0.06]	s_4	s_4	s_3	s_3	s_3	s_2	D_1
C_7	M	32	13.5	[0.05, 0.11]	s_4	s_3	s_4	s_3	s_3	s_3	D_1
C_8	M	36	10.6	[0.01, 0.01]	s_3	s_2	s_3	s_2	s_2	s_2	D_2
C_9	M	41	5.0	[0.02, 0.02]	s_2	s_3	s_1	s_2	s_1	s_2	D_2
C_{10}	M	44	13.0	[0.00, 0.08]	s_3	s_2	s_3	s_2	s_2	s_2	D_1
C_{11}	M	43	4.7	[0.01, 0.01]	s_1	s_2	s_1	s_1	s_0	s_1	D_2
C_{12}	M	48	16.1	[0.10, 0.20]	s_5	s_2	s_5	s_4	s_4	s_4	D_1
C_{13}	F	33	8.7	[0.05, 0.09]	s_3	s_3	s_2	s_2	s_2	s_2	D_1
C_{14}	F	35	12.5	[1.20, 1.28]	s_3	s_5	s_3	s_4	s_3	s_3	D_3
C_{15}	F	42	10.5	[0.20, 0.24]	s_4	s_4	s_4	s_3	s_4	s_3	D_1
C_0	M	41	12.0	[0.05, 0.15]	s_3	s_3	s_2	s_3	s_3	s_2	-

Remark: "M" represents male and "F" represents female.

For target enforcement case C_0, the judgment debtor was 41 years old, male; the detailed information of the judgment debtor is shown in Tabel 4. We assessed whether the judgment debtor concealed property or not by calculating the hybrid similarity measure between the target enforcement case and historical enforcement cases. The recommendation of hidden property analysis mainly includes the judgment debtor's refusal to perform the legal instrument by hiding property (D_1), the judgment debtor's lack of ability to perform the legal instrument (D_2), and the judgment debtor's performance of the legal instrument (D_3). The information on the attributes of historical enforcement cases and the target enforcement case are shown in Table 4.

According to the above information, hidden property analysis of the judgment debtor in the target enforcement case was carried out, and the steps were as follows:

Step 1: using Equations (1)–(7), calculate similarity measure $sim(C_i, C_0)$ under each attribute Q_j between historical enforcement cases C_i and target enforcement case C_0, as shown in Table 5.

Table 5. Similarity measures of attribute Q_j between historical enforcement cases C_i and target enforcement case C_0.

$sim(C_i, C_0)$	Q_1	Q_2	Q_3	Q_4	Q_5	Q_6	Q_7	Q_8	Q_9	Q_{10}
C_1	1.00	0.50	0.61	1.00	0.61	0.92	1.00	0.61	0.72	0.61
C_2	1.00	0.44	0.61	1.00	0.79	1.00	1.00	1.00	0.72	1.00
C_3	1.00	0.57	0.61	0.61	0.99	0.98	0.72	0.61	1.00	0.61
C_4	1.00	0.73	0.37	0.61	0.47	0.97	0.51	0.61	0.72	0.37
C_5	1.00	0.37	1.00	0.37	0.55	0.37	1.00	0.37	0.51	1.00
C_6	1.00	0.88	0.61	0.61	0.96	0.95	0.72	1.00	1.00	1.00
C_7	1.00	0.57	0.61	1.00	0.81	0.98	0.51	1.00	1.00	0.61
C_8	1.00	0.73	1.00	0.61	0.83	0.93	0.72	0.61	0.72	1.00
C_9	1.00	1.00	0.61	1.00	0.38	0.94	0.72	0.61	0.51	1.00
C_{10}	1.00	0.83	1.00	0.61	0.87	0.95	0.72	0.61	0.72	1.00
C_{11}	1.00	0.88	0.37	0.61	0.37	0.93	0.72	0.37	0.37	0.61
C_{12}	1.00	0.65	0.37	0.61	0.57	0.96	0.37	0.61	0.72	0.37
C_{13}	0.37	0.61	1.00	1.00	0.64	0.98	1.00	0.61	0.72	1.00
C_{14}	0.37	0.69	1.00	0.37	0.93	0.40	0.72	0.61	1.00	0.61
C_{15}	0.37	0.94	0.61	0.61	0.81	0.91	0.51	1.00	0.72	0.61

Step 2: calculate hybrid similarity measure $Sim(C_i, C_0)$ between historical enforcement cases C_i and target enforcement case C_0 using Equation (8) as shown in Table 6.

The results show that historical case C_6 was the most similar to target enforcement case C_0, $Sim(C_6, C_0) = 0.87$. The second and third similar cases were C_2 and C_{10}, $Sim(C_2, C_0) = 0.86$, $Sim(C_{10}, C_0) = 0.83$, and the most dissimilar cases were C_{11} and C_{12}, $Sim(C_{11}, C_0) = Sim(C_{12}, C_0) = 0.62$.

Table 6. Hybrid similarity measure $Sim(C_i, C_0)$ between historical enforcement cases C_i and target enforcement case C_0.

Similarity Measure	Historical Cases							
	C_1	C_2	C_3	C_4	C_5	C_6	C_7	C_8
$Sim(C_i, C_0)$	0.76	0.86	0.77	0.63	0.65	0.87	0.81	0.81
Similarity Measure	Historical Cases							
	C_9	C_{10}	C_{11}	C_{12}	C_{13}	C_{14}	C_{15}	
$Sim(C_i, C_0)$	0.78	0.83	0.62	0.62	0.79	0.67	0.71	

Step 3: similarity threshold τ calculated using Equation (9) was 0.79. That is, if similarity measure $Sim(C_i, C_0)$ between historical cases C_i and target case C_0 is more significant than 0.79, it can be added to the set of similar historical cases.

$$\tau = Sim^{(+)} - \frac{Sim^{(+)} - Sim^{(-)}}{3} = 0.87 - \frac{0.87 - 0.62}{3} = 0.79.$$

Step 4: similarity threshold τ was 0.79. Using Equation (10), historical cases with vital reference significance were extracted, and a similar historical enforcement case set was constructed as $C^{Sim} = \{C_2, C_6, C_7, C_8, C_{10}\}$.

Step 5: using Equation (11) or (12), calculate the attribute value of the recommendation and give recommendations.

The recommendation of hidden property analysis includes three kinds: the judgment debtor refuses to perform the legal instrument by hiding property (D_1), the judgment debtor has no ability to perform the legal instrument (D_2), or the judgment debtor performs the legal instrument (D_3), which can be regarded as crisp symbols. According to set C^{Sim} of similar historical cases, there were only two recommendations: D_1 and D_2, as shown in Table 7.

Table 7. Similar historical cases.

Similar Historical Case	Similarity	Recommendation
C_2	0.86	D_1
C_6	0.87	D_1
C_7	0.81	D_1
C_8	0.81	D_2
C_{10}	0.83	D_1

Therefore, the probabilities of these two kinds of recommendations were calculated using Equation (10):

$$p(D_1) = \frac{\sum_{i \in D_1^{Sim}} Sim(C_i, C_0)}{\sum_{i \in N^{Sim}} Sim(C_i, C_0)} = \frac{0.86 + 0.87 + 0.81 + 0.83}{0.86 + 0.87 + 0.81 + 0.81 + 0.83} = 0.81$$

$$p(D_2) = \frac{\sum_{i \in D_2^{Sim}} Sim(C_i, C_0)}{\sum_{i \in N^{Sim}} Sim(C_i, C_0)} = \frac{0.81}{0.86 + 0.87 + 0.81 + 0.81 + 0.83} = 0.19$$

The above analysis shows that the recommendation was that the judgment debtor in the target enforcement case refused to perform the legal instrument by hiding property. According to the detailed information in Table 4, the judgment debtor in the target enforcement case was 41 years old and had unstable work, low credibility. Five similar historical enforcement cases $\{C_2, C_6, C_7, C_8, C_{10}\}$ were extracted using the hybrid similarity measure. Four of those judgment debtors featured a hidden property behavior, and one of them was unable to perform the legal instrument. Therefore, the judgment debtor in the target enforcement case was likely to hide property and needed to be tracked. Actually, the recommendation of CBR-based hidden property analysis was consistent with the practical judicial implementation. The result showed that the developed CBR method can provide a clear and effective way to quickly assess the possibility of property being hidden, reduce the work pressure on law enforcement officers, and improve the efficiency of handling enforcement cases.

4.2. Comparative Analysis

To illustrate effectiveness and novelty of the developed CBR method for hidden property analysis of a judgment debtor, we compared the developed CBR method with the distance-based method for hidden property analysis [8]. The main idea of Wu's method [8] is to judge whether the judgment debtor hides property by calculating the distance between the judgment debtor in the target case and in historical cases. Here, hybrid distance measure $Dis(C_i, C_0)$ between historical enforcement case C_i and target enforcement case C_0 was defined as follows:

$$Dis(C_0, C_i) = \frac{\sum_{j=1}^{M} dis_j(C_0, C_i) w_j}{\sum_{j=1}^{M} w_j} \tag{13}$$

Then, the hybrid distance result was shown in Table 8. The judgment debtor in target case C_0 was closest to the judgment debtor in historical case C_6. Namely, $Dis(C_6, C_0) = 0.13$. The recommendation was D_1—the judgment debtor in C_0 hides property.

Table 8. Hybrid distance measure $Dis(C_i, C_0)$ between historical enforcement cases C_i and target enforcement case C_0.

Distance Measure	Historical Cases							
	C_1	C_2	C_3	C_4	C_5	C_6	C_7	C_8
$d(C_i, C_0)$	0.24	0.14	0.23	0.37	0.35	0.13	0.19	0.19
Distance Measure	Historical Cases							
	C_9	C_{10}	C_{11}	C_{12}	C_{13}	C_{14}	C_{15}	
$d(C_i, C_0)$	0.22	0.17	0.38	0.38	0.21	0.33	0.29	

Although the recommendation obtained by Wu's method [8] was the same as that obtained with the developed CBR method, the developed CBR method was more reasonable than Wu's method. Wu's method suggests extracting only one judgment debtor with the closest distance, while five historical enforcement cases are extracted when using the developed CBR method. The assessment refers to just one judgment debtor's recommendation, which will greatly increase the hidden property analysis error rate. Expert judges will assess whether the judgment debtor hides property according to the similar cases' recommendations, which will improve reliability of the analysis result. Therefore, the analysis result obtained using the developed CBR method was more reasonable than that obtained with Wu's method.

5. Conclusions

Aiming at the hidden property analysis problem, we developed the CBR method for hidden property analysis of a judgment debtor. We introduced the research framework of the developed method, the presentation of enforcement cases, the calculation method for case similarity, the extraction of a similar enforcement case set, and the generation of recommendations. Besides, a case study concerning hidden property analysis of a judgment debtor is provided to illustrate effectiveness of the developed method. The conclusions of our work are as follows.

Firstly, the framework of CBR-based hidden property analysis of a judgment debtor is regarded as a useful tool to assess whether the judgment debtor in the target enforcement case hides property or not. We extracted similar historical cases and used the information and knowledge of similar historical cases to provide the recommendation of hidden property analysis of the judgment debtor. The recommendation of hidden property analysis was consistent with the actual law enforcement. Thus, it can be seen that the developed method has high accuracy.

Secondly, considering the information from the inspection and control system constructed by the Supreme People's Court of China, the enforcement case's attributes are represented by crisp symbols, crisp numbers, interval numbers, and fuzzy linguistic variables, and a hybrid similarity measure between a historical enforcement case and the target enforcement case is developed. The similarity measure method is feasible and straightforward.

Thirdly, the extraction method for similar historical enforcement cases can reduce the slope of case retrieval. The extraction method extracts the five most similar historical enforcement cases out of the 15 enforcement cases selected by manual screening, which can reduce law enforcement officers' work pressure and improve efficiency of handling enforcement cases.

Fourthly, we not only search for similar historical enforcement cases but also give the optimal recommendations. Moreover, the attributes of the recommendations consider different data types and are different from the previous work.

However, many aspects need to be further improved. Firstly, due to the research conditions' limitations, the sample size of the data collected in the research process on hidden property analysis is small. We hope to further improve the research results' accuracy using a sufficiently large data sample. First, we will try nonparametric methods after testing covariability/rejection rates considering real data to make a conclusion about the quality of the results. Second, machine learning or deep learning may solve these problems well. We explore machine learning or deep learning methods to analyze whether the judgment debtor hides property or not provided that there are sufficient data. Third, there still remain many deficiencies in the quantitative presentation of some attributes, such as credibility, which need to be further improved. Fourth, the case presentation method proposed cannot meet the legal instrument description requirements, so it is necessary to study case presentation based on ontology and the method of extraction of similar case sets. Fifth, considering neutrosophic statistics have some advantages in dealing with vague, indecisive, or fuzzy sample data [43–45], we will apply neutrosophic statistics to the hidden property analysis problem.

Author Contributions: Conceptualization, Z.Z. and L.Z.; methodology, S.W.; software, S.W.; validation, Z.Z.; formal analysis, Z.Z.; investigation, S.W.; resources, S.W.; data curation, S.W.; writing—original draft preparation, H.Z., Z.Z. and L.Z.; writing—review and editing, H.Z. and L.Z.; visualization, L.Z.; supervision, H.Z.; project administration, H.Z.; funding acquisition, H.Z. All authors have read and agreed to the published version of the manuscript.

Funding: This work was supported by the National Social Science Foundation of China (No. 18BJY108).

Institutional Review Board Statement: Not applicable.

Informed Consent Statement: Not applicable.

Data Availability Statement: Data sharing not applicable.

Acknowledgments: The authors are thankful to the editors and the reviewers for their comments and suggestions to improve the quality of the manuscript.

Conflicts of Interest: We declare that there are no conflicts of interest.

References

1. Bell, E. Concealing and disguising criminal property. *J. Money Laund. Control.* **2009**, *12*, 268–284. [CrossRef]
2. Dal Pozzolo, A.; Caelen, O.; Le Borgne, Y.A.; Waterschoot, S.; Bontempi, G. Learned lessons in credit card fraud detection from a practitioner perspective. *Expert Syst. Appl.* **2014**, *41*, 4915–4928. [CrossRef]
3. Van Vlasselaer, V.; Bravo, C.; Caelen, O.; Tina, E.; Leman, A.; Monique, S.; Baesens, B. APATE: A novel approach for automated credit card transaction fraud detection using network-based extensions. *Decis. Support Syst.* **2015**, *75*, 38–48. [CrossRef]
4. Dreżewski, R.; Dziuban, G.; Hernik, Ł.; Pączek, M. Comparison of data mining techniques for Money Laundering Detection Sys-tem. In Proceedings of the 2015 International Conference on Science in Information Technology (ICSITech), Yogyakarta, Indonesia, 27–28 October 2015.
5. Van Vlasselaer, V.; Eliassi-Rad, T.; Akoglu, L.; Snoeck, M.; Baesens, B. Gotcha! Network-based fraud detection for social security fraud. *Manag. Sci.* **2017**, *63*, 3090–3110. [CrossRef]
6. Carcillo, F.; Pozzolo, A.D.; Le Borgne, Y.-A.; Caelen, O.; Mazzer, Y.; Bontempi, G. SCARFF: A scalable framework for streaming credit card fraud detection with spark. *Inf. Fusion* **2018**, *41*, 182–194. [CrossRef]
7. Zhang, Z.; Lin, J.; Zhang, H.; Wu, S.; Jiang, D. Hybrid TODIM Method for Law Enforcement Possibility Evaluation of Judgment Debtor. *Mathematics* **2020**, *8*, 1806. [CrossRef]
8. Wu, S.; Lin, J.; Zhang, Z. New distance measures of hesitant fuzzy linguistic term sets. *Phys. Scr.* **2021**, *96*, 015002. [CrossRef]
9. He, J.; Zhang, H.; Zhang, Z.; Zhang, J. Probabilistic Linguistic Three-Way Multi-Attibute Decision Making for Hidden Property Evaluation of Judgment Debtor. *J. Math.* **2021**, *2021*, 9941200. [CrossRef]
10. Aamodt, A.; Plaza, E. Case-Based Reasoning: Foundational Issues, Methodological Variations, and System Approaches. *AI Commun.* **1994**, *7*, 39–59. [CrossRef]
11. Ting, S.L.; Wang, W.M.; Kwok, S.K.; Tsang, A.H.C.; Lee, W.B. RACER: Rule-Associated Case-based Reasoning for supporting General Practitioners in prescription making. *Expert Syst. Appl.* **2010**, *37*, 8079–8089. [CrossRef]
12. Zhuang, Z.Y.; Churilov, L.; Burstein, F.; Sikaris, K. Combining data mining and case-based reasoning for intelligent decision support for pathology ordering by general practitioners. *Eur. J. Oper. Res.* **2009**, *195*, 662–675. [CrossRef]
13. Wu, M.C.; Lo, Y.F.; Hsu, S.H. A fuzzy CBR technique for generating product ideas. *Expert Syst. Appl.* **2008**, *34*, 530–540. [CrossRef]
14. Araz, C.; Ozfirat, P.M.; Ozkarahan, I. An integrated multicriteria decision-making methodology for outsourcing management. *Comput. Oper. Res.* **2007**, *34*, 3738–3756. [CrossRef]
15. Wei, M.; Dai, Q. A prediction model for traffic emission based on interval-valued intuitionistic fuzzy sets and case-based reasoning theory. *J. Intell. Fuzzy Syst.* **2016**, *31*, 3039–3046. [CrossRef]
16. Zheng, J.; Wang, Y.-M.; Lin, Y.; Zhang, K. Hybrid multi-attribute case retrieval method based on intuitionistic fuzzy and evidence reasoning. *J. Intell. Fuzzy Syst.* **2019**, *36*, 271–282. [CrossRef]
17. Somi, S.; Seresht, N.G.; Fayek, A. Framework for Risk Identification of Renewable Energy Projects Using Fuzzy Case-Based Reasoning. *Sustainability* **2020**, *12*, 5231. [CrossRef]
18. Cai, H.; Zhang, X.; Zhang, Y.; Wang, Z.; Hu, B. A Case-Based Reasoning Model for Depression Based on Three-Electrode EEG Data. *IEEE Trans. Affect. Comput.* **2018**, *11*, 383–392. [CrossRef]
19. Hu, X.; Xia, B.; Skitmore, M.; Chen, Q. The application of case-based reasoning in construction management research: An overview. *Autom. Constr.* **2016**, *72*, 65–74. [CrossRef]
20. Pla, A.; López, B.; Gay, P.; Pous, C. eXiT*CBR.v2: Distributed case-based reasoning tool for medical prognosis. *Decis. Support Syst.* **2013**, *54*, 1499–1510. [CrossRef]
21. El-Fakdi, A.; Gamero, F.; Melendez, J.; Auffret, V.; Haigron, P. eXiTCDSS: A framework for a workflow-based CBR for interven-tional Clinical De-cision Support Systems and its application to TAVI. *Expert Syst. Appl.* **2014**, *41*, 284–294. [CrossRef]
22. Ramos-González, J.; López-Sánchez, D.; Castellanos-Garzón, J.A.; de Paz, J.F.; Corchado, J.M. A CBR framework with gradient boosting based feature selection for lung cancer subtype classification. *Comput. Biol. Med.* **2017**, *86*, 98–106. [CrossRef]
23. Herrero-Reder, I.; Urdiales, C.; Peula, J.; Sandoval, F. CBR based reactive behavior learning for the memory-prediction framework. *Neurocomputing* **2017**, *250*, 18–27. [CrossRef]
24. Gilboa, I.; Schmeidler, D. Act similarity in case-based decision theory. *Econ. Theory* **1997**, *9*, 47–61. [CrossRef]
25. Gilboa, I.; Schmeidler, D.; Wakker, P.P. Utility in Case-Based Decision Theory. *J. Econ. Theory* **2002**, *105*, 483–502. [CrossRef]
26. Gilboa, I.; Schmeidler, D. *A Theory of Case-Based Decisions*; Cambridge University Press (CUP): Cambridge, UK, 2001.
27. Caramuta, D.M.; Contiggiani, F.; Tohmé, F. Memory and Similarity: A Graph# Theoretic Model for Case Based Decision Theory. In Proceedings of the XLI Meeting of the Argentina Association of Political Economy, Salta, Argentina, 28 August 2006; Argentina Association of Political Economy: Salta, Argentina, 2006.
28. Fan, Z.P.; Li, Y.H.; Wang, X.; Liu, Y. Hybrid similarity measure for case retrieval in CBR and its application to emergency response towards gas explosion. *Expert Syst. Appl.* **2014**, *41*, 2526–2534. [CrossRef]

29. Fan, Z.P.; Li, Y.H.; Zhang, Y. Generating project risk response strategies based on CBR: A case study. *Expert Syst. Appl.* **2015**, *42*, 2870–2883. [CrossRef]
30. Zhang, Z.; Lin, J.; Miao, R.; Zhou, L. Novel distance and similarity measures on hesitant fuzzy linguistic term sets with application to pattern recognition. *J. Intell. Fuzzy Syst.* **2019**, *37*, 2981–2990. [CrossRef]
31. Zhang, Z.; Li, J.; Sun, Y.; Lin, J. Novel Distance and Similarity Measures on Hesitant Fuzzy Linguistic Term Sets and Their Ap-plication in Clustering Analysis. *IEEE Access* **2019**, *7*, 100231–100242. [CrossRef]
32. Zhang, Z.; Zhao, X.; Qin, Y.; Si, H.; Zhou, L. Interval type-2 fuzzy TOPSIS approach with utility theory for subway station operational risk evaluation. *J. Ambient Intell. Humaniz. Comput.* **2021**, 1–15. [CrossRef]
33. Zhou, L.; Lin, J.; Li, Y.; Zhang, Z. Innovation Diffusion of Mobile Applications in Social Networks: A Multi-Agent System. *Sustainability* **2020**, *12*, 2884. [CrossRef]
34. Zhang, Z.; Zhang, H.; Zhou, L.; Li, Y. Analyzing the Coevolution of Mobile Application Diffusion and Social Network: A Multi-Agent Model. *Entropy* **2021**, *23*, 521. [CrossRef]
35. Chergui, O.; Begdouri, A.; Groux-Leclet, D. Integrating a Bayesian semantic similarity approach into CBR for knowledge reuse in Community Question Answering. *Knowl. Based Syst.* **2019**, *185*, 104919. [CrossRef]
36. Adedoyin, A.; Kapetanakis, S.; Samakovitis, G.; Petridis, M. Predicting fraud in mobile money transfer using case-based reason-ing. In Proceedings of the International Conference on Innovative Techniques and Applications of Artificial Intelligence, Cambridge, UK, 12–14 December 2017; Springer: Cham, Switzerland, 2017; pp. 325–337.
37. Boehmer, W. Analyzing Human Behavior Using Case-Based Reasoning with the Help of Forensic Questions. In Proceedings of the 24th IEEE International Conference on Advanced Information Networking and Applications, Perth, Australia, 1 June 2010; Institute of Electrical and Electronics Engineers (IEEE): Piscataway, NJ, USA; pp. 1189–1194.
38. Chang, C.C.; Hua, K.H. Applying case-based reasoning and expert systems to coastal patrol crime investigation in Tai-wan. In Proceedings of the International Conference on Intelligence and Security Informatics, Taipei, Taiwan, 17 June 2008; Springer: Berlin/Heidelberg, Germany, 2008; pp. 161–170.
39. Han, M.L.; Han, H.C.; Kang, A.R.; Kwak, B.I.; Mohaisen, A.; Kim, H.K. WHAP: Web-Hacking Profiling Using Case-Based Reasoning. In Proceedings of the 2016 IEEE Conference on Communications and Network Security (CNS), Philadelphia, PA, USA, 17–19 October 2016.
40. Guerdjikova, A. Case-based learning with different similarity functions. *Games Econ. Behav.* **2008**, *63*, 107–132. [CrossRef]
41. Shepard R, N. Toward a universal law of generalization for psychological science. *Science* **1987**, *237*, 1317–1323. [CrossRef]
42. Billot, A.; Gilboa, I.; Schmeidler, D. Axiomatization of an exponential similarity function. *Math. Soc. Sci.* **2008**, *55*, 107–115. [CrossRef]
43. Aslam, M.; Rao, G.S.; Khan, N. Single-stage and two-stage total failure-based group-sampling plans for the Weibull distribution under neutrosophic statistics. *Complex Intell. Syst.* **2021**, *7*, 1–10. [CrossRef]
44. Aslam, M. Analyzing wind power data using analysis of means under neutrosophic statistics. *Soft Comput.* **2021**, *25*, 7087–7093. [CrossRef]
45. Aslam, M.; Bantan, R.A.R.; Khan, N. Design of a New Attribute Control Chart Under Neutrosophic Statistics. *Int. J. Fuzzy Syst.* **2019**, *21*, 433–440. [CrossRef]

Article

Energy-Efficient Production Planning Using a Two-Stage Fuzzy Approach

Hsin-Chieh Wu [1], Horng-Ren Tsai [2], Tin-Chih Toly Chen [3,*] and Keng-Wei Hsu [3]

[1] Department of Industrial Engineering and Management, College of Science and Engineering, Chaoyang University of Science and Technology, Taichung 413310, Taiwan; wusteve11@gmail.com
[2] Department of Information Technology, Lingtung University, Taichung 408213, Taiwan; hrt@teamail.ltu.edu.tw
[3] Department of Industrial Engineering and Management, National Yang Ming Chiao Tung University, Hsinchu 30010, Taiwan; ataco.ncsf@msa.hinet.net
* Correspondence: tolychen@ms37.hinet.net

Citation: Wu, H.-C.; Tsai, H.-R.; Chen, T.-C.T.; Hsu, K.-W. Energy-Efficient Production Planning Using a Two-Stage Fuzzy Approach. *Mathematics* **2021**, *9*, 1101. https://doi.org/10.3390/math9101101

Academic Editors: Vassilis C. Gerogiannis and Antonio Francisco Roldán López de Hierro

Received: 25 March 2021
Accepted: 6 May 2021
Published: 13 May 2021

Publisher's Note: MDPI stays neutral with regard to jurisdictional claims in published maps and institutional affiliations.

Copyright: © 2021 by the authors. Licensee MDPI, Basel, Switzerland. This article is an open access article distributed under the terms and conditions of the Creative Commons Attribution (CC BY) license (https://creativecommons.org/licenses/by/4.0/).

Abstract: Analyzing energy consumption is an important task for a factory. In order to accomplish this task, most studies fit the relationship between energy consumption and product design features, process characteristics, or equipment types. However, the energy-saving effects of product yield learning are rarely considered. To bridge this gap, this study proposes a two-stage fuzzy approach to estimate the energy savings brought about by yield improvement. In the two-stage fuzzy approach, a fuzzy polynomial programming approach is first utilized to fit the yield-learning process of a product. Then, the relationship between monthly electricity consumption and increase in yield was fit to estimate the energy savings brought about by the improvement in yield. The actual case of a dynamic random access memory factory was used to illustrate the applicability of the two-stage fuzzy approach. According to the experiment results, product yield learning can greatly reduce electricity consumption.

Keywords: electricity consumption; yield learning; fuzzy forecasting; green manufacturing

1. Introduction

Factories all over the world are striving to reduce energy consumption in order to pursue green and sustainable manufacturing [1–5]. For this reason, evaluating the effects of various treatments on reducing energy consumption is a crucial task [6–9], which is the basis of the necessity for this research.

In the literature, many studies focused on determining the relationship between energy consumption and product design features, process characteristics, or equipment types [10–12]. However, improvement in product yield reduces the amount of rework and additional inputs, thereby saving energy [13,14]. However, this issue was rarely investigated, and this is a research gap that needs to be filled.

This study estimates the reduction in energy consumption on the basis of the reduction in monthly electricity consumption (MEC) brought about by the yield-learning process of a product. The novelty of this research lies in the following: in past studies, other performance measures were used for the same purpose, including production efficiency index (PEI; annual electricity consumption normalized by annual production area) and electrical utilization index (EUI; annual electricity consumption normalized by production units) [15–17]. Most existing indicators are annually measured. However, because the yield of a product is usually tracked on a monthly basis [18], MEC was more suitable for our purposes and replaced the existing annual indicators.

The research question was as follows: taking into account the inherent uncertainty in the yield-learning process of a product, how would one model the effect of improving yield on reducing MEC? To answer this question, a two-stage fuzzy approach is proposed in this study.

In the two-stage fuzzy approach, a fuzzy polynomial-programming (FPP) method is proposed to fit the yield-learning process of a product, so as to predict the future yield in consideration of the inherent uncertainty. In theory, there are other ways to deal with yield uncertainty, such as probabilistic methods or fuzzy rules. However, the planning horizon spans dozens of months, and it is difficult to estimate the probability distribution functions of variables over such a long time. In addition, fuzzy rules are suitable for modelling the effects of multiple factors on yield. When there is only one factor (i.e., time), a fuzzy yield-learning process is more appropriate. Further, the FPP method can generate fuzzy yield forecasts that are very likely to contain actual values [19]. This property may eliminate the need to learn a new example, which is beneficial to the scalability of the two-stage fuzzy approach. For these reasons, the FPP method was applied instead of probabilistic methods or fuzzy rules. Subsequently, in the second stage, the relationship between MEC and yield was fit to estimate the energy savings brought about by the increase in yield. In the two-stage fuzzy approach, polynomial-programming problems were solved that could be easily realized using existing optimization software (e.g., Lingo and MATLAB).

The practical case of a dynamic random-access memory (DRAM) product in a wafer-fabrication (wafer fab) plant was used to illustrate the applicability of the two-stage fuzzy approach. Many researchers attempted to estimate the electricity consumption of DRAM fabs by fabricating DRAM products [18,20]. However, these studies were static because only annual electricity consumption was observed, while long-term electricity consumption was not estimated. In addition, none of the existing methods was able to quantify the reducing effects of yield learning on electricity consumption. Compared with existing methods, the two-stage fuzzy approach has the following advantages:

(1) The original yield value is considered when evaluating forecasting performance. In contrast, existing methods usually consider the logarithmic value of yield.
(2) The reduction in MEC is measured once a month, which is consistent with the progress of yield improvement. In contrast, existing methods usually measure the reduction in power consumption once a year.

The main contributions of this study include:

(1) An FPP method, proposed to improve the precision and accuracy of tracking a yield-improvement process.
(2) A systematic procedure, established to estimate the energy savings brought about by the increase in yield.

The rest of this article is organized as follows: Section 2 is dedicated to a literature review; Section 3 introduces the two-stage fuzzy approach, and a practical case is used to illustrate the applicability of the two-stage fuzzy approach. In addition, existing methods within the field were applied to the case for comparison. In Section 4, experiment results are presented and discussed; then, conclusions are drawn in the last section.

2. Literature Review

There are two ways to analyze the energy consumption of a factory; the top–down and the bottom–up methods [10]. In fact, the energy consumption of a product is affected by many factors, e.g., equipment type, product type, and yield [10,11,13,14].

Reducing energy consumption is an important task for a factory [1]. In order to accomplish this task, factories take the following measures [15,21–32]:

(1) Designing products that require less energy or help to save energy.
(2) Switching to new manufacturing technologies that feature lower energy consumption.
(3) Acquiring new equipment with lower energy consumption.
(4) Solving quality problems that lead to energy waste.
(5) Shifting more production to locations or time periods with lower electricity rates.

(6) Using relatively cheap and environmentally friendly long-term green electricity (such as wind and solar energy).

Many studies used multiple measures at the same time. Table 1 shows the comparison results of some related references.

Table 1. Comparison of relevant references.

Reference	Designing Green Products	Green Manufacturing Technologies	Green Equipment	Solving Quality Problems	Green Production Scheduling	Green Electricity
Gong et al. [21]					√	
Jo et al. [22]			√			
Golpîra et al. [23]						√
Wu and Chen [24]				√		
Dai et al. [25]					√	
Hu et al. [15]	√					
Liang et al. [26]		√				
Gao et al. [27]					√	
Golpîra [28]					√	√
Wang et al. [29]			√		√	
Chang et al. [30]		√				
Kumar et al. [32]			√			√
This study				√		

DRAM is an electronic component that is widely used in computers, mobile phones, medical equipment, robots, etc. [33]. DRAM manufacturing can be divided into four stages: wafer fabrication, sorting, packaging, and final testing [34]. Among these four stages, wafer fabrication is the most energy-consuming stage [35,36]. Wafer fabrication involves very complex and difficult-to-control operations [37,38]. Each job in a wafer fab consists of 20–25 wafers, and goes through hundreds of steps. The processing steps can be divided into several categories, including photolithography, etching, and stripping. Some of these steps are energy-consuming heating and cooling operations. In addition, the same operation is performed on a job many times. As a result, the cycle time for all operations to complete in a job is usually as long as several months, during which a large amount of energy is consumed. Therefore, fabs aim to reduce energy consumption and pursue green manufacturing [39]. The expected benefits include lowering the unit costs of products and reducing the environment impact [30].

3. Two-Stage Fuzzy Approach

The proposed methodology comprises two stages: fitting the uncertain yield-learning process and estimating the reduction in MEC. Figure 1 presents the flowchart of the procedure of the two-stage fuzzy approach. A nomenclature is provided in Appendix A.

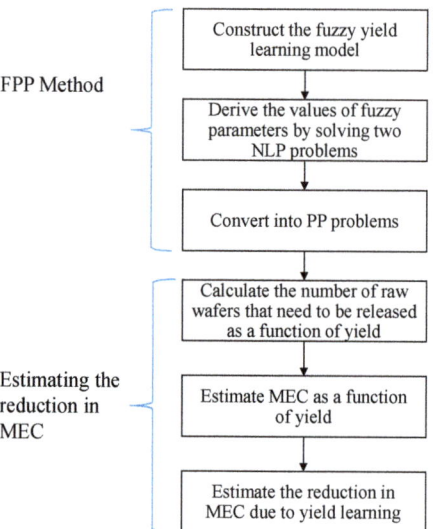

Figure 1. Procedure of two-step fuzzy approach.

3.1. Uncertain Yield-Learning Process

A yield-learning process describes the increase in yield due to various learning activities [40,41]. For example,

- As time goes by, operators become increasingly skilled, which can help to avoid misoperation.
- Quality-control engineers are increasingly experienced in solving quality-related issues.
- Equipment engineers gradually learn how to optimize machine settings.

The general yield model [42] is usually used to describe a yield-learning process:

$$Y_t = Y_0 e^{-\frac{b}{t} + r(t)}, \tag{1}$$

where

- Y_t is the yield at time t; $0 \leq Y_t \leq 1$; $t = 1 - T$;
- Y_0 is the asymptotic or final yield (a real-valued function of the point defect density per unit area, chip area, and a set of parameters unique to the specific yield model); $0 \leq Y_0 \leq 1$;
- b is the learning constant; $b > 0$;
- $r(t)$ is a homoscedastic serially uncorrelated error term that can be ignored.

However, because learning activities are subject to human intervention [43], a yield-learning process involves a lot of uncertainty [44]. This uncertainty can be modelled by defining yield as a probability function or fuzzy set. It is necessary to estimate the parameters of a probability function, which is not easy in the long run. A fuzzy set, on the other hand, is easy to define and calculate. For these reasons, in the two-stage fuzzy approach, the yield is defined as a fuzzy set.

In the two-stage fuzzy approach, parameters in Equation (1) are given as fuzzy values. As a result, the following fuzzy yield-learning model is constructed [45]:

$$\tilde{Y}_t = \tilde{Y}_0 e^{-\frac{\tilde{b}}{t} + r(t)}, \tag{2}$$

where

$$\tilde{Y}_0 = (Y_{01}, Y_{02}, Y_{03}) \tag{3}$$

$$\tilde{b} = (b_1, b_2, b_3) \quad (4)$$

are triangular fuzzy numbers (TFNs). TFNs in this study could be symmetric or asymmetric. In addition, other types of fuzzy numbers are applicable.

According to the fuzzy arithmetic operations of TFNs [46],

$$\begin{aligned}
\tilde{Y}_t &= \tilde{Y}_0 e^{-\frac{\tilde{b}}{t}} \\
&= (Y_{01}, Y_{02}, Y_{03}) e^{-\frac{(b_1, b_2, b_3)}{t}} \\
&\cong (Y_{01}, Y_{02}, Y_{03})(\times)(e^{-\frac{b_3}{t}}, e^{-\frac{b_2}{t}}, e^{-\frac{b_1}{t}}), \\
&\cong (Y_{01} e^{-\frac{b_3}{t}}, Y_{02} e^{-\frac{b_2}{t}}, Y_{03} e^{-\frac{b_1}{t}}) \\
&= (Y_{t1}, Y_{t2}, Y_{t3})
\end{aligned} \quad (5)$$

where ($\times$) indicates fuzzy multiplication. The fuzzy multiplication of TFNs is not a TFN anymore. However, most studies approximated the fuzzy multiplication result with a TFN [47–51]. In Equation (5), fuzzy multiplication result $\tilde{Y}_t$ is also approximated with a TFN. A possible issue is the precision of such approximation. $\tilde{Y}_0$, the final yield of a product, is a value very close to 1. $e^{-\frac{\tilde{b}}{t}}$ is also a value less than 1, and it gradually approaches 1 through learning. The multiplication of the two fuzzy variables can be very precisely approximated with a TFN, as illustrated in Figure 2. Approximation error was less than 0.002. Therefore,

$$Y_{t1} = Y_{01} e^{-\frac{b_3}{t}} \quad (6)$$

$$Y_{t2} = Y_{02} e^{-\frac{b_2}{t}} \quad (7)$$

$$Y_{t3} = Y_{03} e^{-\frac{b_1}{t}}. \quad (8)$$

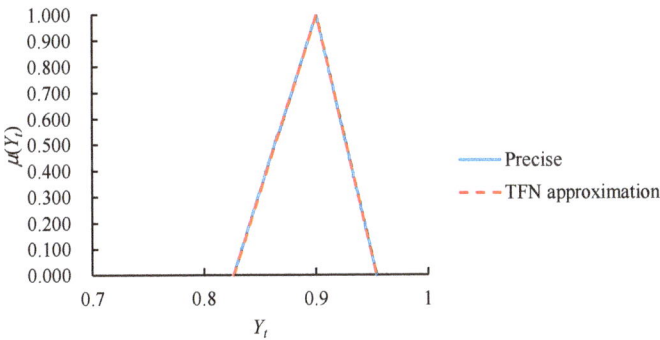

Figure 2. Approximation of fuzzy multiplication result ($\tilde{Y}_0$ = (0.85, 0.92, 0.97); $\tilde{b}$ = (0.10, 0.13, 0.17); t = 6).

To derive the values of fuzzy parameters, the FPP method is proposed, as follows.

3.2. Deriving Values of Fuzzy Parameters

In this research, an FPP method is proposed to derive the values of fuzzy parameters in the fuzzy yield-learning model. This method involves solving two nonlinear-programming (NLP) problems:

(NLP Problem I)

$$\text{Min } Z_1 = \frac{1}{T} \sum_{t=1}^{T} \frac{|Y_t - Y_{t2}|}{Y_t} \quad (9)$$

subject to

$$Y_{t2} = Y_{02} e^{-\frac{b_2}{t}} \quad (10)$$

23

$$b_2 \geq 0 \tag{11}$$

$$0 \leq Y_{02} \leq 1 \tag{12}$$

The objective function is to minimize the mean absolute percentage error (MAPE) to maximize forecasting accuracy.

(NLP Problem II)

$$\text{Min } Z_2 = \frac{1}{T}\sum_{t=1}^{T}(Y_{t3} - Y_{t1}) \tag{13}$$

subject to

$$Y_{t3} = Y_{03}e^{-\frac{b_1}{t}} \tag{14}$$

$$Y_{t1} = Y_{01}e^{-\frac{b_3}{t}} \tag{15}$$

$$Y_t \geq Y_{t1} \tag{16}$$

$$Y_t \leq Y_{t3} \tag{17}$$

$$0 \leq b_1 \leq b_2^* \leq b_3 \tag{18}$$

$$0 \leq Y_{01} \leq Y_{02}^* \leq Y_{03} \leq 1 \tag{19}$$

The objective function minimizes the average range to maximize forecasting precision. However, these two NLP problems include intractable absolute value functions or exponential equations, so they must be converted into more easily solvable forms [52,53].

First, the objective function of NLP Problem I is equivalent to

$$\text{Min } Z_1 = \frac{1}{T}\sum_{t=1}^{T}\frac{\vartheta_t}{Y_t}, \tag{20}$$

where

$$\vartheta_t \geq Y_t - Y_{t2} \tag{21}$$

$$\vartheta_t \geq Y_{t2} - Y_t \tag{22}$$

Subsequently, the exponential function can be approximated as [45]

$$e^x \cong 1 + x + \frac{x^2}{2} + \frac{x^3}{6} + \frac{x^4}{24} \tag{23}$$

when $x \leq 1.97$.

As a result, the two NLP problems are replaced by the following easy-to-solve polynomial-programming (PP) problems [54]:

(PP Problem I)

$$\text{Min } Z_1 = \frac{1}{T}\sum_{t=1}^{T}\frac{\vartheta_t}{Y_t} \tag{24}$$

subject to

$$\vartheta_t \geq Y_t - Y_{t2} \tag{25}$$

$$\vartheta_t \geq Y_{t2} - Y_t \tag{26}$$

$$Y_{02} = Y_{t2} + \frac{b_2 Y_{t2}}{t} + \frac{b_2^2 Y_{t2}}{2t^2} + \frac{b_2^3 Y_{t2}}{6t^3} + \frac{b_2^4 Y_{t2}}{24t^4} \tag{27}$$

$$b_2 \geq 0 \tag{28}$$

$$0 \leq Y_{02} \leq 1 \tag{29}$$

(PP Problem II)

$$\text{Min } Z_2 = \frac{1}{T}\sum_{t=1}^{T}(Y_{t3} - Y_{t1}) \tag{30}$$

subject to

$$Y_{03} = Y_{t3} + \frac{b_1 Y_{t3}}{t} + \frac{b_1^2 Y_{t3}}{2t^2} + \frac{b_1^3 Y_{t3}}{6t^3} + \frac{b_1^4 Y_{t3}}{24t^4} \quad (31)$$

$$Y_{01} = Y_{t1} + \frac{b_3 Y_{t1}}{t} + \frac{b_3^2 Y_{t1}}{2t^2} + \frac{b_3^3 Y_{t1}}{6t^3} + \frac{b_3^4 Y_{t1}}{24t^4} \quad (32)$$

$$Y_t \geq Y_{t1} \quad (33)$$

$$Y_t \leq Y_{t3} \quad (34)$$

$$0 \leq b_1 \leq b_2^* \leq b_3 \quad (35)$$

$$0 \leq Y_{01} \leq Y_{02}^* \leq Y_{03} \leq 1 \quad (36)$$

Table 2 presents the comparison of the FPP method with existing methods for the same purpose. When the original value of yield is considered, only the two-stage fuzzy approach can minimize the forecasting error. In addition, most methods except the artificial-neural-network (ANN) [41] and two-stage fuzzy approaches require defuzzification.

Table 2. Comparison of FPP approach with existing methods for the same purpose.

Method	Type	Objective Functions	Characteristics
Guo and Tanaka [55]	Linear programming (LP)	• Minimization of sum of ranges	• Using symmetric fuzzy parameters • Considering logarithmic yield value
Donoso et al. [56]	Quadratic programming (QP)	• Minimization of the weighted sum of the squared deviations from cores and the squared deviations from the estimated ranges	• Considering logarithmic yield value
Chen [57]	LP	• Minimization of sum of ranges	• Using asymmetric fuzzy parameters • Considering logarithmic yield value
Chen and Lin [58]	Nonlinear programming (NLP)	• Minimization of high-order sum of ranges • Maximization of geometric mean of satisfaction levels	• Considering logarithmic yield value
Peters et al. [59]	LP	• Maximization of average satisfaction level	• Considering logarithmic yield value
Chen and Wang [60]	NLP	• Minimization of high-order sum of ranges • Maximization of geometric mean of satisfaction levels	• Using agents • Considering logarithmic yield value
Chen [61]	Artificial neural network (ANN)	• Minimization of sum of squared errors	• Considering log-sigmoid yield value
Proposed methodology	Polynomial programming (PP)	• Minimization of average range • Maximization of mean absolute percentage error (MAPE)	• Considering original yield value • Defuzzification not required

3.3. Estimating MEC Reduction

Some wafers in a wafer fab are scrapped due to poor quality. Therefore, the number of wafers that could be successfully completed is usually less than the number of wafers that are input into the wafer fab. For this reason, assuming that the monthly production target of a product is Q wafers per month, the number of raw wafers that need to be released into the wafer fab is

$$\tilde{N}_t = \left\lceil \frac{Q}{\tilde{Y}_t} \right\rceil \tag{37}$$

per month.

According to the statistics of historical data, it was assumed that the electricity consumption of each wafer used to fabricate the product is about E. Then, the MEC used to fabricate the product is

$$\begin{aligned} MEC &= E \cdot \tilde{N} \\ &= E \cdot \left\lceil \frac{Q}{\tilde{Y}_t} \right\rceil \\ &= E \cdot (\frac{Q}{\tilde{Y}_t} + \varepsilon_t) \\ &= \frac{EQ}{\tilde{Y}_0} e^{\frac{b}{t}} + E\varepsilon_t \end{aligned} \tag{38}$$

where ε_t is the residue when rounding up the result to the nearest integer; $0 \leq \varepsilon_t \leq 1$. Since Q is usually in the thousands, term $E\varepsilon_t$ is negligible, which leads to

$$MEC \cong \frac{EQ}{\tilde{Y}_0} e^{\frac{b}{t}} \tag{39}$$

This is also a learning process, where the asymptotic value is equal to $EQ/\tilde{Y}_0$ and the learning rate is equal to $\tilde{b}$.

From month t to month $t+1$, yield improves from $\tilde{Y}_t$ to $\tilde{Y}_{t+1}$, so MEC reduces by

$$\Delta MEC = \frac{EQ}{\tilde{Y}_t} (-) \frac{EQ}{\tilde{Y}_{t+1}}, \tag{40}$$

where $(-)$ indicates fuzzy subtraction. ΔMEC is approximated with a TFN as

$$\begin{aligned} \Delta MEC &\cong (\Delta MEC_1, \Delta MEC_2, \Delta MEC_3) \\ &= (\frac{EQ}{Y_{t3}} - \frac{EQ}{Y_{t+1,1}}, \frac{EQ}{Y_{t2}} - \frac{EQ}{Y_{t+1,2}}, \frac{EQ}{Y_{t1}} - \frac{EQ}{Y_{t+1,3}}) \\ &= (\frac{Y_{t+1,1} - Y_{t3}}{Y_{t3} Y_{t+1,1}}, \frac{Y_{t+1,2} - Y_{t2}}{Y_{t2} Y_{t+1,2}}, \frac{Y_{t+1,3} - Y_{t1}}{Y_{t1} Y_{t+1,3}}) EQ \end{aligned} \tag{41}$$

4. Actual Case

4.1. Background

The actual case of a DRAM product [62] was used to illustrate the two-stage fuzzy approach. Because the energy consumed by DRAMs in a large computer system accounts for a large part of the total energy consumption, DRAM has received much attention in energy-saving research [63]. The DRAM product was fabricated in an 8 inch wafer fab located in Hsinchu Scientific Park, Taiwan. There were more than 40 memory products fabricated in the wafer fab. All operators, engineers, and managers were committed to improving the efficiency of the operation and management of the wafer fab, including energy consumption. If the wafer fab was a static environment, then these efforts could reduce total energy consumption. However, the wafer fab was actually a dynamic environment because new products were continuously released into it. New products were usually related to low yields and poor operating efficiency. As a result, there was no significant trend to reduce the total energy consumption of the wafer fab, which was frustrating for the operators, engineers, and managers. It was also difficult to distinguish the energy consumption of old and new products. To solve this problem, the two-stage fuzzy approach was a viable option because it could estimate the energy savings by fabricating a single product.

In order to apply the two-stage fuzzy approach, the following tasks were completed:

(1) The electricity consumption of the wafer fab in the previous year was known.
(2) The number of wafers fabricated in previous years was known.
(3) The latest yield data of the target product were collected.

The actual case included 15 months of yield data, as shown in Table 3. The yield fluctuated greatly, which was caused by machine failures, operator misoperations, lack of experience in solving quality-related problems, unoptimized machine settings, etc. As a result, a crisp yield-learning model could not perfectly fit the collected yield data. As an alternative, many studies [41,42,57–60] used fuzzy-valued parameters to model the learning process of yield to generate fuzzy yield forecasts with ranges. Since there was only one factor (i.e., time) that affected the yield, and all data related to energy consumption were given, the analytical results in this study can be full replicated in another study.

Table 3. Practical case.

t	1	2	3	4	5	6	7	8	9	10	11	12	13	14	15
Y_t	0.789	0.892	0.915	0.87	0.879	0.887	0.892	0.892	0.904	0.939	0.928	0.896	0.883	0.939	0.911

4.2. Fitting the Uncertain Yield-Learning Process

Time-split cross-validation [64] was applied to evaluate forecasting performance as shown in Figure 3.

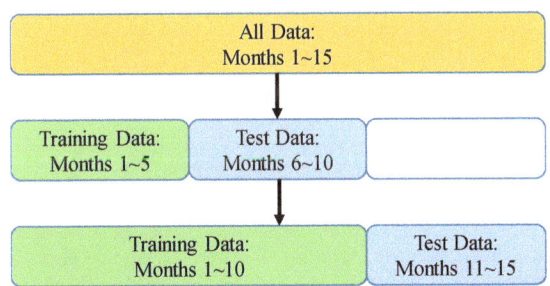

Figure 3. Time-split cross-validation.

When building the PP models using data from the first five months, the optimal solutions are as follows:

(Model PP I) $b_2^* = 0.131$, $Y_{02}^* = 0.948$
(Model PP II) $b_1^* = 0.131$, $b_3^* = 0.131$, $Y_{01}^* = 0.877$, $Y_{03}^* = 0.958$

Fuzzy yield forecasts are compared with actual values in Figure 4. The fitted fuzzy yield-learning model was applied to generate fuzzy yield forecasts for Months 6–10. Then, the forecasting precision was measured in terms of the average range, while the forecasting accuracy was evaluated in terms of mean absolute error (MAE), MAPE, and root mean squared error (RMSE):

$$\text{The average range} = \frac{\sum_{t=1}^{T} |Y_{t3} - Y_{t1}|}{T} \tag{42}$$

$$\text{MAE} = \frac{\sum_{t}^{T} |Y_t - Y_{t2}|}{T} \tag{43}$$

$$\text{MAPE} = \frac{\sum_{t}^{T} \frac{|Y_t - Y_{t2}|}{Y_{t2}}}{T} \cdot 100\% \tag{44}$$

$$\text{RMSE} = \sqrt{\frac{\sum_{t}^{T} (Y_t - Y_{t2})^2}{T}} \tag{45}$$

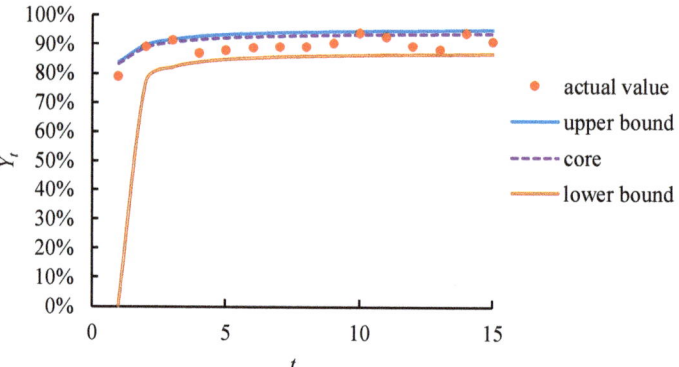

Figure 4. Comparing fuzzy yield forecasts to actual values.

Results are summarized below:

- Average range = 0.080;
- MAE = 0.019;
- MAPE = 2.08%;
- RMSE = 0.019.

Subsequently, the data of the first 10 months were used to construct the PP models to obtain the optimal solutions as

(Model PP I) $b_2^* = 0.101$, $Y_{02}^* = 0.946$
(Model PP II) $b_1^* = 0.101$, $b_3^* = 0.146$, $Y_{01}^* = 0.878$, $Y_{03}^* = 0.946$

Forecasting results are shown in Figure 5. The fitted fuzzy yield-learning model was applied to generate fuzzy yield forecasts for Months 11 to 15. Forecasting performance was evaluated as

- Average range = 0.070;
- MAE = 0.018;
- MAPE = 2.06%;
- RMSE = 0.021.

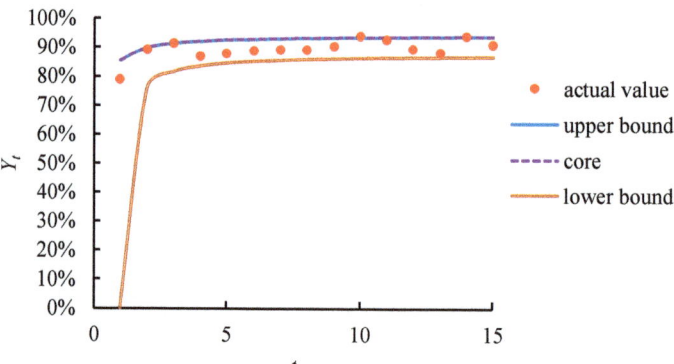

Figure 5. Forecasting results.

After time-split cross-validation, forecasting performance using the two-stage fuzzy approach was evaluated as

- Average range = 0.075;
- MAE = 0.019;
- MAPE = 2.07%;
- RMSE = 0.020.

4.3. Comparison

For comparison, six existing methods in this field, namely, the LP model of Guo and Tanaka [55], the QP model of Donoso et al. [56], the two NLP models of Chen and Lin [58], the QP model of Peters et al. [59], and the ANN approach proposed by Chen [61] were also applied to this case. The two NLP models of Chen and Lin [58] are represented by CL I and CL II. Table 4 summarizes the parameter settings in these methods. A fuzzy yield forecast was defuzzified using the center-of-gravity (COG) method [65,66]. Chen's ANN approach [61] directly compares the core of a fuzzy yield forecast with actual value, so defuzzification is not required. All methods were implemented using MATLAB 2017 on a PC with i7-7700 CPU 3.6 GHz and 8 GB RAM to ensure fair comparison. In addition, the value of the same parameter in various methods was set to the same value. The initial values of solutions (or parameters) in these methods were randomized.

Table 4. Parameter settings in existing methods.

Method	Parameter Setting
Guo and Tanaka [55]	$s = 0.3$, where s is the required satisfaction level.
Donoso et al. [56]	$w_1 = 0.5$ $w_2 = 0.5$ $s = 0.3$, where w_1 and w_2 are the weights of the two terms in the objective function, respectively; s is the required satisfaction level.
CL I [58]	$o = 2$ $s = 0.3$, where o is the order of the range of a fuzzy yield forecast; s is the required satisfaction level.
CL II [58]	$o = 2$ $m = 2$ $d = 0.2$, where o is the order of the range of a fuzzy yield forecast; m is the order of the satisfaction level; d is the required range.
Peters et al. [59]	$d = 0.2$, where d is the required range.
Chen [61]	$\eta = 0.2$ $\omega_1 = 0.7$ $\theta_2 = -0.051$, where η is the learning rate; ω_1 is the connection weight; θ_2 is the threshold on the output node.

Forecasting performance using various methods is compared in Table 5.

Compared with existing methods, the PP models achieved better forecasting performance by minimizing MAE, MAPE, RMSE, and average range, which laid a good foundation for subsequent electricity-consumption estimation. Their complexities and execution times are compared in Table 6.

Table 5. Forecasting performance using various methods.

Method	Average Range	MAE	MAPE	RMSE
Guo and Tanaka [55]	0.082	0.019	2.11%	0.021
Donoso et al. [56]	0.081	0.019	2.12%	0.021
CL I [58]	0.079	0.020	2.17%	0.022
CL II [58]	0.110	0.021	2.33%	0.025
Peters et al. [59]	0.110	0.021	2.33%	0.025
ANN [61]	0.139	0.019	2.10%	0.023
Two-stage fuzzy approach	0.075	0.019	2.07%	0.020

Table 6. Complexity and execution-time comparison results.

Method	Complexity	Computation Time (s)
Guo and Tanaka [55]	LP (global optimal)	<1
Donoso et al. [56]	QP (local optimal)	1
CL I [58]	NLP (local optimal)	2
CL II [58]	NLP (local optimal)	2
Peters et al. [59]	QP (local optimal)	1
ANN [61]	NLP (local optimal)	10
Two-stage fuzzy approach	PP (local optimal)	5

4.4. Estimating MEC Reduction

According to the historical statistics of the wafer fab, the electricity consumption to fabricate an 8 inch wafer was about 1.4 kW-h/cm^2 or 453.8 kW-h per wafer. This product accounted for approximately 60% of the wafer fab's capacity, which is equivalent to 12,000 wafers per month. On the basis of these statistics, MEC reduction due to yield learning was estimated according to Equation (40). The result is shown in Figure 6.

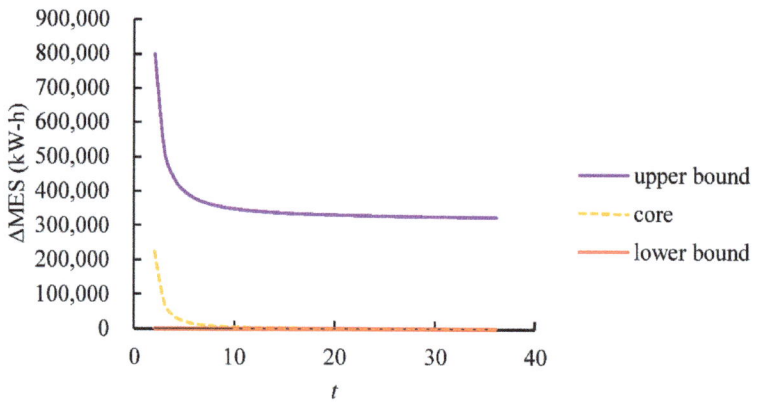

Figure 6. MEC reduction due to yield learning.

According to the experiment results:

(1) As far as yield learning is concerned, the amount of electricity that may be saved by reducing MEC may be as high as 400,000 kW-h per month.
(2) The increase in electricity consumption due to yield loss can be avoided, which means that the MEC reduction estimated in Figure 6 can be achieved.
(3) If yield is already very satisfactory (100%), on the other hand, unless other production conditions are changed, the consumed electricity for fabricating wafers cannot be saved [67,68].
(4) In addition, the reduction in MEC decreased with time, but converged to a certain minimal level.
(5) A larger learning constant means a faster yield-learning process, which can save energy waste owing to quicker yield loss. In this case, MEC drops faster, meaning that more energy can be saved within the planning horizon.
(6) Results here only apply to a single product. By taking into account all products in the wafer fab, it further saves power consumption.

5. Conclusions

There are different levels of green manufacturing. On a higher level of green manufacturing when a certain monthly output is produced, the consumed energy and generated waste should be as low as possible [69]. In low-level green manufacturing, the additional (and unnecessary) consumption of energy and additional (and unnecessary) waste should be avoided by eliminating yield loss, inefficiency, and other aspects [70]. This study estimated the energy-saving effect of the yield-learning process in a wafer fab. To this end, a two-stage fuzzy approach was proposed. In the first stage, an FPP method was proposed to fit the yield-learning process of a product to predict future yield. Subsequently, the relationship between MEC and yield was fit to estimate the energy saving brought by the increase in yield. In addition, there are other factors that affect product energy consumption, such as the type of wafer-fabrication equipment and product type. The same analysis could be performed to model their effects. This study is one of the first attempts to link improvement in product yield with the reduction in electricity consumption, and to quantify the long-term relationship by considering potential uncertainties.

Taking the actual case of a DRAM product as an example, the applicability of the two-stage fuzzy approach is illustrated. According to the experiment results:

(1) The two-stage fuzzy approach was very effective in fitting the yield-learning process of the DRAM product. Compared with existing methods for the same purpose, the FPP approach achieved higher forecasting accuracy in terms of MAE, MAPE, or RMSE.
(2) The two-stage fuzzy approach also established a very narrow range of yield. On the basis of precise and accurate yield forecasts, the energy saved by reducing MEC could be reliably estimated.
(3) Electricity consumption was reduced by fabricating the product in the wafer fab.

However, the focus of this research was to reduce the MEC of a single semiconductor product. There are usually many products in a wafer fab. The MEC reductions of all products need to be aggregated in some way. In addition, the two-stage fuzzy approach can be applied to a situation where the number of released wafers to fabricate a specific product types fluctuates. Further, other data-preprocessing mechanisms can be used, such as input-data analysis mechanisms [71] or outlier-filtering mechanisms [72], to improve the credibility of the input data, thereby enhancing the reliability of the two-stage fuzzy approach.

Author Contributions: All authors contributed equally to the writing of this paper. Data curation, methodology, and writing—original draft, H.-C.W., H.-R.T., and T.-C.T.C.; writing—review and editing, T.-C.T.C., H.-C.W., and K.-W.H. All authors have read and agreed to the published version of the manuscript.

Funding: This research received no external funding.

Institutional Review Board Statement: Not applicable.

Informed Consent Statement: Not applicable.

Conflicts of Interest: The authors declare that there is no conflict of interest regarding the publication of this article.

Appendix A

Table A1. Nomenclature.

Variable/Symbol	Meaning
$(\times)$	Fuzzy multiplication
ε_t	Residue
ϑ_t	Dummy variable
b or $\tilde{b}$	Learning constant
E	Electricity consumption per wafer
MAE	Mean absolute error
$MAPE$	Mean absolute percentage error
MEC	Monthly electricity consumption
ΔMEC	Reduction in MEC
$\tilde{N}_t$	Number of raw wafers that need to be released during period t
Q	Monthly output
$r(t)$	Homoscedastic serially uncorrelated error term
$RMSE$	Root mean squared error
t	Period
T	Planning horizon
Y_0 or $\tilde{Y}_0$	Asymptotic/final yield
Y_t or $\tilde{Y}_t$	Yield at period t

References

1. Gandhi, N.S.; Thanki, S.J.; Thakkar, J.J. Ranking of drivers for integrated lean-green manufacturing for Indian manufacturing SMEs. *J. Clean. Prod.* **2018**, *171*, 675–689. [CrossRef]
2. Chen, T. Competitive and sustainable manufacturing in the age of globalization. *Sustainability* **2017**, *9*, 26. [CrossRef]
3. Lin, C.W.; Chen, T. 3D printing technologies for enhancing the sustainability of an aircraft manufacturing or MRO company—A multi-expert partial consensus-FAHP analysis. *Int. J. Adv. Manuf. Technol.* **2019**, *105*, 4171–4180. [CrossRef]
4. Yin, S.; Zhang, N.; Li, B. Enhancing the competitiveness of multi-agent cooperation for green manufacturing in China: An empirical study of the measure of green technology innovation capabilities and their influencing factors. *Sustain. Prod. Consum.* **2020**, *23*, 63–76. [CrossRef]
5. Chen, T.; Wang, L.C.; Chiu, M.C. A multi-granularity approach for estimating the sustainability of a factory simulation model: Semiconductor packaging as an example. *Oper. Res.* **2018**, *18*, 711–729. [CrossRef]
6. Wang, Y.C.; Chen, T. Modelling and optimization of machining conditions for the multi-pass dry turning process. *Proc. Inst. Mech. Eng. Part. B J. Eng. Manuf.* **2008**, *222*, 1387–1394. [CrossRef]
7. Chen, T. Strengthening the competitiveness and sustainability of a semiconductor manufacturer with cloud manufacturing. *Sustainability* **2014**, *6*, 251–266. [CrossRef]
8. Abualfaraa, W.; Salonitis, K.; Al-Ashaab, A.; Ala'raj, M. Lean-green manufacturing practices and their link with sustainability: A critical review. *Sustainability* **2020**, *12*, 981. [CrossRef]
9. Chen, T.; Wang, Y.C. Long-term load forecasting by a collaborative fuzzy-neural approach. *Int. J. Electr. Power Energy Syst.* **2012**, *43*, 454–464. [CrossRef]
10. Abraham, M.; Nguyen, N. Green engineering: Defining principles—results from the Sandestin conference. *Environ. Prog.* **2004**, *22*, 233–236. [CrossRef]

11. Ershadi, H.; Karimipour, A. Present a multi-criteria modeling and optimization (energy, economic and environmental) approach of industrial combined cooling heating and power (CCHP) generation systems using the genetic algorithm, case study: A tile factory. *Energy* **2018**, *149*, 286–295. [CrossRef]
12. Chen, T. Forecasting the long-term electricity demand in Taiwan with a hybrid FLR and BPN approach. *Int. J. Fuzzy Syst.* **2012**, *14*, 361–371.
13. Sonntag, D.; Kiesmüller, G.P. Disposal versus rework–Inventory control in a production system with random yield. *Eur. J. Oper. Res.* **2018**, *267*, 138–149. [CrossRef]
14. Wang, Y.C.; Chen, T.; Lin, Y.C. A collaborative and ubiquitous system for fabricating dental parts using 3D printing technologies. *Healthcare* **2019**, *7*, 103. [CrossRef]
15. Hu, S.C.; Xu, T.; Chaung, T.; Chan, D.Y.L. Characterization of energy use in 300 mm DRAM (Dynamic Random Access Memory) wafer fabrication plants (fabs) in Taiwan. *Energy* **2010**, *35*, 3788–3792. [CrossRef]
16. Ge, L.; Wang, S.; Jiang, X. A combined interval AHP-entropy method for power user evaluation in Smart Electrical Utilization Systems. In Proceedings of the 2016 IEEE Power and Energy Society General Meeting, Boston, MA, USA, 17–21 July 2016; pp. 1–5.
17. Lakić, E.; Gubian, A.; Fournely, C.; Djokić, S. Introducing system utilization index for energy efficiency evaluation and labelling. In Proceedings of the 2019 16th International Conference on the European Energy Market, Ljubljana, Slovenia, 18–20 September 2019; pp. 1–6.
18. Kumar, N.; Kennedy, K.; Gildersleeve, K.; Abelson, R.; Mastrangelo, C.M.; Montgomery, D.C. A review of yield modelling techniques for semiconductor manufacturing. *Int. J. Prod. Res.* **2006**, *44*, 5019–5036. [CrossRef]
19. Wang, Y.C.; Chen, T. A fuzzy collaborative forecasting approach for forecasting the productivity of a factory. *Adv. Mech. Eng.* **2013**, *5*, 234571. [CrossRef]
20. Chang, C.K.; Hu, S.C.; Liu, V.; Chan, D.Y.L.; Huang, C.Y.; Weng, L.C. Specific energy consumption of dynamic random access memory module supply chain in Taiwan. *Energy* **2012**, *41*, 508–513. [CrossRef]
21. Gong, X.; Van der Wee, M.; De Pessemier, T.; Verbrugge, S.; Colle, D.; Martens, L.; Joseph, W. Integrating labor awareness to energy-efficient production scheduling under real-time electricity pricing: An empirical study. *J. Clean. Prod.* **2017**, *168*, 239–253. [CrossRef]
22. Jo, M.S.; Shin, J.H.; Kim, W.J.; Jeong, J.W. Energy-saving benefits of adiabatic humidification in the air conditioning systems of semiconductor cleanrooms. *Energies* **2017**, *10*, 1774. [CrossRef]
23. Golpîra, H.; Khan, S.A.R.; Zhang, Y. Robust smart energy efficient production planning for a general job-shop manufacturing system under combined demand and supply uncertainty in the presence of grid-connected microgrid. *J. Clean. Prod.* **2018**, *202*, 649–665. [CrossRef]
24. Wu, H.C.; Chen, T.C.T. Quality control issues in 3D-printing manufacturing: A review. *Rapid Prototyp. J.* **2018**, *24*, 607–614. [CrossRef]
25. Dai, M.; Tang, D.; Giret, A.; Salido, M.A. Multi-objective optimization for energy-efficient flexible job shop scheduling problem with transportation constraints. *Robot. Comput. Integr. Manuf.* **2019**, *59*, 143–157. [CrossRef]
26. Liang, J.; Wang, Y.; Zhang, Z.H.; Sun, Y. Energy efficient production planning and scheduling problem with processing technology selection. *Comput. Ind. Eng.* **2019**, *132*, 260–270. [CrossRef]
27. Gao, K.; Huang, Y.; Sadollah, A.; Wang, L. A review of energy-efficient scheduling in intelligent production systems. *Complex. Intell. Syst.* **2020**, *6*, 237–249. [CrossRef]
28. Golpîra, H. Smart energy-aware manufacturing plant scheduling under uncertainty: A risk-based multi-objective robust optimization approach. *Energy* **2020**, *209*, 118385. [CrossRef]
29. Wang, S.; Wang, X.; Chu, F.; Yu, J. An energy-efficient two-stage hybrid flow shop scheduling problem in a glass production. *Int. J. Prod. Res.* **2020**, *58*, 2283–2314. [CrossRef]
30. Chang, K.H.; Sun, Y.J.; Lai, C.A.; Chen, L.D.; Wang, C.H.; Chen, C.J.; Lin, C.M. Big data analytics energy-saving strategies for air compressors in the semiconductor industry—An empirical study. *Int. J. Prod. Res.* **2021**, 1–13. [CrossRef]
31. Wang, Y.C.; Chiu, M.C.; Chen, T. A fuzzy nonlinear programming approach for planning the energy-efficient manufacturing of a wafer fab. *Appl. Soft Comput.* **2020**, *95*, 106506. [CrossRef]
32. Kumar, R.; Mishra, J.S.; Mondal, S.; Meena, R.S.; Sundaram, P.K.; Bhatt, B.P.; Lal, R.; Saurabh, K.; Chandra, N.; Samal, S.K.; et al. Designing an ecofriendly and carbon-cum-energy efficient production system for the diverse agroecosystem of South Asia. *Energy* **2021**, *214*, 118860. [CrossRef]
33. Mandelman, J.A.; Dennard, R.H.; Bronner, G.B.; DeBrosse, J.K.; Divakaruni, R.; Li, Y.; Radens, C.J. Challenges and future directions for the scaling of dynamic random-access memory (DRAM). *IBM J. Res. Dev.* **2002**, *46*, 187–212. [CrossRef]
34. Wang, Y.C.; Chen, T.; Lin, C.W. A slack-diversifying nonlinear fluctuation smoothing rule for job dispatching in a wafer fabrication factory. *Robot. Comput. Integr. Manuf.* **2013**, *29*, 41–47. [CrossRef]
35. Murphy, C.F.; Kenig, G.A.; Allen, D.T.; Laurent, J.P.; Dyer, D.E. Development of parametric material, energy, and emission inventories for wafer fabrication in the semiconductor industry. *Environ. Sci. Technol.* **2003**, *37*, 5373–5382. [CrossRef] [PubMed]
36. Pan, S.Y.; Snyder, S.W.; Ma, H.W.; Lin, Y.J.; Chiang, P.C. Energy-efficient resin wafer electrodeionization for impaired water reclamation. *J. Clean. Prod.* **2018**, *174*, 1464–1474. [CrossRef]
37. Zhang, H.; Jiang, Z.; Guo, C. Simulation-based optimization of dispatching rules for semiconductor wafer fabrication system scheduling by the response surface methodology. *Int. J. Adv. Manuf. Technol.* **2009**, *41*, 110–121. [CrossRef]

38. Chen, T.; Rajendran, C.; Wu, C.W. Advanced dispatching rules for large-scale manufacturing systems. *Int. J. Adv. Manuf. Technol.* **2013**, *67*, 1–3. [CrossRef]
39. Xie, M.; Ruan, J.; Bai, W.; Qiao, Q.; Bai, L.; Zhang, J.; Li, H.; Lv, F.; Fu, H. Pollutant payback time and environmental impact of Chinese multi-crystalline photovoltaic production based on life cycle assessment. *J. Clean. Prod.* **2018**, *184*, 648–659. [CrossRef]
40. Maki, S.; Ashina, S.; Fujii, M.; Fujita, T.; Yabe, N.; Uchida, K.; Ginting, G.; Boer, R.; Chandran, R. Employing electricity-consumption monitoring systems and integrative time-series analysis models: A case study in Bogor, Indonesia. *Front. Energy* **2018**, *12*, 426–439. [CrossRef]
41. Chen, T.C.T.; Lin, C.W. An innovative yield learning model considering multiple learning sources and learning source interactions. *Comput. Ind. Eng.* **2019**, *131*, 455–463. [CrossRef]
42. Nakata, K.; Orihara, R.; Mizuoka, Y.; Takagi, K. A comprehensive big-data-based monitoring system for yield enhancement in semiconductor manufacturing. *IEEE Trans. Semicond. Manuf.* **2017**, *30*, 339–344. [CrossRef]
43. Chiu, M.-C.; Chen, T.; Hsu, K.-W. Modeling an uncertain productivity learning process using an interval fuzzy methodology. *Mathematics* **2020**, *8*, 998. [CrossRef]
44. Chen, T.; Chiu, M.C. An interval fuzzy number-based fuzzy collaborative forecasting approach for DRAM yield forecasting. *Complex. Intell. Syst.* **2021**, *7*, 111–122. [CrossRef]
45. Wang, Y.C.; Chen, T.C.T. A direct-solution fuzzy collaborative intelligence approach for yield forecasting in semiconductor manufacturing. *Procedia Manuf.* **2018**, *17*, 110–117. [CrossRef]
46. Klir, G.J.; Yuan, B. *Fuzzy Sets and Fuzzy Logic: Theory and Applications*; Prentice-Hall Inc.: Hoboken, NJ, USA, 2006.
47. Wang, J.; Ding, D.; Liu, O.; Li, M. A synthetic method for knowledge management performance evaluation based on triangular fuzzy number and group support systems. *Appl. Soft Comput.* **2016**, *39*, 11–20. [CrossRef]
48. Chakraborty, D.; Jana, D.K.; Roy, T.K. A new approach to solve fully fuzzy transportation problem using triangular fuzzy number. *Int. J. Oper. Res.* **2016**, *26*, 153–179. [CrossRef]
49. Zhang, F.; Chen, B. Risk assessment for substation operation based on triangular fuzzy number AHP and cloud model. In Proceedings of the 2018 IEEE/PES Transmission and Distribution Conference and Exposition, Denver, CO, USA, 16–19 April 2018; pp. 1–5.
50. Wang, H.; Lu, X.; Du, Y.; Zhang, C.; Sadiq, R.; Deng, Y. Fault tree analysis based on TOPSIS and triangular fuzzy number. *Int. J. Syst. Assur. Eng. Manag.* **2017**, *8*, 2064–2070. [CrossRef]
51. Irvanizam, I.; Syahrini, I.; Afidh, R.P.F.; Andika, M.R.; Sofyan, H. Applying fuzzy multiple-attribute decision making based on set-pair analysis with triangular fuzzy number for decent homes distribution problem. In Proceedings of the 2018 6th International Conference on Cyber and IT Service Management, Parapat, Indonesia, 7–9 August 2018; pp. 1–7.
52. Lin, Y.C.; Chen, T. A biobjective fuzzy integer-nonlinear programming approach for creating an intelligent location-aware service. *J. Appl. Math.* **2013**, *2013*, 423415. [CrossRef]
53. Tsai, H.R.; Chen, T. A fuzzy nonlinear programming approach for optimizing the performance of a four-objective fluctuation smoothing rule in a wafer fabrication factory. *J. Appl. Math.* **2013**, *2013*, 720607. [CrossRef]
54. Dua, V. Mixed integer polynomial programming. *Comput. Chem. Eng.* **2015**, *72*, 387–394. [CrossRef]
55. Guo, P.; Tanaka, H. Dual models for possibilistic regression analysis. *Comput. Stat. Data Anal.* **2006**, *51*, 253–266. [CrossRef]
56. Donoso, S.; Marin, N.; Vila, M.A. Quadratic programming models for fuzzy regression. In Proceedings of the International Conference on Mathematical and Statistical Modeling in Honor of Enrique Castillo, University of Castilla La Mancha, Ciudad Real, Spain, 28–30 June 2006; pp. 1–12.
57. Chen, T. A fuzzy logic approach for incorporating the effects of managerial actions on semiconductor yield learning. *Int. Conf. Mach. Learn. Cybern.* **2007**, *4*, 1979–1984.
58. Chen, T.; Lin, Y.C. A fuzzy-neural system incorporating unequally important expert opinions for semiconductor yield forecasting. *Int. J. Uncertain. Fuzziness Knowl. Based Syst.* **2008**, *16*, 35–58. [CrossRef]
59. Peters, G.; Crespo, F.; Lingras, P.; Weber, R. Soft clustering–fuzzy and rough approaches and their extensions and derivatives. *Int. J. Approx. Reason.* **2013**, *54*, 307–322. [CrossRef]
60. Chen, T.; Wang, Y.C. An agent-based fuzzy collaborative intelligence approach for precise and accurate semiconductor yield forecasting. *IEEE Trans. Fuzzy Syst.* **2013**, *22*, 201–211. [CrossRef]
61. Chen, T. A heterogeneous fuzzy collaborative intelligence approach for forecasting product yield. *Appl. Soft Comput.* **2017**, *57*, 210–224. [CrossRef]
62. Chen, T. Forecasting the yield of a semiconductor product with a collaborative intelligence approach. *Appl. Soft Comput.* **2013**, *13*, 1552–1560. [CrossRef]
63. Vogelsang, T. Understanding the energy consumption of dynamic random access memories. In Proceedings of the Annual IEEE/ACM International Symposium on Microarchitecture, Atlanta, GA, USA, 4–8 December 2010; pp. 363–374.
64. Sheridan, R.P. Time-split cross-validation as a method for estimating the goodness of prospective prediction. *J. Chem. Inf. Model.* **2013**, *53*, 783–790. [CrossRef]
65. Van Broekhoven, E.; De Baets, B. Fast and accurate center of gravity defuzzification of fuzzy system outputs defined on trapezoidal fuzzy partitions. *Fuzzy Sets Syst.* **2006**, *157*, 904–918. [CrossRef]
66. Huang, D.; Chen, T.; Wang, M.J.J. A fuzzy set approach for event tree analysis. *Fuzzy Sets Syst.* **2001**, *118*, 153–165. [CrossRef]

57. Endo, M.; Nakajima, H.; Hata, Y. Simplified factory energy management system based on operational condition estimation by sensor data. In Proceedings of the IEEE International Conference on Automation Science and Engineering, Seoul, Korea, 20–24 August 2012; pp. 14–19.
58. Makita, H.; Shida, Y.; Nozue, N. Factory energy management system using production information. *Mitsubishi Electr. Adv.* **2012**, *140*, 7–11.
59. Haapala, K.R.; Khadke, K.N.; Sutherland, J.W. Predicting manufacturing waste and energy for sustainable product development via WE-FAB software. In Proceedings of the Global Conference on Sustainable Product Development and Life Cycle Engineering, Berlin, Germany, 29 September 2004; pp. 243–250.
70. Panno, D.; Messineo, A.; Dispenza, A. Cogeneration plant in a pasta factory: Energy saving and environmental benefit. *Energy* **2007**, *32*, 746–754. [CrossRef]
71. Singh, P.K. Granular-based decomposition of complex fuzzy context and its analysis. *Prog. Artif. Intell.* **2019**, *8*, 181–193. [CrossRef]
72. Lazhar, F. Fuzzy clustering-based semi-supervised approach for outlier detection in big text data. *Prog. Artif. Intell.* **2019**, *8*, 123–132. [CrossRef]

Article

Employing Fuzzy Logic to Analyze the Structure of Complex Biological and Epidemic Spreading Models

Nickie Lefevr [1], Andreas Kanavos [1,*], Vassilis C. Gerogiannis [2,*], Lazaros Iliadis [3] and Panagiotis Pintelas [4]

1. Computer Engineering and Informatics Department, University of Patras, 26504 Patras, Greece; nick.lefevr@gmail.com
2. Department of Digital Systems, Geopolis Campus, University of Thessaly, 41500 Larissa, Greece
3. Department of Civil Engineering, School of Engineering, Democritus University of Thrace, 67100 Xanthi, Greece; liliadis@civil.duth.gr
4. Department of Mathematics, University of Patras, 26500 Patras, Greece; ppintelas@gmail.com
* Correspondence: kanavos@ceid.upatras.gr (A.K.); vgerogian@uth.gr (V.C.G.)

Citation: Lefevr, N.; Kanavos, A.; Gerogiannis, V.C.; Iliadis, L.; Pintelas, P. Employing Fuzzy Logic to Analyze the Structure of Complex Biological and Epidemic Spreading Models. *Mathematics* **2021**, *9*, 977. https://doi.org/10.3390/math9090977

Academic Editor: Daniel Gómez Gonzalez

Received: 30 March 2021
Accepted: 25 April 2021
Published: 27 April 2021

Publisher's Note: MDPI stays neutral with regard to jurisdictional claims in published maps and institutional affiliations.

Copyright: © 2021 by the authors. Licensee MDPI, Basel, Switzerland. This article is an open access article distributed under the terms and conditions of the Creative Commons Attribution (CC BY) license (https://creativecommons.org/licenses/by/4.0/).

Abstract: Complex networks constitute a new field of scientific research that is derived from the observation and analysis of real-world networks, for example, biological, computer and social ones. An important subset of complex networks is the biological, which deals with the numerical examination of connections/associations among different nodes, namely interfaces. These interfaces are evolutionary and physiological, where network epidemic models or even neural networks can be considered as representative examples. The investigation of the corresponding biological networks along with the study of human diseases has resulted in an examination of networks regarding medical supplies. This examination aims at a more profound understanding of concrete networks. Fuzzy logic is considered one of the most powerful mathematical tools for dealing with imprecision, uncertainties and partial truth. It was developed to consider partial truth values, between completely true and completely false, and aims to provide robust and low-cost solutions to real-world problems. In this manuscript, we introduce a fuzzy implementation of epidemic models regarding the Human Immunodeficiency Virus (HIV) spreading in a sample of needle drug individuals. Various fuzzy scenarios for a different number of users and different number of HIV test samples per year are analyzed in order for the samples used in the experiments to vary from case to case. To the best of our knowledge, analyzing HIV spreading with fuzzy-based simulation scenarios is a research topic that has not been particularly investigated in the literature. The simulation results of the considered scenarios demonstrate that the existence of fuzziness plays an important role in the model setup process as well as in analyzing the effects of the disease spread.

Keywords: fuzzy models; complex networks; biological networks; neural networks; epidemic models; Acquired Immunodeficiency Syndrome (AIDS); Human Immunodeficiency Virus (HIV)

1. Introduction

Graphs are appropriate mathematical structures to represent and analyze complex networks, and graph theory is a field in mathematics that deals with the study of graphs [1]. Graph theory supports the visualization and analysis of complex network structures. The World Wide Web (WWW) and the human brain, as it is studied in medical informatics, are representative examples of complex networks [2]. The graph representation and analysis of complex networks have been extended in numerous areas, such as biology, computer science, epidemiology, mathematics, physics, sociology and telecommunications [3]. In terms of the human brain, a graph structure represents a network of connected nerve cells, where corresponding cells can make up on their own a network and their task is to cause and create biochemical reactions [4]. Complex networks, represented as graphs, allow researchers to analyze their structural and behavioral properties. The comprehensive knowledge of a complex network structure may contribute to the extraction of valuable information with the aim of further assessing and enhancing methodologies, tools, as well as the outcomes of shaped examinations. All of these reasons contribute to the motivation of the present work, which deals with analyzing the problem of HIV spreading in a sample of needle drug individuals.

In the relevant literature, the epidemic spreading problem has attracted high attention towards the awareness of the dynamic procedures that are generated in corresponding complex networks [5]. The authors of [6] review and present various solved and open problems in the development, analysis, and control of complex epidemic models. Moreover, a detailed review of the extensive research that has been conducted on epidemic procedures is presented in [7]. Another representative research in the same area is presented in [8], where the authors study infections spreading in complex heterogeneous networks based on a Systemic Inflammatory Response Syndrome (SIRS) epidemic model with birth and death rates. The SIRS epidemic model is utilized in clustered networks with the aim of analyzing the impact of the network community structure on the epidemic spreading and dynamics. Besides human epidemic spreading, an additional issue studied with the use of complex network models is related to the impact of different types of animal movements regarding the conditions for the spread of an infectious disease [9].

In a relevant survey [10], the authors review and unify theoretical methods regarding epidemic spreading, in terms of escalating the complexity of the equations used by various methods. In this survey, the authors analyze various methods, including the mean-field approach and various variations of the mean-field approach, such as the heterogeneous mean-field and the quench mean-field. Moreover, the authors examine methods that involve pairwise approximation, link percolation and dynamic message-passing. The authors of [11] introduce effective algorithms for implementing complex networks, which have concrete statistical properties that are non-homogeneous. The authors also suggest a pseudo-code for reproducing complex directed or undirected networks by performing simulations of human brain functions. Regarding sexually transmitted diseases, such as AIDS, the work presented in [12] focuses on the early transmission, the following dissemination, and finally, the establishment of the HIV-1 virus in a human population. The authors claim that the outcomes of their evolutionary analyses are capable of rebuilding the initial dynamics of the HIV-1 virus and, as a result, draw attention to the role of social changes and transport networks within the establishment of this virus in a human population.

Nowadays, within the field of biosciences, a number of levels regarding imprecision and uncertainty, particularly in epidemiological studies, are involved in disease diagnosis [13]. A single disease could affect numerous patients in various ways, and a single symptom may be indicative of various diseases. More importantly, the occurrence of some diseases in a patient may disrupt the expected symptom pattern of any of them. As a result, this may cause a tremendous amount of uncertainty and imprecision towards the interpretation of impact measures. Fuzzy set theory, since its beginning in 1965 [14] as an abstraction of dual rationale and/or classical set theory, has progressed to an effective scientific theory [15]. It contributes a strict scientific (or specifically mathematical) framework in which unclear conceptual phenomena can be absolutely and thoroughly considered [14,16]. Specifically, fuzzy set theory can also be viewed as a modeling language, which is efficient for circumstances where fuzzy criteria and imprecise phenomena are taken into consideration.

In the current work, we analyze the structure and advancement of complex networks by means of an extensive study regarding graph theory by presenting their fundamental types (initially presented in [17]). Concretely, an epidemic model, which is based on fuzzy logic and is expected to set up a relation among the viral load as well as the clinical evolution to Acquired Immunodeficiency Syndrome (AIDS) in HIV contaminated users, is proposed. It is worth mentioning that HIV can be transmitted in different ways, although sexual intercourse is considered the most common and widespread. Nevertheless, HIV can also be transmitted through blood transfusions, through HIV-infected women who transmit the virus to their babies before or during birth, or even later through breastfeeding.

However, in the present study, a special way of transmitting the virus is used, that is, with use of syringes that drug users inject. The proposed model is based on the Erdös–Renyi model and simulates the spread of HIV in an isolated human population. Furthermore, we tried to incorporate the basic principles of random graphs in order to favor certain types of graphs. Although this paper focuses on the context of epidemics, the same model can be directly applied to many different spreading processes in complex networks.

The remainder of the work is structured in the following way: In Section 2, basic preliminaries, complex networks models and epidemic models are introduced. In Section 3, we discuss issues related to fuzzy epidemics, while Section 4 introduces the datasets for validating our framework. Additionally, Section 5 overlooks the experiments that were conducted in order to evaluate our work and claim our findings along with the results assembled. Section 6 concludes the work by focusing on conclusions and considers aspects related to future work. Finally, the notation of this work is summarized in Table 1.

Table 1. Basic notation.

Symbol	Meaning
k	Node's Degree
p_k	Degree Distribution
L	Average Shortest Path Length
b	Betweenness Node
T	Transitivity
C	Clustering Coefficient
c_i	Local Clustering Coefficient of Node i
r	Probability Distribution Function related to Fuzzy Logic Setting
$\mathbb{U}$	Universe of Discourse
F	Fuzzy Set
u	Support Value
$\mu_F(u)$	Membership Function
x	Linguistic Variable
$T(x)$	The Set of Names of x
$M(x)$	Semantic Rule

2. Theoretical Framework

This section presents the basic preliminaries of current work along with an introduction to complex network models and epidemic models that are considered in biological networks.

2.1. Basic Definitions

A graph G presents the connections/associations among the data of a system, which comprises nodes N as well as edges E. Concretely, a graph comprises a collection of data objects, entitled *nodes*. A number of these items are related with links named *edges* [18,19]. Specifically, in the event that the edges are considered towards one direction, then at that point, the graph is regarded as a directed graph [20]; otherwise, the graph is regarded as an *undirected* graph. An undirected graph is a complete graph where all nodes are interconnected in pairs [18].

In numerous applications, each graph is assigned with a related numeric value, entitled *weight*. In this particular case, the edges constitute non-negative integers, and as a result, the graph can be regarded as a weighted graph. In order for the definitions to be correlated, this graph can be directed or undirected while the edge's weight is regularly alluded to as the "cost" of an edge.

In addition, a *path* constitutes a coherence of nodes, which keep the status of each consecutive pair (V_i, V_{i+1}), i.e., a graph's edge. Except for the inclusion of the corresponding nodes, the path involves the coherence of edges that associate these nodes. In a number of cases, paths with repeated nodes can also be considered; however, in most cases, paths with non-repeated nodes are preferred. Specifically, in cases where a non-simple path traverses a particular node, this fact is emphasized as it is referred to as a normal non-simple path [18].

An important aspect that can be derived from graph structure concerns the type of the graph edges; if it is known, a diversity of valuable metrics that depict the graph's characteristics in a more detailed way can be computed. Specifically, the notion of *centrality* is utilized to identify the specific graph nodes that are considered critical [21]. There are a number of possible ways for defining the importance of a node, but the simplest measure of centrality in a network is to observe the number of edges that are associated with each vertex-node. This specific definition is referred to as the *degree centrality*.

In more detail, the node's degree i in an undirected graph consisting of N nodes is denoted by k_i; assuming an adjacency matrix, this degree can be considered as the sum of the ith row of the adjacency matrix [20], as presented in the following Equation (1):

$$k_i = \sum_{j=1}^{N} A_{ij} \qquad (1)$$

In network topology, three measures are considered as the most robust; namely, the degree distribution, the average path length and the clustering coefficient, which will be presented in the following paragraphs. Initially, one of the major properties in terms of a graph is the *degree distribution*, as discussed in [2]. The amount of nodes of the corresponding network maintaining a degree with a number equal to k is indicated with p_k and is presented in Equation (2). The overall fraction of these values p_k produces the degree distribution with the aim of plotting this distribution of a specific network as a function of degree k as follows:

$$p_k = \frac{\text{number of nodes with degree k}}{n} \qquad (2)$$

Another feature that plays a vital part in terms of the graph's dissemination, as well as transmission, is the *shortest path*. The shortest paths are of great importance in characterizing the internal structure of the graph [19]. Thus, the majority of length values of the shortest paths of a given graph G needs to be provided so that when considering a corresponding table A, the input a_{ij} can be associated with its length between nodes i and j. An important aspect of the graph is its *diameter*, which is defined as the maximum value of a_{ij}.

A representative partition among a number of nodes in a concrete graph is identified with the use of the average length of the shortest paths, which is typically introduced as the typical path length. The average path length is considered a concept in network topology that is defined as the average number of steps along the shortest paths for all possible pairs of network nodes. It is a measure of the efficiency of information or mass transport on a network. As an example, one can consider the average number of clicks that will lead you from one website to another. It should not be confused with the diameter of the network, which is defined as the longest geodesic, i.e., the longest shortest path between any two nodes in the network. The average shortest path length L is characterized as the average of the geodetic lengths over all pairs of nodes as presented in Equation (3):

$$L = \frac{\sum_{i,j \in N} d_{ij}}{\sum_{i,j \in N} p_{ij}} \qquad (3)$$

where d_{ij} denotes the shortest distance between nodes i and j; if $i = j$ or j cannot be reached from i then $d_{ij} = 0$. In addition, p_{ij} denotes if there is a path between nodes i and j; if $i = j$ or if there is no path from i to j then $p_{ij} = 0$ and if there is a path from i to j then $p_{ij} = 1$. The value of the all-pairs shortest-path length of a particular graph is denoted by $\sum_{i,j \in N} d_{ij}$, whereas $\sum_{i,j \in N} p_{ij}$ constitutes the number of paths that exist in this graph. For a connected undirected graph, $\sum_{i,j \in N} p_{ij} = N(N-1)$ because paths exist between any pair of nodes [22].

The communication between two non-adjacent nodes depends on the other nodes that belong to each path and connect them. Consequently, we can obtain whether a given node can communicate with a non-neighboring one by measuring the geodetic number, also known as a *betweenness* node.

More importantly, a betweenness node b_i of a node i, often typically referred as load, is computed from the following Equation (4):

$$b_i = \sum_{j,k \in N, j \neq k} \frac{n_{jk}(i)}{n_{jk}} \quad (4)$$

where n_{jk} constitutes the number of the paths that connect faster node j with node k, whereas $n_{jk}(i)$ is the number of paths that connect the same nodes with the detailed information traversing through node i via the shortest path [23].

Furthermore, betweenness is considered as a metric that can be further expanded so as to be applied to the graph's edges. In this case, the definition is slightly alternated, and thus, the *edge betweenness* constitutes the quantity of shortest paths among the pairs of nodes traversing the corresponding edge [24].

The method of clustering, which is as well declared as *transitivity*, constitutes a representative feature of contact networks. As contact networks, one can consider the example of two people having a mutual friend [19]. This may be evaluated by determining the clustering T of a graph as a respective quantity of triplets; namely, the fraction of the three connected triads as in Equation (5) [2]. The factor 3 in the numerator accounts for the aspect that each triangle, consisting of three nodes, is actually contributing three times, which is the connected triads, and guarantees that $0 \leq T \leq 1$, with $T = 1$.

$$T = \frac{3 \times \text{number of triangles in G}}{\text{number of connected triples of vertices in G}} \quad (5)$$

Another option that can be regarded as a factor is the utilization of the *clustering coefficient C* of the corresponding graph [25]. That is, given a concrete node i, this metric is equal to the quantity c_i, which is the local clustering coefficient. This quantity expresses the probability of a_{jm} to become equal to 1 for two connected nodes to node i, namely j and m. More importantly, the definition of the *local clustering coefficient* can be estimated as the fraction among the quantity of edges e_i and the maximum feasible number of edges $\frac{k_i(k_i-1)}{2}$ in one graph, as follows in Equation (6) [26]:

$$c_i = \frac{2e_i}{k_i(k_i-1)} = \frac{\sum_{j,m} a_{ij} a_{jm} a_{mi}}{k_i(k_i-1)} \quad (6)$$

In the following, the clustering coefficient of the graph can be computed as the average of value c_i for the entire number of nodes of the graph, as in Equation (7). By default, $0 \leq c_i \leq 1$, as well as $0 \leq C \leq 1$.

$$C = \langle c \rangle = \frac{1}{N} \sum_{i \in N} c_i \quad (7)$$

2.2. Models of Complex Networks

The structure and the characteristics of complex networks can be analyzed and understood by rigorously examining their corresponding modeling. Specifically, some major issues associated with the analysis and prediction of process behavior in the following simulation are found in the information retrieval, propagation and transmission.

2.2.1. Erdös–Renyi Model

The Erdös–Renyi [27] model is considered among the initial network models with the characteristic that it corresponds to the random graph. Concretely, regarding the model of a random graph, two major aspects of the nodes are represented, namely their quantity as well as the probability that two arbitrarily selected nodes are associated. For every pair of nodes, an equal probability is associated, which is independent of the remaining pairs, as stated in [20,27].

One of the critical reasons for which the Erdös–Renyi model has been widely acceptable is its attributes that encourage the process of modeling the network. Moreover, a special category of graphs, namely random graphs, does not efficiently correspond to the structure of real networks, since the majority of the node degrees in terms of this graph category results from the power-law distribution (Retrieved 27 April 2021, from https://necsi.edu/power-law) [28] rather than from Poisson distribution. In this way, the Erdös–Renyi model does not take into account the impact of the clustering process, while a random graph can be considered as an ideal model option for investigating complex networks [27].

2.2.2. Barabási–Albert Model

The most popular model, having degree distribution in power-law edges, is the Barabási–Albert model [29]. Concretely, the corresponding graphs are constructed under a dynamic process where the edges are added one by one to a core. The probability of a new edge to be linked with an existing one is proportional to the degree of the latter. According to the above, the edges with a high degree of distribution are more likely to be selected as adjacent to the new edges. Once this occurs, the degree of all edges will be increased so that there are more possibilities to be chosen in the future. This process creates a graph with a degree distribution that is characterized by a power-law tail as the number of edges tends to infinity.

The Barabási–Albert model presents a very small average-shortest-path length of a random graph as well as a clustering coefficient. This coefficient decreases with the size of the network and is lower than in real networks. The representation of the community structure of the actual complex networks is properly introduced in Figure 1.

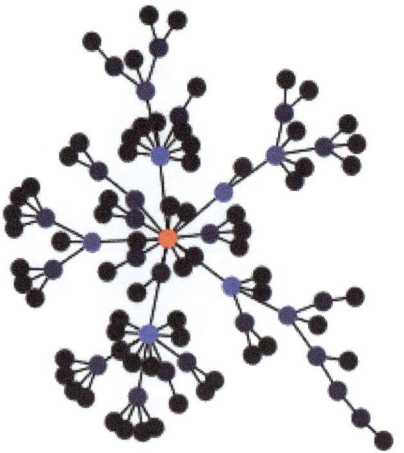

Figure 1. The Barabási–Albert model.

2.3. Epidemic Models in Biological Networks

As a second category of complex networks, biological neural networks of living organisms along with their epidemic networks, are considered. More specifically, two main types of biological networks exist. In addition, we propose a reference to networks based on the heritage/legacy of individuals by utilizing the genetic material (deoxyribonucleic acid—DNA) in conjunction with common attributes that these corresponding individuals come up with from their predecessors. Additionally, the epidemic activity of complex networks utilized by the nodes sensitivity is presented. Furthermore, different scenarios are investigated, like the transferable filial diseases (airborne or sexually transmitted) among humans, which is propagated through different categories of networks, like complex internet ones, or social networks, or even among computers.

This category of networks is also similar to biological networks in terms of utilizing networking either among communities in living organisms or among organism functions. For example, the ecosystem, subsections, and nervous system of the brain, which is perhaps the most studied by scientists.

3. Fuzzy Epidemics

Biological pathogens, such as influenza, measles, as well as sexually transmitted diseases, can result in infectious and contaminating diseases, especially in cases where epidemic diseases are considered. These diseases have the major characteristic of transmitting among individuals. Epidemics are capable of massively contaminating the population or can be dormant for a long time without any evidence of their presence. In extraordinary cases, one unique disease outburst can have a considerable and critical impact on a whole culture; for example, one can consider the entity of epidemics activated by the entry of Europeans in America or even the deadly epidemic of smallpox as featured by the British during the 15th century.

3.1. Transmitted Diseases in Networks

An infectious disease can be spread among individuals within a population of a complex network, as thoroughly displayed in [30]. The network of contacts can lead to the spread and expansion of a corresponding contamination. If these individuals physically encounter each other, then they are likely to catch the disease. Therefore, the precision of the model in terms of the inherent network is of major importance in order to identify the epidemic spreading. A number of comparable works constitute the research of malware spread among computers [31].

3.2. Branching Processes

The branching process is considered as the elementary model of disease propagation, especially with respect to an airborne illness. These kinds of networks are often mentioned as trees, as presented in Figure 2. Transmission waves utilize the specific tree model by taking into consideration the following information: when a number of infections get involved in a healthy population by a group of individuals, at that point there exists a plausibility for the disease to be transmitted to a sensitive portion of this populace, in accordance with a random transmission possibility of the disease [18].

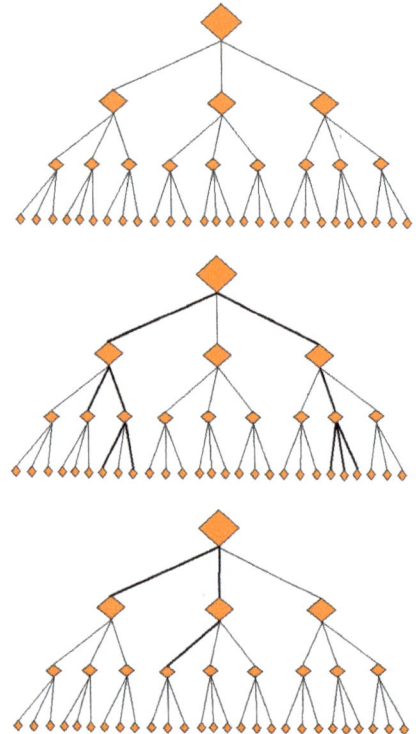

Figure 2. A Tree Network of an Epidemic Spread.

3.3. Susceptible–Infectious–Susceptible Model (SIS)

A basic variation regarding the epidemic models permits the hypothesis that people influenced by an epidemic can be infected a number of times. This characteristic epidemic model is deemed when the nodes interchange among the two phases, namely, the susceptible S and infectious I. In this specific model, there is no third phase and the model returns back to susceptible (S). This is the reason for the naming of the SIS model. More importantly, SIR model information is taken into account when considering this process. More specifically, some individuals of the model are within the infectious phase, while the remaining are within the susceptible phase.

On the other hand, every individual that comes into the infectious phase stays infected for a steady time. For the specific period, the contaminated individuals can maintain the plausibility of reaching the infection from any sensitive neighbor. After this period of time, the infectious individuals, in other words, those that are not infected anymore, can return to the susceptible phase once more.

The SIS model, similar to the above-mentioned SIR model, can be extended so as to efficiently manage more complicated sorts of epidemic cases [5]. Specifically, these types include either diverse transmission possibilities among diverse node individuals, or possibilities of disease reclamation, where each infected node returns to the sensitive situation with some probability, and finally, multiple stages of infection with varying properties of disease between them [18].

3.4. Transient Contact Model

In the previous subsections, we have presented outbreak models that have rapidly evolved. The diseases, for example, sexually transmitted ones (e.g., HIV/AIDS), are expanding into a large portion of individuals over longer time scales. However, this spreading takes several years to evolve in a network. This fact is a direct result of their course and, thus, depends mostly upon the quality of the sexual relationship of each pair. The majority of individuals have occasionally contacted a few times, whereas the properties of these concrete contacts may alternate amid disease propagation. As a result, novel connections and couples are considered, while others are broken up [18].

It is of major importance to identify that the sexual contacts, for this kind of correlating network, are temporary/transient. This fact lasts for a small period of time and through the total life of the epidemic.

3.5. Network Fuzzy Logic

A fuzzy epidemic is considered as a major aspect in disease transmission and epidemiology. More importantly, in recent works, users that are evidently sheltered or not to a specific illness are regarded to be in perilous situations of being categorized as diseased or non-diseased [13,32].

In our present manuscript, a different approach is introduced as we incorporate the concepts of fuzzy logic as well as atomic outcomes. People are deemed to be exposed to a considerable fuzzy aspect in terms of concrete functions of a fuzzy set membership; in the following, their reaction is classified by taking into account supplementary functions of a fuzzy set membership. As a next step, fuzzy set theory along with maximum likelihood were applied, and individual heterogeneity was calculated, thus giving us more realistic estimators than their classical counterparts.

Furthermore, assuming the case where hypothetical possibilities are taken into consideration, hypothetical probabilities under fuzzy logic settings can be determined. A probability distribution function r related to a fuzzy subset F is numerically equivalent to its degree of fuzzy membership function μ_F [33], which is:

$$r(x) = \mu_F(x) \quad \forall x \in X \tag{8}$$

We shall briefly introduce basic components in a traditional fuzzy logic system (for detailed discussion, please refer to [34,35]) and then propose our connectionist model [36]. Such models, also known as parallel distributed processing (PDP) models, are essentially computational models used to model aspects of human thought through the perception, knowledge, and behavior of learning processes [37]. This results in the storage and retrieval of information from the system memory.

Often the architecture of such models substantially differs among different applications; however, all models present specific assumptions that collectively characterize the "connection" approach to cognitive science. It is also important that connectionist models maintain the style of human thinking as in vague logical systems.

We shall define fuzzy sets and linguistic variables. A fuzzy set F defined in a universe of discourse $\mathbb{U}$ is characterized by a fuzzy membership function $\mu_F(x) : \mathbb{U} \to [0,1] | x \in \mathbb{U}$.

Thus, a fuzzy set F in $\mathbb{U}$ may be represented as a set of ordered pairs. Each ordered pair consists of a generic element u and the degree of membership of any element of discourse to the fuzzy set. It is estimated by employing any fuzzy membership function as

$$F = \{(u, \mu_F(u)) | u \in \mathbb{U}\} \tag{9}$$

where u is called a support value if $\mu_F(u) > 0$.

If $\mathbb{U}$ is a continuous universe and F is normal and convex (i.e., $max_{u \in \mathbb{U}} \mu_F(u) = 1$ and $\mu_F(\lambda u_1 + (1-\lambda)u_2) \geq min(\mu_F(u_1), \mu_F(u_2))$, where $(u_1, u_2) \in \mathbb{U}$ and $\lambda \in [0,1]$, then F is a fuzzy number.

A linguistic variable x in a universe of discourse $\mathbb{U}$ is characterized by $T(x) = \{T_x^1, T_x^2, \ldots, T_x^k\}$ and $M(x) = \{M_x^1, M_x^2, \ldots, M_x^k\}$, where $T(x)$ is the term set of x. That is the set of names of linguistic values of x with each value T, where T is a fuzzy number with membership function M_x^i defined on $\mathbb{U}$. So $M(x)$ is a semantic rule for associating each value with its meaning; for example, if x indicates a potential infection, then $T(x)$ may have values equal to {Infected, Susceptible (IS)}.

3.6. Contact Structure and Partnership Dynamics

Numerous utilized models of HIV eco-evolutionary dynamics utilize implied models that include the normal impacts of sexual contact given a concrete couple without impersonating the unequivocal dynamics of the configuration of a partner relationship [38]. Since our motivation stems from the fact that we are interested in exploring the way that issues around virulence evolution rely on the modeled contact structure, we examine a model with growing complexity levels in the contact structure, but at the same time, rearrange several of the remaining epidemiological forms (like the history of HIV as a within-host).

Figure 3 presents a schematic representation of the proposed model with explicit contact structure considering explicitly partnership dynamics [39]. Non-instantaneous partnership formation, which concerns people that are without any partner and spend a period as uncoupled, is presumed in the above schematic representation and comprises five categories related to different types of disease as well as values of partnership. Concretely, the five states are the following:

- Single (uncoupled) susceptible (or sensitive) individuals (S);
- Single infected (or contaminated) individuals (I);
- Concordant negative couples (i.e., susceptible–susceptible, SS) when both partners are susceptible;
- Discordant couples (i.e., susceptible–infected, SI);
- Concordant positive couples (i.e., infected–infected, II) when both partners are infectious.

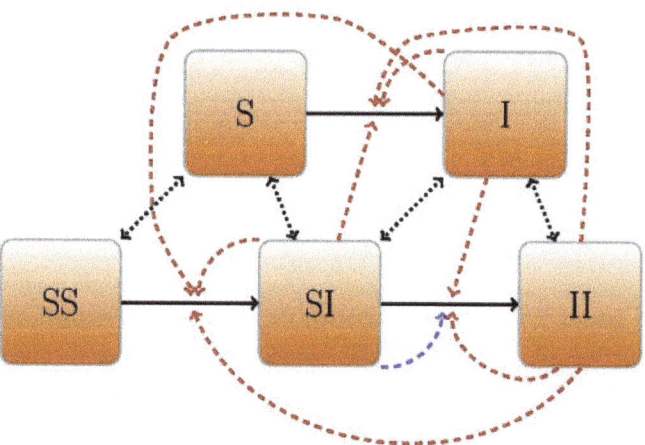

Figure 3. Schematic representation of model with explicit contact structure.

Regarding schematic representation, solid arrows represent infection transitions (e.g., S towards I), dotted arrows exhibit partnership dialysis and configuration (e.g., S towards SI) and dashed arrows represent impacts on the rate of the infection, indicating transmission among the nodes of the pair (with blue color) as well as transmission among the nodes of an uncoupled pair (with red color).

The values of single (i.e., uncoupled) susceptible and infected people generate the rate of the configuration of each pair. Furthermore, associations and relationships among two individuals can either be suspended or even be modified into other types of relationships by infecting one out of two individuals. This corresponding model also incorporates another type of contact, namely when both individuals are uncoupled as well as individuals related to other partnerships. This means that these susceptible partners and susceptible uncoupled individuals in any sort of association can also be contaminated by infected partners or infected uncoupled individuals in any sort of association.

4. HIV Transmission Simulation of Biological Network

The propagation of the AIDS syndrome, triggered by the HIV virus, in a sample of infusing drug users, is introduced and thoroughly discussed in this section. Several virus propagation scenarios with various diverse parametric transmission modes as well as syndrome investigations during this propagation are comprehensively utilized.

4.1. Proposed Model

In the European Union, it has been shown that 18 million of its population are drug users, which is 5% of the entire population (Retrieved 27 April 2021, from https://www.emcdda.europa.eu/). It is worth noting that out of 5%, a percentage equal to 0.63% is attributed to individuals that are HIV infected via shared needles [40]. In light of the above information, the present work examines the propagation of the virus through all injected drug users, with the average transmission of the epidemic being multiple syringes used by various users.

The proposed model addresses the following issues by utilizing Boolean variables:

- Is the individual aware of carrying the infection or not?
- Has the syringe been given to more than one individual or not?
- Is the individual aware of being infected or not?

This proposed model simulates the spread of HIV through sexual transmission within a small isolated human population. HIV can be transmitted in several ways, where sexual contact can be considered as the most common and widespread. However, HIV can also be transmitted with the use of syringes shared through blood transfusions of injecting drug users. Another transmission type could be through women with HIV that can transmit the virus to their babies before or during birth, or even later through breastfeeding.

The proposed method also determines, by means of a variable, the portion of the population that will be manually infected. As a result, when simulating the alternations of input data, new questions and potential problems arise as well as more distinctive outcomes occur. In this study, we based our proposed model by taking into consideration the following aspects:

- For how long will the individual use the syringe?
- How many individuals will use clean (new) needles?
- How many individuals share simultaneously the same needle?
- How often are individuals tested by a physician?

There are auxiliary input variables in the system, which provide the possibility to manually change the data of the model in order to come up with different outcomes and outputs. As a result, the model displays during the simulation the number of infected individuals and is aware of the disease percentage as well as the rate of infection on a weekly basis.

4.2. Random Graph

The equal probability of each pair of individuals concerning the aspect of contact, regardless of the other pairs, is based on the theory of the Erdös–Renyi random graph, as depicted in Algorithm 1. However, an epidemic needs even more time for the spreading to be achieved, so we alternated the transmission of the syndrome into the epidemic transiently contact model accordingly our proposed model, which is more appropriate.

Algorithm 1 Epidemic Transiently Contact Model.

1: **input** All possible edges are considered and included in the graph with equal probability p
2: **input** Variable d that specifies the possibility of the unidirectional edges to be equally modified, i.e., if they are reciprocal
3: **for each** node i **do**
4:    **for each** node $j = i+1 \ldots N$ **do**
5:       Set a random number u between 0 and 1 uniformly
6:       **if** $p > u$ **then**
7:          Create a mutual (reciprocal) edge between node i and node j
8:       **else**
9:          **if** $d > u$ **then**
10:            Create a directed edge from node i to node j
11:            Create a directed edge from node j to node i
12:          **else**
13:            Create a directed edge from node i to node j
14:            Set a randomly chosen node h from the set of all nodes except for i and j uniformly
15:            Create a directed edge from node h to node i
16:          **end if**
17:       **end if**
18:    **end for**
19: **end for**

The overall time complexity of the algorithm to generate a random graph of N nodes under the epidemic transiently contact model is $\Theta(N^2)$ as this is the time complexity to execute the two "for" loops. Specifically, for each new step, the algorithm acts in $\Theta(N)$ if one max directed edge per new node is created; otherwise, the complexity is $\Theta(NM)$ if M the max directed edges per new node is created.

As aforementioned, we have modified the Erdös–Renyi random graph in the way that there is some dependence on whether or not the edges are present. This approach is taken into consideration because in many practical problems, the vertices are in fact randomly positioned in some geometric space (usually Euclidean). Furthermore, two vertices are adjacent if and only if the distance between them (in some specified norm) is less than a certain quantity. These corresponding points are usually uniformly distributed in $[0,1]^n$.

In the present manuscript, we tried to incorporate some basic notations from the random-duster model by biasing the formula for the probability of a set of edges in order to favor certain kinds of graphs arising. In this kind of model, given a graph $G = G(V, E)$ and a set of edges $A \subseteq E$, let $c(V, A)$ denote the number of components of the graph in which the vertices are denoted by V and the corresponding set of edges is denoted by A. Then, the probability that the edges that arise are exactly those in A is [41]:

$$\frac{p^{|A|}(1-p)^{|E|-|A|}q^{c(V,A)}}{\sum_{F \subseteq E} p^{|F|}(1-p)^{|E|-|F|}q^{c(V,F)}} \tag{10}$$

where q is a positive integer used for favoring specific elements of a concrete graph. Namely, observe that when q is equal to 1, the Erdös–Renyi model is recovered. In addition, if $q > 1$, graphs with many components are favored, whereas if $q < 1$, the connected graphs are favored. Notice that the study of this model is closely linked to percolation theory and statistical physics.

4.3. Implementation

In the current paper, the problem of the transmission of HIV through injectable drugs in Europe is presented. Thus, according to the data presented by the European Drug Report, a small sample was adapted to the simulation due to the decrease in percentage of users in Europe in recent years. More specifically, the percentage of injecting drug users diagnosed with AIDS has dropped by almost 40% as compared to the previous decade (Retrieved 27 April 2021, from https://www.emcdda.europa.eu/system/files/publications/11364/2019 1724_TDAT19001ENN_PDF.pdf). The sample used in the implementation is 300 as well as 500 users.

In addition to these samples, according to the study aforementioned [17], we consider a 0.63% disease possibility for the AIDS virus; based on the above, the percentage of the population that is initially infected and enters the model, corresponds to 0.63% of the entity. An important part of the application is considered the sharing of the same needle among drug individuals of the sample, which is implemented by the system's random selection; if a person uses a syringe that "carries" the virus, there is 100% probability of becoming infected. Another issue that has to be taken into account is that after about two years (i.e., 100 weeks), the symptoms of the syndrome begin to appear.

For the verification of our proposed methodology, four different scenarios have been implemented, as shown in Table 2. More specifically, Tables 2 and 3 present the percentages of fuzziness, which has been studied during the experiments. In the first part (out of four) of Table 3, no fuzziness was applied, while in the other three examples, percentages of fuzziness equal to 10%, 30%, and 50%, respectively, were applied. The primary research reason for choosing the specific scenarios is twofold. First, the comparison between the absence of fuzziness and different percentages of fuzziness will provide us with important insights. Second, the three different percentages are thoroughly selected until the percentage of 50% because, if the results exceed this upper bound, the results will not be meaningful in terms of the problem we are trying to resolve.

From the two above-mentioned tables, the results shown in Tables 4–7 are depicted. Concretely, Tables 4 and 5 introduce the outcomes of the first two scenarios where the sample is 300 individuals and they are obliged to carry out one and two tests per year, respectively. On the other hand, Tables 6 and 7 present the results of the last two scenarios where the sample is 500 individuals and are obliged to carry out one and two tests per year, respectively.

Table 2. Four different scenarios.

Scenario	1	2	3	4
Number of Users	300	300	500	500
Number of Tests per Year	1	2	1	2

Table 3. Data of the twelve examples for four different scenarios.

Features	1	2	3	4	5	6	7	8	9	10	11	12
Percentage of Fuzziness	0% Fuzzy			10% Fuzzy			30% Fuzzy			50% Fuzzy		
Shared Syringe	10	0	7	9	0	7	7	0	6	5	0	4
New Syringe	0	10	3	0	9	2	0	7	1	0	5	1
Fuzzy	0	0	0	1	1	1	3	3	3	5	5	5

Table 4. People regarding the first scenario for a different number of weeks.

Option of Illness	100	390	1390	2390	3930
0% Fuzzy—1st example					
AIDS-	298	290	240	142	126
AIDS+	0	2	41	138	174
AIDS?	2	8	19	20	0
0% Fuzzy—2nd example					
AIDS-	298	298	298	298	298
AIDS+	0	2	2	2	2
AIDS?	2	0	0	0	0
0% Fuzzy—3rd example					
AIDS-	297	288	200	135	119
AIDS+	0	5	63	156	181
AIDS?	3	7	37	9	0
10% Fuzzy—4th example					
AIDS-	293	288	191	135	130
AIDS+	3	5	74	162	170
AIDS?	4	7	35	3	0
10% Fuzzy—5th example					
AIDS-	298	298	298	298	298
AIDS+	0	2	2	2	2
AIDS?	2	0	0	0	0
10% Fuzzy—6th example					
AIDS-	296	285	217	148	128
AIDS+	0	9	55	141	172
AIDS?	4	6	28	11	0
30% Fuzzy—7th example					
AIDS-	297	288	234	178	145
AIDS+	0	4	54	109	155
AIDS?	3	8	12	13	0
30% Fuzzy—8th example					
AIDS-	298	298	298	298	298
AIDS+	0	2	2	2	2
AIDS?	2	0	0	0	0
30% Fuzzy—9th example					
AIDS-	292	290	258	189	138
AIDS+	2	4	32	88	162
AIDS?	4	6	10	23	0
50% Fuzzy—10th example					
AIDS-	294	285	213	153	136
AIDS+	2	5	64	134	164
AIDS?	4	10	23	13	0
50% Fuzz—11th example					
AIDS-	298	298	298	298	298
AIDS+	0	2	2	2	2
AIDS?	2	0	0	0	0
50% Fuzzy—12th example					
AIDS-	296	294	277	264	210
AIDS+	0	2	16	31	90
AIDS?	4	4	7	5	0

Table 5. People regarding the second scenario for a different number of weeks.

Option of Illness	100	390	1390	2390	3930
		0% Fuzzy—1st example			
AIDS-	295	294	290	284	284
AIDS+	2	4	4	16	16
AIDS?	3	4	6	0	0
		0% Fuzzy—2nd example			
AIDS-	298	298	298	298	298
AIDS+	0	2	2	2	2
AIDS?	2	0	0	0	0
		0% Fuzzy—3rd example			
AIDS-	295	292	291	291	291
AIDS+	0	5	9	9	9
AIDS?	5	3	0	0	0
		10% Fuzzy—4th example			
AIDS-	295	290	258	254	254
AIDS+	1	4	39	46	46
AIDS?	4	6	3	0	0
		10% Fuzzy—5th example			
AIDS-	298	298	298	298	298
AIDS+	0	2	2	2	2
AIDS?	2	0	0	0	0
		10% Fuzzy—6th example			
AIDS-	296	292	273	273	273
AIDS+	1	3	27	27	27
AIDS?	3	5	0	0	0
		30% Fuzzy—7th example			
AIDS-	296	288	261	244	244
AIDS+	0	5	35	56	56
AIDS?	4	7	4	0	0
		30% Fuzzy—8th example			
AIDS-	298	298	298	298	298
AIDS+	0	2	2	2	2
AIDS?	2	0	0	0	0
		30% Fuzzy—9th example			
AIDS-	294	288	278	278	278
AIDS+	2	5	22	22	22
AIDS?	4	7	0	0	0
		50% Fuzzy—10th example			
AIDS-	295	288	259	253	253
AIDS+	0	5	36	47	47
AIDS?	5	7	5	0	0
		50% Fuzzy—11th example			
AIDS-	298	298	298	298	298
AIDS+	0	2	2	2	2
AIDS?	2	0	0	0	0
		50% Fuzzy—12th example			
AIDS-	296	294	293	293	293
AIDS+	0	4	7	7	7
AIDS?	4	2	0	0	0

Table 6. People regarding the third scenario for a different number of weeks.

Option of Illness	100	390	1390	2390	3930
0% Fuzzy—1st example					
AIDS-	491	489	385	260	211
AIDS+	2	3	78	214	289
AIDS?	7	8	37	26	0
0% Fuzzy—2nd example					
AIDS-	497	497	497	497	497
AIDS+	0	3	3	3	3
AIDS?	3	0	0	0	0
0% Fuzzy—3rd example					
AIDS-	491	483	312	190	172
AIDS+	1	4	131	294	328
AIDS?	8	13	57	16	0
10% Fuzzy—4th example					
AIDS-	492	482	384	235	219
AIDS+	2	5	78	247	281
AIDS?	6	13	38	18	0
10% Fuzzy—5th example					
AIDS-	497	497	497	497	497
AIDS+	0	3	3	3	3
AIDS?	3	0	0	0	0
10% Fuzzy—6th example					
AIDS-	491	477	292	183	171
AIDS+	1	5	141	311	329
AIDS?	8	18	67	6	0
30% Fuzzy—7th example					
AIDS-	491	479	283	169	173
AIDS+	1	4	140	322	329
AIDS?	8	17	77	9	0
30% Fuzzy—8th example					
AIDS-	497	497	497	497	497
AIDS+	0	3	3	3	3
AIDS?	3	0	0	0	0
30% Fuzzy—9th example					
AIDS-	492	475	294	231	223
AIDS+	1	8	151	261	275
AIDS?	7	17	55	8	0
50% Fuzzy—10th example					
AIDS-	491	483	312	190	172
AIDS+	1	4	131	294	328
AIDS?	8	13	57	16	0
50% Fuzzy—11th example					
AIDS-	497	497	497	497	497
AIDS+	0	3	3	3	3
AIDS?	3	0	0	0	0
50% Fuzzy—12th example					
AIDS-	494	487	326	241	221
AIDS+	0	3	114	246	279
AIDS?	6	10	60	13	0

Table 7. People regarding the fourth scenario for a different number of weeks.

Option of Illness	100	390	1390	2390	3930
		0% Fuzzy—1st example			
AIDS-	487	477	417	391	376
AIDS+	3	13	74	106	123
AIDS?	10	10	9	2	0
		0% Fuzzy—2nd example			
AIDS-	497	497	497	497	497
AIDS+	0	3	3	3	3
AIDS?	3	0	0	0	0
		0% Fuzzy—3rd example			
AIDS-	486	481	413	343	318
AIDS+	4	14	70	141	182
AIDS?	10	5	17	16	0
		10% Fuzzy—4th example			
AIDS-	488	487	446	412	395
AIDS+	4	9	45	80	105
AIDS?	8	4	9	8	0
		10% Fuzzy—5th example			
AIDS-	497	497	497	497	497
AIDS+	0	3	3	3	3
AIDS?	3	0	0	0	0
		10% Fuzzy—6th example			
AIDS-	493	485	435	365	331
AIDS+	0	10	57	115	169
AIDS?	7	5	8	17	0
		30% Fuzzy—7th example			
AIDS-	488	485	448	422	400
AIDS+	5	10	43	73	100
AIDS?	7	5	9	5	0
		30% Fuzzy—8th example			
AIDS-	497	497	497	497	497
AIDS+	0	3	3	3	3
AIDS?	3	0	0	0	0
		30% Fuzzy—9th example			
AIDS-	489	486	420	352	340
AIDS+	3	9	62	140	160
AIDS?	8	5	18	8	0
		50% Fuzzy—10th example			
AIDS-	492	478	417	392	380
AIDS+	2	14	74	105	120
AIDS?	6	8	9	3	0
		50% Fuzzy—11th example			
AIDS-	497	497	497	497	497
AIDS+	0	3	3	3	3
AIDS?	3	0	0	0	0
		50% Fuzzy—12th example			
AIDS-	492	486	461	454	443
AIDS+	0	9	36	45	57
AIDS?	8	5	3	1	0

5. Results

In the following, Tables 4–7 present the results for the four above-mentioned scenarios. Please notice the following three categories of users.

- AIDS-: users not infected by HIV.
- AIDS+: users infected by HIV and they know it (they have been tested).
- AIDS?: users who have no knowledge if they are (or not) infected by HIV and they have not passed the one year time limit in order to be tested.

First Scenario: Table 4 shows that examples 2, 5, 8, and 11 achieve the same results. This is due to the fact that all users use a new syringe for every drug use, thus resulting in the same percentage of infection in the sample, for example, 0.67%. Moreover, in examples 1, 4, 7, and 10, users sharing illegal substances are many and no one uses a new syringe. As a result, we can observe that the disease spreading increases rapidly in all four examples, although there is a large percentage of fuzziness in examples 4 (with 10%), 7 (with 30%) and 10 (with 50%). In these examples, the rates of infection range from 40% to 56% as we do not know what the whole sample is doing; that is, when we have a percentage of fuzziness equal to 30%, we actually do not know what 3 out of 10 users are doing (sharing or using a new syringe in each contact).

Regarding examples 3, 6, 9, and 12, the simulation in the sample is closer to reality; that is, some of the users are using illicit substances with a new syringe. An increase in the spread of the virus is depicted, as disease spreading rates range from 25% to 55%. In addition, the largest value is presented in example 6 with the percentage of fuzziness equal to 10%, whereas the lowest value is presented in example 12 with a percentage of fuzziness equal to 50%. These results are justified as the percentage of fuzziness in example 6 is less than the corresponding value in example 12.

It should be noted that, in these examples, each user has been forced to do an HIV test once a year.

Second Scenario: Table 5 shows, similarly to Table 4, that examples 2, 5, 8, and 11 achieve the same results. As a result, the percentage of infection in the sample remained the same, for example, 0.67%. Moreover, in examples 1, 4, 7, and 10, users sharing illegal substances are 10, 9, 7 and 5 out of 10 (according to Table 3 and the corresponding fuzziness) and no one uses a new syringe. Thus, it is observed that the disease spreading increases in an even more rapid way, in all four examples, than in Table 4.

Furthermore, this increase reaches its biggest value in a shorter time, for example, 2390 weeks in all four examples, despite the fact that fuzziness plays an important role in the last three examples. In these examples, the rates of infection range from 5% to 20% and this decrease, compared to Table 4, is due to the number of mandatory HIV test samples submitted over time, which are two instead of one.

As in Table 4, results in examples 3, 6, 9, and 12 present a sharp decrease in virus spreading. The disease spreading values range from 1.3% to 9%, with the largest value being in example 6 with the percentage of fuzziness equal to 10%. On the other hand, the lowest values are presented in examples 1 and 12 with the percentage of fuzziness equal to 0% and 50%, respectively.

Third Scenario: The examples 2, 5, 8, and 11 in Table 6 perform exactly like the corresponding ones in previous Tables 4 and 5. The only difference lies in the rate of infection, which has a value equal to 0.8% (the infection rate has a starting value equal to 0.8% and not 0.63% as the probability of infection lies between 3.15 and 500 under the $500 \times 0.0063 = 3.15$). This is justified as all users use a new syringe in every drug use.

Examples 1, 4, 7, and 10 perform similarly to Table 5, whereas the rates of infection range from 50% to 62%. We also anticipated that examples 3, 6, 9, and 12 would be closer to reality, and the values prove our assumptions. In addition, a marked increase in the spread of the virus is observed where the rates of infection range from 52% to 68%. More specifically, the highest value is achieved in example 9 with the percentage of fuzziness equal to 30%, while the lowest value is achieved in example 12 with the percentage of fuzziness equal to 50%.

Fourth Scenario: As we anticipated, the results in examples 2, 5, 8, and 11 in Table 7 perform in the same way as in previous Tables. Moreover, the rate of infection has a value equal to 0.8%, as in Table 6. In examples 1, 4, 7, and 10, no new syringe is used and the number of users sharing illegal substances is 10, 9, 7 and 5 out of 10, respectively. It is also observed that the increase in the disease spread does not rise in a quick way and thus, it achieves more promising results for all the corresponding examples. The values of infection in the sample range from 13% to 25%, and this is presented due to the two mandatory HIV test samples submitted over time.

Finally, we noticed a pronounced decrease in the spread of the virus in terms of the corresponding results of Table 5, regarding examples 3, 6, 9, and 12. More specifically, the rates of infection range from 9.5% to 36%, where the highest value is achieved when the percentage of fuzziness is equal to 0%, and the lowest value is achieved when the percentage of fuzziness is equal to 50%.

5.1. Comparing All Four Scenarios

Tables 8–11 depict the results from the virus spreading scenarios with the most plausible values (i.e., some users use illegal substances with a new syringe while others share the same); that is, we have used the results from examples 3, 6, 9 and 12. The results are grouped by the value of fuzziness, and both population samples (i.e., 300 and 500 individuals) are displayed in order for the comparison to be manifested.

Table 8. Comparison between the four scenarios for a different number of weeks by considering the 3rd example with 0% fuzzy.

Option of Illness	100	390	1390	2390	3930	100	390	1390	2390	3930
	1st scenario—1 test—300 users					3rd scenario—1 test—500 users				
AIDS-	297	288	200	135	119	491	483	312	190	172
AIDS+	0	5	63	156	181	1	4	131	294	328
AIDS?	3	7	37	9	0	8	13	57	16	0
	2nd scenario—2 tests—300 users					4th scenario—2 tests—500 users				
AIDS-	295	292	291	291	291	486	481	413	343	318
AIDS+	0	5	9	9	9	4	14	70	141	182
AIDS?	5	3	0	0	0	10	5	17	16	0

Table 9. Comparison between the four scenarios for a different number of weeks by considering the 6th example with 10% fuzzy.

Option of Illness	100	390	1390	2390	3930	100	390	1390	2390	3930
	1st scenario—1 test—300 users					3rd scenario—1 test—500 users				
AIDS-	296	285	217	148	128	491	477	292	183	171
AIDS+	0	9	55	141	172	1	5	141	311	329
AIDS?	4	6	28	11	0	8	18	67	6	0
	2nd scenario—2 tests—300 users					4th scenario—2 tests—500 users				
AIDS-	296	292	273	273	273	493	485	435	365	331
AIDS+	1	3	27	27	27	0	10	57	115	169
AIDS?	3	5	0	0	0	7	5	8	17	0

In more detail, in Table 8, with a fuzziness of 0%, the increase in the spread of the virus as the number of weeks increases is clearly visible since this spread in the results concerning the one mandatory blood test per year (scenarios 1 and 3), for both samples, is fairly fast with spread rates ranging from 34% to 52%. On the other hand, assuming two mandatory blood tests per year (scenarios 2 and 4), the rates of the virus spread range from about 1.3% to 36%, respectively.

The results in Table 9 with fuzziness of 10% are almost the same as in Table 8. Specifically, for scenarios 1 and 3, the increase in the virus spreading is fast where the spread percentages present values from about 25% to 55%, respectively. On the other hand, in scenarios 2 and 4, we notice that the virus spreading does not increase so rapidly as it presents values from about 9% to 17%, respectively.

Table 10 presents the results where the percentage of fuzziness is equal to 30%. We can observe that the values are identical with the ones of the previous tables. Concretely, for scenarios 1 and 3, the increase in the spread of the virus in both samples ranges from about 45–68%, respectively. While in scenarios 2 and 4, we notice that these percentages are adequately lower, presenting values from about 1.3–8%, respectively.

Finally, Table 11 depicts the results with a percentage of fuzziness equal to 50%. As mentioned above, the increase for all four scenarios are almost identical, as in the three previous tables. The increase in virus spreading, for scenarios 1 and 3, ranges from about 25–52%, respectively, whereas when considering scenarios 2 and 4, the increase takes values from about 1.3–9.5%.

Table 10. Comparison between the four scenarios for a different number of weeks by considering the 9th example with 30% fuzzy.

Option of Illness	100	390	1390	2390	3930	100	390	1390	2390	3930
	1st scenario—1 test—300 users					3rd scenario—1 test—500 users				
AIDS-	292	290	258	189	138	492	475	294	231	223
AIDS+	2	4	32	88	162	1	8	151	261	275
AIDS?	4	6	10	23	0	7	17	55	8	0
	2nd scenario—2 tests—300 users					4th scenario—2 tests—500 users				
AIDS-	294	288	278	278	278	489	486	420	352	340
AIDS+	2	5	22	22	22	3	9	62	140	160
AIDS?	4	7	0	0	0	8	5	18	8	0

Table 11. Comparison between the four scenarios for a different number of weeks by considering the 12th example with 50% fuzzy.

Option of Illness	100	390	1390	2390	3930	100	390	1390	2390	3930
	1st scenario—1 test—300 users					3rd scenario—1 test—500 users				
AIDS-	296	294	277	264	210	494	487	326	241	221
AIDS+	0	2	16	31	90	0	3	114	246	279
AIDS?	4	4	7	5	0	6	10	60	13	0
	2nd scenario—2 tests—300 users					4th scenario—2 tests—500 users				
AIDS-	296	294	293	293	293	492	486	461	454	443
AIDS+	0	4	7	7	7	0	9	36	45	57
AIDS?	4	2	0	0	0	8	5	3	1	0

5.2. Discussion

Studying complex networks can solve various real-world problems and can be applied to a variety of scientific fields. They make it possible to investigate any scientific network according to the requirements of each real-world area and, of course, based on the input data of each concrete network. Complex networks also provide a view of the composition entities of a network resulting in the creation of arbitrarily configured networks. Additionally, it is possible for these entities to be at any moment removed from the network.

Because of their efficiency described above, complex networks are becoming both popular and attractive.

It is of major importance to notice that studying and understanding the processes utilized in complex networks presents new horizons for researchers to investigate and solve many problems (e.g., diseases diffusion and propagation, mutations) in terms of these networks. The science of molecular biology considers distinct complex networks consisting of numerous interacting parts with different structures, such as enzymes, genes, and proteins. In addition, in the area of epidemiology, beyond the examination of complex networks, the corresponding complex networks are initially analyzed, then modeled and finally simulated in the form of toolboxes.

Any similar approaches in the context of epidemics fail in understanding the principles of random graphs and especially in the corresponding problem we are investigating. Regarding fuzzy estimators, let us assume that we are interested in answering the question "What is the fuzzy probability that a very sexually active individual will develop AIDS?". Then, the fuzzy ratio is considered as we are dealing with the conditional probability that this specific individual will develop AIDS with a certain speed given that he/she is subject to a certain risk due to his/her sexual activity level.

According to the individuals who make up each society (300 and 500 people), a significant difference regarding the results was observed. More specifically, when a run of our proposed technique was performed in a larger sample of people and after many tests, it was found that the sample with the 500 individuals proportionally achieved the greatest improvement in the results in terms of virus transmission with respect to the same conditions and parameters. This results in greater precision of the model in samples approaching the real world.

6. Conclusions and Future Work

In this paper, a fuzzy implementation based on complex network theory was introduced. In particular, the propagation of a corresponding disease (e.g., AIDS) to a sample of individuals with specific characteristics was simulated by implementing two different models of complex networks. The first scheme utilized the Erdös—Renyi model considering that the sample was selected from the original population and assuming that the relationships between individuals follow the random graph; also, in this model, the virus transmission is based on the epidemic contact transient model. On the other hand, in the second scheme utilized, different scenarios were investigated and performed and also different conditions within the sample were measured in order to obtain the results through the process of fuzzy simulations, which cannot be effectively implemented in the real world. These results depict the evolution of formalism among the individuals of the concrete population. Furthermore, we can argue that this tool, according to the information obtained, can also be a preventive application to various diseases.

The study of multi-virus networks as well as the investigation of different epidemic models are some of the future expansions of our work. In addition, another future work that can extend our proposed application is the integration of distinctive algorithmic analytic methods along with the introduction of the theory of dynamic systems. Further analytical experimental evaluation of the application can be considered as a critical point since the system provides new examples through its auxiliary input variables. Finally, after simulating the model, we explored the notion that incorporating effective heuristics in terms of temporal graphs is something to be outlined and attracts a lot of interest.

Author Contributions: N.L., A.K., V.C.G., L.I. and P.P. conceived of the idea, designed and performed the experiments, analyzed the results, drafted the initial manuscript and revised the final manuscript. All authors have read and agreed to the published version of the manuscript.

Funding: This research received no external funding.

Institutional Review Board Statement: Not applicable.

Informed Consent Statement: Not applicable.

Data Availability Statement: Not applicable.

Conflicts of Interest: The authors declare no conflict of interest.

References

1. West, D.B. *Introduction to Graph Theory*; Prentice Hall: Upper Saddle River, NJ, USA, 2001; Volume 2.
2. Newman, M.E.J. The Structure and Function of Complex Networks. *SIAM Rev.* **2003**, *45*, 167–256. [CrossRef]
3. Boccaletti, S.; Latora, V.; Moreno, Y.; Chavez, M.; Hwang, D.U. Complex Networks: Structure and Dynamics. *Phys. Rep.* **2006**, *424*, 175–308. [CrossRef]
4. Power, J.D.; Cohen, A.L.; Nelson, S.M.; Wig, G.S.; Barnes, K.A.; Church, J.A.; Vogel, A.C.; Laumann, T.O.; Miezin, F.M.; Schlaggar, B.L.; et al. Functional Network Organization of the Human Brain. *Neuron* **2011**, *72*, 665–678. [CrossRef]
5. Shang, Y. Mixed SI (R) Epidemic Dynamics in Random Graphs with General Degree Distributions. *Appl. Math. Comput.* **2013**, *219*, 5042–5048. [CrossRef]
6. Nowzari, C.; Preciado, V.; Pappas, G. Analysis and Control of Epidemics: A Survey of Spreading Processes on Complex Networks. *IEEE Control. Syst.* **2016**, *36*, 26–46.
7. Pastor-Satorras, R.; Castellano, C.; Mieghem, P.V.; Vespignani, A. Epidemic Processes in Complex Networks. *Rev. Mod. Phys.* **2015**, *87*, 925–979. [CrossRef]
8. Li, C.H.; Tsai, C.C.; Yang, S.Y. Analysis of Epidemic Spreading of an SIRS Model in Complex Heterogeneous Networks. *Commun. Nonlinear Sci. Numer. Simul.* **2014**, *19*, 1042–1054. [CrossRef]
9. Fofana, A.M.; Hurford, A. Mechanistic Movement Models to Understand Epidemic Spread. *Philos. Trans. R. Soc. Lond. Biol. Sci.* **2017**, *372*, 20160086. [CrossRef]
10. Wang, W.; Tang, M.; Stanley, E.; Braunstein, L.A. Unification of Theoretical Approaches for Epidemic Spreading on Complex Networks. *Rep. Prog. Phys.* **2017**, *80*, 036603. [CrossRef]
11. Prettejohn, B.J.; Berryman, M.J.; McDonnell, M.D. Methods for Generating Complex Networks with Selected Structural Properties for Simulations: A Review and Tutorial for Neuroscientists. *Front. Comput. Neurosci.* **2011**, *2011*. [CrossRef]
12. Faria, N.R.; Rambaut, A.; Suchard, M.A.; Baele, G.; Bedford, T.; Ward, M.J.; Tatem, A.J.; Sousa, J.D.; Arinaminpathy, N.; Pépin, J.; et al. The Early Spread and Epidemic Ignition of HIV-1 in Human Populations. *Science* **2014**, *346*, 56–61. [CrossRef]
13. Massad, E.; Ortega, N.R.S.; Struchiner, C.J.; Burattini, M.N. Fuzzy Epidemics. *Artif. Intell. Med.* **2003**, *29*, 241–259. [CrossRef]
14. Zadeh, L.A. Fuzzy Sets. *Inf. Control.* **1965**, *8*, 338–353. [CrossRef]
15. Zimmermann, H.J. *Fuzzy Set Theory and Its Applications*; Springer Science & Business Media: Berlin/Heidelberg Germany, 2011.
16. Goguen, J.A. The Logic of Inexact Concepts. *Synthese* **1969**, *19*, 325–373. [CrossRef]
17. Lefevr, N.; Margariti, S.; Kanavos, A.; Tsakalidis, A. An Implementation of Disease Spreading over Biological Networks. In Proceedings of the 18th International Conference on Engineering Applications of Neural Networks (EANN), Athens, Greece, 25–27 August 2017; pp. 559–569.
18. Easley, D.A.; Kleinberg, J.M. *Networks, Crowds, and Markets-Reasoning about a Highly Connected World*; Cambridge University Press: Cambridge, UK, 2010.
19. Wasserman, S.; Faust, K. *Social Network Analysis: Methods and Applications*; Cambridge University Press: Cambridge, UK, 1994; Volume 8.
20. Dorogovtsev, S.N. *Lectures on Complex Networks*; Oxford University Press: New York, NY, USA, 2010, Volume 24.
21. Newman, M.E.J. *Networks: An Introduction*; Oxford University Press Inc.: New York, NY, USA, 2010.
22. Mao, G.; Zhang, N. Analysis of Average Shortest-Path Length of Scale-Free Network. *J. Appl. Math.* **2013**, *2013*, 865643:1–865643:5. [CrossRef]
23. Ahuja, R.K.; Magnanti, T.L.; Orlin, J.B. *Network Flows: Theory, Algorithms and Applications*; Prentice Hall: Upper Saddle River, NJ, USA, 1993.
24. Crucitti, P.; Latora, V.; Marchiori, M. Model for Cascading Failures in Complex Networks. *Phys. Rev. E* **2004**, *69*, 045104. [CrossRef] [PubMed]
25. Li, Y.; Shang, Y.; Yang, Y. Clustering Coefficients of Large Networks. *Inf. Sci.* **2017**, *382-383*, 350–358. [CrossRef]
26. Watts, D.J. *Small Worlds: The Dynamics of Networks between Order and Randomness*; Princeton University Press: Princeton, NY, USA, 1999.
27. Erdös, P.; Rényi, A. On Random Graphs I. *Publ. Math. Debr.* **1959**, *6*, 290–297.
28. Adamic, L.A.; Lukose, R.M.; Puniyani, A.R.; Huberman, B.A. Search in Power-Law Networks. *Phys. Rev. E* **2001**, *64*, 046135. [CrossRef] [PubMed]
29. Barabási, A.L.; Albert, R. Emergence of Scaling in Random Networks. *Science* **1999**, *286*, 509–512. [CrossRef]
30. Pastor-Satorras, R.; Vespignani, A. *Evolution and Structure of the Internet: A Statistical Physics Approach*; Cambridge University Press: Cambridge, UK, 2007.
31. Anastasio, T.J. *Tutorial on Neural Systems Modeling*; Sinauer Associates Incorporated Publishers: Sunderland, MA, USA, 2009.
32. Rothman, K.J.; Greenland, S.; Lash, T.L. *Modern Epidemiology*; Wolters Kluwer Health/Lippincott Williams & Wilkins: Philadelphia, PA, USA, 2008.

33. Zadeh, L.A. Fuzzy Sets as a Basis for a Theory of Possibility. *Fuzzy Sets Syst.* **1999**, *100*, 9–34. [CrossRef]
34. Lee, C. Fuzzy Logic in Control Systems: Fuzzy Logic Controller I. *IEEE Trans. Syst. Man, Cybern.* **1990**, *20*, 404–418. [CrossRef]
35. Lee, C. Fuzzy Logic in Control Systems: Fuzzy Logic Controller II. *IEEE Trans. Syst. Man, Cybern.* **1990**, *20*, 419–435. [CrossRef]
36. Lin, C.; Lee, C.S.G. Neural-Network-Based Fuzzy Logic Control and Decision System. *IEEE Trans. Comput.* **1991**, *40*, 1320–1336. [CrossRef]
37. McClelland, J.L.; Cleeremans, A. Consciousness and Connectionist Models. *Oxf. Companion Conscious.* **2009**, *5*, 180–181.
38. Park, S.W.; Bolker, B.M. Effects of Contact Structure on the Transient Evolution of HIV Virulence. *PLoS Comput. Biol.* **2017**, *13*, e1005453. [CrossRef] [PubMed]
39. Champredon, D.; Bellan, S.; Dushoff, J. HIV Sexual Transmission is Predominantly Driven by Single Individuals Rather than Discordant Couples: A Model-Based Approach. *PLoS ONE* **2013**, *8*, e082906. [CrossRef] [PubMed]
40. Patel, P.; Borkowf, C.B.; Brooks, J.T.; Lasry, A.; Lansky, A.; Mermin, J. Estimating Per-Act HIV Transmission Risk: A Systematic Review. *Aids* **2014**, *28*, 1509–1519. [CrossRef] [PubMed]
41. Cannings, C.; Penman, D. Chapter 2: Models of Random Graphs and their Applications. *Handb. Stat.* **2003**, *21*, 51–91.

Article

Elicitation of the Factors Affecting Electricity Distribution Efficiency Using the Fuzzy AHP Method

Vecihi Yiğit [1], Nazlı Nisa Demir [2], Hisham Alidrisi [3] and Mehmet Emin Aydin [4,*]

1. Department of Industrial Engineering, Ataturk University, 25240 Erzurum, Turkey; vyigit@atauni.edu.tr
2. Aras Electric Distribution Company, 25050 Erzurum, Turkey; nazlinisa_demir@hotmail.com
3. Department of Industrial Engineering, King Abdulaziz University, Jeddah 21589, Saudi Arabia; hmalidrisi@kau.edu.sa
4. Department of Computer Science and Creative Technologies, University of the West of England, Bristol BS16 1QY, UK
* Correspondence: mehmet.aydin@uwe.ac.uk

Abstract: Efficient and uninterrupted energy supply plays a crucial role in the quality of modern daily life, while it is obvious that the efficiency and performance of energy supply companies has a significant impact on energy supply itself and on determining and finetuning the future roadmap of the sector. In this study, the performance and efficiency of energy supply companies with respect to productivity is investigated with reference to a case study of an electricity distribution company in Turkey. The factors affecting the company's performance and their corresponding weight have been determined and obtained using the analytical hierarchy process (AHP) and the Fuzzy AHP methods, two well-known multi-criteria decision-making methods, which are widely used in the literature. The results help demonstrate that the criteria obtained to evaluate the company's energy supply performance play a crucial role in developing strategies, policies and action plans to achieve continuous improvement and consistent development.

Keywords: electricity distribution; factor elicitation for efficiency; fuzzy analytical hierarchical process (F-AHP)

Citation: Yiğit, V.; Demir, N.N.; Alidrisi, H.; Aydin, M.E. Elicitation of the Factors Affecting Electricity Distribution Efficiency Using the Fuzzy AHP Method. *Mathematics* **2021**, *9*, 82. https://doi.org/10.3390/math9010082

Received: 30 November 2020
Accepted: 23 December 2020
Published: 31 December 2020

Publisher's Note: MDPI stays neutral with regard to jurisdictional claims in published maps and institutional affiliations.

Copyright: © 2020 by the authors. Licensee MDPI, Basel, Switzerland. This article is an open access article distributed under the terms and conditions of the Creative Commons Attribution (CC BY) license (https://creativecommons.org/licenses/by/4.0/).

1. Introduction

With the developments that took place after the industrial revolution and the rapid growth in the world's population, the need for energy consumption has been increasing on a daily basis, which forces scientific research in this direction and helps to trigger the emergence of new technologies. With the developing forms of technology, electricity has gained functions beyond providing light and has become indispensable for human beings in transportation, communications, industry, education, health, defense and many other fields. With the importance gained, the use of energy, particularly electricity, has become one of the important criteria not only in daily life but also in the progress of civilizations. With this in mind, it is believed that electrical energy will be at the basis of many developments in the future.

The increasing demand for and dependency on electricity has caused the consumption share of electricity to expand rapidly compared to other energy sources. In addition to electrical energy being a type of energy whose demand is rapidly increasing worldwide, it notably must be transmitted quickly and with high quality. With the energy crises in the 1970s and the effects of energy demand on the economy, the importance of electricity production, supply and the supply–demand balance have been recognized by everyone, and the work on the subject has continued [1]. Electricity consumption, with its ever-growing importance, seems to affect many different sectors directly or indirectly. It is often considered as one of the criteria or performance indicators for measuring the development levels and economic growth of countries, as is proved by the case of the Turkish Electricity Joint Stock Company in Turkey.

A privatization process started in the Turkish energy sector two decades ago and finalized in 2008, in which electricity distribution services to customers were delegated to 21 distribution companies in Turkey. Even though distribution companies are in a dominant position given the scope of their licenses, they are audited by different independent and governmental channels such as TEDAŞ, EPDK and the Ministry of Energy and Natural Resources. Hence, the concepts of performance and efficiency have gained more importance for distribution companies [2]. After moving from public ownership to private, energy supply companies started to be exposed to serious competition, which was not in place before. In addition, electricity distribution (energy supply) companies must follow the corporate strategies imposed by the Ministry of Energy and work to reach pre-set efficiency targets in order to ensure customer satisfaction and change public perception towards the companies, as they are no longer public institutions. These energy supply companies have previously been assessed and monitored with respect to financial measures but have never been evaluated with respect to the efficiency of management, performance of operations and customer satisfaction, since they were serving as public companies and were not subject to serious competitions and compliance audits. In order to keep these companies standing firm in the market, all qualitative and quantitative assessments are inevitably required. Following up from this need, this study proposes an approach to identify the performance criteria of energy supply—particularly electricity distribution—companies in performance and efficiency studies as extracted from companies' daily practices. It is paramount to indicate that the best performance and efficiency studies can be conducted through a bottom-up approach, which significantly involves daily practices. There are few studies that have been done on the efficiency of energy companies in different countries—including Turkey—using data-driven techniques such as data envelopment analysis (DEA) [3,4]. It is well-known that the assessments with DEA can only be made with quantitative data and are hard to apply to qualitative data, while non-financial assessments of companies have to rely on qualitative data.

The main aim of this study was to investigate how to assess the performance and efficiency of energy supply companies in the post-privatization Turkish market using expert views, which constitute qualitative data. To the best knowledge of the authors, this is the first study conducted to take qualitative data on board—collected from expert views—for assessing the performance and efficiency of electricity distribution companies in Turkey following the major privatization. Performance and efficiency assessment problems are multi-criteria decision-making (MCDM) problems by their nature. Analytical hierarchy process (AHP) and fuzzy analytical hierarchy process (F-AHP) approaches are known as success-proven and easily implementable qualitative assessment methods for MCDM problems. AHP is a powerful method to identify the impact of the factors affecting the quality of service provided by companies. It is helpful mainly when working with qualitative data and lets the evaluators consider the sub-criteria alongside the main criteria, unlike many other MCDM methods. It is a fact that qualitative data are not crisp by nature and keep overlapping aspects with neighboring value ranges. In order to take such overlapping boundary values into account, which would help contribute to the richness of the data in use, it has previously been decided to use F-AHP in evaluations. It is more reasonable to compare the results gained with a fuzzy model with its crisp version.

This paper reports a study that conducted a comprehensive performance assessment for an electricity distribution company operating in the Eastern Anatolia Region of Turkey. It started by determining the primary factors affecting the efficiency of such a company. Then, the determined factors were prioritized using AHP and F-AHP methods as two prominent multi-criteria decision-making approaches; AHP uniquely and primarily assists in conducting assessments with criteria composed of sub-criteria while F-AHP facilitates encompassing more human expertise with Fuzzy sets and grammar to perform much more realistic assessments. Within the scope of the study, a unique case study has been carried out for one of major energy distribution firms functions in north-east of Turkey, namely Aras Elektrik Dağıtım AŞ (EDAŞ), operating as service provider for 7 provinces: Ağrı, Ardahan, Bayburt, Erzincan, Erzurum, Iğdır and Kars.

The rest of the paper is structured as follows. A relevant literature review is provided in Section 2, while the steps of the Fuzzy AHP method as the proposed approach is introduced in Section 3. The details of expert view capturing process to apply the evaluation and elicit the assessment criteria, and the use of AHP and Fuzzy AHP in conducting the efficiency study is overviewed in Section 4. Section 5 presents the results and findings with relevant discussions while Section 6 briefs the conclusions.

2. Literature Review and Background

The main studies related to electricity distribution companies in Turkey generally, the history of the distribution companies, the privatization process, privatization of electricity companies and examinations before and after their study investigated the structure of the energy sector are [2–5]. The Data Envelopment Analysis (DEA) method was generally used in studies where efficiency analysis of electricity distribution companies was conducted.

Filippini et al. [6] studied the efficiency of electricity distribution companies in Slovenia in which the relationship between efficiency and energy prices was investigated; it was concluded that electricity distribution companies are not efficient, and a more efficient map would be formed by merging small companies. Odyakmaz [7] found that the current performance measurement systems for electricity distribution companies have been set up based on operating costs while the other efficiency and productivity parameters have not been considered. The study uses a DEA approach to calculate the efficiencies and identifies that environmental, structural and quality factors have had impacts on the activities of electricity distribution companies. Duzgün [8] has used a DEA method for measuring the performance of a few electricity distribution companies in Turkey in which the number of personnel, line length and operating expenses were primarily taken as inputs and then the inverse density index and line length index were added to the model in order to measure the impact of environmental factors upon company efficiencies. It concluded the companies with less than 1 million customers or more than 2 million customers in the optimum model are inefficient. In addition, it also found that socio-economic data have a direct effect on the efficiency. Dönmezçelik [9] investigated the efficiency of electricity distribution companies using the DEA method. Two models have been created using 5-year data covering the years 2007–2011. In the first model, data for the factors such as operating costs, loss and leakage rates and income per subscriber are used, while in the second model, input and output values such as the number of personnel, line length, the number of breakdowns and interruptions and transformer power are used. Other studies evaluating the efficiency of electricity distribution companies using the DEA method included: performance evaluation of Iranian electricity distribution companies [10–12]; efficiency analysis of the electricity distribution companies in Turkey [13,14]; efficiency analysis of East and West German electricity distribution companies [15], etc.

Winter et al. [16] have used the KEMIRA-M method to select a warehouse location for an electricity distribution company. Environmental and company-related criteria have been determined for the evaluation of 20 warehouse location alternatives. Janackovic et al. [17] have discussed the selection of key indicators using the F-AHP method to improve the occupational safety system in electricity distribution companies using a number of qualitative factors describing the organizational specificity affecting the safety system. Çelen and Yalçın [18] have studied the quality of service in the electricity distribution companies in Turkey using F-AHP, TOPSIS and DEA methods. The relative importance levels of different quality indicators were determined with a F-AHP method. Then, the TOPSIS method was used to create/estimate the service quality variable. Finally, this variable was used as an output in the DEA stage and the efficiency performances of electricity distribution services were determined, accordingly. Saulo et al. [19] presented an overview of electricity distribution system planning by comparing the short-term planning approach with the long-term vision-oriented planning approach. In the comparison of short- and long-term plans, it has used a simple multi-attribute rating (SMART) technique as a multi-criterion decision-making method. Another recent performance assessment study for energy companies is reported in [20] that used DEA using quantitative data. More recently, Zavadskas et al. [21] have considered F-AHP in procedure development for supplier selection in the steel industry, while Blagojević et al. [22] have merged F-AHP with DEA in a performance assessment and efficiency assessment of a railway company. The authors of [23] have used AHP with other multi criteria decision making state-of-art approaches in displaying the product selection. Recent more studies introduce a few other MCDM approaches including the fuzzy best-worst [24], full-consistency method [25] and fuzzy SWARA methods [26,27], but none of them cover assessments of energy companies, while each seem to be computationally more complicated with AHP for implementation and do not promise a very compromising performance.

AHP has been seen and reviewed as one very prominent multi criteria decision making approach offering qualitative evaluation [28]. The literature review suggests that the majority of performance assessment and efficiency studies covering the post-privatization of the Turkish energy sector have been conducted using the variants of the DEA method as a hard numerical assessment approach using quantitative data. It is known that qualitative data is fuzzy by its nature and that it needs to be quantified to produce consistent and numeric data, but, in many cases, various types of qualitative data could not be satisfactorily converted into numbers. In particular, evaluations based on expert views are preferable to retain in qualitative form; therefore, AHP and its fuzzy form have been usefully and easily implemented for many selection and assessment problems [29–33]. In addition, AHP variants provide assessments without disregarding subcategories and it is not complicated to implement, unlike many other multi-criteria decision-making approaches. All of these facts and reasons have led to the choice to use AHP methods, classical AHP and F-AHP in this study, since all the assessment data used are qualitative and heavily reliant on expert views.

3. Materials and Methods

Case studies on efficiencies with AHP and F-AHP have been examined in the previous section and it is seen that AHP and F-AHP were used in a wide range of subjects [29–33]. Decisions made without concrete data in all sectors with different dynamics pose a significant problem. For example, while determining the criteria that affect productivity, criteria such as operating expenses and income sources can be determined with concrete numbers, but criteria such as workforce opportunities, fringe benefits and the reliability level of the enterprise cannot be expressed with numerical data. Since this situation creates an obstacle preventing the decision makers from reaching a conclusion, it has been observed that the use of multi-criteria decision-making methods in studies on productivity and efficiency contributes to the literature. In addition, reaching a single result in studies with classical AHP sometimes limits the range of action of the decision maker [34]. For example, when an AHP application is made to decide the title of the personnel according to the performance system, the result value for a single title will be reached. However, the decision maker is not given the opportunity to take the initiative in situations that may cause uncertainty, such as the optimum result of the placement of two different personnel for the same title. In the case of similar situations, the solution points with upper and lower values in the solutions made with F-AHP are provided to get rid of the uncertainty for the decision makers. In addition, in previous studies, it was seen that the productivity and efficiency of distribution companies were measured mostly with the DEA method rather than with other MCDM approaches, including the F-AHP method. Following on from this fact, this study has been conducted to determine the efficiency criteria of an energy supply company using data collected on the 2018–2019 form on Aras EDAŞ practices. The data were first evaluated with the AHP method first and then with F-AHP for identifying the factors affecting the efficiency of the company in a wider qualitative sense and under a multiple-criteria decision-making point of view.

Fuzzy AHP plays an important role in establishing a hierarchical structure consisting of main and sub-criteria, addressing the problem clearly and determining the importance of the criteria relative to each other. In addition, it helps to digitize the expressions that belong to a single person or a group of experts, reflecting both subjective and objective views without any numerical value, to reach an analytical solution. Fuzzy AHP, which is used in problem solutions in many different fields, produces simple solutions to complex criteria, while accelerating the decision-making process and offering the opportunity to reach systematic results.

In this study, triangular fuzzy numbers were used to digitize verbal expressions. Since triangular fuzzy numbers allow subjective data to be digitized objectively, they are frequently used in decision problems. In addition, trapezoidal numbers are preferred in fuzzy logic problems due to the fact that they allow operations in a range closer to real values in comparison to other fuzzy numbers, while their graphical representation and operations are easier.

Unlike classical set theory, where the membership of an element in a set is represented by two terms (i.e., 0 or 1), fuzzy set theory allows for partial membership; this means it includes items with varying degrees of membership in the set; it monitors a range of membership functions with values within [0, 1]. Fuzzy Set Theory was proposed by Zadeh in 1965 to reflect reality by using approximate values in ambiguous and uncertain environments due to the nature of human reasoning [35]. Fuzzy set theory has been applied to a wide variety of fields, and produces especially useful results when information is incomplete or uncertain. Fuzzy logic is derived from fuzzy set theory. It is capable of handling concepts that are inherently imprecise (i.e., ambiguous, imprecise, vulgar or false). Both fuzzy set theory and fuzzy logic thus have widespread applications [36].

AHP structures the problem in a hierarchical fashion, from goal to criteria, sub-criteria and alternatives at successive levels [37]. The hierarchy provides experts with an overview of the complex relationships inherent in context and helps them evaluate whether elements of the same level are comparable. The items are then compared in pairs against the 9 level scale to estimate their weights. However, binary comparison, which is the essence of AHP, causes vagueness and uncertainty in experts' judgment. In practical situations, experts may not be able to assign exact numerical values to their preferences due to limited knowledge or ability [38,39]. To overcome the ambiguity in AHP, the exact numbers are replaced by fuzzy numbers that represent linguistic expressions in F-AHP. This tolerates ambiguous judgments by assigning degrees of membership to exact numbers in order to explain that to what extent these numbers belong to an expression [40].

AHP is a multi-criteria decision-making technique. In most cases, it is difficult to measure or prioritize decision-making criteria because they are subjective and not measurable. One of the advantages of AHP is that this method can systematically convert abstract and non-measurable criteria into numerical values [41]. In addition, one of the most important benefits provided by the AHP method is that this method can measure the consistency degree of binary comparisons.

In this study, AHP and F-AHP based on Fuzzy grammar were used in the case study detailed in the next section to help make decisions on the efficiency of the electricity distribution company studied. An algorithm, suggested by Chang and called extent analysis [42,43], has been used for the purpose of implementing F-AHP using fuzzy grammar.

Let $X = \{x_1, x_2, \ldots, x_n\}$ be an object set, and $U = \{u_1, u_2, \ldots, u_m\}$ be a goal set. According to this method, each object is taken and extent analysis for each goal is performed, respectively. Therefore, m extent analysis values for each object can be obtained, with the following signs:

$$M_{gi}^1, M_{gi}^2, \ldots, M_{gi}^m, \ i = 1, 2, \ldots, n \tag{1}$$

where all the $M_{gi}^j (j = 1, 2, \ldots, m)$ are triangular fuzzy numbers. The steps of Chang's extent analysis can be given as follows [44]:

Step 1: The value of fuzzy synthetic extent with respect to the ith object is defined as in Equation (2):

$$S_i = \sum_{j=1}^{m} M_{gi}^j \otimes \left[\sum_{i=1}^{n} \sum_{j=1}^{m} M_{gi}^j \right]^{-1}. \tag{2}$$

To obtain $\sum_{j=1}^{m} M_{gi}^j$, the fuzzy addition operation of m extent analysis values for a particular matrix is performed as in Equation (3):

$$\sum_{j=1}^{m} M_{gi}^j = \left(\sum_{j=1}^{m} l_j, \sum_{j=1}^{m} m_j, \sum_{j=1}^{m} u_j \right). \tag{3}$$

Then to obtain $\left[\sum_{i=1}^{n} \sum_{j=1}^{m} M_{gi}^j \right]^{-1}$, the fuzzy addition operation of M_{gi}^j values is performed as in Equation (4):

$$\sum_{i=1}^{n} \sum_{j=1}^{m} M_{gi}^j = \left(\sum_{i=1}^{n} l_j, \sum_{i=1}^{n} m_j, \sum_{i=1}^{n} u_j \right). \tag{4}$$

Then the inverse of the vector above is computed as in Equation (5):

$$\left[\sum_{i=1}^{n} \sum_{j=1}^{m} M_{gi}^j \right]^{-1} = \left(\frac{1}{\sum_{i=1}^{n} u_i}, \frac{1}{\sum_{i=1}^{n} m_i}, \frac{1}{\sum_{i=1}^{n} l_i} \right). \tag{5}$$

Step 2: As M_1 and M_2 are two triangular fuzzy numbers, the degree of possibility of $M_2 = (l_2, m_2, u_2) \geq M_1 = (l_1, m_1, u_1)$ is defined as

$$V(M_2 \geq M_1) = \sup_{y \geq x}(\min(\mu_{M_1}(x), \mu_{M_2}(y))) \tag{6}$$

and can be equivalently expressed as follows:

$$V(M_2 \geq M_1) = hgt(M_1 \cap M_2) = \mu_{M_2}(d) = \begin{cases} 1 & \text{if } m_2 \geq m_1, \\ 0 & \text{if } l_1 \geq u_2, \\ \frac{l_1 - u_2}{(m_2 - u_2) - (m_1 - l_1)} & \text{otherwise} \end{cases} \tag{7}$$

where d is the ordinate of the highest intersection point D between μ_{M_1} and μ_{M_2}. Equation (8) is illustrated in Figure 1 [44]. The values of both $V(M_1 \geq M_2)$ and $V(M_2 \geq M_1)$ are needed to compare M_1 and M_2.

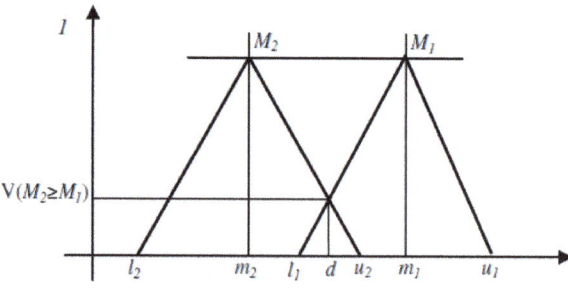

Figure 1. The intersection between M_1 and M_2.

Step 3: The degree of possibility for a convex fuzzy number to be greater than k convex fuzzy numbers $M_i (i = 1, 2, \ldots, k)$ can be defined by Equation (8):

$$V(M \geq M_1, M_2, \ldots, M_k) = V[(M \geq M_1) \text{ and } (M \geq M_2)] \text{ and } \ldots \text{ and } (M \geq M_k) \\ = \min V(M \geq M_i), \ i = 1, 2, 3, \ldots, k \tag{8}$$

Assume that

$$d'(A_i) = \min V(S_i \geq S_k) \tag{9}$$

For $k = 1, 2, \ldots, n;\ k \neq i$. Then the weight vector is given by

$$W' = (d'(A_1), d'(A_2), \ldots, d'(A_n))^T, \tag{10}$$

where $A_i (i = 1, 2, \ldots, n)$ are n elements.

Step 4: With normalization, the normalized weight vectors are

$$W = (d(A_1), d(A_2), \ldots, d(A_n))^T. \tag{11}$$

4. Case Study

This case study aims to implement the F-AHP method explained in the previous section for eliciting factors affecting the efficiency of Aras EDAŞ Co. as an energy supply company operating in the north-east of Turkey. The implementation was endorsed to go through the following steps: (1) Defining the problem and purpose, (2) determining the decision-making group-experts, (3) determining the criteria, (4) creating a hierarchical structure, (5) obtaining the criterion weights with the AHP and F-AHP methods.

4.1. Defining the Problem and Purpose

Electricity is produced by power plants and transported over long distances via transmission lines and short distances via distribution lines and sold/supplied to the end users by retail sales companies.

As a result of the need to manage electricity generation, transmission, distribution and trade from a single source, targets have been set for the electricity sector within the development plans.

Turkey Electricity Distribution Corporation (known as TEDAŞ) was/is a public energy supply company in charge of electricity distribution across the whole country. Its service coverage area has been divided in 21 regions and the decision was made to delegate its distribution service per region to a private distribution company back in 2004 under the scope of privatization established by the Privatization High Council. As part of this process, distribution and retail sales companies were established and started to operate in 21 regions with a license period of 49 years. Aras EDAŞ Co. constitutes one of these distribution regions (Figure 2).

The study was carried out on Aras EDAŞ, an electricity distribution company that provides services in 7 provinces, 58 districts and a 70.554 km² area with 1715 personnel, allowing sample application data to be used in the academic study for the analysis of factors affecting efficiency and productivity in enterprises with the F-AHP method.

Aras EDAŞ Co. operates in one area of activity covering 52 districts, 2033 villages and 1593 settlements (neighborhoods, hamlets, etc.) in an area of 71.007 km² within the borders of the Erzurum, Erzincan, Bayburt, Kars, Ağrı, Ardahan and Iğdır provinces. There are 58 enterprises in total within the 7 provinces in the covered area: 20 are in Erzurum, 9 are in Erzincan, 3 are in Bayburt, 8 are in Kars, 6 are in Ardahan, 8 are in Ağrı and 4 are in Iğdır. The General Directorate, which is affiliated with the board of directors, serves with the Provincial Coordinators in Ağrı, Ardahan, Bayburt, Erzurum, Erzincan Iğdır and Kars provinces and with the District Operation Chiefs in the districts.

Figure 2. Electricity distribution companies in Turkey.

As of 2018, Aras EDAŞ provides electricity distribution services with 1715 personnel, including 462 of its own personnel who work in service procurement. The company had a total of 1,001,044 subscribers in Turkey at that time.

Aras EDAŞ makes investments in network improvement, technological infrastructure, quality and uninterrupted energy in order to increase customer satisfaction and efficiency in its management. After considering the investment needs of the region and the projected investment plans, the distribution service investment expenditure for the 2011–2015 implementation period was approved by the Energy Market Regulatory Board (EPDK) as 352,180,435 TL in total. For the implementation period of 2016–2020, it was approved by EPDK for a total of 595,420,985 TL, or 119,084,197 TL per year.

Although the efficiency aims of distribution companies including Aras EDAŞ are generally focused on cost, they have been directed to work on customer satisfaction by the Ministry of Energy and Natural Resources in recent years. In this context, Aras EDAŞ has moved away from being a public institution and has worked on reorganizing the existing and usual structure for years and ensuring customer satisfaction by reviewing all processes. Examining the studies conducted by Aras EDAŞ and other distribution companies, where customer satisfaction gains more importance day by day, it has been observed that process or person-based efficiency studies are carried out, but there is no work being done to determine the basic criteria that affect the efficiency of the entire company.

The literature review suggests that the studies on the productivity and efficiency of energy supply companies have been mostly conducted using DEA, while the F-AHP method has frequently been used in selection problems such as performance studies of various companies excluding energy supply enterprises. The privatization process has brought a new era to the Turkish energy sector due to the fact that companies supplying energy services have been made subject to competition. In order to address emergent issues during post-privatization, the companies need to measure their efficiency for staying competitive in the market and improving customer satisfaction.

As a relatively new company, Aras EDAŞ sets out an aim to look at its processes and the complete efficiency and productivity; hence, it was revealed that the criteria affecting productivity and their weights should be determined. Once revealed, it is expected to shed light on the actions required to be taken towards improving the efficiency of the entire enterprise.

4.2. Determination of Decision-Making Group-Experts

The large area of activity of Aras EDAŞ and the high number of enterprises to serve and number of personnel within the enterprise require the corporate management to stay firm. In addition, due to the nature of the work performed, it has been observed that the personnel, who generally constitute the management staff, are graduates of technical departments and have a good command of management training. For this reason, a total of 150 managers were interviewed at the levels of Chief, Chief Engineer and Manager and Coordinator in order to benefit from their experience and opinions for the hierarchical structure formed by group decision-making.

4.3. Determination of Criteria

The purpose of this study was to express the productivity in enterprises. The first criteria were expressed as Customer Satisfaction, Uninterrupted Energy and the Quality of Energy, which are the main criteria affecting the efficiency of distribution companies.

Customer Satisfaction (C1): There is an understanding of competition when electricity distribution companies operate for public service purposes but do not focus on profit. Each distribution company is obliged to provide infrastructure services to all its customers in its own service area. Since it is not possible for any distribution company to serve customers in the region of another distribution company, there is no competition between companies. However, the company needs a good customer satisfaction for renewal of their license in the following periods. Although electricity distribution companies operate in a monopoly far from competition, they have adopted a customer satisfaction-oriented approach after privatization. In addition, distribution companies operating under the Ministry of Energy and Natural Resources are evaluated at certain periods in terms of customer satisfaction criteria through surveys and analyses conducted by authorities such as the Ministry, TEDAŞ and EPDK. For this reason, customer satisfaction, which is accepted as an indicator of efficiency in electricity distribution companies, has been included as one of the main criteria in our study.

Uninterrupted Energy (C2): Uninterrupted energy is expressed as the capacity to provide electrical energy to customers served at economically acceptable costs and with the minimum possible downtime. Distribution companies, which have major responsibilities to provide uninterrupted electricity supply for customers, make maximum efforts to provide uninterrupted energy. In addition, all interruptions that occur in all or part of the network must be recorded. This covers all outages regardless of criteria such as the recording duration and number of outages. Notified outages made within the scope of works such as maintenance and repair and shared with customers at the latest 48 hours in advance are subject to inspections by authorities such as TEDAŞ and EPDK in cases of instantaneous interruptions due to failures. For these reasons, uninterrupted energy, which is considered to be an indicator of efficiency in electricity distribution companies, is also one of the main criteria in our study.

Quality of Energy (C3): This refers to the presentation of energy to customers without technical problems such as harmonic disorders and voltage problems with quality energy, also called technical quality. Electricity distribution companies must measure the technical quality of the energy they offer and record this in accordance with the relevant standards. All processes and data belonging to the records received are subject to inspections by authorities such as TEDAŞ and EPDK as efficiency criteria. For these reasons, quality of energy, which is regarded as an indicator of efficiency in electricity distribution companies, is adopted as one of the main criteria in this study.

After the determination of the main criteria, sub-criteria of the main criteria were determined. Its sub-criteria were considered as Service Region, Management and Employees.

Service Area: 21 distribution companies operate across the whole country in Turkey serving customers in different geographic regions. Aras EDAŞ, where the study was conducted, is one of the distribution companies serving the widest geographical area with a service area of 71,007 km^2, which is mostly very mountainous. Such geographical conditions were included in the study as one of the criteria affecting the efficiency of distribution companies due to the fact that field studies are predominant due to the nature of the study.

Similarly, after the determination of the service region criteria, other criteria belonging to the sub-criteria were obtained based on expert opinions. The sub-criteria of the Service

Region criteria were determined as Number of Customers (C11), Geographical Conditions (C12), Climatic Conditions (C13), Network Size (C14), Line Length (C15), Energy Losses (C16) and Investment Amount (C17).

Management: Although many definitions have been developed about management staff and managers in businesses, if we summarize, managers play an auxiliary role in reaching the targets of their enterprise by using all resources with high performance and thus increasing productivity. For this reason, "Management" has been considered as one of the sub-criteria, based on the importance of the role of managers in order for businesses to be successful.

Following the determination of the management criteria other criteria belonging to the sub-criteria similarly were obtained based on expert opinions. The sub-criteria of management are: Determination of Goals (C21), Participation of Personnel in Decision Processes (C22), Ensuring Ergonomic Conditions (C23), Supporting Employee Development (C24), Giving Importance to Occupational Health and Safety (C25), Flexible Working Hours (C26), Existence of Integrated Management System Certificates (C27) and Employee Promotion and Advancement Opportunities (C28).

Employees: No matter how high the technological and technical investments are in the enterprises, it will not be possible to increase productivity unless there are personnel managing these investments and technological infrastructures. As a result of similar opinions expressed by the experts, employees were included in the study as one of the sub-criteria.

After the determination of the employee criteria other criteria belonging to the sub-criteria were similarly obtained based on expert opinions. Sub-criteria of the employee criteria are: Employee Adoption of Goals (C31), Staff Education Level (C32), Employee Motivation (C33), Wages and Benefits (C34), Teamwork (C35), Awareness of Responsibility (C36), Average Service Time of Personnel (C37) and Number of Personnel (C38).

4.4. Creating the Hierarchical Structure

A hierarchical structure was created as a result of the criteria determined by the group decision making method and explained in detail. It is specified as in Figure 3.

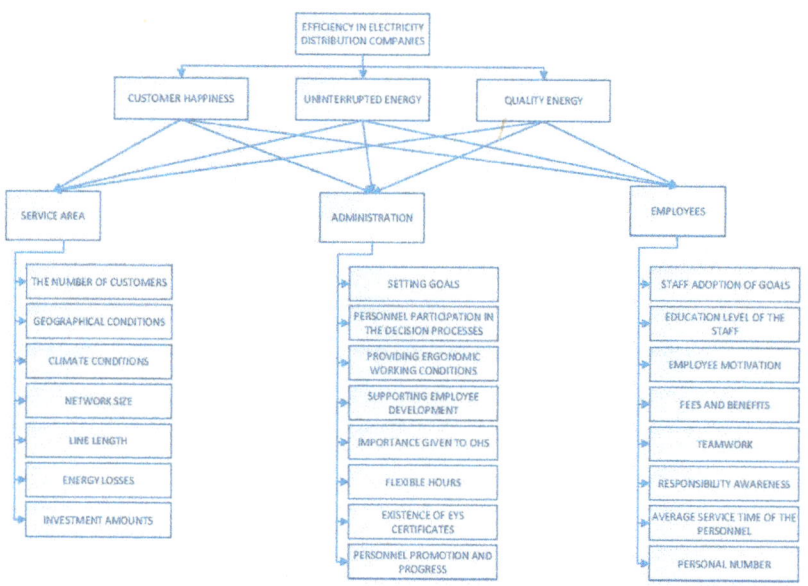

Figure 3. Problem hierarchical structure.

The questionnaire method was used to compare the criteria and sub-criteria, which are indicated in Figure 3 in a hierarchical structure. The questionnaire was sent online to 150 managers at the level of team leads, leads of engineers, managers and coordinators, who previously contributed to the creation of the hierarchical structure by providing expert opinions. While filling in the questionnaire, Aras EDAŞ's internal software survey system was used.

While determining the number of questionnaires to be made, similar studies have been examined and it is seen that although care has been taken to select the sample representing the main population, no special study has been done for the number of questionnaires. For example, in the shipyard efficiency study conducted by Kırdağlı in 2010, the study was completed with only 9 expert opinions [33]. In this study, it was thought that the survey should be conducted with 150 managers or team leads at Aras EDAŞ, while all the personnel at the executive level who were involved in the projects related to efficiency measurements and had an impact on the decision processes were interviewed.

In the survey, experts (managers and team leads in this case) were asked to make pairwise comparisons of the criteria. Verbal expressions, which correspond to fuzzy numbers, were used when taking opinions from the managers. Fuzzy triangle numbers used in binary comparison are given in Table 1.

Table 1. Fuzzy triangular numbers table used for binary comparison.

Point	Verbal Eexpresion	Fuzzy Triangle Numbers					
		Number			Pair		
1	Equally Important	1.000	1.000	1.000	1.000	1.000	1.000
2	A little more important	0.667	1.000	1.500	0.667	1.000	1.500
3	Strongly Important	1.500	2.000	2.500	0.400	0.500	0.667
4	Very Strongly Important	2.500	3.000	3.500	0.286	0.333	0.400
5	Absolutely Important	3.500	4.000	4.500	0.222	0.250	0.286

When the studies conducted with Order Analysis Management were examined, it was seen that the geometric mean was preferred because the arithmetic mean was not sufficient to create comparison matrices. It was observed that geometric mean methods were used to make the survey results similar to triangle fuzzy number values and to include conjugate expressions in the study [45]. Therefore, the views of 150 experts are combined with the geometric mean and the decision matrix formed on these basis is given in Table 2.

Table 2. Pairwise comparison matrix for main criteria.

	C_1 (S_{C_1})	C_2 (S_{C_2})	C_3 (S_{C_3})
C_1 (S_{C_1})	(1.000, 1.000, 1.000)	(1.500, 2.000, 2.500)	(1.500, 2.000, 2.500)
C_2 (S_{C_2})	(0.400, 0.500, 0.667)	(1.000, 1.000, 1.000)	(0.667, 1.000, 1.500)
C_3 (S_{C_3})	(0.400, 0.500, 0.667)	(0.667, 1.000, 1.500)	(1.000, 1.000, 1.000)

The operations performed according to the Rank Analysis steps of Chang's method [43] are given below.

Step 1: The value of the fuzzy synthetic extent with respect to the ith object has been determined in Equation (2) by using Equations (3)–(5). Calculation of the value of C1 criterion is as follows:

$$S_{C_1} = (4.000, 5.000, 6.000) \otimes [8.134, 10.000, 12.334]^{-1} = (0.324, 0.500, 0.738).$$

The S_{C_2} and S_{C_3} values can be calculated in the same way as follows:

$$S_{C_2} = (0.168, 0.250, 0.389)$$

$$S_{C_3} = (0.168, 0.250, 0.389).$$

Step 2: For triangular fuzzy numbers, the degree of possibility is expressed equivalently in Equation (7) and is determined using Equation (6):

- Conditions that satisfy the $V(M_2 \geq M_1) = 1$ property for $m_2 \geq m_1$;

$$V\left(S_{C_1} \geq S_{C_2}\right) = 1 V\left(S_{C_1} \geq S_{C_3}\right) = 1 V\left(S_{C_2} \geq S_{C_3}\right) = 1 V(S_{C_3} \geq S_{C_2}) = 1.$$

- It is seen that there is no case that satisfies the $V(M_2 \geq M_1) = 0$ property for $l_1 \geq u_2$.
- For other cases, the $\frac{l_1 - u_2}{(m_2 - u_2) - (m_1 - l_1)}$ value was calculated using the formula $V(M_2 \geq M_1)$

$$V\left(S_{C_2} \geq S_{C_1}\right) = V\left(S_{C_3} \geq S_{C_1}\right) = (0.324 - 0.389) / ((0.250 - 0.389) - (0.500 - 0.327)) = 0.206$$

Step 3: The degree of possibility for a convex fuzzy number to be greater than k convex fuzzy numbers using Equation (8) is:

$$\min V\left(S_{C_1} \geq S_{C_2}, S_{C_3}\right) = 1; \min V\left(S_{C_2} \geq S_{C_1}, S_{C_3}\right) = 0.206; \min V\left(S_{C_3} \geq S_{C_1}, S_{C_2}\right) = 0.206.$$

Step 4: With normalization, the normalized weight vectors are shown as:

$$W = (0.708, 0.146, 0.146)^T.$$

The F-AHP steps given above have been repeated for the decision matrices given in Tables 3–11.

Table 3. Paired comparison matrix of 'service area' sub-criteria for customer satisfaction.

	C_{11}	C_{12}	C_{13}	C_{14}	C_{15}	C_{16}	C_{17}
C_{11}	(1.000, 1.000, 1.000)	(2.500, 3.000, 3.500)	(1.500, 2.000, 2.500)	(0.667, 1.000, 1.500)	(1.500, 2.000, 2.500)	(0.286, 0.333, 0.400)	(0.222, 0.250, 0.286)
C_{12}	(0.286, 0.333, 0.400)	(1.000, 1.000, 1.000)	(0.667, 1.000, 1.500)	(0.667, 1.000, 1.500)	(0.667, 1.000, 1.500)	(0.286, 0.333, 0.400)	(0.667, 1.000, 1.500)
C_{13}	(0.400, 0.500, 0.667)	(0.667, 1.000, 1.500)	(1.000, 1.000, 1.000)	(0.667, 1.000, 1.500)	(0.400, 0.500, 0.667)	(0.400, 0.500, 0.667)	(0.667, 1.000, 1.500)
C_{14}	(0.667, 1.000, 1.500)	(0.667, 1.000, 1.500)	(0.667, 1.000, 1.500)	(1.000, 1.000, 1.000)	(0.667, 1.000, 1.500)	(0.400, 0.500, 0.667)	(0.400, 0.500, 0.667)
C_{15}	(0.400, 0.500, 0.667)	(0.667, 1.000, 1.500)	(1.500, 2.000, 2.500)	(0.667, 1.000, 1.500)	(1.000, 1.000, 1.000)	(0.667, 1.000, 1.500)	(2.500, 3.000, 3.500)
C_{16}	(2.500, 3.000, 3.500)	(2.500, 3.000, 3.500)	(1.500, 2.000, 2.500)	(1.500, 2.000, 2.500)	(0.667, 1.000, 1.500)	(1.000, 1.000, 1.000)	(0.667, 1.000, 1.500)
C_{17}	(3.500, 4.000, 4.500)	(0.667, 1.000, 1.500)	(0.667, 1.000, 1.500)	(1.500, 2.000, 2.500)	(2.500, 3.000, 3.500)	(0.667, 1.000, 1.500)	(1.000, 1.000, 1.000)

Table 4. Paired comparison matrix of 'management' sub-criteria for customer satisfaction.

	C_{21}	C_{22}	C_{23}	C_{24}	C_{25}	C_{26}	C_{27}	C_{28}
C_{21}	(1.000, 1.000, 1.000)	(1.500, 2.000, 2.500)	(0.400, 0.500, 0.667)	(1.500, 2.000, 2.500)	(0.667, 1.000, 1.500)	(2.500, 3.000, 3.500)	(0.667, 1.000, 1.500)	(0.667, 1.000, 1.500)
C_{22}	(0.400, 0.500, 0.667)	(1.000, 1.000, 1.000)	(0.400, 0.500, 0.667)	(0.400, 0.500, 0.667)	(0.667, 1.000, 1.500)	(2.500, 3.000, 3.500)	(0.667, 1.000, 1.500)	(0.400, 0.500, 0.667)
C_{23}	(1.500, 2.000, 2.500)	(1.500, 2.000, 2.500)	(1.000, 1.000, 1.000)	(1.500, 2.000, 2.500)	(0.667, 1.000, 1.500)	(2.500, 3.000, 3.500)	(1.500, 2.000, 2.500)	(0.667, 1.000, 1.500)
C_{24}	(0.400, 0.500, 0.667)	(1.500, 2.000, 2.500)	(0.400, 0.500, 0.667)	(1.000, 1.000, 1.000)	(1.500, 2.000, 2.500)	(0.400, 0.500, 0.667)	(1.500, 2.000, 2.500)	(1.500, 2.000, 2.500)
C_{25}	(0.667, 1.000, 1.500)	(0.667, 1.000, 1.500)	(0.667, 1.000, 1.500)	(0.400, 0.500, 0.667)	(1.000, 1.000, 1.000)	(0.667, 1.000, 1.500)	(2.500, 3.000, 3.500)	(2.500, 3.000, 3.500)
C_{26}	(0.286, 0.333, 0.400)	(0.286, 0.333, 0.400)	(0.286, 0.333, 0.400)	(1.500, 2.000, 2.500)	(0.667, 1.000, 1.500)	(1.000, 1.000, 1.000)	(1.500, 2.000, 2.500)	(0.667, 1.000, 1.500)
C_{27}	(0.667, 1.000, 1.500)	(0.667, 1.000, 1.500)	(0.400, 0.500, 0.667)	(0.400, 0.500, 0.667)	(0.286, 0.333, 0.400)	(0.400, 0.500, 0.667)	(1.000, 1.000, 1.000)	(0.400, 0.500, 0.667)
C_{28}	(0.667, 1.000, 1.500)	(1.500, 2.000, 2.500)	(0.667, 1.000, 1.500)	(0.400, 0.500, 0.667)	(0.286, 0.333, 0.400)	(0.667, 1.000, 1.500)	(1.500, 2.000, 2.500)	(1.000, 1.000, 1.000)

Table 5. Paired comparison matrix of 'employees' sub-criteria for customer satisfaction.

	C_{31}	C_{32}	C_{33}	C_{34}	C_{35}	C_{36}	C_{37}	C_{38}
C_{31}	(1.000, 1.000, 1.000)	(0.667, 1.000, 1.500)	(0.667, 1.000, 1.500)	(0.667, 1.000, 1.500)	(1.500, 2.000, 2.500)	(0.667, 1.000, 1.500)	(2.500, 3.000, 3.500)	(2.500, 3.000, 3.500)
C_{32}	(0.667, 1.000, 1.500)	(1.000, 1.000, 1.000)	(0.400, 0.500, 0.667)	(1.500, 2.000, 2.500)	(0.400, 0.500, 0.667)	(1.500, 2.000, 2.500)	(1.500, 2.000, 2.500)	(2.500, 3.000, 3.500)
C_{33}	(0.667, 1.000, 1.500)	(1.500, 2.000, 2.500)	(1.000, 1.000, 1.000)	(1.500, 2.000, 2.500)	(0.667, 1.000, 1.500)	(0.400, 0.500, 0.667)	(2.500, 3.000, 3.500)	(2.500, 3.000, 3.500)
C_{34}	(0.667, 1.000, 1.500)	(0.400, 0.500, 0.667)	(0.400, 0.500, 0.667)	(1.000, 1.000, 1.000)	(0.400, 0.500, 0.667)	(0.400, 0.500, 0.667)	(0.400, 0.500, 0.667)	(0.400, 0.500, 0.667)
C_{35}	(0.400, 0.500, 0.667)	(1.500, 2.000, 2.500)	(0.667, 1.000, 1.500)	(1.500, 2.000, 2.500)	(1.000, 1.000, 1.000)	(0.667, 1.000, 1.500)	(1.500, 2.000, 2.500)	(2.500, 3.000, 3.500)
C_{36}	(0.667, 1.000, 1.500)	(0.400, 0.500, 0.667)	(1.500, 2.000, 2.500)	(1.500, 2.000, 2.500)	(0.667, 1.000, 1.500)	(1.000, 1.000, 1.000)	(1.500, 2.000, 2.500)	(1.500, 2.000, 2.500)
C_{37}	(0.286, 0.333, 0.400)	(0.400, 0.500, 0.667)	(0.286, 0.333, 0.400)	(1.500, 2.000, 2.500)	(0.400, 0.500, 0.667)	(0.400, 0.500, 0.667)	(1.000, 1.000, 1.000)	(1.500, 2.000, 2.500)
C_{38}	(0.286, 0.333, 0.400)	(0.286, 0.333, 0.400)	(0.286, 0.333, 0.400)	(1.500, 2.000, 2.500)	(0.286, 0.333, 0.400)	(0.400, 0.500, 0.667)	(0.400, 0.500, 0.667)	(1.000, 1.000, 1.000)

Table 6. Paired comparison matrix of 'service area' sub-criteria for uninterrupted energy.

	C_{11}	C_{12}	C_{13}	C_{14}	C_{15}	C_{16}	C_{17}
C_{11}	(1.000, 1.000, 1.000)	(0.667, 1.000, 1.500)	(0.667, 1.000, 1.500)	(0.400, 0.500, 0.667)	(0.400, 0.500, 0.667)	(0.400, 0.500, 0.667)	(0.400, 0.500, 0.667)
C_{12}	(0.667, 1.000, 1.500)	(1.000, 1.000, 1.000)	(0.667, 1.000, 1.500)	(0.667, 1.000, 1.500)	(0.400, 0.500, 0.667)	(0.286, 0.333, 0.400)	(0.286, 0.333, 0.400)
C_{13}	(0.667, 1.000, 1.500)	(0.667, 1.000, 1.500)	(1.000, 1.000, 1.000)	(2.500, 3.000, 3.500)	(2.500, 3.000, 3.500)	(0.400, 0.500, 0.667)	(2.500, 3.000, 3.500)
C_{14}	(1.500, 2.000, 2.500)	(0.667, 1.000, 1.500)	(0.286, 0.333, 0.400)	(1.000, 1.000, 1.000)	(0.667, 1.000, 1.500)	(0.667, 1.000, 1.500)	(0.667, 1.000, 1.500)
C_{15}	(1.500, 2.000, 2.500)	(1.500, 2.000, 2.500)	(0.286, 0.333, 0.400)	(0.667, 1.000, 1.500)	(1.000, 1.000, 1.000)	(0.400, 0.500, 0.667)	(0.400, 0.500, 0.667)
C_{16}	(1.500, 2.000, 2.500)	(2.500, 3.000, 3.500)	(1.500, 2.000, 2.500)	(0.667, 1.000, 1.500)	(1.500, 2.000, 2.500)	(1.000, 1.000, 1.000)	(0.286, 0.333, 0.400)
C_{17}	(1.500, 2.000, 2.500)	(2.500, 3.000, 3.500)	(0.286, 0.333, 0.400)	(0.667, 1.000, 1.500)	(1.500, 2.000, 2.500)	(2.500, 3.000, 3.500)	(1.000, 1.000, 1.000)

Table 7. Paired comparison matrix of 'management' sub-criteria for uninterrupted energy.

	C_{21}	C_{22}	C_{23}	C_{24}	C_{25}	C_{26}	C_{27}	C_{28}
C_{21}	(1.000, 1.000, 1.000)	(1.500, 2.000, 2.500)	(0.667, 1.000, 1.500)	(0.400, 0.500, 0.667)	(0.667, 1.000, 1.500)	(0.286, 0.333, 0.400)	(1.500, 2.000, 2.500)	(2.500, 3.000, 3.500)
C_{22}	(0.400, 0.500, 0.667)	(1.000, 1.000, 1.000)	(1.500, 2.000, 2.500)	(0.400, 0.500, 0.667)	(0.667, 1.000, 1.500)	(0.286, 0.333, 0.400)	(0.667, 1.000, 1.500)	(0.400, 0.500, 0.667)
C_{23}	(0.667, 1.000, 1.500)	(0.400, 0.500, 0.667)	(1.000, 1.000, 1.000)	(0.400, 0.500, 0.667)	(0.667, 1.000, 1.500)	(0.667, 1.000, 1.500)	(0.400, 0.500, 0.667)	(1.500, 2.000, 2.500)
C_{24}	(1.500, 2.000, 2.500)	(1.500, 2.000, 2.500)	(1.500, 2.000, 2.500)	(1.000, 1.000, 1.000)	(0.667, 1.000, 1.500)	(0.667, 1.000, 1.500)	(2.500, 3.000, 3.500)	(2.500, 3.000, 3.500)
C_{25}	(0.667, 1.000, 1.500)	(0.667, 1.000, 1.500)	(0.667, 1.000, 1.500)	(0.667, 1.000, 1.500)	(1.000, 1.000, 1.000)	(0.667, 1.000, 1.500)	(0.667, 1.000, 1.500)	(2.500, 3.000, 3.500)
C_{26}	(2.500, 3.000, 3.500)	(2.500, 3.000, 3.500)	(0.667, 1.000, 1.500)	(0.667, 1.000, 1.500)	(0.667, 1.000, 1.500)	(1.000, 1.000, 1.000)	(1.500, 2.000, 2.500)	(2.500, 3.000, 3.500)
C_{27}	(0.400, 0.500, 0.667)	(0.667, 1.000, 1.500)	(1.500, 2.000, 2.500)	(0.286, 0.333, 0.400)	(0.667, 1.000, 1.500)	(0.400, 0.500, 0.667)	(1.000, 1.000, 1.000)	(0.400, 0.500, 0.667)
C_{28}	(0.286, 0.333, 0.400)	(1.500, 2.000, 2.500)	(0.400, 0.500, 0.667)	(0.286, 0.333, 0.400)	(0.286, 0.333, 0.400)	(0.286, 0.333, 0.400)	(1.500, 2.000, 2.500)	(1.000, 1.000, 1.000)

Table 8. Paired comparison matrix of 'employees' sub-criteria for uninterrupted energy.

	C_{31}	C_{32}	C_{33}	C_{34}	C_{35}	C_{36}	C_{37}	C_{38}
C_{31}	(1.000, 1.000, 1.000)	(0.400, 0.500, 0.667)	(1.500, 2.000, 2.500)	(0.667, 1.000, 1.500)	(1.500, 2.000, 2.500)	(1.500, 2.000, 2.500)	(2.500, 3.000, 3.500)	(2.500, 3.000, 3.500)
C_{32}	(1.500, 2.000, 2.500)	(1.000, 1.000, 1.000)	(0.667, 1.000, 1.500)	(2.500, 3.000, 3.500)	(0.667, 1.000, 1.500)	(1.500, 2.000, 2.500)	(2.500, 3.000, 3.500)	(2.500, 3.000, 3.500)
C_{33}	(0.400, 0.500, 0.667)	(0.667, 1.000, 1.500)	(1.000, 1.000, 1.000)	(1.500, 2.000, 2.500)	(0.667, 1.000, 1.500)	(0.667, 1.000, 1.500)	(1.500, 2.000, 2.500)	(1.500, 2.000, 2.500)
C_{34}	(0.667, 1.000, 1.500)	(0.286, 0.333, 0.400)	(0.400, 0.500, 0.667)	(1.000, 1.000, 1.000)	(0.667, 1.000, 1.500)	(0.400, 0.500, 0.667)	(0.400, 0.500, 0.667)	(0.400, 0.500, 0.667)
C_{35}	(0.400, 0.500, 0.667)	(0.667, 1.000, 1.500)	(0.667, 1.000, 1.500)	(0.667, 1.000, 1.500)	(1.000, 1.000, 1.000)	(0.667, 1.000, 1.500)	(0.667, 1.000, 1.500)	(0.667, 1.000, 1.500)
C_{36}	(0.400, 0.500, 0.667)	(0.400, 0.500, 0.667)	(0.667, 1.000, 1.500)	(1.500, 2.000, 2.500)	(0.667, 1.000, 1.500)	(1.000, 1.000, 1.000)	(0.667, 1.000, 1.500)	(1.500, 2.000, 2.500)
C_{37}	(0.286, 0.333, 0.400)	(0.286, 0.333, 0.400)	(0.400, 0.500, 0.667)	(1.500, 2.000, 2.500)	(0.667, 1.000, 1.500)	(0.667, 1.000, 1.500)	(1.000, 1.000, 1.000)	(0.400, 0.500, 0.667)
C_{38}	(0.286, 0.333, 0.400)	(0.286, 0.333, 0.400)	(0.400, 0.500, 0.667)	(1.500, 2.000, 2.500)	(0.667, 1.000, 1.500)	(0.400, 0.500, 0.667)	(1.500, 2.000, 2.500)	(1.000, 1.000, 1.000)

Table 9. Paired comparison matrix of 'service area' sub-criteria for quality energy.

	C_{11}	C_{12}	C_{13}	C_{14}	C_{15}	C_{16}	C_{17}
C_{11}	(1.000, 1.000, 1.000)	(0.667, 1.000, 1.500)	(0.667, 1.000, 1.500)	(0.400, 0.500, 0.667)	(0.400, 0.500, 0.667)	(0.400, 0.500, 0.667)	(0.400, 0.500, 0.667)
C_{12}	(0.667, 1.000, 1.500)	(1.000, 1.000, 1.000)	(0.286, 0.333, 0.400)	(0.400, 0.500, 0.667)	(0.400, 0.500, 0.667)	(0.667, 1.000, 1.500)	(0.286, 0.333, 0.400)
C_{13}	(0.667, 1.000, 1.500)	(2.500, 3.000, 3.500)	(1.000, 1.000, 1.000)	(0.667, 1.000, 1.500)	(0.400, 0.500, 0.667)	(0.400, 0.500, 0.667)	(0.400, 0.500, 0.667)
C_{14}	(1.500, 2.000, 2.500)	(1.500, 2.000, 2.500)	(0.667, 1.000, 1.500)	(1.000, 1.000, 1.000)	(0.400, 0.500, 0.667)	(0.400, 0.500, 0.667)	(0.400, 0.500, 0.667)
C_{15}	(1.500, 2.000, 2.500)	(1.500, 2.000, 2.500)	(1.500, 2.000, 2.500)	(1.500, 2.000, 2.500)	(1.000, 1.000, 1.000)	(0.667, 1.000, 1.500)	(0.400, 0.500, 0.667)
C_{16}	(0.667, 1.000, 1.500)	(0.667, 1.000, 1.500)	(1.500, 2.000, 2.500)	(1.500, 2.000, 2.500)	(0.667, 1.000, 1.500)	(1.000, 1.000, 1.000)	(1.500, 2.000, 2.500)
C_{17}	(1.500, 2.000, 2.500)	(2.500, 3.000, 3.500)	(1.500, 2.000, 2.500)	(1.500, 2.000, 2.500)	(1.500, 2.000, 2.500)	(0.400, 0.500, 0.667)	(1.000, 1.000, 1.000)

Table 10. Binary comparison matrix of 'management' sub-criteria for quality energy.

	C_{21}	C_{22}	C_{23}	C_{24}	C_{25}	C_{26}	C_{27}	C_{28}
C_{21}	(1.000, 1.000, 1.000)	(0.667, 1.000, 1.500)	(0.400, 0.500, 0.667)	(0.400, 0.500, 0.667)	(0.667, 1.000, 1.500)	(0.400, 0.500, 0.667)	(2.500, 3.000, 3.500)	(1.500, 2.000, 2.500)
C_{22}	(0.667, 1.000, 1.500)	(1.000, 1.000, 1.000)	(0.400, 0.500, 0.667)	(0.667, 1.000, 1.500)	(0.400, 0.500, 0.667)	(0.286, 0.333, 0.400)	(0.667, 1.000, 1.500)	(0.667, 1.000, 1.500)
C_{23}	(1.500, 2.000, 2.500)	(1.500, 2.000, 2.500)	(1.000, 1.000, 1.000)	(0.400, 0.500, 0.667)	(0.286, 0.333, 0.400)	(0.400, 0.500, 0.667)	(0.286, 0.333, 0.400)	(1.500, 2.000, 2.500)
C_{24}	(1.500, 2.000, 2.500)	(0.667, 1.000, 1.500)	(1.500, 2.000, 2.500)	(1.000, 1.000, 1.000)	(0.667, 1.000, 1.500)	(1.500, 2.000, 2.500)	(2.500, 3.000, 3.500)	(2.500, 3.000, 3.500)
C_{25}	(0.667, 1.000, 1.500)	(1.500, 2.000, 2.500)	(2.500, 3.000, 3.500)	(0.667, 1.000, 1.500)	(1.000, 1.000, 1.000)	(0.400, 0.500, 0.667)	(0.667, 1.000, 1.500)	(2.500, 3.000, 3.500)
C_{26}	(1.500, 2.000, 2.500)	(2.500, 3.000, 3.500)	(1.500, 2.000, 2.500)	(0.400, 0.500, 0.667)	(1.500, 2.000, 2.500)	(1.000, 1.000, 1.000)	(0.667, 1.000, 1.500)	(1.500, 2.000, 2.500)
C_{27}	(0.286, 0.333, 0.400)	(0.667, 1.000, 1.500)	(2.500, 3.000, 3.500)	(0.286, 0.333, 0.400)	(0.667, 1.000, 1.500)	(0.667, 1.000, 1.500)	(1.000, 1.000, 1.000)	(0.286, 0.333, 0.400)
C_{28}	(0.400, 0.500, 0.667)	(0.667, 1.000, 1.500)	(0.400, 0.500, 0.667)	(0.286, 0.333, 0.400)	(0.286, 0.333, 0.400)	(0.400, 0.500, 0.667)	(2.500, 3.000, 3.500)	(1.000, 1.000, 1.000)

Table 11. Paired comparison matrix of 'employees' sub-criteria for quality energy.

	C_{31}	C_{32}	C_{33}	C_{34}	C_{35}	C_{36}	C_{37}	C_{38}
C_{31}	(1.000, 1.000, 1.000)	(0.400, 0.500, 0.667)	(1.500, 2.000, 2.500)	(1.500, 2.000, 2.500)	(1.500, 2.000, 2.500)	(1.500, 2.000, 2.500)	(2.500, 3.000, 3.500)	(2.500, 3.000, 3.500)
C_{32}	(1.500, 2.000, 2.500)	(1.000, 1.000, 1.000)	(2.500, 3.000, 3.500)	(0.667, 1.000, 1.500)	(0.667, 1.000, 1.500)	(1.500, 2.000, 2.500)	(0.667, 1.000, 1.500)	(2.500, 3.000, 3.500)
C_{33}	(0.400, 0.500, 0.667)	(0.286, 0.333, 0.400)	(1.000, 1.000, 1.000)	(0.667, 1.000, 1.500)	(1.500, 2.000, 2.500)	(1.500, 2.000, 2.500)	(2.500, 3.000, 3.500)	(2.500, 3.000, 3.500)
C_{34}	(0.400, 0.500, 0.667)	(0.667, 1.000, 1.500)	(0.667, 1.000, 1.500)	(1.000, 1.000, 1.000)	(0.400, 0.500, 0.667)	(0.400, 0.500, 0.667)	(0.286, 0.333, 0.400)	(0.286, 0.333, 0.400)
C_{35}	(0.400, 0.500, 0.667)	(0.667, 1.000, 1.500)	(0.400, 0.500, 0.667)	(1.500, 2.000, 2.500)	(1.000, 1.000, 1.000)	(0.667, 1.000, 1.500)	(1.500, 2.000, 2.500)	(1.500, 2.000, 2.500)
C_{36}	(0.400, 0.500, 0.667)	(0.400, 0.500, 0.667)	(0.400, 0.500, 0.667)	(1.500, 2.000, 2.500)	(0.667, 1.000, 1.500)	(1.000, 1.000, 1.000)	(2.500, 3.000, 3.500)	(2.500, 3.000, 3.500)
C_{37}	(0.286, 0.333, 0.400)	(0.667, 1.000, 1.500)	(0.286, 0.333, 0.400)	(2.500, 3.000, 3.500)	(0.400, 0.500, 0.667)	(0.286, 0.333, 0.400)	(1.000, 1.000, 1.000)	(0.400, 0.500, 0.667)
C_{38}	(0.286, 0.333, 0.400)	(0.286, 0.333, 0.400)	(0.286, 0.333, 0.400)	(2.500, 3.000, 3.500)	(0.400, 0.500, 0.667)	(0.286, 0.333, 0.400)	(1.500, 2.000, 2.500)	(1.000, 1.000, 1.000)

After applying the F-AHP method steps, criterion weights were obtained in three separate groups: These are the weights of the "Service Region", "Management" and "Employees" sub-criteria for customer satisfaction (1), uninterrupted energy service (2) and quality of energy service provision. In Table 12, "Service Area", "Management" and "Employees" sub-criteria are given weights to cover customer satisfaction towards electricity distribution companies. In Table 13, the weights of "Service Area", "Management" and "Employees" sub-criteria for providing uninterrupted energy service in electricity distribution companies are given.

Table 12. Weights of efficiency criteria for customer satisfaction in electricity distribution companies.

In Terms of Customer Satisfaction								
'Service Region' Sub-criteria	Weight	Rank	'Management' Sub-Criteria	Weight	Rank	'Employees' Sub-Criteria	Weight	Rank
The number of customers (C_{11})	0.173	4	Setting goals (C_{21})	0.184	2	Staff adoption of goals (C_{31})	0.189	2
Geographical conditions (C_{12})	0.050	5	Staff participation in decision processes (C_{22})	0.102	6	Training level of staff (C_{32})	0.167	5
Climatic conditions (C_{13})	0.040	6	Ensuring ergonomic working conditions (C_{23})	0.236	1	Employee motivation (C_{33})	0.198	1
Network size (C_{14})	0.036	7	Supporting employee development (C_{24})	0.129	4	Wages and benefits (C_{34})	0.028	7
Line length (C_{15})	0.177	3	The importance given to OHS (C_{25})	0.137	3	Teamwork (C_{35})	0.179	3–4
Energy losses (C_{16})	0.262	1–2	Flexible hours (C_{26})	0.081	7	Responsibility awareness (C_{36})	0.179	3–4
Investment amounts (C_{17})	0.262	1–2	Presence of EYS certificates (C_{27})	0.006	8	Average service time of the staff (C_{37})	0.046	6
			Employee promotion and advancement opportunities (C_{28})	0.122	5	Personal number (C_{38})	0.015	8

Table 13. Weights of efficiency criteria for uninterrupted energy service in electricity distribution companies.

In Terms of Providing Uninterrupted Energy Service								
'Service Region' Sub-criteria	Weight	Rank	'Management' Sub-Criteria	Weight	Rank	'Employees' Sub-Criteria	Weight	Rank
The number of customers (C_{11})	0.011	6	Setting goals (C_{21})	0.122	4	Staff adoption of goals (C_{31})	0.226	2
Geographical conditions (C_{12})	0.024	5	Staff participation in decision processes (C_{22})	0.078	5–6	Training level of staff (C_{32})	0.259	1
Climatic conditions (C_{13})	0.280	1	Ensuring ergonomic working conditions (C_{23})	0.057	7	Employee motivation (C_{33})	0.153	3
Network size (C_{14})	0.074	4	Supporting employee development (C_{24})	0.211	1–2	Wages and benefits (C_{34})	0.009	8
Line length (C_{15})	0.114	3	The importance given to OHS (C_{25})	0.191	3	Teamwork (C_{35})	0.097	5
Energy losses (C_{16})	0.249	2–3	Flexible hours (C_{26})	0.211	1–2	Responsibility awareness (C_{36})	0.105	4
Investment amounts (C_{17})	0.249	2–3	Presence of EYS certificates (C_{27})	0.078	5–6	Average service time of the staff (C_{37})	0.066	7
			Employee promotion and advancement opportunities (C_{28})	0.053	8	Personal number (C_{38})	0.087	6

The weights of "Service Area", "Management" and "Employees" sub-criteria for providing quality energy service in electricity distribution companies are given in Table 14.

Table 14. Weights of efficiency criteria for quality energy service in electricity distribution companies.

			In Terms of Providing Quality Energy Service					
'Service region' Sub-criteria	Weight	Rank	'Management' Sub-Criteria	Weight	Rank	'Employees' Sub-Criteria	Weight	Rank
The number of customers (C_{11})	0.026	6	Setting goals (C_{21})	0.109	5	Staff adoption of goals (C_{31})	0.235	1
Geographical conditions (C_{12})	0.002	7	Staff participation in decision processes (C_{22})	0.045	8	Training level of staff (C_{32})	0.203	2
Climatic conditions (C_{13})	0.136	4	Ensuring ergonomic working conditions (C_{23})	0.084	6	Employee motivation (C_{33})	0.171	3
Network size (C_{14})	0.074	5	Supporting employee development (C_{24})	0.214	1	Wages and benefits (C_{34})	0.029	7
Line length (C_{15})	0.240	2	The importance given to OHS (C_{25})	0.163	3	Teamwork (C_{35})	0.124	5
Energy losses (C_{16})	0.228	3	Flexible hours (C_{26})	0.204	2	Responsibility awareness (C_{36})	0.133	4
Investment amounts (C_{17})	0.293	1	Presence of EYS certificates (C_{27})	0.115	4	Average service time of the staff (C_{37})	0.057	6
			Employee promotion and advancement opportunities (C_{28})	0.064	7	Personal number (C_{38})	0.007	8

5. Results and Discussions

In this study, the criteria that affect electricity distribution companies and the weights of these criteria are emphasized. Fuzzy logic has been used in distribution companies because efficiency is only understandable with its reflections on customer behavior, and their behavior is complex due to human nature and does not show a clear and linear tendency. However, in order to help validate the achievements, the calculated results should be compared with a state-of-art approach, which is decided in this study to be the classical AHP; the following is the results by AHP determined and comparatively discussed accordingly.

First of all, a hierarchical structure has been established by making interviews with Aras EDAŞ experts, which are the subject of the implementation, and determining the main and sub-criteria affecting productivity. The criteria determined were evaluated on the same group by using the questionnaire method and verbal expressions. Weights were obtained by using unified decision matrices obtained by combining decision makers' opinions with the geometric mean and Chang's Order Analysis Method.

Considering customer satisfaction, uninterrupted energy and quality of energy main criterion weights, it is seen that uninterrupted and high-quality energy is considered to be equal, but rather less important than customer satisfaction. As seen in Figure 4, customer satisfaction has the highest importance for the efficiency of electricity distribution companies, as observed from the studies that the company keeps conducting. In addition, the independent surveys conducted outside of the company suggest that the most important criterion in the measurement of efficiency in distribution companies is customer satisfaction.

Figure 4 reveals that the customer satisfaction criterion has much higher importance over the other two criteria in the solutions made with AHP as well. However, uninterrupted and quality energy criteria were not found to be equal unlike for F-AHP results, where uninterrupted energy is at a higher level of importance than quality of energy.

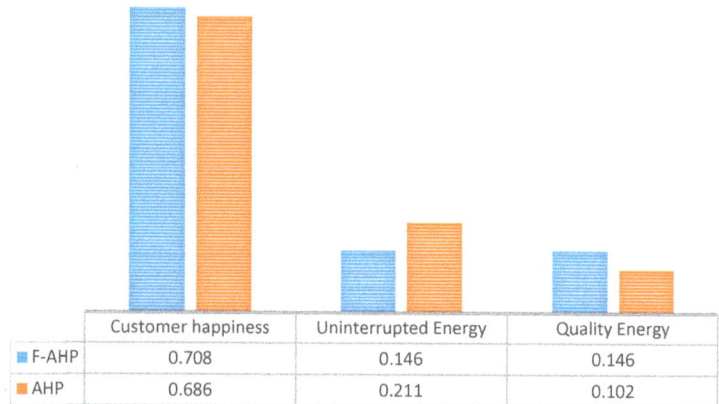

Figure 4. Main criterion weights comparison.

Paired comparisons of the "service region", "management" and "employees" criteria, which are the main customer satisfaction criteria affecting the productivity in distribution companies, were revealed through the analysis. As seen in Figures 5–7, the most important sub-criteria in customer satisfaction are "investment amounts" and "loss and leakage rates". It is seen that the investments made in technical and technological infrastructure work have a priority of ensuring efficiency in customer satisfaction. In addition to the technical investments made in the field services offered to the customers, ensuring that customers can reach the relevant person quickly to solve their problems by increasing the communication channels, appointment systems and online payment facility available will prevent the wasting of consumers' time waiting for service for long hours, the establishment of systems where online requests, complaints and suggestions can be received would be useful. It has been observed that technological investments such as the establishment of management information systems, in which the customer information is kept and customer experiences and trends can be analyzed, have an important priority in customer satisfaction.

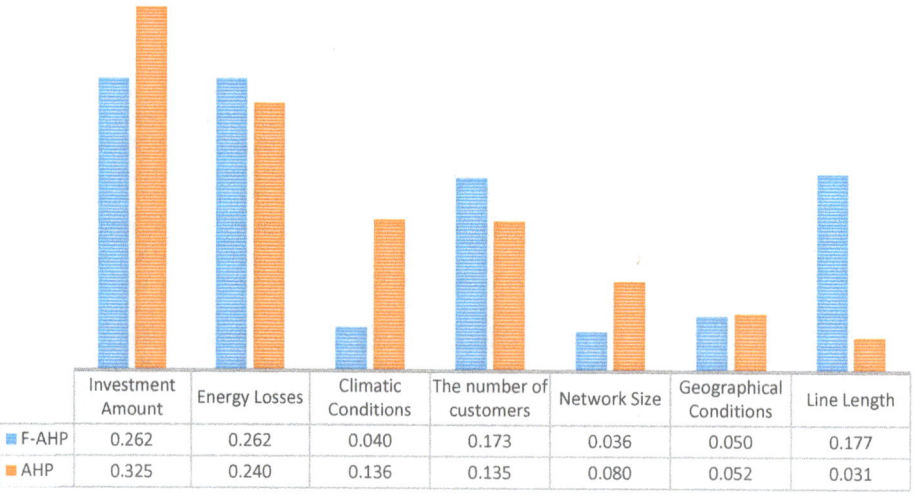

Figure 5. Comparison of 'service area' sub-criterion weights for customer satisfaction.

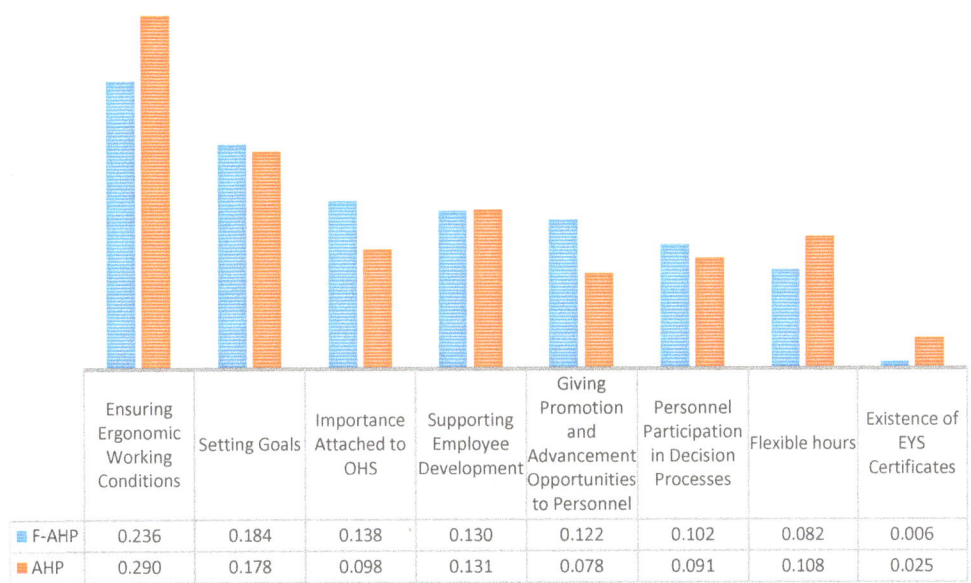

Figure 6. Comparison of 'management' sub-criterion weights for customer satisfaction.

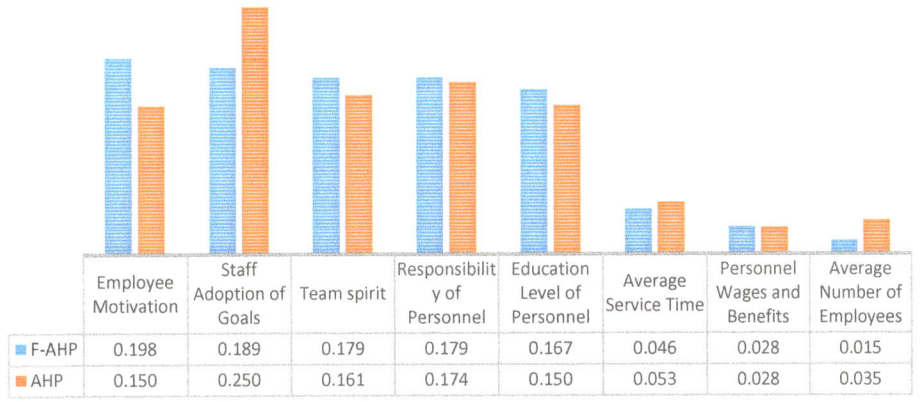

Figure 7. Comparison of 'employees' sub-criterion weights for customer satisfaction.

The issue that the cost of losses and illegal energy use is reflected on customers' bills who pay regularly is frequently mentioned in the national press and causes criticism on social media platforms. This situation creates a prejudice against the service offered by electricity distribution companies in customers and poses a question mark in their minds, no matter how good the service quality is. In addition, the high rate of loss and leakage causes particularly high dissatisfaction in regions where the use of illegal use is intense, while technical scans and technological investments in the field to reduce leakage cause fluctuations in energy demands. For this reason, high loss and leakage rates have become one of the primary criteria affecting customer satisfaction.

Another criterion that has priority is "ergonomic working conditions" as part of the "management" criterion. Employees of the electricity distribution sector, where intense field work is carried out, have to perform breakdown, repair and maintenance works on the powerlines. Depending on the type of pole, it is important to climb from time to time and to provide ergonomic conditions during repair works using basket vehicles from time to time. In addition to working with the help of basket vehicles, most of the employees need to have improved ergonomic conditions in order to provide customer satisfaction to the 75 personnel working in the call centers established to provide faster solutions to customers.

In the electricity distribution sector, field personnel work in shifts, ensuring continuity in field work in order to instantly respond to breakdowns and customer demands, and working overtime from time to time causes a lack of motivation in employees. One of the conditions affecting field workers is that the winter season in provinces such as Erzurum, Ardahan and Kars is difficult. In these provinces, the temperature drops down to −30 degrees centigrade in winter and access to households becomes difficult due to heavy snowfall, making it necessary for the households that cannot be reached by vehicles to be accessed by using tracked vehicles or by walking. Employee motivation is a priority, as the work carried out in electricity distribution services can be achieved by transferring employees who are in direct contact with customers to those customers through correct communication. It is expected that electricity distribution companies will show a positive tendency to increase their efficiency with employee motivation-oriented management approaches.

The results of AHP were analyzed to compare the dual comparisons of "service area", "management" and "employees" criteria, where these are found as the main customer satisfaction criteria affecting the efficiency of distribution companies with F-AHP. As seen in Figure 5, the results of the "service area" sub-criterion for the main criterion of customer satisfaction show similar characteristics with AHP, while the "investment amount", "climatic conditions" and "network size" criteria were found to be more important than F-AHP suggests, where "energy losses", "number of customers" and "line length" were found to be less important. The "Geographical conditions" criterion seems to have approximately the same value suggested by both methods. Figure 6 plots the results of "management" sub-criterion evaluations, where AHP found "ensuring ergonomic work conditions", "determining flexible working hours" and "existence of EYS certificates" to be more important than what F-AHP suggests, while "determining targets", "importance given to OHS", "giving promotion opportunities to personnel" and "personal participation in decision-making processes" to look less important. The criterion of "supporting employee development" seems to have approximately the same importance determined by both methods. In Figure 7, the results of evaluations obtained by both approaches for the "employee" sub-criteria indicate that the "personnel not adopting the targets", "average number of personnel" and "average service time" criteria seem to be more important for AHP than for F-AHP, while "employee motivation", "team spirit", "personnel responsibility awareness" and "education level of the personnel" seem to have the opposite results. The "Staff wages and benefits" criteria has been found to be equally important by both methods.

Binary comparisons were made for the main criteria of "uninterrupted energy" affecting efficiency in distribution companies with the criteria of "service region", "management" and "employees". As seen in Figures 8–10, the most important criteria to achieve "uninterrupted energy" seem to be "climatic conditions", "investment amount" and "loss and leakage ratios", "personnel's adoption of the targets", "education level of the personnel" and "support of employee development", with equally weighted "flexible working hours". Network improvement studies, including the work of taking the cables underground, are among the areas where meticulous work has been carried out by the electricity distribution companies in order to meet the demands of their customers and to provide uninterrupted energy. Heavy rain and snowfall, strong winds and increased soil water levels as a result of melting snow constitute an obstacle to uninterrupted energy. In order to deal with these situations completely independently of human influence, an underground network is emphasized and there is an aim to eliminate malfunctions in a short time by using cable and route detection devices. However, factors such as the height of snow and the number of days that soil spends under the snow negatively affect the uninterrupted energy criteria. For this reason, the primary weighted criterion of "uninterrupted energy" criteria is "climatic conditions".

"Investment amount" and "leakage rate" have a significant impact on "uninterrupted energy" as well as the "customer satisfaction" criteria. Since the increase in "illegal usage" causes excessive load in the network and imbalances in energy demand, it creates an obstacle to "uninterrupted energy". For this reason, distribution companies focus on field scans and technological investments in combating illegal electricity. With the increase in investments, there is an aim to reduce the use of illegal electricity and to provide uninterrupted energy. In Aras EDAŞ Co., where applications are carried out through the PLC project based on communication over electricity lines, investments aimed at protecting the rights of customers, preventing the damage to the country's economy and reducing the use of illegal electricity are being realized.

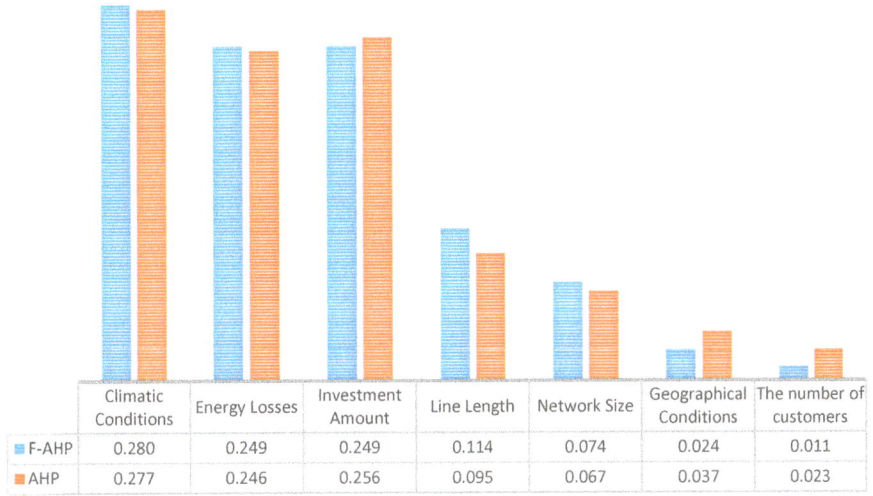

	Climatic Conditions	Energy Losses	Investment Amount	Line Length	Network Size	Geographical Conditions	The number of customers
F-AHP	0.280	0.249	0.249	0.114	0.074	0.024	0.011
AHP	0.277	0.246	0.256	0.095	0.067	0.037	0.023

Figure 8. 'Service region' sub-criterion weights comparison for uninterrupted energy.

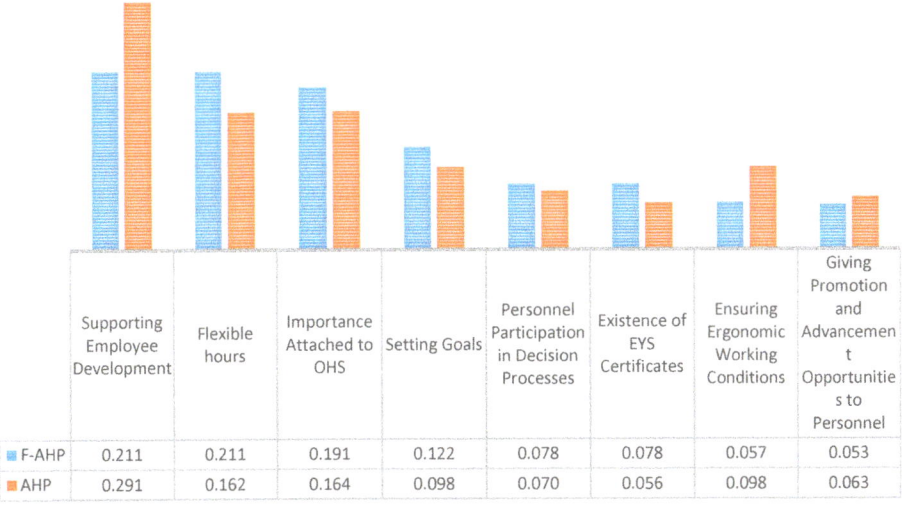

	Supporting Employee Development	Flexible hours	Importance Attached to OHS	Setting Goals	Personnel Participation in Decision Processes	Existence of EYS Certificates	Ensuring Ergonomic Working Conditions	Giving Promotion and Advancement Opportunities to Personnel
F-AHP	0.211	0.211	0.191	0.122	0.078	0.078	0.057	0.053
AHP	0.291	0.162	0.164	0.098	0.070	0.056	0.098	0.063

Figure 9. 'Management' sub-criterion weights for uninterrupted energy.

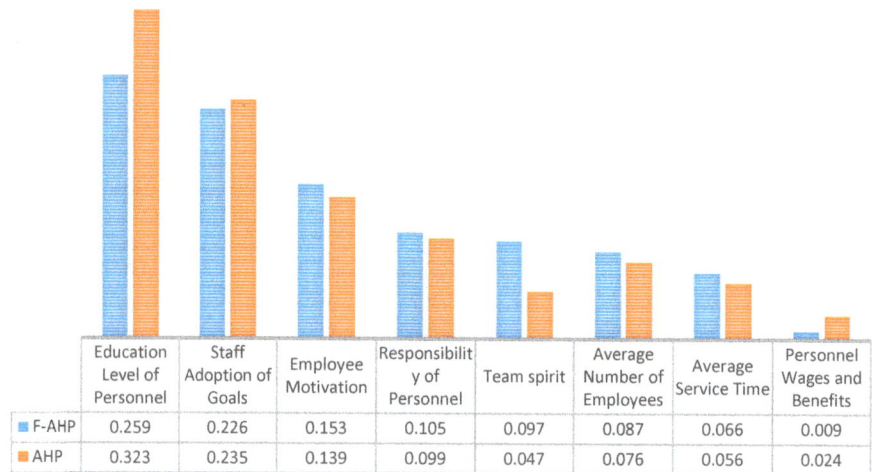

Figure 10. Comparison of 'employees' sub-criterion weights for uninterrupted energy.

The lack of "employee participation" in the enterprises or "lack of knowledge of the targets by the personnel" makes it difficult for the enterprises to reach their goals. Although "uninterrupted energy" is the basic criterion for electricity distribution companies, they have frameworks drawn in accordance with legislation to outline how this should be achieved. For example, these companies need to notify customers in advance of a certain scheduled hour and not conduct any interruptions without notice for beyond a certain hour. However, since these requirements are not adopted by the personnel, this will be reflected in the practices carried out in the field, and it becomes difficult to reach the targets set up within the enterprise or to act in accordance with the legislation. For this reason, the adoption of the rules to be followed or the goals created by the personnel has a high priority weighting.

In order to provide uninterrupted energy, it is necessary to increase maintenance work and to instantly intervene in the uninterrupted energy supply. This situation requires the employees to keep up with developing technologies and to intervene with solution-oriented approaches. This can only be achieved by increasing the technical and personal training of the personnel and supporting their vocational training with trainings suitable for today's conditions. When all these factors are taken into consideration, it has been observed that besides the importance of the education levels of the employees, a parallel approach is needed with the emphasis on supporting employee development over other criteria. In addition, as the standards set the requirements for instant repair of malfunctions and responding to customer requests on a 24/7 basis, flexible working hours are prioritized for uninterrupted energy.

With the analysis made, the AHP results were examined in order to compare the dual comparisons of the "uninterrupted energy" main criterion that affect efficiency in distribution companies with F-AHP and the dual comparisons of the "service region", "management" and "employees" criteria. As seen in Figure 8, the F-AHP results of the "service region" sub-criterion examination for "uninterrupted energy" main criterion are similar to for AHP, while "geographical conditions" and "number of customers" criteria are found to be more important by AHP than by F-AHP, while the criteria for "line length" and "network size" are determined to be less important. It is seen that the criteria for "climatic conditions", "energy losses" and "investment amount" have approximately the same values for both methods. The results of the "management" sub-criterion reviewed for the main criterion of "uninterrupted energy", which is seen in Figure 9, show more importance than the results provided by F-AHP, while "supporting employee development", "providing ergonomic working conditions" and "providing personnel with promotion and advancement opportunities", "flexible working hours", "importance given to OHS", "goals determination", "participation in decision-making processes" and existence of EYS certificates" were all determined as being less important by F-AHP. Figure 10 presents the comparative results provided by both methods, which suggested that "employee" sub-criteria for the main criterion of "uninterrupted energy" prioritizes "education level of the personnel", "personnel wages and benefits", and "not to adopt the personnel targets" obtained higher importance for AHP than for F-AHP. On the other hand, "employee motivation", "team spirit", "personnel responsibility awareness", "average personnel number" and "average service time" were found to be less important for AHP.

Pairwise comparisons were made for the main criterion of "quality of energy" affecting efficiency in distribution companies with the criteria of "service region", "management" and "employees". Figures 11–13 demonstrate the comparative results, where the most important criteria affecting "quality of energy" were weighted as "investment amount", "line length", "energy losses", "staff's adoption of goals", "support of employee development", "training level of the staff" and "flexible working hours", respectively, similar to other comparisons.

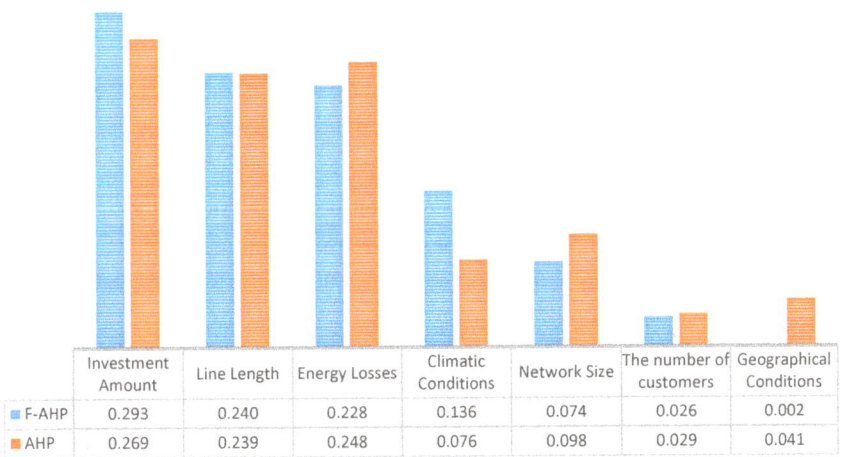

	Investment Amount	Line Length	Energy Losses	Climatic Conditions	Network Size	The number of customers	Geographical Conditions
F-AHP	0.293	0.240	0.228	0.136	0.074	0.026	0.002
AHP	0.269	0.239	0.248	0.076	0.098	0.029	0.041

Figure 11. Comparison of 'service region' sub-criterion weights for quality energy.

	Supporting Employee Development	Flexible hours	Importance Attached to OHS	Existence of EYS Certificates	Setting Goals	Ensuring Ergonomic Working Conditions	Giving Promotion and Advancement Opportunities to Personnel	Personnel Participation in Decision Processes
F-AHP	0.214	0.204	0.163	0.115	0.109	0.084	0.064	0.045
AHP	0.241	0.228	0.209	0.056	0.083	0.092	0.045	0.045

Figure 12. Comparison of 'management' sub-criterion weights for quality energy.

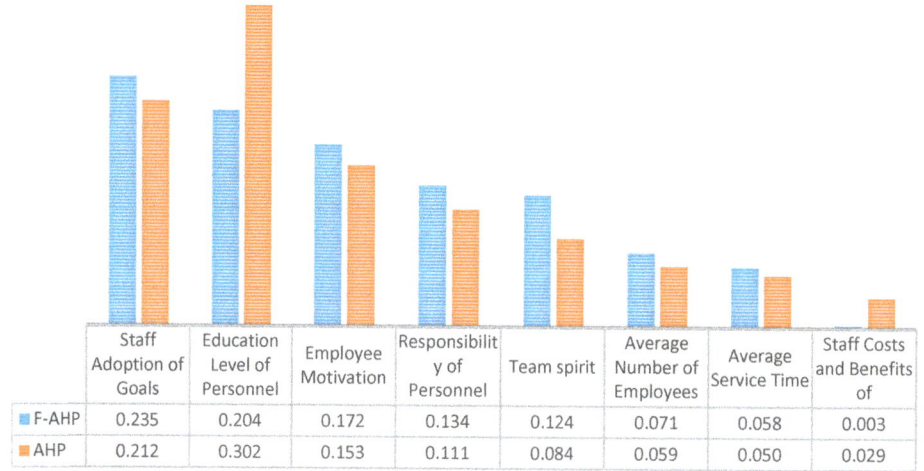

Figure 13. 'Employees' sub-criterion weights for quality energy.

In order to evaluate the pairwise comparisons of "service region", "management" and "employees" criteria for the main criterion of "quality of energy" that affects efficiency in distribution companies, the AHP results were analyzed in comparison with the F-AHP. As presented in Figure 11, the results of "service region" sub-criterion for the "uninterrupted energy" show similar characteristics with AHP, while "energy losses", "network size" and "geographical conditions" criteria seem more important with AHP than with F-AHP, while "investment amount" and" climatic conditions" criteria were determined to be less important. It is seen that the criteria of "line length" and "number of customers" obtained approximately the same values by both methods. While the criteria for "supporting employee development", "flexible working hours", "the importance given to OHS" and "ensuring ergonomic working conditions" are more important under AHP than under F-AHP, as seen in the Figure 12, "giving the personnel the opportunity to promote and progress", "the existence of EYS certificates" have been determined as less important by AHP. As in Figure 13, while "training level of the personnel", "personnel wages and benefits" criteria were more important under the AHP results than the F-AHP results, the evaluation of "employees" sub-criteria for the main criterion of "uninterrupted energy", "personnel's failure to adopt the targets", "employee motivation", "team spirit", "personnel responsibility awareness", "average personnel number" and "average service time" were suggested to be less important by AHP.

6. Conclusions

This study has aimed to investigate the best performance measurement approach and identification of factors affecting the efficiency of electricity distribution companies operating in the post-privatization era in Turkey. The main concern was how to set up competition among the companies operating in the Turkish energy market and to enforce changes in public perception towards distribution companies. Performance assessments with respect to customer satisfaction play the most crucial role in this process. The study has been conducted with an energy supply firm which operates in the north-eastern region of Turkey using AHP and F-AHP methods as two renown qualitative assessment approaches. Each method was separately implemented and used for the case undertaken and the results were compared, where F-AHP demonstrates and exhibits a better qualitative assessment as it let us encompass more expertise within the process.

The results obtained with F-AHP reveals that topmost criterion affecting the efficiency of electricity distribution companies is "customer satisfaction" while the next most prominent one is "sustainable and uninterrupted energy supply". In addition, the other highly prioritized criteria have been observed to be "the amount of investments", "loss and leakage rates", "climatic conditions", "support provided to employees for education and development", "employee motivation" and "flexible working hours". Similarly, it has been determined that criteria such as "employee wages and benefits", "average service duration" and "presence of EYS certificates" have exhibited lower priorities. This study has been conducted for a typical energy supply company operating in Turkey, which can be generalized for all companies in this kind. It can be a guide to apply the same approaches to the firms that are similarly operating, taking the case-specific details, e.g., hierarchies, etc., into account and identifying the impactful factors on efficiency and on performance assessments. The managers have been made aware of the results of the study highlighting the key findings, which are the elicited impactful factors on the company's efficiency and their priority list to help revise and implement strategy and policies for near future, midterm and long term improvements.

The study can be extended by integrating more expert views supplying approaches and incorporating it with other renown multi criteria decision making approaches and their fuzzified forms such as DEMATEL, TOPSIS, SWARA, BWM, etc.

Author Contributions: Conceptualization, V.Y., N.N.D., H.A. and M.E.A.; methodology, V.Y., H.A. and M.E.A.; software, V.Y. and N.N.D.; validation, V.Y., N.N.D. and M.E.A.; investigation, All Authors; resources, V.Y., H.A. and M.E.A.; writing—original draft preparation, V.Y. and N.N.D.; writing—review and editing, V.Y., H.A. and M.E.A.; visualization, N.N.D.; supervision, V.Y. and M.E.A.; funding acquisition, V.Y., H.A. and M.E.A. All authors have read and agreed to the published version of the manuscript.

Funding: This research was funded by the Deanship of Scientific Research (DSR) at King Abdulaziz University, Jeddah, Saudi Arabia under grant number RG-10-34. The APC was jointly funded by the authors.

Institutional Review Board Statement: Not applicable.

Informed Consent Statement: Not applicable.

Data Availability Statement: Restrictions apply to the availability of these data. Data obtained from Aras EDAŞ Co., and are available from the authors by permission of Aras EDAŞ Co.

Acknowledgments: The authors are grateful to Aras EDAŞ Co. for sharing data and offering support in conducting this research.

Conflicts of Interest: The authors declare no conflict of interest. The funders had no role in the design of the study; in the collection, analyses, or interpretation of data; in the writing of the manuscript, or in the decision to publish the results.

References

1. Haliloğlu, E.Y.; Tutu, B.E. Türkiye için Kısa Vadeli Elektrik Enerjisi Talep Tahmini. *J. Yaşar Univ.* **2018**, *13*, 243–255.
2. Odabaşoğlu, E.A. Investigation of Privatization and Distribution of Electricity Distribution Industry Sector in Turkey. Master's Thesis, Türk Hava Kurumu University Social Sciences Institute, Ankara, Turkey, 2016.
3. Ertilay, M. Privatization in Turkey: TEDAŞ (Turkish Electricity Distribution Company) as an Example. Master's Thesis, Süleyman Demirel University Social Sciences Institute, Isparta, Turkey, 2014.
4. Börü, E. Liberalisation in Turkish Electricity Sector and Privatisation of Electricity Distribution Sector. Master's Thesis, Ankara University Social Sciences Institute, Ankara, Turkey, 2009.
5. Alma, H. Examining the Privatized Electricity Distribution and Retail Companies with the Approach of Firm Valuationi. Ph.D. Thesis, Hacettepe University Social Sciences Institute, Ankara, Turkey, 2015.
6. Filippini, M.; Hrovatin, N.; Zoric, J. Efficiency and regulation of the Slovenian electricity distribution companies. *Energy Policy* **2004**, *32*, 335–344. [CrossRef]
7. Odyakmaz, N. Comparative Efficiency Analysis of Turkish Electricity Distribution Firms within the Framework of Performance Based Regulation. Ph.D. Thesis, Hacettepe University Social Sciences Institute, Ankara, Turkey, 2009.
8. Düzgün, M. Efficiency and Productivity Analysis of Electricity Distribution Companies with Data Envelopment Analysis. Master's Thesis, Ankara University Social Sciences Institute, Ankara, Turkey, 2011.
9. Dönmezçelik, O. The Investigation of Electricity Distribution Companies Efficiency in Turkey by the Data Envelopment Analysis. Master's Thesis, Gazi University Institute of Science, Ankara, Turkey, 2014.

10. Omrani, H.; Beiragh, R.G.; Kaleibari, S.S. Performance assessment of Iranian electricity distribution companies by an integrated cooperative game data envelopment analysis principal component analysis approach. *Int. J. Electr. Power Energy Syst.* **2015**, *64*, 617–625. [CrossRef]
11. Sadjadi, S.J.; Omrani, H.; Makui, A.; Shahanaghi, K. An interactive robust data envelopment analysis model for determining alternative targets in Iranian electricity distribution companies. *Expert Syst. Appl.* **2011**, *38*, 9830–9839. [CrossRef]
12. Sadjadi, S.J.; Omrani, H. Data envelopment analysis with uncertain data: An application for Iranian electricity distribution companies. *Energy Policy* **2008**, *36*, 4247–4254. [CrossRef]
13. Çelen, A. Efficiency and productivity (TFP) of the Turkish electricity distribution companies: An application of two–stage (DEA&Tobit) analysis. *Energy Policy* **2013**, *63*, 300–310.
14. Petridis, K.; Ünsal, M.G.; Dey, P.K.; Örkcü, H.H. A novel network data envelopment analysis model for performance measurement of Turkish electric distribution companies. *Energy* **2019**, *174*, 985–998. [CrossRef]
15. Hess, B.; Cullmann, A. Efficiency analysis of East and West German electricity distribution companies—Do the "Ossis" really beat the "Wessis"? *Util. Policy* **2007**, *15*, 206–214. [CrossRef]
16. Kış, Ö.; Can, G.F.; Toktaş, P. Warehouse Location selection for an electricity distribution company by KEMIRA–M method. *Pamukkale Univ. J. Eng. Sci.* **2020**, *26*, 227–240.
17. Janackovic, G.; Stojiljkovic, E.; Grozdanovic, M. Selection of key indicators for the improvement of occupational safety system in electricity distribution companies. *Saf. Sci.* **2020**, *125*, 103654. [CrossRef]
18. Çelen, A.; Yalçın, N. Performance assessment of Turkish electricity distribution utilities: An application of combined FAHP/TOPSIS/DEA methodology to incorporate quality of service. *Util. Policy* **2012**, *23*, 59–71. [CrossRef]
19. Saulo, M.J.; Gaunt, C.T.; Dzobo, O. Comparative Assessment of Short Term Electricity Distribution Planning with Long Term Vision Oriented Planning. In Proceedings of the African Third IASTED African Conference Power and Energy Systems (AfricaPES 2010), Gaborone, Botswana, 6–8 September 2010; pp. 181–187.
20. Alidrisi, H.; Aydin, M.E.; Bafail, A.O.; Abdulal, R.; Karuvatt, S.A. Monitoring the Performance of Petrochemical Organizations in Saudi Arabia Using Data Envelopment Analysis. *Mathematics* **2019**, *7*, 519. [CrossRef]
21. Zavadskas, E.K.; Turskis, Z.; Stević, Ž.; Mardani, A. Modelling procedure for the selection of steel pipes supplier by applying fuzzy AHP method. *Oper. Res. Eng. Sci. Theory Appl.* **2020**, *3*, 39–53. [CrossRef]
22. Blagojević, A.; Vesković, S.; Kasalica, S.; Gojić, A.; Allamani, A. The application of the fuzzy AHP and DEA for measuring the efficiency of freight transport railway undertakings. *Oper. Res. Eng. Sci. Theory Appl.* **2020**, *3*, 1–23. [CrossRef]
23. Uygun, Ö.; Güven, İ.; Şimşir, F.; Aydin, M.E. Selecting display products for furniture stores using fuzzy multi-criteria decision making techniques. In *International Conference on Engineering Applications of Neural Networks*; Springer: Cham, Switzerland, 2018; pp. 181–193.
24. Guo, S.; Zhao, H. Fuzzy best-worst multi-criteria decision-making method and its applications. *Knowl. Based Syst.* **2017**, *121*, 23–31. [CrossRef]
25. Pamučar, D.; Stević, Ž.; Sremac, S. A New Model for Determining Weight Coefficients of Criteria in MCDM Models: Full Consistency Method (FUCOM). *Symmetry* **2018**, *10*, 393. [CrossRef]
26. Rani, P.; Mishra, A.R.; Krishankumar, R.; Mardani, A.; Cavallaro, F.; Soundarapandian Ravichandran, K.; Balasubramanian, K. Hesitant Fuzzy SWARA-Complex Proportional Assessment Approach for Sustainable Supplier Selection (HF-SWARA-COPRAS). *Symmetry* **2020**, *12*, 1152. [CrossRef]
27. Mishra, A.R.; Rani, P.; Pandey, K.; Mardani, A.; Streimikis, J.; Streimikiene, D.; Alrasheedi, M. Novel Multi-Criteria Intuitionistic Fuzzy SWARA–COPRAS Approach for Sustainability Evaluation of the Bioenergy Production Process. *Sustainability* **2020**, *12*, 4155. [CrossRef]
28. Popovic, M.; Kuzmanović, M.; Savić, G. A comparative empirical study of Analytic Hierarchy Process and Conjoint analysis: Literature review. *Decis. Mak. Appl. Manag. Eng.* **2018**, *1*, 153–163. [CrossRef]
29. Kuruüzüm, A.; Atsan, N. The Analytic Hierarchy Process Approach and its Applications in Business. *J. Akdeniz İ.İ.B.F.* **2001**, *1*, 83–105.
30. Dağdeviren, M.; Eren, T. Analytical hierarchy process and use of 0-1 goal programming methods in selecting supplier firms. *J. Fac. Eng. Archit. Gazi Univ.* **2001**, *16*, 41–52.
31. Bal, A. Prioritization of Performance Indicators Using Fuzzy AHP: An Application in Automotive Industry. Master's Thesis, Bahçeşehir University Social Sciences Institute, İstanbul, Turkey, 2014.
32. Güner, H. Fuzzy AHP and the Application for a Company's Supplier Selection Problem. Master's Thesis, Pamukkale University Institute of Science, Denizli, Turkey, 2005.
33. Kırdağlı, M. The Analysis of the Parameters that Affects the Effectiveness of the Shipyards by Fuzzy AHP Method. Ph.D. Thesis, İstanbul Teknik University Institute of Science, İstanbul, Turkey, 2010.
34. Saaty, T.L. *The Analytic Hierarchy Process*; McGraw-Hill: New York, NY, USA, 1980.
35. Zadeh, L.A. Fuzzy sets. *Inf. Control* **1965**, *83*, 338–353. [CrossRef]
36. Maués, L.M.F.; do Nascimento, B.D.M.O.; Lu, W.; Xue, F. Estimating construction waste generation in residential buildings: A fuzzy set theory approach in the Brazilian Amazon. *J. Clean. Prod.* **2020**, *265*, 121779. [CrossRef]
37. Saaty, T.L. How to make a decision: The analytic hierarchy process. *Eur. J. Oper. Res.* **1990**, *48*, 9–26. [CrossRef]

38. Chan, F.T.; Kumar, N. Global supplier development considering risk factors using fuzzy extended AHP-based approach. *Omega* **2007**, *35*, 417–431. [CrossRef]
39. Xu, Z.; Liao, H. Intuitionistic fuzzy analytic hierarchy process. *IEEE Trans. Fuzzy Syst.* **2013**, *22*, 749–761. [CrossRef]
40. Liu, Y.; Eckert, C.M.; Earl, C. A review of fuzzy AHP methods for decision-making with subjective judgements. *Expert Syst. Appl.* **2020**, *161*, 113738. [CrossRef]
41. Kim, Y.S.; Choi, M.K.; Han, S.M.; Lee, C.; Seong, P.H. Development of a method for quantifying relative importance of NPP cyber attack probability variables based on factor analysis and AHP. *Ann. Nucl. Energy* **2020**, *149*, 107790. [CrossRef]
42. Chang, D.Y. *Extent Analysis and Synthetic Decision, Optimization Techniques and Applications*; World Scientific: Singapore, 1992; Volume 1.
43. Chang, D.-Y. Applications of the extent analysis method on fuzzy AHP. *Eur. J. Oper. Res.* **1996**, *95*, 649–655. [CrossRef]
44. Zhu, K.-J.; Jing, Y.; Chang, D.-Y. A discussion on extent analysis method and applications of fuzzy AHP. *Eur. J. Oper. Res.* **1999**, *116*, 450–456. [CrossRef]
45. Yacan, İ. Evaluation of the Factors that Affect the Determination of Quality in Education with Fuzzy AHP and Fuzzy TOPSIS. Master's Thesis, Pamukkale University Social Sciences Institute, Denizli, Turkey, 2016.

Article

Fuzzy Cognitive Maps Optimization for Decision Making and Prediction

Katarzyna Poczeta [1], Elpiniki I. Papageorgiou [2,*] and Vassilis C. Gerogiannis [3,*]

[1] Department of Information Systems, Kielce University of Technology, 25-314 Kielce, Poland; k.piotrowska@tu.kielce.pl
[2] Department of Energy Systems, Faculty of Technology, University of Thessaly, Geopolis Campus, GR 41500 Larissa, Greece
[3] Department of Digital Systems, Faculty of Technology, University of Thessaly, Geopolis Campus, GR 41500 Larissa, Greece
* Correspondence: elpinikipapageorgiou@uth.gr (E.I.P.); vgerogian@uth.gr (V.C.G.)

Received: 19 October 2020; Accepted: 13 November 2020; Published: 18 November 2020

Abstract: Representing and analyzing the complexity of models constructed by data is a difficult and challenging task, hence the need for new, more effective techniques emerges, despite the numerous methodologies recently proposed in this field. In the present paper, the main idea is to systematically create a nested structure, based on a fuzzy cognitive map (FCM), in which each element/concept at a higher map level is decomposed into another FCM that provides a more detailed and precise representation of complex time series data. This nested structure is then optimized by applying evolutionary learning algorithms. Through the application of a dynamic optimization process, the whole nested structure based on FCMs is restructured in order to derive important relationships between map concepts at every nesting level as well as to determine the weights of these relationships on the basis of the available time series. This process allows discovering and describing hidden relationships among important map concepts. The paper proposes the application of the suggested nested approach for time series forecasting as well as for decision-making tasks regarding appliances' energy consumption prediction.

Keywords: fuzzy cognitive maps; optimization; forecasting time series; evolutionary algorithms; decision making; appliances energy prediction

---

1. Introduction

In recent years, fuzzy cognitive maps (FCMs) have become increasingly popular [1]. An FCM can be defined as a type of recurrent neural network, carrying the main aspects of fuzzy logic. An FCM allows mimicking a system or a phenomenon with the use of key concepts and causal relationships among them. FCM models are suitable and particularly useful for modeling and decision-making in the case of complex systems. They have been used in various application domains, e.g., for pattern recognition [2], in risk analysis and crisis management [3], as a decision support tool for political decisions [4], to model an undersea virtual world of dolphins, fish, and sharks [5], for sustainable socio-economic development planning [6], and to support the decision-making process for photovoltaic solar energy sector development [7].

FCMs have also been proved as an effective technique for numerical [8] and linguistic [9] forecasting of time series. In Reference [10], a novel approach based on FCMs and a granular fuzzy set-based model of inputs were proposed for realizing time series prediction at the linguistic and numerical levels. In Reference [11], a methodology that joins FCMs with a moving window approach to time series prediction was developed. The simulation analysis was performed on three different time series datasets: rainfall in London, number of births per month in New York City, and Campito tree rings.

In Reference [12], the analysis of FCMs usage was focused to predict water demand based on historical time series. In addition, recently there have been some novel approaches in the literature attempting to solve time series prediction problems by combining FCMs with neural networks [13,14].

The initial information of an FCM model is based either on expert knowledge or by using learning algorithms. In standard methods of FCM learning, concepts are chosen by experts or selected based on all available data attributes. An enormous amount of data and a big number of concepts may complicate analysis and decision-making. In this direction, various modifications to standard methods have been applied aiming to simplify FCM models by reducing the number of concepts [14–16] and the connections between them [17,18]. These approaches allow obtaining a balance between data accuracy and model readability. To reduce the complexity and increase the readability of FCMs with a large number of concepts, clustering methods have been used with the aim to combine similar concepts based on their dynamic behavior. The related studies have been carried out on ready-made models of FCMs: FCMs initialized by experts [19] or constructed based on data [6]. Simplifying models, by reducing the number of concepts as well as clustering them, allows the creation of legible structures more similar to those created by humans, and making FCMs easier to be analyzed. In the case of a large number of concepts, a decision-making and analysis problem can be described in the form of a nested FCM that allows for a more readable representation of knowledge than the classic FCM [5]. For example, in Reference [20], this type of structure was used to evaluate water quality failures. Nested FCMs could help to understand the underlying problem, support the user to choose at what level of detail he/she wants to analyze the problem of interest, and represent complex systems in a more accurate way. Such an approach, as regards the FCMs construction, can provide more readable and easier to interpret structures, which are closer to human reasoning and inference.

The aim of the current study is to develop an approach for constructing a nested FCM-based structure that will represent a problem's complex data in a more elaborate way. The suggested approach involves the decomposition of each concept at a higher map level into another FCM. The first stage of the proposed methodology is to cluster concepts (data attributes) based on similarities between them with the use of the k-means clustering approach [21]. Next, two popular evolutionary algorithms for learning FCMs (i.e., the Real-Coded Genetic Algorithm (RCGA) [22] and the Structure Optimization Genetic Algorithm (SOGA) [12]) are applied to find important relationships between concepts at every nesting level and determine weights of these relationships on the basis of the available data. The paper recommends applying the proposed nested approach for time series forecasting as well as for decision-making tasks in the field of appliances' energy consumption prediction.

Specifically, energy use forecasting has a vital role in energy planning and energy consumption reduction. As energy costs increase, more effective tools are needed to analyze, manage, and propose energy use reduction and optimization [23]. In Reference [24], support vector machines have been deployed for energy consumption prediction in buildings, while in Reference [25], various regression models were utilized for energy prediction, including multiple linear regression, support vector machines with radial kernel, random forests, and gradient boosting machines. Gradient boosting machines and random forests outperformed the multiple linear regression and support vector machines with the radial kernel, in terms of achieving lower forecasting errors. Additionally, artificial neural network (ANN), autoregressive integrated moving average (ARIMA), and multiple linear regression (MLR) models were used in Reference [26] for energy consumption prediction. In Reference [27], a deep learning model based on an autoencoder was developed that predicts future energy demand according to different situations.

Moreover, evolutionary FCMs have recently found significant applicability in energy forecasting and optimization. For example, in Reference [14], historical time series involving energy consumption data were utilized along with the application of the Structure Optimization Genetic Algorithm (SOGA) [12] for the automatic construction of an evolutionary FCM. SOGA is an extension of the Real-Coded Genetic Algorithm (RCGA) [28], which provided the decision-makers with the ability to identify the most significant concepts of an examined system and the corresponding relationships among them. Considering any available historical data, FCM models can be automatically produced and optimized with the help of the SOGA algorithm application. For example, a two-stage prediction model for forecasting was introduced in Reference [14], which exploits the competent characteristics of evolutionary FCMs enriched with those of SOGA and ANNs. Recently, in Reference [13], a new ensemble-based forecasting approach was proposed for time series analysis, which deals with the problem of natural gas demand prediction, case studying three major cities in Greece. In this study, the outstanding capabilities of FCMs and ANNs were highlighted, through the investigation of an ensemble of the related methods, applied to multivariate time series prediction in natural gas demand forecasting. Moreover, in Reference [29], an approach based on high order FCMs and high order fuzzy time series was developed to predict solar energy. Public data from Brazilian solar stations, from the year 2012 to 2015, were used in simulations. The produced results confirmed the usefulness of the developed approach.

Traditional energy prediction models mainly focus on the prediction accuracy; however, it is also important to determine and monitor various other variables (concepts) that affect energy consumption in order to better understand the energy use behavior and find ways to reduce it. The innovation of the present work lies on the following issues that highlight the research contribution of the article:

- The paper suggests the construction of an efficient FCM-based nested structure in which each concept at a higher map level can be decomposed into another more detailed FCM for analyzing complex data. The proposed approach for optimizing the FCM nested structure is characterized by high performance and flexibility, especially in problems with a large number of variables/concepts.
- The paper proposes the application of the rigorous SOGA algorithm to fine-tune and determine the most appropriate nested FCM architecture aiming at an enhanced prediction performance. Implementing SOGA algorithms allowed the authors to optimize the nested structure by selecting the most significant concepts from all possible concepts at every nesting level.

A simulation analysis regarding the utilization of the nested structure based on FCMs in appliances energy use prediction has been also performed. To evaluate the performance of the developed approach, a detailed comparison between the nested FCM and the standard FCM was conducted. The experiments were performed with the use of an appliances' energy consumption prediction dataset [25].

The outline of the paper is as follows. Section 2 describes an overview of the FCM method. In Section 3, the proposed approach for constructing a nested structure based on FCMs is described. Section 4 presents the simulation analysis results, which were obtained from applying the proposed approach to an appliances' energy prediction dataset. The section also presents a comparative analysis between the proposed technique and the standard FCM in terms of forecasting performance. Section 5 presents a discussion of the results as well as summarizes the main conclusions of the paper.

2. Fuzzy Cognitive Maps Overview

A fuzzy cognitive map (FCM) has the form of a knowledge graph consisting of nodes (concepts) and links among them [1]. The concepts are nonlinear and represent variables in a causal system. They can take values in the range [0, 1]. The directed links that define the relationships between concepts can be positive or negative taking values between [−1,1]. Figure 1 presents an example of an FCM for exploring the development of the photovoltaic solar energy sector in Brazil [30], in economic and political terms.

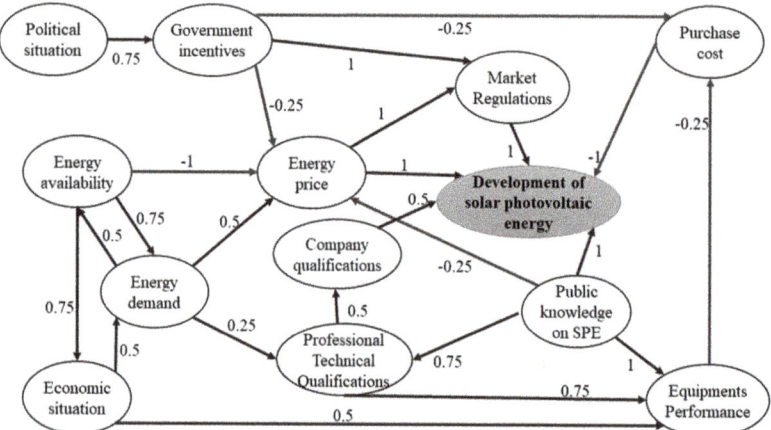

Figure 1. Example of a fuzzy cognitive map created from a group of specialists for Brazilian photovoltaic solar energy development. Republished with permission from Papageorgiou et al. [7]; Published by MDPI, 2020.

Due to the causal nature of the relationships between the concepts, FCMs are an effective tool for modeling decision support systems and time series prediction. Concepts' values undergo a change over time due to the dynamics of the model. In the current research study, the following popular nonlinear dynamics model is applied to calculate the values of concepts:

$$X_i(t+1) = F\left(X_i(t) + \sum_{\substack{j=1 \\ j \neq i}}^{n} X_j(t) \cdot w_{j,i}\right) \qquad (1)$$

where $X_i(t)$ is the value of the i-th concept at the t-th iteration of the FCM execution, t is discrete time, $i,j = 1, 2, \ldots, n$, n is the number of concepts, $w_{j,i}$ is the weight that determines the linkage strength between the j-th concept and the i-th concept taking value in the interval $[-1,1]$, and $F(x)$ is the sigmoidal transformation function normalizing the concept values to the range $[0,1]$. Certain concepts can be defined as decision (output) concepts that should be excluded from further analysis.

FCMs can be created taking into account the experts' knowledge or using machine learning algorithms. FCM learning aims at the determination of the weights of the existing linkages between concepts where data are available. Among the FCM learning methods is the Real-Coded Genetic Algorithm (RCGA) [10,22], in which each individual in a population is determined according to a floating-point vector that contains the weights of the connections (linkages) between concepts. Each individual is then decoded into an FCM model and a fitness function, as described below, is used for its evaluation [10,22]:

$$fitness_p(erorr_l) = \frac{1}{a \cdot erorr_l + 1} \qquad (2)$$

where p is the number of an individual in the population, $p = 1, \ldots, P$, P is the population size, l is the number of a generation, $l = 1, \ldots, L$, L is the maximum number of generations, a is a parameter, and $erorr_l$ is the learning error that can be described as follows:

$$erorr_l = \frac{1}{T} \sum_{t=1}^{T} (Z(t) - X(t))^2 \qquad (3)$$

where $t = 1, \ldots, T$, T is the number of learning records, $X(t)$ is the forecasted value of the decision (output) concept at the t-th iteration, and $Z(t)$ is the actual normalized value of the decision (output) concept at the t-th iteration.

The Structure Optimization Genetic Algorithm (SOGA) constitutes a partial extension of the RCGA algorithm [28]. SOGA allows optimizing the structure of an FCM, during its learning process, by selecting the most significant concepts and the relationships between them. Each individual in SOGA is represented by a floating-point vector containing the weights of the relationships between concepts and by a binary vector of size n containing the information about the concepts incorporated into the candidate FCM model. The evaluation of a candidate FCM is based on a new learning error. A large number of concepts and the non-zero relationships between them increase the FCM complexity providing an additional penalty. The learning error is given by the following function [28]:

$$erorr'_l = erorr_l + b_1 \frac{n_r}{n^2} erorr_l + b_2 \frac{n_c}{n} erorr_l \qquad (4)$$

where $erorr_l$ is the learning error type, b_1, b_2 are the learning parameters, n_r is the number of the existing linkages between concepts, n_c is the number of the concepts in the analyzed fuzzy cognitive map, and n is the number of all possible concepts.

3. The Proposed Approach for Constructing Nested Structure Based on Fuzzy Cognitive Maps

This section describes the proposed approach for constructing a nested FCM structure in which each concept of a higher level can be decomposed into another FCM model illustrating a more detailed image of complex data.

3.1. Data Clustering

The first stage of the proposed approach is to cluster data attributes (concepts) based on the similarity between their values with the use of k-means clustering [21]. It contains the following steps:

1. Determine the number of clusters K via trial and error.
2. Set the output concept as a separate cluster.
3. Initialize $K - 1$ cluster centers from available data attributes (excluding the output concept).
4. Calculate the distance between concepts values and cluster centers based on the Euclidean distance:

$$d(A,C) = \sqrt{\sum_{t=1}^{T}(x_A(t) - x_C(t))^2} \qquad (5)$$

where $t = 1, \ldots, T$, T is the number of records, $x_A(t)$ is the value of concept A at the t-th iteration, and $x_C(t)$ is the value of cluster center C at the t-th iteration. The output concept is omitted in this step.

5. Assign concepts to the closest cluster center.
6. Update the cluster centers based on the values assigned to them.
7. Repeat steps 4–6 until convergence.

3.2. Constructing the First Level of the Nested Structure

The next stage of the proposed approach regards the construction of the most general level of the nested structure (i.e., the first level of the nested structure). It contains the following steps:

1. For each cluster, calculate the average values for concepts within one group according to the following formula:

$$x_k(t) = \frac{1}{n_k} \sum_{i=1}^{n_k} x_i^k(t) \qquad (6)$$

where $t = 1, \ldots, T$, T is the number of records, $x_k(t)$ is the general value of the k-th cluster at the t-th iteration, $k = 1, \ldots, K$, K is the number of clusters, $x_i^k(t)$ is the value of the i-th concept assigned to the k-th cluster at the t-th iteration, and $i = 1, \ldots, n_k$, n_k is the number of concepts assigned to the k-th cluster.

2. Normalize the calculated values into the interval [0,1] using the standard min–max normalization.
3. Divide the averaged normalized data into learning records and testing records.
4. Initialize the general FCM with K concepts based on the clustered data attributes.
5. Learn the general FCM with the use of the RCGA and SOGA algorithms based on learning records in order to determine the relationships between concepts at the first level of the nested structure.

3.3. Constructing the FCM Models for the Second Level of the Nested Structure

The next stage of the proposed approach is to construct the FCM models at the second level of the nested structure (i.e., the more detailed level of the nested structure). A separate FCM model is constructed for each cluster (excluding the cluster that corresponds to the output concept) and is used to predict the output concept. If the first level is sufficient for a given concept, it does not have to be decomposed into another FCM at the second level. The values for the output concept based on the k-th FCM model (i.e., the k-th cluster) are calculated according to the following formula:

$$X^k(t+1) = F\left(X^k(t) + \sum_{i=1}^{n_k} X_i(t) \cdot w_{i,o} + \sum_{\substack{j=1 \\ j \neq k}}^{K-1} X_j(t) \cdot w_{j,o} \right) \quad (7)$$

where $X^k(t)$ is the value of the output concept at the t-th iteration, $t = 1, \ldots, T$, T is the number of learning records, $i = 1, 2, \ldots, n_k$, n_k is the number of concepts assigned to the k-th cluster, $w_{i,o}$ is the weight that determines the strength of the relationship between the i-th concept and the output concept in the k-th FCM model, $X_i(t)$ is the value of the i-th concept in the k-th FCM model, $j = 1, 2, \ldots, K-1$, K is the number of clusters, $w_{j,o}$ is the weight that determines the strength of the relationship between the j-th general concept (cluster j) and the output concept in the k-th FCM model, and $X_j(t)$ is the value of the j-th general concept of the first level at the t-th iteration.

The learning process of the FCM models at the second level is achieved with the use of the RCGA and SOGA algorithms considering learning records, in order to determine the relationships between concepts at the second level of the nested structure [14]. In the case of a large number of concepts in individual FCM models at the second level, we can further extend the nested FCM by another level.

3.4. Calculating the Forecasted Values for the Second Level of the Nested Structure

Additionally, the FCM models from the second level of the nested structure are proposed to be used for the calculation of the forecasted values of the output concept (at the second level). The simple average method was used to calculate the forecasted values of the output concept based on values generated by the FCM models belonging to the second level. This method assigns the same weight to every single model [31], whereas it can improve the average accuracy when increasing the number of the combined single models.

3.5. Testing and Evaluation

The evaluation of the resulting models is accomplished with the use of testing data, which are unknown to the models. In order to evaluate the one-step-ahead prediction, three common statistical indicators were used: mean square error (MSE), root mean square error (RMSE), and mean absolute error (MAE), whose mathematical equations are described below:

1. Mean Squared Error:

$$\text{MSE} = \frac{1}{T}\sum_{t=1}^{T}(Z(t) - X(t))^2 \qquad (8)$$

2. Root Mean Squared Error:

$$\text{RMSE} = \sqrt{\text{MSE}} \qquad (9)$$

3. Mean Absolute Error:

$$\text{MAE} = \frac{1}{T}\sum_{t=1}^{T}|Z(t) - X(t)| \qquad (10)$$

where $X(t)$ is the forecasted value of the output concept at the t-th iteration, $Z(t)$ is the normalized actual value of the output concept at the t-th iteration, and $t = 1, \ldots, T$ is the number of the iteration.

3.6. Software

The simulation analysis of the proposed approach for constructing nested FCMs was implemented in ISEMK (Intelligent Expert System based on Cognitive Maps), a software tool that has been developed to construct and analyze FCMs [14,28]. The ISEMK tool is a C# application that allows users to construct FCMs with the use of evolutionary algorithms. In the context of the current research study, a new module has been implemented in the ISEMK tool, which enables:

- reading data from .data file,
- setting the number of clusters,
- clustering similar concepts with the use of k-means method,
- showing results of clustering,
- calculating the average values for concepts within one group in order to construct the first level (the most general level) of the nested structure,
- exporting these values to the .data file in order to use them to construct the most general FCM model with the use of RCGA and SOGA algorithms, and
- exporting the original values of the concepts in each group to separate .data files in order to construct the FCM models on the second level (the more detailed level) of the nested structure.

Figure 2 presents the implemented module for data clustering.

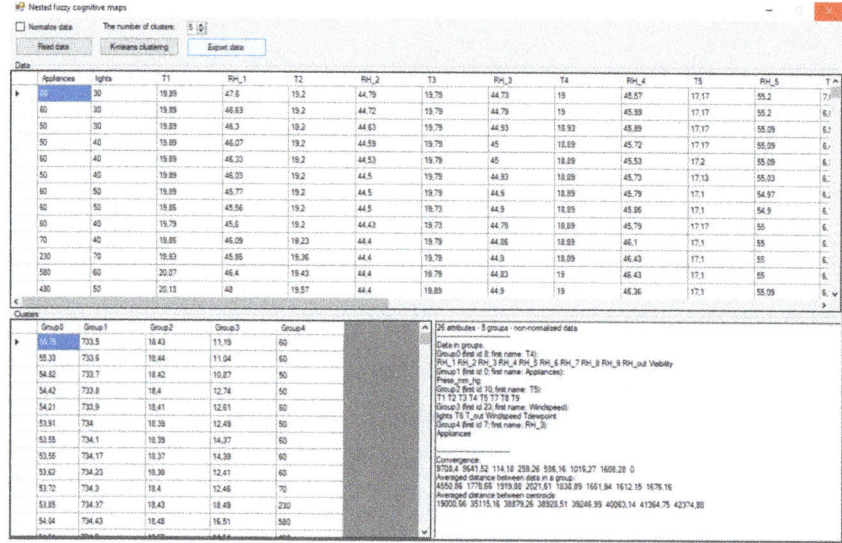

Figure 2. Screenshot of the implemented ISEMK (Intelligent Expert System based on Cognitive Maps) module for data clustering.

4. Case Study

For the purposes of this study, in order to show the functionality of the proposed methodology, a specific appliances' energy prediction dataset was considered and analyzed [25]. This dataset contains energy data recorded for a period of four and a half months from a low energy house, which has been used as a testbed. A wireless sensor network (ZigBee) was used to monitor house temperature and humidity conditions, whereas m-bus energy meters were collecting the energy data every 10 min. Additionally, weather data were provided by a public data repository connected to an airport weather station nearby. The used data contained the following attributes (concepts):

- Appliances—energy consumption (Wh),
- Lights—light fixtures energy consumption (Wh),
- T1—kitchen temperature (Celsius),
- RH1—kitchen humidity (%),
- T2—living room temperature (Celsius),
- RH2—living room humidity (%),
- T3—laundry room temperature (Celsius),
- RH3—laundry room humidity (%),
- T4—office temperature (Celsius),
- RH4—office humidity (%),
- T5—bathroom temperature (Celsius),
- RH5—bathroom humidity (%),
- T6—outside the building temperature (north side) (Celsius),
- RH6—outside the building humidity (north side) (%),
- T7—ironing room temperature (Celsius),
- RH7—ironing room humidity (%),
- T8—teenager room 2 temperature (Celsius),
- RH8—teenager room 2 humidity (%),
- T9—parents room temperature (Celsius),

- RH9—parents room humidity (%),
- Tout—outside temperature (Celsius),
- Pressure—pressure (mm Hg),
- RHout—outside humidity (%),
- Windspeed—wind speed (m/s),
- Visibility (km), and
- Tdewpoint—due point temperature (Celsius).

In what follows, the application of the proposed approach for constructing a nested structure based on FCMs is presented by utilizing this appliances' energy prediction dataset [25]. "Appliances" is set as the output concept of the FCM. The normalized data were divided into learning records (15,000 otal in number) and testing records (4735 total in number). Table 1 presents the sample results of the clustering data related to the use of the appliances' energy dataset into 5 clusters.

Table 1. Results of clustering.

Cluster	Attributes (Concepts)
Cluster 1	T1 T2 T3 T4 T5 T7 T8 T9
Cluster 2	RH1 RH2 RH3 RH4 RH5 RH6 RH7 RH8 RH9 RHout Visibility
Cluster 3	Pressure
Cluster 4	Lights T6 Tout Windspeed Tdewpoint
Cluster 5 (output)	Appliances

The FCM models were constructed with the use of two evolutionary learning algorithms: RCGA and SOGA. The learning parameters were selected by trial and error in order to minimize prediction errors. The learning process was repeated 10 times for each parameter configuration. The average values of the evolution criteria with standard deviation were produced accordingly. Uniform crossover [32] with crossover probability equal to 0.6, random mutation with mutation probability equal to 0.1, and ranking selection for parent selection were used in the simulations. The parents of one generation are completely replaced with the offspring. Elite strategy was applied and the single best individual was kept. Both population size and the maximum number of generations in the respective case study were set equal to 100.

Table 2 shows the calculated prediction errors (MAE, MSE, RMSE) for the first and second levels of the nested FCM. To evaluate the performance of the proposed approach, an extensive comparative analysis between the nested FCM and the standard FCM was performed. The best models in terms of having the lowest MSE value were further analyzed so the forecasted values of energy use of appliances for the second level of the nested structure (second level) would be calculated. Table 3 shows the obtained prediction errors (MAE, MSE, RMSE) for the best FCM models.

Table 2. Comparison results among the nested fuzzy cognitive map and standard fuzzy cognitive map.

Model	Algorithm	MAE	MSE	RMSE
First level	SOGA	0.0423 ± 0.0140	0.0058 ± 0.0017	0.0754 ± 0.0099
	RCGA	**0.0370 ± 0.0015**	**0.0052 ± 0.0006**	**0.0720 ± 0.0039**
Cluster 1	SOGA	0.0454 ± 0.0099	0.0067 ± 0.0019	0.0814 ± 0.0104
	RCGA	0.0424 ± 0.0038	0.0060 ± 0.0006	0.0772 ± 0.0038
Cluster 2	SOGA	0.0453 ± 0.0077	0.0064 ± 0.0009	0.0801 ± 0.0054
	RCGA	0.0409 ± 0.0051	0.0060 ± 0.0007	0.0774 ± 0.0045
Cluster 3	SOGA	0.0423 ± 0.0140	0.0058 ± 0.0017	0.0754 ± 0.0099
	RCGA	**0.0370 ± 0.0015**	**0.0052 ± 0.0006**	**0.0720 ± 0.0039**
Cluster 4	SOGA	0.0414 ± 0.0036	0.0061 ± 0.0008	0.0778 ± 0.0050
	RCGA	0.0373 ± 0.0022	0.0054 ± 0.0005	0.0731 ± 0.0036
Standard FCM	SOGA	0.0485 ± 0.0135	0.0072 ± 0.0015	0.0845 ± 0.0086
	RCGA	0.0426 ± 0.0025	0.0065 ± 0.0007	0.0807 ± 0.0041

Table 3. Best results for the nested fuzzy cognitive map and standard fuzzy cognitive map.

Model	Algorithm	MAE	MSE	RMSE
First level	SOGA	0.0348	0.0045	0.0671
	RCGA	0.0348	0.0045	0.0667
Cluster 1	SOGA	0.0369	0.0048	0.0692
	RCGA	0.0398	0.0053	0.0731
Cluster 2	SOGA	0.0401	0.0053	0.0730
	RCGA	0.0344	0.0052	0.0722
Cluster 3	SOGA	0.0348	0.0045	0.0671
	RCGA	0.0348	0.0045	0.0667
Cluster 4	SOGA	0.0351	0.0048	0.0690
	RCGA	0.0342	**0.0044**	**0.0666**
Second level	SOGA	0.0354	0.0047	0.0682
	RCGA	**0.0334**	0.0045	0.0673
Standard FCM	SOGA	0.0389	0.0055	0.0740
	RCGA	0.0397	0.0054	0.0736

Please notice that the bold values in the above tables represent the best results associated with the least values of prediction error measures.

Figure 3 depicts the sample nested structure obtained with the use of the RCGA and SOGA algorithms. The proposed approach based on a genetic algorithm optimization allowed us to construct the nested fuzzy cognitive map in which each node is an independent FCM model containing similar concepts. The appliances' energy usage prediction can be analyzed at the first (the most general) level or at a more detailed level (with the use of the detailed FCM models constructed for each cluster). Additionally, the use of SOGA allowed the optimization of the nested structure through the selection of the most significant concepts in each cluster.

More specifically, clusters 1, 2, and 4 in Figure 3a contain more variables than those in Figure 3b, which have been selected by applying the SOGA algorithm for FCM learning. Furthermore, the number of weighted relationships among clusters is less in the optimized nested FCM structure as depicted in Figure 3b, producing a less complex model for making a prediction. Figure 3b presents the most significant concepts for the prediction automatically selected by the SOGA algorithm in the sample experiment.

The most important concepts in each cluster in the nested FCM, as they were produced by the SOGA optimization approach, are the following: T1- temperature in the kitchen area, in Celsius, T3- temperature in laundry room area, T5- temperature in bathroom, in Celsius, and T7- temperature in ironing room, in Celsius (Cluster 1), RH9- humidity in parents room, in %, and RHout- humidity outside, in %, (Cluster 2), Press (Cluster 3) and Lights, and T6- temperature outside the building (north side), in Celsius, (Cluster 4). These concepts have a significant impact on appliances to predict their behavior.

Figure 4 presents the sample results for the forecasting of energy use of appliances. The nested FCM outperformed the standard FCM in terms of achieving better forecasting results overall.

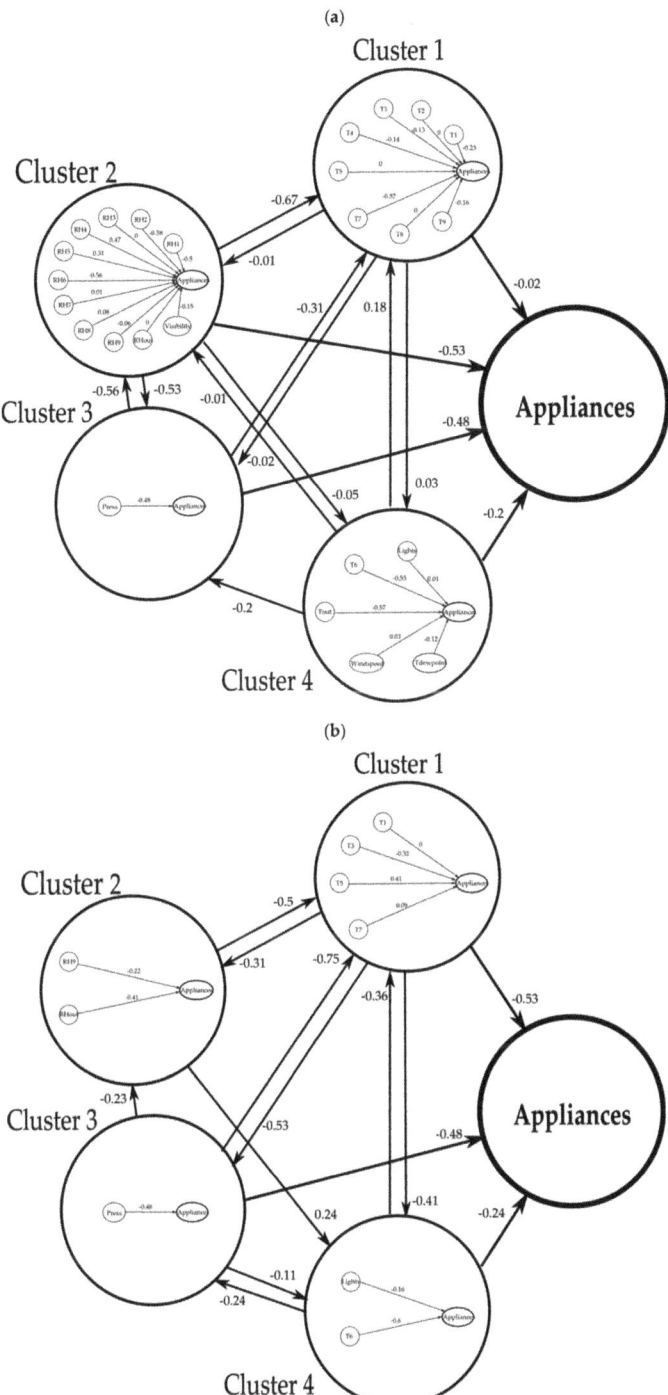

Figure 3. Sample nested fuzzy cognitive map obtained with the use of (**a**) real-coded genetic algorithm (RCGA) and (**b**) structure optimization genetic algorithm (SOGA).

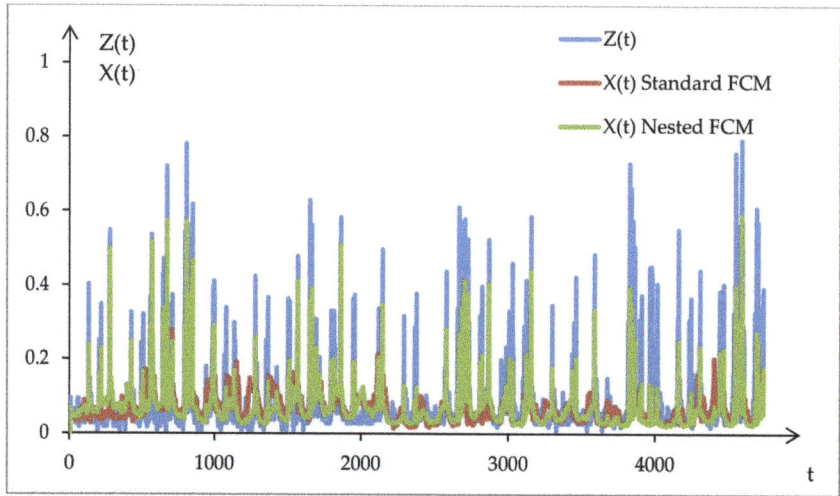

Figure 4. Forecasting results for the best model obtained with the use of the SOGA algorithm.

5. Discussion of Results and Conclusions

In this work, various FCM-based nested architectures were explored, considering the variables that were carefully determined by using the FCM models defined in Section 3. Through the experimental analysis, which involved learning and optimization processes, the optimum nested FCM structure was identified in terms of the overall prediction accuracy.

To further analyze the results of the proposed forecasting approach based on nested FCMs, and assess its effectiveness as well, a comparative analysis has been carried out with respect to the forecasting performance, between the proposed technique and the standard FCM, which has already been applied in similar energy problems as reported in the relevant literature. All the results produced are gathered in the tables and figures cited in the previous section. In particular, from the results shown in Table 1, it emerges that the proposed approach allowed the clustering of 26 concepts related to the use of appliances energy into 5 similar clusters. After a detailed analysis of Tables 2 and 3, as regards the MAE, MSE, and RMSE errors, it can be concluded that the nested structure based on two levels (first level and second level) provided lower errors than the standard approach based on a single FCM.

In Figure 3, it can be noted that the proposed optimization approach allowed the authors to obtain a readable nested structure in which each concept at the first level can be decomposed into another FCM, providing a more detailed representation of appliances' energy time series. Evolutionary algorithms for FCM learning were used to extract important relationships between the concepts at every nesting level and define corresponding weights as regards the available time series. Additionally, the SOGA algorithm helped in the optimization of the nested structure through the selection of the most significant concepts from all possible concepts at every nesting level.

The most important advantageous characteristics of the proposed nested FCM architecture, according to the results as presented in the previous section, are summarized below. More specifically, the nested FCM:

- optimizes the FCM structure by selecting the most proper concepts for decision-making;
- finds out the most important relationships between the concepts at every nesting level and determines the weights of these relationships;
- results in a readable nested structure in which each concept of a first level can be decomposed into another FCM, providing a more detailed representation of time series;
- facilitates understanding of the concepts affecting the forecast;
- clusters available concepts into similar groups

The main limitation of the proposed approach is that it could be time-consuming for large datasets, as it requires the construction of several individual FCM models. However, time series prediction can be limited only to the most general level of the nested structure.

The main outcomes of this research study are outlined as follows:

(i) The proposed nested FCM method demonstrates excellent performance in the case of clustering analysis considering the examined variables/concepts of this case study. For the examined nested structure and after a number of experiments were conducted, a specific configuration was concluded as the best. In general, the optimum nested FCM model is defined through the identification of the most important relationships between the concepts at every nesting level and by determining the weights of these relationships.

(ii) The proposed nested architecture is proven to be superior compared to the standard well-known FCM model, which has been previously used in prediction problems in the energy domain.

(iii) The proposed nested model exhibits remarkable competence when deployed in appliances energy prediction since its performance is better (see Tables 2 and 3) and constitutes a flexible tool to cluster concepts efficiently and, thus, reduce the model complexity.

To sum up, we have developed and suggested a new approach for constructing a nested structure based on fuzzy cognitive maps. The proposed approach seems to be a promising method for time series forecasting and decision-making in many scientific domains. It allows the representation of a readable nested structure in which each concept of a first level can be decomposed into another fuzzy cognitive map for a more detailed presentation of the analyzed time series. Future work is oriented in analyzing the application of the developed approach based on various complex time series. Moreover, we would like to introduce different forecasting models (e.g., artificial neural networks) at the most detailed level of the nested structure in order to achieve higher prediction accuracy.

Author Contributions: Conceptualization, K.P. and E.I.P.; methodology, K.P.; software, K.P.; validation, K.P., E.I.P. and V.C.G.; formal analysis, K.P., E.I.P. and V.C.G.; investigation, K.P. and E.I.P.; resources, K.P.; data curation, K.P.; writing—original draft preparation, K.P., E.I.P. and V.C.G.; writing—review and editing, K.P., E.I.P. and V.C.G.; visualization, K.P.; supervision, E.I.P. and V.C.G. All authors have read and agreed to the published version of the manuscript.

Funding: This research received no external funding.

Conflicts of Interest: The authors declare no conflict of interest.

References

1. Kosko, B. Fuzzy cognitive maps. *Int. J. Man-Mach. Stud.* **1986**, *24*, 65–75. [CrossRef]
2. Papakostas, G.A.; Boutalis, Y.S.; Koulouriotis, D.E.; Mertzios, B.G. Fuzzy cognitive maps for pattern recognition applications. *Int. J. Pattern Recogn. Artif. Intell.* **2008**, *22*, 1461–1468. [CrossRef]
3. Aguilar, J. Dynamic random fuzzy cognitive maps. *Comput. Sist.* **2004**, *7*, 260–271. Available online: http://www.scielo.org.mx/pdf/cys/v7n4/v7n4a5.pdf (accessed on 17 November 2020).
4. Tsadiras, A.K.; Kouskouvelis, I. Using fuzzy cognitive maps as a decision support system for political decisions: The case of Turkey's integration into the European Union. In *Advances in Informatics*; PCI 2005; Lecture Notes in Computer Science; Bozanis, P., Houstis, E.N., Eds.; Springer: Berlin/Heidelberg, Germany, 2005; Volume 3746, pp. 371–381. [CrossRef]
5. Dickerson, J.A.; Kosko, B. Virtual worlds as fuzzy cognitive maps. *Presence* **1994**, *3*, 173–189. [CrossRef]
6. Papageorgiou, K.; Singh, P.K.; Papageorgiou, E.I.; Chudasama, H.; Bochtis, D.; Stamoulis, G. Fuzzy cognitive map-based sustainable socio-economic development planning for rural communities. *Sustainability* **2020**, *12*, 305. [CrossRef]
7. Papageorgiou, K.; Carvalho, G.; Papageorgiou, E.I.; Bochtis, D.; Stamoulis, G. Decision-making process for photovoltaic solar energy sector development using fuzzy cognitive map technique. *Energies* **2020**, *13*, 1427. [CrossRef]
8. Song, H.; Miao, C.; Roel, W.; Shen, Z. Implementation of fuzzy cognitive maps based on fuzzy neural network and application in prediction of time series. *IEEE Trans. Fuzzy Syst.* **2010**, *18*, 233–250. [CrossRef]

9. Lu, W.; Yang, J.; Liu, X. The linguistic forecasting of time series based on fuzzy cognitive maps. In Proceedings of the 2013 Joint IFSA World Congress and NAFIPS Annual Meeting, IFSA/NAFIPS 2013, Edmonton, AB, Canada, 24–28 June 2013; pp. 649–654.
10. Stach, W.; Kurgan, L.; Pedrycz, W. Numerical and linguistic prediction of time series with the use of fuzzy cognitive maps. *IEEE Trans. Fuzzy Syst.* **2008**, *16*, 61–72. [CrossRef]
11. Homenda, W.; Jastrzebska, A.; Pedrycz, W. Modeling time series with fuzzy cognitive maps. In Proceedings of the 2014 IEEE International Conference on Fuzzy Systems, FUZZ-IEEE 2014, Beijing, China, 6–11 July 2014; pp. 2055–2062. [CrossRef]
12. Papageorgiou, E.I.; Poczeta, K.; Laspidou, C. Application of fuzzy cognitive maps to water demand prediction. In Proceedings of the 2015 IEEE International Conference on Fuzzy Systems, FUZZ-IEEE 2015, Istanbul, Turkey, 2–5 August 2015; pp. 1–8. [CrossRef]
13. Papageorgiou, K.; Papageorgiou, E.I.; Poczeta, K.; Gerogiannis, V.C.; Stamoulis, G. Exploring an ensemble of methods that combines fuzzy cognitive maps and neural networks in solving the time series prediction problem of gas consumption in Greece. *Algorithms* **2019**, *12*, 235. [CrossRef]
14. Papageorgiou, E.I.; Poczeta, K. A two-stage model for time series prediction based on fuzzy cognitive maps and neural networks. *Neurocomputing* **2017**, *232*, 113–121. [CrossRef]
15. Homenda, W.; Jastrzebska, A.; Pedrycz, W. Nodes selection criteria for fuzzy cognitive maps designed to model time series. In *Intelligent Systems' 2014. Advances in Intelligent Systems and Computing*; Filev, D., Ed.; Springer: Cham, Switzerland, 2014; Volume 323, pp. 859–870. [CrossRef]
16. Selvin, N.N.; Srinivasaraghavan, A. Dimensionality reduction of inputs for a fuzzy cognitive map for obesity problem. In Proceedings of the 2016 International Conference on Inventive Computation Technologies, ICICT 2016, Coimbatore, Tamilnadu, India, 23–26 August 2016; pp. 1–5. [CrossRef]
17. Chi, Y.; Liu, J. Learning of fuzzy cognitive maps with varying densities using multi-objective evolutionary algorithms. *IEEE Trans. Fuzzy Syst.* **2016**, *24*, 71–81. [CrossRef]
18. Stach, W.; Pedrycz, W.; Kurgan, L.A. Learning of fuzzy cognitive maps using density estimate. *IEEE Trans. Syst. Man Cybern. Part B* **2012**, *42*, 900–912. [CrossRef]
19. Hatwágner, M.F.; Kóczy, L.T. Parameterization and concept optimization of FCM models. In Proceedings of the 2015 IEEE International Conference on Fuzzy Systems, FUZZ-IEEE 2015, Istanbul, Turkey, 2–5 August 2015; pp. 1–8. [CrossRef]
20. Sadiq, R.; Kleiner, Y.; Rajani, B.B. Interpreting fuzzy cognitive maps (FCMs) using fuzzy measures to evaluate water quality failures in distribution networks. In Proceedings of the Joint International Conference on Computation in Civil and Building Engineering, ICCCBE XI, Montreal, QC, Canada, 14–16 June 2006; pp. 1–10.
21. MacQueen, J. Some methods for classification and analysis of multivariate observations. In *Proceedings of the 5th Berkeley Symposium on Mathematical Statistics and Probability*; Le Cam, L.M., Neyman, J., Eds.; University of California Press: Davis, CA, USA, 1967; Volume 1, pp. 281–297. Available online: https://projecteuclid.org/euclid.bsmsp/1200512992 (accessed on 17 November 2020).
22. Stach, W.; Kurgan, L.; Pedrycz, W.; Reformat, M. Genetic learning of fuzzy cognitive maps. *Fuzzy Sets Syst.* **2005**, *153*, 371–401. [CrossRef]
23. Makonin, S.; Ellert, B.; Bajic, I.; Popowich, F. Electricity, water, and natural gas consumption of a residential house in Canada from 2012 to 2014. *Sci. Data* **2016**, *3*, 160037. [CrossRef]
24. Dong, B.; Cao, C.; Lee, S.E. Applying support vector machines to predict building energy consumption in tropical region. *Energy Build.* **2005**, *37*, 545–553. [CrossRef]
25. Candanedo, L.M.; Feldheim, V.; Deramaix, D. Data driven prediction models of energy use of appliances in a low-energy house. *Energy Build.* **2017**, *140*, 81–97. [CrossRef]
26. Kandananond, K. Forecasting electricity demand in Thailand with an artificial neural network approach. *Energies* **2011**, *4*, 1246–1257. [CrossRef]
27. Kim, J.-Y.; Cho, S.-B. Electric energy consumption prediction by deep learning with state explainable autoencoder. *Energies* **2019**, *12*, 739. [CrossRef]
28. Poczeta, K.; Yastrebov, A.; Papageorgiou, E.I. Learning fuzzy cognitive maps using structure optimization genetic algorithm. In Proceedings of the 2015 Federated Conference on Computer Science and Information Systems, FedCSIS 2015, Lodz, Poland, 13–16 September 2015; pp. 547–554. [CrossRef]

29. Orang, O.; Silva, R.; de Lima e Silva, P.C.; Guimarães, F.G. Solar energy forecasting with fuzzy time series using high-order fuzzy cognitive maps. In Proceedings of the 2020 IEEE International Conference on Fuzzy Systems, FUZZ-IEEE 2020, Glasgow, UK, 19–24 July 2020; pp. 1–8. [CrossRef]
30. Papageorgiou, K.; Carvalho, G.; Papageorgiou, E.I.; Papandrianos, N.I.; Mendonça, M.; Stamoulis, G. Exploring Brazilian photovoltaic solar energy development scenarios using the fuzzy cognitive map wizard tool. In Proceedings of the 2020 IEEE International Conference on Fuzzy Systems, FUZZ-IEEE 2020, Glasgow, UK, 19–24 July 2020; pp. 1–8. [CrossRef]
31. Makridakis, S.; Winkler, R.L. Averages of forecasts: Some empirical results. *Manag. Sci.* **1983**, *29*, 987–996. Available online: https://www.jstor.org/stable/2630927 (accessed on 17 November 2020). [CrossRef]
32. De Jong, K.A.; Spears, W.M. A formal analysis of the role of multi-point crossover in genetic algorithms. *Ann. Math. Artif. Intell.* **1992**, *5*, 1–26. [CrossRef]

Publisher's Note: MDPI stays neutral with regard to jurisdictional claims in published maps and institutional affiliations.

© 2020 by the authors. Licensee MDPI, Basel, Switzerland. This article is an open access article distributed under the terms and conditions of the Creative Commons Attribution (CC BY) license (http://creativecommons.org/licenses/by/4.0/).

Article

Extending Fuzzy Cognitive Maps With Tensor-Based Distance Metrics

Georgios Drakopoulos [1,*], Andreas Kanavos [2] and Phivos Mylonas [1] and Panagiotis Pintelas [3]

[1] Humanistic and Social Informatics Lab, Department of Informatics, Ionian University, 49100 Kerkyra, Greece; fmylonas@ionio.gr
[2] Computer Engineering and Informatics Department, University of Patras, 26504 Patras, Greece; kanavos@ceid.upatras.gr
[3] Department of Mathematics, University of Patras, 26504 Patras, Greece; pintelas@math.upatras.gr
* Correspondence: c16drak@ionio.gr

Received: 30 September 2020; Accepted: 26 October 2020; Published: 31 October 2020

Abstract: Cognitive maps are high level representations of the key topological attributes of real or abstract spatial environments progressively built by a sequence of noisy observations. Currently such maps play a crucial role in cognitive sciences as it is believed this is how clusters of dedicated neurons at hippocampus construct internal representations. The latter include physical space and, perhaps more interestingly, abstract fields comprising of interconnected notions such as natural languages. In deep learning cognitive graphs are effective tools for simultaneous dimensionality reduction and visualization with applications among others to edge prediction, ontology alignment, and transfer learning. Fuzzy cognitive graphs have been proposed for representing maps with incomplete knowledge or errors caused by noisy or insufficient observations. The primary contribution of this article is the construction of cognitive map for the sixteen Myers-Briggs personality types with a tensor distance metric. The latter combines two categories of natural language attributes extracted from the namesake Kaggle dataset. To the best of our knowledge linguistic attributes are separated in categories. Moreover, a fuzzy variant of this map is also proposed where a certain personality may be assigned to up to two types with equal probability. The two maps were evaluated based on their topological properties, on their clustering quality, and on how well they fared against the dataset ground truth. The results indicate a superior performance of both maps with the fuzzy variant being better. Based on the findings recommendations are given for engineers and practitioners.

Keywords: cognitive graphs; self organizing maps; tensor distance metrics; higher order data; topological error; Myers-Briggs Type Indicator; MBTI

1. Introduction

Self organizing maps (SOMs) or cognitive maps constitute a class of neural network grids introduced in Reference [1]. In these grids neuron topology is closely related to their functionality. Moreover, the unsupervised training is patterned after a modified Hebbian rule [2]. These two fundamental properties allow SOMs to approximate the shape of a high dimensional manifold, typically represented as a set of selected data points, and subsequently to construct a lower dimensional and continuous topological map thereof. The latter provides an indirect yet efficient clustering of the data points presented to the SOM during the training process. In turn, that makes SOMs important components in many data mining pipelines in dimensionality reduction, clustering, or visualization roles.

Human character dynamics are the focus of many research fields including psychology, sociology, and cognitive sciences. The Myers-Briggs Type Indicator (MBTI) is among the most well-known classifictions of human personality according to four binary fundamental factors, resulting in a total of sixteen possible personality types [3]. Understanding the psychological dynamics of the individual members of a group is instrumental in minimizing or even avoiding non-productive and time consuming frictions, while at the same time maximizing the group potential through efficient task delegation, unperturbed and unambiguous communication, and effective conflict resolution. These skills are crucial among other cases during the formation of startups, even more so when an accelerator or an incubator are involved, in assemblying workgroups for accomplishing specific missions, or during mentorship assignments [4]. These cases are indicative of the potential of such methods.

Despite their increasing significance across a number of fields, the rapid evolution of natural language processing (NLP) algorithms for estimating human emotional states [5,6], and the development of sophisticated image processing algorithms for the identification of a wide spectrum of cognitive tasks [7,8], there are still few algorithms for addressing the topic of inferring personality dynamics from text as reported in Reference [9]. Additionally, the number of applications based on tensor metrics are still few, which is the principal motivation of this work.

The primary research objective of this article is twofold. First, a multilinear weighted function is used is the construction of the topological map as the data point distance metric. Tensors naturally capture higher order interactions between explanatory variables, in this particular case the fundamental personality traits of the MBTI model. Second, each data point is represented as a matrix and not as a vector, which is currently the customary approach. This adds flexibility in at least two ways, as not only inherently two-dimensional objects can be naturally represented but also one-dimensional objects can have simultaneously more than one representations, which can be applied in cases where object representations can be selected adaptively including aspect mining and multilevel clustering. The tensor-based metric and the matrix representations are naturally combined to yield an SOM algorithm operating on two-dimensional representations of personality traits indirectly represented as text attributes. The latter are extracted from short texts from the Kaggle Myers-Briggs dataset. In addition to the main SOM algorithm, a fuzzy one is developed where membership to at most two clusters can be possible, provided that a given data point is close enough to both.

The remaining of this article is structured as follows. In Section 2 the recent scientific literature regarding tensor distance metrics, cognitive maps, and computational cognitive science is briefly reviewed. Section 3 describes the main points behind the MBTI theory. The SOM architecture is the focus of Section 4. Section 5 discusses the attributes extracted from the dataset, the proposed tensor distance metric, and the results of the experiments. Section 6 concludes this work by recapitulating the findings as well as by exploring future research directions. Tensors are represented with capital calligraphic letters, matrices with boldface capital letters, vectors with boldface lowercase letters, and scalars with lowercase letters. When a function requires parameters, they are placed after the arguments following a semicolon. Technical acronyms are explained the first time they are encountered in text. Finally, the notation of this article is summarized in Table 1.

Table 1. Notation of this article.

Symbol	Meaning
$\triangleq$	Definition or equality by definition
$\{s_1,\ldots,s_n\}$ or $\{s_k\}_{k=1}^n$	Set with elements $s_1,\ldots,s_n$
$\|S\|$ or $\|\{s_1,\ldots,s_n\}\|$	Set cardinality
$\times_k$	Tensor multiplication along the k-th direction
$\mathrm{vec}\,(\cdot)$	Vectorize operation for matrices and tensors
$\mathrm{loc}\,(\cdot)$	Location function for data points
$\mathrm{invloc}\,(\cdot)$	Inverse location relationship for neurons
$\mathrm{weight}\,(u)$	Synaptic weights of neuron u
$\mathrm{bias}\,(u)$	Bias of neuron u
$\Gamma(u)$	Neighborhood of neuron u
$\Delta(u)$	Cover of neuron u
$\langle p_1 \| p_2 \rangle$	Kullback-Leibler divergence between discrete distributions p_1 and p_2

2. Previous Work

Cognitive maps or self organizing maps constitute a special class of neural networks which are trained in an unsupervised manner in order to form a low dimensional representation of a higher dimensional manifold with the added property that important topological relationships are maintained [1]. This map is progressively constructed by updating the neuron synaptic weights through a modified Hebbian rule, which eliminates the need for gradient based training methods [10]. Their application to clustering objects in very large databases is thoroughly explored in Reference [11]. Fuzzy cognitive maps are SOMs where clusters are allowed to overlap [12]. Their properties are examined in Reference [13]. Learning the rules of a fuzzy cognitive map can be done through genetic algorithms [14,15], optimization algorithms [16,17], or compressed sensing [18]. SOMs have been applied to clustering massive document collections [19], functional magnetic resonance images (fMRI) based on attributes extracted from the discrete cosine transform (DCT) [20], prediction of distributed denial of service (DDoS) attacks in software defined networks (SDN) [21], factory interdependencies for Industry 4.0 settings [22], task pools for autonomous vehicles [23], and the drivers behind digital innovation [24]. Moreover SOMs have been employed for a hierarchical clustering scheme for discovering latent gene expression patterns [25] and gene regulatory networks [26]. Given that the trained fuzzy cognitive maps can be represented as a fuzzy graph, clustering can be performed by fuzzy community discovery algorithms [27–29]. In Reference [30] fuzzy graphs have been used in a technique for estimating the number of clusters and their respective centroids. C-means fuzzy clustering has been applied to epistasis analysis [31] and image segmentation [32]. An extensive review for software about SOMs is given in Reference [33].

Tensor algebra is the next evolutionary step in linear algebra since it deals primarily with the simultaneous coupling of three or more vector spaces or with vectors of three or more dimensions [34]. Also, tensors can be used in the identification of non-linear systems [35–37]. Tensors and their factorizations have a wide array of applications to various engineering fields. Computationally feasible tensor decompositions are proposed in Reference [38], whereas other applications to machine learning (ML) are the focus of References [39–41]. In Reference [42] a third order tensor represents spatiosocial Twitter data about the Grand Duchy of Luxembourg and is clustered by a genetic algorithm to yield coherent districts both geographically and linguistically. Tensor stack networks (TSNs) are clusters of feedforward neural networks (FFNNs) which can learn not only from their own errors but also from those of other networks in the cluster [43]. TSNs have been applied to large vocabulary speech recognition [44] and graph resiliency assessment [45]. Tensor distance metrics have numerous applications across diverse fields including gene expression [46], dimensionality reduction [47], and face recognition [48].

Distributed processing systems such as Apache Spark play an increasingly important role in data mining (DM) and ML pipelines [49]. In Reference [50] the singular value decomposition (SVD) performs attribute transformation and selection and boosts the performance of various Spark MLlib classifiers in Kaggle datasets. A similar role is played by higher order tensor factorizations [51]. Julia is a high level programming language primarily intended for intense data management and scientific computing applications [52]. Although interpreted, it offers high performance [53] as it is based on the low level virtual machine (LLVM) infrastructure engine [54]. The capabilities and the respective performance of the various ML models of Julia are described in Reference [55] especially over massive graphics processing unit (GPU) arrays [56]. A numerical optimization package for Julia is described in Reference [57], methods for parameter estimation for partial differential equations (PDEs) are discussed in Reference [58], while the potential of a package for the simulation of quantum systems is explained in Reference [59]. Recently a package for seismic inversion was introduced [60].

Emotions are drivers of human actions as well as major components of human personality. The Myers-Briggs type indicator (MBTI) as explained among others in Reference [3] and Reference [61] has been invented in order to create a methodological framework for quantitative personality analysis [62]. This has been used in applications such as brand loyalty [63]. Also taking into account the MBTI and their interactions can lead to significant improvements in teaching [64]. In contrast to emotion models such as Plutchick's emotion wheel [65] or the universal emotion or big five theory proposed by Eckman in Reference [66], frameworks like MBTI offer a more general view of human personality and allow the analysis of interaction between two or more persons. The connection between cognitive functions and personality type is explored in Reference [4]. An overview of the MBTI typology is given among others in Reference [67]. Finally, human emotional state can be estimated in a number of ways. Among the most significant emotional indicators is speech, which is relatively easy to capture and process since one dimensional signal processing methodologies are used [68]. Other emotional state indicators include gait [69], facial cues [70], or a combination thereof [71]. Alternatively, human emotional state can be estimated by brain imaging techniques [72].

The blueprints of a specialized cognitive system aiming at the reconstruction of events and scenes from memory are given in Reference [73]. The role of augmented- (AR) and virtual reality (VR) for cognitive training is investigated in Reference [74]. The principles and properties of cognitive tools are the focus of Reference [75]. A more extensive approach including predictions for future cognitive systems is that of Reference [76]. Brain-computer interface (BCI) collect biosignals related to brain activity [77]. A detailed review of BCI signaling is given in Reference [78]. Convolutional neural network (CNN) architectures in Reference [79] are used to extract temporal information about the brain through BCIs, while age and gender classification with BCI is proposed in Reference [80].

3. Myers-Briggs Type Indicator

The MBTI taxonomy [3] establishes a framework for classifying the personality of an individual along the lines of the theory developed earlier by the pioneering psychologist Karl Jung [67]. It is often now routinely employed by human resources (HR) departments around the globe in order to determine ways to maximize total employee engagement as well as to identify possible friction points arising by different viewpoints and approach to problem solving. At the core of the taxonomy are sixteen archetypal personalities with unique traits. Each such personality type is derived by evaluating the following four fundamental criteria [4]:

- **Approach to socialization**: Introvert (I) vs Extrovert (E). As the name of this variable suggests, it denotes the degree a person is open to others. Introverts tend to work mentally in isolation and rely on indirect cues from others. On the contrary, extroverts share their thoughts frequently with others and ask for explicit feedback.
- **Approach to information gathering**: Sensing (S) vs Intuition (N). Persons who frequently resort to sensory related functions observe the outside world, whether the physical or social environment, in order to collect information about open problems or improve situational awareness belong to the S group. On the other hand, persons labeled as N rely on a less concrete form of information representation for reaching insight.

- **Approach to decision making**: Thinking (T) vs Feeling (F). This variable indicates the primary means by which an individual makes a decision. This may be rational thinking with clearly outlined processes, perhaps in the form of corporate policies of formal problem solving methods such as 5W or TRIZ, or a more abstract and empathy oriented way based on external influences and the emotional implications of past decisions.
- **Approach to lifestyle**: Judging (J) vs Perceiving (P). This psychological function pertains to how a lifestyle is led. Perceiving persons show more understanding to other lifestyles and may not object to open ended evolution processes over a long amount of time. On the contrary, judging persons tend to close open matters as soon as possible and are more likely to apply old solutions to new problems.

As each of the above variables has two possible values, there is a total of sixteen possible personality types in the MBTI model as mentioned earlier. These are listed in Table 2. Each of these personality types is assigned a four-letter acronym which is formed by the corresponding predominant trait of that character type with respect to each of the four basic variables.

Table 2. Myers-Briggs Type Indicator (MBTI) taxonomy (source: [61]).

Type	Attributes	Type	Attributes
ISTJ	Introversion, Sensing, Thinking, Judging	INFJ	Introversion, Intuition, Feeling, Judging
ISTP	Introversion, Sensing, Thinking, Perceiving	INFP	Introversion, Intuition, Feeling, Perceiving
ESTP	Extraversion, Sensing, Thinking, Perceiving	ENFP	Extraversion, Intuition, Feeling, Perceiving
ESTJ	Extraversion, Sensing, Thinking, Judging	ENFJ	Extraversion, Intuition, Feeling, Judging
ISFJ	Introversion, Sensing, Feeling, Judging	INTJ	Introversion, Intuition, Thinking, Judging
ISFP	Introversion, Sensing, Feeling, Perceiving	INTP	Introversion, Intuition, Thinking, Perceiving
ESFP	Extraversion, Sensing, Feeling, Perceiving	ENTP	Extraversion, Intuition, Thinking, Perceiving
ESFJ	Extraversion, Sensing, Feeling, Judging	ENTJ	Extraversion, Intuition, Thinking, Judging

The above personality types are not equally encountered. On the contrary, a few types are more frequently encountered than others. The most common personality type reported is ISFJ with corresponds to 13.8% of the US population [3]. This corresponds to roughly twice the expected frequency of $1/16 \approx 6.25\%$. On the other hand, the less common MBTI type encountered is INTJ with a frequency of 1.5% [64]. Among the reasons explaining this variance are educational system, peer pressure, and adaptation to urban life and its associated socioeconomic conditions. As a sidenote, it is worth mentioning that emotions are not noise in the system but rather complex motivational mechanisms whose evolution has been driven, partly at least, by a combination of factors such as the need for immediate action and cultural norms.

4. Cognitive Maps

Structurally, an SOM is a grid where each point is a neuron u_k with adjustable synaptic weights as well as an optional bias. These weights can be systematically trained to match selected patterns, such as selected points of a manifold of higher dimensions. The latter is represented by a set V of n training vectors or input points denoted as $\mathbf{v}_j$. Thus:

$$V \triangleq \{\mathbf{v}_j\}_{j=1}^n. \tag{1}$$

Functionally, each SOM by construction connects two distinct spaces, namely the data space $\mathcal{V}$ and the coordinate space $\mathcal{C}$. The former space contains V, whereas the latter contains the vectors of the neuron grid coordinates. Thus, SOMs offer dimensionality reduction by mapping points of $\mathcal{V}$ to $\mathcal{C}$. Additionally, $\mathcal{C}$ can be considered as way to cluster the original data points.

The representation of the coordinate space plays an instrumental role in SOM functionality. The following definition describes the structure of $\mathcal{C}$.

Definition 1 (Neuron location). *The location of a neuron u_k is the vector containing the coordinates of the neuron in the grid. The number of components is the dimension of the grid. Thus, for a two dimensional grid:*

$$\text{loc}(u_k) \triangleq \begin{bmatrix} x_k & y_k \end{bmatrix}^T \in \mathcal{C} \tag{2}$$

The set of data points assigned to a particular neuron u_k is denoted by:

$$\text{invloc}(u_k) \triangleq \{\mathbf{v}_j \mid \text{loc}(\mathbf{v}_j) = u_k\} \subseteq \mathcal{V}. \tag{3}$$

There is a key difference between $\text{loc}(\cdot)$ and $\text{invloc}(\cdot)$. The former is a function as it maps one data point to a coordinate vector, but the latter is a relationship since it maps a coordinate vector to a set of data points. The synaptic weight vector $\mathbf{w}_k \in \mathcal{V}$ of neuron u_k is denoted as follows:

$$\text{weight}(u_k) \triangleq \mathbf{w}_k \in \mathcal{V}. \tag{4}$$

The synaptic weight set $\mathbf{w}_k$ for each neuron may also be supplemented with an optional bias b_k which acts as a safeguard against discontinuities in the resulting topological maps by driving inactive neurons closer to active clusters. To this end, biases are not trained in the classic fashion of an FFNN. Instead, they depend on the number of iterations where the neuron did not receive a synaptic weight update. The bias of neuron u_k is typically denoted as $\text{bias}(u_k)$. In contrast to the weight update rule, the bias update does not depend on the proximity to the data points. Instead, as the role of bias is to ensure that no unactivated neurons exist [81]. When a bias mechanism is implemented, then the following two advantages are gained in exchange for a minimal SOM monitoring mechanism:

- All neurons are eventually activated and assigned to clusters, leaving thus no gaps to the topological map. Thus all available neurons are utilized.
- Moreover, in the long run the number of neuron activations is roughly the same for each neuron. For sufficiently large number of epochs each neuron is activated with equal probability.

In this article no such mechanism has been implemented.

Definition 2 (Epoch). *An epoch is defined as the number of iterations necessary to present each input point once to the SOM. Therefore, each epoch is a batch consisting of exactly n iterations.*

During each epoch the order in which each data point is presented to the SOM may well vary. Options proposed in the scientific literature include:

- Random order. In each epoch the data points are selected based on a random permutation of their original order.
- Reverse order. In each epoch the previous order is reversed.

In this article the order of data points remains the same in each epoch.

4.1. Training

The distance function $g(\cdot, \cdot)$ measures distance in the data space $\mathcal{V}$ and, thus, serves as the distance metric between pairs of synaptic weight vectors, data vectors, and between them. Its selection is crucial to both the continuity of the final topological map as well as to the shape of the final clusters. Formally, the distance function is defined as:

$$g(\cdot, \cdot) : \mathcal{V} \times \mathcal{V} \to \mathbb{R}^* \tag{5}$$

Choices for the distance metric may include:

- The ℓ_1 norm or Manhattan distance.

- The ℓ_2 norm of Euclidean distance.

The training process is the algorithmic way for the SOM to learn the primary topological properties of the underlying manifold. True to the long tradition of neural networks, training is indirectly reflected in the change of the synaptic weights of the grid neurons. However, in sharp contrast to other neural network architectures, gradient based methods are not necessary as only the distance between the data point and the synaptic weights of neurons is needed. The SOM training is summarized in Algorithm 1.

The distance function mentioned earlier is central in the synaptic weight update and, hence, in the SOM training process. The latter relies heavily on the Hebbian learning rule. In its original form this rule states that only the winning neuron u^* or best matching unit (BMU), namely the neuron whose synaptic weight vector weight (u^*) is closest to the data point $\mathbf{v}_j$ currently presented to the network. Thus, u^* is defined according to (6):

$$u^* \triangleq \mathrm{argmin}\left\{g\left(\mathrm{weight}\left(u\right),\mathbf{v}_j\right)\right\}. \tag{6}$$

The neighborhood of a neuron are all the neurons in the grid which are found at a distance of one from it. This raises two questions. First what is the pattern and second whether this pattern is allowed to wrap around the grid limits. Options reported in the bibliography are:

- Square.
- Hexagon.
- Cross.

In this work the pattern is a cross formed by the four adjacent neurons located next to the given neuron. Moreover, this pattern cannot wrap around.

Definition 3 (Neighborhood). *For each neuron u the relationship $\Gamma(u)$ returns the set of its neighboring neurons.*

$$\Gamma(u) \triangleq \{u' \mid u' \text{ is adjacent to } u\}. \tag{7}$$

Once the BMU u^* is selected, its synaptic weights are updated as follows:

$$\mathrm{weight}(u^*)[r] \triangleq \mathrm{weight}(u^*)[r-1] + \eta[r] \cdot (\mathbf{v}[r] - \mathrm{weight}(u^*)[r-1]). \tag{8}$$

The *learning rate* $\eta[r]$ during epoch r is a factor which plays a central role in the stability of the training process, since as the epochs gradually progress, each activated neuron receives an increasingly smaller reward in the form of a weight update. This ensures that initially neuron clusters are formed and during later epochs these clusters are finer tuned but not really moved around. Common options for the learning rate include:

- **Constant rate:** This is the simplest case as $\eta[r]$ has a constant positive value of η_0. This imples η_0 should be carefully chosen in order to avoid both a slow synaptic weight convergence and missing the convergence. In some cases a theoretical value of η_0 is given by (9), where $\lambda^\dagger$ is the maximum eigenvalue of the input autocorrelation matrix:

$$\eta_0 = \frac{2}{\lambda^\dagger}. \tag{9}$$

- **Cosine rate:** A common option for the learning rate is the cosine decay rate as shown in (10), which is in general considered flexible and efficient in the sense that the learning rate is initially large enough so that convergence is quickly achieved but also it becomes slow enough so that no overshoot will occur.

$$\eta[r] \triangleq \cos\left(\frac{\pi r}{2r_0}\right), \qquad 0 \le r \le r_0 - 1. \tag{10}$$

In (10) the argument stays in the first quadrant, meaning that the $\eta\,[r]$ is always positive. However, the maximum number of epochs r_0 should be known in advance. This specific learning rate has the advantage that initially it is relatively high but gradually drops with a quadratic rate as seen in Equation (11):

$$\cos\vartheta = \sum_{k=0}^{+\infty}(-1)^k \frac{\vartheta^{2k}}{(2k)!} = 1 - \frac{\vartheta^2}{2} + \frac{\vartheta^4}{4!} - \frac{\vartheta^6}{6!} + \ldots \approx 1 - \frac{\vartheta^2}{2}. \tag{11}$$

To see what this means in practice, let us check when $\eta\,[r]$ drops below 0.5:

$$\eta\,[r] \leq \frac{1}{2} \Leftrightarrow \cos\left(\frac{\pi r}{2r_0}\right) \leq \cos\left(\frac{\pi}{3}\right) \Rightarrow \frac{\pi r}{2r_0} \geq \frac{\pi}{3} \Leftrightarrow r \geq \frac{2r_0}{3}. \tag{12}$$

Thus, for only a third of the total available number of iterations the learning rate is above 0.5. Alternatively, for each iteration where the learning rate is above that threshold there are two where respectively it is below that, provided that the number of iterations is close to the limit r_0. Another way to see this, the learning rate decays with a rate given by (13):

$$\left|\frac{\partial\eta\,[r]}{\partial r}\right| \triangleq \left|\frac{\partial}{\partial r}\cos\left(\frac{\pi r}{2r_0}\right)\right| = \frac{\pi}{2r_0}\left|\sin\left(\frac{\pi r}{2r_0}\right)\right|. \tag{13}$$

- **Inverse linear:** The learning rate scheme of Equation (14) is historically among the first. It has a slow decay which translates in the general case to a slow convergence rate, implying that more epochs are necessary in order for the SOM to achieve a truly satisfactory performance.

$$\eta\,[r;\gamma_0,\gamma_1,\gamma_2] \triangleq \frac{\gamma_2}{\gamma_1 r + \gamma_0}. \tag{14}$$

Now the learning rate decays with a rate of:

$$\left|\frac{\partial\eta\,[r]}{\partial r}\right| \triangleq \frac{\gamma_2\gamma_1}{(\gamma_1 r + \gamma_0)^2} = O\left(\frac{1}{r^2}\right). \tag{15}$$

In order for the learning rate to drop below 0.5 it suffices that:

$$\eta\,[r;\gamma_0,\gamma_1,\gamma_2] \leq \frac{1}{2} \Leftrightarrow r \geq \frac{2\gamma_2 - \gamma_0}{\gamma_1}. \tag{16}$$

From the above equation it follows that γ_1 determines convergence to a great extent.
- **Inverse polynomial:** Equation (17) generalizes the inverse linear learning rate to a higher dimension. In this case there is no simple way to predict its behavior, which may well fluctuate before the dominant term takes over. Also, the polynomial coefficients should be carefully selected in order to avoid negative values. Moreover, although the value at each iteration can be efficiently computed, numerical stability may be an issue especially for large values of p or when r is close to a root. If possible the polynomial should be given in the factor form. Also, ideally polynomials with roots of even moderate multiplicity should be avoided if r can reach their region as the lower order derivatives of the polynomial do not vanish locally. To this end algorithmic techniques such as Horner's schema [82] should be employed. In this case:

$$\eta\left[r;\{\gamma_j\}_{j=0}^{p+1},p\right] \triangleq \frac{\gamma_{p+1}}{\sum_{j=0}^{p}\gamma_j r^j} = \frac{\gamma_{p+1}}{\gamma_p\prod_{j=1}^{p}(r-\tilde{\xi}_j)}. \tag{17}$$

For this option the learning rate decay rate is more complicated compared to the other cases as:

$$\left|\frac{\partial \eta\,[r]}{\partial r}\right| \triangleq \frac{\gamma_{p+1}\left|\sum_{j=1}^{p} j\gamma_j r^{j-1}\right|}{\left(\sum_{j=0}^{p}\gamma_j r^j\right)^2} = O\left(\frac{1}{r^{p+1}}\right). \tag{18}$$

- **Inverse logarithmic:** A more adaptive choice for the learning rate and an intermediate selection between the constant and the inverse linear options is the inverse logarithmic as described by Equation (19). The logarithm base can vary depending on the application and here the Neperian logarithms will be used. Although all logarithms have essentially the same order of magnitude, local differences between iterations may well be observed. In this case:

$$\eta\,[r;\gamma_0,\gamma_1,\gamma_2] \triangleq \frac{\gamma_2}{\gamma_1 \ln(1+r) + \gamma_0}. \tag{19}$$

As r grows, the logarithm tends to behave approximately like a increasing piecewise constant for increasingly large intervals of r. Thus, the learning rate adapts to the number of iterations and does not require a maximum value r_0. Equation (20) gives the rate of this learning rate:

$$\left|\frac{\partial \eta\,[r]}{\partial r}\right| = \left|-\frac{\gamma_2\gamma_1}{(1+r)(\gamma_1 \ln(1+r) + \gamma_0)^2}\right| = O\left(\frac{1}{r\ln^2 r}\right). \tag{20}$$

In order for the learning rate to drop below 0.5 it suffices that:

$$\eta\,[r;\gamma_0,\gamma_1,\gamma_2] \leq \frac{1}{2} \Leftrightarrow r \geq \exp\left(\frac{2\gamma_2 - \gamma_0}{\gamma_1}\right) - 1. \tag{21}$$

Due to the nature of the exponential function all three parameters play their role in determining the number of epochs.
- **Exponential decay:** Finally the learning rate diminishes sharper when the scheme of Equation (22) is chosen, although that depends mainly on the parameter γ_1:

$$\eta\,[r;\gamma_0,\gamma_1] \triangleq \gamma_0 \exp(-\gamma_1 r). \tag{22}$$

The learning rate in this case decays according to:

$$\left|\frac{\partial \eta\,[r]}{\partial r}\right| \triangleq \gamma_0\gamma_1 \exp(-\gamma_1 r) = \gamma_1 \eta\,[r]. \tag{23}$$

Therefore the learning rate decays with a rate proportional to its current value, a well known property of the exponential function, implying this decay is quickly accelerated. Additionally, in order for the learning rate to drop below 0.5 it suffices that:

$$\eta\,[r;\gamma_0,\gamma_1] \leq \frac{1}{2} \Leftrightarrow r \geq \frac{\ln(2\gamma_0)}{\gamma_1}. \tag{24}$$

For each neighboring neuron u to u^* its synaptic weights are also updated as follows:

$$\text{weight}(u)\,[r] \triangleq \text{weight}(u)\,[r-1] + w\,(g\,(u,u^*)) \cdot \eta\,[r] \cdot (\mathbf{v}\,[r] - \text{weight}(u)\,[r-1]). \tag{25}$$

The additional weight $w\,(\cdot)$ depends on the distance between the BMU u^* and the neuron u. Equation (25) implies that the synaptic weight of the neighboring neurons also updated, which is a deviation from the original Hebbian learning rule. This update operation is crucial in formulating clusters in the final topological map. Note that the weight depends on the distance of the neuron u from u^* as measured by $g(\cdot,\cdot)$. Common weight functions for $\mathcal{V}$ include:

- Constant α_0
- Rectangular with rectangle side α_0
- Circular with radius ρ_0
- Triangular with height h_0 and base h_b.
- Gaussian with mean μ_0 and variance σ_0^2

The proximity function $h(\cdot,\cdot)$ measures the distance of two neurons in the coordinate space $\mathcal{C}$. Notice that it differs from $g(\cdot,\cdot)$ since $\mathcal{V}$ and $\mathcal{C}$ are distinct spaces.

$$h(\text{loc}(u), \text{loc}(u')) : \mathcal{C} \times \mathcal{C} \to \mathbb{R}^* \qquad (26)$$

Common proximity functions for $\mathcal{C}$ include:

- Rectangular with rectangle size α_0.
- Circular with radius ρ_0.
- Gaussian with mean μ_0 and variance σ_0^2.

Definition 4 (Cover). *The cover of a neuron u with respect to a threshold η_0 is defined as that set of neurons u' for which the proximity function does not fall under η_0.*

$$\Delta(u;\eta_0) \triangleq \{u' \mid h(u,u') \geq \eta_0\}. \qquad (27)$$

The distinction between the neighborhood $\Gamma(u')$ and cover $\Delta(u';\eta_0)$ of a neuron u' is crucial since the former corresponds to the core of a cluster which can be formed around u' whereas the latter corresponds to a portion of the periphery of that cluster determined by threshold η_0. In most cases it will hold that $\Gamma(u') \subset \Delta(u';\eta_0)$ since the periphery of a cluster is expected to contain more neurons than merely the core.

Selecting the grid dimensions p_0 and q_0 is not a trivial task. There are no criteria in the strict sense of the word, but some rules have been proposed in the literature. Here the following rule is used, which stems from the information content of set V.

$$p_0 = q_0 = b_0 \lceil \log n \rceil + b_1. \qquad (28)$$

4.2. Error Metrics

In this subsection the various performance and error metrics employed to monitor the evolution of an SOM and the correctness of its functionality are explained. They cover various aspects ranging from cluster topology to neuron activation frequency distribution.

Since topology and its partial preservation plays an important role in the training process of an SOM, it makes perfect sense to use it as a performance metric. Specifically, the topological error counts the fraction of data points which have not been assigned to the neighborhood of a neuron.

Definition 5 (Topological error). *During epoch r the topological error is defined as the fraction of data vectors assigned neither to a cluster center nor to its neighboring neurons. Formally, as shown in Equation (29):*

$$e[r] \triangleq \frac{|\{\mathbf{v}_j \in V \mid \text{loc}(\mathbf{v}_j) \notin C[r]\}|}{n}. \qquad (29)$$

Another parameter is the data point density ϵ_0 which acts as an indicator of the average data points corresponding to each grid point. Thus, each cluster is expected to have been approximately assigned a number of data points close to the product of the density by the grid points of the cluster.

Definition 6 (Data point density). *The density is defined as the number of data points divided by the nunber of neurons. In the case of a two dimensional grid this translates to the number of neurons divided by the product of grid dimensions.*

$$\epsilon_0 \triangleq \frac{n}{p_0 q_0} \approx \frac{n}{b_3 \lceil \log n \rceil^2}. \tag{30}$$

Various combinations of neighborhood and weight functions can lead to various cluster shapes. In theory, there is no restriction to their combination, although smooth cluster shapes are more desirable in order to ensure a greater degree of continuity of the topological map. To this end, shapes like squares and triangles are generally avoided in the SOM literary, whereas circles and Gaussian shapes are more common. Known combinations are listed in Table 3.

Table 3. Cluster shapes (source: authors).

Neighborhood	Weight	Shape	Neighborhood	Weight	Shape
Square	Square	Cube	Triangular	Triangular	Pyramid
Square	Triangular	Pyramid	Circular	Semicircular	Dome
Square	Semicircular	Dome	Gaussian	Gaussian	3D Gaussian

Now that all the elements have been explained, the basic SOM training is shown in Algorithm 1.

Algorithm 1 SOM training.

Require: data point selection policy, cognitive map size, and weight initialization policy
Require: termination criterion τ_0 and maximum number of iterations policy τ_1
Require: distance, proximity, and weight functions, cover, neighborhood, and their parameters
Ensure: the resulting cognitive map is continuous and partially preserves topology
1: **initialize** map T
2: **repeat**
3:    **for all** data points $\mathbf{v}_j \in V$ **do**
4:       **select** a $\mathbf{v}_j$ based on the selection policy
5:       **find** the winning neuron u^* as in (6)
6:       **update** weight (u^*) as well as those of $\Delta(u^*)$ based on (8) and (25) respectively
7:    **end for**
8: **until** τ_0 is met **or** iterations dictated by τ_1 are reached
9: **return** T
---

5. Results

5.1. Dataset and Data Point Representation

The Myers-Briggs dataset stored in Kaggle contains short texts from a individuals describing their own characters and describing how they believe others see them, either by mentioning important life events, direct feedback given to them by peers, or self evaluation. Moreover, for each person there is the MBTI taxonomy as given by a domain expert which will be used as the ground truth.

To avoid problems associated with class size imbalance, the original dataset was randomly pruned so that each class had the same number of rows with the smallest class. This resulted in a total of C_0 ground truth classes, one for each MBTI personality, each with $N_0 = 256$ rows.

The attributes extracted from these texts are stored as the entries of the wide matrix $\mathbf{M}$ shown in Equation (31). Table 4 explains each feature. Observe that each value is normalized with respect to the total number of the occurrences in the dataset. This means that for each attribute the respective minimum and maximum values were found and the numerical value of an attribute was expressed as a percentage in that scale. Attributes are organized in two groups of Q_0 features each where the first attribute group is related to how each person writes and the second attribute group pertains to his/her emotional and thinking processes.

$$\mathbf{M} \triangleq \begin{bmatrix} m_{1,1} & m_{1,2} & m_{1,3} & m_{1,4} & m_{1,5} & m_{1,6} \\ m_{2,1} & m_{2,2} & m_{2,3} & m_{2,4} & m_{2,5} & m_{2,6} \end{bmatrix} \in \mathbb{R}^{2 \times Q_0}. \tag{31}$$

Table 4. Extracted attributes.

Attribute	Position in (31)
Normalized number of words	$m_{1,1}$
Normalized number of characters	$m_{1,2}$
Normalized number of punctuation marks	$m_{1,3}$
Normalized number of question marks	$m_{1,4}$
Normalized number of exclamation points	$m_{1,5}$
Normalized number of occurences of two or more '.'	$m_{1,6}$
Normalized number of positive words	$m_{2,1}$
Normalized number of negative words	$m_{2,2}$
Normalized number of self-references	$m_{2,3}$
Normalized number of references to others	$m_{2,4}$
Normalized number of words pertaining to emotion	$m_{2,5}$
Normalized number of words pertaining to reason	$m_{2,6}$

Algorithmic reasons for representing a data point as an attribute matrix instead of a vector include the following:

- A point or even an entire class may be better represented by more than one vectors. Thus, these vectors may be concatenated to yield a matrix.
- Higher order relationships between vectors cannot be represented by other vectors.

5.2. Proposed Metrics

Tensors are direct higher order generalizations of matrices and vectors. From a structural perspective a tensor is a multidimensional array indexed by an array of p integers, where p is termed the tensor order. Formally:

Definition 7 (Tensor). *A p-th order tensor $\mathcal{T}$, where $p \in \mathbb{Z}^*$, is a linear mapping coupling p non necessarily distinct vector spaces $\mathbb{S}_k$, $1 \leq k \leq p$. If $\mathbb{S}_k = \mathbb{R}^{I_k}$, then $\mathcal{T} \in \mathbb{R}^{I_1 \times \ldots \times I_p}$.*

Perhaps the most important operation in tensor algebra is tensor multiplication which defines elementwise the multiplication along the k-th dimension $\mathcal{G} = \mathcal{X} \times_k \mathcal{Y}$ between the tensors $\mathcal{X}$ of order p and $\mathcal{Y}$ of order q, $k \leq \min\{p, q\}$ as shown below, provided that both tensors have the same number of elements I_k along the k-th dimension:

Definition 8 (Tensor multiplication). *The tensor multiplication along the k-th dimension denoted by $\mathcal{X} \times_k \mathcal{Y}$ of two tensors $\mathcal{X} \in \mathbb{R}^{I_1 \times \ldots \times I_{k-1} \times I_k \times I_{k+1} \times \ldots \times I_p}$ and $\mathcal{Y} \in \mathbb{R}^{J_1 \times \ldots \times J_{k-1} \times I_k \times J_{k+1} \times \ldots \times J_q}$ of respective orders p and q with $k \leq \min\{p, q\}$ is a tensor $\mathcal{G}$ of order $p + q - 2$ elementwise defined as:*

$$\mathcal{G}[i_1, \ldots, i_{k-1}, i_{k+1}, \ldots, i_p, j_1, \ldots, j_{k-1}, j_{k+1}, \ldots, j_q] \triangleq \sum_{i_k=1}^{I_k} \mathcal{X}[i_1, \ldots, i_p] \mathcal{Y}[j_1, \ldots, j_q]. \tag{32}$$

For instance, the SVD of an arbitrary data matrix $\mathbf{A} \in \mathbb{R}^{I_1 \times I_2}$ can be recast as:

$$\mathbf{A} = \mathbf{U}\mathbf{\Sigma}\mathbf{V}^T = \mathbf{\Sigma} \times_1 \mathbf{U} \times_2 \mathbf{V}, \quad \mathbf{\Sigma} \in \mathbb{R}^{I_r \times I_r}. \tag{33}$$

As a special case a tensor-vector product $\mathcal{X} \times_k \mathbf{v}$ where $\mathcal{X} \in \mathbb{R}^{I_1 \times \ldots \times I_p}$ and $\mathbf{v} \in \mathbb{R}^{I}_k$ is a tensor $\mathcal{G}$ of order $p - 1$ elementwise defined as:

$$\mathcal{G}\left[i_1, \ldots, i_{k-1}, i_{k+1}, \ldots, i_p\right] \triangleq \sum_{i_k=1}^{I_k} \mathcal{X}\left[i_1, \ldots, i_p\right] \mathbf{v}\left[i_k\right]. \tag{34}$$

The Frobenius norm of a tensor $\mathcal{T}$ is defined as:

$$\|\mathcal{T}\|_F \triangleq \left(\sum_{i_1=1}^{I_1} \ldots \sum_{i_p=1}^{I_p} \mathcal{T}\left[i_1, \ldots, i_p\right]^2 \right)^{\frac{1}{2}}. \tag{35}$$

The proposed distance metric for two data points in $\mathcal{V}$ with the structure shown in (31) is:

$$g\left(\mathbf{M}_1, \mathbf{M}_2\right) \triangleq \|\mathcal{N} \times_1 \left(\mathbf{M}_1 - \mathbf{M}_2\right) \times_2 \left(\mathbf{M}_1 - \mathbf{M}_2\right) \times_3 \left(\mathbf{M}_1 - \mathbf{M}_2\right)\|_F. \tag{36}$$

In Equation (36) the weight tensor $\mathcal{N}$ contains the correlation of each attribute as extracted from the dataset.

For the fuzzy SOM configurations the above distance is computed between each data point and each cluster center. Then the data point is considered to belong to the two closest clusters. A schematic of the proposed tensor metric is depicted at Figure 1.

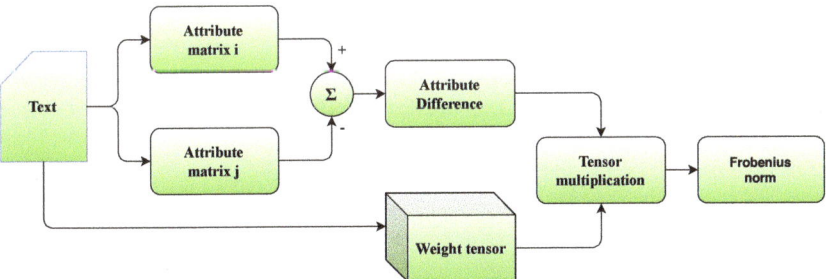

Figure 1. Schematic of the proposed metric (source: authors).

5.3. Experimental Setup

The available options for the various SOM parameters are shown in Table 5.

Given the parameters of Table 5 as a starting point, a number of SOMs were implemented. Their respective configurations are shown in Table 6. In order to reduce complexity the proximity function $h\left(\cdot, \cdot\right)$ has been chosen to be also the weight function $w\left(\cdot\right)$. Each SOM configuration is a tuple with the following structure:

$$\left(p_0, q_0, g\left(\cdot, \cdot\right), h\left(\cdot, \cdot\right), w\left(\cdot\right), \eta\left[\cdot\right]\right). \tag{37}$$

In Figure 2 the architecture of the ML pipeline which has been used in this article is shown. Its linear structure as well as the relatively low number of adjustable parameters leads to a low complexity.

The SOM clustering performance will be evaluated at three distinct levels. From the most general to the most specific these are:

- **Clustering quality**: As SOMs perform clustering general metrics can be used, especially since the dataset contains ground truth classes.
- **Topological map**: It is possible to construct figure of merits based on the SOM operating principles. Although they are by definition SOM-specific, they nonetheless provide insight on how the self-organization of the neurons takes place while adapting to the dataset topology.

- **MBTI permuations**: Finally, the dataset itself provides certain insight. Although no specific formulas can be derived, a qualitative analysis based on findings from the scientific literature.

Table 5. Options for the self organizing map (SOM) parameters (source: authors).

Parameter	Options
Synaptic weight initialization	Random
Bias mechanism	Not implemented
Neighborhood $\Gamma(u)$ shape	Cross
Distance function $g(\cdot,\cdot)$	Tensor (T), Fuzzy tensor (F), ℓ_1 norm (L1), ℓ_2 norm (L2)
Proximity function $h(\cdot,\cdot)$	Gaussian (G), Circular (C), Rectangular (R)
Cover threshold η_0 - Equation (27)	0.5
Weight function in $\mathcal{C}$	Gaussian, Circular, Rectangular (as above)
Gaussian	$\mu_0 = 0, \sigma_0^2 = 8$
Circular	$\rho_0 = 4$
Rectangular	$a_0 = 4$
Learning rate parameter	Cosine (S), Inverse linear (L), Inverse quadratic (Q), Exponential (E)
Cosine	$r_0 = 40$
Inverse linear	$\gamma_2 = 1, \gamma_1 = 0.025, \gamma_0 = 1$
Exponential	$\gamma_0 = 1, \gamma_1 = 0.125$
Grid size b_0 and b_1 - Equation (30)	$b_0 \in \{2,\ldots,8\}, b_1 = 0$
Number of classes C_0	16
Number of rows per class N_0	256
Number of attributes	$2Q_0$
Number of runs R_0	100

Table 6. Indices of SOM configurations (source: authors).

#	Configuration	#	Configuration	#	Configuration	#	Configuration
1	$(p_0, p_0, L1, C, C, S)$	10	$(p_0, p_0, L2, C, C, S)$	19	(p_0, p_0, T, C, C, S)	28	(p_0, p_0, F, C, C, S)
2	$(p_0, p_0, L1, R, R, S)$	11	$(p_0, p_0, L2, R, R, S)$	20	(p_0, p_0, T, R, R, S)	29	(p_0, p_0, F, R, R, S)
3	$(p_0, p_0, L1, G, G, S)$	12	$(p_0, p_0, L2, G, G, S)$	21	(p_0, p_0, T, G, G, S)	30	(p_0, p_0, F, G, G, S)
4	$(p_0, p_0, L1, C, C, L)$	13	$(p_0, p_0, L2, C, C, L)$	22	(p_0, p_0, T, C, C, L)	31	(p_0, p_0, F, C, C, L)
5	$(p_0, p_0, L1, R, R, L)$	14	$(p_0, p_0, L2, R, R, L)$	23	(p_0, p_0, T, R, R, L)	32	(p_0, p_0, F, R, R, L)
6	$(p_0, p_0, L1, G, G, L)$	15	$(p_0, p_0, L2, G, G, L)$	24	(p_0, p_0, T, G, G, L)	33	(p_0, p_0, F, G, G, L)
7	$(p_0, p_0, L1, C, C, E)$	16	$(p_0, p_0, L2, C, C, E)$	25	(p_0, p_0, T, C, C, E)	34	(p_0, p_0, F, C, C, E)
8	$(p_0, p_0, L1, R, R, E)$	17	$(p_0, p_0, L2, R, R, E)$	26	(p_0, p_0, T, R, R, E)	35	(p_0, p_0, F, R, R, E)
9	$(p_0, p_0, L1, G, G, E)$	18	$(p_0, p_0, L2, G, G, E)$	27	(p_0, p_0, T, G, G, E)	36	(p_0, p_0, F, G, G, E)

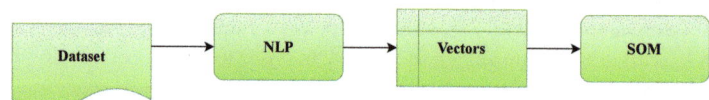

Figure 2. Architecture of the proposed pipeline (source: authors).

5.4. Topological Error

Because of the particular nature of the SOM, certain specialized performance metrics have been developed for it. Perhaps the most important figure of merit of this category is the topological error. The latter is defined in Equation (29). Figure 3 shows the average topological error as a percentage of the total number of data points after R_0 runs for each distance metric using the cosine rate. The reasons for the selection of this particular rate will become apparent later in this subsection. The topological error has been parameterized with respect to the SOM grid size as indexed by the parameter b_0.

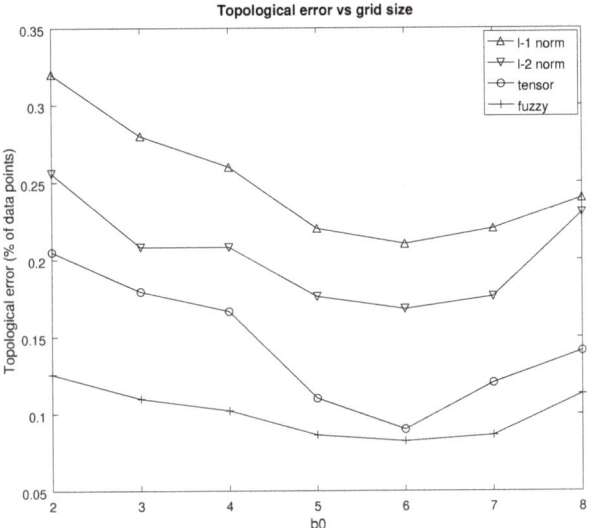

Figure 3. Topological error vs b_0 (source: authors).

From this figure it can be inferred that the fuzzy version of the proposed tensor distance metric achieves the lowest topological error with the original tensor distance metric being a close second for most of the values of b_0. Although ℓ_2 clearly outperforms ℓ_1, the gap from the tensor based metrics is considerable. Representing the topologically incorrectly placed data points as a percentage of the total number of those in the dataset reveals how well the SOM can perform dimensionality reduction. With respect to the parameter b_0 there appears to be a window of $b_0 \in \{5, 6, 7\}$ where the topological error is minimized. Also, it appears that for this particular dataset said window is independent from the distance metric but this needs to be corroborated from further experiments.

An important metric is the distrubution of epochs before a satisfactory topological error is reached. In particular, for each distance metric the deterministic mean I_0 and variance σ^2 are of interest. Assuming for each such metric there were R_0 runs and each run required r_k epochs in total, then the sample mean of the number of epochs is given by Equation (38):

$$I_0 \triangleq \frac{1}{R_0} \sum_{k=1}^{R_0} r_k. \tag{38}$$

Notice that the sample mean of Equation (38) is in fact an estimator of the true stochastic mean of the number of epochs. By computing the average of R_0 samples, the estimation variance is divided by $\sqrt{R_0}$. This is typically enough to ensure convergence based on the weak law of large numbers.

Along a similar line of reasoning, the deterministic variance is similarly defined as in Equation (39). Readers familiar with estimation theory can see this is the squared natural estimator of order two.

$$\sigma_0^2 \triangleq \frac{1}{R_0 - 1} \sum_{k=1}^{R_0} (r_k - I_0)^2. \tag{39}$$

Table 7 contains I_0 and σ_0^2 for each learning parameter rate and each distance metric. The remaining SOM parameters remained the same throughout these experiments in order to ensure fairness. Specifically b_0 was 5 and the proximity function was the Gaussian kernel.

Table 7. Mean and variance of the number of epochs (source: authors).

	Cosine	Inv. linear	Exponential
ℓ_1 norm	$I_0 = 26.4417/\sigma_0^2 = 12.3873$	$I_0 = 27.500/\sigma_0^2 = 16.8865$	$I_0 = 33.1125/\sigma_0^2 = 14.8873$
ℓ_2 norm	$I_0 = 22.3334/\sigma_0^2 = 13.0228$	$I_0 = 24.667/\sigma_0^2 = 14.3098$	$I_0 = 31.8333/\sigma_0^2 = 15.5642$
Tensor	$I_0 = 18.8731/\sigma_0^2 = 11.6686$	$I_0 = 20.2504/\sigma_0^2 = 12.7633$	$I_0 = 26.0021/\sigma_0^2 = 14.6574$
Fuzzy	$I_0 = 14.4457/\sigma_0^2 = 12.1282$	$I_0 = 18.3333/\sigma_0^2 = 12.6645$	$I_0 = 25.3333/\sigma_0^2 = 14.0995$

From the entries of Table 7 the following can be deduced:

- In each case the variance is relatively small, implying that there is a strong concentration of the number of epochs around the respective mean value. In other words, I_0 is a reliable estimator of the true number of epochs of the respective combination of distance metric and learning rate.
- For the same learning rate the fuzzy version of the tensor distance metric consistently requires a lower number of epochs. It is followed closely by the tensor distance metric, whereas the ℓ_2 and ℓ_1 norms are way behind with the former being somewhat better than the latter.
- Conversely, for the same metric the cosine decay rate systematically outperforms the other two options. The inverse linear decay rate may be a viable alternative, although there is a significant gap in the number of epochs. The exponential decay rates results in very slow convergence requiring almost twice the number of epochs compared to the cosine decay rate.

Notice that a lower number of epochs not only translates to quicker total response time, which is of interest when scalability becomes an issue, but also denotes that the distance metric has captured the essence of the underlying domain. This means that the SOM through the distance metric can go beyond the limitation of treating each data point merely as a collection of attributes.

5.5. Clustering Quality

Since SOMs essentially perform clustering, it also makes sense to employ general clustering error metrics in addition to the specialized SOM ones. Since the dataset contains ground truth classes, the cross entropy metric $\bar{H}$ can be used in order to evaluate overall performance by counting the how many data points have been assigned to the wrong cluster. For the fuzzy version if one of the two clusters a data point is assigned to is the correct one, it is considered as correctly classified. In Figure 4 the normalized average cross entropy over R_0 runs is shown.

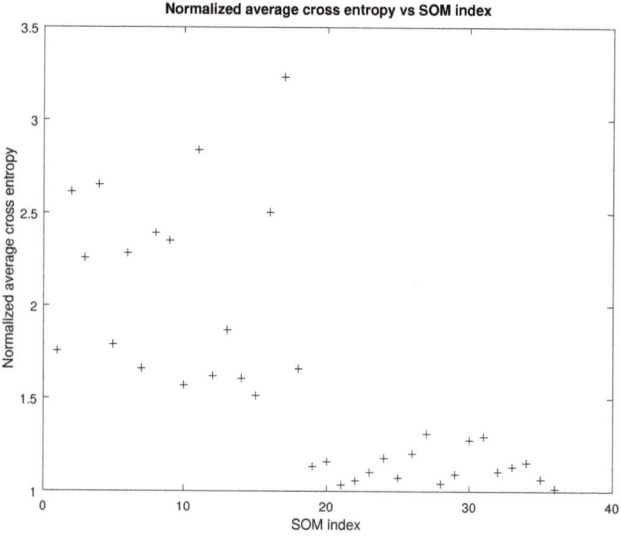

Figure 4. Normalized cross entropy vs SOM index (source: authors).

In case the ground truth classes were not available, as is the case in many clustering scenarios, the average distance $d_{i,j}$ between each possible distinct pair of clusters C_i and C_j is first computed. It is defined as the distance over all points assigned to C_i from each point assigned to C_j as shown in (40):

$$d_{i,j} \triangleq \frac{1}{|C_i||C_j|} \sum_{v \in C_i} \sum_{y \in C_j} g(\mathbf{x}, \mathbf{y}). \tag{40}$$

Then for the SOM configurations of Table 6 the average distance between clusters is defined as the sum of the distances over all distinct cluster pairs averaged over the number of clusters as shown in (41):

$$\bar{d} \triangleq \frac{2}{C_0(C_0-1)} \sum_{i=1}^{C_0} \sum_{j=2}^{i} d_{i,j}. \tag{41}$$

In Figure 5 the normalized $\bar{d}$ averaged over R_0 runs is shown. Observe that SOM configurations which use the proposed tensor metric yield a higher cluster distance, meaning that clusters can be better separated. This can be attributed to the fact that bounds between clusters can have more flexible shapes in comparison to the ℓ_1 and ℓ_2 norms.

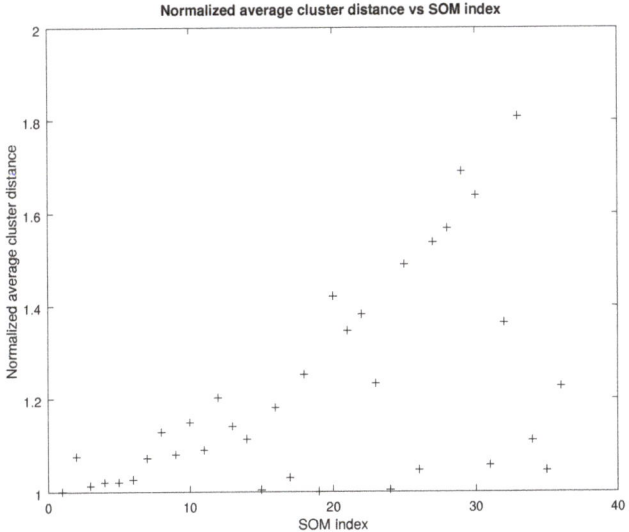

Figure 5. Normalized average cluster distance vs SOM index (source: authors).

5.6. MBTI Permutations

Another way of evaluating the clustering performance is by examining the natural interpretation of the resulting cognitive map based on properties of the dataset. Although this method is the least general since it is confined to the limits of a single dataset, it may lead to insights nonetheless, especially when followed by high level inspection from domain experts. The approach presented here stems from the observation that eventually each topolgical map is a permutation of Table 2. Since topology plays an important role in the continuity of the map and in the overall clustering quality, the form of the final tableau will be used. Specifically, the best map will be considered the one whose distribution of data points is the closest to that of the original dataset. To this end the Kullback-Leibler divergence will be used as shown in Equation (42):

$$\langle p_1 || p_2 \rangle \triangleq \sum_k p_1[k] \log\left(\frac{p_1[k]}{p_2[k]}\right) = \sum_k p_1[k] \log p_1[k] - \sum_k p_1[k] \log p_2[k]. \tag{42}$$

Notice that in Equation (42) the distributions p_1 and p_2 are not interchangeable. Instead, p_1 acts a template, whereas p_2 as a variant or an approximation thereof. In other words, the Kullback-Leibler divergence quantifies the difference of substituting p_1 with p_2. The leftmost part of Equation (42) is the difference of the cross-entropy between p_1 and p_2 from the entropy of p_1. Also, the index k ranges over the union of the events of both probabilities.

As stated earlier, the original Kaggle dataset was randomly sampled such that classes are balanced. Therefore, a proper topological map should have the same number of data points across all clusters. One way to measure that is to compute the Kullback-Leibler divergence of the distribution of data points assigned to clusters from the uniform distribution. Tables 8 and 9 show the topological maps achieving the minimum and the maximum divergence.

Table 8. Clustering attaining the minimum divergence (source: authors).

ISTJ	ISFJ	INFJ	INTJ
ISTP	ISFP	INFP	INTP
ESTP	ESFP	ENFP	ENTP
ESTJ	ESFJ	ENFJ	ENTJ

It comes as no surprise that the topological map achieving the least divergence is in fact the original Briggs-Mayers map, namely Table 2. Notice that in this map each personality differs only by one trait from its neighboring ones. This is reminiscent of the Gray numbering scheme. Perhaps this structure leads to robustness and to higher overall clustering quality. On the contrary, the map with the largest divergence looks more like a random permutation of Table 2. Moreover, the number of traits a type differs from its neighboring ones varies.

Table 9. Clustering attaining the maximum divergence (source: authors).

ENFJ	ISFP	ENFJ	ESFP
ISTJ	INTP	ESTJ	ISFJ
INTJ	INFJ	ENTP	ISTP
ESFJ	ENTJ	ESTP	ISFP

For each SOM configuration and for each of the R_0 runs, each with a different subset of the original dataset, the resulting cognitive map the Kullback-Leibler divergence as described above was recorded. Then for each SOM configuration the average was computed and then each such average was normalized by dividing them with the minimum of them. This provides an insight on the clustering robustness of each map. In Figure 6 the normalized divergences averaged over R_0 runs are shown.

From Figure 6 it follows that the tensor-based SOM configurations have an almost uniform low Kullback-Leibler divergence from the uniform distribution. Therefore, they achieve better clustering of at least most of the R_0 available subsets.

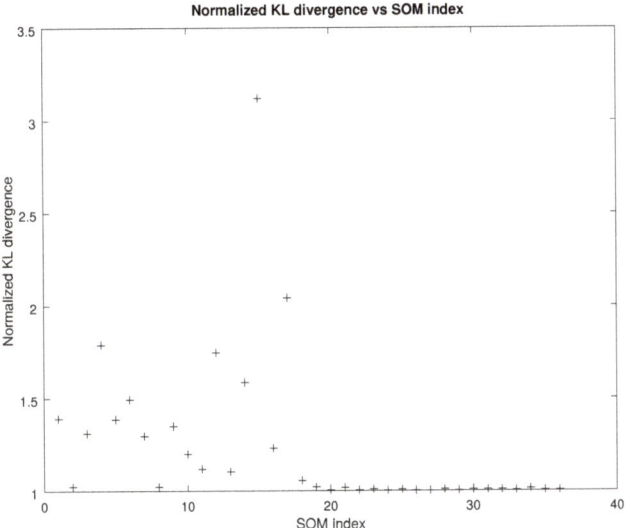

Figure 6. Normalized divergence vs SOM index (source: authors).

5.7. Complexity

The complexity of the proposed method in comparison to that of the norm based methods will be examined here. Figure 7 shows the normalized number of floating point operations for each of the SOM configurations of Table 6 over R_0 iterations. Every operation count has been divided by the minimum one in order to reveal the difference the order of magnitude.

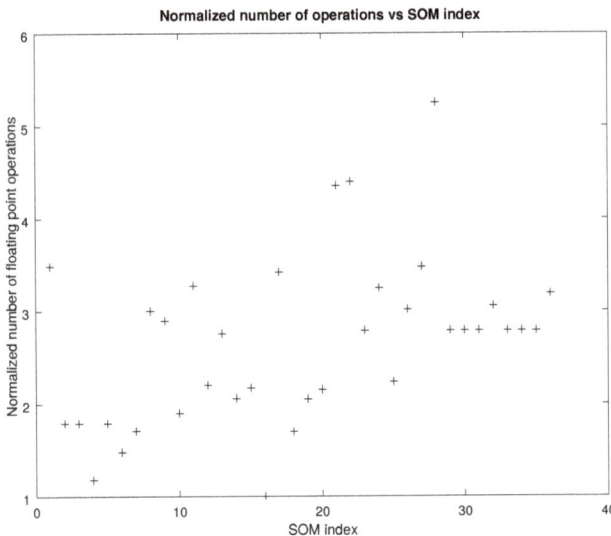

Figure 7. Normalized number of floating point operations vs SOM index (source: authors).

Figure 8 shows the average total execution time for each SOM configuration of Table 6 over R_0 iterations. A similar normalization with that described earlier took place here. Specifically, for each SOM configuration the total execution time averaged over all R_0 subsets of the original dataset was computed. Then, each such average was divided by the minimum one, yielding thus a measure of their relative performance.

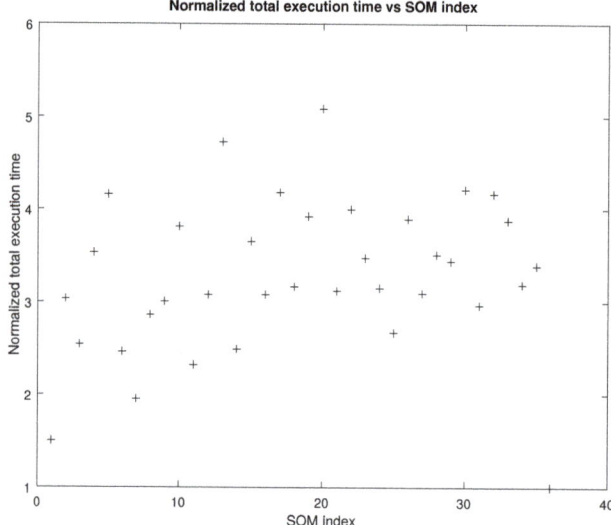

Figure 8. Normalized total execution time vs SOM index (source: authors).

From Figures 7 and 8 it can be deduced that the added cost in floating point operations necessary for the tensor metrics is partially absorbed by the lower number of iterations. Thus, despite their increased nominal complexity, tensor based metrics remain competitive at least in terms of the total execution time.

5.8. Discussion

Based on the results presented earlier, the following can be said about the proposed methodology:

- The cosine decay rate outperforms the inverse linear and the exponential ones. This can be explained by the adaptive nature of the cosine as well as by the fact that the exponential function decays too fast and before convergence is truly achieved.
- Partitioning clusters in Gaussian regions results in lower error in every test case. This is explained by the less sharp shape of these regions compared to cubes or domes. Moreover, with the tensor distance metrics, which can in the general case approximate more smooth shapes, the cluster boundaries can better adapt to the topological properties of the dataset.
- The fuzzy version of the tensor distance metric results in better performance, even a slight one, in all cases. The reason for this may be the additional flexibility since personalities sharing traits from two categories can belong to both up to an extent. On the contrary, all the other distance metrics assign a particular personality to a single cluster.
- The complexity of the tensor metrics in terms of the number of floating point operations involved is clearly more than that of either the ℓ_1 and the ℓ_2 norm. However, because of the lower number of iterations that difference is not evident in the total execution time.

The most evident limitations of the proposed methodology, based on the preceding analysis, are the following:

- The interpretability of the resulting cognitive map is limited by the texts of the original dataset, which in turn are answers to specific questions. Adding more cognitive dimensions to these texts would improve personality clustering quality.
- Although the MBTI map is small, for each cognitive map there is a large number of equivalent permutations. Finding them is a critical step before any subsequent analysis takes place.
- The curent version of the proposed methodology does not utilize neuron bias.

Several approaches have been reported in the cognitive science domain regarding the MBTI taxonomy. It should be noted that the results presented here regarding the distribution of the MBTI permutations are similar to those reported in Reference [83]. Moreover, the computational results agree with the principles for cognitive tools set forth in Reference [75].

Regarding complexity, the number of iterations required to construct the topological maps for similar map sizes are close to those reported in Reference [33]. Also the iterations obtained here are in the same order of magnitude with those of Reference [32], where fuzzy C-means is used for image partitioning, which is a comparable method the SOMs.

5.9. Recommendations

Once the algorithmic tools are available for clustering personalities based on text derived attributes according to the MBTI taxonomy, the following points should be taken into consideration:

- Text, despite being an invaluable source of information about human traits, is not the only one. It is highly advisable that a cross check with other methods utilizing other modalities should take place.
- In case where the personalities of two or more group members are evaluated, it is advisable that their compatibility is checked against the group tasks in order to discover potential conflict points or communication points as early as possible.

6. Conclusions and Future Work

This article focuses on a data mining pipeline for a cognitive application. At its starting stage natural language processing extracts keywords from plain text taken from the Kaggle Myers-Briggs open dataset. Each personality is represented as a wide attribute matrix. At the heart of the pipeline lies a self organizing map which is progressively trained with various combinations of learning rates, neighborhood functions, weight functions, and distance metrics to construct a cognitive map for the sixteen different personality types possible under the Myers-Briggs Type Indicator. The latter is a widespread taxonomy of human personalities based on four primary factors which is frequently used to describe team dynamics and exploit the full potential of interplay among diverse individuals. The novelty of this work comes from separating the linguistic attributes to categories depending on their semantics and using a tensor distance metric to exploit their interplay. Particular emphasis is placed on two aspects of the cognitive map. First, a multilinear distance metric is compared to the ℓ_1 and the ℓ_2 norms, both common options in similar scenarios. Second, a fuzzy version of this metric has been developed, allowing pairwise cluster overlap. The outcome of the experiments suggest that doing so leads to lower error metrics. The latter can be attributed to the added flexibility for personalities sharing traits from up to two archetypal personality types.

The work presented here can be extended in a number of ways. Regarding the algorithmic part, more specialized tensor distance metrics can be developed for various fields. For instance, in a social network analysis application the distance between two accounts can include connectivity patterns or semantic information extracted from the hashtags of the respective tweets. Moreover, clustering robustness should be investigated. The question of unbalanced classes should be addressed, either for the original dataset or in a more general context.

Author Contributions: G.D. created the theoretical framework and run the experiments, P.M. provided intuition and oversight, and A.K. and P.P. provided oversight. All authors have read and agreed to the published version of the manuscript.

Funding: This article is part of Project 451, a long term research initiative whose primary research objective is the development of novel, scalable, numerically stable, and interpretable tensor analytics.

Acknowledgments: The authors gratefully acknowledge the support of NVIDIA corporation with the donation of Titan Xp GPU used in this research.

Conflicts of Interest: The authors declare no conflict of interest.

References

1. Kangas, J.; Kohonen, T.; Laaksonen, J. Variants of self-organizing maps. *IEEE Trans. Neural Netw.* **1990**, *1*, 93–99. [PubMed]
2. Amato, G.; Carrara, F.; Falchi, F.; Gennaro, C.; Lagani, G. Hebbian learning meets deep convolutional neural networks. In *Proceedings of the International Conference on Image Analysis and Processing*; Springer: Berlin/Heidelberg, Germany, 2019; pp. 324–334.
3. Myers, S. Myers-Briggs typology and Jungian individuation. *J. Anal. Psychol.* **2016**, *61*, 289–308. [PubMed]
4. Isaksen, S.G.; Lauer, K.J.; Wilson, G.V. An examination of the relationship between personality type and cognitive style. *Creat. Res. J.* **2003**, *15*, 343–354.
5. Poria, S.; Majumder, N.; Mihalcea, R.; Hovy, E. Emotion recognition in conversation: Research challenges, datasets, and recent advances. *IEEE Access* **2019**, *7*, 100943–100953.
6. Batbaatar, E.; Li, M.; Ryu, K.H. Semantic-emotion neural network for emotion recognition from text. *IEEE Access* **2019**, *7*, 111866–111878.
7. Beliy, R.; Gaziv, G.; Hoogi, A.; Strappini, F.; Golan, T.; Irani, M. From voxels to pixels and back: Self-supervision in natural-image reconstruction from fMRI. In *Proceedings of the 2019 Conference on Neural Information Processing Systems NIPS*, Vancouver, BC, Canada, 8–14 September 2019; pp. 6517–6527.
8. Sidhu, G. Locally Linear Embedding and fMRI feature selection in psychiatric classification. *IEEE J. Transl. Eng. Health Med.* **2019**, *7*, 1–11.
9. Sun, X.; Pei, Z.; Zhang, C.; Li, G.; Tao, J. Design and Analysis of a Human-Machine Interaction System for Researching Human's Dynamic Emotion. *IEEE Trans. Syst. Man Cybern. Syst.* **2019**. [CrossRef]
10. Vesanto, J.; Alhoniemi, E. Clustering of the self-organizing map. *IEEE Trans. Neural Netw.* **2000**, *11*, 586–600.
11. Kohonen, T. Exploration of very large databases by self-organizing maps. In *Proceedings of the International Conference on Neural Networks (ICNN'97)*, Houston, TX, USA, 12 June 1997; Volume 1, pp. PL1–PL6.
12. Kosko, B. Fuzzy cognitive maps. *Int. J. Man-Mach. Stud.* **1986**, *24*, 65–75.
13. Taber, R. Knowledge processing with fuzzy cognitive maps. *Expert Syst. Appl.* **1991**, *2*, 83–87.
14. Stach, W.; Kurgan, L.; Pedrycz, W.; Reformat, M. Genetic learning of fuzzy cognitive maps. *Fuzzy Sets Syst.* **2005**, *153*, 371–401.
15. Yang, Z.; Liu, J. Learning of fuzzy cognitive maps using a niching-based multi-modal multi-agent genetic algorithm. *Appl. Soft Comput.* **2019**, *74*, 356–367.
16. Salmeron, J.L.; Mansouri, T.; Moghadam, M.R.S.; Mardani, A. Learning fuzzy cognitive maps with modified asexual reproduction optimisation algorithm. *Knowl.-Based Syst.* **2019**, *163*, 723–735.
17. Wu, K.; Liu, J. Robust learning of large-scale fuzzy cognitive maps via the lasso from noisy time series. *Knowl.-Based Syst.* **2016**, *113*, 23–38.
18. Wu, K.; Liu, J. Learning large-scale fuzzy cognitive maps based on compressed sensing and application in reconstructing gene regulatory networks. *IEEE Trans. Fuzzy Syst.* **2017**, *25*, 1546–1560.
19. Liu, Y.c.; Wu, C.; Liu, M. Research of fast SOM clustering for text information. *Expert Syst. Appl.* **2011**, *38*, 9325–9333.
20. Drakopoulos, G.; Giannoukou, I.; Mylonas, P.; Sioutas, S. On tensor distances for self organizing maps: Clustering cognitive tasks. In *Proceedings of the International Conference on Database and Expert Systems Applications Part II*; Springer: Berlin/Heidelberg, Germany, 2020; Volume 12392, pp. 195–210. doi:10.1007/978-3-030-59051-2_13. [CrossRef]
21. Nam, T.M.; Phong, P.H.; Khoa, T.D.; Huong, T.T.; Nam, P.N.; Thanh, N.H.; Thang, L.X.; Tuan, P.A.; Dung, L.Q.; Loi, V.D. Self-organizing map-based approaches in DDoS flooding detection using SDN. In *Proceedings of the 2018 International Conference on Information Networking (ICOIN)*, Chiang Mai, Thailand, 10–12 January 2018; pp. 249–254.
22. Hawer, S.; Braun, N.; Reinhart, G. Analyzing interdependencies between factory change enablers applying fuzzy cognitive maps. *Procedia CIRP* **2016**, *52*, 151–156.
23. Zhu, S.; Zhang, Y.; Gao, Y.; Wu, F. A Cooperative Task Assignment Method of Multi-UAV Based on Self Organizing Map. In *Proceedings of the 2018 International Conference on Cyber-Enabled Distributed Computing and Knowledge Discovery (CyberC)*, Zhengzhou, China, 18–20 October 2018; pp. 437–4375.
24. Ladeira, M.J.; Ferreira, F.A.; Ferreira, J.J.; Fang, W.; Falcão, P.F.; Rosa, Á.A. Exploring the determinants of digital entrepreneurship using fuzzy cognitive maps. *Int. Entrep. Manag. J.* **2019**, *15*, 1077–1101.

25. Herrero, J.; Dopazo, J. Combining hierarchical clustering and self-organizing maps for exploratory analysis of gene expression patterns. *J. Proteome Res.* **2002**, *1*, 467–470.
26. Imani, M.; Ghoreishi, S.F. Optimal Finite-Horizon Perturbation Policy for Inference of Gene Regulatory Networks. *IEEE Intell. Syst.* **2020**. [CrossRef]
27. Drakopoulos, G.; Gourgaris, P.; Kanavos, A. Graph communities in Neo4j: Four algorithms at work. *Evol. Syst.* **2019**, doi:10.1007/s12530-018-9244-x. [CrossRef]
28. Gutiérrez, I.; Gómez, D.; Castro, J.; Espínola, R. A new community detection algorithm based on fuzzy measures. In Proceedings of the International Conference on Intelligent and Fuzzy Systems, Istanbul, Turkey, 23–25 July 2019; Springer: Berlin/Heidelberg, Germany, 2019; pp. 133–140.
29. Luo, W.; Yan, Z.; Bu, C.; Zhang, D. Community detection by fuzzy relations. *IEEE Trans. Emerg. Top. Comput.* **2017**, *8*, 478–492. [CrossRef]
30. Drakopoulos, G.; Gourgaris, P.; Kanavos, A.; Makris, C. A fuzzy graph framework for initializing k-means. *IJAIT* **2016**, *25*, 1650031:1–1650031:21, doi:10.1142/S0218213016500317. [CrossRef]
31. Yang, C.H.; Chuang, L.Y.; Lin, Y.D. Epistasis Analysis using an Improved Fuzzy C-means-based Entropy Approach. *IEEE Trans. Fuzzy Syst.* **2019**, *28*, 718–730. [CrossRef]
32. Tang, Y.; Ren, F.; Pedrycz, W. Fuzzy C-means clustering through SSIM and patch for image segmentation. *Appl. Soft Comput.* **2020**, *87*, 105928. [CrossRef]
33. Felix, G.; Nápoles, G.; Falcon, R.; Froelich, W.; Vanhoof, K.; Bello, R. A review on methods and software for fuzzy cognitive maps. *Artif. Intell. Rev.* **2019**, *52*, 1707–1737. [CrossRef]
34. Etingof, P.; Gelaki, S.; Nikshych, D.; Ostrik, V. *Tensor Categories*; American Mathematical Soc.: Providence, RI, USA, 2016; Volume 205.
35. Batselier, K.; Chen, Z.; Liu, H.; Wong, N. A tensor-based volterra series black-box nonlinear system identification and simulation framework. In Proceedings of the 2016 IEEE/ACM International Conference on Computer-Aided Design (ICCAD), Austin, TX, USA, 7–10 November 2016; pp. 1–7.
36. Batselier, K.; Chen, Z.; Wong, N. Tensor Network alternating linear scheme for MIMO Volterra system identification. *Automatica* **2017**, *84*, 26–35. [CrossRef]
37. Batselier, K.; Ko, C.Y.; Wong, N. Tensor network subspace identification of polynomial state space models. *Automatica* **2018**, *95*, 187–196. [CrossRef]
38. Battaglino, C.; Ballard, G.; Kolda, T.G. A practical randomized CP tensor decomposition. *SIAM J. Matrix Anal. Appl.* **2018**, *39*, 876–901. [CrossRef]
39. Sidiropoulos, N.D.; De Lathauwer, L.; Fu, X.; Huang, K.; Papalexakis, E.E.; Faloutsos, C. Tensor decomposition for signal processing and machine learning. *IEEE Trans. Signal Process.* **2017**, *65*, 3551–3582. [CrossRef]
40. Ragusa, E.; Gastaldo, P.; Zunino, R.; Cambria, E. Learning with similarity functions: A tensor-based framework. *Cogn. Comput.* **2019**, *11*, 31–49. [CrossRef]
41. Lu, W.; Chung, F.L.; Jiang, W.; Ester, M.; Liu, W. A deep Bayesian tensor-based system for video recommendation. *ACM Trans. Inf. Syst.* **2018**, *37*, 1–22. [CrossRef]
42. Drakopoulos, G.; Stathopoulou, F.; Kanavos, A.; Paraskevas, M.; Tzimas, G.; Mylonas, P.; Iliadis, L. A genetic algorithm for spatiosocial tensor clustering: Exploiting TensorFlow potential. *Evol. Syst.* **2020**, *11*, 491–501. doi:10.1007/s12530-019-09274-9. [CrossRef]
43. Bao, Y.T.; Chien, J.T. Tensor classification network. In Proceedings of the 2015 IEEE 25th International Workshop on Machine Learning for Signal Processing (MLSP), Boston, MA, USA, 17–20 September 2015; pp. 1–6.
44. Yu, D.; Deng, L.; Seide, F. The deep tensor neural network with applications to large vocabulary speech recognition. *IEEE Trans. Audio Speech Lang. Process.* **2012**, *21*, 388–396. [CrossRef]
45. Drakopoulos, G.; Mylonas, P. Evaluating graph resilience with tensor stack networks: A Keras implementation. *Neural Comput. Appl.* **2020**, *32*, 4161–4176, doi:10.1007/s00521-020-04790-1. [CrossRef]
46. Hore, V.; Viñuela, A.; Buil, A.; Knight, J.; McCarthy, M.I.; Small, K.; Marchini, J. Tensor decomposition for multiple-tissue gene expression experiments. *Nat. Genet.* **2016**, *48*, 1094. [CrossRef] [PubMed]
47. Zhang, C.; Fu, H.; Liu, S.; Liu, G.; Cao, X. Low-rank tensor constrained multiview subspace clustering. In Proceedings of the IEEE international conference on computer vision, Santiago, Chile, 7–13 December 2015; pp. 1582–1590.

48. Cao, X.; Wei, X.; Han, Y.; Lin, D. Robust face clustering via tensor decomposition. *IEEE Trans. Cybern.* **2014**, *45*, 2546–2557. [CrossRef]
49. Zaharia, M.; Xin, R.S.; Wendell, P.; Das, T.; Armbrust, M.; Dave, A.; Meng, X.; Rosen, J.; Venkataraman, S.; Franklin, M.J.; et al. Apache Spark: A unified engine for big data processing. *Commun. ACM* **2016**, *59*, 56–65. [CrossRef]
50. Alexopoulos, A.; Drakopoulos, G.; Kanavos, A.; Mylonas, P.; Vonitsanos, G. Two-step classification with SVD preprocessing of distributed massive datasets in Apache Spark. *Algorithms* **2020**, *13*, 71, doi:10.3390/a13030071. [CrossRef]
51. Yang, H.K.; Yong, H.S. S-PARAFAC: Distributed tensor decomposition using Apache Spark. *J. KIISE* **2018**, *45*, 280–287. [CrossRef]
52. Bezanson, J.; Edelman, A.; Karpinski, S.; Shah, V.B. Julia: A fresh approach to numerical computing. *SIAM Rev.* **2017**, *59*, 65–98. [CrossRef]
53. Bezanson, J.; Chen, J.; Chung, B.; Karpinski, S.; Shah, V.B.; Vitek, J.; Zoubritzky, L. Julia: Dynamism and performance reconciled by design. *Proc. ACM Program. Lang.* **2018**, *2*, 1–23. [CrossRef]
54. Lee, J.; Kim, Y.; Song, Y.; Hur, C.K.; Das, S.; Majnemer, D.; Regehr, J.; Lopes, N.P. Taming undefined behavior in LLVM. *ACM SIGPLAN Not.* **2017**, *52*, 633–647. [CrossRef]
55. Innes, M. Flux: Elegant machine learning with Julia. *J. Open Source Softw.* **2018**, *3*, 602. [CrossRef]
56. Besard, T.; Foket, C.; De Sutter, B. Effective extensible programming: Unleashing Julia on GPUs. *IEEE Trans. Parallel Distrib. Syst.* **2018**, *30*, 827–841. [CrossRef]
57. Mogensen, P.K.; Riseth, A.N. Optim: A mathematical optimization package for Julia. *J. Open Source Softw.* **2018**, *3*, doi:10.21105/joss.00615. [CrossRef]
58. Ruthotto, L.; Treister, E.; Haber, E. jinv–A flexible Julia package for PDE parameter estimation. *SIAM J. Sci. Comput.* **2017**, *39*, S702–S722. [CrossRef]
59. Krämer, S.; Plankensteiner, D.; Ostermann, L.; Ritsch, H. QuantumOptics.jl: A Julia framework for simulating open quantum systems. *Comput. Phys. Commun.* **2018**, *227*, 109–116. [CrossRef]
60. Witte, P.A.; Louboutin, M.; Kukreja, N.; Luporini, F.; Lange, M.; Gorman, G.J.; Herrmann, F.J. A large-scale framework for symbolic implementations of seismic inversion algorithms in Julia. *Geophysics* **2019**, *84*, F57–F71. [CrossRef]
61. Pittenger, D.J. The utility of the Myers-Briggs type indicator. *Rev. Educ. Res.* **1993**, *63*, 467–488. [CrossRef]
62. Gordon, A.M.; Jackson, D. A Balanced Approach to ADHD and Personality Assessment: A Jungian Model. *N. Am. J. Psychol.* **2019**, *21*, 619–646.
63. Lake, C.J.; Carlson, J.; Rose, A.; Chlevin-Thiele, C. Trust in name brand assessments: The case of the Myers-Briggs type indicator. *Psychol.-Manag. J.* **2019**, *22*, 91. [CrossRef]
64. Stein, R.; Swan, A.B. Evaluating the validity of Myers-Briggs Type Indicator theory: A teaching tool and window into intuitive psychology. *Soc. Personal. Psychol. Compass* **2019**, *13*, e12434. [CrossRef]
65. Plutchik, R.E.; Conte, H.R. *Circumplex Models of Personality and Emotions*; American Psychological Association: Washington, DC, USA, 1997.
66. Ekman, P. Darwin, deception, and facial expression. *Ann. N. Y. Acad. Sci.* **2003**, *1000*, 205–221. [CrossRef] [PubMed]
67. Furnham, A. Myers-Briggs type indicator (MBTI). In *Encyclopedia of Personality and Individual Differences*; Springer: Berlin/Heidelberg, Germany, 2020; pp. 3059–3062.
68. Xie, Y.; Liang, R.; Liang, Z.; Huang, C.; Zou, C.; Schuller, B. Speech emotion classification using attention-based LSTM. *IEEE/ACM Trans. Audio Speech Lang. Process.* **2019**, *27*, 1675–1685. [CrossRef]
69. Kim, Y.; Moon, J.; Sung, N.J.; Hong, M. Correlation between selected gait variables and emotion using virtual reality. *J. Ambient. Intell. Humaniz. Comput.* **2019**, 1–8. [CrossRef]
70. Zheng, W.; Yu, A.; Fang, P.; Peng, K. Exploring collective emotion transmission in face-to-face interactions. *PLoS ONE* **2020**, *15*, e0236953. [CrossRef]
71. Nguyen, T.L.; Kavuri, S.; Lee, M. A multimodal convolutional neuro-fuzzy network for emotion understanding of movie clips. *Neural Netw.* **2019**, *118*, 208–219. [CrossRef]
72. Mishro, P.K.; Agrawal, S.; Panda, R.; Abraham, A. A novel type-2 fuzzy C-means clustering for brain MR image segmentation. *IEEE Trans. Cybern.* **2020**. [CrossRef]
73. Sheldon, S.; El-Asmar, N. The cognitive tools that support mentally constructing event and scene representations. *Memory* **2018**, *26*, 858–868. [CrossRef]

74. Zap, N.; Code, J. Virtual and augmented reality as cognitive tools for learning. In *EdMedia+ Innovate Learning*; Association for the Advancement of Computing in Education (AACE): Waynesville, NC, USA, 2016; pp. 1340–1347.
75. Spevack, S.C. Cognitive Tools and Cognitive Styles: Windows into the Culture-Cognition System. Ph.D. Thesis, UC Merced, Merced, CA, USA, 2019.
76. Lajoie, S.P. *Computers As Cognitive Tools: Volume II, No More Walls*; Routledge: London, UK, 2020.
77. Abiri, R.; Borhani, S.; Sellers, E.W.; Jiang, Y.; Zhao, X. A comprehensive review of EEG-based brain–computer interface paradigms. *J. Neural Eng.* **2019**, *16*, 011001. [CrossRef]
78. Ramadan, R.A.; Vasilakos, A.V. Brain computer interface: Control signals review. *Neurocomputing* **2017**, *223*, 26–44. [CrossRef]
79. Sakhavi, S.; Guan, C.; Yan, S. Learning temporal information for brain-computer interface using convolutional neural networks. *IEEE Trans. Neural Netw. Learn. Syst.* **2018**, *29*, 5619–5629. [CrossRef] [PubMed]
80. Kaur, B.; Singh, D.; Roy, P.P. Age and gender classification using brain–computer interface. *Neural Comput. Appl.* **2019**, *31*, 5887–5900. [CrossRef]
81. Beale, M.H.; Hagan, M.T.; Demuth, H.B. *Neural Network Toolbox User's Guide*; The Mathworks Inc.: Natick, MA, USA, 2010.
82. Graillat, S.; Ibrahimy, Y.; Jeangoudoux, C.; Lauter, C. A Parallel Compensated Horner Scheme. In Proceedings of the SIAM Conference on Computational Science and Engineering (CSE), Atlanta, GA, USA, 3 March–27 February 2017.
83. Amirhosseini, M.H.; Kazemian, H. Machine Learning Approach to Personality Type Prediction Based on the Myers–Briggs Type Indicator®. *Multimodal Technol. Interact.* **2020**, *4*, 9. [CrossRef]

Publisher's Note: MDPI stays neutral with regard to jurisdictional claims in published maps and institutional affiliations.

© 2020 by the authors. Licensee MDPI, Basel, Switzerland. This article is an open access article distributed under the terms and conditions of the Creative Commons Attribution (CC BY) license (http://creativecommons.org/licenses/by/4.0/).

Article

Assessing and Comparing COVID-19 Intervention Strategies Using a Varying Partial Consensus Fuzzy Collaborative Intelligence Approach

Hsin-Chieh Wu [1], Yu-Cheng Wang [2] and Tin-Chih Toly Chen [3,*]

[1] Department of Industrial Engineering and Management, Chaoyang University of Technology, Taichung 413310, Taiwan; hcwul@cyut.edu.tw
[2] Department of Aeronautical Engineering, Chaoyang University of Technology, Taichung 413310, Taiwan; tony@cyut.edu.tw
[3] Department of Industrial Engineering and Management National Chiao Tung University 1001, University Road, Hsinchu 30010, Taiwan
* Correspondence: tcchen@g2.nctu.edu.tw

Received: 10 September 2020; Accepted: 26 September 2020; Published: 7 October 2020

Abstract: The COVID-19 pandemic has severely impacted our daily lives. For tackling the COVID-19 pandemic, various intervention strategies have been adopted by country (or city) governments around the world. However, whether an intervention strategy will be successful, acceptable, and cost-effective or not is still questionable. To address this issue, a varying partial consensus fuzzy collaborative intelligence approach is proposed in this study to assess an intervention strategy. In the varying partial consensus fuzzy collaborative intelligence approach, multiple decision makers express their judgments on the relative priorities of factors critical to an intervention strategy. If decision makers lack an overall consensus, the layered partial consensus approach is applied to aggregate their judgments for each critical factor. The number of decision makers that reach a partial consensus varies from a critical factor to another. Subsequently, the generalized fuzzy weighted assessment approach is proposed to evaluate the overall performance of an intervention strategy for tackling the COVID-19 pandemic. The proposed methodology has been applied to compare 15 existing intervention strategies for tackling the COVID-19 pandemic.

Keywords: intervention strategy; COVID-19 pandemic; layered partial consensus; fuzzy analytic hierarchy process

---

1. Introduction

The outbreak of COV-19 was identified in Wuhan, China [1]. Since then, the COVID-19 pandemic has severely affected all aspects of our daily lives [2]. Owing to the high infectivity of COVID-19, governments everywhere have adopted various intervention strategies to curb the spread of COVID-19 [3]. For example, many countries closed their borders to avoid the transnational spread of COVID-19, which was even more meaningful as evidence has shown that COVID-19 mutated differently in different regions [4]. Mass gatherings, especially those held indoors, were discouraged to prevent the spread of COVID through contact [5]. For the same reason, public spaces in which people had close contact, such as movie theaters, churches, and pubs, were also locked down [6]. Samanlioglu and Kaya [7] listed the 15 most common intervention strategies for tackling the COVID-19 pandemic. However, asking people to wear masks was not included, although it had been considered as the most effective intervention strategy [8]. To sum up, the following phenomena have been observed so far:

- Intervention strategies adopted by different governments were not the same [9].
- The effects of various intervention strategies were unequal [10].

- Not all these intervention strategies were acceptable or welcome to people [11].

Therefore, assessing intervention strategies for tackling the COVID-19 pandemic becomes a critical task. Based on the assessment results, the top-performing intervention strategies can be recommended to a country (or city) government. So far, very few attempts have been made to fulfill this task. Samanlioglu and Kaya [7] proposed a hesitant fuzzy analytic hierarchy process (hesitant FAHP) approach, in which hesitant fuzzy numbers [12] were adopted to better consider the subjectivity and uncertainty involved in the judgments of a decision maker.

To sum up, the existing methods for similar purposes are subject to the following problems:

- Fuzzy arithmetic averages are applied to aggregate decision makers' judgements, which may lead to unreasonable results [13,14].
- Decision makers may not reach a consensus about the priorities of factors critical to an intervention strategy [15–17].
- The priority of a critical factor is usually modelled with a crisp value, rather than a fuzzy value. As a result, some meaningful information, such as the possibly highest and lowest priorities of a critical factor, is lost [18–21].

To solve these problems, a varying partial consensus fuzzy collaborative intelligence approach is proposed in this study to assess an intervention strategy for tackling the COVID-19 pandemic. Fuzzy collaborative intelligence methods have rarely been applied to fuzzy group decision-making problems [22–24], because the involved set operations are not easy to calculate [20,25,26]. Fuzzy numerical methods—e.g., fuzzy weighted average (FWA) and its variants [23,24]—are prevalent, but may lead to unreasonable results [20].

The varying partial consensus fuzzy collaborative intelligence approach is a fuzzy group decision-making method in which multiple decision makers assess an intervention strategy for tackling the COVID-19 pandemic collaboratively. In the proposed methodology, the layered partial consensus (LPC) approach proposed by Chen and Wu [27] is applied to aggregate most decision makers' partial consensus, if the overall consensus among all decision makers does not exist. However, Chen and Wu [27] applied the LPC approach to forecast the unit cost of a product, which was a supervised learning problem [25,27,28]. On the contrary, in this study the LPC approach is applied to assess an intervention strategy for tackling the COVID-19 pandemic, which is an unsupervised assessment problem [29,30].

Compared to existing methods in this field, the varying partial consensus fuzzy collaborative intelligence approach has the following novelties:

- The priority of a critical factor is modelled with a fuzzy value.
- When the overall consensus among all decision makers is lacking, the partial consensus among most decision makers [15–17,27] is sought instead.
- The number of decision makers that reach a partial consensus varies when the LPC approach is applied to different critical factors, which is called the "varying" property of the proposed methodology.
- A new assessment method, the generalized fuzzy weighted assessment (GFWA) approach, is proposed to assess an intervention strategy for tackling the COVID-19 pandemic.

In the literature, there have been various methods to aggregate decision makers' fuzzy judgments. The differences between the proposed methodology and some existing methods are summarized in Table 1.

This paper is organized in the following manner. In the next section, the varying partial consensus fuzzy collaborative intelligence approach is introduced. In Section 3, the results of applying the varying partial consensus fuzzy collaborative intelligence approach to assess some intervention strategies for tackling the COVID-19 pandemic are presented. Then, there is a discussion of the experimental results. The conclusions of this study are given in the last section.

Table 1. Differences between the proposed methodology and some existing methods.

Method	Application	Consensus Type	Aggregation Method	Number of Decision Makers Reaching Consensus	Assessment Method
Samanlioglu and Kaya [7]	Intervention strategy assessment	Overall consensus	Fuzzy arithmetic mean	All	Fuzzy arithmetic mean
Lin et al. [22]	Smart technology application assessment	Guaranteed overall consensus	Fuzzy Intersection	All	Fuzzy technique for order preference by similarity to ideal solution
Chen and Wu [27]	Cost forecasting	Layered consensus	Partial consensus fuzzy intersection	Maximum number of decision makers with sufficient consensus	Back propagation network
Chen [31]	Price forecasting	Partial consensus	Partial consensus fuzzy intersection	Maximum number of decision makers with consensus	Back propagation network
Chen and Lin [32]	Yield forecasting	Overall consensus	Fuzzy intersection	All	Back propagation network
Gao et al. [33]	Supplier assessment	Overall consensus	Fuzzy weighted average	All	Fuzzy weighted average
The proposed methodology	Intervention strategy assessment	Varying layered partial consensus	Partial consensus fuzzy intersection	Maximum number of decision makers with sufficient consensus for each critical factor	Generalized fuzzy weighted assessment

2. Literature Review

There are two major trends in the development of fuzzy multiple-criteria decision-making methods. One is to fuzzify an existing crisp multiple-criteria decision-making method by modelling the evaluation result of an alternative, the weight (or relative priority) of a criterion, and/or the weight (or authority level) of each decision maker with fuzzy numbers. For example, Chen [34] applied FWA to aggregate the performances of a hotel along various dimensions, and then defuzzified the aggregation result using a back propagation network. Similarly, fuzzy multi-attribute utility theory (MAUT) methods were applied to select intervention strategies to restore an aquatic ecosystem contaminated by radionuclides [35], assess intelligent buildings [36], and recommend suitable clinics to patients [37]. Sevkli [38] proposed a fuzzy elimination and choice expressing the reality (ELECTRE) method for supplier selection. For a similar purpose, Sachdeva et al. [39] applied the fuzzy preference ranking organization method for enrichment evaluations (PROMETHEE) technique instead. Fuzzy measuring attractiveness by a categorical-based evaluation technique (MACBETH) methods are another type of fuzzy multiple-criteria decision-making method that has been widely applied [40,41]. The other is to adopt new types of fuzzy numbers. For example, Faizi et al. [42] fuzzified the traditional characteristic objects method (COMET), in which the evaluation results of alternatives were given in hesitant fuzzy sets (HFSs). A similar methodology was proposed by Faizi et al. [43] who adopted normalized interval-valued triangular fuzzy numbers instead. Compared to the previous method [42], their methodology considered the difficulty in specifying the membership function, and therefore was more flexible and practicable.

When multiple decision makers are involved, the decision-making problem becomes a group-based one. However, most past studies assumed that there was an overall consensus among all decision makers, and just averaged decision makers' judgements before applying a fuzzy multiple-criteria decision-making method, which was problematic because sometimes it was difficult for decision makers to reach an overall consensus [15–17,27,31]. In addition, the averaging result may be meaningless to decision makers [44]. To address this issue, the partial consensus among some decision makers can be sought instead [15–17]. This study also belongs to this type of research.

3. The Proposed Methodology

3.1. Implementation Procedure

The varying partial consensus fuzzy collaborative intelligence approach is proposed in this study for assessing an intervention strategy for tackling the COVID-19 pandemic. The implementation procedure of the varying partial consensus fuzzy collaborative intelligence approach comprises the following steps:

Step 1. Each decision maker must apply the fuzzy geometric mean (FGM) method [45–47] to evaluate the relative priorities of factors critical to an intervention strategy for tackling the COVID-19 pandemic.

Step 2. Consider the first critical factor.

Step 3. If all the decision makers reached an overall consensus, go to Step 4; otherwise, go to Step 6.

Step 4. Apply fuzzy intersection (FI) [32] to aggregate the relative priorities evaluated by the decision makers.

Step 5. Go to Step 7.

Step 6. Apply the LPC approach to aggregate the relative priorities.

Step 7. If all critical factors have been considered, go to Step 10; otherwise, go to Step 8.

Step 8. Consider the next critical factor.

Step 9. Go to Step 3.

Step 10. Apply the GFWA approach to assess the overall performance of an intervention strategy for tackling the COVID-19 pandemic.

Step 11. Apply the center-of-gravity (COG) method [48,49] to defuzzify the assessment result, so as to generate an absolute ranking of intervention strategies for tackling the COVID-19 pandemic.

A flowchart is provided in Figure 1 to illustrate the implementation procedure of the varying partial consensus fuzzy collaborative intelligence approach.

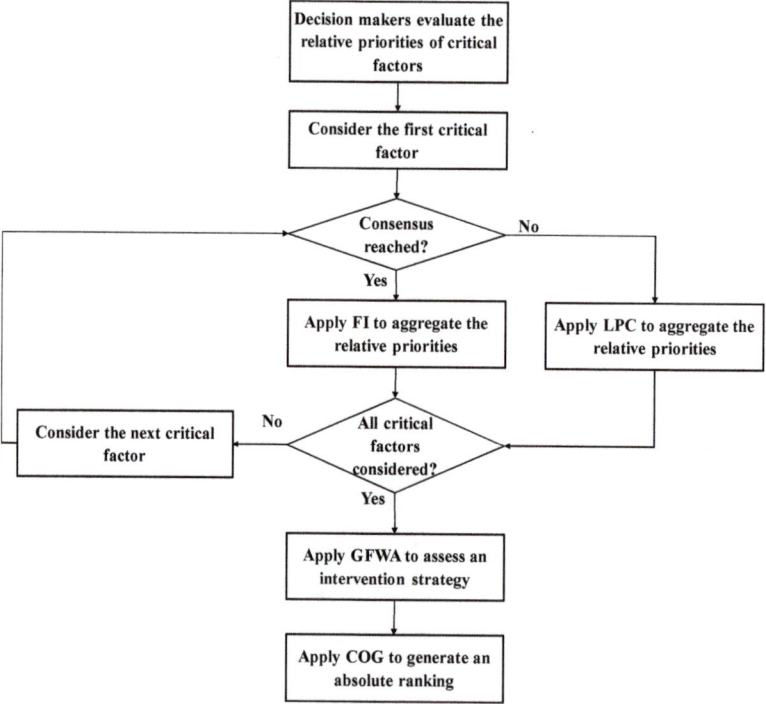

Figure 1. Implementation procedure of the varying partial consensus fuzzy collaborative intelligence approach.

Inputs to the proposed methodology include multiple decision makers' judgments, possible intervention strategies for tackling the COVID-19 pandemic, and critical factors in the intervention strategies. Outputs from the proposed methodology include the relative priorities of critical factors and the ranking result of intervention strategies. The problem structure is illustrated in Figure 2.

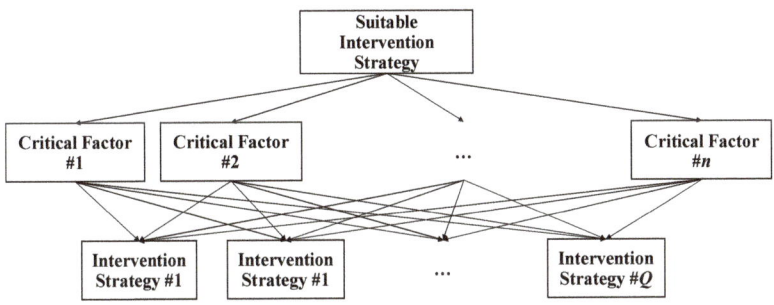

Figure 2. Problem structure.

3.2. FGM Method for Evaluating the Relative Priorities of Critical Factors

In the proposed methodology, first each decision maker evaluates and compares the relative priorities of critical factors in pairs using the FGM method. The comparison results are expressed in linguistic terms such as "as equal as," "weakly more important than," "strongly more important than," "very strongly more important than," "absolutely more important than," etc. A prevalent way is to associate these linguistic terms with triangular fuzzy numbers, as summarized Table 2 [46]. Usually, these triangular fuzzy numbers (TFNs) are within [1,9]. By widening these TFNs, the possibility for decision makers to reach a consensus increases [20]. In addition, restricting these TFNs to be within a narrower range, such as [1,3], elevates the consistency of the pairwise comparison results [7].

Table 2. Linguistic terms for expressing the relative priorities of critical factors.

Symbol	Linguistic Term	TFN
L1	As equal as	(1, 1, 3)
L2	As equal as or weakly more important than	(1, 2, 4)
L3	Weakly more important than	(1, 3, 5)
L4	Weakly or strongly more important than	(2, 4, 6)
L5	Strongly more important than	(3, 5, 7)
L6	Strongly or very strongly more important than	(4, 6, 8)
L7	Very strongly more important than	(5, 7, 9)
L8	Very or absolutely strongly more important than	(6, 8, 9)
L9	Absolutely more important than	(7, 9, 9)

Based on the pairwise comparison results, the fuzzy judgment matrix $\widetilde{\mathbf{A}}_{n \times n} = [\widetilde{a}_{ij}]$ is constructed, in which:

$$\widetilde{a}_{ji} = 1/\widetilde{a}_{ij}. \tag{1}$$

The fuzzy eigenvalue and eigenvector of $\widetilde{\mathbf{A}}$, indicated with $\widetilde{\lambda}$ and $\widetilde{\mathbf{x}}$, respectively, satisfy:

$$det(\widetilde{\mathbf{A}}(-)\widetilde{\lambda}\mathbf{I}) = 0, \tag{2}$$

and

$$(\widetilde{\mathbf{A}}(-)\widetilde{\lambda}\mathbf{I})(\times)\widetilde{\mathbf{x}} = 0, \tag{3}$$

where (−) and (×) denote fuzzy subtraction and multiplication, respectively.

The FGM method [25] is applied to evaluate the relative priority of each critical factor ($\widetilde{w}_i$), as:

$$\widetilde{w}_i \cong \frac{\sqrt[n]{\prod_{j=1}^{n} \widetilde{a}_{ij}}}{\sum_{k=1}^{n} \sqrt[n]{\prod_{j=1}^{n} \widetilde{a}_{kj}}}. \tag{4}$$

The fuzzy maximal eigenvalue $\widetilde{\lambda}_{max}$ can be estimated as:

$$\widetilde{\lambda}_{max} = \frac{1}{n} \sum_{i=1}^{n} \frac{\sum_{j=1}^{n} (\widetilde{a}_{ij}(\times)\widetilde{w}_j)}{\widetilde{w}_i}. \tag{5}$$

The consistency of the pairwise comparison results can be evaluated in terms of the critical ratio (CR):

$$\widetilde{CR} = \frac{\frac{\widetilde{\lambda}_{max}-n}{n-1}}{RI}, \tag{6}$$

where RI is the random consistency index [50]. $\widetilde{CR}$ should be less than 0.1 for a small FAHP problem, or less than 0.3 if the problem size is large or the problem is highly uncertain [51,52].

3.3. LPC Approach for Aggregating the Relative Priorities

When there is no overall consensus among all the decision makers, the partial consensus among some of them can be sought instead [32,53].

Definition 1. *The H/M partial consensus fuzzy intersection (PCFI) of the relative priorities derived by M decision makers for the i-th critical factor, indicated with $\widetilde{w}_i(1) \sim \widetilde{w}_i(M)$, is denoted by $\widehat{PCFI}^{H/M}(\widetilde{w}_i(1), \ldots, \widetilde{w}_i(M))$, such that:*

$$\mu_{\widehat{PCFI}^{H/M}}(x) = \max_{all\ g}(\min(\mu_{\widetilde{w}_1(g(1))}(x), \ldots, \mu_{\widetilde{w}_1(g(H))}(x))), \tag{7}$$

where $g() \in Z^+$; $1 \leq g() \leq M$; $g(p) \cap g(q) = \emptyset \ \forall\ p \neq q$; $H \geq 2$.

An example is given in Figure 3, showing the relative priorities of a critical factor evaluated by five decision makers. If fuzzy intersection is applied to find the common part of the evaluations, the result will be an empty set. As a result, these decision makers lack an overall consensus, because no value is acceptable to all of them.

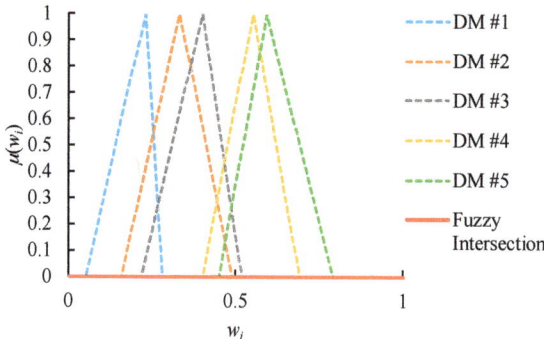

Figure 3. An example.

Nevertheless, (partial) consensus among any four decision makers exists. For illustrating this, the 4/5 PCFI result of the evaluations is derived, as shown in Figure 4. For example, 0.47 is acceptable to decision makers #2, #3, #4, and #5, and has a positive membership. However, the 4/5 PCFI result covers very few possible values.

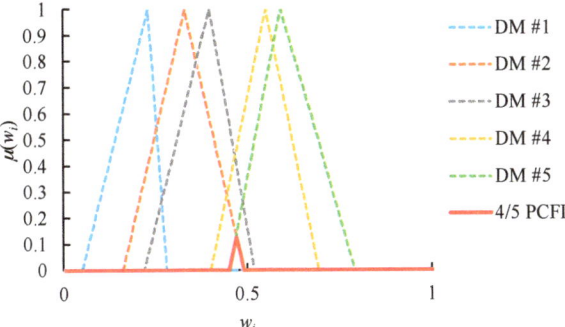

Figure 4. The 4/5 partial consensus fuzzy intersection (PCFI) result.

It is easier to reach a partial consensus among fewer decision makers. For this reason, the 3/5 PCFI result of the fuzzy priorities is derived, as shown in Figure 5. More values are acceptable to three of the five decision makers.

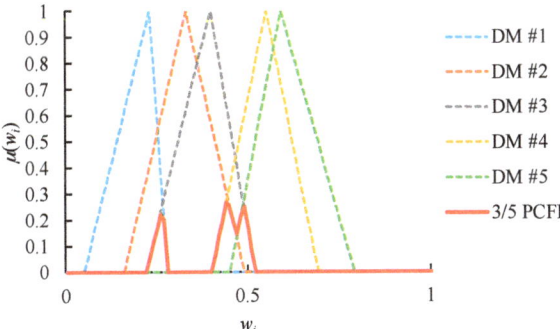

Figure 5. The 3/5 PCFI result.

If the consensus between only two decision makers is sought, there will be much more possible values that are acceptable, as illustrated in Figure 6.

The problem is how to determine the number of decision makers that reach a consensus. According to Chen and Wu [27]:

(1) It is better if more decision makers reach a consensus [54,55].
(2) The PCFI result should cover a sufficient number of possible values: for this purpose, the range of the PCFI result should be wider than a threshold ξ [56].

In the previous example, the ranges of various PCFI results are summarized in Table 3. If ξ is set to 0.3, only the 2/5 PCFI result meets the second requirement, and a partial consensus between any two decision makers will be sought. In contrast, setting ξ to 0.15 makes the 3/5 PCFI result also feasible. In this way, every possible value is acceptable to three decision makers.

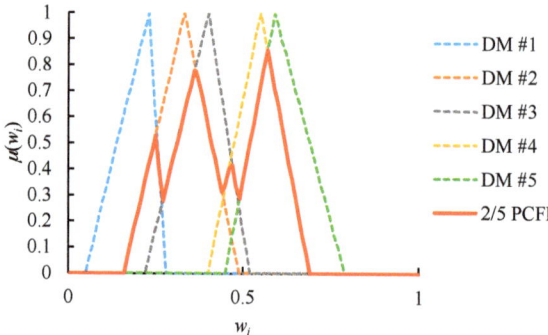

Figure 6. The 2/5 PCFI result.

Table 3. Ranges of various PCFI results.

PCFI	Range
4/5	0.04
3/5	0.18
2/5	0.53

The number of decision makers that reach a partial consensus may vary when the layered partial consensus approach is applied to different critical factors:

$$H_i \neq H_j \ \exists i \neq j, \tag{8}$$

where H_i indicates the number of decision makers that reach a partial consensus, regarding the relative priority of critical factor i.

3.4. GFWA Approach for Assessing an Intervention Strategy

Subsequently, GFWA is proposed to assess an intervention strategy amid the COVID-19 pandemic, for which the varying PCFI result provides the relative weights/priorities of critical factors:

$$\widetilde{S}_q = \sqrt[v]{\sum_{i=1}^{n} \left(\widetilde{PCFI}(\{\widetilde{w}_i(m)\})(\times)\widetilde{p}_{qi}(-)\widetilde{R}_i\right)^v}, \tag{9}$$

where $\widetilde{S}_q$ is the overall performance of the q-th intervention strategy amid the COVID-19 pandemic, $\widetilde{p}_{qi}$ is the performance of the q-th intervention strategy in optimizing the i-th critical factor, $\{\widetilde{R}_i\}$ is the basis reference point, $(-)$ denotes fuzzy subtraction, and $v \in Z^+$.

Theorem 1. *FWA is a special case of GFWA.*

Proof of Theorem 1. The overall performance of the q-th intervention strategy amid the COVID-19 pandemic can be evaluated using FWA as:

$$\widetilde{S}_q = \frac{\sum_{i=1}^{n} \widetilde{PCFI}(\{\widetilde{w}_i(m)\})(\times)\widetilde{p}_{qi}}{\sum_{i=1}^{n} \widetilde{PCFI}(\{\widetilde{w}_i(m)\})} = \frac{\sqrt[1]{\sum_{i=1}^{n} \left(\widetilde{PCFI}(\{\widetilde{w}_i(m)\})(\times)\widetilde{p}_{qi}(-)0\right)^1}}{\sum_{i=1}^{n} \widetilde{PCFI}(\{\widetilde{w}_i(m)\})}. \tag{10}$$

The divisor can be neglected, since it is constant for all intervention strategies amid the COVID-19 pandemic. As a result,

$$\widetilde{S}_q = \sqrt[1]{\sum_{i=1}^{n} \left(\widetilde{PCFI}(\{\widetilde{w}_i(m)\})(\times)\widetilde{p}_{qi}(-)0\right)^1}. \tag{11}$$

which is a special case of GFWA when $v = 1$. □

Theorem 2. *Fuzzy technique for order preference by similarity to ideal solution (FTOPSIS) is a special case of GFWA.*

Proof of Theorem 2. Using FTOPSIS, the distance between the q-th intervention strategy amid the COVID-19 pandemic and two reference points are measured as:

$$\widetilde{d}_q^- = \sqrt{\sum_{i=1}^{n} \left(\widetilde{PCFI}(\{\widetilde{w}_i(m)\})(\times)\widetilde{p}_{qi}(-)\widetilde{R}_i^-\right)^2}, \tag{12}$$

$$\widetilde{d}_q^+ = \sqrt{\sum_{i=1}^{n} \left(\widetilde{PCFI}(\{\widetilde{w}_i(m)\})(\times)\widetilde{p}_{qi}(-)\widetilde{R}_i^+\right)^2}. \tag{13}$$

Both are the special cases of GFWA when $v = 2$. □

However, $\widetilde{PCFI}(\{\widetilde{w}_i(m)\})$ is a polygonal fuzzy number, while $\widetilde{p}_{qi}$ is a TFN. Their combination is not easy to calculate. To tackle such complexity, $\widetilde{PCFI}(\{\widetilde{w}_i(m)\})$ is approximated with a TFN as:

$$\widetilde{PCFI}(\{\widetilde{w}_i(m)\}) \cong (\min(\widetilde{PCFI}(\{\widetilde{w}_i(m)\})),$$
$$3COG(\widetilde{PCFI}(\{\widetilde{w}_i(m)\})) - \max(\widetilde{PCFI}(\{\widetilde{w}_i(m)\})) - \min(\widetilde{PCFI}(\{\widetilde{w}_i(m)\})), \tag{14}$$
$$\max(\widetilde{PCFI}(\{\widetilde{w}_i(m)\})).$$

In this way, the defuzzified value of the approximating TFN is equal to $COG(\widetilde{PCFI}(\{\widetilde{w}_i(m)\}))$, which is calculated as:

$$COG(\widetilde{PCFI}(\{\widetilde{w}_i(m)\})) = \frac{\int_0^1 x \mu_{\widetilde{PCFI}(\{\widetilde{w}_i(m)\})}(x)dx}{\int_0^1 \mu_{\widetilde{PCFI}(\{\widetilde{w}_i(m)\})}(x)dx}. \tag{15}$$

Then, $\widetilde{S}_q$ can be derived using the arithmetic for TFNs. In addition, to generate a crisp ordering of alternatives, the COG method can also be applied to defuzzify $\widetilde{S}_q$.

4. Case Study

Application of the Proposed Methodology

A city government in Taiwan was considering adopting suitable intervention strategies to tackle the COVID-19 pandemic in the city. To this end, the following factors were considered critical:

- Total costs;
- Ease of implementation;
- Acceptability;
- Effectiveness in preventing the spread of COVID-19;
- Irreplaceability by other treatments.

Based on these beliefs, four fuzzy pairwise comparison matrixes were constructed for the decision makers, as shown in Table 4.

Table 4. Fuzzy pairwise comparison matrixes constructed by four decision makers.

	(1, 1, 1)	(3, 5, 7)	-	-	(5, 7, 9)
	-	(1, 1, 1)	-	-	-
Decision maker #1	(2, 4, 6)	(3, 5, 7)	(1, 1, 1)	-	(2, 4, 6)
	(3, 5, 7)	(5, 7, 9)	(3, 5, 7)	(1, 1, 1)	(5, 7, 9)
	-	(1, 3, 5)	-	-	(1, 1, 1)
	(1, 1, 1)	-	-	-	-
	(3, 5, 7)	(1, 1, 1)	(1, 3, 5)	-	(2, 4, 6)
Decision maker #2	(1, 3, 5)	-	(1, 1, 1)	-	(3, 5, 7)
	(2, 4, 6)	(3, 5, 7)	(3, 5, 7)	(1, 1, 1)	(5, 7, 9)
	(1, 3, 5)	-	-	-	(1, 1, 1)
	(1, 1, 1)	-	-	-	-
	(2, 4, 6)	(1, 1, 1)	(1, 3, 5)	-	(1, 3, 5)
Decision maker #3	(3, 5, 7)	-	(1, 1, 1)	-	-
	(5, 7, 9)	(3, 5, 7)	(1, 3, 5)	(1, 1, 1)	(1, 3, 5)
	(1, 3, 5)	-	(1, 3, 5)	-	(1, 1, 1)
	(1, 1, 1)	-	-	-	-
	(1, 3, 5)	(1, 1, 1)	(1, 3, 5)	-	-
Decision maker #4	(1, 3, 5)	-	(1, 1, 1)	-	(1, 3, 5)
	(3, 5, 7)	(2, 4, 6)	(1, 3, 5)	(1, 1, 1)	(1, 3, 5)
	(1, 3, 5)	(1, 3, 5)	-	-	(1, 1, 1)

Each decision maker applied the FGM method to derive the fuzzy maximal eigenvalue and relative priorities from the corresponding fuzzy pairwise comparison matrix. As a result, the derived fuzzy maximal eigenvalues were:

$\widetilde{\lambda}_{max}(1) = (1.89, 5.79, 23.61)$,
$\widetilde{\lambda}_{max}(2) = (1.72, 5.73, 33.01)$,
$\widetilde{\lambda}_{max}(3) = (1.48, 5.60, 46.53)$, and
$\widetilde{\lambda}_{max}(4) = (1.34, 5.87, 62.14)$.

The corresponding consistency ratios were:

$\widetilde{CR}(1) = (-0.67, 0.18, 4.15)$,
$\widetilde{CR}(2) = (-0.73, 0.16, 6.25)$,
$\widetilde{CR}(3) = (-0.79, 0.13, 9.27)$, and
$\widetilde{CR}(4) = (-0.82, 0.19, 12.75)$.

These show certain levels of consistency. In addition, the relative priorities evaluated by the decision makers are summarized in Figure 7.

The overall consensus reached by all the decision makers, represented by the FI results of the relative priorities derived by them, are summarized in Figure 8. Obviously, all the decision makers reached an overall consensus regarding the values of $\widetilde{w}_1$ and $\widetilde{w}_3 \sim \widetilde{w}_5$. However, an overall consensus regarding the value of $\widetilde{w}_2$ was lacking, because the FI result was an empty set. As a result, the existing fuzzy group decision making methods assuming the existence of an overall consensus, such as Chen and Lin [32], Lin et al. [22], Gao et al. [33], Samanlioglu and Kaya [7], and Chen [57], were logically not applicable. To solve this problem, a partial consensus among some of the decision makers was sought instead. For this purpose, the PCFI result of the relative priorities was derived.

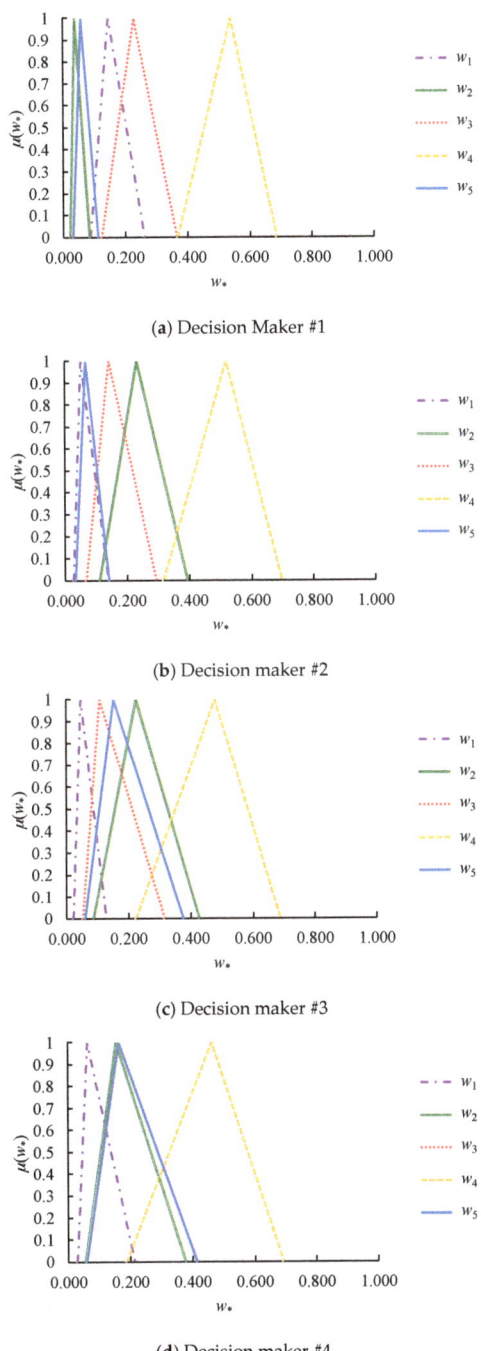

Figure 7. The derived relative priorities.

However, the number of decision makers that reached a partial consensus for each critical factor needed to be determined. To this end, the threshold for the range of the PCFI result, ξ, was set to 0.15—i.e., the range of the PCFI result had to be wider than 0.15 for the partial consensus to be significant. In addition, the decision makers that reached a partial consensus had to be as many as possible. As a result, the number of decision makers that reached a partial consensus for each critical factor was determined, as presented in Table 5. The PCFI results are summarized in Figure 9.

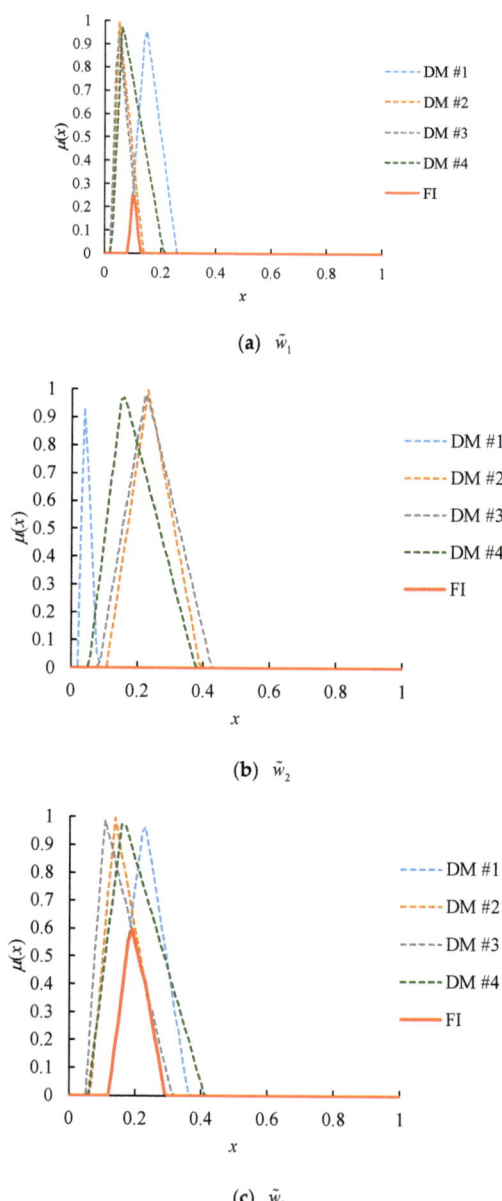

Figure 8. *Cont.*

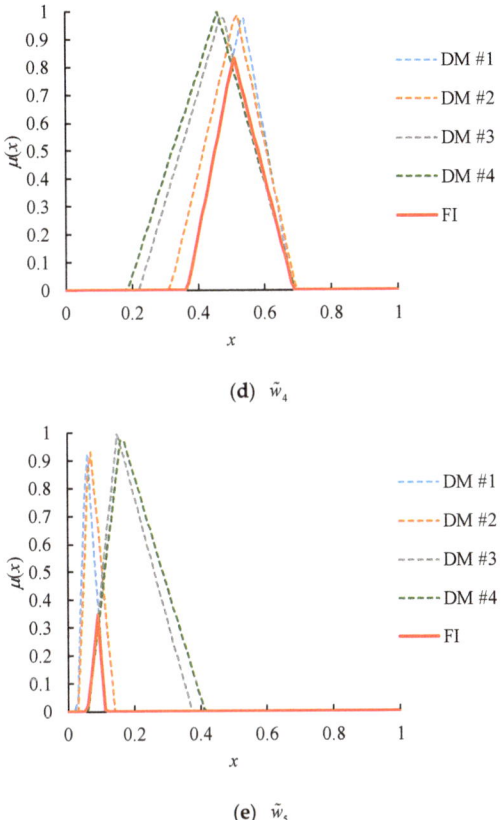

(d) $\tilde{w}_4$

(e) $\tilde{w}_5$

Figure 8. The fuzzy intersection (FI) results of the relative priorities.

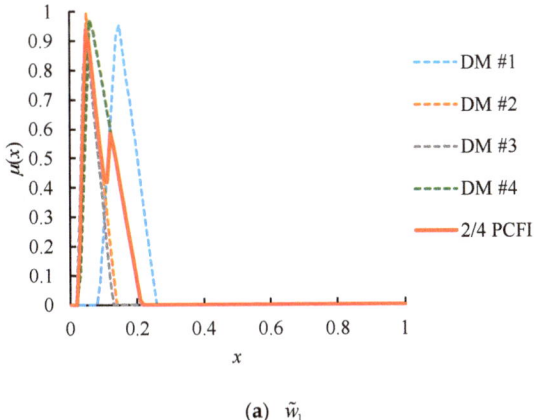

(a) $\tilde{w}_1$

Figure 9. Cont.

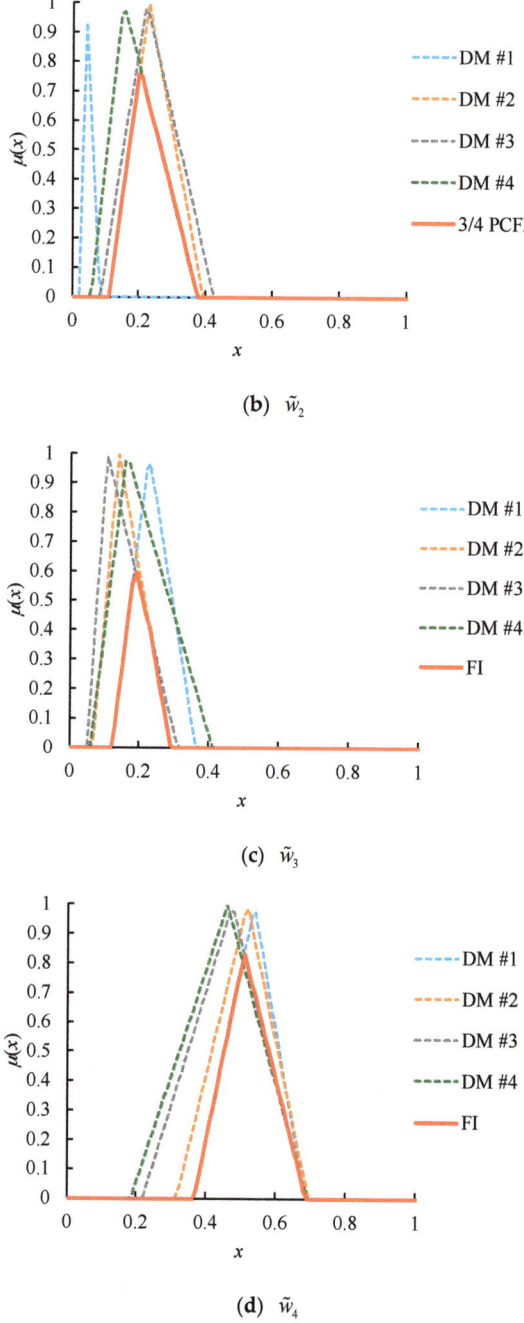

(b) $\tilde{w}_2$

(c) $\tilde{w}_3$

(d) $\tilde{w}_4$

Figure 9. *Cont.*

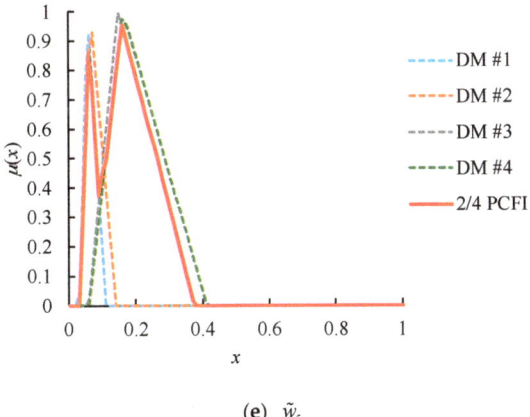

(e) $\tilde{w}_5$

Figure 9. The partial consensus fuzzy intersection (PCFI) results.

Table 5. The number of decision makers achieving a partial consensus for each critical factor.

Critical Factor	Number of Decision Makers	Range of the PCFI Result
$\tilde{w}_1$	2	0.18
$\tilde{w}_2$	3	0.26
$\tilde{w}_3$	4 (overall consensus)	0.16
$\tilde{w}_4$	4 (overall consensus)	0.31
$\tilde{w}_5$	2	0.33

To facilitate the subsequent calculation, the PCFI results were approximated with TFNs according to Equation (14). The approximation results are shown in Figure 10.

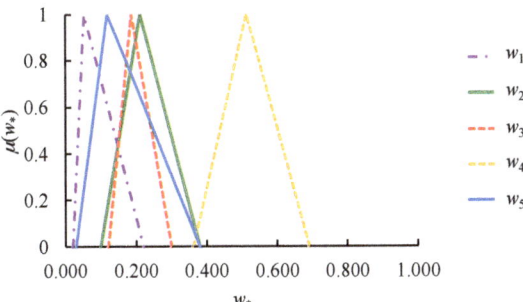

Figure 10. Approximating the partial consensus fuzzy intersection (PCFI) results with triangular fuzzy numbers (TFNs).

Among the five critical factors, only "total costs" was the-lower-the-better performance, whereas the others were the-higher-the-better performances. The performances in optimizing these critical factors were evaluated according to the rules depicted in Table 6.

Table 6. Rules for evaluating the performances in optimizing the critical factors.

Critical Factor	Rule
Total costs	$\widetilde{p}_{q1}(x_q) = \begin{cases} (0, 0, 1) & \text{if} \quad 0.1 \cdot \min_r x_r + 0.9 \cdot \max_r x_r \leq x_k \text{ or data not available} \\ (0, 1, 2) & \text{if} \quad 0.35 \cdot \min_r x_r + 0.65 \cdot \max_r x_r \leq x_k < 0.1 \cdot \min_r x_r + 0.9 \cdot \max_r x_r \\ (1.5, 2.5, 3.5) & \text{if} \quad 0.65 \cdot \min_r x_r + 0.35 \cdot \max_r x_r \leq x_k < 0.35 \cdot \min_r x_r + 0.65 \cdot \max_r x_r \\ (3, 4, 5) & \text{if} \quad 0.9 \cdot \min_r x_r + 0.1 \cdot \max_r x_r \leq x_k < 0.65 \cdot \min_r x_r + 0.35 \cdot \max_r x_r \\ (4, 5, 5) & \text{if} \quad x_k < 0.9 \cdot \min_r x_r + 0.1 \cdot \max_r x_r \end{cases}$ x_q is the estimated total costs.
Ease of implementation	$\widetilde{p}_{q2}(x_q) = \begin{cases} (0, 0, 1) & \text{if} \quad x_k = \text{very difficult} \\ (0, 1, 2) & \text{if} \quad x_k = \text{difficult} \\ (1.5, 2.5, 3.5) & \text{if} \quad x_k = \text{moderate} \\ (3, 4, 5) & \text{if} \quad x_k = \text{easy} \\ (4, 5, 5) & \text{if} \quad x_k = \text{very easy} \end{cases}$ x_q is the ease of implementation.
Acceptability	$\widetilde{p}_{q3}(x_q) = \begin{cases} (0, 0, 1) & \text{if} \quad x_k = \text{very unacceptable} \\ (0, 1, 2) & \text{if} \quad x_k = \text{unacceptable} \\ (1.5, 2.5, 3.5) & \text{if} \quad x_k = \text{neutral} \\ (3, 4, 5) & \text{if} \quad x_k = \text{acceptable} \\ (4, 5, 5) & \text{if} \quad x_k = \text{very acceptable} \end{cases}$ x_q is the acceptability.
Effectiveness in preventing the spread of COVID-19	$\widetilde{p}_{q4}(x_q) = \begin{cases} (0, 0, 1) & \text{if} \quad x_k = \text{very ineffective} \\ (0, 1, 2) & \text{if} \quad x_k = \text{ineffective} \\ (1.5, 2.5, 3.5) & \text{if} \quad x_k = \text{moderate} \\ (3, 4, 5) & \text{if} \quad x_k = \text{effective} \\ (4, 5, 5) & \text{if} \quad x_k = \text{very effective} \end{cases}$ x_q is the effectiveness in preventing the spread of COVID-19.
Irreplaceability by other treatments	$\widetilde{p}_{q5}(x_q) = \begin{cases} (0, 0, 1) & \text{if} \quad x_k = \text{very low} \\ (0, 1, 2) & \text{if} \quad x_k = \text{low} \\ (1.5, 2.5, 3.5) & \text{if} \quad x_k = \text{moderate} \\ (3, 4, 5) & \text{if} \quad x_k = \text{high} \\ (4, 5, 5) & \text{if} \quad x_k = \text{very high} \end{cases}$ x_q is the irreplaceability.

Based on the derived relative priorities, the 15 intervention strategies mentioned by Samanlioglu et al. [7] were compared:

(1) Quarantining patients and those suspected of infection;
(2) Internal border restrictions—i.e., reducing the ability to move/transport freely within a city/country;
(3) Social distancing;
(4) Health monitoring;
(5) Public awareness campaigns;
(6) Restriction of nonessential businesses;
(7) Restrictions of mass gatherings;
(8) External border restrictions—i.e., reducing the ability to exit or enter a city/country;
(9) Closure of schools;
(10) Enhanced control of the country's health resources (materials and health workers);
(11) Formation of an emergency response team;
(12) Common health testing (independent of suspected infection);
(13) Curfew;
(14) Restriction of nonessential government services;
(15) Declaration of emergency.

Samanlioglu et al. [7] did not investigate the critical factors in an intervention strategy, but directly compared all the intervention strategies in pairs using a FAHP approach, which was a rough analysis and limited by too much subjectivity. In contrast, in this study the performances of each intervention strategy in optimizing the critical factors were evaluated. Table 7 presents the evaluation results.

Table 7. Evaluation results.

Intervention Strategy	Total Costs	Ease of Implementation	Acceptability	Effectiveness in Preventing the Spread of COVID-19	Irreplaceability by Other Treatments
Quarantining patients and those suspected of infection	(1.5, 2.5, 3.5)	(1.5, 2.5, 3.5)	(3, 4, 5)	(4, 5, 5)	(4, 5, 5)
Internal border restrictions	(0, 1, 2)	(0, 1, 2)	(0, 1, 2)	(0, 1, 2)	(0, 1, 2)
Social distancing	(4, 5, 5)	(4, 5, 5)	(1.5, 2.5, 3.5)	(1.5, 2.5, 3.5)	(1.5, 2.5, 3.5)
Health monitoring	(3, 4, 5)	(4, 5, 5)	(4, 5, 5)	(1.5, 2.5, 3.5)	(1.5, 2.5, 3.5)
Public awareness campaigns	(3, 4, 5)	(1.5, 2.5, 3.5)	(4, 5, 5)	(0, 1, 2)	(1.5, 2.5, 3.5)
Restriction of nonessential businesses	(0, 1, 2)	(1.5, 2.5, 3.5)	(1.5, 2.5, 3.5)	(1.5, 2.5, 3.5)	(0, 1, 2)
Restrictions of mass gatherings	(1.5, 2.5, 3.5)	(1.5, 2.5, 3.5)	(0, 1, 2)	(1.5, 2.5, 3.5)	(0, 1, 2)
External border restrictions	(0, 1, 2)	(4, 5, 5)	(1.5, 2.5, 3.5)	(3, 4, 5)	(1.5, 2.5, 3.5)
Closure of schools	(1.5, 2.5, 3.5)	(1.5, 2.5, 3.5)	(1.5, 2.5, 3.5)	(1.5, 2.5, 3.5)	(0, 1, 2)
Enhanced control of country's health resources	(1.5, 2.5, 3.5)	(3, 4, 5)	(1.5, 2.5, 3.5)	(1.5, 2.5, 3.5)	(1.5, 2.5, 3.5)
Formation of an emergency response team	(4, 5, 5)	(4, 5, 5)	(4, 5, 5)	(0, 1, 2)	(3, 4, 5)
Common health testing	(0, 1, 2)	(1.5, 2.5, 3.5)	(1.5, 2.5, 3.5)	(4, 5, 5)	(0, 1, 2)
Curfew	(1.5, 2.5, 3.5)	(1.5, 2.5, 3.5)	(0, 0, 1)	(1.5, 2.5, 3.5)	(0, 0, 1)
Restriction of nonessential government services	(1.5, 2.5, 3.5)	(3, 4, 5)	(3, 4, 5)	(1.5, 2.5, 3.5)	(0, 0, 1)
Declaration of emergency	(0, 0, 1)	(0, 1, 2)	(0, 0, 1)	(1.5, 2.5, 3.5)	(0, 0, 1)

Subsequently, the overall performance of an intervention strategy was assessed using the GFWA approach, for which v was set to 3 and for $\widetilde{R}_i$ was set to $\min_q(\widehat{PCFI}(\{\widetilde{w}_i(m)\})(\times)\widetilde{p}_{qi})$. The assessment results are summarized in Table 8. The defuzzification results of the overall performances are also shown in the same table.

According to the experimental results, the following discussion was made:

(1) Intervention strategies with higher overall performances should be adopted earlier than those with lower overall performances. In the experiment, "quarantining patients and those suspected of infection", "common health testing", and "external border restrictions" were the top three intervention strategies. The three intervention strategies have been widely adopted by a number of countries/cities, including the city that the decision makers were located. For example, Taiwan's Center for Disease Control and Prevention monitors all people who travelled to Wuhan within 14 days and developed symptoms of fever or upper respiratory tract infection.

(2) During the peak of the COVID-19 pandemic, as many intervention strategies should be adopted as possible. For guiding this, a threshold for the overall performance could be established—e.g., 1.2. Then, the intervention strategies with overall performances higher than the threshold could be taken, which involved eight intervention strategies.

(3) The overall performances of the intervention strategies were ranked, as shown in Figure 11. For comparison, the ranking result by Samanlioglu et al. [7] was also presented in the same figure. There were considerable differences between the ranking results using the two methods. One possible reason for this was that different national conditions have led to a gap in the preferences of decision makers. Another possible reason was that the ranking result by

Samanlioglu et al. [7] was based on subjective comparisons only, while that using the proposed methodology took the objective performances of intervention strategies into account.

(4) A sensitivity (or parametric) analysis has been conducted by varying the order of the objective function (v) in the GFWA approach, so as to observe changes in the ranking result. The results are summarized in Figure 12. Obviously, the ranking result changed as the value of v varied. Nevertheless, "quarantining patients and those suspected of infection" was always the most suitable intervention strategy. In addition, when v was greater than 5, the ranking result was no longer affected by the value of v, showing the stability of the GFWA approach.

(5) Two more existing methods, FGM-FGM-FWA [14] and FGM-FGM-FTOPSIS [58], have been applied to compare these intervention strategies for tackling the COVID-19 pandemic. In FGM-FGM-FWA, the decision makers' judgments were aggregated using FGM. Then, the relative priorities of the critical factors were also derived from the aggregation result using FGM. Subsequently, FWA was applied to assess the overall performance of each intervention strategy. In FGM-FGM-FTOPSIS, the overall performance of an intervention strategy was assessed using FTOPSIS instead. The ranking results using various methods are compared in Table 9.

(6) Carnero [59] proposed the potentially all pairwise rankings of all possible alternatives (PAPRIKA) method for the failure mode and effects analysis (FMEA) [60] of a waste segregation system. In the PAPRIKA method, the failure rates and weights of risk factors were evaluated with intuitionistic fuzzy numbers (IFNs) that had both membership and nonmembership function values. Then, the intuitionistic fuzzy weighted averaging (IFWA) operator was applied to aggregate the decision makers' evaluation results. However, in Carnero's study, it was assumed that the decision makers reached an overall consensus, while in this study only some decision makers reached a partial consensus. In addition, in Carnero's study, the weights of the decision makers were predetermined and remained unchanged within the decision-making process. In contrast, in the proposed methodology the weights of decision makers varied within the decision-making process. Decision makers that reached a partial consensus about each critical factor had equal weights, while the others had zero weights. For example, when determining the relative priority of "total costs", the weights of the two decision makers who reached a partial consensus were both 0.5. When determining the relative priority of "ease of implementation", three decision makers reached a partial consensus, and their weights were all 0.33.

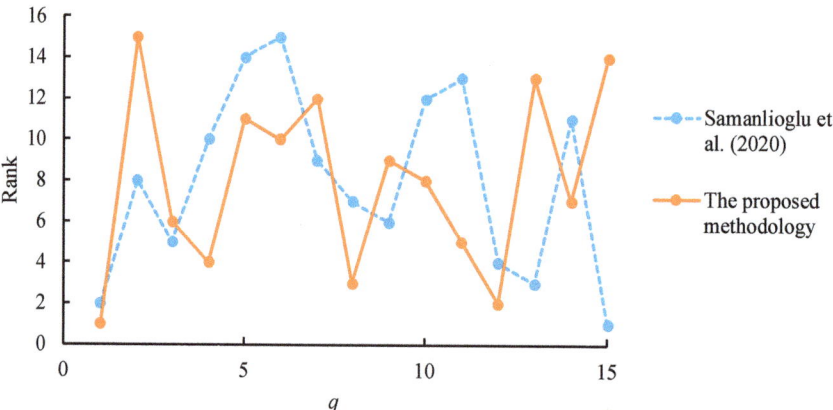

Figure 11. Ranking result.

Table 8. The assessment results.

Intervention Strategy	Overall Performance	Defuzzification Result
Quarantining patients and those suspected of infection	(0.08, 2.09, 3.78)	1.98
Internal border restrictions	(0, 0.2, 1.56)	0.59
Social distancing	(0, 1.06, 2.95)	1.34
Health monitoring	(0.18, 1.23, 3.04)	1.48
Public awareness campaigns	(0.18, 0.95, 2.29)	1.14
Restriction of nonessential businesses	(0, 0.83, 2.63)	1.15
Restrictions of mass gatherings	(0, 0.79, 2.6)	1.13
External border restrictions	(0, 1.63, 3.72)	1.78
Closure of schools	(0, 0.83, 2.64)	1.16
Enhanced control of country's health resources	(0, 0.94, 2.92)	1.29
Formation of an emergency response team	(0.18, 1.14, 2.76)	1.36
Common health testing	(0.06, 2.05, 3.56)	1.89
Curfew	(0, 0.78, 2.57)	1.12
Restriction of nonessential government services	(0.06, 1.03, 2.92)	1.34
Declaration of emergency	(0, 0.77, 2.45)	1.07

Table 9. Ranking results using various methods.

Intervention Strategy	FGM-FGM-FWA	FGM-FGM-FTOPSIS	The Proposed Methodology
Quarantining patients and those suspected of infection	1	1	1
Internal border restrictions	15	15	15
Social distancing	5	6	6
Health monitoring	2	4	4
Public awareness campaigns	9	9	11
Restriction of nonessential businesses	11	11	10
Restrictions of mass gatherings	12	12	12
External border restrictions	3	2	3
Closure of schools	10	10	9
Enhanced control of country's health resources	7	8	8
Formation of an emergency response team	4	5	5
Common health testing	6	3	2
Curfew	13	13	13
Restriction of nonessential government services	8	7	7
Declaration of emergency	14	14	14

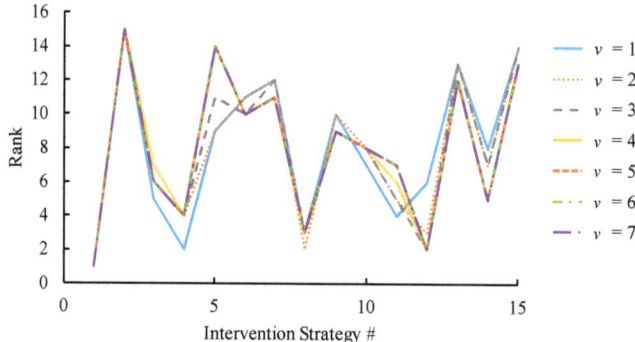

Figure 12. Ranking results with various values of v.

5. Conclusions and Future Research Directions

The COVID-19 pandemic has severely impacted our daily lives. To tackle the COVID-19 pandemic, country (or city) governments around the world have adopted various intervention strategies. Not all intervention strategies will be successful, acceptable, and/or cost-effective. For this reason, the varying partial consensus fuzzy collaborative intelligence approach is proposed in this study to assess an intervention strategy, so that a country (or city) government can choose the top-performing intervention strategies to create synergy. In the varying partial consensus fuzzy collaborative intelligence approach, multiple decision makers express their beliefs on the relative priorities of factors critical to an intervention strategy. If an overall consensus is lacking among the decision makers, the LPC approach is applied to derive a partial consensus among most of the decision makers for each critical factor. Subsequently, the GFWA approach is proposed to evaluate the overall performance of an intervention strategy for tackling the COVID-19 pandemic. Finally, the top-performing intervention strategies can be adopted by or recommended to the country (or city) government to tackle the COVID-19 pandemic.

The proposed methodology has been applied to compare 15 existing intervention strategies for tackling the COVID-19 pandemic to illustrate its applicability. After analyzing the experimental results, the following conclusions were drawn:

(1) Five factors, "total costs", "ease of implementation", "acceptability", "effectiveness in preventing the spread of COVID-19", and "irreplaceability by other treatments", were considered critical to an intervention strategy.
(2) "Quarantining patients and those suspected of infection", "common health testing", and "external border restrictions" were the top three intervention strategies, while "internal border restrictions" performed the worst.
(3) The number of decision makers that reached a partial consensus differed from one.

The proposed methodology has the following advantages over the existing methods:

(1) The proposed methodology does not assume the existence of an overall consensus among all decision makers, which is more practical.
(2) The partial consensus among some decision makers may not be obvious using existing methods, such as Wang and Chen [15], Lin and Chen [16], and Chen et al. [17]. In contrast, the proposed methodology varies the number of decision makers that reach a partial consensus to ensure that the partial consensus is obvious enough.

However, the proposed methodology is also subject to some limits. For example, the partial consensus among decision makers may not be obvious enough, even if the number of decision makers is minimized.

Some future research directions are provided as follows. First, it is difficult to know for how long the COVID-19 pandemic will persist. Therefore, the same analysis needs to be conducted again to see whether the experimental results obtained in this study are still applicable. In addition, intervention strategies for tackling the COVID-19 pandemic can be classified before being compared [61–64]. These constitute some topics for future investigation.

Author Contributions: Data curation, methodology, and writing (original draft): H.-C.W., Y.-C.W., and T.-C.T.C.; writing—review and editing: H.-C.W. and T.-C.T.C. All the authors contributed equally to the writing of this paper. All authors have read and agreed to the published version of the manuscript.

Funding: This study was partly funded by Ministry of Science and Technology, Taiwan, under grant MOST 106-2221-E-009-200-MY3.

Conflicts of Interest: The authors declare no conflict of interest.

References

1. Bloomberg News. What Doctors Treating Covid-19 in Wuhan Say about Coronavirus. Available online: https://www.bloomberg.com/news/articles/2020-03-05/what-doctors-treating-covid-19-in-wuhan-say-about-the-virus (accessed on 30 August 2020).
2. Murray, A. COVID-19 Impact on Daily Life Heightens. Available online: https://www.monmouth.edu/polling-institute/reports/monmouthpoll_US_041320/ (accessed on 28 August 2020).
3. Kalu, A. COVID-19 and Right to Freedom of Movement. Available online: https://www.vanguardngr.com/2020/04/covid-19-and-right-to-freedom-of-movement/ (accessed on 29 August 2020).
4. MacCharles, T. U.S. Border Closed for Another Month as Canada Braces for Fall Surge of COVID-19. Available online: https://www.thestar.com/politics/federal/2020/08/14/us-border-closed-for-another-month-as-canada-braces-for-fall-surge-of-covid-19.html (accessed on 27 August 2020).
5. World Health Organization. WHO Mass Gathering COVID-19 Risk Assessment Tool—Generic Events. Available online: https://www.who.int/publications/i/item/10665-333185 (accessed on 28 August 2020).
6. Carroll, R. Ireland to Extend Europe's Longest Pub Lockdown as Coronavirus Cases Rise. Available online: https://www.theguardian.com/world/2020/aug/28/ireland-pubs-to-remain-shut-coronavirus-cases-rise (accessed on 30 August 2020).
7. Samanlioglu, F.; Kaya, B.E. Evaluation of the COVID-19 pandemic intervention strategies with hesitant F-AHP. *J. Healthc. Eng.* **2020**, *2020*, 8835258. [CrossRef]
8. Ngnenbe, T. Fighting COVID-19: Wear Mask, Maintain Social Distance. Available online: https://www.graphic.com.gh/news/general-news/fighting-covid-19-wear-mask-maintain-social-distance.html (accessed on 28 August 2020).
9. Lu, J. How Different Countries Have Handled COVID-19, Ranked. Available online: https://www.undispatch.com/how-countries-responded-to-covid-19/ (accessed on 30 August 2020).
10. Cullen, P. Covid-19: Temperature Scans at Airports 'Ineffective'. Available online: https://www.irishtimes.com/news/health/covid-19-temperature-scans-at-airports-ineffective-1.4323642 (accessed on 27 August 2020).
11. Andrew, S. The Psychology behind Why Some People Won't Wear Masks. Available online: https://edition.cnn.com/2020/05/06/health/why-people-dont-wear-masks-wellness-trnd/index.html (accessed on 29 August 2020).
12. Riera, J.V.; Massanet, S.; Herrera-Viedma, E.; Torrens, J. Some interesting properties of the fuzzy linguistic model based on discrete fuzzy numbers to manage hesitant fuzzy linguistic information. *Appl. Soft Comput.* **2015**, *36*, 383–391. [CrossRef]
13. Wang, Y.C.; Chen, T.; Yeh, Y.L. Advanced 3D printing technologies for the aircraft industry: A fuzzy systematic approach for assessing the critical factors. *Int. J. Adv. Manuf. Technol.* **2019**, *105*, 4059–4069. [CrossRef]
14. Chen, T. Assessing factors critical to smart technology applications in mobile health care—The FGM-FAHP approach. *Health Policy Technol.* **2020**, *9*, 194–203. [CrossRef]
15. Wang, Y.C.; Chen, T.C.T. A partial-consensus posterior-aggregation FAHP method—Supplier selection problem as an example. *Mathematics* **2019**, *7*, 179. [CrossRef]
16. Lin, C.W.; Chen, T. 3D printing technologies for enhancing the sustainability of an aircraft manufacturing or MRO company—A multi-expert partial consensus-FAHP analysis. *Int. J. Adv. Manuf. Technol.* **2019**, *105*, 4171–4180. [CrossRef]

17. Chen, T.C.T.; Wang, Y.C.; Huang, C.H. An evolving partial consensus fuzzy collaborative forecasting approach. *Mathematics* **2020**, *8*, 554. [CrossRef]
18. Chang, D.Y. Applications of the extent analysis method on fuzzy AHP. *Eur. J. Oper. Res.* **1996**, *95*, 649–655. [CrossRef]
19. Soleimani-Damaneh, M. Fuzzy upper bounds and their applications. *Chaos Solitons Fractals* **2008**, *36*, 217–225. [CrossRef]
20. Chen, T.C.T. Guaranteed-consensus posterior-aggregation fuzzy analytic hierarchy process method. *Neural. Comput. Appl.* **2020**, *32*, 7057–7068. [CrossRef]
21. Chen, T.; Wang, Y.C. A nonlinearly normalized back propagation network and cloud computing approach for determining cycle time allowance during wafer fabrication. *Robot. Comput. Integr. Manuf.* **2017**, *45*, 144–156. [CrossRef]
22. Lin, Y.C.; Wang, Y.C.; Chen, T.C.T.; Lin, H.F. Evaluating the suitability of a smart technology application for fall detection using a fuzzy collaborative intelligence approach. *Mathematics* **2019**, *7*, 1097. [CrossRef]
23. Rahman, K.; Abdullah, S.; Ali, A.; Amin, F. Interval-valued Pythagorean fuzzy Einstein hybrid weighted averaging aggregation operator and their application to group decision making. *Complex Int. Syst.* **2019**, *5*, 41–52. [CrossRef]
24. Yang, W.; Wang, C.; Liu, Y.; Sun, Y. Hesitant Pythagorean fuzzy interaction aggregation operators and their application in multiple attribute decision-making. *Complex Int. Syst.* **2019**, *5*, 199–216. [CrossRef]
25. Chen, T.C.T.; Honda, K. *Fuzzy Collaborative Forecasting and Clustering: Methodology, System Architecture, and Applications*; Springer Nature Switzerland AG: Cham, Switzerland, 2019. [CrossRef]
26. Chen, T.C.T.; Honda, K. Introduction to fuzzy collaborative forecasting systems. In *Fuzzy Collaborative Forecasting and Clustering: Methodology, System Architecture, and Application*; Springer Nature Switzerland AG: Cham, Switzerland, 2019.
27. Chen, T.C.T.; Wu, H.C. Forecasting the unit cost of a DRAM product using a layered partial-consensus fuzzy collaborative forecasting approach. *Complex Int. Syst.* **2020**, *6*, 479–492. [CrossRef]
28. Lippi, M.; Bertini, M.; Frasconi, P. Short-term traffic flow forecasting: An experimental comparison of time-series analysis and supervised learning. *IEEE Trans. Intell. Transp. Syst.* **2013**, *14*, 871–882. [CrossRef]
29. Xavier, A.; Hall, B.; Casteel, S.; Muir, W.; Rainey, K.M. Using unsupervised learning techniques to assess interactions among complex traits in soybeans. *Euphytica* **2017**, *213*, 200. [CrossRef]
30. Perraudin, C.G.; Illiano, V.P.; Calvo, F.; O'Hare, E.; Donnelly, S.C.; Mullan, R.H.; Caulfield, B.; Dorn, J.F. Observational study of a wearable sensor and smartphone application supporting unsupervised exercises to assess pain and stiffness. *Digit. Biomark.* **2018**, *2*, 106–125. [CrossRef]
31. Chen, T. A hybrid fuzzy and neural approach with virtual experts and partial consensus for DRAM price forecasting. *Int. J. Innov. Comput. Inf. Control* **2012**, *8*, 583–597.
32. Chen, T.; Lin, Y.C. A fuzzy-neural system incorporating unequally important expert opinions for semiconductor yield forecasting. *Int. J. Uncertain. Fuzziness Knowl. Based Syst.* **2008**, *16*, 35–58. [CrossRef]
33. Gao, H.; Ju, Y.; Gonzalez, E.D.S.; Zhang, W. Green supplier selection in electronics manufacturing: An approach based on consensus decision making. *J. Clean. Prod.* **2020**, *245*, 118781. [CrossRef]
34. Chen, T. Ubiquitous hotel recommendation using a fuzzy-weighted-average and backpropagation-network approach. *Int. J. Intell. Syst.* **2017**, *32*, 316–341. [CrossRef]
35. Jimenez, A.; Mateos, A.; Sabio, P. Dominance intensity measure within fuzzy weight oriented MAUT: An application. *Omega* **2013**, *41*, 397–405. [CrossRef]
36. Kahraman, C.; Kaya, İ. A fuzzy multiple attribute utility model for intelligent building assessment. *J. Civ. Eng. Manag.* **2012**, *18*, 811–820. [CrossRef]
37. Chen, T.C.T.; Chiu, M.C. A classifying ubiquitous clinic recommendation approach for forming patient groups and recommending suitable clinics. *Comput. Ind. Eng.* **2019**, *133*, 165–174. [CrossRef]
38. Sevkli, M. An application of the fuzzy ELECTRE method for supplier selection. *Int. J. Prod. Res.* **2010**, *48*, 3393–3405. [CrossRef]
39. Sachdeva, A.; Sharma, V.; Bhardwaj, A.; Gupta, R. Selection of logistic service provider using fuzzy PROMETHEE for a cement industry. *J. Manuf. Technol. Manag.* **2012**, *23*, 899–921.
40. Dhouib, D. An extension of MACBETH method for a fuzzy environment to analyze alternatives in reverse logistics for automobile tire wastes. *Omega* **2014**, *42*, 25–32. [CrossRef]

41. Chen, T.; Chuang, Y.H. Fuzzy and nonlinear programming approach for optimizing the performance of ubiquitous hotel recommendation. *J. Ambient. Intell. Humaniz. Comput.* **2018**, *9*, 275–284. [CrossRef]
42. Faizi, S.; Rashid, T.; Sałabun, W.; Zafar, S.; Wątróbski, J. Decision making with uncertainty using hesitant fuzzy sets. *Int. J. Fuzzy Syst.* **2018**, *20*, 93–103. [CrossRef]
43. Faizi, S.; Sałabun, W.; Ullah, S.; Rashid, T.; Więckowski, J. A new method to support decision-making in an uncertain environment based on normalized interval-valued triangular fuzzy numbers and COMET technique. *Symmetry* **2020**, *12*, 516. [CrossRef]
44. Chen, T.C.T.; Wang, Y.C.; Lin, C.W. A fuzzy collaborative forecasting approach considering experts' unequal levels of authority. *Appl. Soft Comput.* **2020**, *94*, 106455. [CrossRef]
45. Buckley, J.J. Fuzzy hierarchical analysis. *Fuzzy Sets Syst.* **1985**, *17*, 233–247. [CrossRef]
46. Zheng, G.; Zhu, N.; Tian, Z.; Chen, Y.; Sun, B. Application of a trapezoidal fuzzy AHP method for work safety evaluation and early warning rating of hot and humid environments. *Saf. Sci.* **2012**, *50*, 228–239. [CrossRef]
47. Sirisawat, P.; Kiatcharoenpol, T. Fuzzy AHP-TOPSIS approaches to prioritizing solutions for reverse logistics barriers. *Comput. Ind. Eng.* **2018**, *117*, 303–318. [CrossRef]
48. Van Broekhoven, E.; De Baets, B. Fast and accurate center of gravity defuzzification of fuzzy system outputs defined on trapezoidal fuzzy partitions. *Fuzzy Sets Syst.* **2006**, *157*, 904–918. [CrossRef]
49. Wu, H.C.; Chen, T.; Huang, C.H. A piecewise linear FGM approach for efficient and accurate FAHP analysis: Smart backpack design as an example. *Mathematics* **2020**, *8*, 1319. [CrossRef]
50. Saaty, T.L. Axiomatic foundation of the analytic hierarchy process. *Manag. Sci.* **1986**, *32*, 841–855. [CrossRef]
51. Lin, Y.C.; Chen, T. A multibelief analytic hierarchy process and nonlinear programming approach for diversifying product designs: Smart backpack design as an example. *Proc. Inst. Mech. Eng. Part B J. Eng. Manuf.* **2020**, *234*, 1044–1056. [CrossRef]
52. Aydogan, E.K. Performance measurement model for Turkish aviation firms using the rough-AHP and TOPSIS methods under fuzzy environment. *Expert Syst. Appl.* **2011**, *38*, 3992–3998. [CrossRef]
53. Kacprzyk, J.; Fedrizzi, M. A 'soft' measure of consensus in the setting of partial (fuzzy) preferences. *Eur. J. Oper. Res.* **1988**, *34*, 316–325. [CrossRef]
54. Chen, T.; Wang, Y.C. An agent-based fuzzy collaborative intelligence approach for precise and accurate semiconductor yield forecasting. *IEEE Trans. Fuzzy Syst.* **2013**, *22*, 201–211. [CrossRef]
55. Sager, K.L.; Gastil, J. The origins and consequences of consensus decision making: A test of the social consensus model. *South. Commun. J.* **2006**, *71*, 1–24. [CrossRef]
56. Chen, T.; Wang, Y.C. An evolving fuzzy planning mechanism for a ubiquitous manufacturing system. *Int. J. Adv. Manuf. Technol.* **2020**, *108*, 2337–2347. [CrossRef]
57. Chen, T. A collaborative fuzzy-neural approach for long-term load forecasting in Taiwan. *Comput. Ind. Eng.* **2012**, *63*, 663–670. [CrossRef]
58. Chen, T.C.T.; Lin, Y.C. Diverse three-dimensional printing capacity planning for manufacturers. *Robot. Comput. Integr. Manuf.* **2021**, *67*, 102052. [CrossRef]
59. Carnero, M.C. Waste segregation FMEA model integrating intuitionistic fuzzy set and the PAPRIKA method. *Mathematics* **2020**, *8*, 1375. [CrossRef]
60. Huang, D.; Chen, T.; Wang, M.J.J. A fuzzy set approach for event tree analysis. *Fuzzy Sets Syst.* **2001**, *118*, 153–165. [CrossRef]
61. Chaffee, E.E. Three models of strategy. *Acad. Manag. Rev.* **1985**, *10*, 89–98. [CrossRef]
62. Chen, T.; Wu, H.C.; Wang, Y.C. Fuzzy-neural approaches with example post-classification for estimating job cycle time in a wafer fab. *Appl. Soft Comput.* **2009**, *9*, 1225–1231. [CrossRef]
63. Guozheng, Y.; Huixian, C.; Yuliang, L.; Yang, X. The Internet network topology probing method based on classified strategy. In Proceedings of the 2012 Second International Conference on Instrumentation, Measurement, Computer, Communication and Control, Harbin, China, 8–10 December 2012; pp. 1156–1159.
64. Chen, T. Estimating job cycle time in a wafer fabrication factory: A novel and effective approach based on post-classification. *Appl. Soft Comput.* **2016**, *40*, 558–568. [CrossRef]

© 2020 by the authors. Licensee MDPI, Basel, Switzerland. This article is an open access article distributed under the terms and conditions of the Creative Commons Attribution (CC BY) license (http://creativecommons.org/licenses/by/4.0/).

Article

Ridge Fuzzy Regression Modelling for Solving Multicollinearity

Hyoshin Kim [1] and Hye-Young Jung [2,*]

[1] Department of Statistics, North Carolina State University, Raleigh, NC 27695, USA; hkim59@ncsu.edu
[2] Department of Applied Mathematics, Hanyang University, Gyeonggi-do 15588, Korea
* Correspondence: hyjunglove@hanyang.ac.kr

Received: 14 August 2020; Accepted: 10 September 2020; Published: 12 September 2020

Abstract: This paper proposes an α-level estimation algorithm for ridge fuzzy regression modeling, addressing the multicollinearity phenomenon in the fuzzy linear regression setting. By incorporating α-levels in the estimation procedure, we are able to construct a fuzzy ridge estimator which does not depend on the distance between fuzzy numbers. An optimized α-level estimation algorithm is selected which minimizes the root mean squares for fuzzy data. Simulation experiments and an empirical study comparing the proposed ridge fuzzy regression with fuzzy linear regression is presented. Results show that the proposed model can control the effect of multicollinearity from moderate to extreme levels of correlation between covariates, across a wide spectrum of spreads for the fuzzy response.

Keywords: ridge fuzzy regression; α-level estimation algorithm; fuzzy linear regression

1. Introduction

Often times in practical applications, the available data may not always be precise. The researcher may be only accessible to minimum and maximum values of data. Sometimes the data may not even be given in numbers. For instance, consider linguistics data such as "young", "tall", or "high", and medicine data such as "healthy" and "not healthy". In such cases where the given data are imprecise and vague, classical representation of numbers may be insufficient. The fuzzy set theory introduced by Zadeh [1,2] can handle such uncertainty in data. In the view of fuzzy set theory, uncertain data are what is called fuzzy. Fuzzy data are prevalent in various fields such as linguistics, survey, medicine and so forth [3–7]. The development of fuzzy set theory has led to statistical methods for analyzing fuzzy data. When the measure of indeterminacy is needed, the neutrosophic set introduced by Smarandache [8] considered the measure of indeterminacy in addition to the fuzzy set. The neutrosophic statistics based on the the neutrosophic set can be applied for the analysis of the data when data are selected from the population with uncertain, fuzzy, and imprecise observations [9].

In 1982, Tanaka et al. [10] proposed the fuzzy linear regression model which generalizes the usual linear regression model to fuzzy data. Fuzzy regression models have been since then widely used to analyze fuzzy data [11–16].

In classical linear regression models, the multicollinearity phenomenon is frequently observed in which two or more explanatory variables are highly linearly related. Common examples of collinear covariates are: a person's height and weight, a person's level of education, gender, race, and starting salary. When multicollinearity occurs, the least squares estimator may not be obtainable or be subject to very high variance. Once the researcher identifies the collinear variables, there are several techniques the researcher can use to handle multicollinearity. Among these techniques, the two most widely used approaches are lasso regression and ridge regression. Lasso regression developed by Tibshirani [17] and ridge regression developed by Hoerl and Kennard [18] improve model performance by adding a penalty term to the classical linear regression model. Both methods aim to shrink the model parameters towards zero. This induces a sparse model which increases the model bias, but decreases the model variance even more, thus improving overall performance. Ridge regression decreases the parameters of low contributing variables towards zero, but not exactly to zero, and stabilizing the parameter variance of the least squares estimator in the presence of multicollinearity. Lasso regression sets the model parameters exactly to zero, removing low contributing variables as well as improving model fitting. However, sometimes the researcher may want to include all the available covariates in the model without having to reduce the dimension of the data. In such cases, ridge regression is preferred to lasso regression.

Similar to classical linear regression models, multicollinearity occurs frequently in fuzzy linear regression models as well, causing problems in the estimation procedure. Often times the number of covariates is not particularly large for fuzzy data. Consequently, dropping any explanatory variables may not be an option. As in the classical statistical setting, we prefer to use ridge regression to lasso regression to handle multicollinearity in such datasets. In this paper, we incorporate fuzzy set theory with ridge regression developed by Hoerl and Kennard [18] to handle multicollinearity observed in fuzzy data. Only some works have suggested ridge estimation methods for fuzzy linear regression, and are limited to obtaining fuzzy ridge estimators which are dependent on the distance between fuzzy numbers [19–21]. We instead propose an α-level estimation algorithm for ridge fuzzy regression modelling. The proposed algorithm is an extension of the ridge regression model introduced in Choi et al. [22]. By applying α-levels to the estimation procedure, we are able to construct a fuzzy ridge estimator which does not depend on the distance between fuzzy numbers. Simulation experiments show the proposed ridge fuzzy regression model can solve moderate to severe degrees of multicollinearity across a wide range of spreads for the fuzzy response. An empirical study using Tanaka's house prices data [10] with multicollinearity, the most widely applied data set in the fuzzy linear regression literature, is conducted to demonstrate the practical implementations.

The rest of this paper is organized as follows. Section 2 introduces key definitions and results from fuzzy set theory. Section 3 describes the classical ridge regression, followed by a step-by-step procedure for the proposed α-level estimation algorithm of ridge fuzzy regression modeling. Sections 4 and 5 illustrates the performance of the model with simulation studies and a numerical example, respectively. Section 6 concludes the paper.

2. Fuzzy Numbers

A fuzzy set is a set of ordered pairs $A = \{(x, \mu_A(x)) : x \in X\}$ where $\mu_A(x) : X \to [0,1]$ is a membership function which represents the degree of membership of x in a set A. Please note that when A is a crisp (classical) set, its membership function can take only the values one or zero depending on whether or not x does or does not belong to A. In this case, $\mu_A(x)$ reduces to the indicator function $I_A(x)$ of a set A. For any α in $[0,1]$, the α-level set of a fuzzy set A is a crisp set $A(\alpha) = \{x \in X : \mu_A(x) \geq \alpha\}$ which contains all the elements in X with membership value in A greater than or equal to α. The α-level set of a fuzzy set A can also be represented by $A(\alpha) = [l_A(\alpha), r_A(\alpha)]$. Here $l_A(\alpha)$ and $r_A(\alpha)$ are the left and right end-points of the α-level set, respectively. Zadeh's [23] resolution identity theorem states that a fuzzy set can represented by its membership function or by its α-level set. Let A be a fuzzy number with membership function $\mu_A(x)$ and α-cut $A(\alpha)$. Then we have $\mu_A(x) = Sup\{\alpha \cdot I_{A(\alpha)}(x) : \alpha \in [0,1]\}$.

A fuzzy number is a normal and convex subset of the real line R with bounded support. The support of a fuzzy set A is defined by $supp(A) = \{x \in R | \mu_A(x) > 0\}$. The following parametric class of fuzzy numbers, the so-called LR-fuzzy numbers denoted by $A = (a_m, s_l, s_r)_{LR}$, is often used as a special case:

$$\mu_A(x) = \begin{cases} L\left(\dfrac{a_m - x}{s_l}\right) & \text{if } x \leq a_m \\ R\left(\dfrac{x - a_m}{s_r}\right) & \text{if } x > a_m \end{cases} \quad \text{for } x \in R \qquad (1)$$

where $L, R : R \to [0, 1]$ are fixed, left-continuous, and non-increasing functions with $R(0) = L(0) = 1$, and $R(1) = L(1) = 0$. L and R are called left and right shape functions of A, respectively. a_m is the mean value of A, and $s_l, s_r > 0$ are each the left and right spreads of A. The spreads s_l and s_r represent the fuzziness of the fuzzy number and can be symmetric or asymmetric. If $s_l = s_r = 0$, the LR-fuzzy number becomes a precise real number with no fuzziness. Thus, a precise real number can be considered to be a special case of a fuzzy number. For a precise observation $a \in R$, its corresponding membership function is $\mu_a(x) = 1$.

In the fuzzy set theory, triangular and trapezoidal fuzzy numbers are special cases of LR-fuzzy numbers and are used extensively [24]. The membership function of a triangular fuzzy number $A = (a_l, a_m, a_r)_T$ is given by

$$\mu_A(x) = \begin{cases} \dfrac{x - a_l}{a_m - a_l} & \text{if } x \leq a_m \\ \dfrac{a_r - x}{a_r - a_m} & \text{if } x > a_m \end{cases} \quad \text{for } x \in R \qquad (2)$$

where a_l, a_m, and a_r are the left end-point, mid-point, and right end-point, respectively.

3. Ridge Fuzzy Regression

In this section, we propose the α-level estimation algorithm for the proposed ridge fuzzy regression model. This algorithm modifies the method based on Choi et al. [22] to estimate the fuzzy parameters. The term α-level estimation indicates that our algorithm uses α-levels to describe fuzzy data. By using α-level, we are able to develop a ridge fuzzy estimator which is not restricted to the distance between fuzzy numbers. We first briefly examine the original formulation of ridge regression model for crisp data.

3.1. Ridge Regression

Given a data set $\{y_i, x_{i1}, x_{i2}, \cdots, x_{ip}\}_{i=1}^N$, a multiple linear regression model assumes that the relationship between a dependent variable y_i, $i = 1, \cdots, N$ and a set of explanatory variables $x_{i1}, x_{i2}, \cdots, x_{ip}$, $i = 1, \cdots, N$ is linear. The model takes the form

$$y_i = \beta_0 + \beta_1 x_{i1} + \cdots \beta_p x_{ip} + \epsilon_i = X_i^t \beta \quad i = 1, \cdots, N \qquad (3)$$

or written alternatively in matrix notation as $Y = X\beta + \epsilon$. A vector $Y = (y_1, \cdots, y_N)^t$ is a vector of observations on the dependent variable, $X = (X_1^t, \cdots, X_N^t)^t$ is a matrix of explanatory variables, $\beta = (\beta_0, \beta_1, \cdots, \beta_p)^t$ is a vector of regression coefficients to be estimated, and $\epsilon = (\epsilon_1, \cdots, \epsilon_N)^t$ is a vector of error terms. The standard estimator for β is the least squares estimator defined by

$$\hat{\beta} = (X^t X)^{-1} X^t Y. \qquad (4)$$

In the presence of multicollinearity, i.e., in state of extreme correlations among the explanatory variables $\hat{\beta}$ is poorly determined and susceptible to high variance. Thus, we may deliberately bias the regression coefficient estimates so as to control their variance. In this manner, the ridge regression estimator was introduced by Hoerl and Kennard [18] as a penalized least squares estimator. It is achieved by minimizing the residual sum of squares (RSS) subject to a constraint on the size of the estimated coefficient vector [25]:

$$RSS(\lambda) = (Y - X\beta)^t(Y - X\beta) + \lambda \beta^t \beta. \tag{5}$$

Here $\lambda \geq 0$ is a shrinkage parameter which controls the size of the coefficients. The larger the value of λ, the greater the amount of shrinkage, and we have coefficients close to zero. The smaller the value of λ is close to 0, we obtain the least squares solutions. Please note that by convention the input matrix X is assumed to be standardized and Y is assumed to be centered before solving RSS(λ). The ridge regression solution is

$$\hat{\beta}^{ridge} = (X^t X + \lambda I)^{-1} X^t Y$$

where I is the $p \times p$ identity matrix. The shrinkage parameter λ is usually selected via K-fold cross validation. Cross validation is a simple and powerful tool often used to calculate the shrinkage parameter and the prediction error in ridge regression. The entire dataset is divided into K parts, and trains the model on all but the kth part. The model is validated on the kth part, iterating for all $k = 1, \cdots, K$. The choice of K is $K = 5$ or $K = 10$ in general.

3.2. Ridge Fuzzy Regression Algorithm

Let us consider a set of observations

$$\{y_i, x_{i1}, x_{i2}, \cdots, x_{ip}\}_{i=1}^N = \{(y_{il}, y_{im}, y_{ir})_T, (x_{1l}, x_{1m}, x_{1r})_T, \cdots, (x_{pl}, x_{pm}, x_{pr})_T\}_{i=1}^N \tag{6}$$

where the dependent variable y_i, $i = 1, \cdots, N$ and the explanatory variables $x_{i1}, x_{i2}, \cdots, x_{ip}$, $i = 1, \cdots, N$ are triangular fuzzy numbers. We assume a linear relationship between the dependent and explanatory variables:

$$y_i = A_0 \oplus A_1 \odot x_{i1} \oplus \cdots \oplus A_p \odot x_{ip} \oplus \epsilon_i, \quad i = 1, \cdots, N \tag{7}$$

where $\{A_j\}_{j=0}^p = \{(A_{jl}, A_{jm}, A_{jr})_T\}_{j=0}^p$ are the fuzzy regression parameters and $\{\epsilon_i\}_{i=1}^N = \{(\epsilon_{il}, \epsilon_{im}, \epsilon_{ir})_T\}_{i=1}^N$ are the fuzzy error terms. $\oplus$ and $\odot$ represent addition and multiplication between two fuzzy numbers, respectively. Often the N equations are stacked together and written in matrix notation as

$$Y = X \odot A \oplus \epsilon. \tag{8}$$

For more details on arithmetic operations between fuzzy numbers, see [10,26]. Please note that the above fuzzy variables can be symmetric or asymmetric, and be extended to various forms such as normal, parabolic, or square root fuzzy data. Since crisp sets are a special case of fuzzy sets, fuzzy inputs and fuzzy outputs, or fuzzy inputs and crisp outputs combinations are also possible. For illustration purposes, in this section, we present our ridge fuzzy regression model using triangular membership functions.

We divide the given data into training and test sets. The model is computed from the training set $\{y_i, x_{i1}, x_{i2}, \cdots, x_{ip}\}_{i=1}^n$, and later its performance is evaluated on the test set $\{y_i, x_{i1}, x_{i2}, \cdots, x_{ip}\}_{i=1}^m$. Note again that N is the total number of observations, n is the number of observations for the training set, and m is the number of observations for the test set, such that $n + m = N$. We fit our ridge fuzzy regression model on the training set by the following estimation algorithm:

Step 1: Create α-level sets of the triangular fuzzy input and output as illustrated in Figure 1. For any α-level in $[0, 1]$,

$$y_i(\alpha) = [l_{y_i}(\alpha), r_{y_i}(\alpha)] \tag{9}$$
$$= [(\alpha-1)s_{il}^y + y_{im}, -(\alpha-1)s_{ir}^y + y_{im}]$$
$$x_{ij}(\alpha) = [l_{x_{ij}}(\alpha), r_{x_{ij}}(\alpha)] \tag{10}$$
$$= [(\alpha-1)s_{ijl}^x + x_{ijm}, -(\alpha-1)s_{ijr}^x + x_{ijm}] \quad i=1,\cdots,n, \quad j=1,\cdots,p$$

where $s_{il}^y, s_{ir}^y, s_{ijl}^x, s_{ijr}^x \geq 0$ are the left and right spreads of the dependent and explanatory variables, respectively. The α-levels are denoted by the sequence $(\alpha_k)_{k=0}^K$ for some K with $\alpha_k \in [0,1]$.

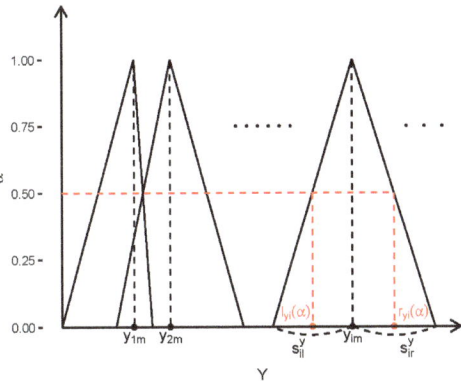

Figure 1. Fuzzy output data.

Step 2: Perform ridge regression of $Y(\alpha_k)$ on $X(\alpha_k)$ for each $k = 0, \cdots, K$. Find the intermediate estimators $\overline{l_A}(\alpha_k)$ and $\overline{r_A}(\alpha_k)$ of $l_A(\alpha_k)$ and $r_A(\alpha_k)$ by minimizing the following respective ridge loss functions (see Figure 2).

$$(l_Y(\alpha_k) - l_X(\alpha_k)l_A(\alpha_k))^t(l_Y(\alpha_k) - l_X(\alpha_k)l_A(\alpha_k)) + \lambda l_A(\alpha_k)^t l_A(\alpha_k) \tag{11}$$
$$(r_Y(\alpha_k) - r_X(\alpha_k)r_A(\alpha_k))^t(r_Y(\alpha_k) - r_X(\alpha_k)r_A(\alpha_k)) + \lambda r_A(\alpha_k)^t r_A(\alpha_k)$$

We assume the endpoints of the α-level set of Y has been centered and the endpoints of α-level set of X has been standardized as is by convention in classical ridge regression [25].

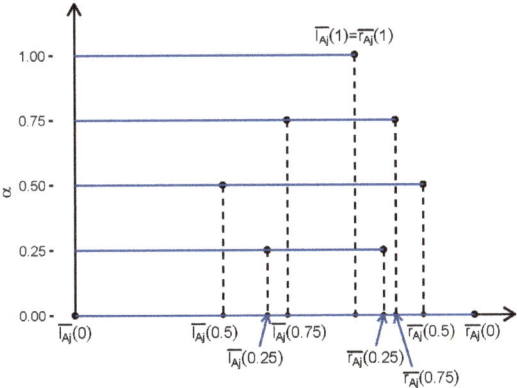

Figure 2. Intermediate estimators $\overline{l_{A_j}}(\alpha_k)$ and $\overline{l_{A_j}}(\alpha_k)$ for the α-level sequence $(0, 0.25, 0.5, 0.75, 1)$.

Step 3: Obtain the estimators $\widetilde{l}_A(\alpha_k)$ and $\widetilde{r}_A(\alpha_k)$ of $l_A(\alpha_k)$ and $r_A(\alpha_k)$ by modifying the intermediate estimators $\overline{l_A}(\alpha_k)$ and $\overline{r_A}(\alpha_k)$ so that the estimated coefficients form the membership function of a triangular fuzzy number. For this the following operations are performed (see Figure 3).

$$\widetilde{l}_A(\alpha_K) = \widetilde{r}_A(\alpha_K) = \overline{l_A}(\alpha_K) = \overline{r_A}(\alpha_K) \tag{12}$$
$$\widetilde{l}_A(\alpha_k) = \min\{\overline{l_A}(\alpha_k), \widetilde{l}_A(\alpha_{k+1})\} \quad k = K-1, K-2, \cdots, 0$$
$$\widetilde{r}_A(\alpha_k) = \max\{\overline{r_A}(\alpha_k), \widetilde{r}_A(\alpha_{k+1})\} \quad k = K-1, K-2, \cdots, 0$$

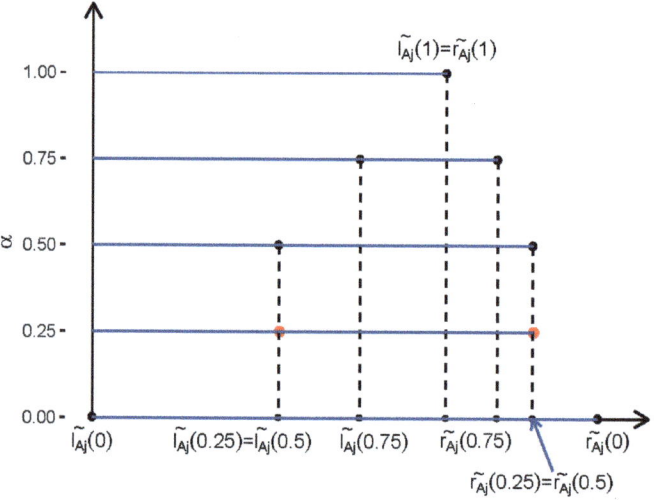

Figure 3. Modified estimators $\widetilde{l}_{A_j}(\alpha_k)$ and $\widetilde{l}_{A_j}(\alpha_k)$ for the α-level sequence $(0, 0.25, 0.5, 0.75, 1)$.

Step 4: Estimate the triangular fuzzy coefficient $\widehat{A} = (\widehat{A}_l, \widehat{A}_m, \widehat{A}_r)_T$ and its membership function $\mu_{\widehat{A}}$ by fitting a linear regression line through $\widetilde{l}_A(\alpha_k)$ and $\widetilde{r}_A(\alpha_k)$ for $k = 0, \cdots, K$, respectively. A constraint is given so that $\mu_{\widehat{A}}$ satisfy the condition of $\mu_{\widehat{A}}(\widetilde{l}_A(1)) = \mu_{\widehat{A}}(\widetilde{r}_A(1)) = 1$ (see Figure 4).

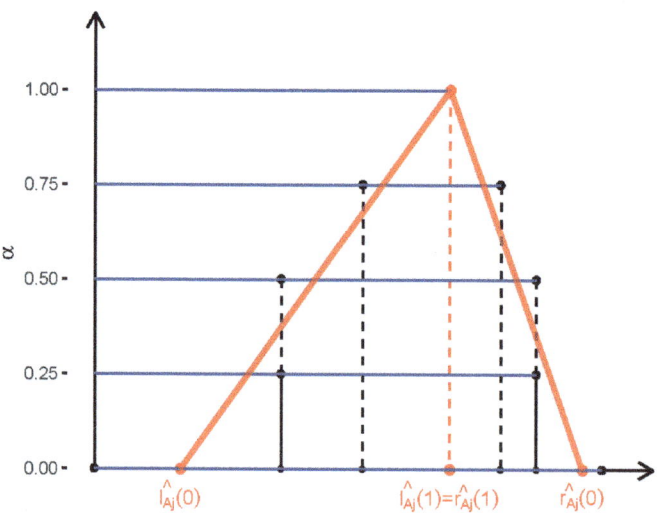

Figure 4. Estimated fuzzy coefficient $\widehat{A}_j = (\widehat{A}_{jl}, \widehat{A}_{jm}, \widehat{A}_{jr})_T$ and its membership function.

Step 5: Symmetric fuzzy inputs or outputs do not always guarantee that the estimated membership function $\mu_{\widehat{A}}$ will also be symmetric. To reduce the difference between the true values with the fitted values we consider the following candidates:

$$\mu_{\widehat{A}}(x) = \begin{cases} \dfrac{x - \widehat{l_A}(0)}{\widehat{l_A}(1) - \widehat{l_A}(0)} & \text{if } x \leq \widehat{l_A}(1) = \widehat{r_A}(1) \\ \dfrac{\widehat{r_A}(0) - x}{\widehat{r_A}(0) - \widehat{r_A}(1)} & \text{if } x > \widehat{l_A}(1) = \widehat{r_A}(1) \end{cases} \quad \text{for } x \in R \tag{13}$$

or

$$\mu_{\widehat{A}}(x) = \begin{cases} \dfrac{x - \widehat{l_A}(0)}{\widehat{l_A}(1) - \widehat{l_A}(0)} & \text{if } x \leq \widehat{l_A}(1) \\ \dfrac{\widehat{l_A}(0) + x}{\widehat{l_A}(1) - \widehat{l_A}(0)} & \text{if } x > \widehat{l_A}(1) \end{cases} \quad \text{for } x \in R \tag{14}$$

where $\widehat{r_A}(0)$ is chosen as $\widehat{r_A}(0) = 2 \times \widehat{l_A}(1) - \widehat{l_A}(0)$, or

$$\mu_{\widehat{A}}(x) = \begin{cases} \dfrac{\widehat{r_A}(0) + x}{\widehat{r_A}(0) - \widehat{r_A}(1)} & \text{if } x \leq \widehat{r_A}(1) \\ \dfrac{\widehat{r_A}(0) - x}{\widehat{r_A}(0) - \widehat{r_A}(1)} & \text{if } x > \widehat{r_A}(1) \end{cases} \quad \text{for } x \in R \tag{15}$$

where $\widehat{l_A}(0)$ is chosen as $\widehat{l_A}(0) = 2 \times \widehat{r_A}(1) - \widehat{r_A}(0)$.

We present two performance criteria based on Diamond's fuzzy distance measure [27] to evaluate the proposed fuzzy estimators. Denote the dependent variable as $y_i = (y_{il}, y_{im}, y_{ir})_T$, $i = 1, \cdots, n$, and its predicted value as $\widehat{y}_i = (\widehat{y_{il}}, \widehat{y_{im}}, \widehat{y_{ir}})_T = (X_{il}^t \widehat{A_l}, X_{im}^t \widehat{A_m}, X_{ir}^t \widehat{A_r})_T$, $i = 1, \cdots, n$. Here n is the number of observations for the training set. We defined RMSE$_F$ (root mean square error for fuzzy numbers) and MAPE$_F$ (mean absolute percentage error for fuzzy numbers) as below.

$$\text{RMSE}_F = \sqrt{\frac{1}{n} \sum_{i=1}^n \{(y_{il} - \widehat{y_{il}})^2 + (y_{im} - \widehat{y_{im}})^2 + (y_{ir} - \widehat{y_{ir}})^2\}} \tag{16}$$

$$\text{MAPE}_F = \frac{100\%}{n} \sum_{i=1}^n (|y_{il} - \widehat{y_{il}}| + |y_{im} - \widehat{y_{im}}| + |y_{ir} - \widehat{y_{ir}}|) \tag{17}$$

Compute the RMSE$_F$ for each of the membership functions, then select the one which minimizes the criterion.

Step 6: Repeat Steps 1–5 for selected α-level sequences $(\alpha_k)_{k=0}^K$ with α_k equally spaced between 0 and 1. Choose the optimal set of α-levels which minimizes RMSE$_F$. Finally, compute the fuzzy ridge coefficient estimate $\widehat{A}$ based on that selected sequence.

4. Simulation Study

A simulation study was conducted to illustrate the performance of the proposed ridge fuzzy regression model in the presence of multicollinearity. Simulation results are compared with the fuzzy linear regression model with varying degrees of correlation. The fuzzy least squares estimator is obtained by setting the tuning parameter λ as zero in Step 2 of Section 3.2.

We generated $N = 100$ observations for each of the $p = 4$ crisp explanatory variables. The number of data dimensions is in line with commonly found fuzzy data. Following Gibbons [28], the explanatory variables x_{ij} are generated by

$$x_{ij} = (1-\rho^2)^{1/2} z_{ij} + \rho z_{ip}, \quad i=1,\cdots,n \quad j=1,\cdots,p \tag{18}$$

where ρ is a given constant and z_{ij} are generated from independent normal distributions with mean 50 and variance 1. Here x_{ij} are assumed to be non-negative so as to reflect the non-negative characteristics of real world fuzzy data. The degree of linear association between explanatory variables is controlled via ρ, where in this case is the correlation between any two explanatory variables is ρ^2. Three different sets of correlation are considered corresponding to $\rho = 0.8$, 0.9, and 0.99. Each value of ρ stands for moderate, high, and very high correlation between the variables. Observations on the fuzzy dependent variable are generated by

$$y_{il} = A_{0l} + A_{1l}x_{i1} + \cdots + A_{pl}x_{ip} + \epsilon_i^1 \tag{19}$$
$$y_{im} = A_{0m} + A_{1m}x_{i1} + \cdots + A_{pm}x_{ip} + \epsilon_i^2$$
$$y_{ir} = A_{0r} + A_{1r}x_{i1} + \cdots + A_{pr}x_{ip} + \epsilon_i^3, \quad i=1,\cdots,N$$

where $\epsilon_i^1, \epsilon_i^2, \epsilon_i^3$ are generated from independent normal distributions with mean 0 and variance σ^2. Four values of σ are investigated in this study: 0.5, 1, 1.5, and 2. Large values of σ correspond to bigger variation in the spreads of the fuzzy dependent variable. $S_l^y = (s_{1l}^y, \cdots, s_{Nl}^y)^t$ the vector of left spreads and $S_r^y = (s_{1r}^y, \cdots, s_{Nr}^y)^t$ the vector of right spreads are determined by

$$s_{il}^y = y_{im} - y_{il} \tag{20}$$
$$s_{ir}^y = y_{ir} - y_{im} \quad i=1,\cdots,N.$$

Cases of asymmetric spreads, $S_l^y \neq S_r^y$, and symmetric spreads, $S_l^y = S_r^y$ are also compared. The supposed parameters of the model are: $A_l = (0, 0.1, 0.15, 0.2, 0.25)$, $A_m = (0, 0.4, 0.45, 0.5, 0.55)$, and $A_r = (0, 0.7, 0.75, 0.8, 0.85)$. In order to analyze the effects of factors ρ and σ, we controlled for the effects of varying α-level sequences in Step 6 of Section 3.2. For both models we fixed the α-level sequence as (0, 0.25, 0.5, 0.75, 1).

200 replicates for each scenario are generated. The explanatory variables and the fuzzy coefficients remain fixed, while the error terms and hence the fuzzy dependent variable changes. We separated the simulated data into training and test sets. Once the ridge fuzzy regression model and the fuzzy linear regression model are fit to the training data, RMSE_F and MAPE_F are computed from the test set for $t=1,\cdots,200$ replicates. Let RMSE_F^t and MAPE_F^t be the performance measures when the fuzzy model is applied to the replicate t. The following quantities are then computed for each fuzzy estimator:

$$\text{Ave. RMSE}_F = \frac{1}{200}\sum_{t=1}^{200}\text{RMSE}_F^t \tag{21}$$

$$\text{Ave. MAPE}_F = \frac{1}{200}\sum_{t=1}^{200}\text{MAPE}_F^t. \tag{22}$$

In addition, we fit the ridge regression model and the linear regression model on the mid-point of our training data $\{y_{im}, x_{i1m}, x_{i2m}, \cdots, x_{ipm}\}_{i=1}^n$ for comparison with fuzzy methods. The test Ave. RMSE and Ave. MAPE values of 200 replicates are recorded for both models. The output from numerical experiments is suggested below in Tables 1–6. Measures of performance are summarized for all combinations of factors ρ, σ and whether the fuzzy output is symmetric or not. The following remarks can be made on the basis of Tables 1–6:

1. Ave. RMSE and Ave. MAPE do not depend on whether the spreads are symmetric or not as they are computed from the mid-points of the generated data. Ridge regression achieves smaller Ave. RMSE than linear regression in all cases. Ridge regression achieves smaller or nearly equal Ave. MAPE with linear regression in all cases. If the Ave. RMSE of ridge regression is smaller

2. Ave. RMSE$_F$ increases as σ increases for both models. As σ and ρ increases, the Ave. RMSE$_F$ difference between ridge fuzzy regression and fuzzy linear regression increases as well. Ave. RMSE$_F$ values are larger when the spreads are symmetric. In all scenarios, ridge fuzzy regression Ave. RMSE$_F$ values almost always outperform those of fuzzy linear regression.
3. Ave. MAPE$_F$ exhibit near identical patterns with Ave. RMSE$_F$. For both ridge fuzzy regression and fuzzy linear regression, Ave. MAPE$_F$ is larger for bigger σ values. The difference between the two models increases as σ and ρ increases. When the fuzzy dependent variable is symmetric the Ave. MAPE$_F$ values are larger than when it is asymmetric. Ave. MAPE$_F$ is in general lower for ridge fuzzy regression than fuzzy linear regression for all σ and ρ combinations and asymmetric, symmetric outputs.

Table 1. The performance measures when $\rho = 0.8$ and the dependent variable is an asymmetric triangular fuzzy number.

	σ:	0.5	1.0	1.5	2.0
Ave. RMSE$_F$	Ridge Fuzzy Reg.	1.161	4.459	10.955	19.419
	Fuzzy Reg.	1.706	8.979	23.130	40.243
Ave. RMSE	Ridge Reg.	0.478	0.957	1.437	1.917
	Linear Reg.	0.481	0.962	1.444	1.925
Ave. MAPE$_F$	Ridge Fuzzy Reg.	1.84%	7.64%	19.26%	34.43%
	Fuzzy Reg.	2.83%	15.81%	41.14%	71.71%
Ave. MAPE	Ridge Reg.	0.31%	0.61%	0.91%	1.21%
	Linear Reg.	0.31%	0.61%	0.92%	1.23%

Table 2. The performance measures when $\rho = 0.8$ and the dependent variable is a symmetric triangular fuzzy number.

	σ:	0.5	1.0	1.5	2.0
Ave. RMSE$_F$	Ridge Fuzzy Reg.	3.604	8.150	19.944	22.572
	Fuzzy Reg.	6.273	19.228	39.020	61.870
Ave. RMSE	Ridge Reg.	0.478	0.957	1.437	1.917
	Linear Reg.	0.481	0.962	1.444	1.925
Ave. MAPE$_F$	Ridge Fuzzy Reg.	5.89%	13.64%	25.52%	38.88%
	Fuzzy Reg.	10.72%	33.72%	69.03%	109.8%
Ave. MAPE	Ridge Reg.	0.31%	0.61%	0.91%	1.21%
	Linear Reg.	0.31%	0.61%	0.92%	1.23%

Table 3. The performance measures when $\rho = 0.9$ and the dependent variable is an asymmetric triangular fuzzy number.

	σ:	0.5	1.0	1.5	2.0
Ave. RMSE$_F$	Ridge Fuzzy Reg.	1.210	4.612	11.625	20.995
	Fuzzy Reg.	2.879	17.321	38.918	63.449
Ave. RMSE	Ridge Reg.	0.478	0.959	1.440	1.921
	Linear Reg.	0.481	0.962	1.444	1.925
Ave. MAPE$_F$	Ridge Fuzzy Reg.	2.02%	8.29%	21.47%	39.05%
	Fuzzy Reg.	5.19%	32.26%	72.62%	118.4%
Ave. MAPE	Ridge Reg.	0.32%	0.64%	0.95%	1.27%
	Linear Reg.	0.32%	0.64%	0.96%	1.28%

Table 4. The performance measures when $\rho = 0.9$ and the dependent variable is a symmetric triangular fuzzy number.

	σ:	0.5	1.0	1.5	2.0
Ave. $RMSE_F$	Ridge Fuzzy Reg.	3.306	8.356	16.036	25.076
	Fuzzy Reg.	8.378	30.691	60.041	91.664
Ave. $RMSE$	Ridge Reg.	0.478	0.959	1.440	1.921
	Linear Reg.	0.481	0.962	1.444	1.925
Ave. $MAPE_F$	Ridge Fuzzy Reg.	5.60%	14.71%	28.85%	45.47%
	Fuzzy Reg.	15.23%	56.89%	111.7%	170.6%
Ave. $MAPE$	Ridge Reg.	0.32%	0.64%	0.95%	1.27%
	Linear Reg.	0.32%	0.64%	0.96%	1.28%

Table 5. The performance measures when $\rho = 0.99$ and the dependent variable is an asymmetric triangular fuzzy number.

	σ:	0.5	1.0	1.5	2.0
Ave. $RMSE_F$	Ridge Fuzzy Reg.	0.952	2.378	6.822	14.514
	Fuzzy Reg.	34.201	101.27	171.70	243.33
Ave. $RMSE$	Ridge Reg.	0.440	0.874	1.310	1.746
	Linear Reg.	0.443	0.885	1.328	1.771
Ave. $MAPE_F$	Ridge Fuzzy Reg.	1.80%	4.70%	14.53%	31.64%
	Fuzzy Reg.	75.07%	222.3%	377.1%	535.0%
Ave.$MAPE$	Ridge Reg.	0.37%	0.74%	1.11%	1.49%
	Linear Reg.	0.38%	0.76%	1.14%	1.52%

Table 6. The performance measures when $\rho = 0.99$ and the dependent variable is a symmetric triangular fuzzy number.

	σ:	0.5	1.0	1.5	2.0
Ave. $RMSE_F$	Ridge Fuzzy Reg.	2.471	6.266	13.195	23.077
	Fuzzy Reg.	55.455	142.97	233.84	325.40
Ave. $RMSE$	Ridge Reg.	0.440	0.874	1.310	1.746
	Linear Reg.	0.443	0.885	1.328	1.771
Ave. $MAPE_F$	Ridge Fuzzy Reg.	4.70%	12.53%	27.65%	49.26%
	Fuzzy Reg.	121.5%	313.5%	513.2%	714.9%
Ave. $MAPE$	Ridge Reg.	0.37%	0.74%	1.11%	1.49%
	Linear Reg.	0.38%	0.76%	1.14%	1.52%

5. Empirical Study

In this section, we demonstrate the performance of the proposed ridge fuzzy regression model on an illustrative example taken from Tanaka [10]. The performance of the ridge fuzzy regression estimator is compared with the fuzzy least squares estimator for crisp explanatory variables and a fuzzy dependent variable. The linear regression fuzzy model from Tanaka [10] is further compared to illustrate the performance of the ridge fuzzy regression model. For both the ridge fuzzy regression and the linear fuzzy model, the α-level sequences $\alpha_k = r \times k, k = 0, \cdots, K$ for some r and K are chosen as candidates for Step 6 of the estimation algorithm in Section 3.2. The list of α-level sequences is presented in Table 7.

Table 7. The list of α-level sequences for Step 6 of the estimation algorithm.

$\alpha_k = r \times k, k = 0, \cdots, K$		
No.	r	K
1	0.01	100
2	0.02	50
3	0.025	40
4	0.04	25
5	0.05	20
6	0.1	10
7	0.15	6
8	0.2	5
9	0.25	4
10	0.3	3
11	0.5	2
12	1	1

Example: House Prices Data

Tanaka et al. [10] presents a data set concerning the price mechanism of prefabricated houses. The relationship between five crisp inputs (rank of material, first floor space (m^2), second first floor space (m^2), number of rooms and number of Japanese-style rooms) and a fuzzy output (house price) is investigated. The complete data is shown in Table 8. The fitted values for the ridge fuzzy model and the linear fuzzy model is shown in Table 9. Results show the predicted values from the ridge fuzzy regression more accurately describes the original data than fuzzy linear regression. This is again clarified in Figure 5. In the triangular fuzzy plot of the observed and fitted values, a comparison of the two models is shown. The black triangles correspond to the observed values, the red triangles in Figure 5a to the ridge fuzzy fitted values, and the blue triangles in Figure 5b to the fuzzy linear fitted values. Both methods estimated the mid-points of the fuzzy dependent variable well. The spreads however, are shorter for the proposed ridge fuzzy regression than the other. The fitted equation for the ridge fuzzy regression is given by

$$\hat{Y} = (-1839.23, -1156.78, -474.32) + (1874.56, 1874.56, 1874.56)x_1 + \qquad (23)$$
$$(73.73, 75.29, 76.85)x_2 + (59.04, 65.57, 72.10)x_3 +$$
$$(-149.93, -149.93, -149.93)x_4 + (543.50, 587.74, 631.98)x_5$$

and for the fuzzy linear regression, the fitted equation is

$$\hat{Y} = (-2038.12, -1129.61, -221.09) + (2386.56, 2386.56, 2386.56)x_1 + \qquad (24)$$
$$(87.13, 93.37, 99.60)x_2 + (71.72, 82.13, 92.54)x_3 +$$
$$(-376.35, -376.35, -376.35)x_4 + (-285.03, -188.25, -91.48)x_5.$$

Please note that the fitted equation for the linear regression fuzzy model shown in Tanaka et al. [10] is

$$\hat{Y} = (10,220, 11,040, 11,860) + (1810, 1810, 1810)x_1 + \qquad (25)$$
$$(1770, 2140, 2510)x_2 + (870, 870, 870)x_3 +$$
$$(-540, -540, -540)x_4 + (-180, -180, -180)x_5.$$

An analysis of the α-level sequences used in Step 6 of the estimation algorithm is presented in Figure 6. The α-level sequence which minimizes RMSE$_F$ was chosen as the optimal α-level sequence for each of the models. The red dots in Figure 6a,b each indicate the chosen α-level sequence based on RMSE$_F$. For the ridge fuzzy regression, $\alpha_k = r \times k, k = 0, \cdots, K$ with $r = 0.01, K = 100$ was chosen. In the case of fuzzy linear regression, $r = 0.5, K = 2$ was selected.

Table 8. Houses prices data.

No.	$Y = (y_m, S_l^y = S_r^y)$	x_1	x_2	x_3	x_4	x_5
1	(6060, 550)	1	38.09	36.43	5	1
2	(7100, 50)	1	62.10	26.50	6	1
3	(8080, 400)	1	63.76	44.71	7	1
4	(8260, 150)	1	74.52	38.09	8	1
5	(8650, 750)	1	75.38	41.40	7	2
6	(8520, 450)	2	52.99	26.49	4	2
7	(9170, 700)	2	62.93	26.49	5	2
8	(10,310, 200)	2	72.04	33.12	6	3
9	(10,920, 600)	2	76.12	43.06	7	2
10	(12,030, 100)	2	90.26	42.64	7	2
11	(13,940, 350)	3	85.70	31.33	6	3
12	(14,200, 250)	3	95.27	27.64	6	3
13	(16,010, 300)	3	105.98	27.64	6	3
14	(16,320, 500)	3	79.25	66.81	6	3
15	(16,990, 650)	3	120.50	32.25	6	3

Table 9. Fitted values of house prices data.

No.	$Y = (y_m, S_l^y = S_r^y)$	Ridge Fuzzy Reg.	Fuzzy Reg.
1	(6060, 550)	(5812.32, 1024.08)	(5735.21, 1621.95)
2	(7100, 50)	(6819.04, 996.70)	(6785.09, 1668.23)
3	(8080, 400)	(7988.07, 1118.22)	(8059.27, 1868.14)
4	(8260, 150)	(8214.21, 1091.78)	(8143.87, 1866.29)
5	(8650, 750)	(9233.67, 1158.99)	(8684.11, 2002.89)
6	(8520, 450)	(8894.65, 1026.66)	(8884.70, 1708.12)
7	(9170, 700)	(9493.11, 1042.17)	(9436.42, 1,770.07)
8	(10,310, 200)	(11,051.53, 1143.94)	(10,266.90, 1992.65)
9	(10,920, 600)	(11,272.79, 1170.98)	(11,276.09, 2024.78)
10	(12,030, 100)	(12,309.87, 1190.31)	(12,561.81, 2108.54)
11	(13,940, 350)	(13,837.21, 1153.57)	(13,781.85, 2059.16)
12	(14,200, 250)	(14,315.80, 1144.40)	(14,372.32, 2080.39)
13	(16,010, 300)	(15,122.16, 1161.12)	(15,372.29, 2147.15)
14	(16,320, 500)	(15,677.92, 1375.23)	(16,093.51, 2388.31)
15	(16,990, 650)	(16,517.66, 1213.89)	(17,106.59, 2285.64)

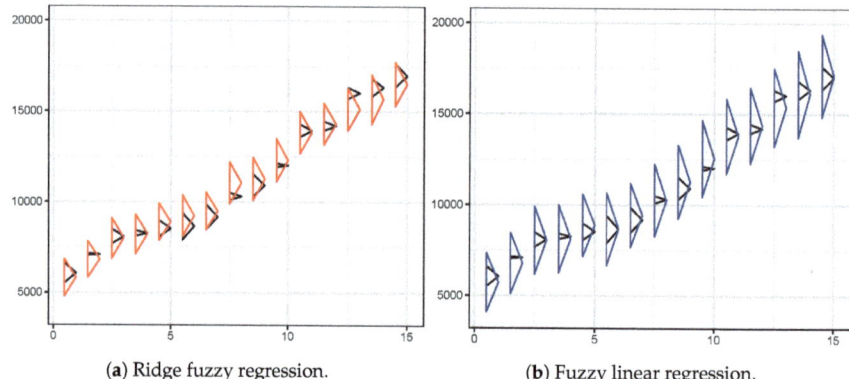

(a) Ridge fuzzy regression. (b) Fuzzy linear regression.

Figure 5. The triangular fuzzy plot of observed and fitted values. (**a**): Ridge fuzzy regression and (**b**): Fuzzy linear regression.

In Table 10 the performance measures $RMSE_F$ and $MAPE_F$ ridge fuzzy regression are compared with the fuzzy linear regression model and the linear regression fuzzy model from Tanaka et al. [10].

Clearly both measures are greatly reduced for the ridge fuzzy regression compared to the other models, suggesting that the proposed ridge fuzzy regression model provides a better fit of the data in comparison to the two methods.

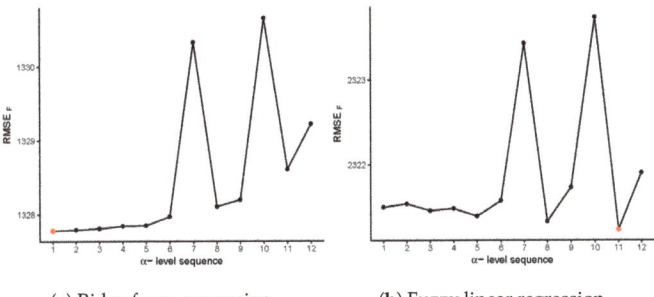

(a) Ridge fuzzy regression. (b) Fuzzy linear regression.

Figure 6. Analysis of the α-level sequences in Step 6 of the estimation algorithm. (**a**): Ridge fuzzy regression and (**b**): Fuzzy linear regression.

Table 10. $RMSE_F$ and $MAPE_F$ fuzzy performance measures for ridge fuzzy regression, fuzzy linear regression, and the linear regression fuzzy model from Tanaka et al. [10].

	$RMSE_F$	$MAPE_F$
Ridge Fuzzy Reg.	1327.78	18%
Fuzzy Reg.	2321.24	33%
Tanaka et al.	349,851.8	55%

6. Conclusions

This paper proposes an α-level estimation algorithm for ridge fuzzy regression modeling, extending the ridge regression model introduced in Choi et al. [22]. As shown in simulation studies and an empirical study, the proposed ridge fuzzy regression model can handle fuzzy data sets with crisp inputs and triangular fuzzy outputs. The same procedure is available with fuzzy inputs and fuzzy outputs, or fuzzy inputs and crisp outputs. In previous works, estimation methods for ridge fuzzy regression depend on the distance between fuzzy numbers. By incorporating α-levels to ridge fuzzy regression, we are able to construct the ridge fuzzy estimator without having to define the distance between fuzzy numbers. Simulation results show the ridge fuzzy regression model reduces the effect of multicollinearity over a wide range of spreads for the fuzzy response, for various levels of correlation between inputs. In the illustrative example taken from Tanaka et al. [10], we have shown the practical implementations of our method. Comparison is made with fuzzy linear regression with respect to RMSE and MAPE for fuzzy numbers. Overall these results demonstrate the effectiveness of ridge regression in fuzzy data.

An importance point to note is that typically ridge regression is preferred over lasso regression when the objective of research is to handle multicollinearity while not wanting to remove low contributing variables. However, when the dimension of the data is large and dropping collinear variables is necessary, one may use lasso regression rather than ridge regression. To manage such cases, in future studies we plan to extend the proposed α-level estimation algorithm for ridge fuzzy models to lasso fuzzy regression models. Lasso fuzzy regression will be especially useful for modeling correlated genetic data sets.

In addition, the present study can be extended for neutrosophic statistics [9,29–35] as future research.

Author Contributions: Conceptualization, H.K. and H.-Y.J.; methodology, H.-Y.J.; software, H.K.; validation, H.K. and H.-Y.J.; formal analysis, H.K.; investigation, H.K.; resources, H.K.; data curation, H.K.; writing–original draft preparation, H.K.; writing–review and editing, H.K. and H.-Y.J.; visualization, H.K.; supervision, H.-Y.J.; project administration, H.-Y.J.; funding acquisition, H.-Y.J. Both authors have read and agreed to the published version of the manuscript.

Funding: This work was supported by the National Research Foundation of Korea (NRF) grant funded by the Korea government (MSIT) (No.2017R1C1B1005069, No.2019R1I1A1A01046810).

Conflicts of Interest: The authors declare no conflict of interest.

References

1. Zadeh, L. Fuzzy sets. *Inf. Control* **1965**, *8*, 338–353. [CrossRef]
2. Zadeh, L. Probability measures of fuzzy events. *J. Math. Anal. Appl.* **1968**, *23*, 421–427. [CrossRef]
3. Barro, S.; Marin, R. *Fuzzy Logic in Medicine*; Springer: Berlin/Heidelberg, Germany, 2002.
4. Bellamy, J.E. Medical diagnosis, diagnostic spaces, and fuzzy systems. *J. Am. Vet. Med. Assoc.* **1997**, *210*, 390–396. [CrossRef] [PubMed]
5. Jung, H.Y.; Choi, H.; Park, T. Fuzzy heaping mechanism for heaped count data with imprecision. *Soft Comput.* **2018**, *22*, 4585–4594. [CrossRef]
6. Jung, H.Y.; Leem, S.; Lee, S.; Park, T. A novel fuzzy set based multifactor dimensionality reduction method for detecting gene-gene interaction. *Comput. Biol. Chem.* **2016**, *65*, 193–202. [CrossRef]
7. Jung, H.Y.; Leem, S.; Park, T. Fuzzy set-based generalized multifactor dimensionality reduction analysis of gene-gene interactions. *BMC Med. Genom.* **2018**, *11*. [CrossRef]
8. Smarandache, F. *A Unifying Field in Logics: Neutrosophic Logic. Neutrosophy, Neutrosophic Set, Neutrosophic Probability: Neutrsophic Logic. Neutrosophy, Neutrosophic Set, Neutrosophic Probability*; Infinite Study: Austin, TX, USA, 2005.
9. Aslam, M.; Arif, O.H.; Sherwani, R.A.K. New diagnosis test under the neutrosophic statistics: An application to diabetic patients. *BioMed Res. Int.* **2020**, *2020*, 2086185.
10. Tanaka, H.; Uejima, S.; Asai, K. Linear regression analysis with fuzzy model. *IEEE Trans. Syst. Man Cybern.* **1982**, *12*, 903–907. [CrossRef]
11. Chang, P.T.; Lee, E. Fuzzy least absolute deviations regression and the conflicting trends in fuzzy parameters. *Comput. Math. Appl.* **1994**, *28*, 89–101. [CrossRef]
12. Choi, S.H.; Jung, H.Y.; Lee, W.J.; Yoon, J.H. Fuzzy regression model with monotonic response function. *Commun. Korean Math. Soc.* **2018**, *33*, 973–983. [CrossRef]
13. Icen, D.; Gunay, S. Design and implementation of the fuzzy expert system in Monte Carlo methods for fuzzy linear regression. *Appl. Soft Comput.* **2019**, *77*, 399–411. [CrossRef]
14. Jung, H.Y.; Yoon, J.H.; Choi, S.H. Fuzzy linear regression using rank transform method. *Fuzzy Sets Syst.* **2015**, *274*, 97–108. [CrossRef]
15. Lee, W.J.; Jung, H.Y.; Yoon, J.H.; Choi, S.H. The statistical inferences of fuzzy regression based on bootstrap techniques. *Appl. Soft Comput.* **2015**, *19*, 883–890. [CrossRef]
16. Sohn, S.Y.; Kim, D.H.; Yoon, J.H. Technology credit scoring model with fuzzy logistic regression. *Appl. Soft Comput.* **2016**, *43*, 150–158. [CrossRef]
17. Tibshirani, R. Regression shrinkage and selection via the lasso. *J. R. Stat. Soc. Ser. (Methodol.)* **1996**, *58*, 267–288. [CrossRef]
18. Hoerl, A.E.; Kennard, R.W. Ridge Regression: Biased Estimation for Nonorthogonal Problems. *Technometrics* **1970**, *12*, 55–67. Available online: http://www.jstor.org/stable/1267351 (accessed on 14 May 2020).
19. Hong, D.H.; Hwang, C. Ridge Regression Procedures For Fuzzy Models Using Triangular Fuzzy Numbers. *Int. J. Uncertain. Fuzziness Knowl.-Based Syst.* **2004**, *12*, 145–159. [CrossRef]
20. Hong, D.H.; Hwang, C.; Ahn, C. Ridge estimation for regression models with crisp inputs and Gaussian fuzzy output. *Fuzzy Sets Syst.* **2004**, *142*, 307–319. [CrossRef]
21. Donoso, S.; Marin, N.; Vila, M.A. Quadratic Programming Models for Fuzzy Regression. In Proceedings of the International Conference on Mathematical and Statistical Modeling in Honor of Enrique Castillo, Ciudad Real, Spain, 28–30 June 2006.
22. Choi, S.H.; Jung, H.Y.; Kim, H. Ridge Fuzzy Regression Model. *Int. J. Fuzzy Syst.* **2019**. [CrossRef]

23. Zadeh, L. The concept of a linguistic variable and its application to approximate reasoning—I. *Inf. Sci.* **1975**, *8*, 199–249. [CrossRef]
24. Dubois, D.; Prade, H. *Fuzzy Sets and Systems: Theory and Applications*; Academic Press: Cambridge, MA, USA, 1980.
25. Hastie, T.; Tibshirani, R.; Friedman, J. *The Elements of Statistical Learning: Data Mining, Inference, and Prediction*, 2nd ed.; Springer: Berlin/Heidelberg, Germany, 2009.
26. Tanaka, H.; Lee, H. Interval regression analysis by quadratic programming approach. *IEEE Trans. Fuzzy Syst.* **1998**, *6*, 473–481. [CrossRef]
27. Diamond, P. Fuzzy least squares. *Inf. Sci.* **1988**, *46*, 141–157. [CrossRef]
28. Gibbons, D.G. A Simulation Study of Some Ridge Estimators. *J. Am. Stat. Assoc.* **1981**, *76*, 131–139. [CrossRef]
29. Aslam, M.; Albassam, M. Application of neutrosophic logic to evaluate correlation between prostate cancer mortality and dietary fat assumption. *Symmetry* **2019**, *11*, 330. [CrossRef]
30. Aslam, M. Introducing Kolmogorov–Smirnov tests under uncertainty: An application to radioactive data. *ACS Omega* **2019**, *5*, 914–917. [CrossRef] [PubMed]
31. Aslam, M.; Al Shareef, A.; Khan, K. Monitoring the temperature through moving average control under uncertainty environment. *Sci. Rep.* **2020**, *10*, 1–8. [CrossRef] [PubMed]
32. Aslam, M. On detecting outliers in complex data using Dixon's test under neutrosophic statistics. *J. King Saud-Univ.-Sci.* **2020**, *32*, 2005–2008.
33. Albassam, M.; Khan, N.; Aslam, M. The W/S test for data having neutrosophic numbers: An application to USA village population. *Complexity* **2020**, *2020*, 3690879.
34. Aslam, M.; Arif, O.H. Test of Association in the Presence of Complex Environment. *Complexity* **2020**, *2020*, 2935435.
35. Aslam, M.; Arif, O.H. Multivariate Analysis under Indeterminacy: An Application to Chemical Content Data. *J. Anal. Methods Chem.* **2020**, *2020*, 1406028.

© 2020 by the authors. Licensee MDPI, Basel, Switzerland. This article is an open access article distributed under the terms and conditions of the Creative Commons Attribution (CC BY) license (http://creativecommons.org/licenses/by/4.0/).

Article

Using the Interval Type-2 Fuzzy Inference Systems to Compare the Impact of Speed and Space Perception on the Occurrence of Road Traffic Accidents

Marjana Čubranić-Dobrodolac [1,2], Libor Švadlenka [1], Svetlana Čičević [2], Aleksandar Trifunović [2] and Momčilo Dobrodolac [2,*]

1. Faculty of Transport Engineering, University of Pardubice, Studentská 95, 532 10 Pardubice, Czech Republic; marjana@sf.bg.ac.rs (M.Č.-D.); libor.svadlenka@upce.cz (L.Š.)
2. Faculty of Transport and Traffic Engineering, University of Belgrade, Vojvode Stepe 305, 11000 Belgrade, Serbia; s.cicevic@sf.bg.ac.rs (S.Č.); a.trifunovic@sf.bg.ac.rs (A.T.)
* Correspondence: m.dobrodolac@sf.bg.ac.rs; Tel.: +381-113091213

Received: 30 July 2020; Accepted: 3 September 2020; Published: 10 September 2020

Abstract: A constantly increasing number of deaths on roads forces analysts to search for models that predict the driver's propensity for road traffic accidents (RTAs). This paper aims to examine a relationship between the speed and space assessment capabilities of drivers in terms of their association with the occurrence of RTAs. The method used for this purpose is based on the implementation of the interval Type-2 Fuzzy Inference System (T2FIS). The inputs to the first T2FIS relate to the speed assessment capabilities of drivers. These capabilities were measured in the experiment with 178 young drivers, with test speeds of 30, 50, and 70 km/h. The participants assessed the aforementioned speed values from four different observation positions in the driving simulator. On the other hand, the inputs of the second T2FIS are space assessment capabilities. The same group of drivers took two types of space assessment tests—2D and 3D. The third considered T2FIS sublimates of all previously mentioned inputs in one model. The output in all three T2FIS structures is the number of RTAs experienced by a driver. By testing three proposed T2FISs on the empirical data, the result of the research indicates that the space assessment characteristics better explain participation in RTAs compared to the speed assessment capabilities. The results obtained are further confirmed by implementing a multiple regression analysis.

Keywords: type-2 fuzzy inference systems; traffic simulator; traffic accidents; road safety; space perception; speed perception

1. Introduction

One of the biggest problems globally nowadays is the rate of road traffic accidents (RTAs) and deaths on roads. Each year, around 1.24 million people are killed in RTAs and up to 20–50 million injured [1,2]. The issue of road safety represents a social and economic concern, resulting in physical and mental injuries and immense loss of property [3]. The costs of the consequences of RTAs vary from 1% to 2% gross national product in underdeveloped and developing countries [2,4]. The current trends indicate that if urgent action is not taken, RTAs could be the seventh leading cause of death by the year 2030. Moreover, 90% of these deaths occur in underdeveloped and developing countries [2,3,5].

Technology development makes vehicles more affordable, which results in a rapid increase in vehicle ownership. On the one hand, this results in an elevated likelihood of the occurrence of RTAs; however, on the other hand, this produces much more RTA data, offering more possibilities to obtain new knowledge in the traffic safety field. With the continuous development of research methods, computer performance, information processing, etc., many universities, research institutes, and safety agencies analyze RTA data in order to propose adequate safety measures [6,7].

The wealth of RTA data inevitably generates more explanatory variables that may provide more accurate models of explaining RTA occurrence. However, it is known that "more is not always better", especially for the prediction of RTAs, considering that a large number of variables may cause model overfitting [8,9]. In addition, this can impact accompanying activities such as long execution time and unreliable prediction results [8,10].

The development of computers and software leads to the development of new types of vehicles. In the current market of new vehicles, safer driving can be recognized through vehicle tracking and smartphone applications that detect risky driving patterns such as speeding or inappropriate lane changing [11]. Furthermore, the appearance of partly or fully autonomous vehicles can significantly contribute to road safety, reducing the frequency of RTAs [11]. However, this is still far from everyday reality, even for the most progressive markets [11,12].

There are many random factors in the occurrence of RTAs; however, they are most often grouped considering the road, vehicle, and driver characteristics, such as vehicle speed, aggressive behavior, skills, etc. If a driver has developed spatial skills while in traffic, his or her attention will be focused on the traffic situation, otherwise, it will be distracted and directed to orientation in space [13,14]. On the other hand, some reports indicate that speeding is a contributing factor in about one-third of all fatal RTAs [15].

Considering all of the above, a motive to carry out the research described in this paper is to offer a model whose implementation would contribute to the explanation of causes of RTAs. The experimental research was conducted to examine the impact of vehicle speed and space assessment capabilities on the occurrence of RTAs.

Speed does not only affect the severity of a crash but is also related to the risk of being involved in an RTA [16]. The dominant forms of improper driving during the late twentieth century were speeding, driving too fast for the existing conditions, improper lane changing, and improper passing [17,18]. Many empirical studies generally confirmed a positive relationship between traffic speed and the frequency of RTAs [19–22]. At the same time, some studies found that higher speeds do not necessarily result in higher accident rates [23,24]. It is suggested that the speed-RTA relationship should be considered in the proper context, accounting for possible additional confounding factors such as traffic exposure and road conditions [24–26], however including a perception of vehicle speed. Speeding, but also an inaccurate vehicle speed, is associated with an increased risk of being involved in a crash.

The current state in the considered field in the Republic of Serbia, the country where our research was carried out, is illustrated by the survey conducted by the state authorities in the period from 2017 to 2019. This survey shows that about half of drivers in urban areas exceed the speed limit (2017—49.4%; 2018—48.4%; 2019—51%) [27]. When it comes to the circumstances and causes of RTAs, the results for this period indicate that the largest number of the worst RTAs, as well as the largest number of fatalities, belong to the category of unadjusted speed (2017—53.14%; 2018—52.14%; 2019—51.41% of the cases where the cause of RTAs with fatalities is unadjusted speed) [28]. According to the Road Traffic Safety Agency in Serbia [27], based on the responses of the participants, every third driver of a passenger car exceeds the speed limit in urban areas by an average of more than 10 km/h. When it comes to the speed of vehicles outside urban areas, the results show that almost two-fifths of the participants drive at a speed that is higher than the limit. A survey of drivers' attitudes to speeding in the Republic of Serbia pointed to the alarming fact that the largest percentage of drivers (41.7) do not agree that speeding in populated areas by 10 km/h increases the risk of being involved in an RTA. The decision on the level of vehicle speed is influenced by the driver's psychological traits, driving skills and limitations, road and environment characteristics, and vehicle characteristics, but also by the space assessment capabilities of the driver.

Driving skills involve processes such as the perception of time, speed, and especially space. How important these skills are for safe participation in traffic is widely explained in the literature.

A well-known term introduced for describing someone's position in traffic related to their skills is situation awareness. This term can be defined as [29,30] "the perception of the elements in the environment within a volume of time and space, the comprehension of their meaning, and the projection of their status in the near future". The aforementioned abilities are connected to the largest number of RTAs that are caused by the human factor. There are findings that the human factor is responsible for 93% of all RTAs [31,32]. From all the above, it can be noticed how important is to examine the perception of speed and space of drivers. A motive to carry out the research described in this paper is to offer a model whose implementation would contribute to the explanation of the causes of RTAs. The experimental research was conducted to examine the impact of vehicle speed and space assessment capabilities on the occurrence of RTAs.

Because the answers of participants related to the assessment of speed and space involve a certain level of imprecision and fuzziness, we assumed that the implementation of fuzzy inference systems would be a convenient tool for data processing. Fuzzy logic is widely used for explaining driver behavior. The previous implementation can be segmented as follows [33]: examination of the interaction between the driver and road infrastructure [34]:, examination of the interaction between the driver and in-vehicle systems [35], testing the psychophysical characteristics of drivers [33,36,37], and determining a driving style [38,39]. The motivation to use fuzzy logic for modeling the propensity for RTAs based on speed assessments and spatial abilities of drivers is actually the introduction of a new field of implementation. This new area can be called the *perception of road traffic conditions and relations*.

In this paper we propose the implementation of the interval Type-2 Fuzzy Inference System (T2FIS). Three T2FIS structures are designed and tested on the empirical data collected in two experiments. The T2FIS that gives the lowest error in the description of data can be considered as the most convenient in explaining the relationship between the inputs—characteristics of the driver, and output—the number of RTAs. The proposed T2FIS can be used as a decision-making tool to calculate the propensity for participation in accidents.

2. Methods

This section is divided into two subsections. The first refers to the description of experiments carried out with the aim of empirical data collection. The second subsection is about the design of T2FIS structures.

2.1. Data Collection

The empirical data are collected in the experiment which consists of two testing sessions, which will be designated as Experiment I and Experiment II in the further text. The task of the respondents in Experiment I was to estimate the passenger car speed. Experiment II was designed to explore the respondent's spatial abilities. Along with the tests related to the assessment of speed and spatial capabilities, the participants also filled the demographic questionnaire and the questionnaire about participation in RTAs. The main purpose of these additional questionnaires was to provide information about the number of RTAs experienced by participants, which were then used as an output variable in the implemented models.

2.1.1. Participants

The experiments were conducted in the Laboratory of Traffic Psychology, Faculty of Transport and Traffic Engineering, in Belgrade. The participants in the experiment were recruited from 178 young drivers (96 males and 82 females). Our participants' mean age was 22.05 years (standard deviation (SD) = 2.12). The experimental procedure (instructions, the method of testing, and data collection) were the same for all participants who took part in both experiments and also completed questionnaires on demographic data and involvement in RTAs. The research adhered to the Code of Ethics and Conduct of the Serbian Psychological Association. The participants also signed a written voluntary informed consent which confirms their willingness to take part in this research. The participants did not receive any compensation for taking part in the survey as well.

2.1.2. Experiment I

For the purpose of this experiment, three different speed levels of a moving vehicle were presented to the participants in the driving simulator. Both experiments were carried out in a PC-based driving simulator, which incorporates three 4200 plasma monitors that provide the respondents a 180° horizontal and 50° vertical field of view of the simulated environment [40,41].

The vehicle used for the experiment was a Peugeot 307. The color of the vehicle was bright yellow. In the literature, it is possible to discover the findings on the relationship between vehicle color and its perception on the road. There is evidence that it is easier to spot the vehicle having a higher contrast between the vehicle color and the environment. More concrete, brighter colored cars provide a lot of contrast between the vehicles and their surroundings; therefore, it is easier to notice them [41–43].

In Experiment I, the vehicle was observed from four positions. These were the following: the first was a front view of the vehicle, which meant that the vehicle was approaching, the second was a back view, which implied that the vehicle was moving away, the third was a side view, indicating that the vehicle was passing by, and the fourth was a view from inside the vehicle, which represented the situation when a driver was behind the wheel, but without information about vehicle speed from the instruments (Figure 1). Every participant estimated all of the three vehicle speed levels, from each viewing position.

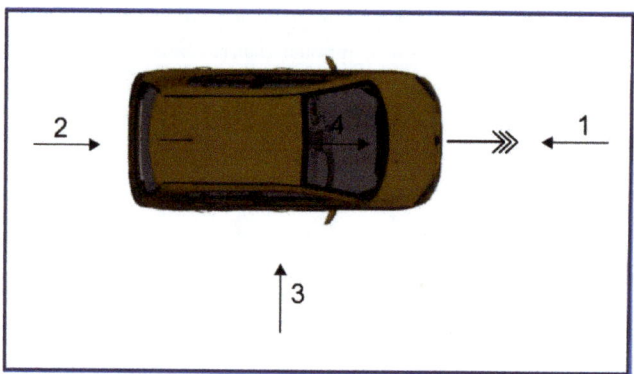

Figure 1. Observation positions in Experiment I: 1—Front view; 2—Back view; 3—Side view; 4—Driver's seat perspective.

In total, each participant made 12 assessments of speed. In the calculation process, to form three input variables based on speed assessment capabilities, the errors in the assessment are grouped around each of three speed levels. This implies a calculation of average assessment error from four positions, per particular speed level. The units for both, speed levels and the errors in the assessments are the same—km/h.

The three test speed levels were 30 km/h, 50 km/h, and 70 km/h. They were chosen due to the most often legal limitations: the limit of 30 km/h is usually set in a school zone; limit of 50 km/h in the inhabited area; and the limit of 70 km/h outside of the inhabited area [41,44,45]. The respondents were asked to report the perceived vehicle speed for each experimental condition. The experimenter entered the declared value into the adequate space in the on-line questionnaire previously prepared for the purpose of this study. The questionnaire also covered demographic variables, as well as those related to participation and the number of experienced RTAs [41,45].

Specific speed/position combination was randomly assigned to each participant, i.e., the stimulus order was determined using a random number generator. This was done in order to avoid the anchoring effect, employing counterbalancing. Counterbalancing was achieved by randomizing the series of presentations of the test stimuli [41].

2.1.3. Experiment II

For Experiment II, 2D and 3D spatial tests were used. The objects were positioned with random orientation in space. All participants had the same viewing position on all tasks. The background was dark, to standardize the local contrasts [46,47]. Examples of 2D and 3D tests are shown in Figure 2.

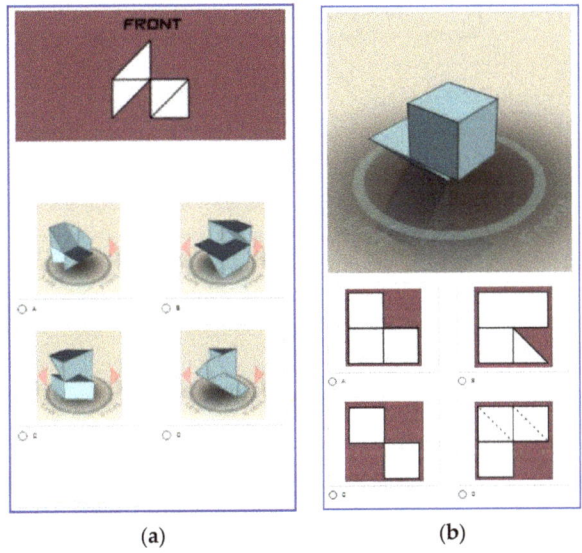

Figure 2. The appearance of the task used in experiment II: (**a**) an example of a 2D test used in the experiment; (**b**) an example of a 3D test used in the experiment.

In the laboratory with reduced environmental light, all participants were placed in the same position with a 58 cm distance between their head and the center of the screen. The tests were displayed on the same monitor that was used in the driving simulator. 2D and 3D tests presentation order was randomized. As in the case of Experiment I, in the beginning, each participant was assigned the specific combination of an experimental test order, which was regulated by using a random number generator. In the 2D test, respondents are asked to find for the given object shown in 2D the appropriate object in 3D (example in Figure 2a). Similarly, when it comes to the 3D task, the respondent had to find an object in 2D for the assigned object shown in 3D (example in Figure 2b).

2.2. Model Development

The models proposed in this paper are based on testing of the Mamdani based T2FIS [48]. The principles of Type-2 fuzzy sets were first proposed and described by Zadeh [49] to expand the possibilities and performance of the standard Type-1 fuzzy sets. The main characteristic of Type-2 fuzzy sets is that they integrate uncertainty about the membership function (MF). For this reason, MF is defined by the corresponding interval bounded by two functions, a lower MF and upper MF, and called the Footprint of Uncertainty (FOU), as illustrated in Figure 3.

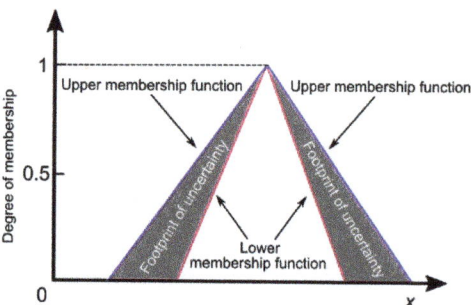

Figure 3. The footprint of uncertainty for an interval Type-2 fuzzy set.

The performance of three T2FIS structures was compared. In the first, there were input variables related to speed assessment capabilities (Figure 4a), in the second, the space assessment capabilities were inputs to the model (Figure 4b), and in the third, the speed and space assessments were jointly considered as inputs (Figure 4c). All three structures had the same output variable—the number of experienced RTAs.

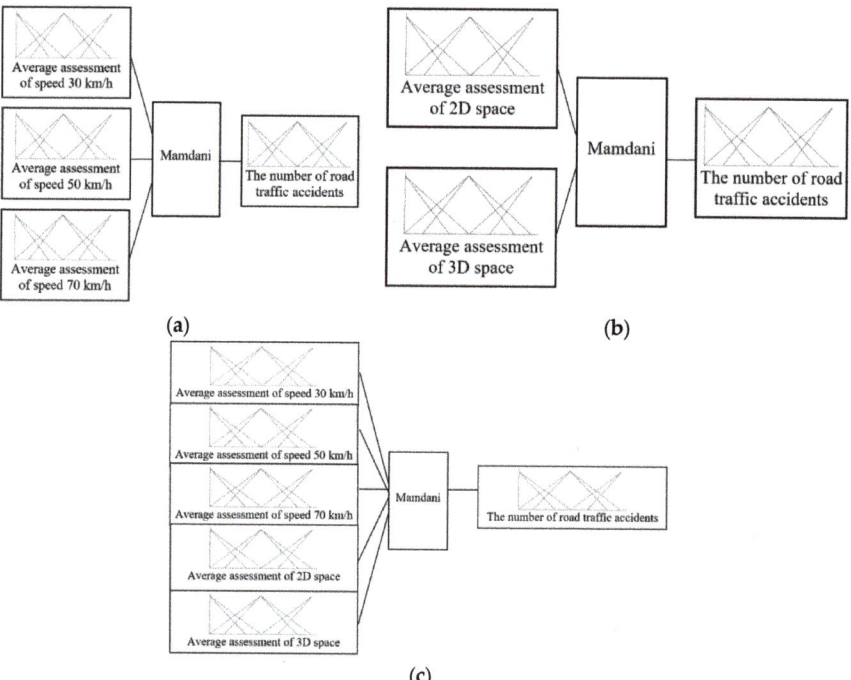

Figure 4. Configuration of the research: (**a**) the model of speed assessment capabilities—*T2FIS_speed*; (**b**) the model of space assessment capabilities—*T2FIS_space*; (**c**) the model that encompasses all considered input variables—*T2FIS_speed_and_space*.

In the figures, as well as in the tables, we use the following notation: T2FIS related to the speed assessment capabilities is designated as *T2FIS_speed*, T2FIS related to the space assessment capabilities is labeled as *T2FIS_space*, and T2FIS that jointly considers both categories is marked as *T2FIS_speed_and_space*.

The first fuzzy inference system has three input variables: *Average assessment of speed 30 km/h*, *Average assessment of speed 50 km/h*, and *Average assessment of speed 70 km/h*. In all three cases, the word "average" is used because the assessments were performed from four positions—front, rear, side view, and from the position of a driver. Therefore, each of the three input variables is the arithmetic mean of four measurements.

Input variables that relate to the speed assessment take the values of average errors that are made when estimating the real speed of the car. The minimum, mean, maximum values, and standard deviation of each variable of the examined sample of 178 young drivers are given in Table 1. It can be noted that in some cases very huge errors in the assessments are recorded. The young age of participants and their humble driving experience may be an explanation for such results.

Table 1. Description of a sample considering errors in speed assessment.

Input Variable	Average Errors in Assessments from Four Different Positions [km/h]			
	Minimum	Mean	Maximum	Standard Deviation
Average assessment of speed 30 km/h	−3.75	21.75	67.50	11.68
Average assessment of speed 50 km/h	−18.75	13.57	62.50	13.51
Average assessment of speed 70 km/h	−54.50	−32.33	15.00	10.06

Input variable *Average assessment of speed 30 km/h* is displayed using five fuzzy sets and their membership functions (Figure 5): U_30—Average assessment is under 30 km/h, A_30—Average assessment is around 30 km/h, MO_30—Average assessment is moderately over 30 km/h, SO_30—Average assessment is significantly over 30 km/h and EO_30—Average assessment is much higher than 30 km/h. This variable is marked as x_1.

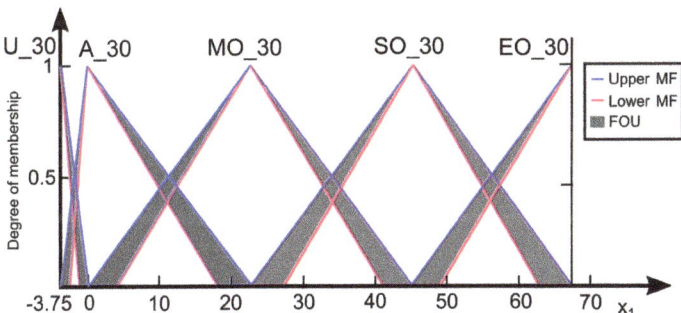

Figure 5. Input variable Average assessment of speed 30 km/h. Used notation: MF—membership function; FOU—footprint of uncertainty.

Input variable *Average assessment of speed 50 km/h* is displayed using five fuzzy sets and their membership functions (Figure 6): U_50—Average assessment is under 50 km/h, A_50—Average assessment is around 50 km/h, MO_50—Average assessment is moderately over 50 km/h, SO_50—Average assessment is significantly over 50 km/h and EO_50—Average assessment is extremely over 50 km/h. This variable is marked as x_2.

Input variable *Average assessment of speed 70 km/h* is displayed using five fuzzy sets and their membership functions (Figure 7): EU_70—Average assessment is greatly under 70 km/h, SU_70—Average assessment is significantly under 70 km/h, MU_70—Average assessment is moderately under 70 km/h, A_70—Average assessment is around 70 km/h, and O_70—Average assessment is over 70 km/h. This variable is marked as x_3.

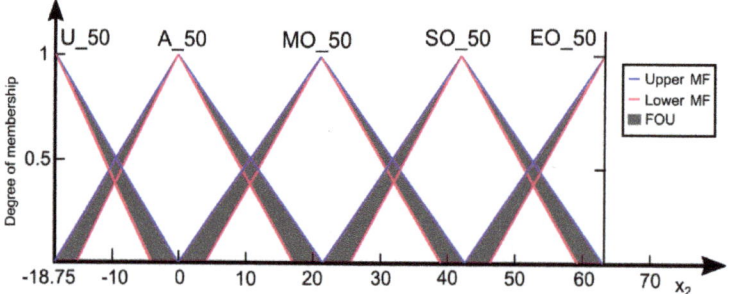

Figure 6. Input variable Average assessment of speed 50 km/h. Used notation: MF—membership function; FOU—footprint of uncertainty.

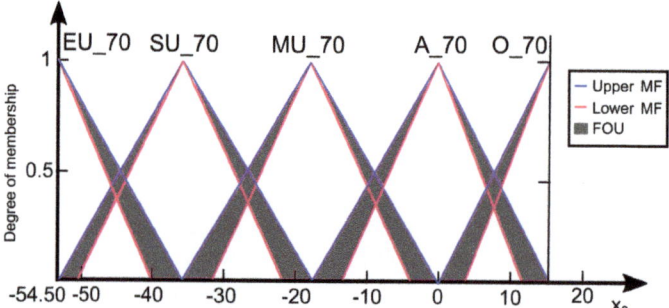

Figure 7. Input variable Average assessment of speed 70 km/h. Used notation: MF—membership function; FOU—footprint of uncertainty.

The output variable named *The number of experienced road traffic accidents* is the same, as previously explained, in both fuzzy inference systems. Since the sample consists of young drivers, the number of reported RTAs is relatively small—the minimum value is 0 and the maximum is 3. Accordingly, the output variable is defined by three fuzzy sets (Figure 8): SNA—a small number of road traffic accidents, MNA—a moderate number of road traffic accidents, and HNA—high number of road traffic accidents. This variable is marked as y.

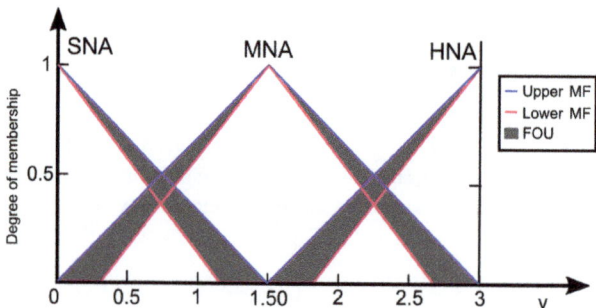

Figure 8. Output variable the number of experienced road traffic accidents. Used notation: MF—membership function; FOU—footprint of uncertainty.

On the other hand, the second fuzzy inference system is based on two input variables that describe the space assessment capabilities. Unlike in the case of speed assessment, where the errors were considered, in this case, each examinee is rated by the grade from 0 to 5 depending on the success on the 2D and 3D spatial abilities test. The minimum, mean, maximum values, and standard deviation of considered variables in the examined sample of 178 young drivers are shown in Table 2.

Table 2. Description of a sample considering errors in space assessments.

Input Variable	Average Marks from the Space Assessments Tests			
	Minimum	Mean	Maximum	Standard Deviation
Average assessment of 2D space	0	1.81	5	1.12
Average assessment of 3D space	0	1.67	5	1.01

Input variable *Average assessment of 2D space* is described using five fuzzy sets and their membership functions (Figure 9): VSM_2—Very small mark, SM_2—Small mark, MM_2—Middle mark, HM_2—High mark, and VHM_2—Very high mark. This variable is marked as x_4.

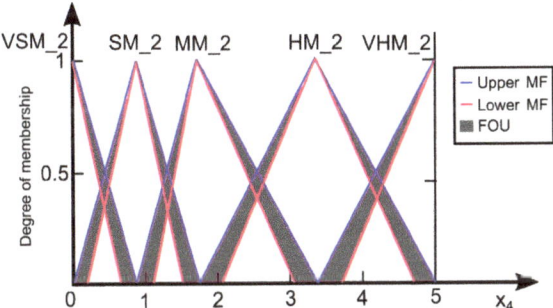

Figure 9. Input variable Average assessment of 2D space. Used notation: MF—membership function; FOU—footprint of uncertainty.

Input variable *Average assessment of 3D space* is described using five fuzzy sets and their membership functions (Figure 10): VSM_3—Very small mark, SM_3—Small mark, MM_3—Middle mark, HM_3—High mark, and VHM_3—Very high mark. This variable is marked as x_5.

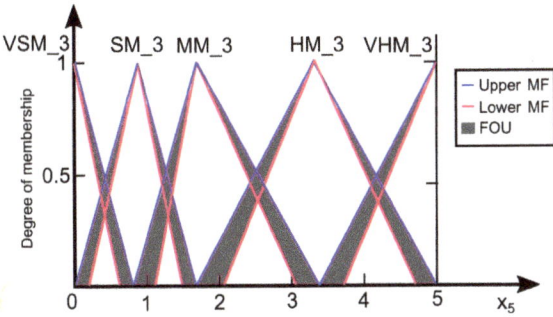

Figure 10. Input variable Average assessment of 3D space. Used notation: MF—membership function; FOU—footprint of uncertainty.

The fuzzy rule base is crucial for the performance of a T2FIS. Here, we use a well-known principle for defining fuzzy rules based on the empirical data introduced by Wang and Mendel (WM) [50].

This approach implies generating one fuzzy rule per one data pair, i.e., per one participant. In our case, there are 178 participants in the sample, and accordingly, 178 fuzzy rules should be formed. However, certain rules are the same or conflicting. The conflicting rules have the same "IF" part, but a different "THEN" part. First, from the same rules, just one should be left. Furthermore, we need to eliminate the conflicting rules. To decide which rules will be retained in the final fuzzy rules database, the procedure involves the calculation of the degree of significance for each of the formed rules. This is done by Equation (1), for the rule defined in the following way: "IF x_1 is A and x_2 is B, THEN y is C". In a group of conflicting rules, only the rule with the maximum degree should be retained. $D(Rule)$ is the importance degree of a rule, $\mu_A(x_1)$ is a value of the membership function of the region A when the input value is x_1, etc.

$$D(Rule) = \mu_A(x_1) * \mu_B(x_2) * \mu_C(y) \tag{1}$$

The implemented programming code for this purpose is based on the code presented in the paper by Čubranić-Dobrodolac et al. [33]. After the required calculations, there are 22 fuzzy rules obtained based on the empirical data, considering the sample of 178 participants, in the case of speed assessment capabilities (Table 3), while as regards spatial abilities assessment, there are 17 fuzzy rules obtained by the same approach (Table 4). Finally, in the T2FIS where all input variables are jointly considered, 84 fuzzy rules are generated from the empirical data based on the WM approach (Table A1 in Appendix A).

Table 3. The fuzzy rules obtained from empirical data in the case of speed capabilities assessment.

$D(Rule)$	Serial No. of MF for Variable x_1	Serial No. of MF for Variable x_2	Serial No. of MF for Variable x_3	Serial No. of MF for Variable y
1	1	1	1	1
0.42682	2	1	1	1
0.25945	2	1	2	1
0.54222	2	2	1	1
0.62963	2	2	2	1
0.29929	3	2	1	1
0.68531	3	2	2	1
0.47288	3	2	3	1
0.35178	3	3	1	1
0.85328	3	3	2	1
0.74074	3	3	3	1
0.33383	3	4	2	1
0.27160	3	4	3	1
0.24294	4	3	2	1
0.30423	4	3	3	1
0.48971	4	4	2	1
0.67901	4	4	3	1
0.50440	4	4	4	1
0.37940	4	5	3	1
0.65040	5	4	5	1
0.10539	5	5	3	2
0.72222	5	5	4	1

Table 4. The fuzzy rules obtained from the empirical data in the case of space capabilities assessment.

$D(Rule)$	Serial No. of MF for Variable x_4	Serial No. of MF for Variable x_5	Serial No. of MF for Variable y
1	1	1	1
0.79518	1	2	1
0.79640	1	3	1
0.80239	1	4	1
0.88888	2	1	1
0.70682	2	2	1
0.70791	2	3	1
0.71324	2	4	1

Table 4. *Cont.*

D(Rule)	Serial No. of MF for Variable x_4	Serial No. of MF for Variable x_5	Serial No. of MF for Variable y
0.87500	3	1	1
0.69578	3	2	1
0.69685	3	3	1
0.70209	3	4	1
0.75000	4	1	1
0.59638	4	2	1
0.59730	4	3	1
0.60179	4	4	1
1	5	5	1

3. Results and Discussion

Finally, the defined T2FIS structures should be tested. This is accomplished based on Equation (2) [51,52]. Cumulative deviation (CD) is a parameter that describes how good a T2FIS describes the empirical data. It represents a sum of absolute values of the difference between the number of RTAs experienced by the drivers from the sample and the corresponding results of T2FIS based on the input values for each driver from the sample. The result of the T2FIS for an examinee number i in Equation (1) is marked as T2FIS(i).

$$CD = \sum_{i=1}^{178} |y^{(i)} - T2FIS(i)| \qquad (2)$$

CD is a cumulative deviation; $y^{(i)}$ represents the number of RTAs experienced by the driver from the sample; T2FIS(i) is the result of the interval Type-2 fuzzy inference system.

Following all the calculations, we are in a position to obtain the final result for the three considered fuzzy inference systems. In the first case, CD value for the interval Type-2 fuzzy inference system related to the speed assessment capabilities is equal to 97.6477. Further, CD value for the T2FIS related to the space assessment capabilities is equal to 91.7891. Finally, testing the T2FIS where all five considered independent variables are entered as inputs showed that CD value is 103.4103. A comparison of empirical data and results of T2FIS structures are graphically shown in Figures 11–13.

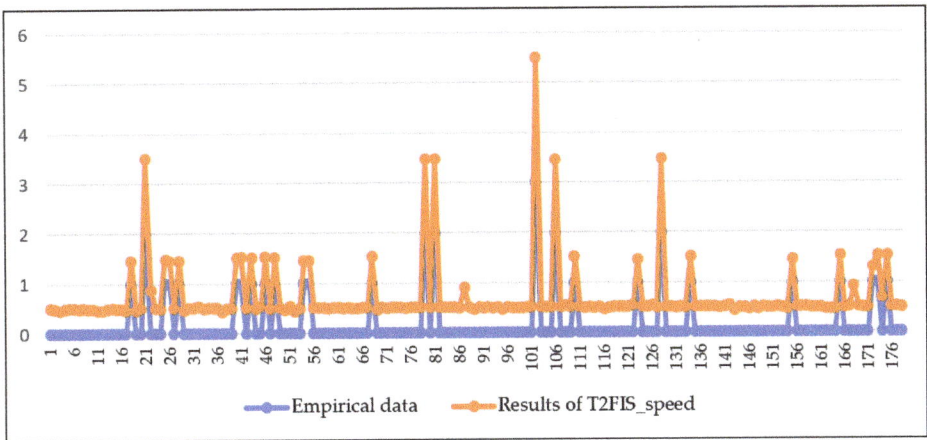

Figure 11. A comparison of empirical data and results of the Type-2 Fuzzy Inference System (T2FIS) in the case of speed capabilities assessment—T2FIS_speed.

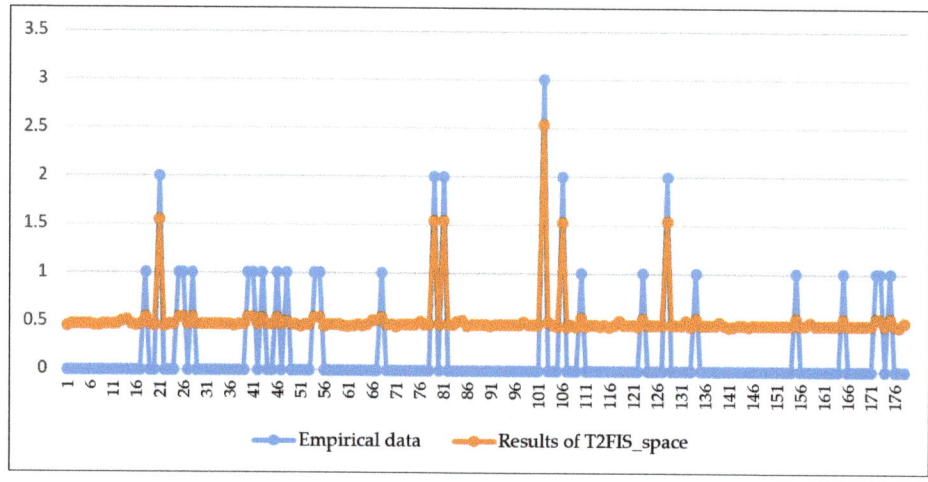

Figure 12. A comparison of empirical data and results of T2FIS in the case of space capabilities assessment—T2FIS_space.

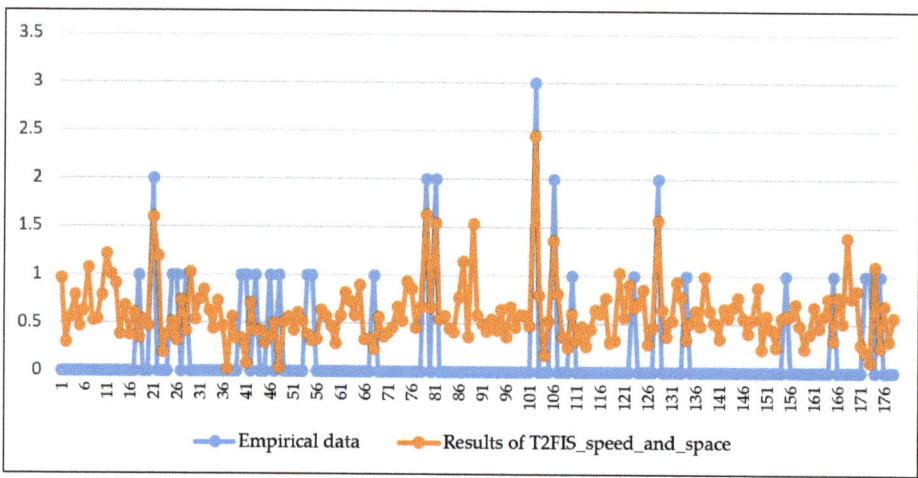

Figure 13. A comparison of empirical data and results of T2FIS in the case of speed and space capabilities assessment—T2FIS_speed_and_space.

It is interesting to note that the T2FIS with five input variables achieved the worst result. As already stated in the introduction of this paper, this can be explained by the fact that introducing more variables in the model does not necessarily lead to better results [8–10]. However, to confirm the conclusions obtained, we performed the paired t-test to examine whether the difference in results between T2FIS structures is statistically significant (Table 5). As is shown, there are significant differences between the results of *T2FIS_space* and the other two T2FIS structures. However, there is no significant difference between *T2FIS_speed* and *T2FIS_speed_and_space*. These results indicate that the space assessment capabilities can better explain the propensity for road traffic accidents of drivers compared to speed assessment capabilities.

Table 5. The difference between cumulative deviation (CD) values per T2FIS tested by paired *t*-test.

	T2FIS_Speed	T2FIS_Space	T2FIS_Speed_and_Space
T2FIS_speed	-		
T2FIS_space	0.048 *	-	
T2FIS_speed_and_space	0.059	0.049 *	-

* $p < 0.05$.

Finally, it is useful to compare the proposed approach with some other method. In this context, we compare the performance of T2FIS with the statistical technique multiple regression analysis. The results are shown in Figure 14. We further implemented a *t*-test to conclude about the statistical significance of the difference between the two approaches; however, the results show that there is no statistically significant difference in all three cases considered. It can be concluded that these two approaches give similar results.

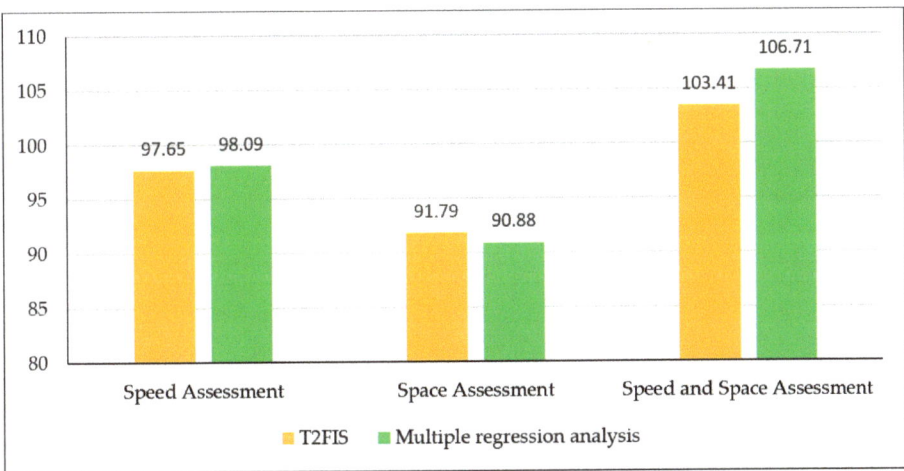

Figure 14. A comparison of T2FIS performance and multiple regression analysis.

Speaking about the performance of T2FIS, further adjustments of membership functions shape, positions, and the design of fuzzy rules can be done using some of the heuristic and metaheuristic algorithms. This would lead to even better results, and accordingly, can be considered as the recommended direction for future research.

Above all, it would be meaningful to implement certain additional methodologies based on fuzzy logic as well. One of the most popular in the literature is the fuzzy regression analysis [53,54]. Here, the main task is to estimate the parameters of the regression model, and these parameters represent fuzzy numbers. To solve this problem, there are three general approaches used [55]: linear and non-linear programming methods (possibilistic regression analysis), fuzzy least squares methods, and machine-learning techniques. Within these approaches, numerous sub directions exist. Having in mind that we apply Type-2 fuzzy sets in this paper, it would be interesting to compare the obtained results with Type-2 fuzzy regression analysis [56–63].

When it comes to the practical implications of this research, in the authors' opinion both speed and space capabilities are important for safe maneuvers in traffic, and this is the reason why both of them are considered in this research. However, the results obtained can be explained in the way that the drivers who record low scores on the spatial abilities test do not possess good skills related to vehicle position in the environment, which in turn could increase the likelihood of RTAs involvement.

The result of this research can be very useful for policy-makers in the field of traffic safety. Modifications have to be undertaken to adapt education and training programs in order to improve space perception which could result in reducing the number of RTAs. The results from numerous studies confirm that spatial cognition can be improved by training [64–67]. This fact can be used when creating the training programs for young drivers applying for a driver's license, for drivers whose driver's license has been revoked, in the recruitment procedures for professional drivers, as well as, in the programs for older drivers whose spatial abilities may decline with aging. All these programs should contribute to lowering the number of RTAs in the whole world and to a higher level of safety on the roads.

4. Conclusions

In this paper, the authors performed the testing of the interval Type-2 fuzzy inference systems to compare the impact of speed and space perception on the occurrence of road traffic accidents. By analyzing three proposed T2FIS structures, the results of the research indicate that the space assessment characteristics better explain the participation in RTAs compared to speed assessment capabilities.

This result may be useful for improving traffic safety. Other authors also support the conclusion from this paper. Conclusions drawn from the results of our study are consistent with research showing that drivers' negligence, speeding, and misperception of space are the main causes of RTAs, while drivers being responsible for about 90% RTAs [68]. Having in mind both human and material losses that all countries globally experience due to RTAs, the need arises for this type of investigation which will contribute to the understanding of the circumstances of RTA occurrence and the development of better traffic safety measures.

The implemented methodology can be further improved in future research. Here, the statistical approach implying the multiple regression analysis and the concept of a Mamdani-based fuzzy inference system are used. It turned out that these two gave similar results. However, other approaches are welcome, such as fuzzy regression analysis, intuitionistic fuzzy sets, Sugeno fuzzy inference systems, etc. Furthermore, the optimization procedure of the current T2FIS structures would be meaningful as well. This would include the implementation of certain metaheuristic algorithms to find as good as possible shapes and positions of membership functions, as well as an adequate fuzzy rules base.

Author Contributions: Conceptualization, M.Č.-D. and L.Š.; methodology, M.Č.-D., L.Š. and S.Č.; software, M.D.; validation, M.Č.-D., L.Š. and A.T.; formal analysis, M.Č.-D. and A.T.; investigation, M.Č.-D.; resources, M.Č.-D., A.T. and S.Č.; data curation, M.Č.-D., A.T. and M.D.; writing—original draft preparation, M.Č.-D.; writing—review and editing, M.Č.-D.; visualization, A.T. and M.D.; supervision, L.Š.; project administration, M.Č.-D. and L.Š.; funding acquisition, M.Č.-D. and L.Š. All authors have read and agreed to the published version of the manuscript.

Funding: The article is supported by the University of Pardubice, SGS_2020_010.

Conflicts of Interest: The authors declare no conflict of interest.

Appendix A

Table A1. The fuzzy rules obtained from the empirical data in the case of joint speed and space capabilities assessment.

D(Rule)	Serial No. of MF for Variable x_1	Serial No. of MF for Variable x_2	Serial No. of MF for Variable x_3	Serial No. of MF for Variable x_4	Serial No. of MF for Variable x_5	Serial No. of MF for Variable y
0.80239	1	1	1	1	4	1
0.30215	2	1	1	2	3	1
0.20504	2	1	1	3	2	1
0.23063	2	1	2	2	1	1

Table A1. Cont.

D(Rule)	Serial No. of MF for Variable x_1	Serial No. of MF for Variable x_2	Serial No. of MF for Variable x_3	Serial No. of MF for Variable x_4	Serial No. of MF for Variable x_5	Serial No. of MF for Variable y
0.12946	2	1	2	2	4	2
0.29663	2	2	1	2	3	1
0.34355	2	2	1	3	3	1
0.32337	2	2	1	4	2	1
0.16547	2	2	1	4	3	1
0.30893	2	2	2	1	2	1
0.29847	2	2	2	1	3	1
0.25239	2	2	2	2	2	1
0.27987	2	2	2	2	4	1
0.55092	2	2	2	3	1	1
0.30552	2	2	2	3	3	1
0.33059	2	2	2	3	4	1
0.32500	2	2	2	4	1	1
0.20980	2	2	2	4	3	1
0.11413	3	2	1	2	3	1
0.15930	3	2	1	2	4	1
0.11327	3	2	1	3	4	1
0.22223	3	2	2	1	2	1
0.33499	3	2	2	1	3	1
0.32831	3	2	2	1	4	1
0.48439	3	2	2	2	2	1
0.28653	3	2	2	2	3	1
0.27443	3	2	2	2	4	1
0.39459	3	2	2	3	2	1
0.33644	3	2	2	3	3	1
0.31541	3	2	2	3	4	1
0.38599	3	2	2	4	1	1
0.35078	3	2	2	4	2	1
0.36788	3	2	2	4	3	1
0.31414	3	2	3	2	2	2
0.20192	3	2	3	2	4	1
0.24565	3	2	3	3	3	1
0.31204	3	2	3	3	4	1
0.28458	3	2	3	4	4	1
0.35178	3	3	1	1	1	1
0.40288	3	3	2	1	1	1
0.40232	3	3	2	1	2	1
0.54969	3	3	2	1	3	1
0.12764	3	3	2	1	4	1
0.55967	3	3	2	2	1	1
0.38411	3	3	2	2	2	1
0.49525	3	3	2	2	3	1
0.44577	3	3	2	2	4	1
0.59369	3	3	2	3	2	1
0.28958	3	3	2	3	3	1
0.51937	3	3	2	4	1	1
0.50663	3	3	2	4	2	1
0.40022	3	3	2	4	3	1
0.40399	3	3	3	1	3	1
0.28975	3	3	3	1	4	2
0.40760	3	3	3	2	1	1
0.17203	3	3	3	2	2	1
0.34380	3	3	3	2	3	1

Table A1. Cont.

D(Rule)	Serial No. of MF for Variable x_1	Serial No. of MF for Variable x_2	Serial No. of MF for Variable x_3	Serial No. of MF for Variable x_4	Serial No. of MF for Variable x_5	Serial No. of MF for Variable y
0.28869	3	3	3	2	4	1
0.51539	3	3	3	3	2	1
0.39328	3	3	3	3	3	1
0.33181	3	3	3	3	4	1
0.16842	3	3	3	4	2	1
0.23263	3	4	2	3	3	1
0.15876	3	4	3	3	2	1
0.16198	3	4	3	4	2	1
0.12092	4	3	2	4	3	1
0.21504	4	3	3	2	2	1
0.19945	4	3	3	2	4	1
0.14372	4	3	3	4	2	1
0.13577	4	3	3	4	3	2
0.29205	4	4	2	4	2	1
0.26880	4	4	3	1	2	1
0.37232	4	4	3	2	2	1
0.38626	4	4	3	2	3	1
0.29795	4	4	3	3	4	1
0.30276	4	4	3	4	1	1
0.40495	4	4	3	4	2	1
0.28480	4	4	3	4	4	1
0.19056	4	4	3	5	5	1
0.30128	4	4	4	4	3	1
0.33724	4	5	3	2	1	1
0.51798	5	4	5	1	3	1
0.07449	5	5	3	2	2	2
0.50251	5	5	4	3	2	1

References

1. World Health Organization. *Global Tuberculosis Report 2013*; World Health Organization: Geneva, Switzerland, 2013.
2. Ihueze, C.C.; Onwurah, U.O. Road traffic accidents prediction modelling: An analysis of Anambra State, Nigeria. *Accid. Anal. Prev.* **2018**, *112*, 21–29. [CrossRef] [PubMed]
3. Chen, T.Y.; Jou, R.C. Using HLM to investigate the relationship between traffic accident risk of private vehicles and public transportation. *Transp. Res. Part A Policy Pract.* **2019**, *119*, 148–161. [CrossRef]
4. Jacobs, G.; Aeron-Thomas, A.; Astrop, A. *Estimating Global Road Fatalities*; Department for International Development: London, UK, 2000.
5. World Health Organization. *Global Status Report on Road Safety 2015*; World Health Organization: Geneva, Switzerland, 2015.
6. Saccomanno, F.F.; Grossi, R.; Greco, D.; Mehmood, A. Identifying black spots along highway SS107 in Southern Italy using two models. *J. Transp. Eng.* **2001**, *127*, 515–522. [CrossRef]
7. Fan, Z.; Liu, C.; Cai, D.; Yue, S. Research on black spot identification of safety in urban traffic accidents based on machine learning method. *Saf. Sci.* **2019**, *118*, 607–616. [CrossRef]
8. Lin, L.; Wang, Q.; Sadek, A.W. A novel variable selection method based on frequent pattern tree for real-time traffic accident risk prediction. *Transp. Res. Part C Emerg. Technol.* **2015**, *55*, 444–459. [CrossRef]
9. Sawalha, Z.; Sayed, T. Traffic accident modeling: Some statistical issues. *Can. J. Civ. Eng.* **2006**, *33*, 1115–1124. [CrossRef]
10. Fernández, A.; Gómez, Á.; Lecumberry, F.; Pardo, Á.; Ramírez, I. Pattern recognition in Latin America in the "Big Data" era. *Pattern Recogn.* **2015**, *48*, 1185–1196. [CrossRef]
11. Ryder, B.; Dahlinger, A.; Gahr, B.; Zundritsch, P.; Wortmann, F.; Fleisch, E. Spatial prediction of traffic accidents with critical driving events–Insights from a nationwide field study. *Transp. Res. Part A Policy Pract.* **2019**, *124*, 611–626. [CrossRef]

12. Ryder, B.; Gahr, B.; Egolf, P.; Dahlinger, A.; Wortmann, F. Preventing traffic accidents with in-vehicle decision support systems-The impact of accident hotspot warnings on driver behavior. *Decis. Support Syst.* **2017**, *99*, 64–74. [CrossRef]
13. Trifunović, A.; Pešić, D.; Čičević, S.; Antić, B. The importance of spatial orientation and knowledge of traffic signs for children's traffic safety. *Accid. Anal. Prev.* **2017**, *102*, 81–92. [CrossRef] [PubMed]
14. Cornoldi, C.; Vecchi, T. *Visuo-Spatial Working Memory and Individual Differences*; Psychology Press: London, UK, 2004. [CrossRef]
15. Trifunović, A.; Čičević, S.; Lazarević, D.; Dragović, M.; Vidović, N.; Mošić, M.; Otat, O. Perception of 3D virtual road markings: Based on estimation of vehicle speed. *FME Trans.* **2019**, *47*, 360–369. [CrossRef]
16. Aarts, L.; Van Schagen, I. Driving speed and the risk of road crashes: A review. *Accid. Anal. Prev.* **2006**, *38*, 215–224. [CrossRef] [PubMed]
17. Dakic, I.; Stevanovic, A. On development of arterial fundamental diagrams based on surrogate density measures from adaptive traffic control systems utilizing stop-line detection. *Transp. Res. Part C Emerg. Technol.* **2018**, *94*, 133–150. [CrossRef]
18. Rudin-Brown, C.M. Vehicle height affects drivers' speed perception: Implications for rollover risk. *Transp. Res. Record.* **2004**, *1899*, 84–89. [CrossRef]
19. Kloeden, C.N.; McLean, A.J.; Moore, V.M.; Ponte, G. *Travelling Speed and the Risk of Crash Involvement Volume 2-Case and Reconstruction Details*; NHMRC Road Accident Research Unit, The University of Adelaide: Adelaide, Australia, 1997.
20. Kloeden, C.N.; McLean, J.; Glonek, G.F.V. *Reanalysis of Travelling Speed and the Risk of Crash Involvement in Adelaide South Australia*; Australian Transport Safety Bureau: Adelaide, Australia, 2002.
21. Kloeden, C.N.; Ponte, G.; McLean, J. *Travelling Speed and Risk of Crash Involvement on Rural Roads*; Australian Transport Safety Bureau: Adelaide, Australia, 2001.
22. Wang, C.; Quddus, M.; Ison, S. The effects of area-wide road speed and curvature on traffic casualties in England. *J. Transp. Geogr.* **2009**, *17*, 385–395. [CrossRef]
23. Baruya, A. Speed-accident relationships on European roads. In Proceedings of the 9th International Conference "Road Safety in Europe", Bergisch Gladbach, Germany, 21–23 September 1998.
24. Gitelman, V.; Doveh, E.; Bekhor, S. The relationship between free-flow travel speeds, infrastructure characteristics and accidents, on single-carriageway roads. *Transp. Res. Proc.* **2017**, *25*, 2026–2043. [CrossRef]
25. Elvik, R.; Christensen, P.; Amundsen, A.H. *Speed and Road Accidents an Evaluation of the Power Model*; Institute of Transport Economics (TØI): Oslo, Norway, 2004.
26. Quddus, M. Exploring the relationship between average speed, speed variation, and accident rates using spatial statistical models and GIS. *J. Transp. Saf. Secur.* **2013**, *5*, 27–45. [CrossRef]
27. Road Traffic Safety Agency. *Statistical Report on the State of Traffic Safety in the Republic of Serbia in 2019*; Road Traffic Safety Agency: Belgrade, Serbia, 2020.
28. Road Traffic Safety Agency. *On Line Statistical Report on the State of Traffic Safety in the Republic of Serbia for the Years from 2017 to 2019*; Road Traffic Safety Agency: Belgrade, Serbia, 2020. Available online: http://195.222.99.60/ibbsPublic/ (accessed on 25 July 2020).
29. Endsley, M.R. Toward a theory of situation awareness in dynamic systems. *Hum. Factors* **1995**, *37*, 32–64. [CrossRef]
30. Day, M.R.; Thompson, A.R.; Poulter, D.R.; Stride, C.B.; Rowe, R. Why do drivers become safer over the first three months of driving? A longitudinal qualitative study. *Accid. Anal. Prev.* **2018**, *117*, 225–231. [CrossRef]
31. Haddon, W., Jr. Advances in the epidemiology of injuries as a basis for public policy. *Public Health Rep.* **1980**, *95*, 411–421.
32. Holmes, B.D.; Haglund, K.; Ameh, E.A.; Olaomi, O.O.; Uthman, U.; Cassidy, L.D. Understanding Etiologies of Road Traffic Crashes, Injuries, and Death for Patients at National Hospital Abuja: A Qualitative Content Analysis Using Haddon's Matrix. *Qual. Rep.* **2020**, *25*, 962–974.
33. Čubranić-Dobrodolac, M.; Švadlenka, L.; Čičević, S.; Dobrodolac, M. Modelling driver propensity for traffic accidents: A comparison of multiple regression analysis and fuzzy approach. *Int. J. Inj. Control Saf. Promot.* **2020**, *27*, 156–167. [CrossRef] [PubMed]
34. Lee, D.; Donnell, E.T. Analysis of nighttime driver behavior and pavement marking effects using fuzzy inference system. *J. Comput. Civ. Eng.* **2007**, *21*, 200–210. [CrossRef]

35. Sentouh, C.; Nguyen, A.-T.; Rath, J.J.; Floris, J.; Popieul, J.-C. Human-machine shared control for vehicle lane keeping systems: A Lyapunov-based approach. *IET Intell. Transp. Syst.* **2019**, *13*, 63–71. [CrossRef]
36. Riaz, F.; Khadim, S.; Rauf, R.; Ahmad, M.; Jabbar, S.; Chaudhry, J. A validated fuzzy logic inspired driver distraction evaluation system for road safety using artificial human driver emotion. *Comput. Netw.* **2018**, *143*, 62–73. [CrossRef]
37. Lin, C.-T.; Tsai, S.-F.; Ko, L.-W. EEG-based learning system for online motion sickness level estimation in a dynamic vehicle environment. *IEEE Trans. Neural Netw. Learn. Syst.* **2013**, *24*, 1689–1700. [CrossRef]
38. Dorr, D.; Grabengiesser, D.; Gauterin, F. Online driving style recognition using fuzzy logic. In Proceedings of the IEEE 17th International Conference on Intelligent Transportation Systems (ITSC), Qingdao, China, 8–11 October 2014; pp. 1021–1026. [CrossRef]
39. Saleh, M.; Aljaafreh, A.; Albdour, N. Fuzzy-based recognition model for driving styles. *(IJEECS) Int. J. Electr. Electron. Comput. Syst.* **2013**, *16*, 816–819.
40. Bıçaksız, P.; Öztürk, İ.; Özkan, T. The differential associations of functional and dysfunctional impulsivity with driving style: A simulator study. *Transp. Res. Part F Traffic Psychol. Behav.* **2019**, *63*, 1–11. [CrossRef]
41. Pešić, D.; Trifunović, A.; Ivković, I.; Čičević, S.; Žunjić, A. Evaluation of the effects of daytime running lights for passenger cars. *Transp. Res. Part F Traffic Psychol. Behav.* **2019**, *66*, 252–261. [CrossRef]
42. Allen, M.J.; Clark, J.R. Automobile running lights—A research report. *Optom. Vis. Sci.* **1964**, *47*, 329–345. [CrossRef]
43. Dahlstedt, S.; Rumar, K. *Vehicle Colour and Front Conspicuity in Some Simulated Rural Traffic Situations*; Traffic Safety Research Group, Department of Psychology, University of Uppsala: Uppsala, Sweden, 1973.
44. Government of the Republic of Serbia. *Law on Road Traffic Safety*; Official Gazette: Belgrade, Serbia, 2019.
45. Čičević, S.; Trifunović, A.; Mitrović, S.; Nešic, M. The usability analysis of a different presentation media design for vehicle speed assessment. In *Ergonomic Design and Assessment of Products and Systems*; Žunjić, A., Ed.; Nova Science: New York, NY, USA, 2017; pp. 195–220.
46. Tse, P.U. Abutting Objects Warp the Three-Dimensional Curvature of Modally Completing Surfaces. *i-Perception* **2020**, *11*, 1–15. [CrossRef] [PubMed]
47. Toscani, M.; Valsecchi, M. Lightness discrimination depends more on bright rather than shaded regions of three-dimensional objects. *i-Perception* **2019**, *10*, 1–10. [CrossRef] [PubMed]
48. Mamdani, E.H.; Assilian, S. An experiment in linguistic synthesis with a fuzzy logic controller. *Int. J. Man-Mach. Stud.* **1975**, *7*, 1–13. [CrossRef]
49. Zadeh, L.A. The Concept of a Linguistic Variable and Its Application to Approximate Reasoning–1. *Inform. Sci.* **1975**, *8*, 199–249. [CrossRef]
50. Wang, L.-X.; Mendel, J.M. Generating fuzzy rules by learning from examples. *IEEE Trans. Syst. Man Cybern.* **1992**, *22*, 1414–1427. [CrossRef]
51. Jovčić, S.; Průša, P.; Dobrodolac, M.; Švadlenka, L. A proposal for a decision-making tool in third-party logistics (3PL) provider selection based on multi-criteria analysis and the fuzzy approach. *Sustainability* **2019**, *11*, 4236. [CrossRef]
52. Čubranić-Dobrodolac, M.; Molkova, T.; Švadlenka, L. The impact of road characteristics assessment on the traffic accidents occurrence. In Proceedings of the Sinteza 2019-International Scientific Conference on Information Technology and Data Related Research, Belgrade, Serbia, 20 April 2019; Singidunum University: Belgrade, Serbia, 2019; pp. 26–31. [CrossRef]
53. Tanaka, H.; Uejima, S.; Asai, K. Linear regression analysis with fuzzy model. *IEEE Trans. Syst. Man Cybern.* **1982**, *12*, 903–907. [CrossRef]
54. Tanaka, H. Fuzzy data analysis by possibilistic linear models. *Fuzzy Sets Syst.* **1987**, *24*, 363–375. [CrossRef]
55. Chukhrova, N.; Johannssen, A. Fuzzy regression analysis: Systematic review and bibliography. *Appl. Soft Comput.* **2019**, *84*, 105708. [CrossRef]
56. Wei, Y.; Watada, J. Building a Type II Fuzzy Qualitative Regression Model. In *Intelligent Decision Technologies*; Smart Innovation, Systems and Technologies; Watada, J., Watanabe, T., Phillips-Wren, G., Howlett, R., Jain, L., Eds.; Springer: Berlin/Heidelberg, Germany, 2012; Volume 15. [CrossRef]
57. Poleshchuk, O.; Komarov, E. A Fuzzy Nonlinear Regression Model for Interval Type-2 Fuzzy Sets. *Int. J. Math. Comput. Sci.* **2014**, *8*, 840–844. [CrossRef]
58. Hosseinzadeh, E.; Hassanpour, H.; Arefi, M. A weighted goal programming approach to fuzzy linear regression with crisp inputs and type-2 fuzzy outputs. *Soft Comput.* **2015**, *19*, 1143–1151. [CrossRef]

59. Darwish, A.; Poleshchuk, O.; Komarov, E. A New Fuzzy Linear Regression Model for a Special Case of Interval Type-2 Fuzzy Sets. *Appl. Math. Inform. Sci.* **2016**, *10*, 1209–1214. [CrossRef]
60. Wei, Y.; Watada, J. Building a type-2 fuzzy regression model based on credibility theory and its application on Arbitrage Pricing theory. *IEEJ Trans. Electr. Electron. Eng.* **2016**, *11*, 720–729. [CrossRef]
61. Bajestani, N.S.; Kamyad, A.V.; Zare, A. A piecewise type-2 fuzzy regression model. *Int. J. Comput. Intell. Syst.* **2017**, *10*, 734–744. [CrossRef]
62. Bajestani, N.S.; Kamyad, A.V.; Esfahani, E.N.; Zare, A. Prediction of retinopathy in diabetic patients using type-2 fuzzy regression model. *Eur. J. Oper. Res.* **2018**, *264*, 859–869. [CrossRef]
63. Gao, P.; Gao, Y. Quadrilateral Interval Type-2 Fuzzy Regression Analysis for Data Outlier Detection. *Math. Probl. Eng.* **2019**, *2019*, 4914593. [CrossRef]
64. Spence, I.; Yu, J.J.; Feng, J.; Marshman, J. Women match men when learning a spatial skill. *J. Exp. Psychol. Learn* **2009**, *35*, 1097–1103. [CrossRef]
65. Spence, I.; Feng, J. Video Games and Spatial Cognitio. *Rev. Gen. Psychol.* **2010**, *14*, 92–104. [CrossRef]
66. Feng, J.; Spence, I.; Pratt, J. Playing an action video game reduces gender differences in spatial cognition. *Psychol. Sci.* **2007**, *18*, 850–855. [CrossRef]
67. Milani, L.; Grumi, S.; Di Blasio, P. Positive Effects of Videogame Use on Visuospatial Competencies: The Impact of Visualization Style in Preadolescents and Adolescents. *Front. Psychol.* **2019**, *10*, 1226. [CrossRef]
68. Ali, G.A.; Tayfour, A. Characteristics and prediction of traffic accident casualties in Sudan using statistical modeling and artificial neural networks. *Int. J. Transp. Sci. Technol.* **2012**, *1*, 305–317. [CrossRef]

© 2020 by the authors. Licensee MDPI, Basel, Switzerland. This article is an open access article distributed under the terms and conditions of the Creative Commons Attribution (CC BY) license (http://creativecommons.org/licenses/by/4.0/).

Article

Waste Segregation FMEA Model Integrating Intuitionistic Fuzzy Set and the PAPRIKA Method

María Carmen Carnero [1,2]

[1] Department of Business Management, Technical School of Industrial Engineering, University of Castilla-la Mancha, 13071 Ciudad Real, Spain; carmen.carnero@uclm.es
[2] CEG-IST, Instituto Superior Técnico, Universidade de Lisboa, 1649-004 Lisboa, Portugal

Received: 8 July 2020; Accepted: 12 August 2020; Published: 17 August 2020

Abstract: Segregation is an important step in health care waste management. If done incorrectly, the risk of preventable infections, toxic effects, and injuries to care and non-care staff, waste handlers, patients, visitors, and the community at large, is increased. It also increases the risk of environmental pollution and prevents recyclable waste from being recovered. Despite its importance, it is acknowledged that poor waste segregation occurs in most health care organizations. This study therefore intends to produce, for the first time, a classification of failure modes related to segregation in the Nuclear Medicine Department of a health care organization. This will be done using Failure Mode and Effects Analysis (FMEA), by combining an intuitionistic fuzzy hybrid weighted Euclidean distance operator, and the multicriteria method Potentially All Pairwise RanKings of all possible Alternatives (PAPRIKA). Subjective and objective weights of risk factors were considered simultaneously. The failure modes identified in the top three positions are: improper storage of waste (placing items in the wrong bins), improper labeling of containers, and bad waste management (inappropriate collection periods and bin set-up).

Keywords: waste segregation; failure mode and effects analysis; intuitionistic fuzzy hybrid weighted Euclidean distance operator; PAPRIKA

1. Introduction

Health care waste (HCW) has increased considerably over recent decades due to the increase in population, number and size of health care organizations, and also through the use of disposable medical products [1]. Furthermore, in middle and low-income countries, health care waste production has increased considerably due to better access to health services. In higher income countries, the rapid ageing of the population has led to an increase in the use of health services [2,3]. This increase in HCW has been calculated at 330% over the 17-year period analyzed in Korkut [4], although the rise in the number of hospital beds was only 10%.

Waste produced as a result of health care activities carries a greater chance of causing infection and injury than other types of waste. Although only 15% of HCW is considered hazardous material that may be infectious, toxic or radioactive [5], improper segregation of health care waste leads to mixing this waste with non-hazardous waste and so to a much higher quantity of potentially hazardous waste [6]. This increases risk of injury and toxic effects, and means more time, more staff, more steps and higher transport costs in order for it to be properly disposed of [7]. If hazardous waste were immediately separated from other waste, however, the amount of dangerous waste could be reduced by 2–5%, and the risk of infection to the workers handling the waste would also be reduced [8]. A simple training program in segregation could lead to savings of 26.3% [9]. If there is no segregation of hazardous from other waste, all health care waste must be considered infectious [10].

Segregation is therefore an important step in HCW management, and consists of separating out the waste flows depending on their hazardous properties, the type of treatment, and the disposal process to be applied [8]. The World Health Organization (WHO) classifies HCW into the categories shown in Table 1. The recommended way of identifying HCW categories is to classify the waste in bags or bins of suitable materials, coded by colors, properly labeled and each in its proper place as described in WHO [5]; the basic recommendations given by the WHO should also be borne in mind [8]:

- The procedure should always take place at the source where the waste is produced.
- It can be easily applied by all care staff and is uniformly applied throughout the country.
- It is safe and guarantees absence of infectious HCW in the domestic waste flow.
- It should be well known and understood by the care staff of the health care organization.
- It should be regularly monitored to make sure that these recommendations are still being met.

Improper HCW segregation increases the risk of preventable infections, toxic effects and injuries to care and non-care staff, waste handlers, patients, visitors and the community at large. The greatest risk posed by infectious waste is accidental needle stick injuries, which can cause hepatitis B and hepatitis C and HIV infection, and recently, COVID-19. There are however numerous other diseases which can be transmitted by contact with infectious health care waste [10]. To this should be added the increase in risk of environmental pollution by cleaning waste (considered dangerous) from combustion gases. This occurs, for instance, in the process of incinerating phthalates in waste disposal sites for HCW [11] made up of polyvinyl chloride (PVC) [7], which is used in tubes and bags for saline solution, plasma and blood for transfusions, dialysis, surgical gloves, etc. It should be further borne in mind that proper segregation has other advantages when applied to non-hazardous waste, since it can be classified into recyclables, biodegradable waste and non-recyclables. If these waste categories are mixed up when they are produced, it may be impossible to prepare the recyclable waste for recovery [5].

The production and segregation of waste in health care facilities is regulated by international, national, and regional legislation, which states that waste holders are responsible for managing it appropriately, in terms both of segregation and of disposal [9]; it is, however, recognized that poor waste segregation is found in most health care organizations [12]. The problems most commonly found are lack of awareness, of health risks associated with HCW, lack of training and competence in the proper handling of waste, lack of waste management and disposal systems, deficiencies in human and economic resources, and the low priority given to the subject [13].

There are a few studies analyzing health care waste management, among which the following should be especially noted. Gai et al. [14] analyzed the results of introducing national regulations and standards for HCW management in China. It showed that the amount produced by primary health care centers is much higher than that of secondary hospitals, which is attributed to the mixing of general waste with medical waste. The study showed that establishing responsibility for medical waste management in departments and treatment rooms, prior education, and experience in learning, can be major factors that determine the knowledge of care staff in HCW management. There is therefore an urgent need for regular training programs and the proper provision of protective measures to improve the safety at work of cleaning staff. With the same goal, Moreira and Gunther [15] analyzed the improvements stemming from a medical waste management plan in Brazil a year after its introduction; the results showed that although total waste generation had increased by 9.8%, the volume of non-recyclable materials fell by 11%, the volume of recyclable materials rose by 4%, and it was also possible to segregate 7% of organic waste to be used as compost. The rate of infectious waste generation in critical areas fell from 0.021 to 0.018 kg/procedure. It was necessary to change the behavior of the staff through training. Abd El-Salam [16] studied HCW management practices in Egypt, and found that 38.9% was considered hazardous waste, and that segregation did not follow the standards, with the result that a certain amount of medical waste was mixed with domestic waste. Thus, the inappropriate practices detected are: ineffective segregation at source, inappropriate collection methods, unsafe storage of waste, inadequate financial and human resources for proper management, and deficient control of waste disposal, lack of suitable protective equipment, and lack of training and clear lines of responsibility between the departments involved in the management of hospital waste. Ferreira and Teixeira [17] suggested that waste segregation is the main deficiency found in healthcare waste practice in Portugal, while the perceptions of risk to health care staff are related to the difficulties of correctly segregating waste, and the lack of knowledge about the importance of this segregation. Manga et al. [18] assessed HCW management systems in Cameroon, highlighting how problems with the most common waste treatment and disposal methods are: dumping in uncontrolled and poorly designed tips, and incineration with inappropriate measures to address emissions to air, soil and water. They noted that the main challenges in developing countries are segregation, collection, inefficient transport of waste flow, lack of suitable training for staff, deficient collection of waste and separation of infectious and general recyclable waste, deficient legislation, management of infectious waste without adequate personal protection equipment, illegal dumping of waste and disposal together with other municipal waste. Sharma and Gupta [19] analyzed HCW management in India, and found that private hospitals produced more HCW than public ones. They saw a great need for human resources departments in hospitals that can optimally design policies and processes related to the management of health care waste. Korkut [4] indicated that to reduce the amount of HCW in Turkey, the mixture of different types of waste should be prevented, and so should the unnecessary use of hospital materials. But the best way to control the impact of HCW is to ensure that only hazardous waste is sent to treatment, while the rest is treated as household waste. Sahiledengle [20] recognized that the key aspect of an effective management of HCW is segregation of the waste at the point of production, regardless of the treatment and disposal of waste. In this study on segregation practices in Ethiopian hospitals, it can be seen that only half of health workers have good segregation practices, and to improve results, it recommends the allocation of sufficient onsite waste containers and regular training. Likewise, Kumar et al. [21] assessed the effectiveness of an intensive training program in HCW management in Pakistan, showing that training is an effective method to improve knowledge, attitudes and practices among healthcare personnel regarding infectious waste management. Along the same lines is the study by Abdo et al. [22], which showed the improvements provided by an educational program in the management of infectious and sharps waste in Kuwait.

Therefore, all the studies analyzed in different countries emphasize the importance of carrying out a proper segregation at source and that the training of health care staff is essential. This is the specific area in which this research is carried out trying to detect the failure modes that contribute most significantly to segregation problems. Although the number of studies analyzing HCW management in different countries is very important, there are no studies that prioritize segregation failure modes using a widely recognized objective method, Failure Mode and Effects Analysis (FMEA). FMEA has been widely and successfully applied in different typologies of industries and products and with different goals [23,24]. However, traditional FMEA presents numerous problems that hinder its applicability to real problems. Intuitionistic Fuzzy Sets (IFS) has been shown to be a very useful tool in FMEA for dealing with vagueness and uncertainty in the real-world risk assessment process [25].

The main contributions of this research are:

- Determining the failure modes related to environmental problems in the Nuclear Medicine Department of a health care organization with a powerful need to improve segregation of the waste produced.
- Prioritizing the various failure modes.
- Solving deficiencies of traditional FMEA by using, for the first time, a combination of an intuitionistic fuzzy hybrid weighted Euclidean distance operator and the multicriteria method Potentially All Pairwise RanKings of all possible Alternatives (PAPRIKA).
- Using a group of experts characterized by assigning an importance weight to each team member, in accordance with the latest trends in the application of FMEA [26].
- Most studies only consider subjective or objective weights of risk factors. This study considers subjective and objective weights of risk factors simultaneously.

Table 1. Categories of health care waste [5].

Non-Hazardous or General Health Care Waste	Hazardous Health Care Waste				
	Infectious Waste	Sharps Waste	Pathological Waste	Pharmaceutical Waste, Cytotoxic Waste	Chemical Waste	Radioactive Waste
Waste that contains no biological, chemical, radioactive or physical hazard.	Waste that contains, or is suspected of containing, pathogens, and poses a risk of transmission of disease, for example, water and other waste contaminated with blood or other bodily fluids, including highly infectious waste such as laboratory cultures and microbiological stocks; excreta and other materials that have been in contact with patients with highly infectious diseases in isolation wards.	Used or unused sharps, for example, hypodermic, intravenous or other needles; auto-disposable syringes; syringes with attached needles; infusion sets; scalpels; pipettes; knives, blades, broken glass.	Human tissues, organs or fluids; body parts, foetuses, unused blood products.	Pharmaceuticals that are past their use-by date or have become unnecessary; items contaminated by or containing pharmaceuticals. Cytotoxic waste containing substances with genotoxic properties, for example, waste containing cytostatic drugs (often used in cancer therapy); genotoxic chemicals.	Waste containing chemical substances, for example laboratory reagents; film developer; disinfectants that are past their use-by date, or that will no longer be necessary; solvents; waste with a high content of heavy metals, such as batteries, broken thermometers and blood pressure gauges.	For example, unused radiotherapy or laboratory research liquids; contaminated glassware, packages or absorbent paper; urine and excreta from patients treated with unsealed radionuclides.

PAPRIKA has been used in place of other multicriteria methods because it involves more judgements than traditional scoring methods, it is simpler to apply, and it reflects the preferences of decision makers more accurately [27]; additionally it is cost-effective, reproducible and it is less cognitively burdensome for decision makers than other methods. Another advantage is that is produce a set of weightings for each decision maker, unlike other MCDM methods, which only give aggregated data. This allows comparisons of weightings between subgroups of participants [28].

The paper is structured as follows. Firstly, it includes a literature review on FMEA and the problems with traditional FMEA, along with multicriteria techniques and intuitionistic fuzzy sets in FMEA. Intuitionistic Fuzzy Failure Model and Effect Analysis methodology is then described. Next, the waste segregation FMEA model integrating Intuitionistic Fuzzy Hybrid Weighted Euclidean Distance Operator and PAPRIKA method applied to the Nuclear Medicine service of a hospital is described. Then the results obtained in the Health Care Organisation are set out. Finally come the discussion, conclusions and references.

2. Literature Review

FMEA is a systematic and analytical technique that combines the technology and experience of experts to identify, analyze and prevent possible failure modes or difficulties in product and process before they take place; the aim is to determine preventive actions in systems, products, processes or services to eliminate or diminish the probability of failures and errors [29]. FMEA is the subjective assessment of risk dependent on expert judgement [30].

Traditional FMEA uses a risk priority number (RPN) to prioritize failure modes in a system, process, design, product or service. In this way, limited company resources can be allocated to the high-risk failure modes. The RPN is obtained by multiplying the probability of occurrence of the failure (O), the severity of the failure (S) and the ability to detect the failure before the impact of the effect occurs (D).

$$RPN = O \times S \times D \quad (1)$$

O, S and D are usually measured on a scale comprising 10 levels from 1 to 10, as shown in the example for the probability of Occurrence in Table 2. Failure modes with higher RPN are considered to be of greater importance, and they should be afforded greater attention with respect to risk mitigation.

Table 2. Ratings of probability of occurrence of a failure mode [1].

Rank	Probability of Failure	Possible Failure Rates
10	Extremely high: failure almost inevitable	≥1 in 2
9	Very high	1 in 3
8	Repeated failures	1 in 8
7	High	1 in 20
6	Moderately high	1 in 80
5	Moderate	1 in 400
4	Relatively low	1 in 2000
3	Low	1 in 15,000
2	Remote	1 in 150,000
1	Nearly impossible	≤1 in 1,500,000

Traditional FMEA employs a risk priority number (RPN) to prioritize failure modes of a system, process, design, product or service. In this way, limited company resources can be allocated to the high-risk failure modes. The RPN is obtained by multiplying the probability of occurrence of the failure (O), the severity of the failure (S) and the ability to detect the failure before the impact of the effect occurs (D).

Traditional FMEA processes use the following procedure [31]: (1) determine the scope of FMEA analysis; (2) designate FMEA team; (3) identify potential failure modes and effects; (4) determine O, S, and D of each failure mode; (5) calculate the RPN of each failure mode; (6) prioritize the failure modes;

(7) report the results of the analysis; and finally (8) calculate the new RPNs when the failure modes have been diminished or eliminated.

Although traditional FMEA has been used successfully since 1960 in different types of companies and real-world examples, the crisp RPN method does, however, have important deficiencies ([1,24,32]):

- O, S and D are considered to have similar importance, which need not be the case in a practical application of the FMEA process.
- Different combinations of O, S and D can generate the same RPN value; however, their hidden risk implications can be totally different. This could cause loss of resources and time, or some high-risk failure modes may go unnoticed.
- O, S and D are difficult to determine precisely by FMEA team members, because a lot of information is often uncertain, vague or expressed in linguistic terms.
- The mathematical formula for calculating RPN is questionable because there is no scientific basis for why O, S and D should be multiplied to obtain RPN.
- The conversion of scores is different for the three risk factors. Thus, while a nonlinear conversion is used between O and the associated ratings, a linear transformation is used for D.
- The RPN only measures risk, but does not take into account the importance or cost of corrective actions in the analysis; Additionally, RPN cannot be used to measure the effectiveness of corrective actions.
- RPNs are not continuous, but rather have many gaps, since many numbers on [1, 1000] cannot be generated from Equation (1). Only 120 of the possible 1000 numbers can be obtained.
- Interdependencies between various failures modes and effects on the same levels and different levels of hierarchical structure of an engineering system are not considered.
- Equation (1) is strongly sensitive to variations in risk factor assessments; that is, a small variation in one rating can lead to a significantly larger effect on the RPN, depending on the values of the other risk factors.
- The RPN elements have many duplicate numbers, for example, 60 RPNs can be formed from 24 different combinations of values of O, S and D.
- The RPN considers only three risk factors related to safety; other important factors such as production cost, quality or other economic aspects are ignored.
- O, S, and D are assessed using discrete ordinal measurement scales. But they are treated as though the numerical operations on them, such as multiplication, were significant. The results are not only meaningless but are in fact misleading.
- The customers' expectations are not usually taken into account during the risk analysis. Severity rates are generally established from the point of view of the organization and not that of its customers [33].

These deficiencies have led to inefficiencies in the practical applications of traditional FMEA [34]. Therefore, variations on traditional FMEA have been proposed, many of which include Multi-Criteria Decision Making (MCDM) analysis because prioritization of failure modes is a topic that considers multiple risk factors [26].

The literature review carried out by Liu [35] between 1992 and 2016 integrating FMEA with uncertainty theories and multicriteria decision making methods identified 56 contributions which have tried to solve the problems of the traditional FMEA. 16 of these studies used distance-based MCDM methods; 11 used compromise-ranking MCDM methods (that is, VIseKriterijumska Optimizacija I Kompromisno Resenje (VIKOR) and Technique for Order of Preference by Similarity to Ideal Solution (TOPSIS)); three papers used our ranking methods (QUALItative FLEXible (QUALIFLEX), ELimination Et Choice Translating REality (ELECTRE) and Preference Ranking Organisation METHod for Enrichment of Evaluations (PROMETHEE)); and eight used pairwise comparison MCDM methods (Analytic Hierarchy Process (AHP) and Analytic Network Process (ANP)). Eighteen other studies used other MCDM methods (Decision-Making Trial and Evaluation Laboratory (DEMATEL), multiple multi-objective optimization by ratio analysis (MULTIMOORA), COPRAS-G, etc.) and Eight used a hybrid MCDM method in which some of the above methods were combined. In addition, based on the 165 papers that included improvements in the application of FMEA, it can be seen how 85 of them used fuzzy sets, with Dempster–Shafer theory a long way behind with 10 contributions. In addition, the evolution of the publication of articles on improvements in FMEA follows a growing exponential trend, with a considerable increase from 2007.

A more recent literature review by Liu et al. [26] looked at 169 studies on FMEA integrated with different typologies of MCDM to counter the disadvantages of the use of RPN. Most of these studies used the risk factors (O, S, D), although in some cases they also use expected cost, cost of failures, profitability, failure mode importance, and weight of corrective actions, or multiple sub-risk factors for O, S, D. The most commonly used technique for the assignment of weights to the criteria is given directly, followed by expert judgement, the entropy method, fuzzy AHP, AHP, ordered weighting, Data Envelopment Analysis (DEA) and a combination of expert judgement and the entropy method.

In FMEA, the most commonly used MCDM methods, with 30.2% of contributions, are distance-based methods, among which Gray Relational Analysis (GRA) and TOPSIS stand out due to their simplicity and robustness, while DEMATEL, DEA, VIKOR, and Fuzzy Weighted Geometric Mean (FWGM) have also been applied frequently to prioritize failure modes in FMEA.

Among the more recent studies with hybrid models combining FMEA and MCDM is Kutlu and Ekmekçioğlu [36], who used fuzzy AHP to compute the weighting vector of three risk factors, and fuzzy TOPSIS to obtain a ranking for the failure modes. Fuzzy TOPSIS was also used by Mangeli et al. [37] for the same purpose. Wang et al. [38] used interval-valued intuitionistic fuzzy sets (IVIFSs) in an ANP method to obtain weightings for the risk factors, and the IVIF-COPRAS method to rank the failure modes. Bao et al. [39] combined FMEA with fuzzy AHP to assess occupational disease. Fattahi and Khalilzadeh [40] used a fuzzy weighted risk priority number instead of traditional RPN; the weightings of these risk factors were calculated via fuzzy AHP. Fuzzy MULTIMOORA was used to calculate the weight of each failure mode from the criteria time, cost, and profit. Tian et al. [41] used the fuzzy best-worst method to obtain weightings for the risk factors, and fuzzy VIKOR to prioritize the failure modes. Boral et al. [42], on the other hand, used fuzzy AHP to calculate the relative importance of the risk factors, and a modified Fuzzy Multi-Attribute Ideal Real Comparative Analysis (MAIRCA) to rank the failure modes. Zhu et al. [43] combined linguistic neutrosophic numbers, regret theory, and PROMETHEE to obtain the risk priorities of failure modes, taking into account psychological behaviors in the approach of the decision makers. Wang et al. [44] used AHP to calculate the weightings of the risk factors, while the failure modes were prioritised via the closeness coefficient. A wide variety of MCDM's are therefore used to carry out FMEA analysis. However, in no prior case has PAPRIKA been used, despite its greater precision, and the ease with which it obtains judgements from the decision makers.

Numerous methods have combined fuzzy sets with FMEA to configure fuzzy FMEA; fuzzy sets based on triangular fuzzy numbers is the method most commonly preferred in the studies reviewed by Liu et al. [26] for risk assessment, such as [25,31,33–35,45–50].

However, the number of contributions using intuitionistic fuzzy sets in the field of FMEA is smaller despite the improvements they represent compared to fuzzy FMEA. Among these are Chang and Cheng [51], which integrated intuitionistic fuzzy sets and DEMATEL to prioritize failure modes in a 0.15 µm DRAM engraving process. Liu et al. [52] used the Intuitionistic Fuzzy Hybrid Weighted Euclidean Distance (IFHWED) operator for the prioritization of failure modes, while the uncertain assessments given by FMEA team members are treated as linguistic terms expressed in Intuitionistic Fuzzy Numbers (IFNs), and the Intuitionistic Fuzzy Weighted Averaging (IFWA) operator is used to add the FMEA team members individual judgements into a group assessment. Liu et al. [53] used the Interval 2-Tuple Hybrid Weighted Distance (ITHWD) operator and assignments provided by the FMEA team members are included using interval 2-tuple linguistic variables; additionally, subjective and objective weights of risk factors have been taken into account in the prioritization of the failure modes that appear in the blood transfusion process. Liu et al. [25] applied the intuitionistic fuzzy hybrid TOPSIS method to prioritize failure modes in super-twisted nematic color. The IFWA operator is employed to aggregate the trials of the FMEA team members. The IFHWED operator is then used to obtain the distances of each failure mode from intuitionistic fuzzy positive ideal and negative ideal solutions. Finally, a relative closeness coefficient is used to compute the risk priority of the failure modes. Both subjective and objective weights of risk factors are taken into account in the study. Guo [54] used linguistic variables and intuitionistic fuzzy numbers to evaluate S, O, and D and transform them into basic probability assignment functions; the Jousselme distance is then used to obtain the weightings of the decision makers. The weighted trial average is obtained and the classical Dempster combination rule is used to combine the modified mass functions. Tooranloo and Ayatollah [55] calculated the weight of risk factors using intuitionistic fuzzy linguistic terms and the IFWA operator to aggregate weighting factors while the failure modes of the quality of internet banking services have been prioritized using the intuitionistic fuzzy TOPSIS technique. Yazdi [56] used the IFHWED operator together with TOPSIS to prioritize hazards occurring in a gas refinery for welding and lamination processes. A heterogeneous group of experts was used to assign a level of confidence or weight to each expert for which AHP has been used. Mirghafoori et al. [57] analyze the quality of the electronic library services in a university library using entropy based on FMEA model in the intuitionistic fuzzy environment. Tooranloo et al. [58] evaluated 16 failure modes related with knowledge management in organizations in an oil and gas company. To do this, they determined the weight of each decision maker using linguistic expressions and intuitionistic fuzzy numbers. Next, an aggregated matrix of intuitionistic fuzzy decisions, based on the decision-makers' judgements, was generated using the IFWA operator. The weight of each risk factor was calculated using linguistic expressions and intuitionistic fuzzy numbers through the IFWA operator. Since TOPSIS is being used in this intuitionistic environment, it is necessary to determine the intuitionistic fuzzy positive and negative ideal amounts for, then to compute the distance between failure items through positive and negative ideals. This was done using normalized Euclidean distance. Finally, the relative proximity ratio was calculated. The results were that the priority failure modes were identified to be lack of management commitment and leadership. Can [59] ranked corrective-preventive strategies through the combination of FMEA and Weighted Aggregated Sum Product Assessment (WASPAS). Intuitionistic fuzzy risk priority numbers, duration of exposure, occurrence, detection, severity, cost, and system safety factors were used.

Therefore, although the number of contributions that use an intuitionistic fuzzy set in FMEA is very limited, it has been successfully applied to different fields with the use of different distance operators. However, in no case has it been applied with the aim of prioritizing segregation failure modes in a health care organization. In the specific area of HCW, only the research by Liu et al. [60] used fuzzy set theory and VIKOR method selection for the appropriate treatment method in HCW. Linguistic variables are used to assign the ratings and weights to the criteria, while the Ordered Weighted Averaging (OWA) operator is used to aggregate individual opinions of decision makers into a group assessment.

3. Intuitionistic Fuzzy Failure Model and Effect Analysis Methodology

A risk classification procedure was designed using risk analysis techniques together with multicriteria techniques, and an FMEA methodology applied using the Intuitionistic Fuzzy Hybrid Weighted Euclidean Distance (IFHWED) Operator and the multicriteria method PAPRIKA.

This methodology has the advantage that when using linguistic terms for the assignment of values to the risk factors, these assessments are much more precise. For this purpose, the Intuitionistic Fuzzy Set (IFS) concept will be used. IFS was introduced by Atanassov [61] considering a generalization of fuzzy and more exhaustive elements than fuzzy conventional sets, which only have a membership function [62]; in addition, they allow the hesitation and the indeterminacy that are generally found in decision-making processes to be considered, something that is not taken into account in the fuzzy set [63]. They have a more logical mathematical framework to deal with inaccurate facts or incomplete information [55]. IFSs are characterized by a membership function, a non-membership function, and an indeterminacy function. Therefore, IFS is recognized as a suitable approach to deal with the ambiguities and uncertainties present in the realization of FMEA [51].

The methodology set out below allows the limitations of the traditional FMEA to be overcome, and its effectiveness to be improved. The uncertainty in the assessments of the team in the FMEA study is handled using linguistic terms expressed with intuitionistic fuzzy numbers.

If X is considered a fixed set, an IFS S in X is introduced in accordance with Equation (2) [35]:

$$S = \{\langle x, \mu_s(x), v_s(x) \rangle x \in X\} \qquad (2)$$

where $\mu_s(x) : X \to [0,1]$ is a membership function and $v_s(x) : X \to [0,1]$ a non-membership function and $0 \leq \mu_s(x) + v_s(x) \leq 1, \forall x \in X$ is satisfied. Furthermore, $\pi_s(x) = 1 - \mu_s(x) - v_s(x)$ is called the hesitation degree of $x \in X$ and represents the degree of uncertainty or hesitancy of x to S, satisfying $0 \leq \pi_s(x) \leq 1, \forall x \in X$ [64].

Whether $\pi_s(x)$ is higher or lower is an indication that x is more or less uncertain respectively. If $\mu_s(x)$ and $v_s(x)$ are continuous functions, IFS regresses to traditional fuzzy sets when $\mu_s(x) = 1 - v_s(x)$, while when $\mu_s(x) = 1 - v_s(x)$ is equal to 0 or 1, it is a crisp set.

$(\mu_s(x), v_s(x))$ is known as an Intuitionistic Fuzzy Number (IFN) and can be denoted by $\alpha = (\mu_\alpha, v_\alpha)$ where $\mu_\alpha \in [0,1], v_\alpha \in [0,1]$, and satisfying $\mu_\alpha + v_\alpha \leq 1$. $\alpha^+ = (1,0)$ and $\alpha^- = (0,1)$ are respectively the largest and smallest IFNs.

Let $\alpha_1 = (\mu_{\alpha_1}, v_{\alpha_1})$, $\alpha_2 = (\mu_{\alpha_2}, v_{\alpha_2})$ be two IFNs, the operational laws of IFNs are expressed by Equations (3) to (5) [65]:

$$\alpha_1 + \alpha_2 = (\mu_{\alpha_1} + \mu_{\alpha_2} - \mu_{\alpha_1}\mu_{\alpha_2}, v_{\alpha_1}v_{\alpha_2}) \qquad (3)$$

$$\alpha_1 \times \alpha_2 = (\mu_{\alpha_1}\mu_{\alpha_2}, v_{\alpha_1} + v_{\alpha_2} - v_{\alpha_1}v_{\alpha_2}) \qquad (4)$$

$$\lambda\alpha_1 = (1 - (1 - \mu_{\alpha_1})^\lambda, v_{\alpha_1}^\lambda), \lambda > 0$$
$$\alpha_1^\lambda = (\mu_{\alpha_1}^\lambda, 1 - (1 - v_{\alpha_1})^\lambda), \lambda > 0 \qquad (5)$$

Table 3 shows the linguistic terms and the IFNs used to assess the failure modes [56].

Table 3. Linguistic terms for assessing failure modes.

Linguistic Terms	IFN
Extremely low (EL)	(0.10, 0.90)
Very low (VL)	(0.25, 0.70)
Low (L)	(0.30, 0.60)
Medium low (ML)	(0.40, 0.50)
Medium (M)	(0.50, 0.50)
Medium high (MH)	(0.60, 0.30)
High (H)	(0.70, 0.20)
Very high (VH)	(0.75, 0.20)
Extremely high (EH)	(0.90, 0.10)

Most FMEA methods consider only objective or subjective risk weights independently. To overcome this problem, objective and subjective weightings of risk factors are considered simultaneously in this methodology, as suggested in Liu et al. [25] and Liu [35]. Subjective weights are evaluated by a decision-making group using the linguistic terms shown in Table 4 [56]. Objective weights are determined using the ordered weights of the risk factors, which are derived from the method based on the normal distribution.

Table 4. Linguistic terms for assessing subjective weights of risk factors.

Linguistic Terms	IFN
Very low (VL)	(0.10, 0.85)
Low (L)	(0.25, 0.70)
Moderate (M)	(0.50, 0.50)
High (H)	(0.75, 0.20)
Very high (VH)	(0.90, 0.05)

The decision group must provide individual assessments of failure modes using the linguistic terms defined by IFNs.

The Intuitionistic Fuzzy Distance (IFD) between two IFNs, $\alpha_1 = (\mu_{\alpha_1}, \nu_{\alpha_1})$ and $\alpha_2 = (\mu_{\alpha_2}, \nu_{\alpha_2})$ will be defined as shown in Equation (6) [25].

$$d_{IFD}(\alpha_1, \alpha_2) = \frac{1}{2} \times (|\mu_{\alpha_1} - \mu_{\alpha_2}| + |\nu_{\alpha_1} - \nu_{\alpha_2}|) \quad (6)$$

There are assumed to be l members in the decision group responsible for the assessment of m failure modes with respect to n risk factors. Each member of the decision group will have an assigned weighting $\lambda_k > 0$ ($k = 1, 2, \ldots, l$) satisfying $\sum_{k=1}^{l} \lambda_k = 1$ to reflect the relative importance of each member of the group.

Let $\alpha_{ij}^k = (\mu_{ij}^k, \nu_{ij}^k)$ be an IFN provided by each member of the group to assess each failure mode with respect to each risk factor, and $w_j^k = (\mu_j^k, \nu_j^k)$ is the subjective weighting of each risk factor given by each member of the decision group. The Intuitionistic Fuzzy Weighted Averaging (IFWA) operator (see Equations (7) and (8)) will be used to aggregate the judgements and derive a consensus judgement stemming from the decision group [35].

$$\alpha_{ij} = IFWA\left(\alpha_{ij}^1, \alpha_{ij}^2, \ldots, \alpha_{ij}^l\right) = \sum_{k=1}^{l} \lambda_k \alpha_{ij}^k = \left[1 - \prod_{k=1}^{l}\left(1 - \mu_{ij}^k\right)^{\lambda_k}, \prod_{k=1}^{l}\left(\nu_{ij}^k\right)^{\lambda_k}\right], \quad (7)$$
$$i = 1, 2, \ldots, m; j = 1, 2, \ldots, n$$

$$w_j = IFWA\left(w_j^1, w_j^2, \ldots, w_j^l\right) = \sum_{k=1}^{l} \lambda_k w_j^k = \left[1 - \prod_{k=1}^{l}\left(1 - \mu_j^k\right)^{\lambda_k}, \prod_{k=1}^{l}\left(\nu_j^k\right)^{\lambda_k}\right], \quad (8)$$
$$j = 1, 2, \ldots, n$$

where $\alpha_{ij} = (\mu_{ij}, \nu_{ij})$ are the assessments of the group comprising l members for the failure modes with respect to the risk factors, and $w_j = (\mu_j, \nu_j)$ are the subjective weightings of the group for the risk factors of the l members of the group.

The subjective weightings of the risk factors will be determined using the subjective weightings of the group $w_j = (\mu_j, \nu_j)$ obtained from Equation (8). These weightings will be normalised using Equation (9) [35].

$$\overline{w}_j = \frac{\mu_j + \pi_j\left(\frac{\mu_j}{\mu_j + \nu_j}\right)}{\sum_{j=1}^{n}\left(\mu_j + \pi_j\left(\frac{\mu_j}{\mu_j + \nu_j}\right)\right)}, \quad j = 1, 2, \ldots, n \quad (9)$$

where $\pi_j = 1 - \mu_j - \nu_j$ is the hesitation degree, and $\sum_{j=1}^{n} \overline{w}_j = 1$.

The objective weightings of the risk factors were determined using the normal distribution-based method developed by Xu [66].

Next, reference series for risk factors should be established. These reference series should be the optimal level of all risk factors for failure modes in FMEA. When FMEA is being performed, the smaller score represents a lower risk, therefore, the minimum value $\alpha^- = (0, 1)$ can be used as a reference series. This can be expressed as shown in Equation (10).

$$\widetilde{A}_0 = [\alpha_{01}, \alpha_{02}, \ldots, \alpha_{0n}] = [\alpha^-, \alpha^-, \ldots, \alpha^-] \tag{10}$$

The IFHWED operator is used to calculate the distances between the reference series and the aggregated results (see Equation (11)).

$$IFHWED\left(\widetilde{A}_i, \widetilde{A}_0\right) = \varphi(\sum_{j=1}^{n} \overline{w}_j(d_{IFD}(\alpha_{ij}, \alpha_{0j}))^2)^{\frac{1}{2}} + (1-\varphi)(\sum_{j=1}^{n} \omega_j(d_{IFD}(\alpha_{i\sigma(j)}, \alpha_{0\sigma(j)}))^2)^{1/2} \quad i = 1, 2, \ldots, m \tag{11}$$

where $(\alpha(1), \ldots, \alpha(n))$ is any permutation of $(1, 2, \ldots, n)$ such that $d_{IFD}(\alpha_{i\sigma(j-1)}, \alpha_{0\sigma(j-1)}) \geq d_{IFD}(\alpha_{i\sigma(j)}, \alpha_{0\sigma(j)})$, $j = 1, 2, \ldots, n$ and $\varphi \in [0, 1]$.

Next, all failure modes are classified in descending order of the IFHWEDs obtained. The greater distance implies a higher overall risk of failure mode.

The relative weights of the decision group members were provided in the form of non-fuzzy values because they are relatively easy to determine in the study. However, other methods, such as fuzzy AHP or the Delphi method, could be used. The linguistic terms included in Table 4 can also be applied and Equation (9) can be used to calculate them.

4. Waste Segregation FMEA Model Integrating Intuitionistic Fuzzy Sets and the PAPRIKA Method

The application of the methodology outlined in the previous section to prioritizing failure modes related to HCW segregation problems in a Hospital is shown below.

From the Central Services of the Health Service of Castilla-La Mancha (Spain) there is a great concern for reducing the amount of waste generated in a hospital. To do this, they consider the need to improve the segregation of hospital waste. For this study, the Nuclear Medicine Service is selected as a pilot unit in which to analyze the problems and solutions to be proposed. The choice of this service instead of others is because it generates a large amount of waste (it is the 11th service in terms of annual waste generation of the 41 into which the hospital is organized) and, in addition, it can generate waste of all the different possible typologies such as [67]:

- Group I: general, no risk.
- Group II: sanitary, assimilated to urban.
- Group III: sanitary, potentially infectious.
- Group IV: bodies and human remains.
- Group V: dangerous chemical waste.
- Group VI: cytotoxic with carcinogenic, mutagenic and teratogenic risk.
- Group VII: radioactive.

Radioactive waste is low and medium activity, does not generate heat and has a relatively short radioactive life (about 30 years as a limit). It is mainly about operating material such as gloves, rags, syringes, filters, etc.

The goal is to extend the improvement plans and actions to the other areas, units and services of the hospital.

The flow chart with the steps that have been followed in this investigation are shown in Figure 1.

In order to identify the failure modes related to waste segregation, surveys were carried out with personnel who work in the Nuclear Medicine Department: the head of department, a nuclear medicine specialist doctor, service supervisor, senior technicians, nurses and administrative assistants and caretakers. The results of the survey were that 60% of respondents believed that the service did not have adequate containers for type II waste, 62.5% of care and non-care staff did not perform correct segregation of type II waste, 56.25% of the respondents do not know the maximum time that elapses in the collection of waste, 93.75% of the staff do not know the weight thresholds (minimum and maximum) per container, 87.5% believe that there is no documentation with the action procedures in waste management, and 50% consider that the presence of intermediate waste containers in the department is necessary. From the complete results obtained from the survey, the failure modes shown in Table 5 were established.

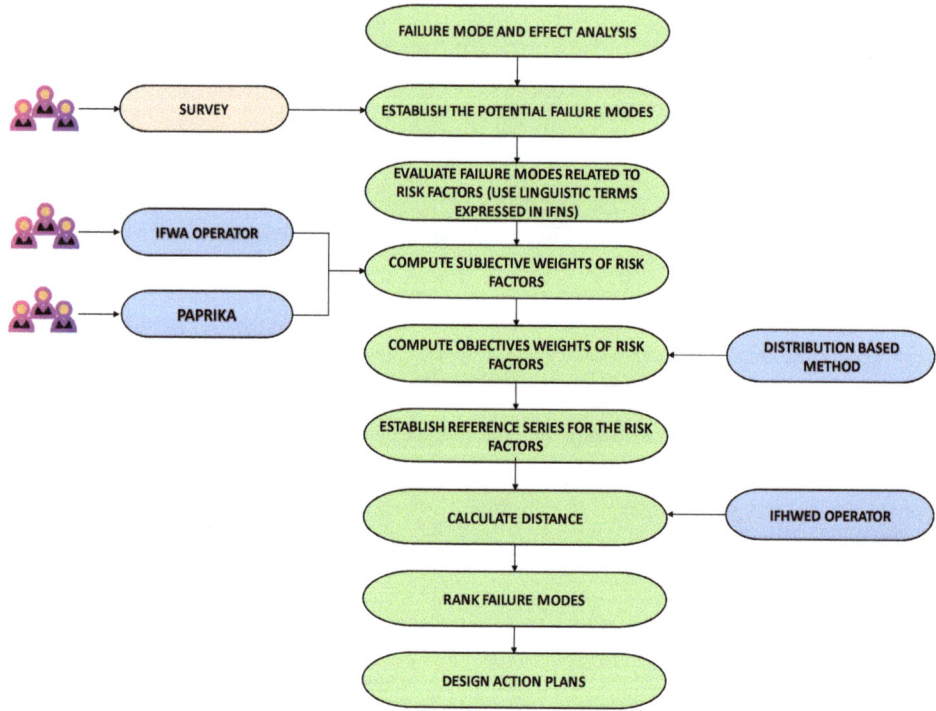

Figure 1. Flowchart of the study.

Table 5. Nuclear Medicine Department segregation failure modes.

Failure Mode	Description
Failure mode 1	Incorrect labeling; for example, marking a container as organic material when in fact it is a container for glass
Failure mode 2	Poor waste management; for example: putting bags inside a container implying that a container is permanent when it is not, lack of collection with the necessary frequency
Failure mode 3	Improperly stored waste; deposit items in containers that do not correspond; for example, organic matter to a glass container
Failure mode 4	Collection of containers when they reach minimum weights per container
Failure mode 5	Lack of space for correct placement of containers or new containers
Failure mode 6	Lack of information from healthcare staff on: collection time, container location, weight thresholds, maximum and minimum container
Failure mode 7	Lack of signage/posters on environmental risks
Failure mode 8	Lack of training of health personnel on environmental risks
Failure mode 9	Lack of continuous control of data on quantities/weights/elements generated

Visual documents on non-conformities were also collected, such as, for example, Figure 2 shows how tweezers had been disposed of in a container for storing needles, the correct action being sterilization of the tweezers.

Figure 2. Incorrect segregation of waste documented in the Nuclear Medicine Service.

The judgements necessary for the application of this methodology were made by two Decision Makers (DM_i). One of them has had the role of Deputy Director of Technical Services of the Hospital, whose responsibility included the Environment Area of the Hospital. The other Decision Maker is an external expert, although he is knowledgeable about the environmental problems of the Hospital. Like [56], the experts used in the allocation of occurrence, severity and detectability in this research have very different knowledge and experiences in the area analyzed, being very positive for the allocation process. Table 6 shows the judgements given by both DMs evaluating the different failure modes described with respect to the criteria: occurrence, severity and detectability. A number of different linguistic term scales were gathered from the literature [35,52,55,68], to provide linguistic terms for assessing subjective weights of risk factors and for assessing failure modes. The linguistic scales were chosen from among the different options available by means of a questionnaire given to the decision makers about their preferences. The scales chosen were the nine-point rating scale shown in Table 3, and the same scale was used for the three risk criteria to avoid confusion in the assessment of failure modes, and the scale in Table 4. The results of the aggregation of the judgements using Equations (7) and (8) are shown in Table 7. A weight of 0.25 has been assigned to DM_1 and 0.75 to DM_2.

Table 6. Evaluation of the failure modes in each criterion by the DMs.

Criteria	Occurrence		Severity		Detectability	
Decision Maker	DM_1	DM_2	DM_1	DM_2	DM_1	DM_2
Failure mode 1	EH	H	EH	MH	VH	M
Failure mode 2	VH	H	VH	MH	M	H
Failure mode 3	EH	MH	EH	MH	VH	H
Failure mode 4	M	H	MH	H	VH	M
Failure mode 5	ML	ML	ML	M	MH	ML
Failure mode 6	H	MH	MH	MH	M	H
Failure mode 7	MH	M	MH	H	VL	H
Failure mode 8	VH	MH	H	MH	M	H
Failure mode 9	M	H	ML	MH	M	MH

Table 7. Evaluation of the failure modes in each criterion by the DMs.

Criteria	Occurrence		Severity		Detectability	
Decision Maker	DM_1	DM_2	DM_1	DM_2	DM_1	DM_2
Failure mode 1	0.444	0.168	0.411	0.228	0.293	0.398
Failure mode 2	0.362	0.200	0.324	0.271	0.292	0.251
Failure mode 3	0.411	0.228	0.411	0.228	0.362	0.200
Failure mode 4	0.292	0.251	0.315	0.221	0.293	0.398
Failure mode 5	0.164	0.500	0.194	0.500	0.213	0.440
Failure mode 6	0.305	0.271	0.274	0.300	0.292	0.251
Failure mode 7	0.241	0.440	0.315	0.221	0.247	0.274
Failure mode 8	0.324	0.271	0.305	0.271	0.292	0.251
Failure mode 9	0.215	0.251	0.229	0.341	0.250	0.341

Applying the method based on the normal distribution of Xu [66], the objective weights of the risk factors are obtained. For this, the Ordered Weighted Averaging (OWA) operator is used to determine their associated weightings. The OWA operator has been used in many applications, especially in environmental problems [60,69]. This operator has the advantage that the input data are rearranged in descending order, and the weights associated with the OWA operator are the weights of the ordered positions of the input data rather than of the input data itself [60].

If μ_n is the mean of the collection of 1, 2, ..., n, and σ_n ($\sigma_n > 0$) is the standard deviation of the collection 1, 2, ..., n and both can be calculated from the expressions:

$$\mu_n = \frac{1+n}{2} \qquad (12)$$

$$\sigma_n = \left(\frac{1}{n}\sum_{i=1}^{n}(i-\mu_n)^2\right)^{1/2} \qquad (13)$$

Then the weight vector of the OWA operator can be calculated from the equation [66]:

$$w_i = \frac{e^{-[\frac{(1-\frac{1+n}{2})^2}{2\sigma_n^2}]}}{\sum_{j=1}^{n} e^{-[\frac{(j-\frac{1+n}{2})^2}{2\sigma_n^2}]}}, \quad i = 1, 2, \ldots, n \qquad (14)$$

The order of the criteria, Occurrence (O), Severity (S) and Detectability (D), and thus the weighting assigned to each of them, was decided by one of the decision makers used in the study. Therefore, for $n = 3$ we obtain:

$$\mu_3 = 2; \sigma_n = \sqrt{\frac{2}{3}}$$

$$w_O = \frac{e^{-3/4}}{1+2e^{-3/4}} = 0.243$$

$$w_S = \frac{1}{1+2e^{-3/4}} = 0.514$$

$$w_D = \frac{e^{-3/4}}{1+2e^{-3/4}} = 0.243$$

Therefore, the vector of objective weightings obtained is the following:

$$\omega = (0.243, 0.514, 0.243)$$

Next, the PAPRIKA multicriteria technique [27] will be used to obtain the subjective weightings of the risk factors. PAPRIKA has been successfully applied in numerous real-world problems particularly related to the health care field, for example in patient prioritization [70,71], health technology prioritization [28,72], disease classification and diagnosis [73], disease prioritization for R&D [74], assessment of non-clinical hospital services [75], to analyze preferences for physical activity attributes in adults with chronic knee pain [76], or to value health states worse than dead [77].

PAPRIKA has been used, implemented through 1000minds software, since, in real time and very efficiently, it tracks all the potentially millions of pair rankings of the options made by decision makers. Furthermore, unlike other methods based on ratio measurements of the decision makers' preferences, for example the ratio-scale measurement of 1 to 9 used by AHP, PAPRIKA selects an option from just two possibilities. This is a much simpler and more natural selection method [28]. All this provides great confidence in the answers provided by the decision makers [78].

PAPRIKA allows a ranking of alternatives to be obtained by comparing pairs of all potentially non-dominated pairs with respect to all possible alternatives in the model. A non-dominated pair is a pair of alternatives in which one of them has a higher rank in at least one criterion and a lower rank in at least one other criterion, and therefore a judgement of the decision maker is necessary for the alternatives to be classified by pairwise comparisons. On the other hand, a dominated pair is a pair of alternatives in which one of them has a higher rank category in at least one criterion and none of a lower rank in the other criterion, so it is not necessary to make the comparison. The number of pairwise comparisons is minimized by a method that identifies all pairs classified as evident within the explicit pair ranking [27].

The steps to be followed to apply this technique are:

1. Definition of the criteria and the levels of each criterion.
2. Definition of possible alternatives and obtaining of total scores.
3. Identification of undominated pairs.
4. Classification of non-dominated pairs and identification of all implicitly ranked pairs.
5. Obtaining the global ranking of alternatives.

PAPRIKA starts out by identifying all the pairs of options defined for two criteria simultaneously, and which involve compensation. Each decision maker must choose in random order between pairs of options. Each time the decision maker classifies a pair of options, all the remaining hypothetical options that could be classified by pairs by transitivity are identified and eliminated. For example, if a decision maker prefers A to B, and then B to C, then by transitivity, A has priority over C. This procedure guarantees that the number of questions put to the decision maker is minimized. However, the decision maker classifies by pairs all the alternatives differentiated in two criteria simultaneously, both explicitly and implicitly, that is, by transitivity. The number of questions put to the decision maker depends on the number of criteria and on the levels associated to each criterion. As an example, with four criteria and three or four levels per criterion, approximately 30 judgements are required [78]. Some questions are repeated as an internal consistency check [79]. From the classifications by explicit pairs, 1000Minds using linear programming, which can be consulted in Hansen and Ombler [27], to calculate the weightings of the criteria. The decision makers' weights are averaged to obtain mean weights and standard deviations for the decision makers as a set. Significant differences in the mean weights for the criteria ($p < 0.05$) are assessed by variance analysis for the normally distributed variables, and by the Kruskal-Wallis rank test when the normality criterion was not satisfied [79].

According to [79], the global values for risk S_{Rj}, and value S_{Vj}, are calculated from Equations (15) and (16) respectively. For each alternative j, the normalised means of the weightings w_i for each criterion i, are multiplied by the performance scores for the risk $R_{i,j}$, and value-based criteria $V_{i,j}$.

$$S_{Rj} = \sum_i w_i \times R_{ij} \qquad (15)$$

$$S_{Vj} = \sum_i w_i \times V_{ij} \tag{16}$$

Comparing two of the methods most widely used in the literature, AHP and TOPSIS, and one of the newly-created MCDM, the Characteristic Objects METhod (COMET) [80] with PAPRIKA, shows the following. AHP uses a hierarchical, multilevel structure to conceptualize how the alternatives can achieve the main goal. The weights of the criteria are established based on pairwise comparisons. Pairwise comparisons are used at each level to provide estimates for the weights of the criteria and also for the alternatives, resulting in a pairwise comparison matrix. The criteria weights are determined by the principal eigenvector method, and a consistency ratio is defined to assess the consistency of judgements. TOPSIS uses a rational, intuitive logic, which allows the best alternatives to be sought for each criterion, with a simple mathematical formula which takes into account the values of the weights of each criterion in the calculation process, as well as whether the criterion is a cost or a benefit. The order of the alternatives is calculated from the geometric distance to the positive and negative ideal solutions. However, it does not have a specific procedure for obtaining the weightings of the criteria, and so many studies use AHP to obtain these weightings, causing similar problems to AHP.

AHP and TOPSIS have the problem that they may undergo all the types of rank reversal caused by change of local priorities before and after an alternative is added or deleted. In the case of TOPSIS this is due to the calculation of the norm and the choice of the ideal positive and negative solutions. Although modifications have been introduced into these techniques to avoid this rank reversal, the phenomenon has not been perfectly resolved [81] and it may be considered as the main flaw in most MCDM methods [82]. COMET, on the other hand, completely avoids rank reversal because there is no comparison between the decision variants assessed. It also allows a relatively simple identification of linear and non-linear decision-maker functions, increasing its applicability to both linear and non-linear problems [83]. This method accounts for correlation between the components of an MCDM function, and comparisons between the characteristic objects are simpler than comparisons between alternatives [80]. Thus, when a decision maker compares two characteristic objects, the more preferred is given one point, and the second gets nil point, whereas if the preferences are equal, both objects are awarded half a point. After the final object comparison, the complete fuzzy rule base is obtained. The preference of alternative is calculated as the sum of the product of all activated rules, their degrees of fulfilment, and their preference values.

In PAPRIKA, weightings between criteria are obtained by comparing the preference or equality of one criterion relative to another, while in COMET the comparison is carried out between characteristic objects (relative to all criteria at once), choosing the best each time. The accuracy obtained with COMET and PAPRIKA may therefore be considered better than with AHP and TOPSIS, which are based on the use of a scale from 1 to 9, and its inverse, and so the comparison requires a greater number of options than COMET and PAPRIKA. An example of use described in Sałabun and Piegat [82] shows that COMET has a lower root mean square error (RMSE) and a higher ratio of correct answers than AHP and TOPSIS, and therefore gives greater accuracy.

Furthermore, the comparison process used by both COMET and PAPRIKA leads to low biased results, since participants can express their true preferences more freely, and in both cases, software is needed to apply it. AHP, PAPRIKA and COMET all come with very intuitive software for applying the method, but only in the case of COMET is the associated software capable of calculating the behavior of the arithmetic intervals, hesitant fuzzy sets and intuitionistic fuzzy sets [84]. In this regard, COMET is an intuitionistic approach, unlike the other methods previously mentioned.

In the case of PAPRIKA, the number of further necessary questions is reduced dynamically, as a function of the decisions already made, by eliminating the dominated alternatives. Although any number of criteria and scale levels can be included, as their number increases the number of potential alternatives (combinations) increases exponentially. In the case of COMET, the number of required questions increases polynomially relative to the number of characteristic objects; even in the most optimistic case, which assumes that each linguistic variable will have two characteristic values, the number of questions increases exponentially with the number of criteria [84]; however, by creating a hierarchical structure, the number of pairwise comparisons in the COMET technique is considerably reduced.

The main advantage of the PAPRIKA methodology is that the criteria weights can be constructed without explicitly asking decision makers about them. This technique also provides information on the value functions related to the different criteria, which requires greater effort by the analysts and decision makers than with the other methods [85]. Furthermore, care must be taken to guarantee that the number of sets of options used (combining the various criteria and scale levels) gives sufficient data for the statistical analysis.

The results obtained with the help of the 1000Minds software are shown below, taking into account the assessments of four decision makers who constitute a heterogeneous group: two of them belong to the Hospital staff, one of them being in charge of the Hospital's Environment service, and the other two are university experts. Decision makers are identified as DM_1 to DM_4. The preference values obtained by the DM_i are shown in Table 8. Three categories or scale levels have been considered in each risk criterion. The ranking of the criteria or risk factors is shown in Table 9. Table 10 shows the relative importance between the criteria in a pairwise comparison. The weights of the risk criteria or normalized criteria and the scores of each criterion (means) are shown in Table 11.

Table 8. Preferential values given by decision makers.

	DM_1	DM_2	DM_3	DM_4	Median	Mean
			Occurrence			
High	0%	0%	0%	0%	0%	0%
Medium	12.1%	16.0%	14.3%	12.5%	13.4%	13.7%
Low	24.2%	20.0%	28.6%	16.7%	22.1%	22.4%
			Severity			
Very severe	0%	0%	0%	0%	0%	0%
Severe	24.2%	12.0%	14.3%	20.8%	17.6%	17.8%
Not severe	39.4%	48.0%	50.0%	50.0%	49.0%	46.8%
			Detectability			
Not detected	0%	0%	0%	0%	0%	0%
Sometimes detected	18.2%	8.0%	7.1%	8.3%	8.2%	10.4%
High capacity for detection	36.4%	32.0%	21.4%	33.3%	32.7%	30.8%

Table 9. Ranking of risk factors.

Risk Criteria	dm_1	DM_2	DM_3	DM_4	Median	Mean
Occurrence	1st	1st	1st	1st	1.000	1.000
Severity	3rd	3rd	2nd	3rd	3.000	2.750
Detectability	2nd	2nd	3rd	2nd	2.000	2.250

Table 10. Relative importance of risk factors in comparison by pairs.

Risk Criteria	Severity	Occurrence	Detectability
Occurrence	1.0	2.1	1.5
Severity	0.5	1.0	0.7
Detectability	0.7	1.4	1.0

Table 11. Weightings of risk criteria.

Risk Criteria	Weightings ($\sum w_i = 1$)	Categories	Individual Valuation (0–100)
Occurrence	0.468	High	0.0
		Medium	61.4
		Low	100.0
Severity	0.224	Very severe	0.0
		Severe	38.1
		Not severe	100.0
Detectability	0.308	Not detected	0.0
		Sometimes detected	33.8
		High capacity for detection	100.0

5. Results

$\varphi = 0.6$ was established following the recommendation of Liu [35]. Regarding the reference series for the risk factors, considering that the lower the score, the lower the risk, the minimum value $\alpha^- = (0, 1)$ can be used, thus, taking $A_0 = [\alpha^-, \alpha^-, \ldots, \alpha^-] = [(0, 1), (0, 1), \ldots, (0, 1)]$. Once the reference series of the risk factors, the objective and subjective weightings of the risk factors were obtained, the calculation of the distances between the reference series and the aggregated results using the IFHWED operator, defined in Equation (11), were established. Table 12 shows the final ranking of failure modes to be treated in the Nuclear Medicine Department of the hospital. It can be seen that the failure mode ranked first is waste mismanagement, followed by incorrect labeling and incorrect storage of the waste.

Table 12. Ranking of failure modes using IFHWED and subjective weights in risk criteria using PAPRIKA.

Failure Modes	IFHWED ($\varphi = 0.6$) + PAPRIKA	Ranking
Failure mode 1	0.574	2nd
Failure mode 2	0.546	3rd
Failure mode 3	0.589	1st
Failure mode 4	0.511	5th
Failure mode 5	0.353	9th
Failure mode 6	0.508	6th
Failure mode 7	0.479	7th
Failure mode 8	0.522	4th
Failure mode 9	0.462	8th

The sensitivity analysis gives the results shown in Table 13. As can be seen, the methodology is robust since there is only an inversion in the classification of the failure modes 4 and 6, which are in 5th and 6th positions, in the case of $\varphi = 0.2$ and $\varphi = 0.8$. The same full ranking of failure modes was maintained for the remaining cases.

Table 13. Sensitivity analysis using IFHWED and subjective weightings of risk factors using PAPRIKA.

Failure Modes	IFHWED + PAPRIKA ($\varphi = 0.2$)	Ranking	IFHWED + PAPRIKA ($\varphi = 0.4$)	Ranking	IFHWED + PAPRIKA ($\varphi = 0.8$)	Ranking
Failure mode 1	0.573	2nd	0.574	2nd	0.575	2nd
Failure mode 2	0.542	3rd	0.544	3rd	0.549	3rd
Failure mode 3	0.589	1st	0.589	1st	0.589	1st
Failure mode 4	0.516	6th	0.513	5th	0.508	6th
Failure mode 5	0.354	9th	0.353	9th	0.353	9th
Failure mode 6	0.505	5th	0.506	6th	0.510	5th
Failure mode 7	0.493	7th	0.486	7th	0.471	7th
Failure mode 8	0.521	4th	0.521	4th	0.522	4th
Failure mode 9	0.458	8th	0.460	8th	0.464	8th

6. Validation

The methodology described was validated in two ways. Firstly, linguistic terms are used to assess the subjective weights of risk factors, rather than PAPRIKA. Secondly, using fuzzy TOPSIS, a recognized and widely used technique, which has also been used successfully in various studies where it is combined with FMEA.

To validate the proposed methodology, the linguistic terms in Table 4 were used to assess the subjective weights of risk factors, rather than PAPRIKA. Two DMs were used for this, the same ones who provided the linguistic assessments of the failure modes and who also provided the judgements in the PAPRIKA method. The resulting judgements are shown in Table 14.

Table 14. Risk criteria judgements.

Criteria	Occurrence	Severity	Detectability
DM_1	(0.75, 0.2)	(0.9, 0.05)	(0.5, 0.5)
DM_2	(0.9, 0.05)	(0.75, 0.2)	(0.5, 0.5)

To determine the subjective weightings of the risk factors, the subjective weightings of the group $w_j = (\mu_j, \nu_j)$, obtained from Equation (8), will be used.

$$w_1 = (0.874, 0.071); \ w_2 = (0.801, 0.141); \ w_3 = (0.500, 0.500)$$

These weights are to be normalized according to Equation (8), giving the weights:

$$\overline{w}_1 = 0.407; \ \overline{w}_2 - 0.374; \ \overline{w}_3 = 0.220$$

Once the reference series of the risk factors were established, the calculation of the distances between the reference series and the aggregated results using the IFHWED operator, defined in Equation (11), the final ranking of failure modes is obtained (see Table 15). $\varphi = 0.6$ was used again in this case, as with PAPRIKA.

Table 15. Ranking of failure modes.

Failure Modes	IFHWED ($\varphi = 0.6$)	Ranking
Failure mode 1	0.579	2nd
Failure mode 2	0.545	3rd
Failure mode 3	0.590	1st
Failure mode 4	0.517	5th
Failure mode 5	0.352	9th
Failure mode 6	0.505	6th
Failure mode 7	0.488	7th
Failure mode 8	0.522	4th
Failure mode 9	0.460	8th

The sensitivity analysis gives the results shown in Table 16. The methodology can be seen to be robust, since the same complete ranking of failure modes was maintained for all the assessed values of φ.

Table 16. Sensitivity analysis.

Failure Modes	IFHWED ($\varphi = 0.2$)	Ranking	IFHWED ($\varphi = 0.4$)	Ranking	IFHWED ($\varphi = 0.8$)	Ranking
Failure mode 1	0.575	2nd	0.577	2nd	0.582	2nd
Failure mode 2	0.541	3rd	0.543	3rd	0.547	3rd
Failure mode 3	0.589	1st	0.590	1st	0.590	1st
Failure mode 4	0.518	5th	0.517	5th	0.517	5th
Failure mode 5	0.353	9th	0.352	9th	0.351	9th
Failure mode 6	0.504	6th	0.505	6th	0.506	6th
Failure mode 7	0.496	7th	0.492	7th	0.483	7th
Failure mode 8	0.521	4th	0.521	4th	0.522	4th
Failure mode 9	0.457	8th	0.459	8th	0.461	8th

It can be seen that the ranking using PAPRIKA or linguistic terms to evaluate the subjective weights of risk factors is the same, and there is no change in ranking of the failure modes between the two methodologies. The differences between the values obtained with linguistic terms and those from PAPRIKA are 0.289% on average. Five values are found to be slightly higher with PAPRIKA compared to linguistic terms, and one value is the same with the two methodologies. The valuations with PAPRIKA are therefore very slightly higher than when only IFHWED and linguistic terms are used. Thus, PAPRIKA slightly increases the risk assessment in the failure modes compared to IFHWED and linguistic terms.

The methodology that combines IFHWED and PAPRIKA with a methodology that includes the weightings obtained via fuzzy linguistic terms and fuzzy TOPSIS was also checked, to obtain the classification of the failure modes. The fuzzy linguistic scale for weightings traditionally used in fuzzy TOPSIS is shown in Table 17 (see [36]). The linguistic variables for the ratings are shown in Table 18. Using the linguistic variables from Table 17 on the risk factors, from the two decision makers previously used in this study, the values shown in Table 19 are obtained. A weight of 0.25 is assigned to DM_1 and 0.75 to DM_2 as in the methodology described in our study. The weighted normalised decision matrix is shown in Table 20.

Table 17. Linguistic scale for the weights.

Linguistic Terms	Triangular Fuzzy Number
Very Low (VL)	(0, 0, 0.1)
Low (L)	(0, 0.1, 0.3)
Medium Low (ML)	(0.1, 0.3, 0.5)
Medium (M)	(0.3, 0.5, 0.7)
Medium High (MH)	(0.5, 0.7, 0.9)
High (H)	(0.7, 0.9, 1.0)
Very High (VH)	(0.9, 1.0, 1.0)

Table 18. Linguistic scale for the ratings.

Linguistic Terms	Triangular Fuzzy Number
Very Poor (VP)	(0, 0, 1)
Poor (P)	(0, 1, 3)
Medium Poor (MP)	(1, 3, 5)
Fair (F)	(3, 5, 7)
Medium Good (MG)	(5, 7, 9)
Good (G)	(7, 9, 10)
Very Good (VG)	(9, 10, 10)

Table 19. Risk criteria judgements.

Criteria	Occurrence	Severity	Detectability
DM_1	(0.7, 0.9, 1)	(0.9, 1, 1)	(0.3, 0.5, 0.7)
DM_2	(0.9, 1, 1)	(0.7, 0.9, 1)	(0.3, 0.5, 0.7)

Table 20. Weighted normalized decision matrix.

Alternative	Occurrence	Severity	Detectability
Failure mode 1	(0.340, 0.464, 0.500)	(0.276, 0.414, 0.500)	(0.090, 0.188, 0.298)
Failure mode 2	(0.319, 0.439, 0.500)	(0.257, 0.390, 0.500)	(0.075, 0.175, 0.298)
Failure mode 3	(0.298, 0.415, 0.475)	(0.276, 0.414, 0.500)	(0.120, 0.238, 0.350)
Failure mode 4	(0.234, 0.342, 0.425)	(0.237, 0.390, 0.500)	(0.090, 0.188, 0.298)
Failure mode 5	(0.043, 0.146, 0.250)	(0.079, 0.195, 0.316)	(0.045, 0.125, 0.245)
Failure mode 6	(0.255, 0.390, 0.475)	(0.197, 0.341, 0.474)	(0.075, 0.175, 0.298)
Failure mode 7	(0.298, 0.415, 0.475)	(0.237, 0.390, 0.500)	(0.053, 0.113, 0.193)
Failure mode 8	(0.213, 0.342, 0.425)	(0.119, 0.244, 0.369)	(0.075, 0.175, 0.298)
Failure mode 9	(0.313, 0.437, 0.500)	(0.225, 0.347, 0.425)	(0.060, 0.150, 0.280)

The distances d_i^+ and d_i^- of each weighted alternative obtained from the fuzzy positive ideal solution (FPIS) and the farthest distance from a fuzzy negative ideal solution (FNIS) are shown in Table 21. The Table also includes the Closeness Coefficient (CC) of each failure mode, and the resulting ranking.

Table 21. The distances, Closeness Coefficients and ranking of failure modes.

Alternatives	Distances		CC	Ranking
	d_i^+	d_i^-		
Failure mode 1	11.9923	1.0573	0.08102	2nd
Failure mode 2	12.0335	1.0252	0.07851	3rd
Failure mode 3	11.9886	1.0640	0.08152	1st
Failure mode 4	12.1169	0.9435	0.07224	5th
Failure mode 5	12.5326	0.5491	0.04197	9th
Failure mode 6	12.1278	0.9441	0.07222	6th
Failure mode 7	12.1242	0.9263	0.07098	7th
Failure mode 8	12.2642	0.8068	0.06172	8th
Failure mode 9	12.1027	0.9529	0.07299	4th

If the ranking obtained with the methodology described here is compared with that found using fuzzy TOPSIS, it is seen that the rankings is similar. The only change is between failure modes 8 and 9, in 4th and 8th position.

Since this difference exists in the classification of alternatives, the most frequently-used measures of the analysis of the ranking similarity in decision-making problems were applied: Spearman, Kendall and Goodman-Kruskal coefficients [86–88]. Spearman's coefficient, ρ, is interpreted as a percentage of the rank variance of one variable, explained by the other variable [88]. Equation (17) was used to calculate Spearman's coefficient, where d_i is the difference between the rankings obtained via the MCDM methods and the number of elements in the ranking. The Kendall, τ, and Goodman-Kruskal, G, coefficients are calculated from Equations (18) and (19) respectively, where N_s is the number of compatible pairs, N_d the number of non-compliant pairs, and n the number of all pairs. These coefficients represent the difference between the probability that the variables compared will be in the same order for both variables and the probability that they will be in the opposite order.

$$\rho = 1 - \frac{6 \times \sum d_i^2}{n \times (n^2 - 1)} \qquad (17)$$

$$\tau = \frac{2(N_s - N_d)}{n \times (n-1)} \tag{18}$$

$$G = \frac{N_s - N_d}{N_s + N_d} \tag{19}$$

The values obtained for these coefficients are: $\rho = 0.733$; $\tau = 0.389$; $G = 0.389$; therefore, Spearman's coefficient suggests strong or high association, as it is between 0.7 and 0.9. As expected, Spearman's coefficient is greater than the other coefficients, since the latter are more sensitive to error, or discrepancies in the data. The Kendall and Goodman-Kruskal coefficients show some positive relation, in that knowing the order of the independent variable assists in predicting the order of the dependent variable, but there is not high concordance. However, the difference at the top should be more significant than an error at the bottom of the ranking. To solve this problem, therefore, the Value of Similarity (WS) coefficient suggested in Sałabun and Urbaniak [88] is also calculated. This WS coefficient is strongly related to the difference between two rankings at particular positions, and the top of the ranking has a more significant influence on similarity than the bottom. Equation (20) is used to calculate the WS coefficient.

$$WS = 1 - \sum_{i=1}^{n} 2^{-R_{xi}} \times \frac{|R_{xi} - R_{yi}|}{max\{|1 - R_{yi}|, |N - R_{yi}|\}} \tag{20}$$

where N is a ranking length, R_{xi} and R_{yi} are defined as the positions in the ranking of the ith element in ranking x and ranking y respectively. If the WS coefficient is less than 0.234, then the similarity is low, while if the value is higher than 0.808, then the similarity is high [88]. In the case checked, WS = 0.934, and therefore the similarity is high. This is because of the similar in the rankings with only two variations of the nine alternatives, and because the three top positions in the ranking do not undergo change.

Thus, the proposed methodology using FMEA in the segregation of health care waste is considered to be validated by two different methodologies.

7. Discussion

Although there are many papers analyzing health waste management problems in different countries, especially in middle and low-income countries, they are descriptive studies at the country or wide geographical area level, so they do not focus on the problems of a specific hospital. However, as can be seen in this study, health waste management problems also exist in high-income countries. Although the problems may have different failure modes in middle and low-income countries than in high income countries, the results cause similar risks for health personnel and other staff working in the health care organization, for patients and visitors, and for the environment. Therefore, it should be analyzed in detail not only in low-income countries where it seems that the studies are focused on this topic, but in all countries.

In addition, it should be noted that in no case studied in the literature on health waste management have risk assessment techniques such as FMEA been used. Such techniques are, however, not uncommon in risk assessment in other areas such as assessing machinery and device failures, improving the decision process of the emergency department of a hospital, evaluating safety risks in organizations, evaluating options of the production process, improving the process of purchasing in a hospital, etc.

Therefore, this study focuses on a higher level of precision than the current literature, although at the hospital level studied, improvement actions may be strategic.

The use of the intuitionistic fuzzy FMEA methodology, in addition to solving the problems derived from using classical FMEA, prioritizes failure modes in the segregation of health care waste in a very practical way, always based on expert judgement. By using linguistic terms, the significance of each failure mode can be readily established, and when weighting each decision maker, a reliability can be assigned to each judgement issued, which is highly advisable when, for example, decision makers have different levels of knowledge about the specific facility being assessed.

The goal of the hospital at the first stage was to maintain the number of containers used, but to obtain a weight per container higher than that achieved up to that point, since that would be a hallmark of better segregation and compliance with the regulations regarding minimum weights per container (since it had been observed that containers have sometimes been collected without meeting the stipulated minimums). Once this first step was taken, the second part consisted of reducing the number of containers and the total weight. For this, the amount of waste (kg) and the number of containers generated by the Nuclear Medicine Departments were monitored on a monthly basis.

In view of the prioritization of the failure modes obtained, the incorrectness in the placing of material in the containers is in first place. To address this, especially regarding hazardous waste, a poka-yoke system was designed. Poka-yoke are systems originally devised at Toyota, to avoid mistakes in the operation of a system. This is a sticker (see Figure 3) to be placed on the lids of the 3-litre containers. This sticker will serve a dual purpose: on the one hand, it will serve to remind the user of what parts to insert for correct segregation and, on the other, it will prevent the erroneous insertion of certain objects (for example, syringes). Figure 3a) shows the profiles of the lid of the 3-litre container (red), the thickness of a poorly segregated syringe (blue) and the final design of a sticker (green). Although the sticker can remain attached to the container when it is collected, it has a strategically placed tab to enable it to be removed at any time.

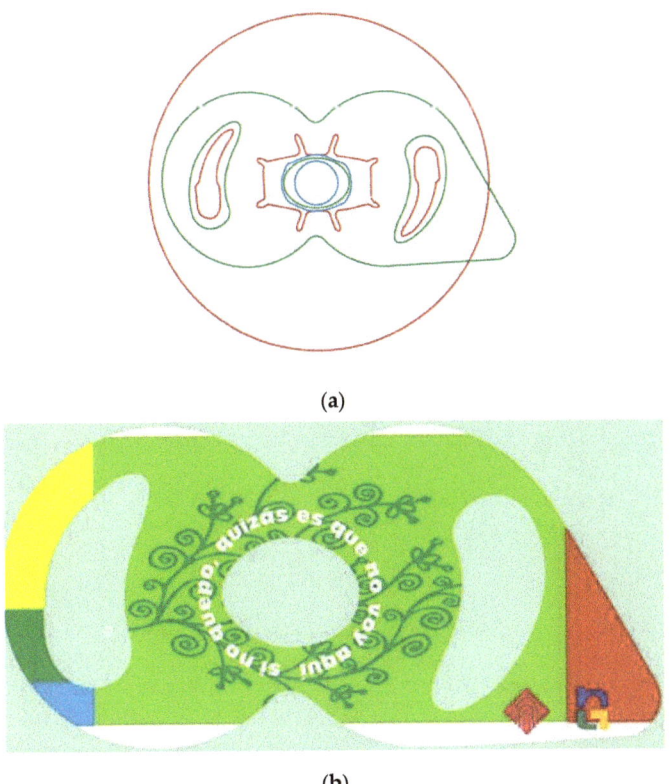

Figure 3. Sticker to be placed on 3-litre containers (**a**) Design; (**b**) Final sticker.

In addition, an informative brochure has been produced to make the care staff of the Nuclear Medicine Department aware of the importance of a good segregation and the improvement that it would mean for their working conditions and risk reduction. The brochure consists of 24 sides (in Spanish); Attempts have been made, in a casual way, to make the user aware of the problems in their environment and to visualize different correct and incorrect segregation actions. As an example, two pages of the brochure are shown (see Figures 4 and 5 with the text in Spanish). Information about the collection time, its location and cleaning times has also been included in the brochure. Posters have also been created. The brochure was distributed digitally and on paper, while the posters are put up at the Nuclear Medicine Department, to provide information for both workers and patients. The information campaign has been reinforced with a series of training talks at the department. There is also an intention to certify the research, so the Quality Unit would look at the possibility of offering these talks, not as a mere instrument of information, but also for training.

Failure mode 5, which occupies the last position in the ranking, despite being one of the problems that is clearest according to the view of human resources, could be solved with a proper relocation of containers. Although there is a lack of space for the placement of new containers, these would not be necessary if the healthcare staff make proper use of those that are currently available.

Since this research began, changes have been observed in the worker's culture in this regard, and thus, the Environmental Technician announced that, after obtaining the latest data on recycling and collection of waste material in the department, a significant decrease had been seen in waste generated.

Figure 4. Information on identification of containers and signage.

Figure 5. Correct and incorrect segregation actions.

8. Conclusions

Segregation is recognized as an important step in health care waste management; however, it is also observed that poor waste segregation exists in health care organizations in a generalized way, with the lack of awareness about related health risks with health care waste, the lack of education and training in proper waste management, the absence of waste management and disposal systems, insufficient human and economic resources, and the low priority assigned to the topic being perceived as the most common problems.

Incorrect segregation can affect hospital care staff, but also non-care staff, for example, facility maintenance or cleaning personnel, waste handlers, and patients and companions, until it becomes a public health problem. It also has implications for the environment and reduces the possible amount of waste to be recycled. In addition, it increases the amount of hazardous waste generated, since the wrong mix means that all mixed waste has to be treated as hazardous. However, despite the importance of segregation, the number of studies that prioritize the failure modes related to segregation is non-existent, with only descriptive studies associated with countries being found. However, the literature does show multiple examples of using FMEA for risk prioritization in other areas.

Therefore, this study has designed a prioritization of failure modes related to segregation in the Nuclear Medicine Department of a hospital. For this, an intuitive fuzzy FMEA methodology was used to avoid the many problems presented by crisp FMEA. PAPRIKA has been used to obtain the subjective risk criteria weights, while the distribution-based method has been used to calculate the objective weights.

The methodology described has been validated in two ways: using linguistic terms, rather than PAPRIKA, to assess the subjective weights of risk factors, and with fuzzy TOPSIS. In the first case the ranking is the same, and in the second, there is only one change between the classification of two failure modes. WS coefficient is used to calculate the level of similarity between the models, and WS = 0.934, and therefore the similarity is high. A sensitivity analysis was also carried out to show the robustness of the methodology.

The proposed methodology can help other health care organizations to classify their failure modes relative to health care waste management and focus improvement efforts on the most critical failure modes. In addition, it can be seen how, by initiating a study in the Hospital on the problem of segregation, the staff becomes more aware and the segregation data of the department analyzed improves.

As future research, the aim is to incorporate additional risk factors to the O, S, and D considered in this study and use them to build a hierarchical structure that contributes to a better prioritization of failures modes. Furthermore, PAPRIKA has not been tested on the decision-making paradox, where different decision-making methods can yield different results, when applied to exactly the same decision problem and data, but it could exhibit this phenomenon; therefore, other techniques such as Measuring Attractiveness by a Categorical Based Evaluation Technique (MACBETH) or the more up-to-date COMET method, could be used to assign subjective weights to said risk criteria and sub-criteria.

Also, future research will use methods different from the OWA operator to determine the objective weights and compare the results obtained.

The research described was performed using the results of a survey carried out with personnel who work in the Nuclear Medicine Department of a specific Hospital; due to the subjective nature of surveys, it is proposed that the failure modes related to health care segregation be generated using data from government sources or national private agencies to make the results more objective. In this way, the failure modes generated will affect not just the care services at one hospital, but will also be more generally characteristic of behavior throughout the country.

Funding: This research was funded by the University of Castilla-La Mancha and the European Union through the European Regional Development Fund to the Predictive Analysis Laboratory (PREDILAB) group (2020-GRIN-28770).

Conflicts of Interest: The author declares no conflict of interest.

References

1. Liu, H.C.; Liu, L.; Liu, N. Risk evaluation approaches in failure mode and effects analysis: A literature review. *Expert Syst. Appl.* **2013**, *40*, 828–838. [CrossRef]
2. Minoglou, M.; Gerassimidou, S.; Komilis, D. Healthcare Waste Generation Worldwide and Its Dependence on Socio-Economic and Environmental Factors. *Sustainability* **2017**, *9*, 220. [CrossRef]
3. Vaccari, M.; Tudor, T.; Perteghella, A. Costs associated with the management of waste from healthcare facilities: An analysis at national and site level. *Waste Manag. Res.* **2018**, *36*, 39–47. [CrossRef] [PubMed]
4. Korkut, E.N. Estimations and analysis of medical waste amounts in the city of Istanbul and proposing a new approach for the estimation of future medical waste amounts. *Waste Manag.* **2018**, *81*, 168–176. [CrossRef] [PubMed]
5. *Safe Management of Wastes from Health-Care Activities*, 2nd ed.; Chartier, Y.; Emmanuel, J.; Pieper, U.; Prüss, A.; Rushbrook, P.; Stringer, R.; Townend, W.; Wilburn, S.; Zghondi, R. (Eds.) World Health Organization: Geneva, Switzerland, 2014; Available online: https://apps.who.int/iris/bitstream/handle/10665/85349/9789241548564_eng.pdf;jsessionid=DB89B73BACE6CA03F815F758C29D4726?sequence=1 (accessed on 26 June 2020).
6. Kanbar, A.; Abdessater, M.; Dabal, C.; El Khoury, J.; Akl, H.; El Hachem, C.; Halabi, R.; Elias, S.; Boustany, J.; El Khoury, R. Health-care waste segregation among surgical team groups: A new assessment method. *Perioper. Care Oper. Room Manag.* **2020**, *20*. [CrossRef]
7. Thornton, J.; McCally, M.; Orris, P.; Weinberg, J. Hospitals and plastics. Dioxin prevention and medical waste incinerators. *Public Health Rep.* **1996**, *111*, 298–313. [PubMed]
8. *Preparation of National Health-Care Waste Management Plans in Sub-Saharan Countries Guidance Manual*; World Health Organization: Geneva, Switzerland, 2005; Available online: https://apps.who.int/iris/bitstream/handle/10665/43118/924154662X.pdf (accessed on 26 June 2020).
9. Mosquera, M.; Andrés-Prado, M.J.; Rodríguez-Caravaca, G.; Latasa, P.; Mosquera, M.E.G. Evaluation of an education and training intervention to reduce health care waste in a tertiary hospital in Spain. *Am. J. Infect. Control* **2014**, *42*, 894–897. [CrossRef]
10. *Management of Solid Health-Care Waste at Primary Health-Care Centres: A Decision-Making Guide*; World Health Organization: Geneva, Switzerland, 2005; Available online: https://apps.who.int/iris/handle/10665/43123 (accessed on 22 June 2020).
11. *Libro Verde. Cuestiones Medioambientales Relacionadas con el PVC*; Comisión de las Comunidades Europeas: Bruselas, Belgium, 26 July 2000; Available online: https://ec.europa.eu/environment/waste/pvc/pdf/es.pdf (accessed on 16 June 2020).
12. Mbongwe, B.; Mmereki, B.T.; Magashula, A. Healthcare waste management: Current practices in selected healthcare facilities, Botswana. *Waste Manag.* **2008**, *28*, 226–233. [CrossRef]
13. *Health-Care Waste*; World Health Organization: Geneva, Switzerland, 2018; Available online: https://www.who.int/news-room/fact-sheets/detail/health-care-waste (accessed on 17 June 2020).
14. Gai, R.Y.; Xu, L.Z.; Li, H.J.; Zhou, C.C.; He, J.J.; Shirayama, Y.; Tang, W.; Kuroiwa, C. Investigation of health care waste management in Binzhou District, China. *Waste Manag.* **2010**, *30*, 246–250.
15. Moreira, A.M.; Gunther, W.M. Assessment of medical waste management at a primary health-care center in Sao Paulo, Brazil. *Waste Manag.* **2013**, *33*, 162–167. [CrossRef]
16. Abd El-Salam, M.M. Hospital waste management in El-Beheira Governorate, Egypt. *J. Environ. Manag.* **2010**, *91*, 618–629. [CrossRef] [PubMed]
17. Ferreira, V.; Teixeira, M.R. Healthcare waste management practices and risk perceptions: Findings from hospitals in the Algarve region, Portugal. *Waste Manag.* **2010**, *30*, 2657–2663. [CrossRef] [PubMed]
18. Manga, V.E.; Forton, O.T.; Mofor, L.A.; Woodard, R. Health care waste management in Cameroon: A case study from the Southwestern Region. *Resour. Conserv. Recycl.* **2011**, *57*, 108–116. [CrossRef]
19. Sharma, S.K.; Gupta, S. Healthcare waste management scenario: A case of Himachal Pradesh (India). *Clin. Epidemiol. Glob. Health* **2017**, *5*, 169–172. [CrossRef]
20. Sahiledengle, B. Self-reported healthcare waste segregation practice and its correlate among healthcare workers in hospitals of Southeast Ethiopia. *BMC Health Serv. Res.* **2019**, *19*, 591. [CrossRef]

21. Kumar, R.; Somrongthong, R.; Shaikh, B.T. Effectiveness of intensive healthcare waste management training model among health professionals at teaching hospitals of Pakistan: A quasi-experimental study. *BMC Health Serv. Res.* **2015**, *15*, 81. [CrossRef]
22. Abdo, N.M.; Hamza, W.S.; Al-Fadhli, M.A. Effectiveness of education program on hospital waste management. *Int. J. Workplace Health Manag.* **2019**, *12*, 457–468. [CrossRef]
23. Yang, J.; Huang, H.Z.; He, L.P.; Zhu, S.P.; Wen, D. Risk evaluation in failure mode and effects analysis of aircraft turbine rotor blades using Dempster–Shafer evidence theory under uncertainty. *Eng. Fail. Anal.* **2011**, *18*, 2084–2092. [CrossRef]
24. Zheng, H.; Tang, Y. Deng Entropy Weighted Risk Priority Number Model for Failure Mode and Effects Analysis. *Entropy* **2020**, *22*, 280. [CrossRef]
25. Liu, H.C.; You, J.X.; Shan, M.M.; Shao, L.N. Failure mode and effects analysis using intuitionistic fuzzy hybrid TOPSIS approach. *Soft Comput.* **2015**, *19*, 1085–1098. [CrossRef]
26. Liu, H.C.; Chen, X.Q.; Duan, C.Y.; Wang, Y.M. Failure mode and effect analysis using multi-criteria decision making methods: A systematic literature review. *Comput. Ind. Eng.* **2019**, *135*, 881–897. [CrossRef]
27. Hansen, P.; Ombler, F. A new method for scoring additive multi-attribute value models using pairwise rankings of alternatives. *J. Multi-Criteria Decis. Anal.* **2009**, *15*, 87–107. [CrossRef]
28. Martelli, N.; Hansen, P.; van den Brink, H.; Boudard, A.; Cordonnier, A.L.; Devaux, C.; Pineau, J.; Prognon, P.; Borget, I. Combining multi-criteria decision analysis and mini-health technology assessment: A funding decision-support tool for medical devices in a university hospital setting. *J. Biomed. Informatiz.* **2016**, *59*, 201–208. [CrossRef] [PubMed]
29. Balaraju, J.; Raj, M.G.; Murthy, C.S. Fuzzy-FMEA risk evaluation approach for LHD machine-A case study. *J. Sustain. Min.* **2019**, *18*, 257–268. [CrossRef]
30. Moubray, J. *Reliability-Centered Maintenance*; Industrial Press Inc.: New York, NY, USA, 1992.
31. Liu, H.C.; Chen, Y.Z.; You, J.X.; Li, H. Risk evaluation in failure mode and effects analysis using fuzzy digraph and matrix approach. *J. Intell. Manuf.* **2016**, *27*, 805–816. [CrossRef]
32. Kumru, M.; Kumru, P.Y. Fuzzy MFEA application to improve purchasing process in a public hospital. *Appl. Soft Comput.* **2013**, *13*, 721–733. [CrossRef]
33. Braglia, M.; Frosolini, M.; Montanari, R. Fuzzy TOPSIS approach for failure mode, effects and criticality analysis. *Qual. Reliab. Eng. Int.* **2003**, *19*, 425–443. [CrossRef]
34. Huang, J.; Li, Z.S.; Liu, H.C. New approach for failure mode and effect analysis using linguistic distribution assessments and TODIM method. *Reliab. Eng. Syst. Saf.* **2017**, *167*, 302–309. [CrossRef]
35. Liu, H.C. FMEA Using Uncertainty Theories and MCDM Methods. In *FMEA Using Uncertainty Theories and MCDM Methods*; Springer: Singapore, 2016.
36. Kutlu, A.C.; Ekmekçioğlu, M. Fuzzy failure modes and effects analysis by using fuzzy TOPSIS-based fuzzy AHP. *Expert Syst. Appl.* **2012**, *39*, 61–67. [CrossRef]
37. Mangeli, M.; Shahraki, A.; Saljooghi, F.H. Improvement of risk assessment in the FMEA using nonlinear model, revised fuzzy TOPSIS, and support vector machine. *Int. J. Ind. Ergon.* **2019**, *69*, 209–216. [CrossRef]
38. Wang, L.; Liu, H.; Quan, M. Evaluating the risk of failure modes with a hybrid MCDM model under interval-valued intuitionistic fuzzy environment. *Comput. Ind. Eng.* **2016**, *102*, 175–185. [CrossRef]
39. Bao, J.; Johansson, J.; Zhang, J. An occupational disease assessment of the mining industry's occupational health and safety management system based on FMEA and an improved AHP model. *Sustainability* **2017**, *9*, 94. [CrossRef]
40. Fattahi, R.; Khalilzadeh, M. Risk evaluation using a novel hybrid method based on FMEA, extended MULTIMOORA, and AHP methods under fuzzy environment. *Saf. Sci.* **2018**, *102*, 290–300. [CrossRef]
41. Tian, Z.P.; Wang, J.Q.; Zhang, H.Y. An integrated approach for failure mode and effects analysis based on fuzzy best-worst, relative entropy, and VIKOR methods. *Appl. Soft Comput.* **2018**, *72*, 636–646. [CrossRef]
42. Boral, S.; Howard, I.; Chaturvedi, S.K.; McKee, K.; Naikan, V.N.A. An integrated approach for fuzzy failure modes and effects analysis using fuzzy AHP and fuzzy MAIRCA. *Eng. Fail. Anal.* **2020**, *108*, 104195. [CrossRef]
43. Zhu, J.; Shuai, B.; Li, G.; Chin, K.S.; Wang, R. Failure mode and effect analysis using regret theory and PROMETHEE under linguistic neutrosophic context. *J. Loss Prev. Process. Ind.* **2020**, *64*, 104048. [CrossRef]
44. Wang, Z.; Ran, Y.; Chen, Y.; Yu, H.; Zhang, G. Failure mode and effects analysis using extended matter-element model and AHP. *Comput. Ind. Eng.* **2020**, *140*, Article 106233. [CrossRef]

45. Dong, C. Failure mode and effects analysis based on fuzzy utility cost estimation. *Int. J. Qual. Reliab. Manag.* **2007**, *24*, 958–971. [CrossRef]
46. Ilangkumaran, M.; Shanmugam, P.; Sakthivel, G.; Visagavel, K. Failure mode and effect analysis using fuzzy analytic hierarchy process. *Int. J. Product. Qual. Manag.* **2014**, *14*, 296–313. [CrossRef]
47. Safari, H.; Faraji, Z.; Majidian, S. Identifying and evaluating enterprise architecture risks using FMEA and fuzzy VIKOR. *J. Intell. Manuf.* **2016**, *27*, 475–486. [CrossRef]
48. Shi, J.L.; Wang, Y.J.; Jin, H.H.; Fan, S.J.; Ma, Q.Y.; Zhou, M.J. A modified method for risk evaluation in failure mode and effects analysis. *J. Appl. Sci. Eng.* **2016**, *19*, 177–186.
49. Carpitella, S.; Certa, A.; Izquierdo, J.; La Fata, C.M. A combined multi-criteria approach to support FMECA analyses: A real-world case. *Reliab. Eng. Syst. Saf.* **2018**, *169*, 394–402. [CrossRef]
50. Sakthivel, G.; Saravanakumar, D.; Muthuramalingam, T. Application of failure mode and effect analysis in manufacturing industry—An integrated approach with FAHP-fuzzy TOPSIS and FAHP-fuzzy VIKOR. *Int. J. Product. Qual. Manag.* **2018**, *24*, 398–423. [CrossRef]
51. Chang, K.H.; Cheng, C.H. A risk assessment methodology using intuitionistic fuzzy set in FMEA. *Int. J. Syst. Sci.* **2010**, *41*, 1457–1471. [CrossRef]
52. Liu, H.C.; Liu, L.; Li, P. Failure mode and effects analysis using intuitionistic fuzzy hybrid weighted Euclidean distance operator. *Int. J. Syst. Sci.* **2014**, *45*, 2012–2030. [CrossRef]
53. Liu, H.C.; You, J.X.; You, X.Y. Evaluating the risk of healthcare failure modes using interval 2-tuple hybrid weighted distance measure. *Comput. Ind. Eng.* **2014**, *78*, 249–258. [CrossRef]
54. Guo, J. A risk assessment approach for failure mode and effects analysis based on intuitionistic fuzzy sets and evidence theory. *J. Intell. Fuzzy Syst.* **2016**, *30*, 869–881. [CrossRef]
55. Tooranloo, H.S.; Ayatollah, A.S. A model for failure mode and effects analysis based on intuitionistic fuzzy approach. *Appl. Soft Comput.* **2016**, *49*, 238–247. [CrossRef]
56. Yazdi, M. Risk assessment based on novel intuitionistic fuzzy-hybrid-modified TOPSIS approach. *Saf. Sci.* **2018**, *110*, 438–448. [CrossRef]
57. Mirghafoori, S.H.; Izadi, M.R.; Daei, A. Analysis of the barriers affecting the quality of electronic services of libraries by VIKOR, FMEA and entropy combined approach in an intuitionistic-fuzzy environment. *J. Intell. Fuzzy Syst.* **2018**, *34*, 2441–2451. [CrossRef]
58. Tooranloo, H.S.; Ayatollah, A.S.; Alboghobish, S. Evaluating knowledge management failure factors using intuitionistic fuzzy FMEA approach. *Knowl. Inf. Syst.* **2018**, *57*, 1–23.
59. Can, G.F. An intuitionistic approach based on failure mode and effect analysis for prioritizing corrective and preventive strategies. *Hum. Factors Ergon. Manuf.* **2018**, *28*, 130–147. [CrossRef]
60. Liu, H.C.; Wu, J.; Li, P. Assessment of health-care waste disposal methods using a VIKOR-based fuzzy multi-criteria decision making method. *Waste Manag.* **2013**, *33*, 2744–2751. [CrossRef] [PubMed]
61. Atanassov, K.T. Intuitionistic Fuzzy Sets. *Fuzzy Sets Syst.* **1986**, *20*, 87–96. [CrossRef]
62. Xu, Z. Approaches to multiple attribute group decision making based on intuitionistic fuzzy power aggregation operators. *Knowl.-Based Syst.* **2011**, *24*, 749–760. [CrossRef]
63. Xu, Z.; Zhao, N. Information fusion for intuitionistic fuzzy decision making: An overview. *Inf. Fusion* **2016**, *28*, 10–23. [CrossRef]
64. Liu, H.C.; You, J.X.; Lin, Q.L.; Li, H. Risk assessment in system FMEA combining fuzzy weighted average with fuzzy decision-making trial and evaluation laboratory. *Int. J. Comput. Integr. Manuf.* **2015**, *28*, 701–714. [CrossRef]
65. Xu, Z. Intuitionistic Fuzzy Aggregation Operators. *IEEE Trans. Fuzzy Syst.* **2007**, *15*, 1179–1187.
66. Xu, Z.S. An overview of methods for determining OWA weights. *Int. J. Intell. Syst.* **2005**, *20*, 843–865. [CrossRef]
67. Carnero, M.C. Assessment of Environmental Sustainability in Health Care Organizations. *Sustainability* **2015**, *7*, 8270–8291. [CrossRef]
68. Zhao, J.; You, X.Y.; Liu, H.C.; Wu, S.M. An Extended VIKOR Method Using Intuitionistic Fuzzy Sets and Combination Weights for Supplier Selection. *Symmetry* **2017**, *9*, 169. [CrossRef]
69. Llopis-Albert, C.; Palacios-Marques, D. Applications of ordered weighted averaging (OWA) operators in environmental problems. *Multidiscip. J. Educ. Soc. Technol. Sci.* **2017**, *4*, 52–63. [CrossRef]

70. Fitzgerald, A.; de Coster, C.; McMillan, S.; Naden, R.; Armstrong, F.; Barber, A.; Cunning, L.; Conner-Spady, B.; Hawker, G.; Lacaille, D.; et al. Relative urgency for referral from primary care to rheumatologists: The Priority Referral Score. *Arthritis Care Res.* **2011**, *63*, 231–239. [CrossRef] [PubMed]
71. Hansen, P.; Hendry, A.; Naden, R.; Ombler, F.; Stewart, R. A new process for creating points systems for prioritising patients for elective health services. *Clin. Gov. Int. J.* **2012**, *17*, 200–209. [CrossRef]
72. Sullivan, T.; Hansen, P. Determining criteria and weights for prioritizing health technologies based on the preferences of the general population: A New Zealand pilot study. *Value Health* **2017**, *20*, 679–686. [CrossRef] [PubMed]
73. Shiboski, C.H.; Shiboski, S.C.; Seror, R.; Criswell, L.A.; Labetoulle, M.; Lietman, T.M.; Rasmussen, A.; Scofield, H.; Vitali, C.; Bowman, S.J.; et al. 2016 American College of Rheumatology/European League against Rheumatism classification criteria for primary Sjögren's syndrome: A consensus and data-driven methodology involving three international patient cohorts. *Arthritis Rheumatol.* **2017**, *69*, 35–45. [CrossRef]
74. Tacconelli, E.; Carrara, E.; Savoldi, A.; Harbarth, S.; Mendelson, M.; Monnet, D.L.; Pulcini, C.; Zorzet, A. Discovery, research, and development of new antibiotics: The WHO priority list of antibiotic-resistant bacteria and tuberculosis. *Lancet Infect. Dis.* **2018**, *18*, 318–327. [CrossRef]
75. Lasorsa, I.; Padoano, E.; Marceglia, S.; Accardo, A. Multi-criteria decision analysis for the assessment of non-clinical hospital services: Methodology and case study. *Oper. Res. Health Care* **2019**, *23*. [CrossRef]
76. Pinto, D.; Bockenholt, U.; Lee, J.; Chang, R.W.; Hansen, P. Preferences for physical activity: A conjoint analysis involving people with chronic knee pain. *Osteoarthr. Cartil.* **2019**, *27*, 240–247. [CrossRef]
77. Sullivan, T.; Hansen, P.; Ombler, F.; Derrett, S.; Devlin, N. A new tool for creating personal and social EQ-5D-5L value sets, including valuing 'dead'. *Soc. Sci. Med.* **2020**, *246*. [CrossRef]
78. PAPRIKA Method. Available online: https://www.1000minds.com/about/paprika (accessed on 22 July 2020).
79. De Nardo, P.; Gentilotti, E.; Mazzaferri, F.; Cremonini, E.; Goossens, H.; Tacconelli, E.; The Members of the COVID-19 MCDA Group. Multi-Criteria Decision Analysis to prioritize hospital admission of patients affected by COVID-19 in low-resource settings with hospital-bed shortage. *Int. J. Infect. Dis.* **2020**. [CrossRef]
80. Sałabun, W. The Characteristic Objects Method: A New Distance based approach to multicrieria decision making problems. *J. Multi-Criteria Decis. Anal.* **2015**, *22*, 37–50.
81. Wang, Y.M.; Elhag, T.M.S. An approach to avoiding rank reversal in AHP. *Decis. Support. Syst.* **2006**, *42*, 1474–1480. [CrossRef]
82. Sałabun, W.; Piegat, A. Comparative analysis of MCDM methods for the assessment of mortality in patients with acute coronary syndrome. *Artif. Intell. Rev.* **2017**, *48*, 557–571.
83. Sałabun, W.; Piegat, A.; Wątróbski, J.; Karczmarczyk, A.; Jankowski, J. *The COMET Method: The First MCDA Method Completely Resistant to Rank Reversal Paradox*; European Working Group "Multiple Criteria Decision Aiding" Series 3, n° 39; Spring: Berlin/Heidelberg, Germany, 2019.
84. Sałabun, W.; Karczmarczyk, A. Using the COMET Method in the Sustainable City Transport Problem: An Empirical Study of the Electric Powered Cars. *Procedia Comput. Sci.* **2018**, *126*, 2248–2260. [CrossRef]
85. Németh, B.; Molnár, A.; Bozóki, S.; Wijaya, K.; Inotai, A.; Campbell, J.D.; Kaló, Z. Comparison of weighting methods used in multicriteria decision analysis frameworks in healthcare with focus on low- and middle-income countries. *J. Comp. Eff. Res.* **2019**, *8*. [CrossRef]
86. Mulliner, E.; Malys, N.; Maliene, V. Comparative analysis of MCDM methods for the assessment of sustainable housing affordability. *Omega* **2016**, *59*, 146–156. [CrossRef]
87. Faizi, S.; Rashid, T.; Salabun, W.; Zafar, S.; Wątróbski, J. Decision making with uncertainty using hesitant fuzzy sets. *Int. J. Fuzzy Syst.* **2017**, *20*, 93–103. [CrossRef]
88. Sałabun, W.; Urbaniak, K. A New Coefficient of Rankings Similarity in Decision-Making Problems. In *Computational Science—ICCS 2020*; Lecture Notes in Computer Science; Krzhizhanovskaya, V., Závodszky, G., Lees, M.H., Dongarra, J.J., Sloot, P.M.A., Brissos, S., Teixeira, J., Eds.; Springer: Cham, Switzerland, 2020; Volume 12138. [CrossRef]

© 2020 by the author. Licensee MDPI, Basel, Switzerland. This article is an open access article distributed under the terms and conditions of the Creative Commons Attribution (CC BY) license (http://creativecommons.org/licenses/by/4.0/).

Article

A Piecewise Linear FGM Approach for Efficient and Accurate FAHP Analysis: Smart Backpack Design as an Example

Hsin-Chieh Wu [1], Toly Chen [2,*] and Chin-Hau Huang [2,3]

[1] Department of Industrial Engineering and Management, Chaoyang University of Technology, Taichung 41349, Taiwan; hcwul@cyut.edu.tw
[2] Department of Industrial Engineering and Management, National Chiao Tung University, 1001, University Road, Hsinchu 300, Taiwan; sasa76130@hotmail.com
[3] Department of Computer-Aided Industrial Design, Overseas Chinese University, 100, Chiao Kwang Road, Seatwen, Taichung City 407, Taiwan
* Correspondence: tolychen@ms37.hinet.net

Received: 16 July 2020; Accepted: 6 August 2020; Published: 8 August 2020

Abstract: Most existing fuzzy AHP (FAHP) methods use triangular fuzzy numbers to approximate the fuzzy priorities of criteria, which is inaccurate. To obtain accurate fuzzy priorities, time-consuming alpha-cut operations are usually required. In order to improve the accuracy and efficiency of estimating the fuzzy priorities of criteria, the piecewise linear fuzzy geometric mean (PLFGM) approach is proposed in this study. The PLFGM method estimates the α cuts of fuzzy priorities and then connects these α cuts with straight lines. As a result, the estimated fuzzy priorities will have piecewise linear membership functions that resemble the real shapes. The PLFGM approach has been applied to the identification of critical features for a smart backpack design. According to the experimental results, the PLFGM approach improved the accuracy and efficiency of estimating the fuzzy priorities of these critical features by 33% and 80%, respectively.

Keywords: fuzzy analytic hierarchy process; fuzzy geometric mean; alpha-cut operations; piecewise linear

1. Introduction

The analytic hierarchy process (AHP), proposed by Saaty [1], is a well-known multi-criteria decision-making method. AHP is based on the pairwise comparison of criteria, which is a subjective process. To better consider such subjectivity, fuzzy logic has been incorporated into AHP, which resulted in various fuzzy AHP (FAHP) methods [2]. FAHP have been extensively applied to a number of topics in various fields, e.g., supplier selection [3–6], project selection and risk assessment/management [7,8], personnel selection [9,10], failure mode and effect analysis [11,12], strategy analysis and technology selection [13–16], etc.

In a FAHP problem, deriving the values of fuzzy eigenvalue and eigenvector requires a number of fuzzy multiplication operations, which is a time-consuming task [17]. For this reason, most existing FAHP methods [18–26] estimate, rather than derive, the values of fuzzy eigenvalue and eigenvector. To improve both the efficiency and accuracy of solving a FAHP problem, a piecewise linear fuzzy geometric mean (PLFGM) approach is proposed in this study. The PLFGM approach can be viewed as a hybrid of alpha-cut operations (ACO) [18] and fuzzy geometric mean (FGM) [22]. In the PLFGM approach, some α cuts of fuzzy eigenvalue and eigenvector are estimated using FGM. Then, these α cuts are connected with straight lines. As a result, the membership functions of the estimated fuzzy eigenvalue and eigenvector become piecewise linear functions, rather than triangular functions. In this way, the estimated fuzzy eigenvalue and eigenvector better approximate their exact values. In addition, the required calculations can be done quickly, even for a large-scale FAHP problem. The novelty of the proposed methodology resides in the following:

(1) The priority of a criterion is approximated with a polygon fuzzy number, rather than a triangular fuzzy number (TFN).
(2) The commonly used FGM method is modified, and the PLFGM approach is proposed to improve the accuracy of deriving the priorities of criteria.
(3) The proposed PLFGM approach is similar in nature to the ACO method, but much more efficient than it.
(4) The center-of-gravity (COG) [27] of a polygon fuzzy number is derived.

The remainder of this paper is organized as follows. Section 2 is dedicated to the literature review. Section 3 is a preliminary of some existing FAHP methods. Section 4 introduces the proposed PLFGM approach. Section 5 details the application of the PLFGM approach to the identification of critical features of a smart backpack design. Several existing methods were also applied to the same problem for comparison. Section 6 concludes this study and puts forth some topics for future investigation.

2. Related Work

In theory, the fuzzy eigenvalue and eigenvector of a fuzzy judgment matrix can be derived using ACO [18]. To enhance the computational efficiency, some researchers modified the definition of consistency, so as to derive fuzzy eigenvalue and vector in a different way (i.e., not fuzzy eigenanalysis) [19,20]. In addition, many existing FAHP methods approximate, rather than derive, the values of fuzzy eigenvalue and eigenvector using techniques such as fuzzy extent analysis (FEA) [21], FGM [22], and the fuzzy inverse of column sum (FICSM) [23]. However, such approximation may lead to incorrect decisions [24,25]. To address this problem, Chen et al. [26] modified the ACO method and proposed the approximating alpha-cut operations (xACO) method that derived the values of fuzzy eigenvalue and eigenvector without enumerating all possible α cuts of a fuzzy judgment matrix. However, Chen et al.'s method was still time-consuming for a large-scale FAHP problem.

In the recent literature, Sirisawat and Kiatcharoenpol [28] ranked a few solutions for reverse logistics barriers using technique for order preference by similarity to ideal solution (TOPSIS). Factors critical to the ranking process were prioritized by solving a FAHP problem using the FEA method. Chen et al. [29] considered a FAHP problem as a fuzzy collaborative forecasting process [30–33], in which the fuzzy priorities of criteria, rather than experts' fuzzy pairwise comparison results, were aggregated. Lyu et al. [34] compared the effects of various risks on constructing a metro tunnel, for which the FEA method was applied to solve the FAHP problem. Chen and Wu [35] decomposed an inconsistent fuzzy judgment matrix into several consistent fuzzy subjudgment matrixes, so as to assess the suitability of a smart technology application for e-health. Boral et al. [36] combined FAHP and fuzzy multi-attribute ideal deal comparative analysis (fuzzy MAIRCA) for comparing risk factors in conducting a failure mode and effect analysis. For evaluating the sustainability of a smart technology application to mobile health care, Chen [37] applied the FGM method to aggregate the pairwise comparison results by multiple experts, and then derived the fuzzy priorities of criteria using the ACO method. The differences between the proposed methodology and some existing methods are summarized in Table 1.

Table 1. Differences between the proposed methodology and some existing methods.

Method	Type of Eigenvalue and Eigenvector	Shape of Membership Functions	Efficiency	Accuracy
FGM [22]	Fuzzy	Triangular	Very high	Low
FEA [21,28,34]	Crisp	-	Very high	Very low
FICSM [23]	Fuzzy	Triangular	Very high	Low
ACO [18,37]	Fuzzy	Nonlinear	Very low	Very high
xACO [26]	Fuzzy	Logarithmic	Low ~ moderate	High
The proposed methodology	Fuzzy	Piecewise Linear	Very high	Moderate ~ High

3. Preliminary

3.1. FAHP

In a FAHP problem, a decision maker compares the relative priority of a criterion over that of another using linguistic terms such as "as equal as," "weakly more important than," "strongly more important than," "very strongly more important than," and "absolutely more important than." These linguistic terms are usually mapped to TFNs within [1,9] (see Table 2) [38,39].

Table 2. Linguistic terms for expressing relative priorities.

Symbol	Linguistic Term	TFN
L1	As equal as	(1, 1, 3)
L2	As equal as or weakly more important than	(1, 2, 4)
L3	Weakly more important than	(1, 3, 5)
L4	Weakly or strongly more important than	(2, 4, 6)
L5	Strongly more important than	(3, 5, 7)
L6	Strongly or very strongly more important than	(4, 6, 8)
L7	Very strongly more important than	(5, 7, 9)
L8	Very or absolutely strongly more important than	(6, 8, 9)
L9	Absolutely more important than	(7, 9, 9)

Based on pairwise comparison results, the fuzzy judgment matrix $\widetilde{\mathbf{A}}_{n \times n} = [\widetilde{a}_{ij}]$ is constructed as:

$$\begin{aligned} \widetilde{a}_{ji} &= (a_{ji1}, a_{ji2}, a_{ji3}) \\ &= 1/\widetilde{a}_{ij} \\ &\cong (1/a_{ij3}, 1/a_{ij2}, 1/a_{ij1}) \end{aligned} \quad (1)$$

$$\widetilde{a}_{ii} = 1 \quad (2)$$

The fuzzy eigenvalue and eigenvector of $\widetilde{\mathbf{A}}$, indicated with $\widetilde{\lambda}$ and $\widetilde{\mathbf{x}}$ respectively, satisfy [40]:

$$det(\widetilde{\mathbf{A}}(-)\widetilde{\lambda}\mathbf{I}) = 0 \quad (3)$$

and

$$(\widetilde{\mathbf{A}}(-)\widetilde{\lambda}\mathbf{I})(\times)\widetilde{\mathbf{x}} = 0 \quad (4)$$

where (−) and (×) denote fuzzy subtraction and multiplication, respectively. To derive the values of $\widetilde{\lambda}$ and $\widetilde{\mathbf{x}}$, a number of fuzzy multiplication operations need to be performed. However, the multiplication of TFNs does not yield a TFN [41]. Therefore, $\widetilde{\lambda}$ and $\widetilde{\mathbf{x}}$ are not TFNs anymore, as illustrated in Figure 1. Approximating them with TFNs may lead to incorrect decisions.

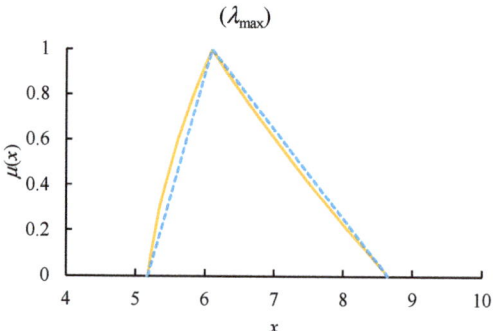

Figure 1. Non-TFN nature of a fuzzy eigenvalue.

3.2. ACO

In the ACO method, fuzzy parameters and variables in Equations (3) and (4) are replaced with their α cuts:

$$\det(\widetilde{A}(\alpha) - \widetilde{\lambda}(\alpha)\mathbf{I}) = 0 \tag{5}$$

$$(\widetilde{A}(\alpha) - \widetilde{\lambda}(\alpha)\mathbf{I})\widetilde{\mathbf{x}}(\alpha) = 0 \tag{6}$$

Each α cut is an interval:

$$\widetilde{a}_{ij}(\alpha) = [a_{ij}^L(\alpha),\ a_{ij}^R(\alpha)] \tag{7}$$

$$\widetilde{\lambda}(\alpha) = [\lambda^L(\alpha),\ \lambda^R(\alpha)] \tag{8}$$

$$\widetilde{\mathbf{x}}(\alpha) = [\mathbf{x}^L(\alpha),\ \mathbf{x}^R(\alpha)] \tag{9}$$

If α takes 11 possible values $(0, 0.1, \ldots, 1)$, Equations (5) and (6) must be solved $11 \cdot 2^{C_2^n}$ times to derive the membership functions of fuzzy eigenvalue and eigenvector as [26]:

$$\lambda^L(\alpha) = \min_{\det([a_{ij}^*(\alpha)] - \lambda_t(\alpha)I) = 0} (\lambda_t(\alpha)) \tag{10}$$

$$\lambda^R(\alpha) = \max_{\det([a_{ij}^*(\alpha)] - \lambda_t(\alpha)I) = 0} (\lambda_t(\alpha)) \tag{11}$$

$$\mathbf{x}^L(\alpha) = \min_{([a_{ij}^*(\alpha)] - \lambda_t(\alpha)\mathbf{I})\mathbf{x}_t(\alpha) = 0} (\mathbf{x}_t(\alpha)) \tag{12}$$

$$\mathbf{x}^R(\alpha) = \max_{([a_{ij}^*(\alpha)] - \lambda_t(\alpha)\mathbf{I})\mathbf{x}_t(\alpha) = 0} (\mathbf{x}_t(\alpha)) \tag{13}$$

where $* = L$ or R. $\lambda_t^L(\alpha)$, $\lambda_t^R(\alpha)$, $\mathbf{x}_t^L(\alpha)$, and $\mathbf{x}_t^R(\alpha)$ are the results derived from the t-th combination; $t = 1 \sim 11 \cdot 2^{C_2^n}$. Although the ACO method can derive the membership functions of fuzzy eigenvalue and eigenvector accurately, it is time-consuming.

Based on $\widetilde{\mathbf{x}}$, the fuzzy priorities of criteria can be derived as [40]:

$$\widetilde{w}_i = \frac{\widetilde{x}_i}{\sum_{j=1}^n \widetilde{x}_j} = \frac{1}{1 + \sum_{j \neq i} \frac{\widetilde{x}_j}{\widetilde{x}_i}} \tag{14}$$

In addition, based on $\tilde{\lambda}_{max}$, fuzzy consistency ratio can be assessed as [40]:

$$\widetilde{CR} = \frac{\frac{\tilde{\lambda}_{max}-n}{n-1}}{RI} \quad (15)$$

where RI random consistency index. If $\widetilde{CR} \leq 0.1$, then the decision maker's pairwise comparison results are consistent. Neither $\tilde{w}_i$ nor $\widetilde{CR}$ are TFNs [26].

The COG method can be applied to defuzzify a fuzzy priority as [27]:

$$COG(\tilde{w}_i) = \frac{\int_0^1 x \mu_{\tilde{w}_i}(x)dx}{\int_0^1 \mu_{\tilde{w}_i}(x)dx} \quad (16)$$

However, the ACO method takes samples uniformly along the y axis, while COG requires that samples be taken regularly along the x axis [26]. To resolve this discrepancy, the range of $\tilde{w}_i$ can be partitioned into Γ equal intervals [42]:

$$\tilde{w}_i = \{[\frac{\Gamma-\eta+1}{\Gamma}w_i^L(0) + \frac{\eta-1}{\Gamma}w_i^R(0).., \frac{\Gamma-\eta}{\Gamma}w_i^L(0) + \frac{\eta}{\Gamma}w_i^R(0)] \Big| \eta = 1 \sim \Gamma\} \quad (17)$$

The center of the η-th interval is indicated with $C_i(\eta)$:

$$\begin{aligned} C_i(\eta) &= \tfrac{1}{2}(\tfrac{\Gamma-\eta+1}{\Gamma}w_i^L(0) + \tfrac{\eta-1}{\Gamma}w_i^R(0) + \tfrac{\Gamma-\eta}{\Gamma}w_i^L(0) + \tfrac{\eta}{\Gamma}w_i^R(0)) \\ &= \tfrac{2\Gamma-2\eta+1}{2\Gamma}w_i^L(0) + \tfrac{2\eta-1}{2\Gamma}w_i^R(0) \end{aligned} \quad (18)$$

The membership of $C_i(\eta)$ is determined by interpolating those of the two closest α cuts of $\tilde{w}_i$:

$$\mu_{\tilde{w}_i}(C_i(\eta)) = \frac{C_i(\eta) - \max\limits_{w_i^*(\alpha) \leq C_i(\eta)} w_i^*(\alpha)}{\min\limits_{w_i^*(\alpha) \geq C_i(\eta)} w_i^*(\alpha) - \max\limits_{w_i^*(\alpha) \leq C_i(\eta)} w_i^*(\alpha)} \cdot \min\limits_{w_i^*(\alpha) \geq C_i(\eta)} \alpha \\ + \frac{\min\limits_{w_i^*(\alpha) \geq C_i(\eta)} w_i^*(\alpha) - C_i(\eta)}{\min\limits_{w_i^*(\alpha) \geq C_i(\eta)} w_i^*(\alpha) - \max\limits_{w_i^*(\alpha) \leq C_i(\eta)} w_i^*(\alpha)} \cdot \max\limits_{w_i^*(\alpha) \leq C_i(\eta)} \alpha \quad (19)$$

where * can be R or L. Then, the COG of $\tilde{w}_i$ is calculated based on the centers of the intervals:

$$COG(\tilde{w}_i) = \frac{\sum\limits_{\eta=1}^{\Gamma}(\mu_{\tilde{w}_i}(C_i(\eta))C_i(\eta))}{\sum\limits_{\eta=1}^{\Gamma}\mu_{\tilde{w}_i}(C_i(\eta))} \quad (20)$$

3.3. FGM

The FGM method estimates the fuzzy priority of criterion i as [38]:

$$\tilde{w}_i \cong \frac{\sqrt[n]{\prod\limits_{j=1}^{n}\tilde{a}_{ij}}}{\sum\limits_{k=1}^{n}\sqrt[n]{\prod\limits_{j=1}^{n}\tilde{a}_{kj}}} \quad (21)$$

When $\tilde{w}_i$ is approximated with a TFN, i.e., $\tilde{w}_i = (w_{i1}, w_{i2}, w_{i3})$, the following theorem holds.

Theorem 1 ([39]).

$$w_{i1} \cong \frac{1}{1 + \sum_{k \neq i} \frac{\sqrt[n]{\prod_{j=1}^{n} a_{kj3}}}{\sqrt[n]{\prod_{j=1}^{n} a_{ij1}}}} \tag{22}$$

$$w_{i2} \cong \frac{1}{1 + \sum_{k \neq i} \frac{\sqrt[n]{\prod_{j=1}^{n} a_{kj2}}}{\sqrt[n]{\prod_{j=1}^{n} a_{ij2}}}} \tag{23}$$

$$w_{i3} \cong \frac{1}{1 + \sum_{k \neq i} \frac{\sqrt[n]{\prod_{j=1}^{n} a_{kj1}}}{\sqrt[n]{\prod_{j=1}^{n} a_{ij3}}}} \tag{24}$$

The COG method can be applied to defuzzify a TFN-based fuzzy priority as [27]

$$COG(\widetilde{w}_i) = \frac{w_{i1} + w_{i2} + w_{i3}}{3} \tag{25}$$

The fuzzy maximal eigenvalue $\widetilde{\lambda}_{max}$ can be estimated as [38]

$$\widetilde{\lambda}_{max} \cong \frac{1}{n} \sum_{i=1}^{n} \frac{\sum_{j=1}^{n} (\widetilde{a}_{ij}(\times)\widetilde{w}_j)}{\widetilde{w}_i}. \tag{26}$$

The following theorem holds if $\widetilde{\lambda}_{max}$ is approximated with a TFN.

Theorem 2 ([39]).

$$\lambda_{max,1} \cong 1 + \frac{1}{n} \sum_{i=1}^{n} \sum_{j \neq i} \frac{a_{ij1} w_{j1}}{w_{i3}} \tag{27}$$

$$\lambda_{max,2} \cong 1 + \frac{1}{n} \sum_{i=1}^{n} \sum_{j \neq i} \frac{a_{ij2} w_{j2}}{w_{i2}} \tag{28}$$

$$\lambda_{max,3} \cong 1 + \frac{1}{n} \sum_{i=1}^{n} \sum_{j \neq i} \frac{a_{ij3} w_{j3}}{w_{i1}}. \tag{29}$$

Based on $\widetilde{\lambda}_{max}$, fuzzy consistency ratio, in terms of a TFN, can be evaluated according to Equation (15) as

$$CR_1 = \frac{\frac{\lambda_{max,1} - n}{n-1}}{RI} \tag{30}$$

$$CR_2 = \frac{\frac{\lambda_{max,2} - n}{n-1}}{RI} \tag{31}$$

$$CR_3 = \frac{\frac{\lambda_{max,3} - n}{n-1}}{RI}. \tag{32}$$

4. The PLFGM Approach

4.1. Assumptions and Limitations

The following assumptions are made in this study:

(1) The decision-maker is able to compare the relative priorities of criteria in pairs.
(2) Pairwise comparison results are consistent.
(3) An efficient ACO-based method for solving large-scale FAHP problems is still lacking.

In addition, the proposed PLFGM approach is subject to the following limitations:

(1) The PLFGM approach can only improve the accuracy of α cuts when α is not equal to 0 or 1.
(2) When pairwise comparison results are inconsistent, the effect of the PLFGM method is limited.
(3) When the uncertainty of pairwise comparison results is not high, the effect of the PLFGM method is also limited.

A flowchart is provided in Figure 2 to illustrate the procedure of the PLFGM approach.

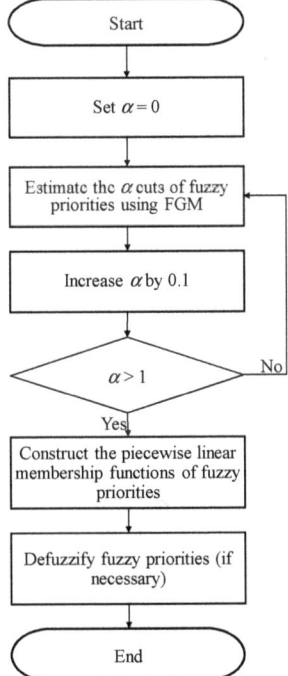

Figure 2. Procedure of the proposed methodology.

4.2. Piecewise Linear Membership Functions

Letting the left and right α cuts of $\tilde{w}_i$ be indicated with $w_i^L(\alpha)$ and $w_i^R(\alpha)$, respectively. According to Theorem 1:

$$w_i^L(\alpha) \cong \frac{1}{1 + \sum_{k \neq i} \frac{\sqrt[n]{\prod_{j=1}^{n} a_{kj}^R(\alpha)}}{\sqrt[n]{\prod_{j=1}^{n} a_{ij}^L(\alpha)}}} \qquad (33)$$

$$w_i^R(\alpha) \cong \frac{1}{1 + \sum_{k \neq i} \frac{\sqrt[n]{\prod_{j=1}^{n} a_{kj}^L(\alpha)}}{\sqrt[n]{\prod_{j=1}^{n} a_{ij}^R(\alpha)}}} \tag{34}$$

In PLFGM, a fuzzy priority is estimated by connecting some of its α cuts with straight lines, as illustrated in Figure 3, in which the membership function on either side is approximated by connecting four α cuts with straight lines [43]. FGM is a special case of PLFGM because only the α cuts when $\alpha = 0$ and 1 are connected.

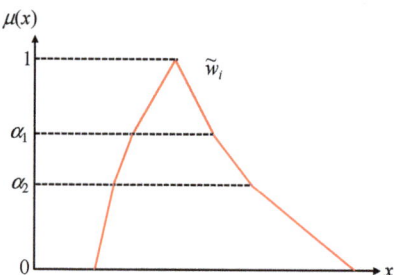

Figure 3. A fuzzy priority estimated using PLFGM.

An example is provided in Figure 4 that illustrates the differences among ACO, xACO, FGM, and PLFGM.

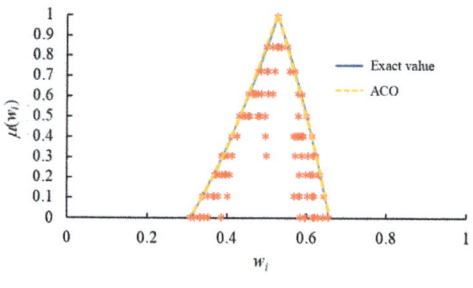

(**a**) ACO

Figure 4. *Cont.*

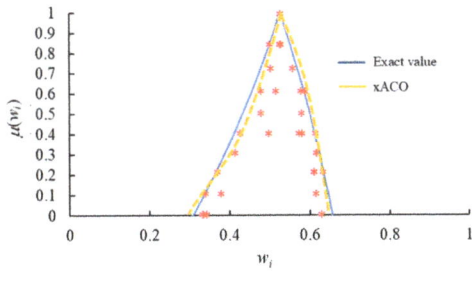

(b) xACO

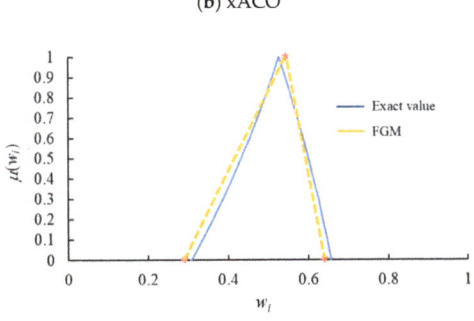

(c) FGM

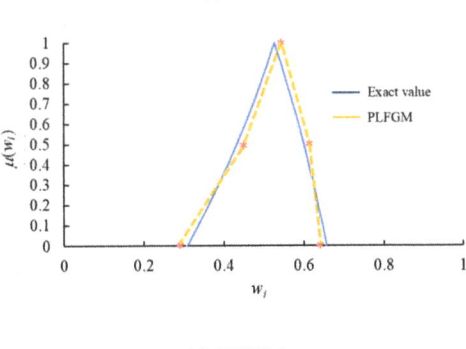

(d) PLFGM

Figure 4. Differences among ACO, xACO, FGM, and PLFGM (* denotes a data point) (**a**) ACO; (**b**) xACO; (**c**) FGM; (**d**) PLFGM.

4.3. Defuzzification

To defuzzify a fuzzy priority estimated using the PLFGM approach, the following theorems are helpful:

Theorem 3 ([6]). *The integral of a non-normal trapezoidal fuzzy number (TrFN) $\widetilde{P}$, shown in Figure 5, is:*

$$\int_{x_1}^{x_2} \mu_{\widetilde{P}(x)}(x)dx = \frac{\mu_2 x_2^2 + \mu_1 x_2^2 - 2\mu_2 x_1 x_2 + \mu_1 x_1^2 - 2\mu_1 x_1 x_2 + \mu_2 x_1^2}{2(x_2 - x_1)} \tag{35}$$

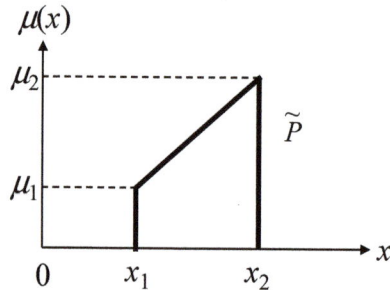

Figure 5. A non-normal TrFN.

Theorem 4 ([6]).

$$\int_{x_1}^{x_2} x\mu_{\widetilde{P}(x)}(x)dx = \frac{2\mu_2 x_2^3 + \mu_1 x_2^3 - 3\mu_2 x_1 x_2^2 + \mu_2 x_1^3 + 2\mu_1 x_1^3 - 3\mu_1 x_1^2 x_2}{6(x_2 - x_1)}. \tag{36}$$

A fuzzy priority estimated using the PLFGM approach can be decomposed into several non-normal TrFNs, as illustrated in Figure 6. In this figure, there are four non-normal TrFNs, whose corner data are summarized in Table 3. Then, the defuzzified value of $\widetilde{w}_i$ can be derived by applying Theorems 3 and 4 as follows.

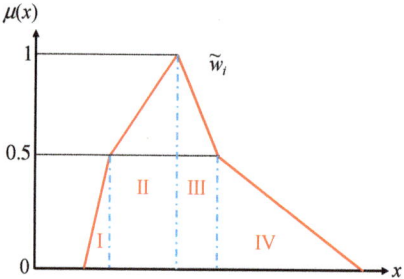

Figure 6. Decomposing a fuzzy priority estimated using PLFGM into several non-normal TrFNs.

Table 3. Corner data of the non-normal TrFNs.

	I	II	III	IV
x_1	$w_i^L(0)$	$w_i^L(0.5)$	$w_i^*(1)$	$w_i^R(0.5)$
x_2	$w_i^L(0.5)$	$w_i^*(1)$	$w_i^R(0.5)$	$w_i^R(0)$
μ_1	0	0.5	1	0.5
μ_2	0.5	1	0.5	0

Theorem 5. Let $\widetilde{w}_i$ be a polygonal fuzzy number as shown in Figure 6. Then the COG of $\widetilde{w}_i$ is:

$$COG(\widetilde{w}_i) = \frac{\begin{array}{c} w_i^L(0.5)^3\gamma_2\gamma_3\gamma_4 - 1.5w_i^L(0)w_i^L(0.5)^2\gamma_2\gamma_3\gamma_4 + 0.5w_i^L(0)^3\gamma_2\gamma_3\gamma_4 + 2.5w_i^*(1)^3\gamma_1\gamma_3\gamma_4 \\ -3w_i^L(0.5)w_i^*(1)^2\gamma_1\gamma_3\gamma_4 + 2w_i^L(0.5)^3\gamma_1\gamma_3\gamma_4 - 1.5w_i^L(0.5)^2w_i^*(1)\gamma_1\gamma_3\gamma_4 + 2w_i^R(0.5)^3\gamma_1\gamma_2\gamma_4 \\ -1.5w_i^*(1)w_i^R(0.5)^2\gamma_1\gamma_2\gamma_4 + 2.5w_i^*(1)^3\gamma_1\gamma_2\gamma_4 - 3w_i^*(1)^2w_i^R(0.5)\gamma_1\gamma_2\gamma_4 + 0.5w_i^R(0)^3\gamma_1\gamma_2\gamma_3 \\ +w_i^R(0.5)^3\gamma_1\gamma_2\gamma_3 - 1.5w_i^R(0.5)^2w_i^R(0)\gamma_1\gamma_2\gamma_3 \end{array}}{\begin{array}{c} 1.5w_i^L(0.5)^2\gamma_2\gamma_3\gamma_4 - 3w_i^L(0)w_i^L(0.5)\gamma_2\gamma_3\gamma_4 + 1.5w_i^L(0)^2\gamma_2\gamma_3\gamma_4 + 7.5w_i^*(1)^2\gamma_1\gamma_3\gamma_4 \\ -9w_i^L(0.5)w_i^*(1)\gamma_1\gamma_3\gamma_4 + 4.5w_i^L(0.5)^2\gamma_1\gamma_3\gamma_4 + 7.5w_i^R(0.5)^2\gamma_1\gamma_2\gamma_4 - 9w_i^*(1)w_i^R(0.5)\gamma_1\gamma_2\gamma_4 \\ +4.5w_i^*(1)^2\gamma_1\gamma_2\gamma_4 + 1.5w_i^R(0)^2\gamma_1\gamma_2\gamma_3 + 1.5w_i^R(0.5)^2\gamma_1\gamma_2\gamma_3 - 3w_i^R(0.5)w_i^R(0)\gamma_1\gamma_2\gamma_3 \end{array}} \tag{37}$$

where $\gamma_1 = w_i^L(0.5) - w_i^L(0);\ \gamma_2 = w_i^*(1) - w_i^L(0.5);\ \gamma_3 = w_i^R(0.5) - w_i^*(1);\ \gamma_4 = w_i^R(0) - w_i^R(0.5)$.

Proof.

$$\begin{aligned}
COG(\widetilde{w}_i) &= \frac{\int x\mu_{\widetilde{w}_i}(x)dx}{\int \mu_{\widetilde{w}_i}(x)dx} \\
&= \frac{\int_{x\in I} x\mu_{\widetilde{w}_i}(x)dx + \int_{x\in II} x\mu_{\widetilde{w}_i}(x)dx + \int_{x\in III} x\mu_{\widetilde{w}_i}(x)dx + \int_{x\in IV} x\mu_{\widetilde{w}_i}(x)dx}{\int_{x\in I} \mu_{\widetilde{w}_i}(x)dx + \int_{x\in II} \mu_{\widetilde{w}_i}(x)dx + \int_{x\in III} \mu_{\widetilde{w}_i}(x)dx + \int_{x\in IV} \mu_{\widetilde{w}_i}(x)dx} \\
&= \frac{\dfrac{w_i^L(0.5)^3 - 1.5w_i^L(0)w_i^L(0.5)^2 + 0.5w_i^L(0)^3}{6w_i^L(0.5) - 6w_i^L(0)}}{} \\
&\quad + \frac{2.5w_i^*(1)^3 - 3w_i^L(0.5)w_i^*(1)^2 + 2w_i^L(0.5)^3 - 1.5w_i^L(0.5)^2 w_i^*(1)}{6w_i^*(1) - 6w_i^L(0.5)} \\
&\quad + \frac{2w_i^R(0.5)^3 - 1.5w_i^*(1)w_i^R(0.5)^2 + 2.5w_i^*(1)^3 - 3w_i^*(1)^2 w_i^R(0.5)}{6w_i^R(0.5) - 6w_i^*(1)} \\
&\quad + \frac{0.5w_i^R(0)^3 + w_i^R(0.5)^3 - 1.5w_i^R(0.5)^2 w_i^R(0)}{6w_i^R(0) - 6w_i^R(0.5)}
\end{aligned}$$

$$= \frac{\begin{array}{c}\dfrac{0.5w_i^L(0.5)^2 - w_i^L(0)w_i^L(0.5) + 0.5w_i^L(0)^2}{2w_i^L(0.5) - 2w_i^L(0)} \\ + \dfrac{2.5w_i^*(1)^2 - 3w_i^L(0.5)w_i^*(1) + 1.5w_i^L(0.5)^2}{2w_i^*(1) - 2w_i^L(0.5)} \\ + \dfrac{2.5w_i^R(0.5)^2 - 3w_i^*(1)w_i^R(0.5) + 1.5w_i^*(1)^2}{2w_i^R(0.5) - 2w_i^*(1)} \\ + \dfrac{0.5w_i^R(0)^2 + 0.5w_i^R(0.5)^2 - w_i^R(0.5)w_i^R(0)}{2w_i^R(0) - 2w_i^R(0.5)} \end{array}}{} \tag{38}$$

$$= \frac{\begin{array}{c} w_i^L(0.5)^3\gamma_2\gamma_3\gamma_4 - 1.5w_i^L(0)w_i^L(0.5)^2\gamma_2\gamma_3\gamma_4 + 0.5w_i^L(0)^3\gamma_2\gamma_3\gamma_4 + 2.5w_i^*(1)^3\gamma_1\gamma_3\gamma_4 \\ -3w_i^L(0.5)w_i^*(1)^2\gamma_1\gamma_3\gamma_4 + 2w_i^L(0.5)^3\gamma_1\gamma_3\gamma_4 - 1.5w_i^L(0.5)^2w_i^*(1)\gamma_1\gamma_3\gamma_4 + 2w_i^R(0.5)^3\gamma_1\gamma_2\gamma_4 \\ -1.5w_i^*(1)w_i^R(0.5)^2\gamma_1\gamma_2\gamma_4 + 2.5w_i^*(1)^3\gamma_1\gamma_2\gamma_4 - 3w_i^*(1)^2w_i^R(0.5)\gamma_1\gamma_2\gamma_4 + 0.5w_i^R(0)^3\gamma_1\gamma_2\gamma_3 \\ +w_i^R(0.5)^3\gamma_1\gamma_2\gamma_3 - 1.5w_i^R(0.5)^2w_i^R(0)\gamma_1\gamma_2\gamma_3 \end{array}}{\begin{array}{c} 1.5w_i^L(0.5)^2\gamma_2\gamma_3\gamma_4 - 3w_i^L(0)w_i^L(0.5)\gamma_2\gamma_3\gamma_4 + 1.5w_i^L(0)^2\gamma_2\gamma_3\gamma_4 + 7.5w_i^*(1)^2\gamma_1\gamma_3\gamma_4 \\ -9w_i^L(0.5)w_i^*(1)\gamma_1\gamma_3\gamma_4 + 4.5w_i^L(0.5)^2\gamma_1\gamma_3\gamma_4 + 7.5w_i^R(0.5)^2\gamma_1\gamma_2\gamma_4 - 9w_i^*(1)w_i^R(0.5)\gamma_1\gamma_2\gamma_4 \\ +4.5w_i^*(1)^2\gamma_1\gamma_2\gamma_4 + 1.5w_i^R(0)^2\gamma_1\gamma_2\gamma_3 + 1.5w_i^R(0.5)^2\gamma_1\gamma_2\gamma_3 - 3w_i^R(0.5)w_i^R(0)\gamma_1\gamma_2\gamma_3 \end{array}}$$

where $\gamma_1 = w_i^L(0.5) - w_i^L(0);\ \gamma_2 = w_i^*(1) - w_i^L(0.5);\ \gamma_3 = w_i^R(0.5) - w_i^*(1);\ \gamma_4 = w_i^R(0) - w_i^R(0.5)$. This completes the proof. □

Based on the derived (or estimated) fuzzy priorities of criteria, fuzzy weighted average (FWA) [16], multi-attribute utility theory (MAUT) [44], fuzzy technique for order preference by similarity to ideal solution (fuzzy TOPSIS) [42], or fuzzy VIseKriterijumska Optimizacija I Kompromisno Resenje (fuzzy VIKOR) [45] can be applied to evaluate the overall performances of alternatives.

5. Smart Backpack Design Case

5.1. Application of the Proposed Methodology

A smart backpack, also known as an enhanced backpack, is an innovative application of smart technologies, with functions such as motion detection, navigation, and power generation [46]. However, most of the research and development focus is on rechargeable backpacks with a variety of compartments, that is, placing a mobile power supply in a backpack and connecting the power to the USB plug of each compartment [47]. Although it is very convenient to record activities and navigation using a smart phone, there are still occasions when a smart backpack with functions such as motion detection, navigation, and power generation is required. For example, sometimes it is inconvenient to hold a smart phone, a smart phone is out of power, a mobile power supply is out of power, there is no base station signal, or there is no offline map [48].

The research and development of smart backpacks is still in a nascent stage. As a result, it is a challenging task to identify factors that are critical to a smart backpack design. After reviewing the relevant literature and current practices, the following five factors were considered critical to a smart backpack design:

(1) C1: sleek design;
(2) C2: low price;
(3) C3: many smart technologies;
(4) C4: high practicability;
(5) C5: lightweight.

A designer first compared the relative priorities of these critical factors with linguistic terms. The results are summarized in Table 4.

Table 4. Results of pairwise comparisons.

Critical Factor #1	Critical Factor #2	Relative Priority of Critical Factor #1 Over Critical Factor #2
Low price	Sleek design	Weakly more important than
Many smart technologies	Sleek design	Strongly more important than
Sleek design	High practicability	Weakly more important than
Lightweight	Sleek design	Weakly more important than
Many smart technologies	Low price	Weakly more important than
Low price	High practicability	Weakly more important than
Lightweight	Low price	As equal as
Many smart technologies	High practicability	Strongly more important than
Many smart technologies	Lightweight	Weakly or strongly more important than
High practicability	Lightweight	As equal as

The following fuzzy judgment matrix was constructed:

$$\tilde{A} = \begin{bmatrix} 1 & 1/(1,3,5) & 1/(3,5,7) & (1,3,5) & 1/(1,3,5) \\ (1,3,5) & 1 & 1/(1,3,5) & (1,3,5) & 1/(1,1,3) \\ (3,5,7) & (1,3,5) & 1 & (3,5,7) & (2,4,6) \\ 1/(1,3,5) & 1/(1,3,5) & 1/(3,5,7) & 1 & (1,1,3) \\ (1,3,5) & (1,1,3) & 1/(2,4,6) & 1/(1,1,3) & 1 \end{bmatrix}$$

At first, the ACO method was applied to derive the exact values of fuzzy maximal eigenvalue and fuzzy priorities from this fuzzy judgment matrix. The results are shown in Figures 7 and 8, respectively. The fuzzy consistency ratio was around 0.096 with a minimum of 0 and a maximum of 0.611. After applying COG to defuzzify fuzzy priorities, the results were 0.121, 0.196, 0.443, 0.11, and 0.174.

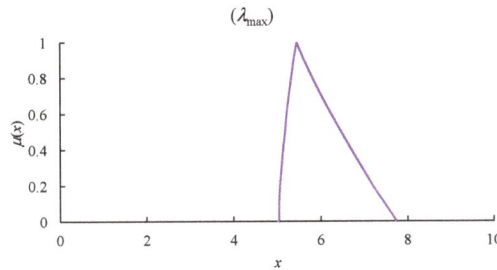

Figure 7. Values of fuzzy maximal eigenvalue derived using ACO.

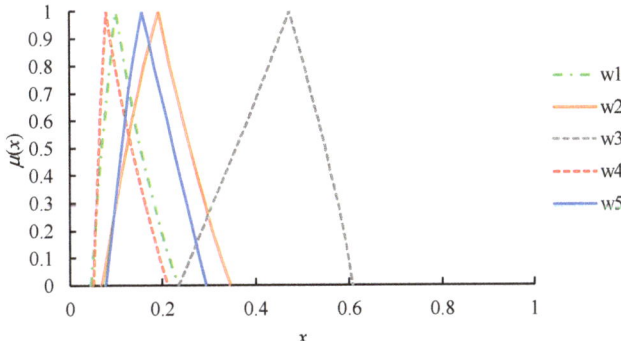

Figure 8. Values of fuzzy priorities derived using ACO.

The ACO method was implemented using MATLAB on a PC with an i7-7700 CPU 3.6 GHz and 8 GB RAM. The execution time was up to 20 s. To enhance computational efficiency, the PLFGM approach was applied.

In the PLFGM approach, the α-cuts of fuzzy priorities when α is in $\{0, 0.5, 1\}$ were estimated according to Equations (33) and (34) and then connected, which resulted in their piecewise-linear membership functions, as shown in Figure 9. Obviously, most of the fuzzy priorities estimated using the PLFGM approach resembled their exact values. Subsequently, COG is applied to defuzzify these fuzzy priorities. The results were 0.121, 0.209, 0.482, 0.11, and 0.174. Three of the estimated priorities were equal to the corresponding exact values, showing the effectiveness of the PLFGM approach.

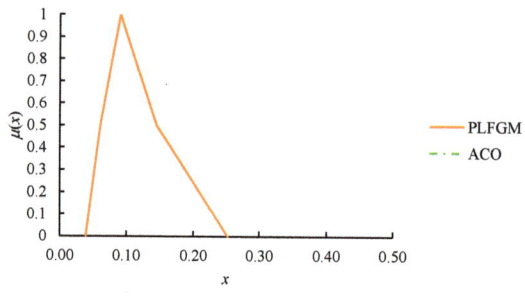

(a) w_1.

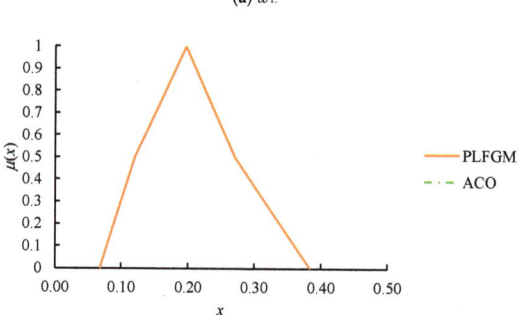

(b) w_2.

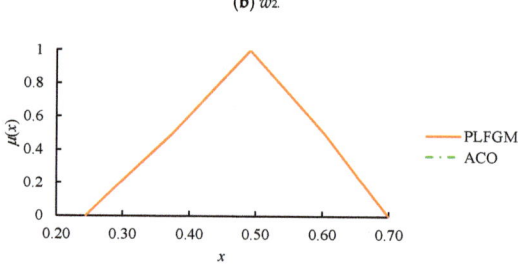

(c) w_3.

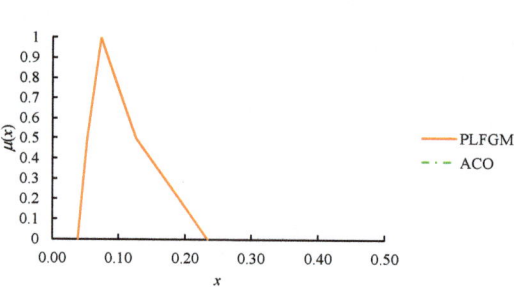

(d) w_4.

Figure 9. *Cont.*

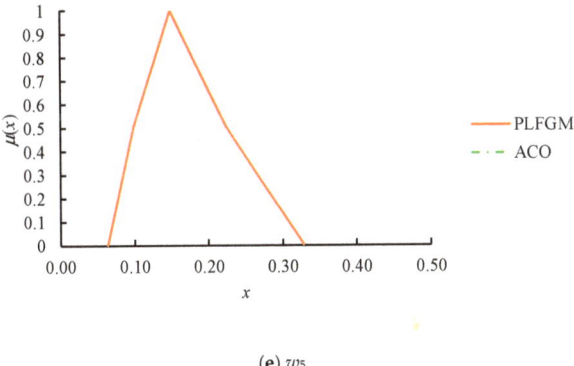

(e) w_5.

Figure 9. Fuzzy priorities estimated using PLFGM (a) w_1; (b) w_2; (c) w_3; (d) w_4; (e) w_5.

5.2. Comparison with Existing Methods

For comparison, three existing methods, FGM, FEA, and xACO were also applied to this case. In the FGM method, fuzzy priorities were approximated with TFNs. In the FEA method, priorities were given in crisp values. In the xACO method, about 20% of the α-cut combinations required by the ACO method were enumerated, which shortened the execution time to about 5 s. Subsequently, the COG method was applied to defuzzify fuzzy priorities. To compare the accuracy achieved using various methods, the average deviation (AD) from exact values was measured:

$$AD = \frac{\sum_{i=1}^{n} |COG_{method}(w_i) - COG_{ACO}(w_i)|}{n} \quad (39)$$

The results are summarized in Table 5. The execution time for each method was also shown in this table.

Table 5. Performances of various methods.

Method	AD	Execution Time (seconds)
FGM	0.015	1
FEA	0.031	1
xACO	0.01	5
PLFGM	0.01	1

5.3. Discussion

According to the experimental results,

(1) Both xACO and PLFGM achieved the highest estimation accuracy, followed by FGM. The prevalent FEA method was the least accurate method. Compared to FEA, PLFGM improved the estimation accuracy, in terms of AD, by 33%.
(2) On the other hand, the execution time of xACO was considerably longer than that of PLFGM, FEA, or FGM. If the size of a FAHP problem becomes larger, xACO will take much more time, while other methods can still be completed instantaneously. Compared to xACO, PLFGM improved the estimation efficiency, in terms of the execution time, by 80%.
(3) In this case, the PLFGM approach was considered to be superior to the three existing methods, since it achieved the highest estimation accuracy within the shortest execution time.
(4) The most obvious advantage of the proposed methodology is that it improves the estimation accuracy and efficiency at the same time.

(5) One disadvantage of the PLFGM approach is the complexity of the formula for calculating the defuzzification value.

6. Conclusions

In a FAHP problem, deriving the fuzzy priorities of criteria is a time-consuming task. As a result, most existing FAHP methods estimate, rather than derive, the values of fuzzy priorities of criteria. In this way, fuzzy priorities are approximated with TFNs. However, the edges of fuzzy priorities are actually curved. Such inaccuracy may lead to incorrect decisions. To address this problem, the PLFGM approach is proposed in this study. The PLFGM approach is a hybrid of ACO and FGM, so it is expected to have the advantages of these two methods. In the PLFGM approach, some α cuts of fuzzy priorities are estimated using the FGM method and connected with straight lines. As a result, the estimated fuzzy priorities have piecewise linear membership functions that resemble the real shapes. In addition, since FGM is much faster than ACO and xACO, the PLFGM approach can greatly improve the efficiency of estimating fuzzy priorities.

The PLFGM approach has been applied to identify the critical features of a smart backpack design. The following conclusions were drawn from the experimental results:

(1) "Many smart technologies" and "low price" were the two most important features of a smart backpack design. In contrast, "high practicability" was the least important feature.
(2) Compared to the FGM method, the PLFGM approach improved the estimation accuracy, in terms of AD, by 33%.
(3) In addition, the efficiency of the PLFGM approach, in terms of the execution time, was 80% higher than that of the xACO method.
(4) The efficiency of the xACO method deteriorates rapidly as the size of the FAHP problem increases. Therefore, the advantage of the PLFGM approach over the xACO method will be more significant for a larger-scale FAHP problem.

The PLFGM approach needs to be applied to more real cases to further elaborate its effectiveness. In addition, a simpler formula for defuzzifying a polygon fuzzy number must be proposed to enhance the practicability of the PLFGM approach. These constitute some directions for future research.

Author Contributions: Data curation, methodology and writing original draft: H.-C.W., T.C. and C.-H.H.; writing—review and editing: H.-C.W. and T.C. All authors contributed equally to the writing of this paper. All authors read and approved the final manuscript.

Funding: This study was partly funded by Ministry of Science and Technology, Taiwan.

Conflicts of Interest: The authors declare no conflict of interest.

References

1. Saaty, T.L. Axiomatic foundation of the analytic hierarchy process. *Manag. Sci.* **1986**, *32*, 841–855. [CrossRef]
2. Ruoning, X.; Xiaoyan, Z. Extensions of the analytic hierarchy process in fuzzy environment. *Fuzzy Sets Syst.* **1992**, *52*, 251–257. [CrossRef]
3. Shaw, K.; Shankar, R.; Yadav, S.S.; Thakur, L.S. Supplier selection using fuzzy AHP and fuzzy multi-objective linear programming for developing low carbon supply chain. *Expert Syst. Appl.* **2012**, *39*, 8182–8192. [CrossRef]
4. Junior, F.R.L.; Osiro, L.; Carpinetti, L.C.R. A comparison between Fuzzy AHP and Fuzzy TOPSIS methods to supplier selection. *Appl. Soft Comput.* **2014**, *21*, 194–209. [CrossRef]
5. Awasthi, A.; Govindan, K.; Gold, S. Multi-tier sustainable global supplier selection using a fuzzy AHP-VIKOR based approach. *Int. J. Prod. Econ.* **2018**, *195*, 106–117. [CrossRef]
6. Wang, Y.C.; Chen, T.C.T. A partial-consensus posterior-aggregation FAHP method—Supplier selection problem as an example. *Mathematics* **2019**, *7*, 179. [CrossRef]
7. Abdelgawad, M.; Fayek, A.R. Risk management in the construction industry using combined fuzzy FMEA and fuzzy AHP. *J. Constr. Eng. Manag.* **2010**, *136*, 1028–1036. [CrossRef]

8. Taylan, O.; Bafail, A.O.; Abdulaal, R.M.; Kabli, M.R. Construction projects selection and risk assessment by fuzzy AHP and fuzzy TOPSIS methodologies. *Appl. Soft Comput.* **2014**, *17*, 105–116. [CrossRef]
9. Erdem, M.B. A fuzzy analytical hierarchy process application in personnel selection in it companies: A case study in a spin-off company. *Acta Phys. Pol. A* **2016**, *130*, 331–334. [CrossRef]
10. Ozdemir, Y.; Nalbant, K.G. Personnel selection for promotion using an integrated consistent fuzzy preference relations-fuzzy analytic hierarchy process methodology: A real case study. *Asian J. Interdiscip. Res.* **2020**, *3*, 219–236. [CrossRef]
11. Kutlu, A.C.; Ekmekçioğlu, M. Fuzzy failure modes and effects analysis by using fuzzy TOPSIS-based fuzzy AHP. *Expert Syst. Appl.* **2012**, *39*, 61–67. [CrossRef]
12. Sakthivel, G.; Saravanakumar, D.; Muthuramalingam, T. Application of failure mode and effect analysis in manufacturing industry-an integrated approach with FAHP-fuzzy TOPSIS and FAHP-fuzzy VIKOR. *Int. J. Product. Qual. Manag.* **2018**, *24*, 398–423. [CrossRef]
13. Büyüközkan, G.; Çifçi, G. A combined fuzzy AHP and fuzzy TOPSIS based strategic analysis of electronic service quality in healthcare industry. *Expert Syst. Appl.* **2012**, *39*, 2341–2354. [CrossRef]
14. Kirubakaran, B.; Ilangkumaran, M. Selection of optimum maintenance strategy based on FAHP integrated with GRA–TOPSIS. *Ann. Oper. Res.* **2016**, *245*, 285–313. [CrossRef]
15. Chen, T. Assessing factors critical to smart technology applications in mobile health care—The FGM-FAHP approach. *Health Policy Technol.* **2020**, *9*, 194–203. [CrossRef]
16. Wang, Y.C.; Chen, T.; Yeh, Y.L. Advanced 3D printing technologies for the aircraft industry: A fuzzy systematic approach for assessing the critical factors. *Int. J. Adv. Manuf. Technol.* **2019**, *105*, 4059–4069. [CrossRef]
17. Patil, S.K.; Kant, R. A fuzzy AHP-TOPSIS framework for ranking the solutions of Knowledge Management adoption in Supply Chain to overcome its barriers. *Expert Syst. Appl.* **2014**, *41*, 679–693. [CrossRef]
18. Cheng, C.H.; Mon, D.L. Evaluating weapon system by analytical hierarchy process based on fuzzy scales. *Fuzzy Sets Syst.* **1994**, *63*, 1–10. [CrossRef]
19. Leung, L.C.; Cao, D. On consistency and ranking of alternatives in fuzzy AHP. *Eur. J. Oper. Res.* **2000**, *124*, 102–113. [CrossRef]
20. Yu, C.S. A GP-AHP method for solving group decision-making fuzzy AHP problems. *Comput. Oper. Res.* **2002**, *29*, 1969–2001. [CrossRef]
21. Chang, D.Y. Applications of the extent analysis method on fuzzy AHP. *Eur. J. Oper. Res.* **1996**, *95*, 649–655. [CrossRef]
22. Wang, X.; Kerre, E.E.; Ruan, D. Consistency of judgement matrix and fuzzy weights in fuzzy analytic hierarchy process. *Int. J. Uncertain. Fuzziness Knowledge-Based Syst.* **1995**, *3*, 35–46. [CrossRef]
23. Ahmed, F.; Kilic, K. Fuzzy Analytic Hierarchy Process: A performance analysis of various algorithms. *Fuzzy Sets Syst.* **2019**, *362*, 110–128. [CrossRef]
24. Kumar, N.V.; Ganesh, L.S. A simulation-based evaluation of the approximate and the exact eigenvector methods employed in AHP. *Eur. J. Oper. Res.* **1996**, *95*, 656–662. [CrossRef]
25. Wang, Y.M.; Luo, Y.; Hua, Z. On the extent analysis method for fuzzy AHP and its applications. *Eur. J. Oper. Res.* **2008**, *186*, 735–747. [CrossRef]
26. Chen, T.; Lin, Y.C.; Chiu, M.C. Approximating alpha-cut operations approach for effective and efficient fuzzy analytic hierarchy process analysis. *Appl. Soft Comput.* **2019**, *85*, 105855. [CrossRef]
27. Talon, A.; Curt, C. Selection of appropriate defuzzification methods: Application to the assessment of dam performance. *Expert Syst. Appl.* **2017**, *70*, 160–174. [CrossRef]
28. Sirisawat, P.; Kiatcharoenpol, T. Fuzzy AHP-TOPSIS approaches to prioritizing solutions for reverse logistics barriers. *Comput. Ind. Eng.* **2018**, *117*, 303–318. [CrossRef]
29. Chen, T.C.T.; Wang, Y.C.; Lin, Y.C.; Wu, H.C.; Lin, H.F. A fuzzy collaborative approach for evaluating the suitability of a smart health practice. *Mathematics* **2019**, *7*, 1180. [CrossRef]
30. Chen, T.C.T.; Honda, K. *Fuzzy Collaborative Forecasting and Clustering: Methodology, System Architecture, and Applications*; Springer Nature Switzerland AG: Cham, Switzerland, 2019.
31. Chen, T.C.T.; Honda, K. Introduction to fuzzy collaborative forecasting systems. In *Fuzzy Collaborative Forecasting and Clustering: Methodology, System Architecture, and Application*; Springer Nature Switzerland AG: Cham, Switzerland, 2019.

32. Lin, Y.C.; Chen, T. An advanced fuzzy collaborative intelligence approach for fitting the uncertain unit cost learning process. *Complex Intell. Syst.* **2019**, *5*, 303–313. [CrossRef]
33. Chen, T.C.T.; Wang, Y.C.; Huang, C.H. An evolving partial consensus fuzzy collaborative forecasting approach. *Mathematics* **2020**, *8*, 554. [CrossRef]
34. Lyu, H.M.; Sun, W.J.; Shen, S.L.; Zhou, A.N. Risk assessment using a new consulting process in fuzzy AHP. *J. Constr. Eng. Manag.* **2020**, *146*, 04019112. [CrossRef]
35. Chen, T.; Wu, H.C. Assessing the suitability of smart technology applications for e-health using a judgment-decomposition analytic hierarchy process approach. *Health Technol.* **2020**, *10*, 767–776. [CrossRef]
36. Boral, S.; Howard, I.; Chaturvedi, S.K.; McKee, K.; Naikan, V.N.A. An integrated approach for fuzzy failure modes and effects analysis using fuzzy AHP and fuzzy MAIRCA. *Eng. Fail. Anal.* **2020**, *108*, 104195. [CrossRef]
37. Chen, T. Evaluating the sustainability of a smart technology application to mobile health care—The FGM-ACO-FWA approach. *Complex Intell. Syst.* **2020**, *6*, 109–121. [CrossRef]
38. Zheng, G.; Zhu, N.; Tian, Z.; Chen, Y.; Sun, B. Application of a trapezoidal fuzzy AHP method for work safety evaluation and early warning rating of hot and humid environments. *Saf. Sci.* **2012**, *50*, 228–239. [CrossRef]
39. Chen, T.C.T. Guaranteed-consensus posterior-aggregation fuzzy analytic hierarchy process method. *Neural Comput. Appl.* **2020**, *32*, 7057–7068. [CrossRef]
40. Saaty, T.L. Decision making with the analytic hierarchy process. *Int. J. Serv. Sci.* **2008**, *1*, 83–98. [CrossRef]
41. Hanss, M. *Applied Fuzzy Arithmetic*; Springer: Berlin/Heidelberg, Germany, 2005.
42. Lin, Y.C.; Wang, Y.C.; Chen, T.C.T.; Lin, H.F. Evaluating the suitability of a smart technology application for fall detection using a fuzzy collaborative intelligence approach. *Mathematics* **2019**, *7*, 1097. [CrossRef]
43. Antoni, L.; Krajči, S.; Krídlo, O. Representation of fuzzy subsets by Galois connections. *Fuzzy Sets Syst.* **2017**, *326*, 52–68. [CrossRef]
44. Ashour, O.M.; Kremer, G.E.O. A simulation analysis of the impact of FAHP–MAUT triage algorithm on the Emergency Department performance measures. *Expert Syst. Appl.* **2013**, *40*, 177–187. [CrossRef]
45. Gul, M.; Guven, B.; Guneri, A.F. A new Fine-Kinney-based risk assessment framework using FAHP-FVIKOR incorporation. *J. Loss Prev. Process Ind.* **2018**, *53*, 3–16. [CrossRef]
46. Lin, Y.C.; Chen, T. A multibelief analytic hierarchy process and nonlinear programming approach for diversifying product designs: Smart backpack design as an example. *Proc. Inst. Mech. Eng. Part B: J. Eng. Manuf.* **2020**, *234*, 1044–1056. [CrossRef]
47. Coronado, A. 10 Best Smart Backpacks for Work, Travel, and Play. Available online: https://ideaing.com/ideas/best-smart-backpacks/ (accessed on 16 July 2020).
48. Sharon, U. Smart Backpack|What To Consider When Choosing One In [2020]? Available online: https://www.trvltrend.com/gadgets/smart-backpack/ (accessed on 16 July 2020).

© 2020 by the authors. Licensee MDPI, Basel, Switzerland. This article is an open access article distributed under the terms and conditions of the Creative Commons Attribution (CC BY) license (http://creativecommons.org/licenses/by/4.0/).

Article

Supportiveness of Low-Carbon Energy Technology Policy Using Fuzzy Multicriteria Decision-Making Methodologies

Konstantinos Kokkinos [1] and Vayos Karayannis [2,*]

[1] Energy Systems Department, University of Thessaly, 41110 Larissa, Greece; kokkinos@uth.gr
[2] Chemical Engineering Department, University of Western Macedonia, 50100 Kozani, Greece
* Correspondence: vkarayannis@uowm.gr

Received: 3 June 2020; Accepted: 8 July 2020; Published: 17 July 2020

Abstract: The deployment of low-carbon energy (LCE) technologies and management of installations represents an imperative to face climate change. LCE planning is an interminable process affected by a multitude of social, economic, environmental, and health factors. A major challenge for policy makers is to select a future clean energy strategy that maximizes sustainability. Thus, policy formulation and evaluation need to be addressed in an analytical manner including multidisciplinary knowledge emanating from diverse social stakeholders. In the current work, a comparative analysis of LCE planning is provided, evaluating different multicriteria decision-making (MCDM) methodologies. Initially, by applying strengths, weaknesses, opportunities, and threats (SWOT) analysis, the available energy alternative technologies are prioritized. A variety of stakeholders is surveyed for that reason. To deal with the ambiguity that occurred in their judgements, fuzzy goal programming (FGP) is used for the translation into fuzzy numbers. Then, the stochastic fuzzy analytic hierarchical process (SF-AHP) and fuzzy technique for order performance by similarity to ideal solution (F-TOPSIS) are applied to evaluate a repertoire of energy alternative forms including biofuel, solar, hydro, and wind power. The methodologies are estimated based on the same set of tangible and intangible criteria for the case study of Thessaly Region, Greece. The application of FGP ranked the four energy types in terms of feasibility and positioned solar-generated energy as first, with a membership function of 0.99. Among the criteria repertoire used by the stakeholders, the SF-AHP evaluated all the criteria categories separately and selected the most significant category representative. Finally, F-TOPSIS assessed these criteria ordering the energy forms, in terms of descending order of ideal solution, as follows: solar, biofuel, hydro, and wind.

Keywords: low-carbon energy (LCE); clean energy technology; policy; multicriteria decision making (MCDM); fuzzy methodologies; SWOT; FGP; SF-AHP; F-TOPSIS

1. Introduction

The use of energy is one of the most critical aspects in today's society, as it participates in all expressions of human development (industrial, economic, urban, and rural). For competent authorities, it is also of great importance to develop clean technologies, mechanisms, and policies that control regional resources and direct the regional development via the use of renewable and environment-friendly energy forms. Thus, energy conservation and sustainability are equally important in energy planning decision making. For that reason, the European Commission has suggested, consequently, from 2014 and every year, a guideline to create a sustainable energy action plan (SEAP) to include actions for the transition towards sustainable energy technologies. Via this European level action, the body of European Governors had agreed to reduce atmospheric CO_2 at least 20% by 2020, a goal which was never reached.

The key action for the modern regions is, therefore, to determine trajectories for establishing policies in order to advance the use of renewable low-carbon resources for clean power generation systems with techno-commercial viability, including solar, wind, hydro, and even hydrogen energy conversion and storage installations capacity and response for efficient utilization [1–4], while also minimizing the reliance on non-renewable fossil energy resources. Another primary goal is to promote initiatives that would lead to bioenergy development in biomass and waste biorefineries for increased production and use of sustainable biofuels [5–9]. Adopting an energy shift towards multifaceted low-carbon technologies with sustainable nature and related policies would be to positively contribute to slow down greenhouse gas cumulative emissions for addressing the climate change crucial problem [10–12].

At the same time, the following critical question arises: Is it feasible from an economical point of view to accomplish these energy transitions? Investors surely understand the environmental gain from such a shift to renewable energy usage, but certain reluctance still remains due to the lack of an optimal solution to this problem [13]. The aforementioned conditions and restrictions make the problem of energy planning and decision making a more complex one [14]. The conventional multicriteria decision-making (MCDM) methodologies are not convenient to deal with this problem, as a participatory modeling fuzzy environment is needed where all criteria in decision making, all uncertainties related to energy form selection, and all subjectivities would be expressed with linguistic variables instead of crisp-valued quantities [15,16]. The application of MCDM methods with participation of fuzzy variables is promising in dealing with the vagueness in the process and revealing the most influential factors associated with the embedded uncertainties in decision making.

Most of the studies that include fuzzy methodologies in the energy MCDM problem focus on the following: (a) evaluation of a certain type of energy resource [17], (b) determination of an energy policy for an energy usage alternative [18–20], and (c) power plant selection towards renewable energies [21–23].

The main objective of the present original research is to evaluate participatory modeling as a primary methodology for supporting a policy making process for the implementation of low-carbon energy technologies. Using this method, first, competent authorities design a multitude of scenarios based on regional environmental, economic, social, political, and health factors. The interoperability of these parameters is not always constructive, as there can be negative or inverse causalities between any two of these factors. In participatory modeling, regional stakeholders contribute to the buildup of these causalities. Their opinion is obtained either by surveys or focus groups. Thus, linguistic or intuitionistic variables are used for capturing this information. After all data are acquainted, fuzzy methodologies are employed for evaluating the various scenarios and also selecting a specific energy technology alternative. The application of participation modeling via surveys and focus groups succeeds to record stakeholder preferences as fuzzy numbers initially. Four different candidate energy types (solar, hydro, biofuel, and wind) are first evaluated by the fuzzy goal programming methodology in terms of their feasibility according to the criteria set by the stakeholders. This succeeds in transforming the problem from multiple objective into a single goal, i.e., to rank the energy types according to the primary criteria. For this reason, the stochastic fuzzy analytic hierarchical process (SF-AHP) is involved for evaluating the interrelations among the criteria and computing the pairwise fuzzy weight matrices. Later, the fuzzy technique for order performance by similarity to ideal solution (F-TOPSIS) methodologies is used to find near optimal solutions based on the predefined criteria that were used for the evaluation. The aim is to optimize the achievement of this decision-making process relative to the preset criteria, their pairwise relations, and the preset goals.

The structure of the paper is as follows: In the following section, we present all the material and methods related to SWOT (strengths, weaknesses, opportunities, and threats), FGP (fuzzy goal programming), SF-AHP, and F-TOPSIS methodologies, each one covering its own subsection. At the same time, we provide the necessary literature review in each subsection when we lay out each one and every methodology. In section three, we use a combined analysis for the SWOT and the SF-AHP to determine priorities of criteria or alternative policies in the decision matrix. The steps in this analysis are the same as in conventional AHP studies, i.e., (i) setting up the hierarchy, (ii) setting up the weight scale, and (iii) creating the decision matrix. The last is also created for the F-TOPSIS methodology with the use of triangular fuzzy numbers. In addition, FGP previously computed the importance of the criteria used in SF-AHP and F-TOPSIS method. Our results and discussion follow in the next section with the application of the methodology in Thessaly Region, Greece. In the final section, we discuss conclusions and future challenges for the issue.

2. Material and Methods

2.1. Strengths, Weaknesses, Opportunities, and Threats (SWOT) Analysis

Strengths, weaknesses, opportunities, and threats (SWOT) analysis (see Figure 1) is a planning methodology for project managers and decision makers to organize and highlight all above characteristics in a use case of decision making or a project. This analysis is at a preliminary stage, at the very first high level, and it is intended to mark all the objectives, as well as the internal and external factors that affect the process achieving these objectives. The interoperability and interrelationship between the internal and external factors are usually handled by means of the strategic fit of the decision making and affect later steps in this planning analysis to achieve the objective (such as AHP). The SWOT analysis is usually the first step applied in most of the energy planning methodologies [24,25]. Furthermore, the SWOT analysis is used to analyze stakeholder perceptions according to the decision-making process at hand [26], moving from a top-down to a bottom-up approach.

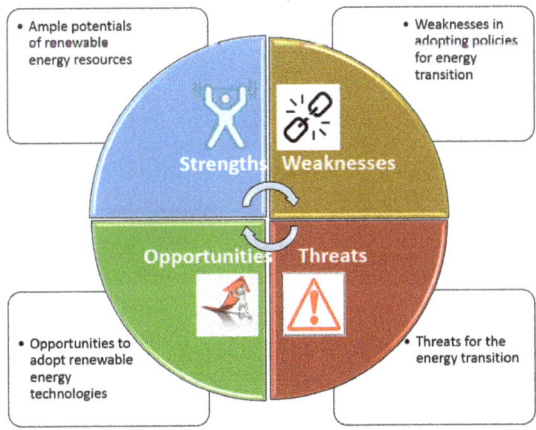

Figure 1. Cognitive map of the strengths, weaknesses, opportunities, and threats (SWOT) analysis.

2.2. Stochastic Fuzzy Set Theory and Fuzzy Analytic Hierarchal Process

Introduced by Zadeh [27], fuzzy sets are the means to present uncertainty due to imprecision or vagueness. Fuzzy sets are able to present data of linguistic variables and imprecise values. A fuzzy set is characterized by the notion of membership as a function which assigns a grade of membership to each entity in the set (a normalized value between 0 and 1). Fuzzy theory also includes the necessary mathematical operators and programming to apply to the fuzzy domain [28–32].

The AHP was introduced by Saaty [33] and has become the most popular method used for MCDM. However, AHP has shown some noticeable drawbacks because the variables involved in the method must be valued with exact crisp numbers. For that reason, fuzzy AHP (FAHP) was developed as an extension to AHP [34]. Special note here is given to the triangular fuzzy number which is defined by the triplet (l, m, u) where $(l \leq m \leq u)$, (see Figure 2).

$$\mu(x) = \begin{cases} \frac{x-l}{m-l} & l \leq x \leq m \\ \frac{u-x}{u-m} & m \leq x \leq u \\ 0 & otherwise \end{cases} \quad (1)$$

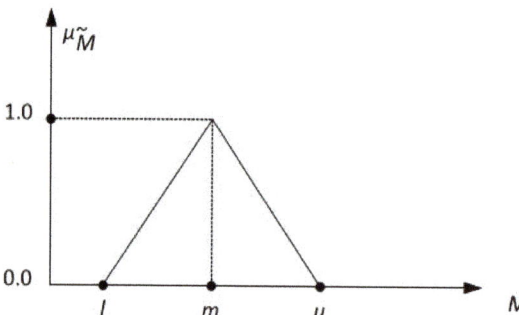

Figure 2. The presentation of a triangular fuzzy number.

Note that m indicates the mean and the most possible value, where l and u denote the smallest and the largest possible value, respectively.

According to the method, first, the experts recommend natural linguistic terms (e.g., equally important and weakly important) to express their judgments in fuzzy AHP and compare any two criteria pairs [35,36] (see Table 1). The pairwise comparison between any two criteria is based on a nine-integer scale shown where vales in between can be used. Table 1 presents the corresponding fuzzy value of this linguistic comparison.

Table 1. Equivalence between linguistic values and triangular fuzzy numbers.

Definition	Crisp Values (Intensity of Importance)	Fuzzy Triangular Scale $\tilde{M}=(l,m,u)$
Equally important	1	(1,1,1)
Weakly important	3	(1,3,5)
Fairly important	5	(3,5,7)
Strongly important	7	(5,7,9)
Absolutely important	9	(7,9,9)

(Values 2,4,6,8 correspond to intermediate values to compromise between the previous ones).

According to the previous notation, it is worthwhile to present the most common algebraic operations between any two fuzzy numbers and a compact description of how the judgement matrix is calculated in the SF-AHP [37–40].

$$\tilde{M} = (l, m, u) \quad (2)$$

$$(\tilde{M})^{-1} = (l, m, u)^{-1} = \left(\frac{1}{u'}, \frac{1}{m'}, \frac{1}{l}\right) \quad (3)$$

$$\tilde{M}_1 \oplus \tilde{M}_2 = (l_1, m_1, u_1) \oplus (l_2, m_2, u_2) = (l_1 + l_2, m_1 + m_2, u_1 + u_2) \quad (4)$$

$$\tilde{M}_1 - \tilde{M}_2 = (l_1, m_1, u_1) - (l_2, m_2, u_2) = (l_1 - l_2, m_1 - m_2, u_1 - u_2) \quad (5)$$

$$\tilde{M}_1 \otimes \tilde{M}_2 = (l_1, m_1, u_1) \otimes (l_2, m_2, u_2) = (l_1 l_2, m_1 m_2, u_1 u_2) \quad (6)$$

240

Using the equations above for the addition and the multiplication of fuzzy numbers, we also show the formulas for the inner product and the summation of multiple fuzzy numbers needed for the calculation of the judgement matrix:

$$\prod_{i=1}^{n} \widetilde{M}_i = \left(\prod_{i=1}^{n} l, \prod_{i=1}^{n} m, \prod_{i=1}^{n} u \right) \quad (7)$$

$$\sum_{i=1}^{n} \widetilde{M}_i = \left(\sum_{i=1}^{n} l, \sum_{i=1}^{n} m, \sum_{i=1}^{n} u \right) \quad (8)$$

Using the answers (values) for the criteria under judgement for reaching the goal of the SF-AHP, the judgement matrix must be calculated according to the following equation:

$$\widetilde{M}_{ij} = \begin{bmatrix} \widetilde{M}_{11} & \widetilde{M}_{12} & \cdots & \widetilde{M}_{1n} \\ \widetilde{M}_{21} & \widetilde{M}_{22} & \cdots & \widetilde{M}_{2n} \\ \vdots & \vdots & \cdots & \vdots \\ \widetilde{M}_{n1} & \widetilde{M}_{n2} & \cdots & \widetilde{M}_{nn} \end{bmatrix} = \begin{bmatrix} l_{11}m_{11}u_{11} & l_{12}m_{12}u_{12} & \cdots & l_{1n}m_{1n}u_{1n} \\ l_{21}m_{21}u_{21} & l_{22}m_{22}u_{22} & \cdots & l_{2n}m_{2n}u_{2n} \\ \vdots & \vdots & \cdots & \vdots \\ l_{n1}m_{n1}u_{n1} & l_{n2}m_{n2}u_{n2} & \cdots & l_{nn}m_{nn}u_{nn} \end{bmatrix} \quad (9)$$

for $i = 1..n$, $j = 1..n$

For each one of the criteria under study we also have to calculate the geometric mean of the values of the matrix above, because it is needed to convert the fuzzy numbers back to crisp numbers and to normalize them. This is via the equation:

$$\widetilde{F}_i = \widetilde{R} \otimes \widetilde{G}_i = \left(\sum_{i=1}^{n} \sqrt[n]{\prod_{j=1}^{n} \widetilde{M}_{ij}} \right)^{-1} \otimes \sqrt[n]{\prod_{j=1}^{n} \widetilde{M}_{ij}}, \quad (10)$$

where $\widetilde{G}_i$ is the fuzzy geometric mean of the criterion C_i, R is the reciprocal of the sum of the geometric mean of fuzzy comparison values, and $\widetilde{F}_i$ represents the fuzzy weight for criterion C_i. The last step of the algorithm to compute the weights for each one of the criteria in this methodology is to find the normalized value of the mean of the fuzzy weights above so that for all criteria these weights must add up to 1. We must also add, for the case in which we have more than one expert that we contribute to the decision-making process, the previous methodology must be repeated each time.

In the last few years, the method has started to be widely used in the decision-making processes regarding supplier evaluations. There is a plethora of research works which have just been published also in relation to the subject at hand and for which we include, here. a synoptic reference:

In a recent work [41], the authors investigated supply chain sustainability by using the Pythagorean fuzzy analytic hierarchy process for the Indian manufacturing industry using the engagement of stakeholders. The study proved that the sustainable supply chain innovation along with social, environmental, and economic advancements were the key factors in improvement of the manufacturing industries. Towards the same line, other researchers [42] used the SF-AHP method to explore dilemmas regarding the solar energy in Taiwan buildings and analyzed the economic development of energy exploiting and environmental protection as the main categories of setting up criteria. Their findings indicated that the method used provided an operational evaluation decision-making system model. Furthermore, 15 representative energy enterprises in China were investigated and their performance was evaluated [43]. SF-AHP for F-TOPSIS was applied to rank the enterprises accordingly and they recommended differentiated subsidy policies for uncertainty evaluation to increase the credibility of the results. Since the problem at hand is of an international nature and it is a reality for most undergrown countries, another work [44] dealt with the evaluation of the renewable resource alternatives in Pakistan employing SWQIT analysis with SF-AHP to assess the internal and external factors which affect the renewable energy technologies. More specifically the SF-AHP was used as a multi-perspective approach to study the solar, wind, and biomass energy types identifying that economic and socio-political were the two most important criteria, thus suggesting that there must be a priority of the government to exploit renewable resources to mitigate the current energy crisis. In addition, other researchers agreed with the aforementioned conclusion when they dealt with similar problems referring to Serbia [45,46]. These authors dealt mostly with measuring energy security, but they applied the same methodology, since it was simply evaluation of another set of criteria. The authors claimed that SF-AHP operates with numerical and linguistic data and there is universality of its application concluding to an experimentally verified assessment of energy security and its trend in the future of the natural gas sector.

2.3. Fuzzy Technique for Order Performance by Similarity to Ideal Solution

The basic idea behind the technique for order performance by similarity to ideal solution (TOPSIS) is the use of the heuristic that any candidate decision among all candidates must have the minimum distance from the positive ideal candidate decision and the longest distance from the negative ideal candidate decision [47–49]. Although the method was developed in 1981 [50], it is heavily used for almost every decision-making process, which is based on linguistic variables after the fuzzy extension was proposed [51]. This extension gives the decision maker the ability to define each criterion, its weight, and every decision alternative with triangular based fuzzy numbers as they were defined in (1). Assuming any two fuzzy numbers $\tilde{M}_1 = (l_1, m_1, u_1)$ and $\tilde{M}_2 = (l_2, m_2, u_2)$ and using the vertex method for F-TOPSIS, the distance between $\tilde{M}_1$ and $\tilde{M}_2$ is given as:

$$d(\tilde{M}_1, \tilde{M}_2) = \sqrt{\frac{1}{3}\left[(l_1 - l_2)^2 + (m_1 - m_2)^2 + (u_1 - u_2)^2\right]} \quad (11)$$

In relation to finding near optimal or suboptimal solutions for the renewable type energy selection problem, lately, there exists some new research [52–57].

Here, we present the step-by-step algorithm of the F-TOPSIS procedure as follows:

Step 1 Define and classify the weights of the criteria involved. Each of the decision maker experts assigns a linguistic weight to all of the predetermined criteria. The assignment is subjective to each expert, but the linguistic values used are similar to a five-Likert scale, which is given in Table 1. Typical values can be "very low importance", "low importance", "medium importance", "high importance" and "very high importance" and the corresponding normalized fuzzy numbers are shown in Table 2.

Table 2. Expert linguistic values and corresponding normalized triangular fuzzy numbers.

Linguistic Value	Normalized Fuzzy Triangular Number
Very low importance	(0,0.1,0.3)
Low importance	(0.1,0.3,0.5)
Medium importance	(0.3,0.5,0.7)
High importance	(0.5,0.7,0.9)
Very high importance	(0.7,0.9,1)

Step 2 Creation of the judgement matrix. The judgement matrix refers to each decision maker and it is constructed by the available alternative decisions D_i in combination with the available criteria C_j.

$$JM = \begin{array}{c} \\ D_1 \\ D_2 \\ \vdots \\ D_n \end{array} \begin{bmatrix} C_1 & C_2 & \cdots & C_m \\ \tilde{r}_{11} & \tilde{r}_{12} & \cdots & \tilde{r}_{1m} \\ \tilde{r}_{21} & \tilde{r}_{22} & \cdots & \tilde{r}_{2m} \\ \vdots & \vdots & \cdots & \vdots \\ \tilde{r}_{n1} & \tilde{r}_{n2} & \cdots & \tilde{r}_{nm} \end{bmatrix} \quad (12)$$

Step 3 Creation of the normalized judgement matrix. To achieve this transformation, we first classify the criteria set into two subsets, namely (a) the benefit criteria (BC) subset and (b) the cost criteria (CC) subset. The normalized judgement matrix NJM is created using JM, BC, and CC where

$$NJM = \begin{bmatrix} \tilde{x}_{11} & \tilde{x}_{12} & \cdots & \tilde{x}_{1m} \\ \tilde{x}_{21} & \tilde{x}_{22} & \cdots & \tilde{x}_{2m} \\ \vdots & \vdots & \cdots & \vdots \\ \tilde{x}_{n1} & \tilde{x}_{n2} & \cdots & x_{nm} \end{bmatrix} \tag{13}$$

$$\tilde{x}_{ij} = \left(\frac{a_{ij}}{c_j^*}, \frac{b_{ij}}{c_j^*}, \frac{c_{ij}}{c_j^*} \right), \quad j \in BC, \quad \tilde{x}_{ij} = \left(\frac{a_j^-}{c_{ij}}, \frac{a_j^-}{b_{ij}}, \frac{a_j^-}{a_{ij}} \right), \quad j \in CC \tag{14}$$

$$c_j^* = max_i\, c_{ij}, \quad j \in BC, \quad a_j^- = max_i\, a_{ij}, \quad j \in CC \tag{15}$$

Step 4 Construct the weighted NJM. The weighted NJM denoted as WNJM is constructed as

$$\tilde{V} = \left[\tilde{v}_{ij}\right]_{n \times m} \quad \tilde{v}_{ij} = \tilde{x}_{ij}(.)\tilde{w}_i \quad i = 1 \ldots n \quad j = 1 \ldots m \tag{16}$$

Step 5 Calculate the fuzzy positive ideal solution (FPIS) and the fuzzy negative ideal solution (FNIS). These solutions are given by the calculation of two vectors respectively A^* and A^- where

$$A^* = \left(\tilde{v}_1^*, \tilde{v}_2^*, \ldots, \tilde{v}_n^*\right) \quad A^- = \left(\tilde{v}_1^-, \tilde{v}_2^-, \ldots, \tilde{v}_n^-\right) \tag{17}$$

and $\tilde{v}_i^* = (1,1,1)$ and $\tilde{v}_i^- = (0,0,0)$ $i = 1 \ldots n.g$

Step 6 Calculate the distance between FPIS and FNIS, that is, the distance between A^* and A^- where

$$\tilde{d}_i^* = \sum_{i=1}^n d\left(\tilde{v}_{ij}, \tilde{v}_i^*\right), \quad i = 1 \ldots n \tag{18}$$

$$\tilde{d}_i^- = \sum_{i=1}^n d\left(\tilde{v}_{ij}, \tilde{v}_i^-\right), \quad i = 1 \ldots n \tag{19}$$

Step 7 Calculate the closeness coefficient of each of the alternative decisions and order them in descending order.

$$COEF_i = \frac{\tilde{d}_i^-}{\tilde{d}_i^* + \tilde{d}_i^-} \tag{20}$$

When dealing with the energy suppliers' problem, we must investigate the selection of the best supplier under conditions and criteria. Some authors [58] have claimed that the selection became difficult because in order to choose they needed to achieve the balance between criteria which were not of the same morphological type (i.e., ordinal, cardinal, categorical values, etc.) Therefore, they used the F-TOPSIS method in a two-phase model, with FAHP as the first step, to evaluate and select suppliers. This model could be used as a decision support and making tool since it succeeded to optimize the savings choosing the optimal supplier. In a similar study [59], criteria for solar energy were evaluated, but mostly technological, using intuitionistic fuzzy TOPSIS with a trigonometric entropy vector weight. In addition, another researcher [60] dealt with the renewable energy power deployment in various systems that used electrical power and claimed that the sustainability study of energy storage systems was of critical significance. Therefore, the author did an extensive analysis, evaluation, and ranking of eight criteria in economic, social, environmental, and technological pillars that affected the aforementioned problem. The author initially used the Bayesian best–worst method to determine the weights of the criteria, and then the fuzzy TOPSIS method was used to rank the sustainability performance of different electrochemical energy storage technologies according to the criteria participating in the process. As for the integrating energy type selection planning, a latest work [61] showed the integration of SWOT analysis, SF-AHP, and F-TOPSIS to evaluate energy strategies for energy sustainability. Initially, SWOT was deployed to determine the important factors for sustainable energy planning. Then, SF-AHP was used to calculate the weights of each factor and sub-factor, and in the last step F-TOPSIS ranked the various energy strategies studied. The methodology was very clear and very similar to the proposed methodology in this paper since it guaranteed a systematic approach for energy strategy sustainability evaluation. On the other hand, the same problem was approached with multi-criteria decision-making (MCDM) methods [62]. By using participatory modeling and surveying, the authors identified all relevant criteria that had quantitative and qualitative characteristics and used a decision-making process to calculate the criteria weights [63]. Specifically, SF-AHP was used for the weights, and then fuzzy VIKOR and F-TOPSIS were utilized for result comparisons. Finally, the most proper energy systems in Saudi Arabia were investigated using SF-AHP, fuzzy VIKOR, and F-TOPSIS methods to select the most eligible system among eight alternatives [64]. The priority of the investment for energy systems was computed by doing sensitivity analysis, and pairwise comparison of the alternatives was implemented using the weight of group utility and fuzzy DEA (data envelopment analysis) approaches. The results showed that solar energy was the most productive.

2.4. Fuzzy Goal Programming

Goal programming (GP) is a well-known method introduced by Charnes and Cooper [65] and later on extended by other researchers [66–70]. This methodology aims at optimizing (minimizing) the achievement of a decision relative to the preset goal levels. The mathematical definition of GP is [65]:

$$\text{Min} \left(\sum_{i=1}^{K} (p_i + n_i) \right) \quad \text{s.t.} \quad \begin{array}{l} (AX)_i + n_i - p_i = b_i \\ X \in C_s \\ n_i, p_i \geq 0 \end{array} \quad i = 1..K \tag{21}$$

where n_i, p_i, b_i, X, C_s are the set of positive deviations, the set of negative deviations, the preset level of goal, the decision, and the constrains or criteria, respectively. There are many differentiations to the method sometimes focusing on the problem at hand such as: (a) weighted GP (WGP) [68], (b) lexicographic GP (LGP) [71] and (c) MINMAX GP (MGP) [72]. The introduction of fuzzy representation of variables in GP was presented by Narasimhan [73] who created the fuzzy goal programming (FGP) method. This author involved fuzzy subsets to formulate imprecision in defining goals for the decision making.

The problem is a multi-objective and multi constraint problem which consists of the following set of optimization functions along with the rich set of constraints:

$$\text{Min} \sum_{i=1}^{i_0} w_i \frac{p_i}{\Delta_i^R} + \sum_{i=i_0+1}^{j_0} w_i \frac{n_i}{\Delta_i^L} + \sum_{i=j_0+1}^{K} w_i \left(\frac{n_i}{\Delta_i^L} + \frac{p_i}{\Delta_i^R} \right)$$

$$\begin{array}{ll}
\text{s.t.} \ (AX)_i - p_i \leq b_i & i = 1, \ldots, i_0 \\
(AX)_i + n_i \geq b_i & i = i_0 + 1, \ldots, j_0 \\
(AX)_i + n_i - p_i = b_i & i = j_0 + 1, \ldots, k_0 \\
(AX)_i - p_i \leq b_i^u & i = k_0 + 1, \ldots, K \\
(AX)_i + n_i \geq b_i^l & i = k_0 + 1, \ldots, K \\
\mu_i + \frac{p_i}{\Delta_i^R} = 1 & i = 1, \ldots, i_0 \\
\mu_i + \frac{n_i}{\Delta_i^L} = 1 & i = i_0 + 1, \ldots, j_0 \\
\mu_i + \frac{n_i}{\Delta_i^L} + \frac{p_i}{\Delta_i^R} = 1 & i = j_0 + 1, \ldots, K \\
\mu_i, n_i, p_i \geq 0 & i = 1, \ldots, K \\
X \in C_s &
\end{array} \tag{22}$$

Relatively to decision making in energy-oriented problems, lately, there has been substantial research that has utilized various versions of the GP and the FGP methodologies. In other work [74], FGP was adapted to accommodate changes in energy costs and future advances in technology maturity for the type of energy selection problem, in the case of Oregon, USA. This model also took under consideration the preferences of the stakeholders to reveal the costs and benefits of complex decisions regarding renewable energy. In a similar work also presented [75], the authors proposed an FGP model that integrates optimal resource allocation for the development of policies related to setting goals such as the minimization of energy consumption and the reduction of greenhouse emissions, while at the same time there exists economic development for the United Arab Emirates. As for renewable energy, a research [76] applied the FGP methodology to evaluate the policies related to biodiesel production in the Philippines using as objectives the maximization of feedstock production, the overall revenue, and minimization of energy. In that work, we see the innovative involvement of several agricultural, rural, environmental and social criteria and constraints, such as the availability of land, labor, water, and machine time, using fuzzy linguistic values for their representations. Towards this direction, a fairly recent research [77] evaluated suitable sustainable feedstocks considering them as the key factor for the optimum renewable products allocation. Their study proposed a hybrid adaptive framework based on a participatory modeling approach, with a process to produce weights of evaluation criteria and their ranking, using dynamic hesitant fuzzy sets. Each of the criteria sets was assigned a weight based on the dynamic hesitant fuzzy entropy method. Using F-TOPSIS, the criteria were ranked in descending order with respect to the FPIS and the FNIS. However, all policies must base their methodology on the optimal mix of different plant types, where in the country these new plants must be built, and finally, what their capacity should be. According to these additional criteria, from the administrative point of view, the interoperability between the available types of renewable energy plants was analyzed [78], synthesizing a variety of additional factors such as geographical, climatic and ecological. The authors applied the FGP model for the case study of the Algeria focusing on the generation of electricity using renewable energy resources. An increasing number of researchers have conducting similar research referring to their own country territory and this has interested emanates due to the huge economic and environmental advantages accrued by the process [79].

Additional research attempts relating to fuzzy goal programming and energy alternatives, types, and suppliers have also been shown recently. First, on the one hand, a priority-based FGP method was presented [80], to deal with the congestion management problem in electric power transmissions and their formulation was via the use of genetic algorithms to determine the membership functions that correspond to the criteria of their analysis. On the other hand, other authors [81] claimed that hybrid energy systems are the future of earth consisting of different types of conventional and renewable resources. After they categorized these systems into grid and stand-alone, they tried to formulate the total profit obtained by their operation utilizing the ratio of renewable energies with the load demand for consumption using FGP. Additionally, previous research was extended [82] on macroeconomic growth models and introduced new criteria variables for investment into the energy sector for the use case of Kazakhstan. Their method was based on FGP and it contributed significant findings in terms of the impact made by R&D on the long-run economic sustainable growth of Kazakhstan regarding energy decision making. Similarly, in a work for the country of Morocco [83], the author proposed an FGP methodology to calculate a sustainable solution, while keeping in mind the unpredictable fluctuations of price, demand, and uncertainty in the energy sector and more specifically for the biodiesel production. In terms also of other renewable energy types, a recent work [84] investigated the potential of exploiting wind energy in India. More specifically, the authors explored various decision-making approaches in relation to fuzzy analysis with the perspective of justification of major factors that influence the effective use of wind energy. Their findings indicated that India had the maximum potential for taping wind energy via a set of suggested policies that would need to be established to maximize the use of renewable source of energy. Finally, an innovative weighted-additive fuzzy multi-choice goal programming (WA-FMCGP) model was proposed [85], introducing energy relating goals with multiple-choice aspiration levels (MCALs). Although their work was mostly presented as a proof-of-concept, application to energy sector numerical problems could help as a supplementary method, in contrast to the multi-attribute decision making for fuzzy programming and multi-choice goal programming related problems.

2.5. Research Comparison and Novelty of our Approach

In this subsection, we summarize the existed literature depicted in the previous section in a comparative table and we discussion the novelty of our research as compared with the exiting literature. We concentrate only on the research that relates the models of SF-AHP, FGP, and F-TOPSIS to energy (giving focus to renewable energy sector) as the amount of research in the general application of the aforementioned models is beyond limits and out of the scope of this work. Table 3 presents a multitude of popular MCDM fuzzy oriented techniques for sustainable and renewable energy planning related studies.

Table 3. Comparison of research results related to renewable energy selection using stochastic fuzzy analytic hierarchical process (SF-AHP), fuzzy goal programming (FGP), and fuzzy technique for order performance by similarity to ideal solution (F-TOPSIS).

Studies	Case Study	Energy Strategies	Criteria	MCDM Methods	Best Strategy
[52]	Lagos Central District	Numerical illustrations	Energy selection	IF-TOPSIS	Only TOPSIS
[81]	Numerical example of small town	Multiobjective decision via function optimization	Collaboration of multiple energy types	GP	GP
[83]	Numerical example	Biodiesel	classification	FGP	Only one is considered
[62]	Turkey	Select the best energy	Multicriteria	FAHP, F-VICOR, F-TOPSIS	Collaboration
[53]	Turkey	Selection among all, not only renewable	Strengths, opportunities, weaknesses, threats	F-TOPSIS, SWOT, ANP	ANP
[74]	Oregon	Min and max of criteria	Construction cost, Production cost, land use, environmental impact	FGP	FGP
[54]	N/A	Biomass	Profit, sales, customization, affordability, participation, experience, technology	HF-DEMATEL, HF-TOPSIS	HF-TOPSIS
[85]	N/A	Electrochemical energy storage	Economic, social, environmental, and technological	F-TOPSIS, FGP	F-TOPSIS
[55]	Numerical Example	Renewable energy policy selection	Technology, environmental, social, economical	VIKOR, IVPLTS	IVPLTS
[42]	Taiwan	Solar energy	Economic development, energy exploiting, environmental protection	SEA, FDM, SAM, Fuzzy AHP	FAHP
[76]	Philippines	Biodiesel	Max feedstock production and revenue, min of energy used and working capital, availability of land, labor, water and machine time	FGP	FGP
[56,57]	India	Selection between nuclear, solar, hydropower, biomass, heat, and power	Efficiency, investment-operation cost, water pollution, pollutant emission, land, social acceptance, job creation	F-TOPSIS	F-TOPSIS
[56]	India	Determine the potentiality indices for healthier exploration of wind energy resources in India	Wind power density, availability of suitable, land, government initiatives, grid connectivity, technical prowess	TOPSIS VIKOR FAHP	Combination of F-TOPSIS and F-VIKOR

Table 3. Cont.

Studies	Case Study	Energy Strategies	Criteria	MCDM Methods	Best Strategy
[61]	Pakistan	Rank 13 energy strategies	Multitude of criteria in MCDM process	SWOT FAHP and F-TOPSIS	Integration of the two methods
[64]	Saudi Arabia	Eight energy strategies as candidates	Power generation, capacity, efficiency, storability, safety, air pollution, net present value	Integrated FAHP F-VIKOR, F-TOPSIS	Solar energy is the most profitable according to both F-VIKOR and F-TOPSIS
[44]	Pakistan	solar, wind, and biomass	4 Basic criteria (economic, environmental, technical, and socio-political), and 17 subcriteria	SWOT FAHP	SWOT FAHP

We claim that our research is novel as compared with the most related (state of the art) research because of the following arguments:

- Most of the research attempts concentrate on a specific MCDM methodology and they do not integrate a plethora of methodologies to produce a "holistic" result based on more than one mode.
- There is not any other research work on the Greek case study to the best of our knowledge.
- Our methodology extends the conventional AHP, GP, and TOPSIS methodologies in terms of integrating the opinions of most critical stakeholder bodies as fuzzy values of their linguistic values in order to solve the MCDM problem of selecting renewable energy sources.
- The proposed methodology explores the validity and applicability of FAHP, FGP, and F-TOPSIS under the existed divergence.
- The only previous research works [62,74] that have some similarity to our methods and findings systematically try to select the best energy type under criteria.

3. Case Study: Thessaly Region, Greece

3.1. Characteristics of the Region and Methodological Roadmap of the Study

Thessaly Region is located in the middle mainland of Greece (see map in Figure 3) extending with a total area of 14,036.64 km^2 and a population of 725,874 inhabitants (2018). Lately, the region exhibits a sharp turn to manufacturing and industrialization from the conventional agricultural activities.

Figure 3. Map of the region of the case study.

Regional sustainability (especially energy sustainability) has become a major concern of competent authorities. It participates in several initiatives in relation to urban planning actions, transition to renewable energies, and boosting of the establishment of solar energy production plants. Following

Europe's post-petroleum actions, most of the regional municipalities initiated several actions towards bio-energy transition, always under the precondition of succeeding economic growth at the same time. Apart from competent authorities, however, this energy conversion depends on the interoperability and the interplay between the regional stakeholders and the various regional social groups.

The methodological organization framework of this work is depicted in Figure 4. Initially, we set the scope of the study, which is the evaluation of low-carbon energy technology alternatives, to select the most suitable for the region under examination. The ultimate goal is the conversion to electricity, the most commonly used energy form. This would provide proof to competent authorities for supporting future policy making. The first step to achieve this goal is to perform the SWOT analysis for establishing all the relevant advantages and disadvantages, as well as any opportunities or threats that can occur due to the decision of choosing an energy alternative. Data for the SWOT analysis comes after selecting the stakeholders, conducting thorough interviews, and organizing all responses setting up all the criteria which they believe that affect the selection. The criteria can be clustered in various categories according to what they refer to. In most of the studies, these criteria are categorized into technological, social, economic, and environmental. Then, the FGP methodology is engaged to find the degrees of memberships of these criteria. We have a bidirectional process of the FGP and FAHP, as seen in Figure 4, as the most important criteria have to be discovered for participating in FAHP, and later in F-TOPSIS. Thus, first, FGP is attended, and then FAHP produces the normalized crisp weight distribution of the criteria. Then, FGP is again involved to provide the degrees of memberships in order to ensure that the selection among all criteria is adequate to provide reliable input for F-TOPSIS. Note, that the criteria are organized for pairwise comparisons based on the FAHP approach that succeeds in ranking them on a predefined importance scale, and therefore weight assignment is possible. Further comparisons between results from FAHP are done after the F-TOPSIS application. Following the FGP, FAHP, and F-TOPSIS application, the policy maker can use the TOWS analysis that can define various strategies attacking the problem at hand.

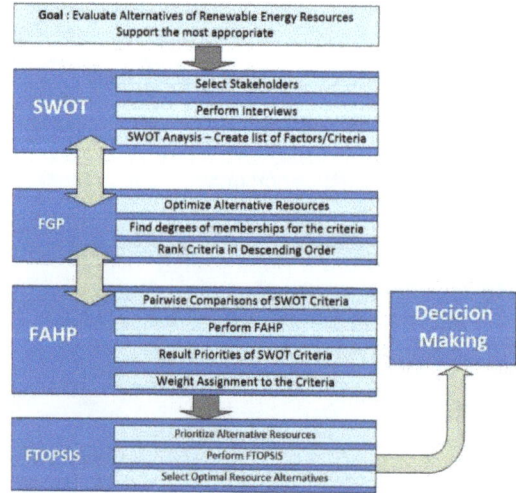

Figure 4. Methodological map in evaluating renewable energies.

3.2. SWOT Analysis

We use the SWOT analysis to strategically integrate all strengths, weaknesses, opportunities, and threats in relation to the energy planning problem.

Recently, many similar studies have been conducted to solve this problem, with typical interests in renewable energy [86], bio-energy [87] and regional energy planning [88,89]. We have utilized 17 experts/stakeholders to set up the SWOT matrix coming from a diverse environment of education, research, government, and energy production utilities according to the recommended expert sampling methodologies [90,91]. The result of their interviews is depicted in Figure 5, where, after amalgamation of similar factors in one, we summarize all the strengths, weaknesses, opportunities, and threats. Following this survey, we asked the experts, in a second stage, to identify all the relevant criteria in selecting one of the candidate types of renewable energy (biofuel, wind, hydro and solar). The interview was conducted under the pre-assumption of clustering these criteria into the aforementioned categories of technological, economic, social, and environmental. The categories of criteria from this survey are shown in Table 4 and the quantification of the stakeholders' importance of these criteria before fuzzification are shown in Figure 6. More specifically, according to the four categories of experts coming from the education, research, government, and energy production utilities sectors, we obtain four average series for the 21 criteria emanated from the survey. The value of each curve is an average evaluation of each criterion from the corresponding stakeholder body.

Figure 5. SWOT analysis, setup of strengths, opportunities, weaknesses, and threats.

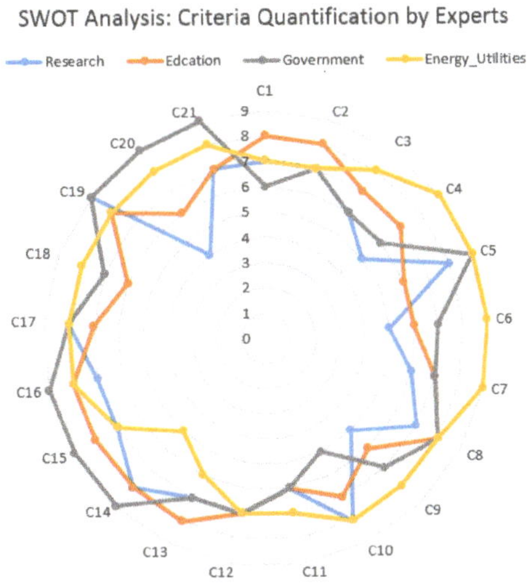

Figure 6. SWOT analysis, criteria quantification by experts before fuzzification.

Table 4. Expert stakeholder criteria setup for the energy type selection.

Criteria No.	Description
TECHNOLOGICAL	
C1	Availability of the technological resources for application of the type
C2	Human capital expertise
C3	Robustness and reliability of the energy type
C4	Electricity supply
C5	Safety
ECONOMIC	
C6	Capital cost
C7	Fuel or energy cost
C8	Life expectancy of the system
C9	Cost to connect to the electricity network
C10	Research and development cost
C11	Marketing and other cost
ENVIRONMENTAL	
C12	Waste production
C13	Hazardous aerial emissions
C14	Ecology preservation
C15	Land use
SOCIAL	
C16	New jobs
C17	Quantification of the (not in my back yard) NIMBY phenomenon
C18	Social perception and acceptance
C19	Impact on residents' everyday life and health
C20	Feasibility of the energy plant
C21	Impact to regional sustainability

Using the previous model, we also apply the TOWS analysis (a reverse approach to SWOT), to identify potential strategies for the problem resolution. The set of strengths, weaknesses, opportunities, and threats, remains the same, but the morphology of the TOWS matrix is altered as to the prioritization of the pairwise strategies chosen. More specifically, we choose the following: (a) To minimize both threats and weaknesses as the strategy of the highest priority, therefore the WT (weakness-threat) as a (min-min) strategy can be used to reduce the threats simultaneously with the overcoming weaknesses and shortcomings; (b) to minimize weaknesses while at the same time try to maximize the opportunities (Strategy WO) to new and well-established energy portfolio alternatives is another promising strategy used in order to mitigate the weakness; (c) Strategy ST (max-min) to maximize the strengths of each alternative energy portfolio while at the same time minimizing the threats and risks taken choosing a specific energy type; and (d) Strategy SO (max-max), the most optimistic approach, to attempt to maximize the strengths while at the same time maximizing the opportunities.

3.3. Fuzzy Goal Programming Analysis

In this section, we provide the mathematical formulation of the use case of Thessaly attacking the problem from the fuzzy goal programming point of view. Policy makers, competent authorities, and regional stakeholders have determined, via the participatory modeling (surveys and focus groups), the criteria for alternative resource energies. Let:

- X_1 be the solar annual electricity generation;
- X_2 be the biofuel annual electricity generation;
- X_3 be the hydro annual electricity generation; and
- X_4 be the wind annual electricity generation.

Note that all aforementioned electricity amounts are in GWh units.

Because the survey participants gave fuzzy evaluations of the criteria above, we also used questions that relate the fuzzy intervals on the hard or approximate values. For example, in relation to criterion C1 (availability of technological resources), participants could easily answer the question "How many technological resources are needed of solar/hydro/wind/biofuel conversion to electricity?" with answers such as "medium", "large", or "low", but could not specify a specific or hard number in such amounts. The idea of specifying intervals (lower and higher thresholds) for set/crisp values on the criteria alleviated the problem. The problem, however, of determining the initial values of the fixed criteria values remains, as it depends on the entity each time. For example, the amount of technological resources is difficult to be determined in moneys as opposed to capital costs or fuel or energy costs. At the same time, wide ranges of intervals initiate higher uncertainties and need to initially go through a sensitivity analysis or need to be predicted accordingly [92,93].

In addition, it is possible to retrieve a solution with adequate results using deviation variables and deviation quantities.

According to international studies [85,94] and the Thessaly Region authorities, the crisp values and the intervals for the criteria under study are given in Table 5.

Table 5. Crisp criteria values and intervals.

Criteria	Solar	Wind	Biofuel	Hydro	Aspiration Level	Tolerance
C1	$4{,}048{,}112 \leq y_{11} \leq 4{,}648{,}112$	$2{,}098{,}741 \leq y_{12} \leq 3{,}098{,}741$	$8{,}683{,}567 \leq y_{13} \leq 9{,}500{,}000$	$650{,}000 \leq y_{14} \leq 750{,}000$	18,000,000	1,000,000
C2	$40{,}481 \leq y_{21} \leq 46{,}481$	$82{,}962 \leq y_{22} \leq 92{,}962$	$605{,}571 \leq y_{23} \leq 645.571$	$10{,}000 \leq y_{24} \leq 15{,}000$	6,000,000	600,000
C6	467,925	1,814,470	9,292,500	375,000	41,000,000	4,100,000
C7	N/A	N/A	N/A	N/A	N/A	N/A
C12	14,190	57,178	68,950	52,000	4,000,000	4,000,000
C16	$1500 \leq y_{61} \leq 2000$	$900 \leq y_{62} \leq 1200$	$500 \leq y_{63} \leq 800$	$500 \leq y_{64} \leq 800$	1500	350

Due to the fact that there is not available data in terms of the criterion C7 (fuel or energy cost), this criterion does not participate in the goal programming calculations. The problem is, then, formulated as an optimization problem that is described by the following goals:

$$G_1: y_{11}X_1 + y_{12}X_2 + y_{13}X_3 + y_{14}X_4 \leq 18{,}000{,}000$$
$$G_2: y_{21}X_1 + y_{22}X_2 + y_{23}X_3 + y_{24}X_4 \leq 6{,}000{,}000$$
$$G_3: 467925X_1 + 1814470X_2 + 9292500X_3 + 375{,}000X_4 \leq 6{,}000{,}000 \quad (23)$$
$$G_4: 14190X_1 + 57178X_2 + 68950X_3 + 52{,}000X_4 \leq 18{,}000{,}000$$
$$G_5: y_{61}X_1 + y_{62}X_2 + y_{63}X_3 + y_{64}X_4 \leq 1500,$$

where the variables X represent the solar, wind, hydro, and biofuel conversions to electricity (annual amounts) in GWh.

Assuming the following hard constraints set by the policy makers given by the inequalities:

$$X_1 + X_2 + X_3 + X_4 \geq 40$$
$$X_1 + X_3 \geq 22$$
$$X_2 \geq 12 \quad (24)$$
$$X_3 \geq 10$$
$$X_4 \geq 10$$

For the above constraints we can find a variety of solution sets for the variables X_1, X_2, X_3, X_4 (for example, a solution set is 10, 12, 10, 10) can produce a set of membership functions for the fuzzy goal programming model. A set that corresponds to the previous solution set is as follows:

$$(\mu_1, \mu_2, \mu_3, \mu_4, \mu_5) = (0.37, 1, 0.45, 0.67, 1)$$

Solving the problem with LINGO [95], yields the following near optimal solution for the decision variables and the degree of the membership functions:

$$(X_1, X_2, X_3, X_4) = (17.173256, 12, 12.826744, 10)$$

$$(\mu_1, \mu_2, \mu_3, \mu_4, \mu_5) = (0.99, 0.99, 0.99, 0.67, 1),$$

showing that the goal, G_4 (membership function degree 0.67), that corresponds to the waste production minimization is not fully achieved.

3.4. Stochastic Fuzzy AHP Analysis

The main objective using AHP is to order the importance of criteria and factors that directly affect the goal of the problem solution. Thus, the prioritization of the criteria weights effectively determines the operational energy measures that a policy maker must take within the scope of energy sustainability in a region. Coming from the SWOT analysis, we have categorized these criteria into technological, economic environmental, and social. For the completion of the reciprocal pairwise comparison matrix in SF-AHP, we followed the method of producing separate matrices for each criteria category instead of a single one. There are two reasons for doing this. The first reason is the introduced bias by the experts, who unconsciously prioritize criteria of their own expertise higher than of other expertise. Secondly, studies have shown that as the number of criteria increases, the accuracy of determining the exact defuzzified value of the importance weight of each criteria decreases [96,97]. Tables 6–9 are depicted in pairs, namely Table 6a,b to Table 9a,b, accordingly. Each of these pair are devoted to each one of the aforementioned criteria categories. Specifically, the (a) part of each table shows the fuzzified pairwise comparison matrix. The second part illustrates the following results: (a) the computation of the fuzzy geometric mean, (b) the final fuzzified value of each criteria using the normalized value its own fuzzy geometric mean, (c) the defuzzified crisp value, and finally (d) the normalized crisp numeric percentage weight of the criteria. The method of calculating the fuzzy geometric mean is introduced by Buckley [98]. More specifically:

- Table 6a shows the calculation of the fuzzified pairwise comparison matrix for the technological category of criteria used in the survey.
- Table 6b shows the technological criteria fuzzy and defuzzified weights.
- Table 7a, above, shows the calculation of the fuzzified pairwise comparison matrix for the economics category of criteria used in the survey, whereas Table 7b, below, shows the economics criteria fuzzy and defuzzified weights computed.
- Table 8a, above, shows the calculation of the fuzzified pairwise comparison matrix for the environmental category of criteria used in the survey, whereas Table 8b, below, shows the environmental criteria fuzzy and defuzzified weights computed.
- And finally, Table 9a, above, shows the calculation of the fuzzified pairwise comparison matrix for the social category of criteria used in the survey, whereas Table 9b, below, shows the social criteria fuzzy and defuzzified weights computed.

Table 6. SF-AHP results per criteria category for the category technological. (**a**) Fuzzified pairwise comparison matrix; (**b**) Criteria fuzzy and defuzzified weights.

(a)

	Fuzzified Pairwise Comparison Matrix				
	C1	C2	C3	C4	C5
C1	(1,1,1)	(1,2,3)	(2,3,4)	(2,3,4)	(0.166,0.2,0.25)
C2	(0.333,0.5,1)	(1,1,1)	(6,7,8)	(2,3,4)	(6,7,8)
C3	(0.25,0.333,0.5)	(0.125,0.142,0.166)	(1,1,1)	(0.166,0.2,0.25)	(0.25,0.333,0.5)
C4	(0.25,0.333,0.5)	(0.25,0.333,0.5)	(4,5,6)	(1,1,1)	(1,1,1)
C5	(4,5,6)	(0.125,0.142,0.166)	(2,3,4)	(1,1,1)	(1,1,1)

(b)

	Criteria Fuzzy and Defuzzified Weights				
Fuzzy Geometric Mean	Lower	Middle	Upper	Crisp	Norm Crisp
(0.9213, 1.2919, 1.6437)	0.1232	0.2145	0.3402	0.2260	0.2123
(1.8877, 2.3618, 3.0314)	0.2524	0.3922	0.6275	0.4240	0.3983
(0.2645, 0.3159, 0.4010)	0.0354	0.0525	0.0830	0.0569	0.0535
(0.7578, 0.8887, 1.0844)	0.1013	0.1476	0.2245	0.1578	0.1482
(1, 1.1632, 1.3184)	0.1337	0.1932	0.2729	0.1999	0.1878

Table 7. SF-AHP results per criteria category for the category economic. (**a**) Fuzzified pairwise comparison matrix; (**b**) Criteria fuzzy and defuzzified weights.

(a)

	Fuzzified Pairwise Comparison Matrix					
	C6	C7	C8	C9	C10	C11
C6	(1,1,1)	(6,7,8)	(6,7,8)	(7,8,9)	(7,8,9)	(6,7,8)
C7	(0.125,0.142,0.166)	(1,1,1)	(4,5,6)	(4,5,6)	(6,7,8)	(7,8,9)
C8	(0.125,0.142,0.166)	(0.142,0.2,0.25)	(1,1,1)	(3,4,5)	(2,3,4)	(3,4,5)
C9	(1.111,0.125,0.142)	(0.142,0.2,0.25)	(0.2,0.25,0.333)	(1,1,1)	(3,4,5)	(3,4,5)
C10	(1.111,0.125,0.142)	(0.125,0.142,0.166)	(0.25,0.333,0.5)	(0.2,0.25,0.333)	(1,1,1)	(0.25,0.333,0.5)
C11	(0.125,0.142,0.166)	(1.111,0.125,0.142)	(0.2,0.25,0.333)	(0.2,0.25,0.333)	(2,3,4)	(1,1,1)

(b)

	Criteria Fuzzy and Defuzzified Weights				
Fuzzy Geometric Mean	Lower	Middle	Upper	Crisp	Norm Crisp
(4.6857, 5.2915, 5.8836)	0.4058	0.5233	0.6331	0.5207	0.5127
(2.6367, 2.4183, 2.7495)	0.2283	0.2392	0.2958	0.2544	0.2505
(0.8492, 1.0541, 1.2685)	0.0735	0.1043	0.1365	0.1048	0.1032
(0.5673, 0.6813, 0.8171)	0.0491	0.0674	0.0879	0.0681	0.067
(0.2362, 0.2814, 0.3545)	0.0205	0.0278	0.0381	0.0288	0.0284
(0.3218, 0.3868, 0.4686)	0.0279	0.0383	0.0504	0.0389	0.0383

Table 8. SF-AHP results per criteria category for the category environmental. (**a**) Fuzzified pairwise comparison matrix; (**b**) Criteria fuzzy and defuzzified weights.

(a)

	Fuzzified Pairwise Comparison Matrix			
	C12	C13	C14	C15
C12	(1,1,1)	(1,2,3)	(3,4,5)	(2,3,4)
C13	(0.333,0.5,1)	(1,1,1)	(1,2,3)	(0.333,0.5,1)
C14	(0.2,0.25,0.333)	(0.333,0.5,1)	(1,1,1)	(2,3,4)
C15	(0.25,0.333,0.5)	(1,2,3)	(0.25,0.333,0.5)	(1,1,1)

(b)

	Criteria Fuzzy and Defuzzified Weights				
Fuzzy Geometric Mean	Lower	Middle	Upper	Crisp	Norm Crisp
(1.5651, 2.2134, 2.7832)	0.2564	0.4892	0.8569	0.5342	0.4698
(0.5774, 0.8409, 1.3161)	0.0946	0.1858	0.4052	0.2285	0.2010
(0.6043, 0.7825, 1.0746)	0.0990	0.1729	0.3309	0.2009	0.1767
(0.5000, 0.6866, 0.9306)	0.0819	0.1517	0.2865	0.1734	0.1525

Table 9. SF-AHP results per criteria category for the category social. (**a**) Fuzzified pairwise comparison matrix; (**b**) Criteria fuzzy and defuzzified weights.

(a)

	Fuzzified Pairwise Comparison Matrix					
	C16	C17	C18	C19	C20	C21
C16	(1,1,1)	(1,2,3)	(3,4,5)	(1,2,3)	(6,7,8)	(3,4,5)
C17	(0.333,0.5,1)	(1,1,1)	(1,1,1)	(1,2,3)	(2,3,4)	(3,4,5)
C18	(0.2,0.25,0.333)	(1,1,1)	(1,1,1)	(0.25,0.333,0.5)	(1,1,1)	(1,2,3)
C19	(0.333,0.5,1)	(0.333,0.5,1)	(2,3,4)	(1,1,1)	(5,6,7)	(3,4,5)
C20	(0.125,0.142,0.166)	(0.25,0.333,0.5)	(1,1,1)	(0.142,0.166,0.2)	(1,1,1)	(0.333,0.5,1)
C21	(0.2,0.25,0.333)	(0.2,0.25,0.333)	(0.333, 0.5,1)	(0.2,0.25,0.333)	(1,2,3)	(1,1,1)

(b)

	Criteria Fuzzy and Defuzzified Weights				
Fuzzy Geometric Mean	Lower	Middle	Upper	Crisp	Norm Crisp
(1.9442, 2.7662, 3.4878)	0.2003	0.3776	0.6111	0.3963	0.3615
(1.1225, 1.2988, 1.9786)	0.1156	0.1773	0.3467	0.2132	0.1945
(0.7071, 0.7418, 0.7647)	0.0728	0.1013	0.1340	0.1027	0.0937
(1.2222, 1.6189, 2.2787)	0.1259	0.2210	0.3992	0.2487	0.2269
(0.3379, 0.3979, 0.5054)	0.0348	0.0543	0.0885	0.0592	0.0540
(0.3724, 0.500, 0.6934)	0.0384	0.0683	0.1215	0.0760	0.0694

3.5. Fuzzy TOPSIS Analysis

As explained in the previous section, the norm crisp values for each criterion have been calculated in the SF-AHP process. For the case of F-TOPSIS, we choose to at least use one criterion from each of the categories provided by the participation modeling and the SWOT analysis (categories are: technological, economics, environmental, and social). The one chosen is the one performing with the maximum normalized crisp value obtained from the SF-AHP calculation. To enrich the F-TOPSIS analysis with more criteria, we choose another two out of all performing with the largest of the remaining normalized crisp vales (i.e., C1 and C7). Table 10 is the summary of the normalized fuzzy weights of all participating criteria in the F-TOPSIS.

Table 10. Normalized fuzzy weights of criteria used in fuzzy TOPSIS.

Criteria ID	Lower	Middle	Upper
C16	0.059532	0.168872987	0.416734861
C12	0.076205	0.218783542	0.584356247
C6	0.120609	0.234033989	0.431737589
C2	0.075016	0.175402504	0.427918712
C1	0.036617	0.095930233	0.231996727
C7	0.067854	0.106976744	0.201718494

Table 11 calculates the fuzzy decision matrix and the fuzzy positive ideal solution, as well as the fuzzy negative ideal solution (where H, hydro; S, solar; B, biofuel; W, wind; N, FNIS; and P, FPIS).

Table 11. Calculation of the fuzzy decision matrix and the fuzzy positive ideal solution (FPIS) and fuzzy negative ideal solution (FNIS).

	Normalized Fuzzy Decision Matrix Using the c_j^* and a_j^-					
S	(0.555, 0.805, 1)	(0.666, 0.833, 1)	(0.444, 0.592, 1)	(0.444, 0.533, 0.8)	(0.25, 0.444, 1)	(0.777, 0.888, 1)
B	(0.777, 0.888, 1)	(0.777, 0.888, 1)	(0.444, 0.64, 0.869)	(0.571, 0.695, 1)	(0.25, 0.266, 1)	(0.111, 0.222, 0.333)
H	(0.666, 0.833, 1)	(0.666, 0.833, 1)	(0.444, 0.533, 0.8)	(0.444, 0.5, 0.571)	(0.25, 0.4, 1)	(0.222, 0.444, 0.666)
W	(0.666, 0.805, 1)	(0.666, 0.833, 1)	(0.444, 0.592, 1)	(0.571, 0.727, 1)	(0.25, 0.444, 1)	(0.222, 0.388, 0.666)
	Weighted Normalized Fuzzy Decision Matrix					
S	(0.019, 0.076, 0.231)	(0.049, 0.145, 0.427)	(0.053, 0.138, 0.431)	(0.029, 0.056, 0.160)	(0.019, 0.096, 0.584)	(0.045, 0.149, 0.416)
B	(0.028, 0.084, 0.231)	(0.058, 0.155, 0.427)	(0.053, 0.149, 0.374)	(0.038, 0.073, 0.201)	(0.019, 0.057, 0.584)	(0.006, 0.037, 0.138)
H	(0.023, 0.079, 0.231)	(0.049, 0.145, 0.427)	(0.053, 0.124, 0.344)	(0.029, 0.053, 0.114)	(0.019, 0.087, 0.584)	(0.013, 0.074, 0.277)
W	(0.023, 0.076, 0.231)	(0.049, 0.145, 0.427)	(0.053, 0.138, 0.431)	(0.038, 0.077, 0.201)	(0.019, 0.096, 0.584)	(0.013, 0.065, 0.277)
	FNIS and FPIS					
N	(0.028, 0.084, 0.231)	(0.058, 0.155, 0.427)	(0.053, 0.138, 0.431)	(0.038, 0.077, 0.201)	(0.019, 0.096, 0.584)	(0.045, 0.149, 0.416)
P	(0.019, 0.076, 0.231)	(0.049, 0.145, 0.427)	(0.053, 0.138, 0.431)	(0.029, 0.056, 0.160)	(0.019, 0.057, 0.584)	(0.006, 0.037, 0.138)

H, hydro; S, solar; B, biofuel; W, wind; N, FNIS; P, FPIS.

Finally, the distance from the FNIS and the FPIS, as well as the ranking of the four energy alternatives is given in Tables 12 and 13, respectively, ranking the solar energy as the best performing with the biofuel as the least performing alternative.

Table 12. Calculation of the distance from FNIS and FPIS.

Distance of Weighted Normalized Fuzzy Decision Matrix from FNIS						
Solar	0	0	0	0	0.02240119	0.174605594
Biofuel	0.006699751	0.007370663	0.033285032	0.026082561	0	0
Hydro	0.002786276	0	0.050800427	0.026688137	0.016916363	0.082897105
Wind	0.002309401	0	0	0.026891263	0.02240119	0.081655598
Distance of Weighted Normalized Fuzzy Decision Matrix from FPIS						
Solar	0.006699751	0.007370663	0	0.026891263	0	0
Biofuel	0	0	0.033651548	0	0.02240119	0.174605594
Hydro	0.003970306	0.007370663	0.050800427	0.052336253	0.005484828	0.093375746
Wind	0.005249127	0.007370663	0	0	0	0.095999878

Table 13. Ranking of the energy alternative types.

Energy Type	$\tilde{d}_i^*$	$\tilde{d}_i^-$	$CC_i = d_i^-/(d_i^- + d_i^*)$	RANK
Solar	0.040961676	0.197006784	0.827869306	1
Biofuel	0.230658332	0.073438007	0.24149586	4
Hydro	0.213338222	0.180088307	0.457743172	3
Wind	0.108619668	0.133257452	0.550930373	2

$\tilde{d}_i^*$ and $\tilde{d}_i^-$ distance between FPIS and FNIS (Equations (18) and (19))

4. Discussion of Results

The FGP methodology is extensively used with the aim to mitigate the ambiguity introduced by the participatory modeling. Unfortunately, the limitation of no availability of set values for the criterion C7 (fuel or energy cost) cannot fully support the translation into fuzzy numbers for all the criteria under concern. However, the results of the GP methodology show a great degree of membership functions for the rest of the participating criteria. Therefore, assuming at least five out of the six criteria are well taken, FAHP was applied for each one of the four criteria categories, based on the results of FAHP as follows:

- For the technological oriented criteria, criteria C2 (human capital expertise) was calculated to be the most important criterion with a normalized crisp weight of 0.3983, with the second in order criterion C1 (availability of the technological resources for application of the type) with a normalized crisp weight of 0.2123. The strategy is to, first, gain the human capital needed to build and manage the energy conversion establishments, and then think about which resources are available. Robustness of the projects is thought to be the least important factor. However, safety and the amount of electricity (GWh) that would be directed to the market are almost equally important criteria.

- For the economically oriented criteria, criteria C6 (capital cost), C7 (fuel and energy cost), and C8 (life expectancy of the system) by far are the most important factors in this specific order, with C6 obtaining a normalized crisp weight of 0.5127 and the other two obtaining weights of 0.2505 and 0.1032, respectively. As expected, the issue of initial capital is the most important factor in investing, especially in such investments of regional level and high cost. The second factor of importance is the energy costs for such factories to operate. Usually, this is calculated as a percentage of the outcome in electricity, but it is a key performance indicator for the overall operation trustworthiness. The lack of obtaining a degree of membership for C7 from the FGP methodology diminishes the trustworthiness of the FAHP method, especially relatively to the outcome of the C7 criterion. However, the value of importance of C7 is still undisputed because of its rating within the category and because of the high score received. Note, for example, that criteria C8, C9, C10, and C11 are all well below the range of 0.10 normalized weight, therefore, we can argue that the rate of C7 within the category cannot be changed and that was the reason that C7 was included in the F-TOPSIS.

- For the environmentally oriented criteria, similarly, clear weight ordering appears in this category with criterion C12 (waste production) performing much higher than the other criteria gaining a normalized crisp weight of 0.4698 and with criterion C13 (hazardous aerial emissions) in second place with a normalized crisp weight of 0.2010, outperforming criteria C14 and C15. The results show that stakeholders want to explore the opportunity to experience green and renewable energy exploitation via policies that minimize the waste production. Moreover, competent authorities and the final policy makers should integrate this approach horizontally and vertically to try to incorporate the appropriate strategic alliances towards low carbon economy.

- For the socially oriented criteria, relative to social acceptance and supportiveness of the low carbon energy policy making, the results of FAHP indicate that the primary factor for the Greek society is the creation of new jobs and how this is going to affect the regional economy with criterion C16 (new jobs) outperforming the other criteria of the category (normalized crisp weight of 0.3615). At the same time, criteria C17 (quantification of the (not in my back yard) NIMBY phenomenon) and C19 (impact on residents' everyday life and health) are almost equally important for the social bodies of Thessaly Region with normalized crisp weights of 0.1947 and 0.2269, respectively. The remaining category criteria participate in the distribution of weights with very low percentages. Thus, although the society wants new jobs and is aware of the health and environmental benefits of the conversion into low carbon practices, people are still afraid to reside close to such energy production plants.

Using the outcomes of SF-AHP, the application of the F-TOPSIS methodology was performed only on the most important criteria of each category, as aforementioned. The method ranks solar energy plants and investments as the most preferable (CC_i of 0.827869306) and wind parks (CC_i of 0.550930373) are ranked second. The substantial difference between the first and second choice is justified by the geographic location of the region and the social perception that solar energy is the least expensive form of producing electricity, while not affecting the environment. However, further investigation has shown that solar energy systems deployment must agree with specific locations. For example, in Thessaly, there are locations in the eastern part, which are more preferable than locations in the western part that occasionally suffers from floods. As to the equipment to be used, there is a need for equipment synchronization in order to become beneficial for the process.

This research offers an original contribution to knowledge by applying a hybrid methodology of three fuzzy MCDM models that can be used as a decision-making tool by competent authorities and investment groups for investing in the energy industry. Using input from the basic pillars of society, the selection of the best renewable energy type fitted in a region is succeeded by the steps of this research paradigm. As it has shown in Sections 3.3–3.5, the amalgamation of the SF-AHP, FGP and F-TOPSIS analyses highlighted the criteria of (a) new job generation, (b) capital cost, (c) availability of technological resources, and (d) waste production, which prevail in the decision-making of competent authorities and private investors when deciding to establish a new energy plant. Thus, the hybrid application of AHP and TOPSIS with the assistance of experts produces a decision-making methodology which can be applicable to the renewable energy industry.

5. Conclusions and Future Challenges

The use of the appropriate form of energy technology is crucial for human society, as it directly affects the regional economy and the industrial and rural development. On top of the critical effects, health and environmental indicators became significant in energy planning decision making, since they affect the sustainable use of regional resources. Therefore, any regional policy making must be focused on designing technologies for the safe management of regional resources and direct investors towards the exploitation of renewable and environment-friendly energy forms.

In this work, we applied the participatory modeling methodology for visioning and strategy development in terms of selecting the most appropriate energy type for regional investments. Available forms were the solar, wind, hydro, and biofuel energy. Initially, a SWOT analysis was performed to mark all the objectives, as well as the internal and external factors that affect the energy form selection process and the establishment of policies to support this selection. The interoperability and interrelationships among the internal and external factors were thoroughly examined. A well-designed effort of polling the public opinion, and most importantly, the stakeholders was also developed via surveys and focus groups. This process highlighted a set of important criteria spanning from technology, economics, environment, and society. Through the interaction between FGP and SF-AHP, we selected the criteria with a high degree of trustworthiness in the process, which are the principal components in the decision-making process, and we calculated the pairwise comparisons matrices making individual runs for each criteria category. This approach provided the most significant criteria/factors according to their normalized crisp weight. The highest weight criterion for each category, as well as the two other criteria with the highest among the rest weights, participated in the F-TOPSIS calculation of ranking the energy types. The result showed that solar energy ranked as the first preference with wind, hydro, and biofuel following, in this order.

Except for the good results emanated from our research, the application of the most popular fuzzy MCDM methodologies such as SF-AHP, FGP, and F-TOPSIS also faced a few, yet memorable limitations, in terms of the planning process, the refinement of fuzzified values, and the combination of the models used [99]. More specifically, the non-existence of budget constraints in the application of the FGP model and the use of budget constraints coming from the literature are a major limitation that leads to doubts in terms of experimental verification of the results of the model. At a second level, on the one hand, involvement of fuzzy modeling always initiates limitations of results as opposed to crisp value measurements. On the other hand, this deficiency is also beneficial in terms of the ability of the stakeholders to express their opinions with linguistic terms as opposed to crisp evaluations. Finally, any use of SF-AHP to find the weights of the criteria used for all the energy alternatives introduces a limitation as to the unidirectional application of only one method as opposed to a comparative approach involving more techniques.

Further investigation must be undertaken for other energy forms and also alternatives. The inclusion of new renewable energy technologies would add confidence in integrated energy policy modeling and decision making. Additionally, a comparative analysis with other fuzzy and soft computing methodologies would also be appropriate to provide a holistic study. Fuzzy cognitive maps, for example, is also a useful tool that could introduce causalities between the criteria, thus, taking into account their interrelations.

Author Contributions: Conceptualization, K.K. and V.K.; methodology, K.K.; validation, K.K. and V.K.; formal analysis, K.K.; investigation, K.K. and V.K.; resources, K.K.; data curation, K.K.; writing—original draft preparation, K.K.; writing—review and editing, K.K. and V.K.; visualization, K.K.; supervision, V.K. All authors have read and agreed to the published version of the manuscript.

Funding: This research received no external funding.

Conflicts of Interest: The authors declare no conflict of interest.

References

1. Sampaio, P.G.V.; González, M.O.A.; De Vasconcelos, R.M.; Dos Santos, M.A.T.; Vidal, P.D.C.J.; Pereira, J.P.P.; Santi, E. Prospecting technologies for photovoltaic solar energy: Overview of its technical-commercial viability. *Int. J. Energy Res.* **2020**, *44*, 651–668. [CrossRef]
2. Mahmoud, M.; Ramadan, M.; Olabi, A.-G.; Pullen, K.; Naher, S. A review of mechanical energy storage systems combined with wind and solar applications. *Energy Convers. Manag.* **2020**, *210*, 112670. [CrossRef]
3. Athanasiou, C.; Garagounis, I.; Kyriakou, V.; Vourros, A.; Marnellos, G.E.; Stoukides, M. Demonstration of hydrogen production in a hybrid lignite-assisted solid oxide electrolysis cell. *Int. J. Hydrogen Energy* **2019**, *44*, 22770–22779. [CrossRef]
4. Nautiyal, H.; Goel, V. Sustainability assessment of hydropower projects. *J. Clean. Prod.* **2020**, *265*, 121661. [CrossRef]
5. Kokkinos, K.; Lakioti, E.; Papageorgiou, E.; Moustakas, K.; Karayannis, V. Fuzzy cognitive map-based modeling of social acceptance to overcome uncertainties in establishing waste biorefinery facilities. *Front. Energy Res.* **2018**, *6*, 112. [CrossRef]
6. Nikolopoulos, I.; Kogkos, G.; Kordouli, E.; Bourikas, K.; Kordulis, C.; Lycourghiotis, A. Waste cooking oil transformation into third generation green diesel catalyzed by nickel—Alumina catalysts. *Mol. Catal.* **2020**, *482*, 110697. [CrossRef]
7. De Vrieze, J.; Verbeeck, K.; Pikaar, I.; Boere, J.; Van Wijk, A.; Rabaey, K.; Verstraete, W. The hydrogen gas bio-based economy and the production of renewable building block chemicals, food and energy. *New Biotechnol.* **2020**, *55*, 12–18. [CrossRef]
8. Gerogiannis, V.C.; Kazantzi, V.; Anthopoulos, L. A hybrid method for evaluating biomass suppliers—Use of intuitionistic fuzzy sets and multi-periodic optimization. *IFIP Adv. Inf. Commun. Technol.* **2012**, *381 Pt 1*, 217–223. [CrossRef]
9. Zabaniotou, A.; Fytili, D.; Lakioti, E.; Karayannis, V. Transition to bioenergy: Engineering and technology undergraduate students' perceptions of and readiness for agricultural waste-based bioenergy in Greece. *Glob. Transit.* **2019**, *1*, 157–170. [CrossRef]
10. Nyambuu, U.; Semmler, W. Climate change and the transition to a low carbon economy—Carbon targets and the carbon budget. *Econ. Model.* **2020**, *84*, 367–376. [CrossRef]
11. Lee, C.T.; Rozali, N.E.M.; Klemeš, J.J.; Towprayoon, S. Advancing low-carbon emissions in Asia: Mitigation of greenhouse gases and enhancing economic feasibility for major sectors. *Clean Technol. Environ. Policy* **2018**, *20*, 441–442. [CrossRef]
12. Maiorova, T.V.; Belik, I.S.; Ponomareva, O.S.; Kolyada, L.G. Low carbon global economy: Scenarios of sustainable development, power consumption and greenhouse gas emission control. *IOP Conf. Ser. Earth Environ. Sci.* **2019**, *315*. [CrossRef]
13. Alizadeh, R.; Soltanisehat, L.; Lund, P.D.; Zamanisabzi, H. Improving renewable energy policy planning and decision-making through a hybrid MCDM method. *Energy Policy* **2020**, *137*, 111174. [CrossRef]
14. Kaya, I.; Holak, M.; Terzi, F. A comprehensive review of fuzzy multi criteria decision making methodologies for energy policy making. *Energy Strat. Rev.* **2019**, *24*, 207–228. [CrossRef]
15. Lak Kamari, M.; Isvand, H.; Alhuyi Nazari, M. Applications of Multi-Criteria Decision-Making (MCDM) Methods in Renewable Energy Development: A Review. *Renew. Energy Res. Appl.* **2020**, *1*, 47–54. [CrossRef]
16. Zhao, N.; Xu, Z.; Ren, Z. Hesitant fuzzy linguistic prioritized superiority and inferiority ranking method and its application in sustainable energy technology evaluation. *Inf. Sci.* **2019**, *478*, 239–257. [CrossRef]
17. OECD ILibrary. Innovation Policies for Sustainable Development: Low-Carbon Energy and Smart-City Initiatives. Available online: https://www.oecd-ilibrary.org/science-and-technology/innovation-policies-for-sustainable-development_6287ddb2-en (accessed on 24 March 2020).

18. Awodumi, O.; Adewuyi, A.O. The role of non-renewable energy consumption in economic growth and carbon emission: Evidence from oil producing economies in Africa. *Energy Strat. Rev.* **2020**, *27*, 100434. [CrossRef]
19. Papapostolou, A.; Karakosta, C.; Kourti, K.-A.; Doukas, H.; Psarras, J. Supporting Europe's Energy Policy Towards a Decarbonised Energy System: A Comparative Assessment. *Sustainability* **2019**, *11*, 4010. [CrossRef]
20. Demir, C.; Cergibozan, R. Does alternative energy usage converge across Oecd countries? *Renew. Energy* **2020**, *146*, 559–567. [CrossRef]
21. Wu, Y.; Sun, X.; Lu, Z.; Zhou, J.; Xu, C. Optimal site selection of straw biomass power plant under 2-dimension uncertain linguistic environment. *J. Clean. Prod.* **2019**, *212*, 1179–1192. [CrossRef]
22. Shah, B.; Lakhani, H.; Abhishek, K.; Kumari, S. Application of Fuzzy Linguistic Modeling Aggregated with VIKOR for Optimal Selection of Solar Power Plant Site: An Empirical Study. In *Renewable Energy and Climate Change. In Smart Innovation, Systems and Technologies*; Dipankar, D., Ambesh, D., Laltu, C., Eds.; Springer: Singapore, 2020; pp. 119–127. [CrossRef]
23. Shorabeh, S.N.; Firozjaei, M.K.; Nematollahi, O.; Firozjaei, H.K.; Jelokhani-Niaraki, M. A Risk-Based Multi-Criteria Spatial Decision Analysis for Solar Power Plant Site Selection in Different Climates: A Case Study in Iran. *Renew. Energy* **2019**, *143*, 958–973. [CrossRef]
24. Bas, E. The integrated framework for analysis of electricity supply chain using an integrated SWOT-fuzzy TOPSIS methodology combined with AHP: The case of Turkey. *Int. J. Electr. Power Energy Syst.* **2013**, *44*, 897–907. [CrossRef]
25. Fertel, C.; Bahn, O.; Vaillancourt, K.; Waaub, J.-P. Canadian energy and climate policies: A SWOT analysis in search of federal/provincial coherence. *Energy Policy* **2013**, *63*, 1139–1150. [CrossRef]
26. Helms, M.M.; Nixon, J. Exploring SWOT analysis—Where are we now? *J. Strat. Manag.* **2010**, *3*, 215–251. [CrossRef]
27. Zadeh, L. Fuzzy sets. *Inf. Control.* **1965**, *8*, 338–353. [CrossRef]
28. Kokkinos, K.; Lakioti, E.; Samaras, P.; Karayannis, V. Evaluation of public perception on key sustainability indicators for drinking water quality by fuzzy logic methodologies. *Desalin. Water Treat.* **2019**, *170*, 378–393. [CrossRef]
29. Wang, W.-M.; Peng, H.-H. A fuzzy multi-criteria evaluation framework for urban sustainable development. *Mathematics* **2020**, *8*, 330. [CrossRef]
30. Gerogiannis, V.C.; Tzikas, G. Using fuzzy linguistic 2-Tuples to collectively prioritize software requirements based on stakeholders' evaluations. In Proceedings of the 21st Pan-Hellenic Conference on Informatics, Larissa, Greece, 28–30 September 2017. [CrossRef]
31. Rong, Y.; Liu, Y.; Pei, Z. Novel multiple attribute group decision-making methods based on linguistic intuitionistic fuzzy information. *Mathematics* **2020**, *8*, 322. [CrossRef]
32. Papageorgiou, K.I.; Poczeta, K.; Papageorgiou, E.; Gerogiannis, V.C.; Stamoulis, G. Exploring an ensemble of methods that combines fuzzy cognitive maps and neural networks in solving the time series prediction problem of gas consumption in Greece. *Algorithms* **2019**, *12*, 235. [CrossRef]
33. Saaty, T.L. An Exposition of the AHP in Reply to the Paper "Remarks on the Analytic Hierarchy Process". *Manag. Sci.* **1990**, *36*, 259–268. [CrossRef]
34. Chang, D.Y. Extent analysis and synthetic decision. In Proceedings of the International Conference on Optimization Techniques and Applications, Singapore, 3–5 June 1992; Volume 1, pp. 352–355. [CrossRef]
35. Altintas, K.; Vayvay, O.; Apak, S.; Cobanoglu, E. An Extended GRA Method Integrated with Fuzzy AHP to Construct a Multidimensional Index for Ranking Overall Energy Sustainability Performances. *Sustainability* **2020**, *12*, 1602. [CrossRef]
36. Saaty, T.L.; Vargas, L.G. International Series in Operations Research & Management Science. In *Models, Methods, Concepts & Applications of the Analytic Hierarchy Process*, 2nd ed.; Springer: New York, NY, USA, 2012. [CrossRef]
37. Chamodrakas, I.; Batis, D.; Martakos, D. Supplier selection in electronic marketplaces using satisficing and fuzzy AHP. *Expert Syst. Appl.* **2010**, *37*, 490–498. [CrossRef]
38. Chan, F.T.S.; Kumar, N.; Tiwari, M.K.; Lau, H.C.W.; Choy, K.L. Global supplier selection: A fuzzy-AHP approach. *Int. J. Prod. Res.* **2008**, *46*, 3825–3857. [CrossRef]
39. Kahraman, C.; Cebeci, U.; Ulukan, Z. Multi-Criteria supplier selection using fuzzy AHP. *Logist. Inf. Manag.* **2003**, *16*, 382–394. [CrossRef]

40. Noorul Haq, A.; Kannan, G. Fuzzy analytical hierarchy process for evaluating and selecting a vendor in a supply chain model. *Int. J. Adv. Manuf. Technol.* **2006**, *29*, 826–835. [CrossRef]
41. Shete, P.C.; Ansari, Z.N.; Kant, R. A Pythagorean fuzzy AHP approach and its application to evaluate the enablers of sustainable supply chain innovation. *Sustain. Prod. Consum.* **2020**, *23*, 77–93. [CrossRef]
42. Liu, S.-Y.; Lee, R.-S. Analysis of the dilemmas of solar energy application for Taiwan building with Fuzzy AHP approach. *IOP Conf. Ser. Earth Environ. Sci.* **2019**, *237*, 042006. [CrossRef]
43. Wang, X.; Song, Y.; Zhang, X.; Liu, H. Optimization of Subsidy Policy for New Energy Automobile Industry in China Based on an Integrated Fuzzy-AHP-TOPSIS Methodology. *Math. Probl. Eng.* **2019**, *2019*, 4304806. [CrossRef]
44. Wang, Y.; Xu, L.; Solangi, Y.A. Strategic renewable energy resources selection for Pakistan: Based on SWOT-Fuzzy AHP approach. *Sustain. Cities Soc.* **2020**, *52*, 101861. [CrossRef]
45. Madžarević, A.R.; Ivezić, D.D.; Tanasijević, M.L.; Živković, M.A. The Fuzzy–AHP Synthesis Model for Energy Security Assessment of the Serbian Natural Gas Sector. *Symmetry* **2020**, *12*, 908. [CrossRef]
46. Blagojević, A.; Vesković, S.; Kasalica, S.; Gojić, A.; Allamani, A. The application of the fuzzy AHP and DEA for measuring the efficiency of freight transport railway undertakings. *Oper. Res. Eng. Sci. Theory Appl.* **2020**, 1–23. [CrossRef]
47. Gerogiannis, V.C.; Fitsilis, P.; Kameas, A.D. Using a combined intuitionistic fuzzy set-TOPSIS method for evaluating project and portfolio management information systems. *IFIP Adv. Inf. Commun. Technol.* **2011**, *364 Pt 2*, 67–81. [CrossRef]
48. Chen, S.J.; Hwang, C.L. *Fuzzy Multiple Attribute Decision-Making Methods and Application*; Springer: Berlin/Heidelberg, Germany; New York, NY, USA, 1992.
49. Yoon, K.P.; Hwang, C.L. Multiple attributes decision-making: An introduction. In *Sage University Paper Series on Quantitative Applications in the Social Science, 07–104*; Sage: Thousand Oaks, CA, USA, 1995.
50. Hwang, C.-L.; Yoon, K. Methods for Multiple Attribute Decision Making. In *Multiple Attribute Decision Making: Methods and Applications A State-Of-The-Art Survey*; Springer: Berlin, Germany, 1981; pp. 58–191. [CrossRef]
51. Chen, C.-T. Extensions of the TOPSIS for group decision-making under fuzzy environment. *Fuzzy Sets Syst.* **2000**, *114*, 1–9. [CrossRef]
52. Aikhuele, D.O.; Ighravwe, D.E.; Akinyele, D. Evaluation of Renewable Energy Technology Based on Reliability Attributes Using Hybrid Fuzzy Dynamic Decision-Making Model. *Technol. Econ. Smart Grids Sustain. Energy* **2019**, *4*, 16. [CrossRef]
53. Cayir Ervural, B.; Zaim, S.; Demirel, O.F.; Aydin, Z.; Delen, D. An ANP and fuzzy TOPSIS-based SWOT analysis for Turkey's energy planning. *Renew. Sustain. Energy Rev.* **2018**, *82*, 1538–1550. [CrossRef]
54. Dinçer, H.; Yüksel, S. Multidimensional evaluation of global investments on the renewable energy with the integrated fuzzy decision-making model under the hesitancy. *Int. J. Energy Res.* **2019**, *43*, 1775–1784. [CrossRef]
55. Krishankumar, R.; Mishra, A.R.; Ravichandran, K.S.; Peng, X.; Zavadskas, E.K.; Cavallaro, F.; Mardani, A. A Group Decision Framework for Renewable Energy Source Selection under Interval-Valued Probabilistic linguistic Term Set. *Energies* **2020**, *13*, 986. [CrossRef]
56. Rani, P.; Mishra, A.R.; Mardani, A.; Cavallaro, F.; Alrasheedi, M.; Alrashidi, A. A novel approach to extended fuzzy TOPSIS based on new divergence measures for renewable energy sources selection. *J. Clean. Prod.* **2020**, *257*, 120352. [CrossRef]
57. Rani, P.; Mishra, A.R.; Pardasani, K.R.; Mardani, A.; Liao, H.; Streimikiene, D. A novel VIKOR approach based on entropy and divergence measures of Pythagorean fuzzy sets to evaluate renewable energy technologies in India. *J. Clean. Prod.* **2019**, *238*, 117936. [CrossRef]
58. Chatterjee, P.; Stević, Ž. A two-phase fuzzy AHP-fuzzy TOPSIS model for supplier evaluation in manufacturing environment. *Oper. Res. Eng. Sci. Theory Appl.* **2019**, *2*, 72–90. [CrossRef]
59. Cavallaro, F.; Zavadskas, E.K.; Streimikiene, D.; Mardani, A. Assessment of concentrated solar power (CSP) technologies based on a modified intuitionistic fuzzy topsis and trigonometric entropy weights. *Technol. Forecast. Soc. Change* **2019**, *140*, 258–270. [CrossRef]
60. Guo, S. Chapter 14—Life Cycle Sustainability Decision-Making Framework for the Prioritization of Electrochemical Energy Storage under Uncertainties. In *Life Cycle Sustainability Assessment for Decision-Making*; Ren, J., Toniolo, S., Eds.; Elsevier: Amsterdam, The Netherlands, 2020; pp. 291–308. [CrossRef]

61. Solangi, Y.A.; Tan, Q.; Mirjat, N.H.; Ali, S. Evaluating the strategies for sustainable energy planning in Pakistan: An integrated SWOT-AHP and Fuzzy-TOPSIS approach. *J. Clean. Prod.* **2019**, *236*, 117655. [CrossRef]
62. Büyüközkan, G.; Havle, C.A.; Feyzioğlu, O.; Uztürk, D. Integrated Fuzzy Multi Criteria Decision Making Approach for Sustainable Energy Technology Selection. In *Proceedings of the 9th International Conference on Informatics, Environment, Energy and Applications, IEEA 2020, Amsterdam, The Netherlands, 13–16 March 2020*; Association for Computing Machinery: Amsterdam, The Netherlands, 2020; pp. 93–98. [CrossRef]
63. Deveci, M.; Cali, U.; Kucuksari, S.; Erdogan, N. Interval type-2 fuzzy sets based multi-criteria decision-making model for offshore wind farm development in Ireland. *Energy* **2020**, *198*, 117317. [CrossRef]
64. Taylan, O.; Alamoudi, R.; Kabli, M.; AlJifri, A.; Ramzi, F.; Herrera-Viedma, E. Assessment of Energy Systems Using Extended Fuzzy AHP, Fuzzy VIKOR, and TOPSIS Approaches to Manage Non-Cooperative Opinions. *Sustainability* **2020**, *12*, 2745. [CrossRef]
65. Charnes, A.; Cooper, W.W. *Management Models and Industrial Application of Linear Programming*; Wiley: New York, NY, USA, 1961.
66. Lee, S.M. *Goal Programming for Decision Analysis*; Auerbach: Philadelphia, PA, USA, 1972.
67. Ignizio, J.P. *Goal Programming and Extensions (Health (Lexington Books))*; Lexington Books: Lanham, MD, USA, 1976.
68. Tamiz, M.; Jones, D.; Romero, C. *European Journal of Operational Research*; Elsevier: Amsterdam, The Netherlands, 1998; Volume 111, pp. 569–581.
69. Romero, C. A general structure of achievement function for a goal programming model. *Eur. J. Oper. Res.* **2004**, *153*, 675–686. [CrossRef]
70. Aouni, A.; Ben Abdelaziz, F.; La Torre, D. The stochastic goal programming model: Theory and applications. In *Journal of Multicriteria Decision Analysis*; Wiley: Hoboken, NJ, USA, 2012; Volume 19, pp. 185–200.
71. Flavell, R.B. *A New Goal Programming Formulation*; Elsevier: Amsterdam, The Netherlands, 1976; Volume 4, pp. 731–732.
72. Lai, Y.J.; Hwang, C.L. Multiple Objective Decision Making. In *Fuzzy Multiple Objective Decision Making. Lecture Notes in Economics and Mathematical Systems*; Springer: Berlin/Heidelberg, Germany, 1994; Volume 404.
73. Narasimhan, R. Goal Programming in a Fuzzy Environment. *Decis. Sci.* **1980**, *11*, 325–336. [CrossRef]
74. Daim, T.U.; Kayakutlu, G.; Cowan, K. Developing Oregon's renewable energy portfolio using fuzzy goal programming model. *Comput. Ind. Eng.* **2010**, *59*, 786–793. [CrossRef]
75. Jayaraman, R.; Liuzzi, D.; Colapinto, C.; Malik, T. A fuzzy goal programming model to analyze energy, environmental and sustainability goals of the United Arab Emirates. *Ann. Oper. Res.* **2017**, *251*, 255–270. [CrossRef]
76. Lutero, D.S.; Pangue, E.; Tubay, J.M.; Lubag, S.P. A fuzzy goal programming model for biodiesel production. *J. Phys. Conf. Ser.* **2016**, *693*, 012007. [CrossRef]
77. Gitinavard, H.; Shirazi, M.A.; Fazel Zarandi, M.H. Sustainable feedstocks selection and renewable products allocation: A new hybrid adaptive utility-based consensus model. *J. Environ. Manag.* **2020**, *264*, 110428. [CrossRef]
78. Ghouali, S.; Guellil, M.S.; Belmokaddem, M. Looking over the Horizon 2030: Efficiency of Renewable Energy Base Plants in Algeria Using Fuzzy Goal Programming. In *Smart Energy Empowerment in Smart and Resilient Cities, Lecture Notes in Networks and Systems*; Hatti, M., Ed.; Springer International Publishing: Cham, Switzerland, 2020; pp. 329–337. [CrossRef]
79. Yu, S.; Zhou, S.; Zheng, S.; Li, Z.; Liu, L. Developing an optimal renewable electricity generation mix for China using a fuzzy multi-objective approach. *Renew. Energy* **2019**, *139*, 1086–1098. [CrossRef]
80. Biswas, P.; Pal, B.B. A fuzzy goal programming method to solve congestion management problem using genetic algorithm. *Decis. Mak. Appl. Manag. Eng.* **2019**, *2*, 36–53. [CrossRef]
81. Aktas, A.; Kabak, M. A goal programming model for grid-connected hybrid energy system operations. *SN Appl. Sci.* **2019**, *2*, 71. [CrossRef]
82. Colapinto, C.; Jayaraman, R.; La Torre, D. A goal programming model to study the impact of R&D expenditures on sustainability-related criteria: The case of Kazakhstan. Management Decision ahead-of-print. *Manag. Decis* **2020**. [CrossRef]
83. Alaoui, M.E. Fuzzy goal programming for biodiesel production. *Int. J. Green Energy* **2020**, 1–8. [CrossRef]

84. Rathi, R.; Prakash, C.; Singh, S.; Krolczyk, G.; Pruncu, C.I. Measurement and analysis of wind energy potential using fuzzy based hybrid MADM approach. *Energy Rep.* **2020**, *6*, 228–237. [CrossRef]
85. Hocine, A.; Zhuang, Z.-Y.; Kouaissah, N.; Li, D.-C. Weighted-additive fuzzy multi-choice goal programming (WA-FMCGP) for supporting renewable energy site selection decisions. *Eur. J. Oper. Res.* **2020**, *285*, 642–654. [CrossRef]
86. Chen, W.M.; Kim, H.; Yamaguchi, H. Renewable energy in eastern Asia: Renewable energy policy review and comparative SWOT analysis for promoting renewable energy in Japan, South Korea, and Taiwan. *Energy Policy* **2014**, *74*, 319–329. [CrossRef]
87. Cavicchi, B.; Bryden, J.M.; Vittuari, M. A comparison of bioenergy policies and institutional frameworks in the rural areas of Emilia Romagna and Norway. *Energy Policy* **2014**, *67*, 355–363. [CrossRef]
88. Markovska, N.; Taseska, V.; Pop-Jordanov, J. SWOT analyses of the national energy sector for sustainable energy development. *Energy* **2009**, *34*, 752–756. [CrossRef]
89. Terrados, J.; Almonacid, G.; Hontoria, L. Regional energy planning through SWOT analysis and strategic planning tools: Impact on renewables development. *Renew. Sustain. Energy Rev.* **2007**, *11*, 1275–1287. [CrossRef]
90. Büyüközkan, G.; Ilıcak, Ö. Integrated SWOT analysis with multiple preference relations: Selection of strategic factors for social media. *Kybernetes* **2019**, *48*, 451–470. [CrossRef]
91. Powell, B.J.; Waltz, T.J.; Chinman, M.J.; Damschroder, L.J.; Smith, J.L.; Matthieu, M.M.; Proctor, E.K.; Kirchner, J.E. A refined compilation of implementation strategies: Results from the Expert Recommendations for Implementing Change (ERIC) project. *Implement. Sci.* **2015**, *10*, 21. [CrossRef]
92. Chatfield, C. Model uncertainty, data mining and statistical inference. *J. R. Stat. Soc. A* **1993**, *158*, 419–466. [CrossRef]
93. Christoffersen Peter, F. Evaluating Interval Forecasts. *Int. Econ. Rev.* **1998**, *39*, 841–862. [CrossRef]
94. Hocine, A.; Kouaissah, N.; Bettahar, S.; Benbouziane, M. Optimizing renewable energy portfolios under uncertainty: A multi-segment fuzzy goal programming approach. *Renew. Energy* **2018**, *129*, 540–552. [CrossRef]
95. Schrage, L. *Optimization Modelling with LINGO*; Lindo Systems Inc.: Chicago, IL, USA, 2009.
96. Promentilla, M.A.B.; Aviso, K.B.; Tan, R.R. A Fuzzy Analytic Hierarchy Process (fahp) Approach for Optimal Selection of Low-Carbon Energy Technologies. 2015. Available online: https://www.semanticscholar.org/paper/A-Fuzzy-Analytic-Hierarchy-Process-(fahp)-Approach-Promentilla-Aviso/52c4733a0ddd91add7ca1651efcb08c3005600b1 (accessed on 8 April 2020).
97. Beşikçi, E.B.; Kececi, T.; Arslan, O.; Turan, O. An application of fuzzy-AHP to ship operational energy efficiency measures. *Ocean Eng.* **2016**, *121*, 392–402. [CrossRef]
98. Buckley, J.J.; Uppuluri, V.R.R. Fuzzy Hierarchical Analysis. In *Uncertainty in Risk Assessment, Risk Management, and Decision Making, Advances in Risk Analysis*; Covello, V.T., Lave, L.B., Moghissi, A., Uppuluri, V.R.R., Eds.; Springer: Boston, MA, USA, 1987; pp. 389–401. [CrossRef]
99. Ioannou, A.; Angus, A.; Brennan, F. Risk-Based methods for sustainable energy system planning: A review. *Renew. Sustain. Energy Rev.* **2017**, *74*, 602–615. [CrossRef]

© 2020 by the authors. Licensee MDPI, Basel, Switzerland. This article is an open access article distributed under the terms and conditions of the Creative Commons Attribution (CC BY) license (http://creativecommons.org/licenses/by/4.0/).

Article

Three-Way Decisions Making Using Covering Based Fractional Orthotriple Fuzzy Rough Set Model

Shougi S. Abosuliman [1], Saleem Abdullah [2,*] and Muhammad Qiyas [2]

1. Department of Transportation and Port Management, Faculty of Maritime Studies, King Abdulaziz University, Jeddah 21588, Saudi Arabia; sabusulaiman@kau.edu.sa
2. Department of Mathematics, Abdul Wali Khan University, Mardan 23200, Pakistan; muhammadqiyas@awkum.edu.pk
* Correspondence: saleemabdullah@awkum.edu.pk

Received: 9 May 2020; Accepted: 29 June 2020; Published: 9 July 2020

Abstract: On the basis of decision-theoretical rough sets (DTRSs), the three-way decisions give new model of decision approach for deal with the problem of decision. This proposed model of decision method is based on the loss function of DTRSs. First, the concept of fractional orthotriple fuzzy β-covering (FOF β-covering) and fractional orthotriple fuzzy β-neighborhood (FOF β-neighborhood) was introduced. We combined loss feature of DTRSs with covering-based fractional orthotriple fuzzy rough sets (CFOFSs) under the fractional orthotriple fuzzy condition. Secondly, we proposed a new FOF-covering decision-theoretical rough sets model (FOFCDTRSs) and developed related properties. Then, based on the grade of positive, neutral and negative membership of fractional orthotriple fuzzy numbers (FOFNs), five methods are established for addressing the expected loss expressed in the form of FOFNs and the corresponding three-way decisions are also derived. Based on this, we presented a FOFCDTRS-based algorithm for multi-criteria decision making (MCDM). Then, an example verifies the feasibility of the five methods for solving the MCDM problem. Finally, by comparing the results of the decisions of five methods with different loss functions.

Keywords: covering-based fractional orthotriple fuzzy rough sets; fractional orthotriple fuzzy β-covering decision-theoretic rough sets; fractional orthotriple fuzzy β-neighborhood; multi-attribute decision making; decision-theoretic rough sets

1. Introduction

Multi-criteria decision making analysis is also used in different contexts [1,2]. Intuitionistic fuzzy set (IFS) [3], a vital extension of fuzzy set (FS) [4], is considered as suitable tool to handle these information. An IFS contains two membership grades $\rho_\theta(\hbar) \in [0,1]$ and $\check{n}_\theta(\hbar) \in [0,1]$ in a finite universe of discourse $\beth$ with $\rho_\theta(\hbar) + \check{n}_\theta(\hbar) \leq 1$, for each $\hbar \in \beth$. Since the introduction of IFS, the theories and applications of IFS have been studied comprehensively, including its' applications in decision making problems (DMPs). These researches are very appropriate to tackle DMPs under IFS environment only owing to the condition $0 \leq \rho_\theta + \check{n}_\theta \leq 1$. However, in practical DMPs, the experts provide evaluation-value in the form of $(\rho_\theta, \check{n}_\theta)$, but it may be not satisfy the condition $\rho_\theta(\hbar) + \check{n}_\theta(\hbar) \leq 1$ and beyond the upper bound 1.

As IFSs have only two kinds of responses, i.e., "yes" and "no" but there is some issue with three types of reply in the case of election, e.g., "yes", "no" and "refusal", and the ambitious answer is "refusal". In order to overcome this defect, Cuong [5,6] developed the idea of picture fuzzy set (PFS), which dignified the positives, neutral and negative membership grades in three different functions. Cuong [7] addressed some PFSs characteristics and also accepted distance measurements. Cuong & Hai [8] defined fuzzy logic operators and specify basic operations in the picture fuzzy logic for fuzzy derivation types. Cuong et al. [9] analyzed the features of the blurry t-norm and t-conorm picture. Phong et al. [10] discussed some configuration of picture fuzzy relationships. Wei et al. [11–13] have identified several procedures for calculating the closeness between picture fuzzy sets. Many authors have currently built more models in the condition of PF sets: Singing [14] proposes the correlation coefficient of PFS and apply it to the clustering analysis. Son et al. [15,16] give time and temperature estimates based on the PF sets domain. Son [17,18] describes PF as isolation, distance and association measurements, often combined with the condition of PFSs. Van Viet and Van Hai [19] described a novel PFS fluid derivation structure and improved a classic fluid inference technique. Thong et al. [20,21] using the PF clustering technique for the optimization of complex & particle clumps. Wei [22] defined some basic leadership methodology using the PF weighted cross-entropy principle and used this method to rate the alternative. Yang et al. [23] described flexible soft matrix of decision making using PFSs. In [24], Garg feature aggregation of MCDM problems with PFSs. Peng et al. introduced the PFSs solution in [25] and apply in decision making. For the PF-set, readers see also [26–28]. Ashraf et al. [29] extend cubic set structure to PFSs.

Three-way decisions are one of the important ways in solving the decision making problems under uncertainty. Their key strategy is to consider a decision making problem as a ternary classification one labeled by three decision actions of acceptance, rejection and non-commitment in practice. In general, many theories can be utilized for inducing three-way decisions such as shadowed sets [30,31], modal logic [32] and orthopairs [33]. The essential idea of three-way decisions is to divide a universal set into three pairwise disjoint regions named as the positive, negative and boundary regions. The three regions are then processed to make different decisions with accept, reject and deferment [34]. The general framework of three-way decisions was outlined by Yao [35,36].

Zakowski's [37] Covering-based fuzzy rough sets (CRS) is a variant of the classical rough sets (RS) generalization. It is an extension of Pawlak RS partition to RS cover. Two rough approximation operators are built on this basis, and several conclusions are drawn. Many scholars then studied several types of RS models based on reporting from different angles. In 2003, Zhu & Wang [38] introduced the generalized rough set cover model, and studied the model's reduction and axiomatic properties. They then introduced three different types of CRS models based on the known models and identified several important features. Safari et al. [39] introduced twelve types of coverage approximation operators in 2016, and studied the structural properties and interrelations of these twelve CRS models. In addition, Ma [40] substitutes for the classical equivalence relationship with the general binary relationship (neighborhood relationship), thus generalizing the CRS. Many scholars have applied the classical CRS to the fuzzy world in recent years. The rough fuzzy set (RFS) and the fuzzy rough set (FRS) were introduced in Dubios et al. [41]. Researchers have done some researches on CFRS. The generalized CFRS structure was introduced by Ma [42] Deer et al. [43,44] introduced the fuzzy β-neighborhoods and fuzzy neighborhoods definition. Hussain [45] introduced the q-rung orthopair fuzzy TOPSIS method for the MCDM problem which depends on the Cq-ROFRS model. Quek et al. [46] defined the concept of Plithogenic set is an extension of the crisp set, fuzzy set, intuitionistic fuzzy set, and neutrosophic sets, whose elements are characterized by one or more attributes, and each attribute can assume many values. Zeng [47] proposed a framework for solving MADM problem based on complex Spherical fuzzy rough set (CSFRS) models and created a TOPSIS method for dealing with MADM problem.

In recent years, research on decision-theoretical rough sets (DTRSs) has made great progress. Many scholars have studied this theory. The key directions for research include the reduction of attributes, loss feature and some new extended models focused on DTRSs [48–59]. Yao suggested three-way decisions which are modern DTRS theories. Three-way decisions divide the universal set into three disjoint parts: positive area, boundary area and negative region. The Three-way decisions are a combination of DTRSs and Bayesian decision process, which has solved several classification problems successfully. The theory of three-way decisions has been extended to many specific areas, such as cluster analysis [60,61], risk decision taking by the government [62], medical evaluation [63], investment decision making [64], multi-attribute community decision making (MAGDM) [65], etc.

Current work has concentrated on conditional likelihood and loss function to extend the idea of three-way decisions. Yao & Zhou [66] determined the conditional probability on the basis of Bayes' theorem and the naive probabilistic independence. Liu [67] calculated the conditional probability through logistic regression. In order to address the problem that it is difficult to calculate the loss accurately in a specific situation, there is a trend towards reducing the precision of loss calculation by some kind of fluid method. Liang & Liu [68] have developed a new model of three-way decisions that calculates the loss function by using hesitant fuzzy sets. Liang & Liu [69] also considered IFSs as a new framework for evaluating the loss feature in Three-way decisions and then developed a new Three-way decision model. Mandal & Ranadive [70] introduced PFNs into the loss function and developed three methods with Pythagorean fuzzy decision-theoretical rough sets (PFDTRSs) to extract Three-way decisions. These studies have encouraged widespread application of DTRS and Three-way Decisions. While Mandal & Ranadive [70] introduced PFNs into the loss function and proposed the concept of PFDTRSs. The factional orthotriple fuzzy set is new generalized tool to describe the uncertainty and Pythagorean fuzzy set (PyFS) and q-rung orthopair fuzzy set is particulars cases. In case, we have $f = \frac{p}{q} = 2$, then the fractional orthotriple fuzzy set is reduced a Pythagorean fuzzy set, and if $f = \frac{p}{q} = p$ and $q = 1$, then the fractional orthotriple fuzzy set is reduced to q-rung orthopair fuzzy set. The model of [70] did not implement on the fractional orthotriple fuzzy environment. To fill this research space, this paper tries to study the model of (fractional orthotriple fuzzy covering-based decision-theoretical rough sets (FOFCDTRSs) through fractional orthotriple fuzzy (FOF) β-neighborhood structures and Three-way decisions. Using the positive, neutral and negative characteristics of FOFNs, we develop five methods to resolve fractional orthotriple fuzzy numbers (FOFNs) and deduce appropriate Three-way decisions. We focus on the determination of loss functions, using the opinions of multiple experts. We compare the five approaches (Methods), summarize their advantages and drawbacks and establish a corresponding algorithm for deriving FOF β-covering Three-way decisions with DTRSs. In real life, the FOFCDTRS model is a critical instrument for coping with ambiguity and confusion. In addition, by adjusting the value of $0 \leq \rho_\theta(\hbar)^2, \check{n}_\theta(\hbar)^2, \nu_\theta(\hbar)^2 \leq 1$, it is found that FOFCDTRSs is an important extension of covering-based Spherical fuzzy decision-theoretic rough sets (CSFDTRSs). And by adjusting $0 \leq \rho_\theta(\hbar), \check{n}_\theta(\hbar), \nu_\theta(\hbar) \leq 1$, it is an important extension of covering-based picture fuzzy decision-theoretic rough sets (CPFDTRSs). This shows that the FOFCDTRS model is more capable of dealing with uncertainty than the CPFDTRSs and CSFDTRSs.

The factional orthotriple fuzzy set is new generalized tool to describe the uncertainty and Pythagorean fuzzy set and q-rung orthopair fuzzy set is particulars cases. In case, we have $f = p/q = 2$, then the fractional orthotriple fuzzy set is reduced a Pythagorean fuzzy set, and if $f = p/q = p$ and $q = 1$, then the fractional orthotriple fuzzy set is reduced to q-rung orthopair fuzzy set. The model of [70] did not implement on the fractional orthotriple fuzzy environment.

The role of the fractional orthotriple fuzzy sets (FOFSs) in the decision making problem is very important among the other extension of fuzzy sets. In the FOFS, the opinion is not only restricted to yes or no, also having some sort of refusal or abstinence. The best example for representing the FOFS as, voting systems, in voting systems, there are four type of voters, i.e vote in favor, or against vote, refuse to vote, or neutral for vote. In FOFS, the MD is used for vote in favor, NMD is used for against vote, ND is used for neutral for vote and RD is used for refuse to vote. In many cases of real life, we have exist situation where the experts plans for best decision by using more accurate tools. The FOFS is a very important tool to describe the object with no uncertainty, and in other tool the information diverse and having uncertainty. For example, we consider a country want build or start a project for the medical treatment or health care center. The government party will give high favor for his project, Govt assigned MD 0.8, while the opposition party will show it, the same project is not good, they will highly against. The opposition party will assigned NMD 0.75. The other small party will remain neutral and they will assigned NM is 0.2, in case of picture fuzzy set, $0.8 + 0.75 + 0.2 = 1.75 > 1$, in this case the picture fuzzy set failed to explain such information. Now consider SFS, $(0.8)^2 + (0.75)^2 + (0.2)^2 = 1.243 > 1$, also in this case the SFS failed to explain the such information, In case of FOFS, $(0.8)^f + (0.75)^f + (0.2)^f \leq 1$, where $f \in Q^+$.

In order to handle such problem of uncertainty, we need a comprehensive tool to describe such type of problem during the decision making process.

The rest of this paper is arranged as follows: the basic concepts of FOFSs and their generalization are introduced in Section 2. In Section 3, the concept of CFOFRSs based on FOF β-neighborhoods is proposed along with the corresponding axiomatic system. Apart from these, the method of obtaining conditional probability is discussed in this section. In Section 4, we propose the FOFCDTRSs model and give the minimum cost decision rules under FOF environment, and further study the decision rules $(P_1) - (N_1)$ according to different comparison methods of FOFNs, and propose five methods to deduce Three-way decisions with FOFCDTRS. Then, an application algorithm based on FOFCDTRSs model to solve MCDM is designed in Section 5, and also an example shows the implementation of the latest three-way decisions, and contrasts and analyzes the five approaches proposed. Section 6, concludes the paper and discusses future research.

2. Preliminaries

The fuzzy set theory was first time defined by Zadeh [4], which contribute a fruitful scheme for representing and manipulating uncertainty in the form of gradualness. In 1986, Atanassov update the FS into IFS [3], by developing the notion of negative membership grade along with a positive membership grade.

This section presented the briefly remembrance the rudiments of IFS, PyFS, PFS and SFS.

Definition 1 ([3]). *Let $\beth \neq \phi$ are the genral set. An intuitionistic fuzzy set ϑ is described as;*

$$\beth = \{(\hbar, \rho_\vartheta(\hbar), \nu_\vartheta(\hbar) | \hbar \in \beth\}. \tag{1}$$

where the functions $\rho_\vartheta(\hbar) : \beth \to [0,1]$ and $\nu_\vartheta(\hbar) : \mathbb{R} \to [0,1]$ represent the grade of positive and negative membership of each number, with $0 \leq \rho_\vartheta(\hbar) + \nu_\vartheta(\hbar) \leq 1$ for all $\hbar \in \mathbb{R}$.

Definition 2 ([71]). *For any fixed set $\beth$. A PyFS ϑ on $\beth$ is described with the pair of mappings $\rho_\vartheta : \beth \to [0,1]$ and $\check{n}_\vartheta : \beth \to [0,1]$ where each $\hbar \in \beth$, $\rho_\vartheta(\hbar)$, $\check{n}_\vartheta(\hbar)$ and $\nu_\vartheta(\hbar)$ are said to be positive and negative membership grades of $\hbar$, respectively, and $\rho_\vartheta^2(\hbar) + \check{n}_\vartheta^2(\hbar) \leq 1$. That is,*

$$\vartheta = \{(\hbar, \rho_\vartheta(\hbar), \check{n}_\vartheta(\hbar))\}.$$

Conventionally, $\pi_\vartheta(\hbar) = \sqrt{1 - s_\vartheta^2(\hbar)}$, where $s^2(\hbar) = \rho_\vartheta^2(\hbar) + \check{n}_\vartheta^2(\hbar) + \nu_\vartheta^2(\hbar)$ is said to be the hesitancy grade of $\hbar$, and $\rho_\vartheta^2(\hbar) + \check{n}_\vartheta^2(\hbar) \leq 1$ for each $\hbar \in \beth$.

Definition 3 ([72]). *For any fixed set $\beth$. A q-rung orthopair fuzzy set (q-ROFS) ϑ on $\beth$ is described with the pair of mappings $\rho_\vartheta : \beth \to [0,1]$, $\check{n}_\vartheta : \beth \to [0,1]$ and $\nu_\vartheta : \beth \to [0,1]$, where each $\hbar \in \beth$, $\rho_\vartheta(\hbar)$, $\check{n}_\vartheta(\hbar)$ and $\nu_\vartheta(\hbar)$ are said to be positive and negative grades of $\hbar$, correspondingly, and $0 \leq \rho_\vartheta(\hbar)^f + \nu_\vartheta(\hbar)^f \leq 1, (f \geq 1)$. That is*

$$\vartheta = \left\{(\hbar, \rho_\vartheta(\hbar), \nu_\vartheta(\hbar)) : \rho_\vartheta(\hbar)^f + \nu_\vartheta(\hbar)^f \leq 1 \text{ for each } \hbar \in \beth\right\}$$

Conventionally, $\pi_\vartheta(\hbar) = \left(1 - \rho_\vartheta(\hbar)^f - \nu_\vartheta(\hbar)^f\right)^{\frac{1}{f}}$ is said to be the indeterminacy membership grade of $\hbar$.

Definition 4 ([5]). *For any fixed set* ℶ. *An picture fuzzy set (PFS)* ϑ *on* ℶ *is described with the pair of mappings* $\rho_\vartheta : ℶ \to [0,1]$, $\check{n}_\vartheta : ℶ \to [0,1]$ *and* $v_\vartheta : ℶ \to [0,1]$, *where each* $\hbar \in ℶ$, $\rho_\vartheta(\hbar)$, $\check{n}_\vartheta(\hbar)$ *and* $v_\vartheta(\hbar)$ *are said to be positive, neutral and negative membership grades of* $\hbar$, *respectively, and* $\rho_\vartheta(\hbar) + \check{n}_\vartheta(\hbar) + v_\vartheta(\hbar) \leq 1$. *That is*

$$\vartheta = \{(\hbar, \rho_\vartheta(\hbar), \check{n}_\vartheta(\hbar), v_\vartheta(\hbar)) : \rho_\vartheta(\hbar) + \check{n}_\vartheta(\hbar) + v_\vartheta(\hbar) \leq 1 \text{ for each } \hbar \in ℶ\}.$$

Conventionally, $\pi_\vartheta(\hbar) = 1 - \rho_\vartheta(\hbar) - \check{n}_\vartheta(\hbar) - v_\vartheta(\hbar)$ *is said to be the indeterminacy membership grade of* $\hbar$. *We note that a standard membership grade is a special case of an picture positive membership grade where* $\check{n}_\vartheta(\hbar) = 1 - \rho_\vartheta(\hbar) - v_\vartheta(\hbar)$. *Also, standard membership grade has* $\pi_\vartheta(\hbar) = 0$.

Definition 5 ([73]). *For any fixed set* ℶ. *A Spherical fuzzy set (SFS)* ϑ *on* ℶ *is described with the pair of mappings* $\rho_\vartheta : ℶ \to [0,1]$, $\check{n}_\vartheta : ℶ \to [0,1]$ *and* $v_\vartheta : ℶ \to [0,1]$ *where each* $\hbar \in ℶ$, $\rho_\vartheta(\hbar)$, $\check{n}_\vartheta(\hbar)$ *and* $v_\vartheta(\hbar)$ *are said to be positive, neutral and negative membership grades of* $\hbar$, *respectively, and* $\rho_\vartheta^2(\hbar) + \check{n}_\vartheta^2(\hbar) + v_\vartheta^2(\hbar) \leq 1$. *That is*

$$\vartheta = \{(\hbar, \rho_\vartheta(\hbar), \check{n}_\vartheta(\hbar), v_\vartheta(\hbar)) : \rho_\vartheta^2(\hbar) + \check{n}_\vartheta^2(\hbar) + v_\vartheta^2(\hbar) \leq 1 \text{ for each } \hbar \in ℶ\}.$$

Conventionally, $\pi_\vartheta(\hbar) = \sqrt{1 - s_\vartheta^2(\hbar)}$, *where* $s^2(\hbar) = \rho_\vartheta^2(\hbar) + \check{n}_\vartheta^2(\hbar) + v_\vartheta^2(\hbar)$ *is said to be the hesitancy grade of* $\hbar$.

Definition 6 ([74]). *A fuzzy-rough set is the pair of lower and upper approximations of a fuzzy set* ϑ *in a universe* ℶ *on which a fuzzy relation R is defined. The fuzzy-rough model is obtained by fuzzifying the definitions of the crisp lower and upper approximation. Recall that the condition for an element to belong to the crisp lower approximation is*

$$\forall y \in ℶ(x,y) \in R \to y \in \vartheta$$

The equivalence relation R is now a fuzzy relation, and ϑ *is a fuzzy set. The values* $R(x,y)$ *and* $\vartheta(y)$ *are connected by a fuzzy implication* Γ, *so* $\Gamma(R(x,y), \vartheta(y))$ *expresses to what extent elements that are similar x to belong to* ϑ. *The membership value of an element* $x \in ℶ$ *to the lower approximation is high if these values* $\Gamma(R(x,y), \vartheta(y))$ *are high for all* $y \in \vartheta$:

$$\forall y \in ℶ(R \downarrow \vartheta)(x) = \min_{y \in ℶ} \Gamma(R(x,y), \vartheta(y))$$

$$\forall y \in ℶ(R \uparrow \vartheta)(x) = \max_{y \in ℶ} \Gamma(R(x,y), \vartheta(y))$$

This upper approximation expresses to what extent there exist instances that are similar to x and belong to ϑ.

Definition 7 ([47]). *(1) Consider a universal set* ℶ *and* $\mathcal{S} = \{\mathcal{S}_1, \mathcal{S}_2, \mathcal{S}_3, ... \mathcal{S}_n\}$ *and each* $\mathcal{S}_i \in SFS(ℶ)$. *Then,* $\mathcal{S}$ *is called spherical* β-*covering(SF* β-*covering) of* ℶ, *if there is another SFS* β *of* ℶ *such that* $\left(\bigcup_{i=1}^{n} \mathcal{S}_i\right)(x) \succcurlyeq \beta$ *for all* $x \in ℶ$. *Thus, the pair* $(ℶ, \mathcal{S})$ *is said to a be SFCAS.*

(2) Consider $(ℶ, \mathcal{S})$ *be a SFCAS, for* β *and SF* β-*covering* $\mathcal{S} = \{\mathcal{S}_1, \mathcal{S}_2, \mathcal{S}_3, ... \mathcal{S}_n\}$ *of* ℶ. *Then*

$$\mathbb{N}_{\mathcal{S}(x)}^\beta = \bigcap \{\mathcal{S}_i \in \mathcal{S}/\mathcal{S}_i(x)\} \succcurlyeq \beta, i = 1, 2, 3, ..., n$$

is called an SF β-*covering neighborhood of* ℶ.

(3) Consider $\mathbb{N}_{\mathcal{S}}^\beta = \{\mathbb{N}_{\mathcal{S}(x)}^\beta / x \in ℶ\}$ *denote an SF* β-*covering neighborhood system induced by an SF* β-*covering* $\mathcal{S}$. *Further, we have the representation of SF* β-*neighborhood systems as following;*

$$M_{\mathcal{S}}^\beta = \left[\mathbb{N}_{\mathcal{S}(x)}^\beta(x)\right]_{(x_1, x_2) \in ℶ \times ℶ}$$

Definition 8 ([75]). *Decision-theoretic rough set models are a probabilistic extension of the algebraic rough set model. The required parameters for defining probabilistic lower and upper approximations are calculated based on more familiar notions of costs (risks) through the well-known Bayesian decision procedure.*

3. Fractional Orthotriple Fuzzy Set

Definition 9. *For any fixed set $\beth$. A fractional orthotriple fuzzy set (FOFS) ϑ on $\beth$ is described with the triple of mappings $\rho_\vartheta : \beth \to [0,1]$, $\check{n}_\vartheta : \beth \to [0,1]$ and $\nu_\vartheta : \beth \to [0,1]$, where each $\hbar \in \beth$, $\rho_\vartheta(\hbar)$, $\check{n}_\vartheta(\hbar)$ and $\nu_\vartheta(\hbar)$ are said to be positive, neutral and negative grades of $\hbar$, correspondingly, and $0 \leq \rho_\vartheta(\hbar)^f + \check{n}_\vartheta(\hbar)^f + \nu_\vartheta(\hbar)^f \leq 1, (f \geq 1)$. That is*

$$\vartheta = \left\{ (\hbar, \rho_\vartheta(\hbar), \check{n}_\vartheta(\hbar), \nu_\vartheta(\hbar)) : \rho_\vartheta(\hbar)^f + \check{n}_\vartheta(\hbar)^f + \nu_\vartheta(\hbar)^f \leq 1 \text{ for each } \hbar \in \beth \right\}. \tag{2}$$

Conventionally, $\pi_\vartheta(\hbar) = \left(1 - \rho_\vartheta(\hbar)^f - \check{n}_\vartheta(\hbar)^f - \nu_\vartheta(\hbar)^f\right)^{\frac{1}{f}}$ *is said to be the indeterminacy membership grade of $\hbar$.*

For convenience, fractional orthotriple fuzzy number (FOFN) is denoted as $(\rho_\vartheta(\hbar), \check{n}_\vartheta(\hbar), \nu_\vartheta(\hbar))$ for all $\hbar \in \beth$, and the collection of all FOFSs on $\beth$ is written by $FOF(\beth)$.

Definition 10. *Suppose $\vartheta_1(\hbar) = (\rho_{\vartheta_1}(\hbar), \check{n}_{\vartheta_1}(\hbar), \nu_{\vartheta_1}(\hbar))$ and $\vartheta_2(\hbar) = (\rho_{\vartheta_2}(\hbar), \check{n}_{\vartheta_2}(\hbar), \nu_{\vartheta_2}(\hbar))$ are two FOFNs. Then, one has the following properties;*

1. $\vartheta_1(\hbar) \subseteq \vartheta_2(\hbar)$ if $\rho_{\vartheta_1}(\hbar) \leq \rho_{\vartheta_2}(\hbar), \check{n}_{\vartheta_1}(\hbar) \geq \check{n}_{\vartheta_2}(\hbar)$ and $\nu_{\vartheta_1}(\hbar) \geq \nu_{\vartheta_2}(\hbar)$;
2. $\vartheta_1(\hbar) = \vartheta_2(\hbar)$ if $\rho_{\vartheta_1} = \rho_{\vartheta_2}, \check{n}_{\vartheta_1} = \check{n}_{\vartheta_2}$ and $\nu_{\vartheta_1} = \nu_{\vartheta_2}$;
3. $\vartheta_1(\hbar) \cap \vartheta_2(\hbar) = \{\min(\rho_{\vartheta_1}(\hbar), \rho_{\vartheta_2}(\hbar)), \max(\check{n}_{\vartheta_1}(\hbar), \check{n}_{\vartheta_2}(\hbar)), \max(\nu_{\vartheta_1}(\hbar), \nu_{\vartheta_2}(\hbar))\}$;
4. $\vartheta_1(\hbar) \cup \vartheta_2(\hbar) = \{\max(\rho_{\vartheta_1}(\hbar), \rho_{\vartheta_2}(\hbar)), \min(\check{n}_{\vartheta_1}(\hbar), \check{n}_{\vartheta_2}(\hbar)), \min(\nu_{\vartheta_1}(\hbar), \nu_{\vartheta_2}(\hbar))\}$;
5. $\vartheta_1^c(\hbar) = (\nu_{\vartheta_1}(\hbar), \check{n}_{\vartheta_1}(\hbar), \rho_{\vartheta_1}(\hbar))$;
6. $\vartheta_1(\hbar) \oplus \vartheta_2(\hbar) = \left\{ \begin{array}{l} \left(\rho_{\vartheta_1}(\hbar)^f + \rho_{\vartheta_2}(\hbar)^f - \rho_{\vartheta_1}(\hbar)^f \cdot \rho_{\vartheta_2}(\hbar)^f\right)^{\frac{1}{f}}, \\ \check{n}_{\vartheta_1}(\hbar) \cdot \check{n}_{\vartheta_2}(\hbar), \nu_{\vartheta_1}(\hbar) \cdot \nu_{\vartheta_2}(\hbar) \end{array} \right\}$;
7. $\vartheta_1(\hbar) \otimes \vartheta_2(\hbar) = \left\{ \begin{array}{l} \rho_{\vartheta_1}(\hbar) \cdot \rho_{\vartheta_2}(\hbar), \left(\check{n}_{\vartheta_1}(\hbar)^f + \check{n}_{\vartheta_2}(\hbar)^f - \check{n}_{\vartheta_1}(\hbar)^f \cdot \check{n}_{\vartheta_2}(\hbar)^f\right)^{\frac{1}{f}}, \\ \left(\nu_{\vartheta_1}(\hbar)^f + \nu_{\vartheta_2}(\hbar)^f - \nu_{\vartheta_1}(\hbar)^f \cdot \nu_{\vartheta_2}(\hbar)^f\right)^{\frac{1}{f}} \end{array} \right\}$;
8. $\Psi \vartheta_1(\hbar) = \left\{ \left(1 - \left(1 - \rho_{\vartheta_1}(\hbar)^f\right)^\Psi\right)^{\frac{1}{f}}, \check{n}_{\vartheta_1}(\hbar)^\Psi, \nu_{\vartheta_1}(\hbar)^\Psi \right\}, \Psi > 0$;
9. $(\vartheta_1(\hbar))^\Psi = \left\{ (\rho_{\vartheta_1}(\hbar))^\Psi, \left(1 - \left(1 - \check{n}_{\vartheta_1}(\hbar)^f\right)^\Psi\right)^{\frac{1}{f}}, \left(1 - \left(1 - \nu_{\vartheta_1}(\hbar)^f\right)^\Psi\right)^{\frac{1}{f}} \right\}$.

Definition 11. *Consider two FOFNs $\vartheta_1(\hbar) = (\rho_{\vartheta_1}(\hbar), \check{n}_{\vartheta_1}(\hbar), \nu_{\vartheta_1}(\hbar))$ and $\vartheta_2(\hbar) = (\rho_{\vartheta_2}(\hbar), \check{n}_{\vartheta_2}(\hbar), \nu_{\vartheta_2}(\hbar))$. Then, there are a natural quasi-ordering on the FOFNs is defined as follows;*

$$\vartheta_1(\hbar) \geq \vartheta_2(\hbar) \Leftrightarrow \rho_{\vartheta_1}(\hbar) \geq \rho_{\vartheta_2}(\hbar), \check{n}_{\vartheta_1}(\hbar) \leq \check{n}_{\vartheta_2}(\hbar) \text{ and } \nu_{\vartheta_1}(\hbar) \leq \nu_{\vartheta_2}(\hbar) \tag{3}$$

Remark 1. *It is easy observed from Definition (11) that the FOFN $f^+ = (1,0,0)$ is the largest FOFN and the $f^- = (0,0,1)$ is the smallest FOFN, correspondingly. We called f^+, the positive ideal FOFN and f^-, the negative ideal FOFN.*

Definition 12. *Let $\vartheta(\hbar) = (\rho_\vartheta(\hbar), \check{n}_\vartheta(\hbar), \nu_\vartheta(\hbar))$ be a FOFN, the score $S(\vartheta(\hbar))$ and the corresponding accuracy function $H(\vartheta(\hbar))$ are defined as follows;*

$$S(\vartheta(\hbar)) = \rho_\vartheta(\hbar)^f - \check{n}_\vartheta(\hbar)^f - \nu_\vartheta(\hbar)^f \tag{4}$$

and
$$H(\vartheta(\hbar)) = \rho_\vartheta(\hbar)^f + \check{n}_\vartheta(\hbar)^f + v_\vartheta(\hbar)^f \tag{5}$$

Obviously, $-1 \leq S(\vartheta(\hbar)) \leq 1$ and $0 \leq H(\vartheta(\hbar)) \leq 1$.

According to the Definition (12), the comparison rules for FOFNs as follows;

1. If $S(\vartheta_1(\hbar)) > S(\vartheta_2(\hbar))$, then $(\vartheta_1(\hbar)) > (\vartheta_2(\hbar))$;
2. If $S(\vartheta_1(\hbar)) < S(\vartheta_2(\hbar))$, then $(\vartheta_1(\hbar)) < (\vartheta_2(\hbar))$;
3. If $S(\vartheta_1(\hbar)) = S(\vartheta_2(\hbar))$, then;

   (a) If $H(\vartheta_1(\hbar)) > H(\vartheta_2(\hbar))$, then $(\vartheta_1(\hbar)) > (\vartheta_2(\hbar))$;

   (b) If $H(\vartheta_1(\hbar)) < H(\vartheta_2(\hbar))$, then $(\vartheta_1(\hbar)) < (\vartheta_2(\hbar))$;

   (c) If $H(\vartheta_1(\hbar)) = H(\vartheta_2(\hbar))$, then $(\vartheta_1(\hbar)) = (\vartheta_2(\hbar))$;

Definition 13. Let $\vartheta_1(\hbar) = \left(\rho_{\vartheta_1}(\hbar), \check{n}_{\vartheta_1}(\hbar), v_{\vartheta_1}(\hbar)\right)$ and $\vartheta_2(\hbar) = \left(\rho_{\vartheta_2}(\hbar), \check{n}_{\vartheta_2}(\hbar), v_{\vartheta_2}(\hbar)\right)$ are two FOFNs, the generalized distance between $\vartheta_1(\hbar)$ and $\vartheta_2(\hbar)$ is defined as follows;

$$d(\vartheta_1(\hbar), \vartheta_2(\hbar)) = \left\{ \frac{1}{2}(1-p) \left(\begin{array}{c} \left|\rho_{\vartheta_1}(\hbar)^f - \rho_{\vartheta_2}(\hbar)^f\right|^\lambda \\ + \left|\check{n}_{\vartheta_1}(\hbar)^f - \check{n}_{\vartheta_2}(\hbar)^f\right|^\lambda \\ + \left|v_{\vartheta_1}(\hbar)^f - v_{\vartheta_2}(\hbar)^f\right|^\lambda \end{array} \right) + p\left|\pi_{\vartheta_1}(\hbar)^f - \pi_{\vartheta_2}(\hbar)^f\right|^\lambda \right\}^{\frac{1}{\lambda}} \tag{6}$$

where

$$\pi_{\vartheta_1}(\hbar) = \left(1 - \rho_{\vartheta_1}(\hbar)^f - \check{n}_{\vartheta_1}(\hbar)^f - v_{\vartheta_1}(\hbar)^f\right)^{\frac{1}{q}},$$

$$\pi_{\vartheta_2}(\hbar) = \left(1 - \rho_{\vartheta_2}(\hbar)^f - \check{n}_{\vartheta_2}(\hbar)^f - v_{\vartheta_2}(\hbar)^f\right)^{\frac{1}{q}},$$

$\lambda > 0$ and $p \in [0,1]$. When the parameters λ and p take different values, we will get some different distance measures.

Case 1. When $\lambda = 1$ and $f = 2$, the distance will be reduced to Hamming-indeterminacy degree-preference distance.

$$d(\vartheta_1(\hbar), \vartheta_2(\hbar)) = \left\{ \frac{1}{2}(1-p) \left(\begin{array}{c} \left|\rho_{\vartheta_1}(\hbar)^2 - \rho_{\vartheta_2}(\hbar)^2\right| \\ + \left|\check{n}_{\vartheta_1}(\hbar)^2 - \check{n}_{\vartheta_2}(\hbar)^2\right| \\ + \left|v_{\vartheta_1}(\hbar)^2 - v_{\vartheta_2}(\hbar)^2\right| \end{array} \right) + p\left|\pi_{\vartheta_1}(\hbar)^2 - \pi_{\vartheta_2}(\hbar)^2\right| \right\}$$

In case 1, if $p = 0$, the effect of the indeterminacy grade is not considered. The distance will be reduced to metric distance.

$$d(\vartheta_1(\hbar), \vartheta_2(\hbar)) = \left\{ \frac{1}{2}(1-p) \left(\begin{array}{c} \left|\rho_{\vartheta_1}(\hbar)^2 - \rho_{\vartheta_2}(\hbar)^2\right| + \left|\check{n}_{\vartheta_1}(\hbar)^2 - \check{n}_{\vartheta_2}(\hbar)^2\right| \\ + \left|v_{\vartheta_1}(\hbar)^2 - v_{\vartheta_2}(\hbar)^2\right| \end{array} \right) \right\}$$

Case 2. When $\lambda = 2$ and $f = 2$, the distance will be reduced to Euclidean-indeterminacy grade-preference distance.

$$d(\vartheta_1(\hbar), \vartheta_2(\hbar)) = \left\{ \begin{array}{c} \frac{1}{2}(1-p) \left(\begin{array}{c} \left|\rho_{\vartheta_1}(\hbar)^2 - \rho_{\vartheta_2}(\hbar)^2\right|^2 \\ + \left|\check{n}_{\vartheta_1}(\hbar)^2 - \check{n}_{\vartheta_2}(\hbar)^2\right|^2 \\ + \left|\nu_{\vartheta_1}(\hbar)^2 - \nu_{\vartheta_2}(\hbar)^2\right|^2 \end{array} \right) \\ + p \left|\pi_{\vartheta_1}(\hbar)^2 - \pi_{\vartheta_2}(\hbar)^2\right|^{\frac{1}{2}} \end{array} \right\}$$

In the Case 2, if $p = 0$, the distance will be reduced to Euclidean distance.

$$d(\vartheta_1(\hbar), \vartheta_2(\hbar)) = \left\{ \frac{1}{2}(1-p) \left(\begin{array}{c} \left|\rho_{\vartheta_1}(\hbar)^2 - \rho_{\vartheta_2}(\hbar)^2\right|^2 \\ + \left|\check{n}_{\vartheta_1}(\hbar)^2 - \check{n}_{\vartheta_2}(\hbar)^2\right|^2 \\ + \left|\nu_{\vartheta_1}(\hbar)^2 - \nu_{\vartheta_2}(\hbar)^2\right|^2 \end{array} \right) \right\}^{\frac{1}{2}}$$

Definition 14. Let $\vartheta_1(\hbar) = (\rho_{\vartheta_1}(\hbar), \check{n}_{\vartheta_1}(\hbar), \nu_{\vartheta_1}(\hbar))$ and $\vartheta_2(\hbar) = (\rho_{\vartheta_2}(\hbar), \check{n}_{\vartheta_2}(\hbar), \nu_{\vartheta_2}(\hbar))$ are two FOFNs, the distance d satisfied the following properties;

1. $d(\vartheta_1(\hbar), \vartheta_2(\hbar)) \geq 0$;
2. $d(\vartheta_1(\hbar), \vartheta_2(\hbar)) = d(\vartheta_2(\hbar), \vartheta_1(\hbar))$;
3. $d(\vartheta_1(\hbar), \vartheta_2(\hbar)) = 0 \Leftrightarrow d(\vartheta_1(\hbar)) = d(\vartheta_2(\hbar))$.

According to the Definition (13), it is easy to find the distance of FOFN $\vartheta(\hbar) = (\rho_\vartheta(\hbar), \check{n}_\vartheta(\hbar), \nu_\vartheta(\hbar))$ and the positive ideal FOFN $f^+ = (1, 0, 0)$ as follows;

$$d(\vartheta(\hbar), f^+) = \left\{ \frac{1}{2}(1-p) \left(\left|1 - \rho_\vartheta(\hbar)^f\right|^\lambda + \left|\check{n}_\vartheta(\hbar)^f\right|^\lambda + \left|\nu_\vartheta(\hbar)^f\right|^\lambda \right) \right\}^{\frac{1}{\lambda}} \quad (7)$$

and distance between the FOFN $\vartheta(\hbar) = (\rho_\vartheta(\hbar), \check{n}_\vartheta(\hbar), \nu_\vartheta(\hbar))$ and the negative ideal FOFN $f^- = (0, 0, 1)$ as follows;

$$d(\vartheta(\hbar), f^-) = \left\{ \frac{1}{2}(1-p) \left(\left|\rho_\vartheta(\hbar)^f\right|^\lambda + \left|1 - \check{n}_\vartheta(\hbar)^f\right|^\lambda + \left|1 - \nu_\vartheta(\hbar)^f\right|^\lambda \right) \right\}^{\frac{1}{\lambda}} \quad (8)$$

Usually, the smaller the distance $d(\vartheta(\hbar), f^+)$ is the bigger the FOFN $\vartheta(\hbar)$ is; and on the contrary the larger the distance $d(\vartheta(\hbar), f^-)$ is, the bigger the FOFN $\vartheta(\hbar)$ is. Inspire by the concept of TOPSIS [76], we developed the idea of closeness index for the FOFN.

Definition 15. Let $\vartheta(\hbar) = (\rho_\vartheta(\hbar), \check{n}_\vartheta(\hbar), \nu_\vartheta(\hbar))$ be a FOFN, $f^+ = (1, 0, 0)$ be the positive ideal FOFN and $f^- = (0, 0, 1)$ be the negative ideal FOFN, then the closeness index of $\vartheta(\hbar)$ is defined as following;

$$\zeta(\vartheta(\hbar)) = \frac{d(\vartheta(\hbar), f^-)}{d(\vartheta(\hbar), f^-) + d(\vartheta(\hbar), f^+)} \quad (9)$$

Apparently, if $\vartheta(\hbar) = f^-$, then $\zeta(\vartheta(\hbar)) = 0$; if $\vartheta(\hbar) = f^+$, then $\zeta(\vartheta(\hbar)) = 1$. Meanwhile, it is easily noticed that the closeness index $\zeta(\vartheta(\hbar)) \in [0, 1]$.

And for two FOFNs $\vartheta_1(\hbar) = (\rho_{\vartheta_1}(\hbar), \check{n}_{\vartheta_1}(\hbar), \nu_{\vartheta_1}(\hbar))$ and $\vartheta_2(\hbar) = (\rho_{\vartheta_2}(\hbar), \check{n}_{\vartheta_2}(\hbar), \nu_{\vartheta_2}(\hbar))$, if $\zeta(\vartheta_1(\hbar)) \geq \zeta(\vartheta_2(\hbar))$, then $\vartheta_1(\hbar) \geq \vartheta_2(\hbar)$.

4. Covering Based Fractional Orthotriple Fuzzy Rough Set

In this section, we defined some new concept of fractional orthotriple fuzzy β-covering (FOF β-covering), fractional orthotriple fuzzy covering approximation space (FOFCAS) and FOF β-neighborhood.

Definition 16.

1. Assume $\beth$ is a universe set, $\widetilde{E} = \left(\widetilde{E}_1, ..., \widetilde{E}_n \right)$, where $\widetilde{E}_i \in FOF(\beth)$ and $k = 1, ..., n$. For any FOFN $\beta = \left(\rho_\beta(\hbar), \check{n}_\beta(\hbar), \nu_\beta(\hbar) \right)$, then $\widetilde{E}$ is called a FOF β-covering of $\beth$ if

$$\left(\bigcup_{k=1}^{n} \widetilde{E}_k \right)(\hbar) \geq \beta \tag{10}$$

for all $\hbar \in \beth$. The $\left(\beth, \widetilde{E} \right)$ is called a FOFCAS.

2. Let $\left(\beth, \widetilde{E} \right)$ be a FOFCAS and $\widetilde{E} = \left(\widetilde{E}_1, ..., \widetilde{E}_n \right)$ be a FOF β-covering of $\beth$ for some $\beta = \left(\rho_\beta(\hbar), \check{n}_\beta(\hbar), \nu_\beta(\hbar) \right)$. Then,

$$\widetilde{N}^\beta_{\widetilde{E}(\hbar)} = \left(\widetilde{E}_k \in \widetilde{E} | \widetilde{E}_k(\hbar) \geq \beta, k = 1, ..., n \right) \tag{11}$$

is called a FOF β-neighborhood of $\hbar$ in $\beth$.

Based on the above FOF β-neighborhood $\widetilde{N}^\beta_{\widetilde{E}(\hbar)}$, a crisp set called fractional orthotriple β-neighborhood (FOF β-neighborhood) is introduced as follows;

Definition 17. Given that $\widetilde{E} = \left(\widetilde{E}_1, ..., \widetilde{E}_n \right)$ is a FOF β-covering on $\beth$. $\widetilde{N}^\beta_{\widetilde{E}(\hbar)}$ is a FOF β-neighborhood of $\hbar$ in $\beth$. For a FOFN $\beta = \left(\rho_\beta(\hbar), \check{n}_\beta(\hbar), \nu_\beta(\hbar) \right)$, if each $\hbar \in \beth$, FO β-neighborhood $\widehat{N}^\beta_{\widetilde{E}(\hbar)}$ of $\hbar$ is defined as;

$$\widehat{N}^\beta_{\widetilde{E}(\hbar)} = \left\{ z \in \beth : \rho_{\widetilde{N}^\beta_{\widetilde{E}(\hbar)}}(z) \geq \rho_\beta(\hbar), \check{n}_{\widetilde{N}^\beta_{\widetilde{E}(\hbar)}}(z) \leq \check{n}_\beta(\hbar), \nu_{\widetilde{N}^\beta_{\widetilde{E}(\hbar)}}(z) \leq \nu_\beta(\hbar) \right\} \tag{12}$$

Definition 18. Let $\left(\beth, \widetilde{E} \right)$ be a FOFCAS. The conditional probability in which the object $\hbar$ belongs to $\hat{H}$ with respect to $\widehat{N}^\beta_{\widetilde{E}(\hbar)}$, denoted by $P_r \left(\hat{H} | \widehat{N}^\beta_{\widetilde{E}(\hbar)} \right)$ for every $\hat{H} \subseteq \beth$, is defined as;

$$P_r \left(\hat{H} | \widehat{N}^\beta_{\widetilde{E}(\hbar)} \right) = \frac{\left| \hat{H} \cap \widehat{N}^\beta_{\widetilde{E}(\hbar)} \right|}{\left| \widehat{N}^\beta_{\widetilde{E}(\hbar)} \right|} \tag{13}$$

Clearly, for all $\hbar \in \beth$, $0 \leq P_r \left(\hat{H} | \widehat{N}^\beta_{\widetilde{E}(\hbar)} \right) \leq 1$.

Example 1. *Suppose that* $(\vartheta, \beth)$ *be a FOFCAS and* $\tilde{E} = (\tilde{E}_1, ..., \tilde{E}_4)$ *is a set of FOFSs*, $f \geq 4$, *where* $\beth = (\hbar_1, ..., \hbar_5)$, $\beta = (0.8.0.6.0.4)$. *Details are shown in Table 1.*

Table 1. FOF β—covering $\tilde{E}$ in Example 1.

	$\tilde{E}_1$	$\tilde{E}_2$	$\tilde{E}_3$	$\tilde{E}_4$
$\hbar_1$	(0.9, 0.1, 0.2)	(0.7, 0.3, 0.5)	(0.6, 0.3, 0.5)	(0.8, 0.5, 0.2)
$\hbar_2$	(0.5, 0.3, 0.4)	(0.9, 0.3, 0.1)	(0.8, 0.1, 0.4)	(0.7, 0.2, 0.4)
$\hbar_3$	(0.9, 0.4, 0.3)	(0.3, 0.2, 0.1)	(0.8, 0.2, 0.4)	(0.5, 0.4, 0.6)
$\hbar_4$	(0.8, 0.1, 0.4)	(0.5, 0.2, 0.1)	(0.9, 0.3, 0.4)	(0.8, 0.3, 0.1)
$\hbar_5$	(0.8, 0.4, 0.3)	(0.9, 0.4, 0.3)	(0.7, 0.3, 0.1)	(0.4, 0.2, 0.1)

Therefore, $\tilde{E}$ is FOF β—covering of $\beth$. Then, $\tilde{N}_{\tilde{E}(\hbar_1)}^{(0.8.0.6.0.4)} = \tilde{E}_1 \cap \tilde{E}_4$, $\tilde{N}_{\tilde{E}(\hbar_2)}^{(0.8.0.6.0.4)} = \tilde{E}_2 \cap \tilde{E}_3$, $\tilde{N}_{\tilde{E}(\hbar_3)}^{(0.8.0.6.0.4)} = \tilde{E}_1 \cap \tilde{E}_3$, $\tilde{N}_{\tilde{E}(\hbar_4)}^{(0.8.0.6.0.4)} = \tilde{E}_3 \cap \tilde{E}_4$, $\tilde{N}_{\tilde{E}(\hbar_5)}^{(0.8.0.6.0.4)} = \tilde{E}_1 \cap \tilde{E}_2$.

By calculations, we have the FOF β—neighborhood $\tilde{N}_{\tilde{E}}^{(0.8.0.6.0.4)}$ as shown in Table 2.

Table 2. FOF β—neighborhood $\tilde{N}_{\tilde{E}}^{(0.8.0.6.0.4)}$ in Example 1.

	$\hbar_1$	$\hbar_2$	$\hbar_3$	$\hbar_4$	$\hbar_5$
$\hbar_1$	(0.8, 0.1, 0.2)	(0.5, 0.2, 0.4)	(0.5, 0.4, 0.6)	(0.8, 0.1, 0.4)	(0.4, 0.2, 0.3)
$\hbar_2$	(0.6, 0.3, 0.5)	(0.8, 0.1, 0.4)	(0.3, 0.2, 0.4)	(0.5, 0.2, 0.4)	(0.7, 0.3, 0.3)
$\hbar_3$	(0.6, 0.1, 0.5)	(0.5, 0.1, 0.4)	(0.8, 0.2, 0.4)	(0.8, 0.1, 0.4)	(0.7, 0.3, 0.3)
$\hbar_4$	(0.6, 0.3, 0.5)	(0.7, 0.1, 0.4)	(0.5, 0.2, 0.6)	(0.8, 0.3, 0.4)	(0.4, 0.2, 0.1)
$\hbar_5$	(0.7, 0.1, 0.5)	(0.5, 0.3, 0.4)	(0.3, 0.2, 0.3)	(0.5, 0.1, 0.4)	(0.8, 0.4, 0.3)

$\tilde{N}_{\tilde{E}(\hbar_1)}^{(0.8.0.6.0.4)} = (\hbar_1)$, $\tilde{N}_{\tilde{E}(\hbar_2)}^{(0.8.0.6.0.4)} = (\hbar_2)$, $\tilde{N}_{\tilde{E}(\hbar_3)}^{(0.8.0.6.0.4)} = (\hbar_3)$, $\tilde{N}_{\tilde{E}(\hbar_4)}^{(0.8.0.6.0.4)} = (\hbar_1, \hbar_3, \hbar_4)$, $\tilde{N}_{\tilde{E}(\hbar_5)}^{(0.8.0.6.0.4)} = (\hbar_5)$.

Let the decision set $\hat{H} = (\hbar_1, \hbar_4, \hbar_5)$, so we have the conditional probability as;

$$P_r\left(\hat{H} | \hat{N}_{\tilde{E}(\hbar_1)}^\beta\right) = \frac{|(\hbar_1) \cap (\hbar_1, \hbar_4, \hbar_5)|}{|(\hbar_1)|} = 1,$$

$$P_r\left(\hat{H} | \hat{N}_{\tilde{E}(\hbar_2)}^\beta\right) = \frac{|(\hbar_2) \cap (\hbar_1, \hbar_4, \hbar_5)|}{|(\hbar_2)|} = 0,$$

$$P_r\left(\hat{H} | \hat{N}_{\tilde{E}(\hbar_3)}^\beta\right) = \frac{|(\hbar_3) \cap (\hbar_1, \hbar_4, \hbar_5)|}{|(\hbar_3)|} = 1,$$

$$P_r\left(\hat{H} | \hat{N}_{\tilde{E}(\hbar_4)}^\beta\right) = \frac{|(\hbar_1, \hbar_3, \hbar_4) \cap (\hbar_1, \hbar_4, \hbar_5)|}{|(\hbar_1, \hbar_3, \hbar_4)|} = \frac{2}{3},$$

$$P_r\left(\hat{H} | \hat{N}_{\tilde{E}(\hbar_5)}^\beta\right) = \frac{|(\hbar_5) \cap (\hbar_1, \hbar_4, \hbar_5)|}{|(\hbar_5)|} = 1.$$

5. FOF β-Covering Decision-Theoretic Rough Set Model

In this section, we discuss the loss function of DTRS with FOFNs in view of the new uncertainty measurement of FOFSs, and construct a FOFCDTRS as per Bayesian decision procedure [53,68,69].

According to the results of Liang and Liu [69] and Bayesian decision procedure, the q- ROFCDTRS consists of two states and three actions. The family of states is denoted by $\Gamma = (D, \neg D)$, which means that an object is in the state D or not in the state D. And, the collection of three actions is denoted by $\mathbb{Z} = (b_P, b_B, b_N)$, in which b_P, b_B and b_N stand for the three actions in classifying an object $\hbar$, namely, deciding $\hbar \in POS(D)$, deciding $\hbar \in BND(D)$ and deciding $\hbar \in NEG(D)$, respectively. At the moment, $POS(D), BND(D)$ and $NEG(D)$ correspond the decision rules of three-way decisions. Using the idea Liang and Liu [69] and Bayesian decision procedure, under the fractional orthotriple fuzzy information, We create a loss function matrix for the risk or cost of behavior in the various states. The results are given in Table 3.

Table 3. The loss function matrix with FOFNs.

	D
b_P	$\vartheta(\lambda_{PP}) = (\rho_\theta(\lambda_{PP}), \check{n}_\theta(\lambda_{PP}), \nu_\theta(\lambda_{PP}))$
b_B	$\vartheta(\lambda_{BP}) = (\rho_\theta(\lambda_{BP}), \check{n}_\theta(\lambda_{BP}), \nu_\theta(\lambda_{BP}))$
b_N	$\vartheta(\lambda_{NP}) = (\rho_\theta(\lambda_{NP}), \check{n}_\theta(\lambda_{NP}), \nu_\theta(\lambda_{NP}))$
	$\neg D$
b_P	$\vartheta(\lambda_{PN}) = (\rho_\theta(\lambda_{PN}), \check{n}_\theta(\lambda_{PN}), \nu_\theta(\lambda_{PN}))$
b_B	$\vartheta(\lambda_{BN}) = (\rho_\theta(\lambda_{BN}), \check{n}_\theta(\lambda_{BN}), \nu_\theta(\lambda_{BN}))$
b_N	$\vartheta(\lambda_{NN}) = (\rho_\theta(\lambda_{NN}), \check{n}_\theta(\lambda_{NN}), \nu_\theta(\lambda_{NN}))$

In Table 3, the loss function $\vartheta(\lambda..)$ is FOFN $(\cdot = P; B; N)$. When the object $\hbar$ is in the state D, its loss degrees with FOFNs are $\vartheta(\lambda_{PP}), \vartheta(\lambda_{BP})$ and $\vartheta(\lambda_{NP})$ incurred for taking actions of b_P, b_B and b_N, correspondingly. In the same way, when the object $\hbar$ does not belong to D, its loss degrees with FOFNs are $\vartheta(\lambda_{PP}), \vartheta(\lambda_{BP})$ and $\vartheta(\lambda_{NP})$ incurred for taking the same actions. Utilizing the property of FOFN and the semantics of three-way decisions, the loss functions of Table 3, have the following relationship:

$$\rho_\theta(\lambda_{PP}) \leq \rho_\theta(\lambda_{BP}) < \rho_\theta(\lambda_{NP}); \tag{14}$$

$$\check{n}_\theta(\lambda_{NP}) \leq \check{n}_\theta(\lambda_{BP}) < \check{n}_\theta(\lambda_{PP}); \tag{15}$$

$$\nu_\theta(\lambda_{NP}) \leq \nu_\theta(\lambda_{BP}) < \nu_\theta(\lambda_{PP}); \tag{16}$$

$$\rho_\theta(\lambda_{NN}) \leq \rho_\theta(\lambda_{BN}) < \rho_\theta(\lambda_{PN}); \tag{17}$$

$$\check{n}_\theta(\lambda_{PN}) \leq \check{n}_\theta(\lambda_{BN}) < \check{n}_\theta(\lambda_{NN}); \tag{18}$$

$$\nu_\theta(\lambda_{PN}) \leq \nu_\theta(\lambda_{BN}) < \nu_\theta(\lambda_{NN}). \tag{19}$$

Proposition 1. *Using the relationship of loss functions (14)–(19), we can obtain the following results;*

$$\vartheta(\lambda_{PP}) \leq \vartheta(\lambda_{BP}) < \vartheta(\lambda_{NP}) \tag{20}$$

$$\vartheta(\lambda_{NN}) \leq \vartheta(\lambda_{BN}) < \vartheta(\lambda_{PN}) \tag{21}$$

From Proposition (1), Equation (20) shows that the loss of classifying the object $\hbar$ belonging to D into the positive region $POS(D)$ is less than or equal to the loss of classifying it into the boundary region $BND(D)$, and both of them are less than the loss of classifying $\hbar$ into the negative region $NEG(D)$. The relationship (21) can be explained in the same way.

Assume that $P_r\left(D|\widehat{N}^\beta_{\widetilde{E}(\hbar)}\right)$ is the conditional probability in which the object $\hbar$ belonging to D is described by its FO β-neighborhood $\widehat{N}^\beta_{\widetilde{E}(\hbar)}$. Then, there exists a relationship $P_r\left(D|\widehat{N}^\beta_{\widetilde{E}(\hbar)}\right) + P_r\left(\neg D|\widehat{N}^\beta_{\widetilde{E}(\hbar)}\right) = 1$. Now, for every $\hbar \in \beth$, the corresponding expected losses $R\left(b.|\widehat{N}^\beta_{\widetilde{E}(\hbar)}\right)$ ($\cdot = P, B, N$) can be shown as;

$$R\left(b_P|\widehat{N}^\beta_{\widetilde{E}(\hbar)}\right) = \vartheta\left(\lambda_{PP}\right) P_r\left(D|\widehat{N}^\beta_{\widetilde{E}(\hbar)}\right) \oplus \vartheta\left(\lambda_{PN}\right) P_r\left(D|\widehat{N}^\beta_{\widetilde{E}(\hbar)}\right); \tag{22}$$

$$R\left(b_B|\widehat{N}^\beta_{\widetilde{E}(\hbar)}\right) = \vartheta\left(\lambda_{BP}\right) P_r\left(D|\widehat{N}^\beta_{\widetilde{E}(\hbar)}\right) \oplus \vartheta\left(\lambda_{BN}\right) P_r\left(D|\widehat{N}^\beta_{\widetilde{E}(\hbar)}\right); \tag{23}$$

$$R\left(b_N|\widehat{N}^\beta_{\widetilde{E}(\hbar)}\right) = \vartheta\left(\lambda_{NP}\right) P_r\left(D|\widehat{N}^\beta_{\widetilde{E}(\hbar)}\right) \oplus \vartheta\left(\lambda_{NN}\right) P_r\left(D|\widehat{N}^\beta_{\widetilde{E}(\hbar)}\right); \tag{24}$$

Proposition 2. *According to* $P_r\left(D|\widehat{N}^\beta_{\widetilde{E}(\hbar)}\right) + P_r\left(\neg D|\widehat{N}^\beta_{\widetilde{E}(\hbar)}\right) = 1$, *Equations* (22)–(24), *can be expressed as follows;*

$$R\left(b_P|\widehat{N}^\beta_{\widetilde{E}(\hbar)}\right) = \left\{\begin{array}{c}\left(\begin{array}{c}\left(1-\left(1-\rho_\vartheta\left(\lambda_{PP}\right)^f\right)^{P_r\left(D|\widehat{N}^\beta_{\widetilde{E}(\hbar)}\right)}\right)^{\frac{1}{f}},\\ \check{n}_\vartheta\left(\lambda_{PP}\right)^{P_r\left(D|\widehat{N}^\beta_{\widetilde{E}(\hbar)}\right)},\\ \nu_\vartheta\left(\lambda_{PP}\right)^{P_r\left(D|\widehat{N}^\beta_{\widetilde{E}(\hbar)}\right)}\end{array}\right)\\ \oplus\\ \left(\begin{array}{c}\left(1-\left(1-\rho_\vartheta\left(\lambda_{PP}\right)^f\right)^{P_r\left(\neg D|\widehat{N}^\beta_{\widetilde{E}(\hbar)}\right)}\right)^{\frac{1}{f}},\\ \check{n}_\vartheta\left(\lambda_{PP}\right)^{P_r\left(\neg D|\widehat{N}^\beta_{\widetilde{E}(\hbar)}\right)},\\ \nu_\vartheta\left(\lambda_{PP}\right)^{P_r\left(\neg D|\widehat{N}^\beta_{\widetilde{E}(\hbar)}\right)}\end{array}\right)\end{array}\right. \tag{25}$$

$$R\left(b_B|\widehat{N}^\beta_{\widetilde{E}(\hbar)}\right) = \left\{\begin{array}{c}\left(\begin{array}{c}\left(1-\left(1-\rho_\vartheta\left(\lambda_{BP}\right)^f\right)^{P_r\left(D|\widehat{N}^\beta_{\widetilde{E}(\hbar)}\right)}\right)^{\frac{1}{f}}, \check{n}_\vartheta\left(\lambda_{BP}\right)^{P_r\left(D|\widehat{N}^\beta_{\widetilde{E}(\hbar)}\right)},\\ \nu_\vartheta\left(\lambda_{BP}\right)^{P_r\left(D|\widehat{N}^\beta_{\widetilde{E}(\hbar)}\right)}\end{array}\right)\\ \oplus\\ \left(\begin{array}{c}\left(1-\left(1-\rho_\vartheta\left(\lambda_{BP}\right)^f\right)^{P_r\left(\neg D|\widehat{N}^\beta_{\widetilde{E}(\hbar)}\right)}\right)^{\frac{1}{f}},\\ \check{n}_\vartheta\left(\lambda_{BP}\right)^{P_r\left(\neg D|\widehat{N}^\beta_{\widetilde{E}(\hbar)}\right)},\\ \nu_\vartheta\left(\lambda_{BP}\right)^{P_r\left(\neg D|\widehat{N}^\beta_{\widetilde{E}(\hbar)}\right)}\end{array}\right)\end{array}\right. \tag{26}$$

$$R\left(b_N|\widehat{N}^\beta_{\widetilde{E}(\hbar)}\right) = \left\{ \begin{pmatrix} \left(1 - \left(1 - \rho_\theta\left(\lambda_{NP}\right)^f\right)^{P_r\left(D|\widehat{N}^\beta_{\widetilde{E}(\hbar)}\right)}\right)^{\frac{1}{f}}, \\ \check{n}_\theta\left(\lambda_{NP}\right)^{P_r\left(D|\widehat{N}^\beta_{\widetilde{E}(\hbar)}\right)}, \\ \nu_\theta\left(\lambda_{NP}\right)^{P_r\left(D|\widehat{N}^\beta_{\widetilde{E}(\hbar)}\right)} \end{pmatrix} \oplus \begin{pmatrix} \left(1 - \left(1 - \rho_\theta\left(\lambda_{NP}\right)^f\right)^{P_r\left(\neg D|\widehat{N}^\beta_{\widetilde{E}(\hbar)}\right)}\right)^{\frac{1}{f}}, \\ \check{n}_\theta\left(\lambda_{NP}\right)^{P_r\left(\neg D|\widehat{N}^\beta_{\widetilde{E}(\hbar)}\right)}, \\ \nu_\theta\left(\lambda_{NP}\right)^{P_r\left(\neg D|\widehat{N}^\beta_{\widetilde{E}(\hbar)}\right)} \end{pmatrix} \right\} \quad (27)$$

Proposition 3. *The expected losses* $R\left(b.|\widehat{N}^\beta_{\widetilde{E}(\hbar)}\right)$ $(\cdot = P, B, N)$ *are expressed as follows;*

$$R\left(b_P|\widehat{N}^\beta_{\widetilde{E}(\hbar)}\right) = \left\{ \begin{pmatrix} \left(1 - \left(1 - \rho_\theta\left(\lambda_{PP}\right)^f\right)^{P_r\left(D|\widehat{N}^\beta_{\widetilde{E}(\hbar)}\right)} \left(1 - \rho_\theta\left(\lambda_{PN}\right)^f\right)^{P_r\left(\neg D|\widehat{N}^\beta_{\widetilde{E}(\hbar)}\right)}\right)^{\frac{1}{f}}, \\ \left(\check{n}_\theta\left(\lambda_{PP}\right)^{P_r\left(D|\widehat{N}^\beta_{\widetilde{E}(\hbar)}\right)} \check{n}_\theta\left(\lambda_{PN}\right)^{P_r\left(\neg D|\widehat{N}^\beta_{\widetilde{E}(\hbar)}\right)}\right), \\ \left(\nu_\theta\left(\lambda_{PP}\right)^{P_r\left(D|\widehat{N}^\beta_{\widetilde{E}(\hbar)}\right)} \nu_\theta\left(\lambda_{PN}\right)^{P_r\left(\neg D|\widehat{N}^\beta_{\widetilde{E}(\hbar)}\right)}\right) \end{pmatrix} \right\} \quad (28)$$

$$R\left(b_B|\widehat{N}^\beta_{\widetilde{E}(\hbar)}\right) = \left\{ \begin{pmatrix} \left(1 - \left(1 - \rho_\theta\left(\lambda_{BP}\right)^f\right)^{P_r\left(D|\widehat{N}^\beta_{\widetilde{E}(\hbar)}\right)} \left(1 - \rho_\theta\left(\lambda_{BN}\right)^f\right)^{P_r\left(\neg D|\widehat{N}^\beta_{\widetilde{E}(\hbar)}\right)}\right)^{\frac{1}{f}}, \\ \left(\check{n}_\theta\left(\lambda_{BP}\right)^{P_r\left(D|\widehat{N}^\beta_{\widetilde{E}(\hbar)}\right)} \check{n}_\theta\left(\lambda_{BN}\right)^{P_r\left(\neg D|\widehat{N}^\beta_{\widetilde{E}(\hbar)}\right)}\right), \\ \left(\nu_\theta\left(\lambda_{BP}\right)^{P_r\left(D|\widehat{N}^\beta_{\widetilde{E}(\hbar)}\right)} \nu_\theta\left(\lambda_{BN}\right)^{P_r\left(\neg D|\widehat{N}^\beta_{\widetilde{E}(\hbar)}\right)}\right) \end{pmatrix} \right\} \quad (29)$$

$$R\left(b_N|\widehat{N}^\beta_{\widetilde{E}(\hbar)}\right) = \left\{ \begin{pmatrix} \left(1 - \left(1 - \rho_\theta\left(\lambda_{PP}\right)^f\right)^{P_r\left(D|\widehat{N}^\beta_{\widetilde{E}(\hbar)}\right)} \left(1 - \rho_\theta\left(\lambda_{PN}\right)^f\right)^{P_r\left(\neg D|\widehat{N}^\beta_{\widetilde{E}(\hbar)}\right)}\right)^{\frac{1}{f}}, \\ \left(\check{n}_\theta\left(\lambda_{NP}\right)^{P_r\left(D|\widehat{N}^\beta_{\widetilde{E}(\hbar)}\right)} \check{n}_\theta\left(\lambda_{NN}\right)^{P_r\left(\neg D|\widehat{N}^\beta_{\widetilde{E}(\hbar)}\right)}\right), \\ \left(\nu_\theta\left(\lambda_{NP}\right)^{P_r\left(D|\widehat{N}^\beta_{\widetilde{E}(\hbar)}\right)} \nu_\theta\left(\lambda_{NN}\right)^{P_r\left(\neg D|\widehat{N}^\beta_{\widetilde{E}(\hbar)}\right)}\right) \end{pmatrix} \right\}. \quad (30)$$

As can be seen from Proposition (3), the following results hold.

Proposition 4. Based on (28)–(30), the expected losses $R\left(b.|\widehat{N}^{\beta}_{\widetilde{E}(\hbar)}\right)$ $(\cdot = P, B, N)$ are calculated as follows;

$$R\left(b_N|\widehat{N}^{\beta}_{\widetilde{E}(\hbar)}\right) = \left\{\begin{array}{c} \left(1-\left(1-\rho_\theta\left(\lambda.p\right)^f\right)^{P_r\left(D|\widehat{N}^{\beta}_{\widetilde{E}(\hbar)}\right)}\left(1-\rho_\theta\left(\lambda.N\right)^f\right)^{P_r\left(\neg D|\widehat{N}^{\beta}_{\widetilde{E}(\hbar)}\right)}\right)^{\frac{1}{f}}, \\ \left(\check{n}_\theta\left(\lambda.p\right)^{P_r\left(D|\widehat{N}^{\beta}_{\widetilde{E}(\hbar)}\right)}\check{n}_\theta\left(\lambda.N\right)^{P_r\left(\neg D|\widehat{N}^{\beta}_{\widetilde{E}(\hbar)}\right)}\right), \\ \left(\nu_\theta\left(\lambda.p\right)^{P_r\left(D|\widehat{N}^{\beta}_{\widetilde{E}(\hbar)}\right)}\nu_\theta\left(\lambda.N\right)^{P_r\left(\neg D|\widehat{N}^{\beta}_{\widetilde{E}(\hbar)}\right)}\right) \end{array}\right\}$$

$$= (\rho., \check{n}., \nu.) \,(\cdot = P, B, N)$$

We give the following minimum cost decision rules under FOF environment as per the Bayesian decision-making process;

(P). If $R\left(b_P|\widehat{N}^{\beta}_{\widetilde{E}(\hbar)}\right) \leq R\left(b_B|\widehat{N}^{\beta}_{\widetilde{E}(\hbar)}\right)$ and $R\left(b_P|\widehat{N}^{\beta}_{\widetilde{E}(\hbar)}\right) \leq R\left(b_N|\widehat{N}^{\beta}_{\widetilde{E}(\hbar)}\right)$, decide $\hbar \in POS\,(D)$;

(B). If $R\left(b_B|\widehat{N}^{\beta}_{\widetilde{E}(\hbar)}\right) \leq R\left(b_P|\widehat{N}^{\beta}_{\widetilde{E}(\hbar)}\right)$ and $R\left(b_B|\widehat{N}^{\beta}_{\widetilde{E}(\hbar)}\right) \leq R\left(b_N|\widehat{N}^{\beta}_{\widetilde{E}(\hbar)}\right)$, decide $\hbar \in BND\,(D)$;

(N). If $R\left(b_N|\widehat{N}^{\beta}_{\widetilde{E}(\hbar)}\right) \leq R\left(b_B|\widehat{N}^{\beta}_{\widetilde{E}(\hbar)}\right)$ and $R\left(b_N|\widehat{N}^{\beta}_{\widetilde{E}(\hbar)}\right) \leq R\left(b_P|\widehat{N}^{\beta}_{\widetilde{E}(\hbar)}\right)$, decide $\hbar \in NEG\,(D)$;

where $R\left(b_P|\widehat{N}^{\beta}_{\widetilde{E}(\hbar)}\right)$, $R\left(b_B|\widehat{N}^{\beta}_{\widetilde{E}(\hbar)}\right)$ and $R\left(b_N|\widehat{N}^{\beta}_{\widetilde{E}(\hbar)}\right)$ are FOFNs. According to the above results, the researches on the decision rules $(P) - (N)$ are further conducted by using (28)–(30), as per the operations of FOFNs.

5.1. Decision-Making Analysis of FOFCDTRS

In Section 4, we construct a FOFCDTRS model. At the same time, the decision rules $(P) - (N)$ are put forward. Since the expected losses of FOFCDTRS cannot be directly compared, we need to further investigate the decision rules $(P) - (N)$ as per the operations of FOFNs. A FOFN characterized both by positive, neutral and negative, gives a way to calculate the decision problem with the positive, neutral and the negative viewpoints. In this section, we defined five methods to deduce Three-way decisions with FOFCDTRS.

5.1.1. Method 1: A Positive Viewpoint

For decision rules $(P) - (N)$, the expected losses $R\left(b.|\widehat{N}^{\beta}_{\widetilde{E}(\hbar)}\right) = (\rho., \check{n}., \nu.)\,(\cdot = P, B, N)$ are FOFNs. With regard to the positive viewpoint, we directly utilize the positive degree of FOFNs to represent the expected losses. When we compare the expected losses, the positive degree of the expected losses keep in step with them. According to this scenario, decision rules $(P) - (N)$ can be re-expressed as;

(P_1). If $\rho^f_P \leq \rho^f_B$ and $\rho^f_P \leq \rho^f_N$, decide $\hbar \in POS\,(D)$;
(B_1). If $\rho^f_B \leq \rho^f_P$ and $\rho^f_B \leq \rho^f_N$, decide $\hbar \in BND\,(D)$;
(N_1). If $\rho^f_N \leq \rho^f_P$ and $\rho^f_N \leq \rho^f_B$, decide $\hbar \in NEG\,(D)$;

where, $\rho. = \left(1-\left(1-\rho_\theta\left(\lambda.p\right)^f\right)^{P_r\left(D|\widehat{N}^{\beta}_{\widetilde{E}(\hbar)}\right)}\left(1-\rho_\theta\left(\lambda.N\right)^f\right)^{P_r\left(\neg D|\widehat{N}^{\beta}_{\widetilde{E}(\hbar)}\right)}\right)^{\frac{1}{f}}$ $(\cdot = P, B, N)$. With the conditions (14) and (17), we simplify the decision rules $(P_1) - (N_1)$. For the rule (P_1), the first condition is expressed as:

$$\rho_P^f \leq \rho_B^f \Leftrightarrow 1 - \left(1 - \rho_\theta\left(\lambda_{PP}\right)^f\right)^{\Pr\left(D|\hat{N}_{\tilde{E}(\hbar)}^\beta\right)} \left(1 - \rho_\theta\left(\lambda_{PN}\right)^f\right)^{\Pr\left(\neg D|\hat{N}_{\tilde{E}(\hbar)}^\beta\right)}$$

$$\leq 1 - \left(1 - \rho_\theta\left(\lambda_{BP}\right)^f\right)^{\Pr\left(D|\hat{N}_{\tilde{E}(\hbar)}^\beta\right)} \left(1 - \rho_\theta\left(\lambda_{BN}\right)^f\right)^{\Pr\left(\neg D|\hat{N}_{\tilde{E}(\hbar)}^\beta\right)}$$

$$\Leftrightarrow \left(1 - \rho_\theta\left(\lambda_{PP}\right)^f\right)^{\Pr\left(D|\hat{N}_{\tilde{E}(\hbar)}^\beta\right)} \left(1 - \rho_\theta\left(\lambda_{PN}\right)^f\right)^{\Pr\left(\neg D|\hat{N}_{\tilde{E}(\hbar)}^\beta\right)}$$

$$\geq \left(1 - \rho_\theta\left(\lambda_{BP}\right)^f\right)^{\Pr\left(D|\hat{N}_{\tilde{E}(\hbar)}^\beta\right)} \left(1 - \rho_\theta\left(\lambda_{BN}\right)^f\right)^{\Pr\left(\neg D|\hat{N}_{\tilde{E}(\hbar)}^\beta\right)}$$

$$\Leftrightarrow \log\left(\left(1 - \rho_\theta\left(\lambda_{PP}\right)^f\right)^{\Pr\left(D|\hat{N}_{\tilde{E}(\hbar)}^\beta\right)} \left(1 - \rho_\theta\left(\lambda_{PN}\right)^f\right)^{\Pr\left(\neg D|\hat{N}_{\tilde{E}(\hbar)}^\beta\right)}\right)$$

$$\geq \log\left(\left(1 - \rho_\theta\left(\lambda_{BP}\right)^f\right)^{\Pr\left(D|\hat{N}_{\tilde{E}(\hbar)}^\beta\right)} \left(1 - \rho_\theta\left(\lambda_{BN}\right)^f\right)^{\Pr\left(\neg D|\hat{N}_{\tilde{E}(\hbar)}^\beta\right)}\right)$$

$$\Leftrightarrow \log\left(\left(1 - \rho_\theta\left(\lambda_{PP}\right)^f\right)^{\Pr\left(D|\hat{N}_{\tilde{E}(\hbar)}^\beta\right)}\right) + \left(\log\left(1 - \rho_\theta\left(\lambda_{PN}\right)^f\right)^{\Pr\left(\neg D|\hat{N}_{\tilde{E}(\hbar)}^\beta\right)}\right)$$

$$\geq \log\left(\left(1 - \rho_\theta\left(\lambda_{BP}\right)^f\right)^{\Pr\left(D|\hat{N}_{\tilde{E}(\hbar)}^\beta\right)}\right) + \left(\log\left(1 - \rho_\theta\left(\lambda_{BN}\right)^f\right)^{\Pr\left(\neg D|\hat{N}_{\tilde{E}(\hbar)}^\beta\right)}\right)$$

$$\Leftrightarrow \Pr\left(D|\hat{N}_{\tilde{E}(\hbar)}^\beta\right) \log\left(1 - \rho_\theta\left(\lambda_{PP}\right)^f\right) + \Pr\left(\neg D|\hat{N}_{\tilde{E}(\hbar)}^\beta\right) \log\left(1 - \rho_\theta\left(\lambda_{PN}\right)^f\right)$$

$$\geq \Pr\left(D|\hat{N}_{\tilde{E}(\hbar)}^\beta\right) \log\left(1 - \rho_\theta\left(\lambda_{BP}\right)^f\right) + \Pr\left(\neg D|\hat{N}_{\tilde{E}(\hbar)}^\beta\right) \log\left(1 - \rho_\theta\left(\lambda_{BN}\right)^f\right)$$

$$\Leftrightarrow \Pr\left(D|\hat{N}_{\tilde{E}(\hbar)}^\beta\right) \geq \log\left(\frac{1 - \rho_\theta\left(\lambda_{BN}\right)^f}{1 - \rho_\theta\left(\lambda_{PN}\right)^f}\right) \Big/ \log\left(\frac{1 - \rho_\theta\left(\lambda_{PP}\right)^f * 1 - \rho_\theta\left(\lambda_{BN}\right)^f}{1 - \rho_\theta\left(\lambda_{PN}\right)^f * 1 - \rho_\theta\left(\lambda_{BP}\right)^f}\right)$$

Similarly, the second condition of rule (P_1) can be expressed as:

$$\rho_P^f \leq \rho_N^f \Leftrightarrow 1 - \left(1 - \rho_\theta\left(\lambda_{PP}\right)^f\right)^{\Pr\left(D|\hat{N}_{\tilde{E}(\hbar)}^\beta\right)} \left(1 - \rho_\theta\left(\lambda_{PN}\right)^f\right)^{\Pr\left(\neg D|\hat{N}_{\tilde{E}(\hbar)}^\beta\right)}$$

$$\leq 1 - \left(1 - \rho_\theta\left(\lambda_{NP}\right)^f\right)^{\Pr\left(D|\hat{N}_{\tilde{E}(\hbar)}^\beta\right)} \left(1 - \rho_\theta\left(\lambda_{NN}\right)^f\right)^{\Pr\left(\neg D|\hat{N}_{\tilde{E}(\hbar)}^\beta\right)}$$

$$\Leftrightarrow \Pr\left(D|\hat{N}_{\tilde{E}(\hbar)}^\beta\right) \geq \log\left(\frac{1 - \rho_\theta\left(\lambda_{NN}\right)^f}{1 - \rho_\theta\left(\lambda_{PN}\right)^f}\right) \Big/ \log\left(\frac{1 - \rho_\theta\left(\lambda_{PP}\right)^f * 1 - \rho_\theta\left(\lambda_{NN}\right)^f}{1 - \rho_\theta\left(\lambda_{PN}\right)^f * 1 - \rho_\theta\left(\lambda_{NP}\right)^f}\right)$$

The first condition of rule (B_1) is the converse of the first condition of rule (P_1). It follows,

$$\rho_B^f \leq \rho_P^f \Leftrightarrow \Pr\left(D|\hat{N}_{\tilde{E}(\hbar)}^\beta\right) \geq \log\left(\frac{1 - \rho_\theta\left(\lambda_{BN}\right)^f}{1 - \rho_\theta\left(\lambda_{PN}\right)^f}\right) \Big/ \log\left(\frac{1 - \rho_\theta\left(\lambda_{PP}\right)^f * 1 - \rho_\theta\left(\lambda_{BN}\right)^f}{1 - \rho_\theta\left(\lambda_{PN}\right)^f * 1 - \rho_\theta\left(\lambda_{BP}\right)^f}\right).$$

For the second condition of rule (B_1), we have;

$$\rho_B^f \leq \rho_N^f \Leftrightarrow 1 - \left(1 - \rho_\theta\left(\lambda_{BP}\right)^f\right)^{P_r\left(D|\hat{N}_{\tilde{E}(\hbar)}^\beta\right)} \left(1 - \rho_\theta\left(\lambda_{BN}\right)^f\right)^{P_r\left(\neg D|\hat{N}_{\tilde{E}(\hbar)}^\beta\right)}$$

$$\leq 1 - \left(1 - \rho_\theta\left(\lambda_{NP}\right)^f\right)^{P_r\left(D|\hat{N}_{\tilde{E}(\hbar)}^\beta\right)} \left(1 - \rho_\theta\left(\lambda_{NN}\right)^f\right)^{P_r\left(\neg D|\hat{N}_{\tilde{E}(\hbar)}^\beta\right)}$$

$$\Leftrightarrow P_r\left(D|\hat{N}_{\tilde{E}(\hbar)}^\beta\right) \geq \log\left(\frac{1 - \rho_\theta\left(\lambda_{NN}\right)^f}{1 - \rho_\theta\left(\lambda_{BN}\right)^f}\right) / \log\left(\frac{1 - \rho_\theta\left(\lambda_{BP}\right)^f \ast 1 - \rho_\theta\left(\lambda_{NN}\right)^f}{1 - \rho_\theta\left(\lambda_{BN}\right)^f \ast 1 - \rho_\theta\left(\lambda_{NP}\right)^f}\right)$$

The first condition of rule (N_1) is the converse of the second condition of rule (P_1) and the second condition of rule (N_1) is the converse of the second condition of rule (B_1). It follows,

$$\rho_N^f \leq \rho_P^f \Leftrightarrow$$

$$P_r\left(D|\hat{N}_{\tilde{E}(\hbar)}^\beta\right) \geq \log\left(\frac{1 - \rho_\theta\left(\lambda_{NN}\right)^f}{1 - \rho_\theta\left(\lambda_{PN}\right)^f}\right) / \log\left(\frac{1 - \rho_\theta\left(\lambda_{PP}\right)^f \ast 1 - \rho_\theta\left(\lambda_{NN}\right)^f}{1 - \rho_\theta\left(\lambda_{PN}\right)^f \ast 1 - \rho_\theta\left(\lambda_{NP}\right)^f}\right)$$

$$\rho_N^f \leq \rho_B^f \Leftrightarrow$$

$$P_r\left(D|\hat{N}_{\tilde{E}(\hbar)}^\beta\right) \geq \log\left(\frac{1 - \rho_\theta\left(\lambda_{NN}\right)^f}{1 - \rho_\theta\left(\lambda_{BN}\right)^f}\right) / \log\left(\frac{1 - \rho_\theta\left(\lambda_{BP}\right)^f \ast 1 - \rho_\theta\left(\lambda_{NN}\right)^f}{1 - \rho_\theta\left(\lambda_{BN}\right)^f \ast 1 - \rho_\theta\left(\lambda_{NP}\right)^f}\right)$$

On basis of the derivation of decision rules $(P_1) - (N_1)$, we denote the three expressions in these conditions by the following three thresholds;

$$\alpha_1 = \log\left(\frac{1 - \rho_\theta\left(\lambda_{BN}\right)^f}{1 - \rho_\theta\left(\lambda_{PN}\right)^f}\right) / \log\left(\frac{1 - \rho_\theta\left(\lambda_{PP}\right)^f \ast 1 - \rho_\theta\left(\lambda_{BN}\right)^f}{1 - \rho_\theta\left(\lambda_{PN}\right)^f \ast 1 - \rho_\theta\left(\lambda_{BP}\right)^f}\right) \quad (31)$$

$$\beta_1 = \log\left(\frac{1 - \rho_\theta\left(\lambda_{NN}\right)^f}{1 - \rho_\theta\left(\lambda_{BN}\right)^f}\right) / \log\left(\frac{1 - \rho_\theta\left(\lambda_{BP}\right)^f \ast 1 - \rho_\theta\left(\lambda_{NN}\right)^f}{1 - \rho_\theta\left(\lambda_{BN}\right)^f \ast 1 - \rho_\theta\left(\lambda_{NP}\right)^f}\right) \quad (32)$$

$$\gamma_1 = \log\left(\frac{1 - \rho_\theta\left(\lambda_{NN}\right)^f}{1 - \rho_\theta\left(\lambda_{PN}\right)^f}\right) / \log\left(\frac{1 - \rho_\theta\left(\lambda_{PP}\right)^f \ast 1 - \rho_\theta\left(\lambda_{NN}\right)^f}{1 - \rho_\theta\left(\lambda_{PN}\right)^f \ast 1 - \rho_\theta\left(\lambda_{NP}\right)^f}\right) \quad (33)$$

Then, the decision rules $(P_1) - (N_1)$, can be re-expressed concisely as;

(P_1). If $P_r\left(D|\hat{N}_{\tilde{E}(\hbar)}^\beta\right) \geq \alpha_1$ and $P_r\left(D|\hat{N}_{\tilde{E}(\hbar)}^\beta\right) \geq \gamma_1$, decide $\hbar \in POS(D)$;

(B_1). If $P_r\left(D|\hat{N}_{\tilde{E}(\hbar)}^\beta\right) \leq \alpha_1$ and $P_r\left(D|\hat{N}_{\tilde{E}(\hbar)}^\beta\right) \geq \beta_1$, decide $\hbar \in BND(D)$;

(N_1). If $P_r\left(D|\hat{N}_{\tilde{E}(\hbar)}^\beta\right) \leq \beta_1$ and $P_r\left(D|\hat{N}_{\tilde{E}(\hbar)}^\beta\right) \leq \gamma_1$, decide $\hbar \in NEG(D)$;

From the positive viewpoint, we finally determine the decision rule of the object $\hbar$ by comparing the conditional probability $P_r\left(D|\hat{N}_{\tilde{E}(\hbar)}^\beta\right)$ and the thresholds $(\alpha_1, \beta_1, \gamma_1)$.

5.1.2. Method 2: A Neutral Viewpoint

For decision rules $(P) - (N)$, the expected losses are $R\left(b.|\hat{N}_{\tilde{E}(\hbar)}^\beta\right) = (\rho., \check{n}., \nu.)$ $(\cdot = P, B, N)$. With regard to the neutral viewpoint, we straightly adopt the neutral degree of FOFNs to analyze decision rules $(P) - (N)$. Under this situation, the neutral degree of the expected loss have opposite directions with the expected losses. Following this scenario decision rules $(P) - (N)$ can be expressed as:

(P_2). If $\check{n}_P^f \leq \check{n}_B^f$ and $\check{n}_P^f \leq \check{n}_N^f$, decide $\hbar \in POS(D)$;
(B_2). If $\check{n}_B^f \leq \check{n}_P^f$ and $\check{n}_B^f \leq \check{n}_N^f$, decide $\hbar \in BND(D)$;
(N_2). If $\check{n}_N^f \leq \check{n}_P^f$ and $\check{n}_N^f \leq \check{n}_B^f$, decide $\hbar \in NEG(D)$;

where, $\check{n}. = \check{n}_\theta(\lambda.p)^{P_r(D|\hat{N}^\beta_{\tilde{E}(\hbar)})} \check{n}_\theta(\lambda.N)^{P_r(\neg D|\hat{N}^\beta_{\tilde{E}(\hbar)})}$ $(· = P, B, N)$. Under conditions of (15) and (18), we simplify the decision rules $(P_2) - (N_2)$. For the rule (P_2), the first condition is expressed as:

$$\check{n}^f_P \leq \check{n}^f_B \Leftrightarrow \check{n}_\theta(\lambda_{PP})^{f.P_r(D|\hat{N}^\beta_{\tilde{E}(\hbar)})} \check{n}_\theta(\lambda_{PN}) f.^{P_r(\neg D|\hat{N}^\beta_{\tilde{E}(\hbar)})}$$

$$\geq \check{n}_\theta(\lambda_{BP})^{f.P_r(D|\hat{N}^\beta_{\tilde{E}(\hbar)})} \check{n}_\theta(\lambda_{BN}) f.^{P_r(\neg D|\hat{N}^\beta_{\tilde{E}(\hbar)})}$$

$$\Leftrightarrow \check{n}_\theta(\lambda_{PP})^{f.P_r(D|\hat{N}^\beta_{\tilde{E}(\hbar)})} \check{n}_\theta(\lambda_{PN})^{f.P_r(\neg D|\hat{N}^\beta_{\tilde{E}(\hbar)})}$$

$$\geq \check{n}_\theta(\lambda_{BP})^{f.P_r(D|\hat{N}^\beta_{\tilde{E}(\hbar)})} \check{n}_\theta(\lambda_{BN})^{f.P_r(\neg D|\hat{N}^\beta_{\tilde{E}(\hbar)})}$$

$$\Leftrightarrow \log\left(\check{n}_\theta(\lambda_{PP})^{f.P_r(D|\hat{N}^\beta_{\tilde{E}(\hbar)})} \check{n}_\theta(\lambda_{PN})^{f.P_r(\neg D|\hat{N}^\beta_{\tilde{E}(\hbar)})}\right)$$

$$\geq \log\left(\check{n}_\theta(\lambda_{BP})^{f.P_r(D|\hat{N}^\beta_{\tilde{E}(\hbar)})} \check{n}_\theta(\lambda_{BN})^{f.P_r(\neg D|\hat{N}^\beta_{\tilde{E}(\hbar)})}\right)$$

$$\Leftrightarrow \log\left(\check{n}_\theta(\lambda_{PP})^{f.P_r(D|\hat{N}^\beta_{\tilde{E}(\hbar)})}\right) + \log\left(\check{n}_\theta(\lambda_{PN})^{f.P_r(\neg D|\hat{N}^\beta_{\tilde{E}(\hbar)})}\right)$$

$$\geq \log\left(\check{n}_\theta(\lambda_{BP})^{f.P_r(D|\hat{N}^\beta_{\tilde{E}(\hbar)})}\right) + \log\left(\check{n}_\theta(\lambda_{BN})^{f.P_r(\neg D|\hat{N}^\beta_{\tilde{E}(\hbar)})}\right)$$

$$\Leftrightarrow f.P_r\left(D|\hat{N}^\beta_{\tilde{E}(\hbar)}\right) \log(\check{n}_\theta(\lambda_{PP})) + f.P_r\left(\neg D|\hat{N}^\beta_{\tilde{E}(\hbar)}\right) \log(\check{n}_\theta(\lambda_{PN}))$$

$$\geq f.P_r\left(D|\hat{N}^\beta_{\tilde{E}(\hbar)}\right) \log(\check{n}_\theta(\lambda_{BP})) + f.P_r\left(\neg D|\hat{N}^\beta_{\tilde{E}(\hbar)}\right) \log(\check{n}_\theta(\lambda_{BN}))$$

$$\Leftrightarrow P_r\left(D|\hat{N}^\beta_{\tilde{E}(\hbar)}\right) \geq \log\left(\frac{\check{n}_\theta(\lambda_{BN})}{\check{n}_\theta(\lambda_{PN})}\right) / \log\left(\frac{\check{n}_\theta(\lambda_{PP}) * \check{n}_\theta(\lambda_{BN})}{\check{n}_\theta(\lambda_{PN}) * \check{n}_\theta(\lambda_{BP})}\right)$$

Similarly, the second condition of rule (P_2) can be expressed as:

$$\check{n}^f_P \leq \check{n}^f_N \Leftrightarrow \check{n}_\theta(\lambda_{PP})^{f.P_r(D|\hat{N}^\beta_{\tilde{E}(\hbar)})} \check{n}_\theta(\lambda_{PN})^{f.P_r(\neg D|\hat{N}^\beta_{\tilde{E}(\hbar)})}$$

$$\leq \check{n}_\theta(\lambda_{NP})^{f.P_r(D|\hat{N}^\beta_{\tilde{E}(\hbar)})} \check{n}_\theta(\lambda_{NN})^{f.P_r(\neg D|\hat{N}^\beta_{\tilde{E}(\hbar)})}$$

$$\Leftrightarrow P_r\left(D|\hat{N}^\beta_{\tilde{E}(\hbar)}\right) \geq \log\left(\frac{\check{n}_\theta(\lambda_{NN})}{\check{n}_\theta(\lambda_{PN})}\right) / \log\left(\frac{\check{n}_\theta(\lambda_{PP}) * \check{n}_\theta(\lambda_{NN})}{\check{n}_\theta(\lambda_{PN}) * \check{n}_\theta(\lambda_{NP})}\right)$$

The first condition of rule (B_2) is the converse of the first condition of rule (P_2). It follows,

$$\check{n}^f_B \leq \check{n}^f_P \Leftrightarrow P_r\left(D|\hat{N}^\beta_{\tilde{E}(\hbar)}\right) \geq \log\left(\frac{\check{n}_\theta(\lambda_{BN})}{\check{n}_\theta(\lambda_{PN})}\right) / \log\left(\frac{\check{n}_\theta(\lambda_{PP}) * \check{n}_\theta(\lambda_{BN})}{\check{n}_\theta(\lambda_{PN}) * \check{n}_\theta(\lambda_{BP})}\right).$$

For the second condition of rule (B_2), we have;

$$\check{n}^f_B \leq \check{n}^f_N \Leftrightarrow \check{n}_\theta(\lambda_{BP})^{f.P_r(D|\hat{N}^\beta_{\tilde{E}(\hbar)})} \check{n}_\theta(\lambda_{BN})^{f.P_r(\neg D|\hat{N}^\beta_{\tilde{E}(\hbar)})}$$

$$\leq \check{n}_\theta(\lambda_{NP})^{f.P_r(D|\hat{N}^\beta_{\tilde{E}(\hbar)})} \check{n}_\theta(\lambda_{NN})^{f.P_r(\neg D|\hat{N}^\beta_{\tilde{E}(\hbar)})}$$

$$\Leftrightarrow P_r\left(D|\hat{N}^\beta_{\tilde{E}(\hbar)}\right) \geq \log\left(\frac{\check{n}_\theta(\lambda_{NN})}{\check{n}_\theta(\lambda_{BN})}\right) / \log\left(\frac{\check{n}_\theta(\lambda_{BP}) * \check{n}_\theta(\lambda_{NN})}{\check{n}_\theta(\lambda_{BN}) * \check{n}_\theta(\lambda_{NP})}\right)$$

The first condition of rule (N_2) is the converse of the second condition of rule (P_2) and the second condition of rule (N_2) is the converse of the second condition of rule (B_2). It follows,

$$\check{n}_N^f \leq \check{n}_P^f \Leftrightarrow$$

$$P_r\left(D|\widehat{N}_{\tilde{E}(\hbar)}^\beta\right) \geq \log\left(\frac{\check{n}_\theta(\lambda_{NN})}{\check{n}_\theta(\lambda_{PN})}\right) / \log\left(\frac{\check{n}_\theta(\lambda_{PP}) * \check{n}_\theta(\lambda_{NN})}{\check{n}_\theta(\lambda_{PN}) * \check{n}_\theta(\lambda_{NP})}\right)$$

$$\check{n}_N^f \leq \check{n}_B^f \Leftrightarrow$$

$$P_r\left(D|\widehat{N}_{\tilde{E}(\hbar)}^\beta\right) \geq \log\left(\frac{\check{n}_\theta(\lambda_{NN})}{\check{n}_\theta(\lambda_{BN})}\right) / \log\left(\frac{\check{n}_\theta(\lambda_{BP}) * \check{n}_\theta(\lambda_{NN})}{\check{n}_\theta(\lambda_{BN}) * \check{n}_\theta(\lambda_{NP})}\right)$$

For the decision rules $(P_2) - (N_2)$, the three thresholds in these conditions are deduced as follows;

$$\alpha_2 = \log\left(\frac{\check{n}_\theta(\lambda_{BN})}{\check{n}_\theta(\lambda_{PN})}\right) / \log\left(\frac{\check{n}_\theta(\lambda_{PP}) * \check{n}_\theta(\lambda_{BN})}{\check{n}_\theta(\lambda_{PN}) * \check{n}_\theta(\lambda_{BP})}\right) \tag{34}$$

$$\beta_2 = \log\left(\frac{\check{n}_\theta(\lambda_{NN})}{\check{n}_\theta(\lambda_{BN})}\right) / \log\left(\frac{\check{n}_\theta(\lambda_{BP}) * \check{n}_\theta(\lambda_{NN})}{\check{n}_\theta(\lambda_{BN}) * \check{n}_\theta(\lambda_{NP})}\right) \tag{35}$$

$$\gamma_2 = \log\left(\frac{\check{n}_\theta(\lambda_{NN})}{\check{n}_\theta(\lambda_{PN})}\right) / \log\left(\frac{\check{n}_\theta(\lambda_{PP}) * \check{n}_\theta(\lambda_{NN})}{\check{n}_\theta(\lambda_{PN}) * \check{n}_\theta(\lambda_{NP})}\right) \tag{36}$$

Then, the decision rules $(P_2) - (N_2)$, can be re-expressed concisely as;

(P_2). If $P_r\left(D|\widehat{N}_{\tilde{E}(\hbar)}^\beta\right) \geq \alpha_2$ and $P_r\left(D|\widehat{N}_{\tilde{E}(\hbar)}^\beta\right) \geq \gamma_2$, decide $\hbar \in POS(D)$;

(B_2). If $P_r\left(D|\widehat{N}_{\tilde{E}(\hbar)}^\beta\right) \leq \alpha_2$ and $P_r\left(D|\widehat{N}_{\tilde{E}(\hbar)}^\beta\right) \geq \beta_2$, decide $\hbar \in BND(D)$;

(N_2). If $P_r\left(D|\widehat{N}_{\tilde{E}(\hbar)}^\beta\right) \leq \beta_2$ and $P_r\left(D|\widehat{N}_{\tilde{E}(\hbar)}^\beta\right) \leq \gamma_2$, decide $\hbar \in NEG(D)$;

From the neutral viewpoint, we finally determine the decision rule of the object $\hbar$ by comparing the conditional probability $P_r\left(D|\widehat{N}_{\tilde{E}(\hbar)}^\beta\right)$ and the thresholds $(\alpha_2, \beta_2, \gamma_2)$.

5.1.3. Method 3: A Negative Viewpoint

For decision rules $(P) - (N)$, the expected losses are $R\left(b.|\widehat{N}_{\tilde{E}(\hbar)}^\beta\right) = (\rho., \check{n}., \nu.)$ $(\cdot = P, B, N)$. With regard to the negative viewpoint, we straightly adopt the negative degree of FOFNs to analyze decision rules $(P) - (N)$. Under this situation, the negative degree of the expected losses have opposite directions with the expected losses. Following this scenario decision rules $(P) - (N)$ can be expressed as:

(P_3). If $\nu_P^f \leq \nu_B^f$ and $\nu_P^f \leq \nu_N^f$, decide $\hbar \in POS(D)$;

(B_3). If $\nu_B^f \leq \nu_P^f$ and $\check{n}_B^f \leq \nu_N^f$, decide $\hbar \in BND(D)$;

(N_3). If $\nu_N^f \leq \nu_P^f$ and $\nu_N^f \leq \nu_B^f$, decide $\hbar \in NEG(D)$;

where, $\nu. = \nu_\theta(\lambda_{\cdot P})^{P_r\left(D|\widehat{N}_{\tilde{E}(\hbar)}^\beta\right)} \nu_\theta(\lambda_{\cdot N})^{P_r\left(\neg D|\widehat{N}_{\tilde{E}(\hbar)}^\beta\right)}$ $(\cdot = P, B, N)$. Under conditions of (16) and (19), we simplify the decision rules $(P_3) - (N_3)$. For the rule (P_3), the first condition is written as:

$$v_P^f \leq v_B^f \Leftrightarrow v_\theta(\lambda_{PP})^{f.P_r\left(D|\hat{N}_{\bar{E}(\hbar)}^\beta\right)} v_\theta(\lambda_{PN}) f.^{P_r\left(\neg D|\hat{N}_{\bar{E}(\hbar)}^\beta\right)}$$

$$\geq v_\theta(\lambda_{BP})^{f.P_r\left(D|\hat{N}_{\bar{E}(\hbar)}^\beta\right)} v_\theta(\lambda_{BN})^{f.P_r\left(\neg D|\hat{N}_{\bar{E}(\hbar)}^\beta\right)}$$

$$\Leftrightarrow v_\theta(\lambda_{PP})^{f.P_r\left(D|\hat{N}_{\bar{E}(\hbar)}^\beta\right)} v_\theta(\lambda_{PN})^{f.P_r\left(\neg D|\hat{N}_{\bar{E}(\hbar)}^\beta\right)}$$

$$\geq v_\theta(\lambda_{BP})^{f.P_r\left(D|\hat{N}_{\bar{E}(\hbar)}^\beta\right)} v_\theta(\lambda_{BN})^{f.P_r\left(\neg D|\hat{N}_{\bar{E}(\hbar)}^\beta\right)}$$

$$\Leftrightarrow \log\left(v_\theta(\lambda_{PP})^{f.P_r\left(D|\hat{N}_{\bar{E}(\hbar)}^\beta\right)} v_\theta(\lambda_{PN})^{f.P_r\left(\neg D|\hat{N}_{\bar{E}(\hbar)}^\beta\right)}\right)$$

$$\geq \log\left(v_\theta(\lambda_{BP})^{f.P_r\left(D|\hat{N}_{\bar{E}(\hbar)}^\beta\right)} v_\theta(\lambda_{BN})^{f.P_r\left(\neg D|\hat{N}_{\bar{E}(\hbar)}^\beta\right)}\right)$$

$$\Leftrightarrow \log\left(v_\theta(\lambda_{PP})^{f.P_r\left(D|\hat{N}_{\bar{E}(\hbar)}^\beta\right)}\right) + \log\left(v_\theta(\lambda_{PN})^{f.P_r\left(\neg D|\hat{N}_{\bar{E}(\hbar)}^\beta\right)}\right)$$

$$\geq \log\left(v_\theta(\lambda_{BP})^{f.P_r\left(D|\hat{N}_{\bar{E}(\hbar)}^\beta\right)}\right) + \log\left(v_\theta(\lambda_{BN})^{f.P_r\left(\neg D|\hat{N}_{\bar{E}(\hbar)}^\beta\right)}\right)$$

$$\Leftrightarrow f.P_r\left(D|\hat{N}_{\bar{E}(\hbar)}^\beta\right) \log(v_\theta(\lambda_{PP})) + f.P_r\left(\neg D|\hat{N}_{\bar{E}(\hbar)}^\beta\right) \log(v_\theta(\lambda_{PN}))$$

$$\geq f.P_r\left(D|\hat{N}_{\bar{E}(\hbar)}^\beta\right) \log(v_\theta(\lambda_{BP})) + f.P_r\left(\neg D|\hat{N}_{\bar{E}(\hbar)}^\beta\right) \log(v_\theta(\lambda_{BN}))$$

$$\Leftrightarrow P_r\left(D|\hat{N}_{\bar{E}(\hbar)}^\beta\right) \geq \log\left(\frac{v_\theta(\lambda_{BN})}{v_\theta(\lambda_{PN})}\right) / \log\left(\frac{v_\theta(\lambda_{PP}) * v_\theta(\lambda_{BN})}{v_\theta(\lambda_{PN}) * v_\theta(\lambda_{BP})}\right)$$

Similarly, the second condition of rule (P_3) can be expressed as:

$$v_P^f \leq v_N^f \Leftrightarrow v_\theta(\lambda_{PP})^{f.P_r\left(D|\hat{N}_{\bar{E}(\hbar)}^\beta\right)} v_\theta(\lambda_{PN})^{f.P_r\left(\neg D|\hat{N}_{\bar{E}(\hbar)}^\beta\right)}$$

$$\leq v_\theta(\lambda_{NP})^{f.P_r\left(D|\hat{N}_{\bar{E}(\hbar)}^\beta\right)} \check{n}_\theta(\lambda_{NN})^{f.P_r\left(\neg D|\hat{N}_{\bar{E}(\hbar)}^\beta\right)}$$

$$\Leftrightarrow P_r\left(D|\hat{N}_{\bar{E}(\hbar)}^\beta\right) \geq \log\left(\frac{v_\theta(\lambda_{NN})}{v_\theta(\lambda_{PN})}\right) / \log\left(\frac{v_\theta(\lambda_{PP}) * v_\theta(\lambda_{NN})}{\check{n}_\theta(\lambda_{PN}) * v_\theta(\lambda_{NP})}\right)$$

The first condition of rule (B_3) is the converse of the first condition of rule (P_3). It follows,

$$v_B^f \leq v_P^f \Leftrightarrow P_r\left(D|\hat{N}_{\bar{E}(\hbar)}^\beta\right) \geq \log\left(\frac{v_\theta(\lambda_{BN})}{v_\theta(\lambda_{PN})}\right) / \log\left(\frac{v_\theta(\lambda_{PP}) * v_\theta(\lambda_{BN})}{v_\theta(\lambda_{PN}) * v_\theta(\lambda_{BP})}\right).$$

For the second condition of rule (B_3), we have;

$$v_B^f \leq v_N^f \Leftrightarrow v_\theta(\lambda_{BP})^{f.P_r\left(D|\hat{N}_{\bar{E}(\hbar)}^\beta\right)} v_\theta(\lambda_{BN})^{f.P_r\left(\neg D|\hat{N}_{\bar{E}(\hbar)}^\beta\right)}$$

$$\leq v_\theta(\lambda_{NP})^{f.P_r\left(D|\hat{N}_{\bar{E}(\hbar)}^\beta\right)} v_\theta(\lambda_{NN})^{f.P_r\left(\neg D|\hat{N}_{\bar{E}(\hbar)}^\beta\right)}$$

$$\Leftrightarrow P_r\left(D|\hat{N}_{\bar{E}(\hbar)}^\beta\right) \geq \log\left(\frac{v_\theta(\lambda_{NN})}{v_\theta(\lambda_{BN})}\right) / \log\left(\frac{v_\theta(\lambda_{BP}) * v_\theta(\lambda_{NN})}{v_\theta(\lambda_{BN}) * v_\theta(\lambda_{NP})}\right)$$

The first condition of rule (N_3) is the converse of the second condition of rule (P_3) and the second condition of rule (N_3) is the converse of the second condition of rule (B_3). It follows,

$$v_N^f \leq v_P^f \Leftrightarrow P_r\left(D|\widehat{N}_{\widetilde{E}(\hbar)}^\beta\right) \geq \log\left(\frac{v_\theta(\lambda_{NN})}{v_\theta(\lambda_{PN})}\right) / \log\left(\frac{v_\theta(\lambda_{PP}) * v_\theta(\lambda_{NN})}{v_\theta(\lambda_{PN}) * v_\theta(\lambda_{NP})}\right)$$

$$v_N^f \leq v_B^f \Leftrightarrow P_r\left(D|\widehat{N}_{\widetilde{E}(\hbar)}^\beta\right) \geq \log\left(\frac{v_\theta(\lambda_{NN})}{v_\theta(\lambda_{BN})}\right) / \log\left(\frac{v_\theta(\lambda_{BP}) * v_\theta(\lambda_{NN})}{v_\theta(\lambda_{BN}) * v_\theta(\lambda_{NP})}\right)$$

For the decision rules $(P_3) - (N_3)$, the three thresholds in these conditions are deduced as follows;

$$\alpha_3 = \log\left(\frac{v_\theta(\lambda_{BN})}{v_\theta(\lambda_{PN})}\right) / \log\left(\frac{v_\theta(\lambda_{PP}) * v_\theta(\lambda_{BN})}{v_\theta(\lambda_{PN}) * v_\theta(\lambda_{BP})}\right) \tag{37}$$

$$\beta_3 = \log\left(\frac{v_\theta(\lambda_{NN})}{v_\theta(\lambda_{BN})}\right) / \log\left(\frac{v_\theta(\lambda_{BP}) * v_\theta(\lambda_{NN})}{v_\theta(\lambda_{BN}) * v_\theta(\lambda_{NP})}\right) \tag{38}$$

$$\gamma_3 = \log\left(\frac{v_\theta(\lambda_{NN})}{v_\theta(\lambda_{PN})}\right) / \log\left(\frac{v_\theta(\lambda_{PP}) * v_\theta(\lambda_{NN})}{v_\theta(\lambda_{PN}) * v_\theta(\lambda_{NP})}\right) \tag{39}$$

Then, the decision rules $(P_3) - (N_3)$, can be re-expressed concisely as;

(P_3). If $P_r\left(D|\widehat{N}_{\widetilde{E}(\hbar)}^\beta\right) \geq \alpha_3$ and $P_r\left(D|\widehat{N}_{\widetilde{E}(\hbar)}^\beta\right) \geq \gamma_3$, decide $\hbar \in POS(D)$;

(B_3). If $P_r\left(D|\widehat{N}_{\widetilde{E}(\hbar)}^\beta\right) \leq \alpha_3$ and $P_r\left(D|\widehat{N}_{\widetilde{E}(\hbar)}^\beta\right) \geq \beta_3$, decide $\hbar \in BND(D)$;

(N_3). If $P_r\left(D|\widehat{N}_{\widetilde{E}(\hbar)}^\beta\right) \leq \beta_3$ and $P_r\left(D|\widehat{N}_{\widetilde{E}(\hbar)}^\beta\right) \leq \gamma_3$, decide $\hbar \in NEG(D)$;

From the negative viewpoint, we finally drive the decision rule of the object $\hbar$ by comparing the conditional probability $P_r\left(D|\widehat{N}_{\widetilde{E}(\hbar)}^\beta\right)$ and the thresholds $(\alpha_3, \beta_3, \gamma_3)$.

5.1.4. Method 4–5: Based on Composite Viewpoint

With regards to Method 1, 2 and 3, it merely uses the positive neutral and negative degrees of FOFNs to generate decision rules with the positive viewpoint. From the Example 2, we find the inconsistency of Method 1, 2 and 3. For solving this problem, we required to synchronously consider the positive degree, neutral degree and the negative degree of FOFNs, which is known as a composite viewpoint. In order to compare the expected losses $R\left(b_\cdot|\widehat{N}_{\widetilde{E}(\hbar)}^\beta\right) = (\rho_\cdot, \check{n}_\cdot, v_\cdot)$ $(\cdot = P, B, N)$, we introduce three different functions that compare the size of FOFNs. The first one is the score and the accuracy function, the second one is closeness index. These two methods are introduced as follows:

Method 4

In light of Definition (12), the score functions of the expected losses can be obtained as follows;

$$S\left(R\left(b_P|\widehat{N}_{\widetilde{E}(\hbar)}^\beta\right)\right) = \rho_P(\hbar)^f - \check{n}_P(\hbar)^f - v_P(\hbar)^f \tag{40}$$

$$S\left(R\left(b_B|\widehat{N}_{\widetilde{E}(\hbar)}^\beta\right)\right) = \rho_B(\hbar)^f - \check{n}_B(\hbar)^f - v_B(\hbar)^f \tag{41}$$

$$S\left(R\left(b_N|\widehat{N}_{\widetilde{E}(\hbar)}^\beta\right)\right) = \rho_N(\hbar)^f - \check{n}_N(\hbar)^f - v_N(\hbar)^f \tag{42}$$

where $\rho.$ = $\left(1-\left(1-\rho_\theta\left(\lambda.p\right)^f\right)^{P_r\left(D|\widehat{N}^\beta_{\widetilde{E}(\hbar)}\right)}\left(1-\rho_\theta\left(\lambda.N\right)^f\right)^{P_r\left(\neg D|\widehat{N}^\beta_{\widetilde{E}(\hbar)}\right)}\right)^{\frac{1}{f}}$, $\check{n}.$ =

$\check{n}_\theta\left(\lambda.p\right)^{P_r\left(D|\widehat{N}^\beta_{\widetilde{E}(\hbar)}\right)}\check{n}_\theta\left(\lambda.N\right)^{P_r\left(\neg D|\widehat{N}^\beta_{\widetilde{E}(\hbar)}\right)}$ and $v.$ = $v_\theta\left(\lambda.p\right)^{P_r\left(D|\widehat{N}^\beta_{\widetilde{E}(\hbar)}\right)}v_\theta\left(\lambda.N\right)^{P_r\left(\neg D|\widehat{N}^\beta_{\widetilde{E}(\hbar)}\right)}$

$(\cdot = P, B, N)$. Meanwhile, the accuracy functions of the expected losses can also be computed:

$$H\left(R\left(b_P|\widehat{N}^\beta_{\widetilde{E}(\hbar)}\right)\right) = \rho_P\left(\hbar\right)^f + \check{n}_P\left(\hbar\right)^f + v_P\left(\hbar\right)^f \tag{43}$$

$$H\left(R\left(b_B|\widehat{N}^\beta_{\widetilde{E}(\hbar)}\right)\right) = \rho_B\left(\hbar\right)^f + \check{n}_B\left(\hbar\right)^f + v_B\left(\hbar\right)^f \tag{44}$$

$$H\left(R\left(b_N|\widehat{N}^\beta_{\widetilde{E}(\hbar)}\right)\right) = \rho_N\left(\hbar\right)^f + \check{n}_N\left(\hbar\right)^f + v_N\left(\hbar\right)^f \tag{45}$$

For the rule (P), the first condition $R\left(b_P|\widehat{N}^\beta_{\widetilde{E}(\hbar)}\right) \leq R\left(b_B|\widehat{N}^\beta_{\widetilde{E}(\hbar)}\right)$ implies the following prerequisites:

$(C_1).S\left(R\left(b_P|\widehat{N}^\beta_{\widetilde{E}(\hbar)}\right)\right) < S\left(R\left(b_B|\widehat{N}^\beta_{\widetilde{E}(\hbar)}\right)\right)$

$(C_2).S\left(R\left(b_P|\widehat{N}^\beta_{\widetilde{E}(\hbar)}\right)\right) = S\left(R\left(b_B|\widehat{N}^\beta_{\widetilde{E}(\hbar)}\right)\right) \wedge H\left(R\left(b_P|\widehat{N}^\beta_{\widetilde{E}(\hbar)}\right)\right)$
$\leq H\left(R\left(b_B|\widehat{N}^\beta_{\widetilde{E}(\hbar)}\right)\right)$

In the same way, the prerequisites for the second condition $R\left(b_P|\widehat{N}^\beta_{\widetilde{E}(\hbar)}\right) \leq R\left(b_N|\widehat{N}^\beta_{\widetilde{E}(\hbar)}\right)$ of rule (P) are

$(C_3).S\left(R\left(b_P|\widehat{N}^\beta_{\widetilde{E}(\hbar)}\right)\right) < S\left(R\left(b_N|\widehat{N}^\beta_{\widetilde{E}(\hbar)}\right)\right)$

$(C_4).S\left(R\left(b_P|\widehat{N}^\beta_{\widetilde{E}(\hbar)}\right)\right) = S\left(R\left(b_N|\widehat{N}^\beta_{\widetilde{E}(\hbar)}\right)\right) \wedge H\left(R\left(b_P|\widehat{N}^\beta_{\widetilde{E}(\hbar)}\right)\right)$
$\leq H\left(R\left(b_N|\widehat{N}^\beta_{\widetilde{E}(\hbar)}\right)\right)$

For the rule (B), we have

$(C_5).S\left(R\left(b_B|\widehat{N}^\beta_{\widetilde{E}(\hbar)}\right)\right) < S\left(R\left(b_P|\widehat{N}^\beta_{\widetilde{E}(\hbar)}\right)\right)$

$(C_6).S\left(R\left(b_B|\widehat{N}^\beta_{\widetilde{E}(\hbar)}\right)\right) = S\left(R\left(b_P|\widehat{N}^\beta_{\widetilde{E}(\hbar)}\right)\right) \wedge H\left(R\left(b_B|\widehat{N}^\beta_{\widetilde{E}(\hbar)}\right)\right)$
$\leq H\left(R\left(b_P|\widehat{N}^\beta_{\widetilde{E}(\hbar)}\right)\right)$

$(C_7).S\left(R\left(b_B|\widehat{N}^\beta_{\widetilde{E}(\hbar)}\right)\right) < S\left(R\left(b_N|\widehat{N}^\beta_{\widetilde{E}(\hbar)}\right)\right)$

$(C_8).S\left(R\left(b_B|\widehat{N}^\beta_{\widetilde{E}(\hbar)}\right)\right) = S\left(R\left(b_N|\widehat{N}^\beta_{\widetilde{E}(\hbar)}\right)\right) \wedge H\left(R\left(b_B|\widehat{N}^\beta_{\widetilde{E}(\hbar)}\right)\right)$
$\leq H\left(R\left(b_N|\widehat{N}^\beta_{\widetilde{E}(\hbar)}\right)\right)$

And for the rule (N), we have

$(C_9).S\left(R\left(b_N|\widehat{N}^\beta_{\widetilde{E}(\hbar)}\right)\right) < S\left(R\left(b_P|\widehat{N}^\beta_{\widetilde{E}(\hbar)}\right)\right)$

$(C_{10}).S\left(R\left(b_N|\widehat{N}^\beta_{\widetilde{E}(\hbar)}\right)\right) = S\left(R\left(b_P|\widehat{N}^\beta_{\widetilde{E}(\hbar)}\right)\right) \wedge H\left(R\left(b_N|\widehat{N}^\beta_{\widetilde{E}(\hbar)}\right)\right)$
$\leq H\left(R\left(b_P|\widehat{N}^\beta_{\widetilde{E}(\hbar)}\right)\right)$

$(C_{11}) . S\left(R\left(b_N | \hat{N}^{\beta}_{\tilde{E}(\hbar)}\right)\right) < S\left(R\left(b_B | \hat{N}^{\beta}_{\tilde{E}(\hbar)}\right)\right)$

$(C_{12}) . S\left(R\left(b_N | \hat{N}^{\beta}_{\tilde{E}(\hbar)}\right)\right) = S\left(R\left(b_B | \hat{N}^{\beta}_{\tilde{E}(\hbar)}\right)\right) \wedge H\left(R\left(b_N | \hat{N}^{\beta}_{\tilde{E}(\hbar)}\right)\right)$
$\leq H\left(R\left(b_B | \hat{N}^{\beta}_{\tilde{E}(\hbar)}\right)\right)$

Therefore, the decision rules $(P) - (N)$ can be re-expressed as $(P_4) - (N_4)$

(P_4). If $((C_1) \vee (C_2)) \wedge ((C_3) \vee (C_4))$, decide $\hbar \in POS(D)$;
(B_4). If $((C_5) \vee (C_6)) \wedge ((C_7) \vee (C_8))$, decide $\hbar \in POS(D)$;
(N_4). If $((C_9) \vee (C_{10})) \wedge ((C_{11}) \vee (C_{12}))$, decide $\hbar \in POS(D)$.

Method 5

In light of Definition (15), the closeness index of the expected losses can be determined as follows;

$$\Im\left(R\left(b_P | \hat{N}^{\beta}_{\tilde{E}(\hbar)}\right)\right) = \frac{1}{3}\left(1 + \rho_P(\hbar)^f - \check{n}_P(\hbar)^f - \nu_P(\hbar)^f\right) \tag{46}$$

$$\Im\left(R\left(b_B | \hat{N}^{\beta}_{\tilde{E}(\hbar)}\right)\right) = \frac{1}{3}\left(1 + \rho_B(\hbar)^f - \check{n}_B(\hbar)^f - \nu_B(\hbar)^f\right) \tag{47}$$

$$\Im\left(R\left(b_N | \hat{N}^{\beta}_{\tilde{E}(\hbar)}\right)\right) = \frac{1}{3}\left(1 + \rho_N(\hbar)^f - \check{n}_N(\hbar)^f - \nu_N(\hbar)^f\right) \tag{48}$$

where $\rho. = \left(1 - \left(1 - \rho_\theta(\lambda.P)^f\right)^{P_r\left(D|\hat{N}^{\beta}_{\tilde{E}(\hbar)}\right)}\left(1 - \rho_\theta(\lambda.N)^f\right)^{P_r\left(\neg D|\hat{N}^{\beta}_{\tilde{E}(\hbar)}\right)}\right)^{\frac{1}{f}}$, $\check{n}. =$

$\check{n}_\theta(\lambda.P)^{P_r\left(D|\hat{N}^{\beta}_{\tilde{E}(\hbar)}\right)} \check{n}_\theta(\lambda.N)^{P_r\left(\neg D|\hat{N}^{\beta}_{\tilde{E}(\hbar)}\right)}$ and $\nu. = \nu_\theta(\lambda.P)^{P_r\left(D|\hat{N}^{\beta}_{\tilde{E}(\hbar)}\right)} \nu_\theta(\lambda.N)^{P_r\left(\neg D|\hat{N}^{\beta}_{\tilde{E}(\hbar)}\right)}$
$(\cdot = P, B, N)$.

Therefore, the decision rules $(P) - (N)$ can be expressed as $(P_5) - (N_5)$:

(P_5). If

$\Im\left(R\left(b_P | \hat{N}^{\beta}_{\tilde{E}(\hbar)}\right)\right) \leq \Im\left(R\left(b_B | \hat{N}^{\beta}_{\tilde{E}(\hbar)}\right)\right)$ and
$\Im\left(R\left(b_P | \hat{N}^{\beta}_{\tilde{E}(\hbar)}\right)\right) \leq \Im\left(R\left(b_N | \hat{N}^{\beta}_{\tilde{E}(\hbar)}\right)\right)$, decide $\hbar \in POS(D)$;

(B_5). If

$\Im\left(R\left(b_B | \hat{N}^{\beta}_{\tilde{E}(\hbar)}\right)\right) \leq \Im\left(R\left(b_P | \hat{N}^{\beta}_{\tilde{E}(\hbar)}\right)\right)$ and
$\Im\left(R\left(b_B | \hat{N}^{\beta}_{\tilde{E}(\hbar)}\right)\right) \leq \Im\left(R\left(b_N | \hat{N}^{\beta}_{\tilde{E}(\hbar)}\right)\right)$, decide $\hbar \in BND(D)$;

(N_5). If

$\Im\left(R\left(b_N | \hat{N}^{\beta}_{\tilde{E}(\hbar)}\right)\right) \leq \Im\left(R\left(b_P | \hat{N}^{\beta}_{\tilde{E}(\hbar)}\right)\right)$ and
$\Im\left(R\left(b_N | \hat{N}^{\beta}_{\tilde{E}(\hbar)}\right)\right) \leq \Im\left(R\left(b_B | \hat{N}^{\beta}_{\tilde{E}(\hbar)}\right)\right)$, decide $\hbar \in NEG(D)$.

6. Algorithm for the Multi-Attribute Decision Making with FOFCDTRSs

Input Decision-making table with FOF information and loss functions with FOFNs for risk or cost of actions in different states;

Step 1. Obtain FOF β-neighborhood $\tilde{N}^{\beta}_{\tilde{E}(\hbar)}$ and FO β-neighborhood $\hat{N}^{\beta}_{\tilde{E}(\hbar)}$ from the given decision-making table with FOF information by using Definitions (1) and (17);

Step 2. Calculate the conditional probability $P_r\left(D | \hat{N}^{\beta}_{\tilde{E}(\hbar)}\right)$ by the Formula (13).

Step 3. Give loss function with FOFNs for risk or cost of actions in different states, and then calculate the values of the thresholds $(\alpha_1, \beta_1, \gamma_1), (\alpha_2, \beta_2, \gamma_2)$ and $(\alpha_3, \beta_3, \gamma_3)$ according to Formulas (31)–(39), respectively.

Step 4. Obtain the expected losses $R\left(b.|\widehat{N}^{\beta}_{\widetilde{E}(\hbar)}\right)$ $(\cdot = P, B, N)$ by using the Formulas (28)–(30). According to the Formulas (40)–(45) and (46)–(48), we further acquire the values of the score and the accuracy function $H\left(R\left(b.|\widehat{N}^{\beta}_{\widetilde{E}(\hbar)}\right)\right)$ and the closeness index function $\Im\left(R\left(b.|\widehat{N}^{\beta}_{\widetilde{E}(\hbar)}\right)\right)$.

Step 5. Based on the five methods in Section 5, the corresponding decision rules are used to calculate the positive domain POS (D), negative domain NEG (D) and boundary domain BND (D), respectively.

Step 6. Find and compare the optimal decision results.

6.1. An Illustrative Example

In this section, we will present the proposed MADM method based on FOFS models related to the evaluation and rank of heavy rainfall in the district of Lasbella district and adjoining areas of the Baluchistan, Pakistan.

A recent storm caused a spell of heavy rainfall in the Lasbella district, and adjoining areas of Baluchistan, Pakistan were hit with unprecedented flash floods in February 2019. In this flood a large number of roads which link the district of Lasbella with other parts of Baluchistan were destroyed. In this flood a large number of roads which link the district of Lasbella with other parts of Baluchistan were destroyed.

Such projects were carried out by a small number of well-established contractors, and the selection process was based solely on the tender price. In recent years, rising project complexity, technological capability, higher performance, security and financial requirements have demanded the use of multi-attribute decision-making methods. Pakistan's government has released a newspaper notice for this, and one construction company is responsible for choosing the best construction firm from a selection of six potential alternatives, $\hbar_1$ = Ahmed Construction, $\hbar_2$ = Matracon Pakistan Private (Pvt) Limited (Ltd), $\hbar_3$ = Eastern Highway Company, $\hbar_4$ = Banu Mukhtar Concrete Pvt. Ltd., $\hbar_5$ = Khyber Grace Pvt. Ltd., $\hbar_6$ = Experts Engineering services on the basis of the attributes, $\widetilde{E}_1$ = Technical capability, $\widetilde{E}_2$ = Higher performance, $\widetilde{E}_3$ = Safety, $\widetilde{E}_4$ = Financial requirements, $\widetilde{E}_5$ = Time saving, that is bid for these projects, and all criteria are of the type of benefit, so no need to normalized it. Then the Government's goal is to choose among them the best construction company for the task. Hence, as shown below, the following decision matrix was constructed given in Table 4:

Table 4. A tabular representation of FOFSs for $\widetilde{E}$.

	$\widetilde{E}_1$	$\widetilde{E}_2$	$\widetilde{E}_3$	$\widetilde{E}_4$	$\widetilde{E}_5$
$\hbar_1$	(0.9, 0.1, 0.2)	(0.8, 0.2, 0.5)	(0.7, 0.3, 0.5)	(0.8, 0.2, 0.5)	(0.9, 0.1, 0.3)
$\hbar_2$	(0.8, 0.2, 0.4)	(0.3, 0.4, 0.5)	(0.7, 0.5, 0.3)	(0.6, 0.2, 0.1)	(0.5, 0.6, 0.2)
$\hbar_3$	(0.9, 0.3, 0.1)	(0.6, 0.3, 0.5)	(0.7, 0.2, 0.4)	(0.3, 0.4, 0.1)	(0.5, 0.4, 0.6)
$\hbar_4$	(0.8, 0.1, 0.5)	(0.6, 0.2, 0.7)	(0.5, 0.3, 0.4)	(0.7, 0.3, 0.2)	(0.8, 0.4, 0.3)
$\hbar_5$	(0.6, 0.5, 0.2)	(0.9, 0.4, 0.3)	(0.5, 0.3, 0.7)	(0.3, 0.2, 0.1)	(0.8, 0.5, 0.2)
$\hbar_6$	(0.8, 0.3, 0.5)	(0.6, 0.3, 0.1)	(0.9, 0.3, 0.2)	(0.6, 0.2, 0.3)	(0.5, 0.1, 0.4)

Now, take the threshold $\beta = (0.6, 0.5, 0.4)$, then $\widetilde{E}$ is a FOF β-covering. Then, $\widetilde{N}^{(0.6,0.5,0.4)}_{\widetilde{E}(\hbar_1)} = \widetilde{E}_1 \cap \widetilde{E}_5$, $\widetilde{N}^{(0.6,0.5,0.4)}_{\widetilde{E}(\hbar_2)} = \widetilde{E}_1 \cap \widetilde{E}_3 \cap \widetilde{E}_4$, $\widetilde{N}^{(0.6,0.5,0.4)}_{\widetilde{E}(\hbar_3)} = \widetilde{E}_1 \cap \widetilde{E}_3$, $\widetilde{N}^{(0.6,0.5,0.4)}_{\widetilde{E}(\hbar_4)} = \widetilde{E}_4 \cap \widetilde{E}_5$, $\widetilde{N}^{(0.6,0.5,0.4)}_{\widetilde{E}(\hbar_5)} = \widetilde{E}_1 \cap \widetilde{E}_2 \cap \widetilde{E}_5$, $\widetilde{N}^{(0.6,0.5,0.4)}_{\widetilde{E}(\hbar_6)} = \widetilde{E}_2 \cap \widetilde{E}_3 \cap \widetilde{E}_4$

According to the Definition (1), we get the FOF β-neighborhood as shown in Table 5.

Assume that the decision makers gives a evaluation threshold $\beta = (0.6, 0.5, 0.4)$. As a result, based on Table 5, and Equation (12), we have $\widehat{N}^{(0.6,0.5,0.4)}_{\widetilde{E}(\hbar_1)} = (\hbar_1), \widehat{N}^{(0.6,0.5,0.4)}_{\widetilde{E}(\hbar_2)} = (\hbar_2, \hbar_3), \widehat{N}^{(0.6,0.5,0.4)}_{\widetilde{E}(\hbar_3)} = (\hbar_3), \widehat{N}^{(0.6,0.5,0.4)}_{\widetilde{E}(\hbar_4)} = (\hbar_4), \widehat{N}^{(0.6,0.5,0.4)}_{\widetilde{E}(\hbar_5)} = (\hbar_1, \hbar_2, \hbar_5), \widehat{N}^{(0.6,0.5,0.4)}_{\widetilde{E}(\hbar_6)} = (\hbar_6)$.

Let the state set $D = (\hbar_1, \hbar_3, \hbar_5)$. By Equation (13), we have $P_r\left(D|\widehat{N}^\beta_{\tilde{E}(\hbar_1)}\right) = 1$, $P_r\left(D|\widehat{N}^\beta_{\tilde{E}(\hbar_2)}\right) = \frac{1}{2}$, $P_r\left(D|\widehat{N}^\beta_{\tilde{E}(\hbar_3)}\right) = 1$, $P_r\left(D|\widehat{N}^\beta_{\tilde{E}(\hbar_4)}\right) = 0$, $P_r\left(D|\widehat{N}^\beta_{\tilde{E}(\hbar_5)}\right) = \frac{2}{3}$, $P_r\left(D|\widehat{N}^\beta_{\tilde{E}(\hbar_6)}\right) = 0$.

Table 5. A tabular representation of FOF β-neighborhood.

$\widetilde{N}^\beta_{\tilde{E}(\hbar)}$	$\hbar_1$	$\hbar_2$	$\hbar_3$
$\widetilde{N}^\beta_{\tilde{E}(\hbar_1)}$	(0.9, 0.1, 0.3)	(0.5, 0.2, 0.4)	(0.5, 0.3, 0.6)
$\widetilde{N}^\beta_{\tilde{E}(\hbar_2)}$	(0.7, 0.1, 0.5)	(0.6, 0.2, 0.4)	(0.3, 0.2, 0.4)
$\widetilde{N}^\beta_{\tilde{E}(\hbar_3)}$	(0.7, 0.1, 0.5)	(0.7, 0.2, 0.4)	(0.7, 0.2, 0.4)
$\widetilde{N}^\beta_{\tilde{E}(\hbar_4)}$	(0.8, 0.1, 0.5)	(0.5, 0.2, 0.2)	(0.3, 0.4, 0.6)
$\widetilde{N}^\beta_{\tilde{E}(\hbar_5)}$	(0.9, 0.1, 0.5)	(0.3, 0.2, 0.5)	(0.5, 0.3, 0.6)
$\widetilde{N}^\beta_{\tilde{E}(\hbar_6)}$	(0.7, 0.2, 0.5)	(0.3, 0.2, 0.5)	(0.3, 0.2, 0.5)

	$\hbar_4$	$\hbar_5$	$\hbar_6$
$\widetilde{N}^\beta_{\tilde{E}(\hbar_1)}$	(0.8, 0.1, 0.5)	(0.6, 0.5, 0.2)	(0.5, 0.1, 0.5)
$\widetilde{N}^\beta_{\tilde{E}(\hbar_2)}$	(0.5, 0.1, 0.5)	(0.6, 0.5, 0.2)	(0.6, 0.2, 0.5)
$\widetilde{N}^\beta_{\tilde{E}(\hbar_3)}$	(0.5, 0.1, 0.5)	(0.3, 0.2, 0.7)	(0.8, 0.3, 0.5)
$\widetilde{N}^\beta_{\tilde{E}(\hbar_4)}$	(0.7, 0.3, 0.3)	(0.3, 0.2, 0.2)	(0.5, 0.1, 0.4)
$\widetilde{N}^\beta_{\tilde{E}(\hbar_5)}$	(0.6, 0.1, 0.7)	(0.6, 0.4, 0.3)	(0.5, 0.1, 0.5)
$\widetilde{N}^\beta_{\tilde{E}(\hbar_6)}$	(0.5, 0.2, 0.7)	(0.3, 0.2, 0.7)	(0.6, 0.2, 0.3)

Assume that the loss function for risk or cost of functions in different states D and $\neg D$ are in Table 6.

Table 6. The loss function 1 matrix in this Example.

	D	$\neg D$
b_P	$\vartheta(\lambda_{PP}) = (0, 0.1, 0.9)$	$\vartheta(\lambda_{PN}) = (0.85, 0.7, 0.1)$
b_B	$\vartheta(\lambda_{BP}) = (0.4, 0.4, 0.5)$	$\vartheta(\lambda_{BN}) = (0.7, 0.6, 0.3)$
b_N	$\vartheta(\lambda_{NP}) = (0.85, 0.8, 0.1)$	$\vartheta(\lambda_{NN}) = (0.02, 0.5, 0.75)$

Let $RP(\hbar) = R\left(b_P|\widehat{N}^\beta_{\tilde{E}(\hbar)}\right)$, $RB(\hbar) = R\left(b_B|\widehat{N}^\beta_{\tilde{E}(\hbar)}\right)$ and $RN(\hbar) = R\left(b_N|\widehat{N}^\beta_{\tilde{E}(\hbar)}\right)$. Based on the Table 6 and Equations (28)–(30), we can get the expected losses $R\left(b.|\widehat{N}^\beta_{\tilde{E}(\hbar)}\right)(\cdot = P, B, N)$, which are shown in Table 7.

Table 7. Expected losses $R\left(b.|\widehat{N}^\beta_{\tilde{E}(\hbar)}\right)(\cdot = P, B, N)$.

	$RP(\hbar)$	$RB(\hbar)$	$RN(\hbar)$
$\hbar_1$	(0, 0.1, 0.9)	(0.4, 0.4, 0.5)	(0.85, 0.8, 0.1)
$\hbar_2$	(0.745, 0.269, 0.299)	(0.529, 0.489, 0.387)	(0.746, 0.632, 0.274)
$\hbar_3$	(0, 0.1, 0.9)	(0.4, 0.4, 0.5)	(0.85, 0.8, 0.1)
$\hbar_4$	(0.85, 0.7, 0.1)	(0.7, 0.6, 0.3)	(0.02, 0.5, 0.75)
$\hbar_5$	(0.683, 0.199, 0.432)	(0.497, 0.458, 0.422)	(0.789, 0.684, 0.195)
$\hbar_6$	(0.85, 0.7, 0.1)	(0.7, 0.6, 0.3)	(0.02, 0.5, 0.75)

In what follows, we shall adopt the above five decision methods to deal with this problem.

6.1.1. Decision-Making Based on Method 1

According to the Equations (31)–(33), we calculate the thresholds $\alpha_1, \beta_1, \gamma_1$, respectively. Concretely, $\alpha_1 = 0.889$, $\beta_1 = 0.321$, $\gamma_1 = 0.499$. Based on the Method 1, according to the decision rules $(P_1) - (N_1)$, we have $POS(D) = (\hbar_3)$, $BND(D) = (\hbar_1, \hbar_2, \hbar_5)$, $NEG(D) = (\hbar_4, \hbar_6)$.

6.1.2. Decision-Making Based on Method 2

According to the Equations (34)–(36), we calculate the thresholds $\alpha_2, \beta_2, \gamma_2$, respectively. Concretely, $\alpha_2 = 1, \beta_2 = 0.208, \gamma_2 = 0.139$. Based on the Method 2, according to the decision rules $(P_2) - (N_2)$, we have
$POS(D) = (\hbar_3), BND(D) = (\hbar_1, \hbar_2, \hbar_5), NEG(D) = (\hbar_4, \hbar_6)$.

6.1.3. Decision-Making Based on Method 3

According to the Equations (37)–(39), we calculate the thresholds $\alpha_3, \beta_3, \gamma_3$, respectively. Concretely, $\alpha_2 = 0.652, \beta_2 = 0.363, \gamma_2 = 0.478$. Based on the Method 3, according to the decision rules $(P_3) - (N_3)$, we have $POS(D) = (\hbar_3), BND(D) = (\hbar_1, \hbar_{2,\hbar_5}), NEG(D) = (\hbar_4, \hbar_6)$.

6.1.4. Decision-Making Based on Method 4

Let $RP(\hbar) = R\left(b_P | \widehat{N}^\beta_{\widetilde{E}(\hbar)}\right), RB(\hbar) = R\left(b_B | \widehat{N}^\beta_{\widetilde{E}(\hbar)}\right)$ and $RN(\hbar) = R\left(b_N | \widehat{N}^\beta_{\widetilde{E}(\hbar)}\right)$. Based on the Method 4, according to the Equations (40)–(45), we calculate the score and accuracy function of expected losses, respectively. And the result are shown in Table 8.

Table 8. The score and accuracy functions of expected losses in this Example.

	$S(RP(\hbar))$	$S(RB(\hbar))$	$S(RN(\hbar))$	$H(RP(\hbar))$	$H(RB(\hbar))$	$H(RN(\hbar))$
$\hbar_1$	−0.656	−0.063	0.121	0.656	0.113	0.923
$\hbar_2$	0.295	−0.002	0.141	0.321	0.157	0.465
$\hbar_3$	−0.656	−0.063	0.121	0.656	0.113	0.923
$\hbar_4$	0.282	0.104	−0.064	0.762	0.378	0.064
$\hbar_5$	0.181	−0.015	0.151	0.253	0.136	0.606
$\hbar_6$	0.282	0.104	−0.064	0.762	0.378	0.064

So, according to the decision rules $(P_4) - (N_4), POS(D) = (\hbar_1, \hbar_3), BND(D) = (\hbar_2, \hbar_5), NEG(D) = (\hbar_4, \hbar_6)$.

6.1.5. Decision-Making Based on Method 5

Let $RP(\hbar) = R\left(b_P | \widehat{N}^\beta_{\widetilde{E}(\hbar)}\right), RB(\hbar) = R\left(b_B | \widehat{N}^\beta_{\widetilde{E}(\hbar)}\right)$ and $RN(\hbar) = R\left(b_N | \widehat{N}^\beta_{\widetilde{E}(\hbar)}\right)$. Based on the Method 5, according to the Equations (46)–(48), we calculate the closeness index of the expected losses, respectively. And the result are shown as Table 9.

Table 9. The closeness index in this Example.

	$\Im(RP(\hbar))$	$\Im(RB(\hbar))$	$\Im(RN(\hbar))$
$\hbar_1$	0.115	0.312	0.373
$\hbar_2$	0.432	0.309	0.378
$\hbar_3$	0.115	0.312	0.373
$\hbar_4$	0.427	0.368	0.312
$\hbar_5$	0.394	0.328	0.389
$\hbar_6$	0.427	0.368	0.312

So, according to the decision rules $(P_5) - (N_5)$, we have $POS(D) = (\hbar_3), BND(D) = (\hbar_1, \hbar_2, \hbar_5), NEG(D) = (\hbar_4, \hbar_6)$.

In the following, we orderly used five methods of Section 6 for deriving Three way-decsions.

(1) The contraction company selection with Method 1, 2, 3 (Positive, neutral and negative viwepoint): With the aid of the general method of Section 6, we first compute the FOF β-neighborhood $\widetilde{N}^\beta_{\widetilde{E}(\hbar)}$ and FO β-neighborhood $\widehat{N}^\beta_{\widetilde{E}(\hbar)}$ from the given decision-making Table 4 by using the Definitions (1) and (17). We also, calculate the conditional probability $P_r\left(D | \widehat{N}^\beta_{\widetilde{E}(\hbar)}\right)$ by the Equation (13), and give loss function with FOFNs for risk or cost of actions in different states.

After that, find the values of the thresholds $(\alpha_1, \beta_1, \gamma_1), (\alpha_2, \beta_2, \gamma_2)$ and $(\alpha_3, \beta_3, \gamma_3)$ according to Formulsa (31)–(39), respectively. On the basis of the decision rules $(P_1) - (N_1)$ to $(P_3) - (N_3)$, we can judge the corresponding decision rule for each company. At the moment, using the decision rules $(P_1) - (N_1)$ to $(P_3) - (N_3)$, we can predict that $(\hbar_3) \in POS(D), (\hbar_1, \hbar_2, \hbar_5) \in BND(D)$ and $(\hbar_4, \hbar_6) \in NEG(D)$.

(2) The contraction company selection with Method 4 (Score and Accuracy function): Based on the Method 4, according to the Equations (40)–(45), we calculate the score and accuracy function of expected losses, respectively. Then, using the decision rules $(P_4) - (N_4)$, we can predict that $(\hbar_1, \hbar_3) \in POS(D), (\hbar_2, \hbar_5) \in BND(D)$ and $(\hbar_4, \hbar_6) \in NEG(D)$.

(3) The contraction company selection with Method 5 (Closness index): We use the ranking method of the closness index function for the selection of construction company. Based on the Method 5, according to the Equations (46)–(48), we calculate the closeness index of the expected losses, respectively. Then, using the decision rules $(P_5) - (N_5)$, we can predict that $(\hbar_3) \in POS(D), (\hbar_1, \hbar_2) \in BND(D)$ and $(\hbar_4, \hbar_5, \hbar_6) \in NEG(D)$.

6.1.6. Sensitivity Analysis

When the $\beta = (0.6, 0.5, 0.4)$ and $f = 3$. The decision result of multi-attribute decision making will change with the change of loss function. Assume that there are three different loss functions as shown in Tables 6, 10 and 11. The decision results obtained by five methods under different loss functions are shown in Table 12 as follows.

Table 10. The loss function 2 matrix.

	D	¬D
b_P	$\vartheta(\lambda_{PP}) = (0.3, 0.1, 0.7)$	$\vartheta(\lambda_{PN}) = (0.3, 0.2, 0.4)$
b_B	$\vartheta(\lambda_{BP}) = (0.4, 0.3, 0.3)$	$\vartheta(\lambda_{BN}) = (0.5, 0.4, 0.1)$
b_N	$\vartheta(\lambda_{NP}) = (0.1, 0.8, 0.1)$	$\vartheta(\lambda_{NN}) = (0.7, 0.3, 0.2)$

Table 11. The loss function 3 matrix.

	D	¬D
b_P	$\vartheta(\lambda_{PP}) = (0.6, 0.2, 0.3)$	$\vartheta(\lambda_{PN}) = (0.3, 0.5, 0.1)$
b_B	$\vartheta(\lambda_{BP}) = (0.5, 0.1, 0.4)$	$\vartheta(\lambda_{BN}) = (0.4, 0.6, 0.3)$
b_N	$\vartheta(\lambda_{NP}) = (0.2, 0.7, 0.2)$	$\vartheta(\lambda_{NN}) = (0.2, 0.1, 0.7)$

According to the two different loss functions described in Tables 6, 10 and 11, we can use the five different decision methods in Section 5 to get different decision results, as shown in Table 12.

Table 12. Comparison of decision results of five methods (LF = loss function).

Loss Function	Method	POS(D)	BND(D)	NEG(D)
The LF-1 in Table 6	Method 1	$(\hbar_3)$	$(\hbar_1, \hbar_2, \hbar_5)$	$(\hbar_4, \hbar_6)$
	Method 2	$(\hbar_3)$	$(\hbar_1, \hbar_2, \hbar_5)$	$(\hbar_4, \hbar_6)$
	Method 3	$(\hbar_1, \hbar_3)$	$(\hbar_2, \hbar_5)$	$(\hbar_4, \hbar_6)$
	Method 4	$(\hbar_3)$	$(\hbar_1, \hbar_2,)$	$(\hbar_4, \hbar_5, \hbar_6)$
	Method 5	$(\hbar_3)$	$(\hbar_1, \hbar_2, \hbar_3)$	$(\hbar_4, \hbar_6)$
The LF-2 in Table 10	Method 1	$(\hbar_3)$	$(\hbar_1, \hbar_2, \hbar_5)$	$(\hbar_4, \hbar_6)$
	Method 2	$(\hbar_3)$	$(\hbar_1, \hbar_2, \hbar_5)$	$(\hbar_4, \hbar_6)$
	Method 3	$(\hbar_3)$	$(\hbar_1, \hbar_2, \hbar_5, \hbar_6)$	$(\hbar_4)$
	Method 4	$(\hbar_1, \hbar_3)$	$(\hbar_2, \hbar_4)$	$(\hbar_5, \hbar_6)$
	Method 5	$(\hbar_3)$	$(\hbar_1, \hbar_2)$	$(\hbar_4, \hbar_5, \hbar_6)$
The LF-3 in Table 11	Method 1	$(\hbar_3)$	$(\hbar_1, \hbar_2, \hbar_5)$	$(\hbar_4, \hbar_6)$
	Method 2	$(\hbar_3)$	$(\hbar_1, \hbar_2, \hbar_5)$	$(\hbar_4, \hbar_6)$
	Method 3	$(\hbar_3)$	$(\hbar_1, \hbar_2)$	$(\hbar_4, \hbar_6)$
	Method 4	$(\hbar_3)$	$(\hbar_1, \hbar_2, \hbar_5)$	$(\hbar_4 \hbar_6)$
	Method 5	$(\hbar_3)$	$(\hbar_2, \hbar_5)$	$(\hbar_4, \hbar_6)$

It can be seen from Table 12, that on the basis of loss function 1, 2, 3 the decision results of the five methods are the same, but only changes occur in the method 4 on the basis of loss function 3, thn the decision results of loss function 1 and loss function 2. Thus, Eastern Highway Company $\hbar_3$ is the best construction company for the selection of project.

6.1.7. Comparison and Analysis

To elaborate the validity and practicability of the created method in this essay, we conduct a collection of comparative analyzing with other previous decision methodologies including the method based upon covering-based Spherical fuzzy rough set Model hybrid with TOPSIS method proposed by Zeng et al. [77], the method based upon Spherical fuzzy Dombi aggregation operators proposed by Ashraf et al. [78], Spherical aggregation operators proposed by Ashraf and Abdullah [79] and the method based upon Spherical fuzzy Graphs proposed by Akram et al. [80]. We utilize these methods to cope with the Example in this paper, the score values and ranking of alternatives are displayed in Table 13. From it, we can attain the same sorting results of alternatives based on the previous methods and the designed method in this article, which can demonstrate the effectiveness of the propounded methods.

Table 13. Comparison Information.

Approaches	Score Value of Alternative						Ranking
	$\hbar_1$	$\hbar_2$	$\hbar_3$	$\hbar_4$	$\hbar_5$	$\hbar_6$	
Zeng et al. [77]	0.027	0.024	0.062	0.017	0.010	0.009	$\hbar_3 > \hbar_1 > \hbar_2 > \hbar_4 > \hbar_5 > \hbar_6$
Ashraf et al. [78]	0.603	0.520	0.823	0.391	0.476	0.314	$\hbar_3 > \hbar_1 > \hbar_2 > \hbar_5 > \hbar_4 > \hbar_6$
Ashraf & Abdullah [79]	0.293	0.463	0.537	0.235	0.114	0.079	$\hbar_3 > \hbar_2 > \hbar_1 > \hbar_4 > \hbar_5 > \hbar_6$
Akram et al. [80]	1.734	1.498	1.893	1.528	1.384	1.272	$\hbar_3 > \hbar_1 > \hbar_4 > \hbar_2 > \hbar_5 > \hbar_6$

It is noteworthy that the class of FOFSs extends the classes of PFSs and SFSs. Thus, it can express vague information more flexibly and accurately with increasing fraction. When $f = 1$, this model reduces to the PF model, and when $f = 2$, it becomes the SF model. Thus, a wider range of uncertain information can be expressed using the methods proposed in this paper, which are closer to real decision-making. This helps us to deal with MCDM problems and to sketch real scenarios more accurately. Hence our approach towards MCDM is more flexible and generalized, which provides a vast space of acceptable triplets given by decision-makers, according to the different attitudes, as compared to the PF model.

7. Conclusions

The FOFCDTRS model is an important tool in real life for handling uncertainties. In this paper, we combine the loss functions of DTRSs with CFOFSs in the fractional orthotriple fuzzy context. Therefore, a new approach is adopted to fractional orthotriple fuzzy sets with notions of covering rough set to presented the new method of FOFCDTRS through FOF β-neighborhoods. Then, we propose a new FOFCDTRS model and elaborate its respective properties. We set out five methods for resolving the predicted loss in the form of FOFNs and extract the related three-way decisions. At the same time we present an algorithm based on FOFCDTRSs for decision making with multiple attributes. Through example analysis, it is proved that the five methods proposed are correct and effective. Among them, Methods 1, 2 and 3 have better stability.

In the next researches, we mainly focus on the following topics: (1) Extend FOFCDTRSs to the multi-period situation. (2) The application of FOFCDTRSs in big data processing and analysis. (3) Use the developed concept on new multi-attribute evaluation models to deal with fuzziness and uncertainty in multiple criteria decision- making topics such as planning choices, construction options, site selection, and decision-making problem in many other areas.

Author Contributions: Data curation, M.Q.; Funding acquisition, S.S.A.; Resources, S.S.A.; Supervision, S.A.; Writing—original draft, M.Q.; Writing, review, editing, S.A. All authors have read and agreed to the published version of the manuscript.

Funding: This work was supported by the Deanship of Scientific Research (DSR), King Abdulaziz University, Jeddah, under the grant No. (DF-189-980-1441).

Acknowledgments: This work was supported by the Deanship of Scientific Research (DSR), King Abdulaziz University, Jeddah, under the grant No. (DF-189-980-1441). The authors, therefore, gratefully acknowledge DSR technical and financial support.

Conflicts of Interest: The authors declare no conflict of interest.

References

1. Ghandour, R.; Shoaibi, A.; Khatib, R.; Rmeileh, N.A.; Unal, B.; Sözmen, K.; Kılıç, B.; Fouad, F.; Al Ali, R.; Romdhane, H.B.; et al. Priority setting for the prevention and control of cardiovascular diseases: Multi-criteria decision analysis in four eastern Mediterranean countries. *Int. J. Public Health* **2015**, *60*, 73–81. [CrossRef] [PubMed]
2. Tromp, N.; Baltussen, R. Mapping of multiple criteria for priority setting of health interventions: An aid for decision makers. *BMC Health Serv. Res.* **2012**, *12*, 454. [CrossRef]
3. Atanassov, K.T. Intuitionistic fuzzy sets. In *Intuitionistic Fuzzy Sets*; Physica: Heidelberg, Germany, 1986; pp. 87–96.
4. Zadeh, L.A. Fuzzy sets. *Inf. Control.* **1965**, *8*, 338–353. [CrossRef]
5. Cuong, B.C. *Picture Fuzzy Sets-First Results. Part 1 "Seminar" Neuro-Fuzzy Systems with Applications*; Preprint 04/2013; Institute of Mathematics: Hanoi, Vietnam, 2013.
6. Cuong, B.C. *Picture Fuzzy Sets-First results. Part 2 "Seminar" Neuro-Fuzzy Systems with Applications*; Preprint 04/2013; Institute of Mathematics: Hanoi, Vietnam, 2013.
7. Cuong, B.C. Picture fuzzy sets. *J. Comput. Cybern.* **2014**, *30*, 409.
8. Cuong, B.C.; Van Hai, P. Some fuzzy logic operators for picture fuzzy sets. In Proceedings of the 2015 Seventh International Conference on Knowledge and Systems Engineering (KSE), Ho Chi Minh City, Vietnam, 8–10 October 2015.
9. Cuong, B.C.; Kreinovitch, V.; Ngan, R.T. A classification of representable t-norm operators for picture fuzzy sets. In Proceedings of the 2016 Eighth International Conference on Knowledge and Systems Engineering, Hanoi, Vietnam, 6–8 October 2016.
10. Phong, P.H.; Hieu, D.T.; Ngan, R.T.; Them, P.T. Some compositions of picture fuzzy relations. In Proceedings of the 7th National Conference on Fundamental and Applied Information Technology Research (FAIR'7), Thai Nguyen, 19–20 June 2014; pp. 19–20.
11. Wei, G.; Gao, H. The generalized Dice similarity measures for picture fuzzy sets and their applications. *Informatica* **2018**, *29*, 107–124. [CrossRef]
12. Wei, G. Some similarity measures for picture fuzzy sets and their applications. *Iran. J. Fuzzy Syst.* **2018**, *15*, 77–89.
13. Wei, G.; Alsaadi, F.E.; Hayat, T.; Alsaedi, A. Projection models for multiple attribute decision making with picture fuzzy information. *Int. J. Mach. Learn. Cybern.* **2018**, *9*, 713–719. [CrossRef]
14. Singh, P. Correlation coefficients for picture fuzzy sets. *J. Intell. Fuzzy Syst.* **2015**, *28*, 591–604. [CrossRef]
15. Son, L.H. DPFCM: A novel distributed picture fuzzy clustering method on picture fuzzy sets. *Expert Syst. Appl.* **2015**, *2*, 51–66. [CrossRef]
16. Thong, P.H. A new approach to multi-variable fuzzy forecasting using picture fuzzy clustering and picture fuzzy rule interpolation method. In *Knowledge and Systems Engineering*; Springer: Cham, Switzerland, 2015; pp. 679–690.
17. Son, L.H. Generalized picture distance measure and applications to picture fuzzy clustering. *Appl. Soft Comput.* **2016**, *46*, 284–295. [CrossRef]
18. Son, L.H. Measuring analogousness in picture fuzzy sets: from picture distance measures to picture association measures. *Fuzzy Optimization Decis. Mak.* **2017**, *16*, 359–378. [CrossRef]
19. Van Viet, P.; Van Hai, P. Picture inference system: A new fuzzy inference system on picture fuzzy set. *Appl. Intell.* **2017**, *46*, 652–669.

20. Thong, P.H. Picture fuzzy clustering for complex data. *Eng. Appl. Artif. Intell.* **2016**, *56*, 121–130. [CrossRef]
21. Thong, P.H. A novel automatic picture fuzzy clustering method based on particle swarm optimization and picture composite cardinality. *Knowl. Based Syst.* **2016**, *109*, 48–60. [CrossRef]
22. Wei, G. Picture fuzzy cross-entropy for multiple attribute decision making problems. *J. Bus. Econ. Manag.* **2016**, *17*, 491–502. [CrossRef]
23. Yang, Y.; Liang, C.; Ji, S.; Liu, T. Adjustable soft discernibility matrix based on picture fuzzy soft sets and its applications in decision making. *J. Intell. Fuzzy Syst.* **2015**, *29*, 1711–1722. [CrossRef]
24. Garg, H. Some picture fuzzy aggregation operators and their applications to multicriteria decision-making. *Arab. J. For. Sci. Eng.* **2017**, *42*, 5275–5290. [CrossRef]
25. Peng, X.; Dai, J. Algorithm for picture fuzzy multiple attribute decision-making based on new distance measure. *Int. J. Uncertain. Quantif.* **2017**, *7*, 177–187. [CrossRef]
26. Phuong, P.T.M.; Thong, P.H. Theoretical analysis of picture fuzzy clustering: Convergence and property. *J. Comput. Cybern.* **2018**, *34*, 17–32. [CrossRef]
27. Thong, P.H.; Fujita, H. Interpolative picture fuzzy rules: A novel forecast method for weather nowcasting. In Proceedings of the 2016 IEEE International Conference on Fuzzy Systems (FUZZ-IEEE), Vancouver, BC, Canada, 24–29 July 2016; pp. 86–93.
28. Van Viet, P.; Chau, H.T.M.; Van Hai, P. Some extensions of membership graphs for picture inference systems. In Proceedings of the 2015 Seventh International Conference on Knowledge and Systems Engineering (KSE), Ho Chi Minh City, Vietnam, 8–10 October 2015; pp. 192–197.
29. Ashraf, S.; Abdullah, S.; Qadir, A. Novel concept of cubic picture fuzzy sets. *J. New Theory* **2018**, *24*, 59–72.
30. Pedrycz, W. Shadowed sets: representing and processing fuzzy sets. *IEEE Trans. Syst. Man Cybern. Part B (Cybern.)* **1998**, *28*, 103–109. [CrossRef] [PubMed]
31. Pedrycz, W. *Granular Computing: Analysis and Design of Intelligent Systems*; CRC Press: Boca Raton, FL, USA, 2018.
32. Cattaneo, G.; Ciucci, D.; Dubois, D. Algebraic models of deviant modal operators based on de Morgan and Kleene lattices. *Inf. Sci.* **2011**, *181*, 4075–4100. [CrossRef]
33. Ciucci, D. Orthopairs: A simple and widely usedway to model uncertainty. *Fundam. Inform.* **2011**, *108*, 287–304.
34. Yao, Y. Three-way conflict analysis: Reformulations and extensions of the Pawlak model. *Knowl. Based Syst.* **2019**, *180*, 26–37. [CrossRef]
35. Yao, Y. The superiority of three-way decisions in probabilistic rough set models. *Inf. Sci.* **2011**, *181*, 1080–1096. [CrossRef]
36. Yao, Y. Three-way decision and granular computing. *Int. J. Approx. Reason.* **2018**, *103*, 107–123. [CrossRef]
37. Zakowski, W. Approximations in the space (U, π). *Demon Stration Math.* **1983**, *16*, 761–769. [CrossRef]
38. Zhu, W.; Wang, F.Y. Reduction and axiomization of covering generalized rough sets. *Inf. Sci.* **2003**, *152*, 217–230.
39. Safari, S.; Hooshmandasl, M.R. On twelve types of covering-based rough sets. *SpringerPlus* **2016**, *5*, 1003. [CrossRef]
40. Ma, L. On some types of neighborhood-related covering rough sets. *Int. J. Approx. Reason.* **2012**, *5*, 901–911. [CrossRef]
41. Dubois, D.; Prade, H. Rough fuzzy sets and fuzzy rough sets. *Int. J. Gen. Syst.* **1990**, *17*, 191–209. [CrossRef]
42. Ma, L. Two fuzzy covering rough set models and their generalizations over fuzzy lattices. *Fuzzy Sets Syst.* **2016**, *294*, 1–17. [CrossRef]
43. D'eer, L.; Restrepo, M.; Cornelis, C.; Gomez, J. Neighborhood operators for covering-based rough sets. *Inf. Sci.* **2016**, *336*, 21–44. [CrossRef]
44. D'eer, L.; Cornelis, C.; Godo, L. Fuzzy neighborhood operators based on fuzzy coverings. *Fuzzy Sets Syst.* **2017**, *312*, 17–35. [CrossRef]
45. Hussain, A.; Irfan Ali, M.; Mahmood, T. Covering based q-rung orthopair fuzzy rough set model hybrid with TOPSIS for multi-attribute decision making. *J. Intell. Fuzzy Syst.* **2019**, *37*, 981–993. [CrossRef]
46. Quek, S.G.; Selvachandran, G.; Smarandache, F.; Vimala, J.; Le, S.H.; Bui, Q.T.; Gerogiannis, V.C. Entropy Measures for Plithogenic Sets and Applications in Multi-Attribute Decision Making. *Mathematics* **2020**, *8*, 965.

47. Zeng, S.; Hussain, A.; Mahmood, T.; Irfan Ali, M.; Ashraf, S.; Munir, M. Covering-Based Spherical Fuzzy Rough Set Model Hybrid with TOPSIS for Multi-Attribute Decision-Making. *Symmetry* **2019**, *11*, 547. [CrossRef]
48. Bagga, P.; Hans, R.; Joshi, A. QoS based Web Service Selection and Multi-Criteria Decision Making Methods. *Int. J. Interact. Multimed. Artif. Intell.* **2019**, 113–121. [CrossRef]
49. Borhani, M.; Akbari, K.; Matkan, A.; Tanasan, M. A Multicriteria Optimization for Flight Route Networks in Large-Scale Airlines Using Intelligent Spatial Information. *Int. J. Interact. Multimed. Artif. Intell.* **2020**, 123–131. [CrossRef]
50. Deng, X.; Yao, Y. Decision-theoretic three-way approximations of fuzzy sets. *Inf. Sci.* **2014**, *279*, 702–715. [CrossRef]
51. Jia, X.; Liao, W.; Tang, Z.; Shang, L. Minimum cost attribute reduction in decision-theoretic rough set models. *Inf. Sci.* **2013**, *219*, 151–167. [CrossRef]
52. Li, H.; Zhou, X.; Zhao, J.; Liu, D. Attribute reduction in decision-theoretic rough set model: A further investigation. In *International Conference on Rough Sets and Knowledge Technology*; Springer: Berlin/Heidelberg, Germany, 2011; pp. 466–475.
53. Liang, D.; Liu, D.; Pedrycz, W.; Hu, P. Triangular fuzzy decision-theoretic rough sets. *Int. J. Approx.* **2013**, *54*, 1087–1106.
54. Liu, D.; Li, T.; Ruan, D. Probabilistic model criteria with decision-theoretic rough sets. *Inf. Sci.* **2011**, *181*, 3709–3722.
55. Li, W.; Xu, W. Double-quantitative decision-theoretic rough set. *Inf. Sci.* **2015**, *316*, 54–67. [CrossRef]
56. Liang, D.; Liu, D. Systematic studies on three-way decisions with interval-valued decision-theoretic rough sets. *Inf. Sci.* **2014**, *276*, 186–203. [CrossRef]
57. Min, F.; Zhu, W. Attribute reduction of data with error ranges and test costs. *Inf. Sci.* **2012**, *211*, 48–67. [CrossRef]
58. Yao, Y.; Zhao, Y. Attribute reduction in decision-theoretic rough set models. *Inf. Sci.* **2008**, *178*, 3356–3373. [CrossRef]
59. Zhao, Y.; Wong, S.M.; Yao, Y. A note on attribute reduction in the decision-theoretic rough set model. In *Transactions on Rough Sets XIII*; Springer: Berlin/Heidelberg, Germany, 2011; pp. 260–275.
60. Yu, H.; Wang, Y. Three-way decisions method for overlapping clustering. In *International Conference on Rough Sets and Current Trends in Computing*; Springer: Berlin/Heidelberg, Germany, 2012; pp. 277–286.
61. Yu, H.; Zhang, C.; Wang, G. A tree-based incremental overlapping clustering method using the three-way decision theory. *Knowl. Based Syst.* **2016**, *91*, 189–203. [CrossRef]
62. Liu, D.; Li, T.; Liang, D. Three-way government decision analysis with decision-theoretic rough sets. *Int. J. Uncertain. Fuzziness Knowl. Based Syst.* **2012**, *20*, 119–132. [CrossRef]
63. Chen, Y.; Yue, X.; Fujita, H.; Fu, S. Three-way decision support for diagnosis on focal liver lesions. *Knowl. Based Syst.* **2017**, *127*, 85–99. [CrossRef]
64. Liu, D.; Yao, Y.; Li, T. Three-way investment decisions with decision-theoretic rough sets. *Int. J. Comput. Intell. Syst.* **2011**, *4*, 66–74. [CrossRef]
65. Liang, D.; Pedrycz, W.; Liu, D.; Hu, P. Three-way decisions based on decision-theoretic rough sets under linguistic assessment with the aid of group decision making. *Appl. Soft Comput.* **2015**, *29*, 256–269. [CrossRef]
66. Yao, Y.; Zhou, B. Naive Bayesian rough sets. In *International Conference on Rough Sets and Knowledge Technology*; Springer: Berlin/Heidelberg, Germany, 2010; pp. 719–726.
67. Liu, D.; Li, T.; Liang, D. Incorporating logistic regression to decision-theoretic rough sets for classifications. *Int. J. Approx. Reason.* **2014**, *55*, 197–210. [CrossRef]
68. Liang, D.; Liu, D. A novel risk decision making based on decision-theoretic rough sets under hesitant fuzzy information. *IEEE Trans. Fuzzy Syst.* **2014**, *23*, 237–247. [CrossRef]
69. Liang, D.; Liu, D. Deriving three-way decisions from intuitionistic fuzzy decision-theoretic rough sets. *Inf. Sci.* **2015**, *300*, 28–48. [CrossRef]
70. Mandal, P.; Ranadive, A.S. Decision-theoretic rough sets under Pythagorean fuzzy information. *Int. J. Intell. Syst.* **2018**, *33*, 818–835. [CrossRef]
71. Yager, R.R.; Abbasov, A.M. Pythagorean membership grades, complex numbers, and decision making. *Int. J. Intell. Syst.* **2013**, *28*, 436–452. [CrossRef]
72. Yager, R.R. Generalized orthopair fuzzy sets. *IEEE Trans. Fuzzy Syst.* **2016**, *25*, 1222–1230. [CrossRef]

73. Ashraf, S.; Abdullah, S.; Mahmood, T.; Ghani, F.; Mahmood, T. Spherical fuzzy sets and their applications in multi-attribute decision making problems. *J. Intell. Fuzzy Syst.* **2019**, *36*, 2829–2844. [CrossRef]
74. Antucheviciene, J.; Tavana, M.; Nilashi, M.; Bausys, R. Managing information uncertainty and complexity in decision-making. *Complexity* **2017**, *2017*, 1268980. [CrossRef]
75. Yao, Y. Decision-theoretic rough set models. In *International Conference on Rough Sets and Knowledge Technology*; Springer: Berlin/Heidelberg, Germany, 2007; pp. 1–12.
76. Yoon, K. *Multiple Attribute Decision Making: Methods and Applications*; Springer: New York, NY, USA, 1981.
77. Zeng, S.; Munir, M.; Mahmood, T.; Naeem, M. Some T-Spherical Fuzzy Einstein Interactive Aggregation Operators and Their Application to Selection of Photovoltaic Cells. *Math. Probl. Eng.* **2020**, *2020*, 1904362. [CrossRef]
78. Ashraf, S.; Abdullah, S.; Mahmood, T. Spherical fuzzy Dombi aggregation operators and their application in group decision making problems. *J. Ambient. Intell. Humaniz. Comput.* **2019**. [CrossRef]
79. Ashraf, S.; Abdullah, S. Spherical aggregation operators and their application in multiattribute group decision-making. *Int. J. Intell. Syst.* **2019**, *34*, 493–523. [CrossRef]
80. Akram, M.; Saleem, D.; Al-Hawary, T. Spherical Fuzzy Graphs with Application to Decision-Making. *Math. Comput. Appl.* **2020**, *25*, 8. [CrossRef]

© 2020 by the authors. Licensee MDPI, Basel, Switzerland. This article is an open access article distributed under the terms and conditions of the Creative Commons Attribution (CC BY) license (http://creativecommons.org/licenses/by/4.0/).

Article

Modeling an Uncertain Productivity Learning Process Using an Interval Fuzzy Methodology

Min-Chi Chiu [1], Tin-Chih Toly Chen [2],* and Keng-Wei Hsu [2]

[1] Department of Industrial Engineering and Management, National Chin-Yi University of Technology, 57, Sec. 2, Zhongshan Rd., Taiping, Taichung City 411, Taiwan; mcchiu@ncut.edu.tw
[2] Department of Industrial Engineering and Management, National Chiao Tung University, 1001, University Road, Hsinchu 300, Taiwan; ataco.ncsf@msa.hinet.net
* Correspondence: tolychen@ms37.hinet.net

Received: 20 May 2020; Accepted: 16 June 2020; Published: 18 June 2020

Abstract: Existing methods for forecasting the productivity of a factory are subject to a major drawback—the lower and upper bounds of productivity are usually determined by a few extreme cases, which unacceptably widens the productivity range. To address this drawback, an interval fuzzy number (IFN)-based mixed binary quadratic programming (MBQP)–ordered weighted average (OWA) approach is proposed in this study for modeling an uncertain productivity learning process. In the proposed methodology, the productivity range is divided into the inner and outer sections, which correspond to the lower and upper membership functions of an IFN-based fuzzy productivity forecast, respectively. In this manner, all actual values are included in the outer section, whereas most of the values are included within the inner section to fulfill different managerial purposes. According to the percentages of outlier cases, a suitable forecasting strategy can be selected. To derive the values of parameters in the IFN-based fuzzy productivity learning model, an MBQP model is proposed and optimized. Subsequently, according to the selected forecasting strategy, the OWA method is applied to defuzzify a fuzzy productivity forecast. The proposed methodology has been applied to the real case of a dynamic random access memory factory to evaluate its effectiveness. The experimental results indicate that the proposed methodology was superior to several existing methods, especially in terms of mean absolute error, mean absolute percentage error, and root mean square error in evaluating the forecasting accuracy. The forecasting precision achieved using the proposed methodology was also satisfactory.

Keywords: productivity; learning; interval fuzzy number; mixed binary quadratic programming; ordered weighted average

1. Introduction

Productivity is a measure of how efficient a system is in converting inputs into outputs and is usually measured by dividing the quantity or value of outputs by that of inputs [1–3]. Productivity can be measured at different levels, such as for a factory (or store), city, or even country [4]. This study focuses on the productivity of a factory. In a factory, productivity increases with time because of operators becoming more familiar with their tasks, equipment engineers becoming skilled in maintaining and repairing machines, product engineers becoming more experienced in solving product quality problems, and other reasons [5].

Factories are adopting an increasing number of information technologies (ITs) that include software, hardware, and artificial intelligence [6,7]. For example, factories rely on transaction processing systems (TPSs) to automate routine operations, which obviously elevates productivity [8–11]. Consequently, human workers are now trained to be familiar with MISs rather than with routine operations. The emergence of Industry 4.0 has created opportunities for further enhancing productivity. For example, when wireless sensors are incorporated in a machine, the sensors can detect abnormal operating conditions before a serious shutdown that results in the loss of productivity, thereby enabling predictive maintenance [12]. Although some researchers have asserted that artificial intelligence will eventually replace human workers for performing many tasks, the applications of artificial intelligence do not necessarily enhance productivity due to reasons such as false hopes, mismeasurement, redistribution, and implementation lags [13]. Nevertheless, productivity improves as users learn to master IT. Although productivity improves by conducting activities involving substantial human intervention, productivity is subject to considerable uncertainty [14,15]. To address this problem, fuzzy logic [16] has been extensively applied to model productivity. For example, in a study by Hougaard [17], the inputs and outputs of a production plan were given in or estimated with fuzzy numbers. After enumerating all possible values of fuzzy inputs and outputs, the α cuts of fuzzy productivity were derived. Finally, a triangular fuzzy number was used to approximate fuzzy productivity. Similarly, Emrouznejad et al. [18] modeled inputs, outputs, and prices through fuzzy numbers. The α cuts of fuzzy parameters were fed as interval data into a data envelopment analysis model to calculate the overall profit Malmquist productivity index. Wang and Chen [19] proposed a fuzzy collaborative forecasting approach for forecasting the productivity of a factory. In the fuzzy collaborative forecasting approach, multiple experts fitted a fuzzy productivity learning process with quadratic or nonlinear programming models to forecast productivity. The fuzzy productivity forecasts by experts were aggregated using fuzzy intersection. Then, the aggregation result was defuzzified using a back propagation network. In a study by Chen and Wang [20], fuzzy productivity forecasts were compared with a competitive region to assess the productivity competitiveness of a factory. Recently, Chen et al. [21] proposed a heterogeneous fuzzy collaborative forecasting approach in which experts constructed either mathematical programming models or artificial neural networks to forecast productivity. The adoption of different fuzzy forecasting methods contributed to the diversification of fuzzy productivity forecasts, which was considered a favorable property for a multiple-expert forecasting problem.

However, a problem associated with existing methods is that the lower and upper bounds on a fuzzy productivity forecast are usually determined by a few extreme cases [20]. Moreover, other cases may lie considerably close to cores (or centers), which unreasonably widens the range of a fuzzy productivity forecast, as illustrated in Figure 1, in which red circles represent extreme cases. There exist two types of extreme cases, namely better-than-anticipated (BTA) and poorer-than-expected (PTE) cases.

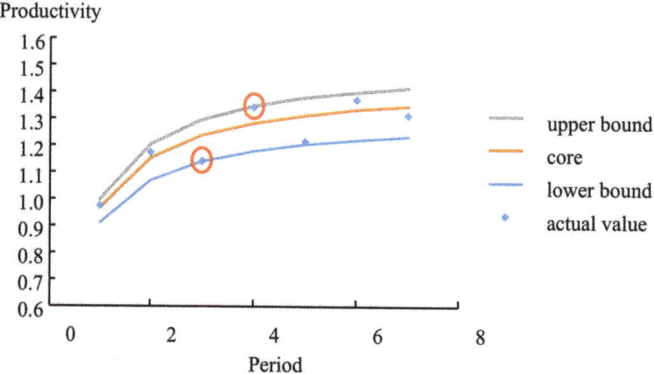

Figure 1. Lower and upper bounds determined by extreme cases.

Therefore, a desirable option is to form a narrow interval that contains most of the collected data by excluding extreme cases, as illustrated in Figure 2. To this end, an interval fuzzy number (IFN) [22–24] is a viable option. There exist two membership functions in an IFN, one of which is suitable for modeling the inner part of a fuzzy productivity forecast, whereas the other is suitable for modeling the outer part.

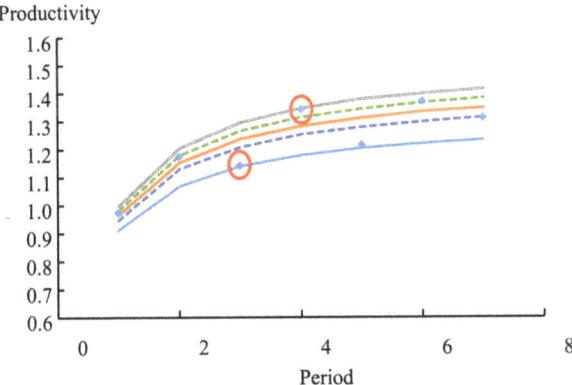

Figure 2. Narrow interval that contains most of the collected data.

Due to the aforementioned reasons, an IFN-based mixed binary quadratic programming (MBQP)–ordered weighted average (OWA) approach is proposed in this study for modeling an uncertain productivity learning process by distinguishing between BTA and PTE cases. The motives for this study are explained as follows:

(1) Owing to the existence of extreme cases, fuzzy productivity forecasts generated using an existing fuzzy forecasting method are not sufficiently precise.
(2) Fuzzy productivity forecasts generated using existing fuzzy forecasting methods are usually type-1 fuzzy numbers [2,15,19]. Compared with type-1 fuzzy numbers, IFNs can better consider uncertainty [25,26]. However, fuzzy forecasting methods that generate IFN-based fuzzy productivity forecasts are not widely used.
(3) A special defuzzifier needs to be proposed for an IFN-based fuzzy productivity forecast that separates extreme cases from normal cases.

To the best of our knowledge, the present study is the first attempt of its kind. The parameters of the IFN-based fuzzy productivity learning model are given in the form of IFNs. Consequently, fuzzy productivity forecasts generated by the IFN-based fuzzy productivity learning model are also in the form of IFNs. In the proposed methodology, the range of productivity is divided into the inner and outer sections that correspond to the lower and upper membership functions of an IFN-based fuzzy productivity forecast, respectively. In this manner, all actual values are included in the outer section, whereas most of the values lie within the inner section. Moreover, the ratio of the number of PTE cases to the number of BTA cases is a useful factor for selecting a suitable forecasting strategy. To derive the values of parameters in the IFN-based fuzzy productivity learning model, an MBQP model is proposed and optimized. Finally, according to the selected forecasting strategy, the OWA method [27] was applied to defuzzify a fuzzy productivity forecast.

The remainder of this paper is organized as follows. First, some arithmetic operations on IFNs are introduced in Section 2. The proposed methodology is detailed in Section 3. To illustrate the applicability of the proposed methodology, a real case is discussed in Section 4. The performance of the proposed methodology is also compared with those of several existing methods. Finally, the conclusions of this study and some directions for future research are provided in Section 5.

2. Preliminary

IFNs have been extensively applied in multiple-criteria decision-making problems. For example, Hu et al. [28] considered a multiple-criteria decision-making problem in which criteria took the values of IFNs. Moreover, some of the weights assigned to criteria were unknown. To address this problem, an expected value function was optimized through a maximizing deviation method. However, in existing studies on IFN applications, the motives for adopting IFNs are not clear or strong. By contrast, in this study, the motive for adopting an IFN to represent a fuzzy productivity forecast is clear.

This section introduces some arithmetic operations on IFNs. First, the definition of an IFN is given as follows [29]:

Definition 1. *An IFN $\widetilde{A}$ is a subset of real numbers R and is defined as the set of ordered pairs $\widetilde{A} = \{(x, \mu_{\widetilde{A}}(x)) \mid x\mu_{\widetilde{A}}(x) \in R\}$, where $\mu_{\widetilde{A}}(x) : R \to [0, 1]$ is the interval-valued membership function of $\widetilde{A}$.*

If $\widetilde{A}$ is Moore-continuous, then there exist two membership functions for $\widetilde{A}$, namely the lower membership function (LMF) $\mu_{\widetilde{A}_l}(x)$ and the upper membership function (UMF) $\mu_{\widetilde{A}_u}(x)$, such that $\mu_{\widetilde{A}}(x) = [\mu_{\widetilde{A}_l}(x), \mu_{\widetilde{A}_u}(x)]$. An IFN is a special case of type-II fuzzy sets [30].

Some attributes of an IFN are defined as follows:

Definition 2. *The inner support, outer support, and core of an IFN $\widetilde{A}$ of R are defined, respectively, as follows:*

$$isupp_{\widetilde{A}} = \{x \in R \mid \mu_{\widetilde{A}_l}(x) > 0\} \quad (1)$$

$$osupp_{\widetilde{A}} = \{x \in R \mid \mu_{\widetilde{A}_u}(x) > 0\} \quad (2)$$

$$core_{\widetilde{A}} = \{x \in R \mid \mu_{\widetilde{A}_l}(x) = \mu_{\widetilde{A}_u}(x) = 1\} \quad (3)$$

Definition 3. *An IFN $\widetilde{A}$ is an interval triangular fuzzy number (ITFN) if both the LMF and UMF of $\widetilde{A}$ are triangular functions,*

$$\mu_{\widetilde{A}_l}(x) = \begin{cases} \frac{x - A_{l1}}{A_2 - A_{l1}} & \text{if} \quad A_{l1} \leq x < A_2 \\ \frac{A_{l3} - x}{A_{l3} - A_2} & \text{if} \quad A_2 \leq x < A_{l3} \\ 0 & \text{otherwise} \end{cases} \quad (4)$$

$$\mu_{\widetilde{A}_u}(x) = \begin{cases} \frac{x - A_{u1}}{A_2 - A_{u1}} & \text{if} \quad A_{u1} \leq x < A_2 \\ \frac{A_{u3} - x}{A_{u3} - A_2} & \text{if} \quad A_2 \leq x < A_{u3} \\ 0 & \text{otherwise} \end{cases} \quad (5)$$

$\widetilde{A}$ can be briefly denoted by $((A_{l1}, A_2, A_{l3}), (A_{u1}, A_2, A_{u3}))$ or $(A_{u1}, A_{l1}, A_2, A_{l3}, A_{u3})$.

An ITFN is shown in Figure 3, in which $\widetilde{A} = ((5, 9, 12), (2, 8, 13))$ or $(2, 5, 9, 12, 13)$.

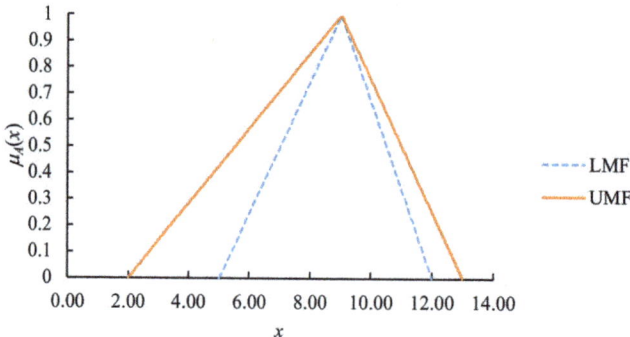

Figure 3. An ITFN.

Property 1. *The inner support, outer support, and core of an ITFN $\widetilde{A}$ can be derived as follows:*

$$isupp_{\widetilde{A}} = [A_{l1}, A_{l3}] \tag{6}$$

$$osupp_{\widetilde{A}} = [A_{u1}, A_{u3}] \tag{7}$$

$$core_{\widetilde{A}} = A_2 \tag{8}$$

Some arithmetic operations on ITFNs are summarized in the following theorem [31–33].

Theorem 1. *(Arithmetic Operations on ITFNs)*

(1) Fuzzy addition: $\widetilde{A}(+)\widetilde{B} = (A_{u1} + B_{u1}, A_{l1} + B_{l1}, A_2 + B_2, A_{l3} + B_{l3}, A_{u3} + B_{u3})$.
(2) Fuzzy subtraction: $\widetilde{A}(-)\widetilde{B} = (A_{u1} - B_{u3}, A_{l1} - B_{l3}, A_2 - B_2, A_{l3} - B_{l1}, A_{u3} - B_{u1})$.
(3) Fuzzy product (or multiplication): $\widetilde{A}(\times)\widetilde{B} \cong (A_{u1}B_{u1}, A_{l1}B_{l1}, A_2B_2, A_{l3}B_{l3}, A_{u3}B_{u3})$ whenever $0 \notin \widetilde{B}$.
(4) Fuzzy division: $\widetilde{A}(/)\widetilde{B} = (A_{u1}/B_{u3}, A_{l1}/B_{l3}, A_2/B_2, A_{l3}/B_{l1}, A_{u3}/B_{u1})$ whenever $0 \notin \widetilde{B}$.
(5) Exponential function: $e^{\widetilde{A}} \cong (e^{A_{u1}}, e^{A_{l1}}, e^{A_2}, e^{A_{l3}}, e^{A_{u3}})$.
(6) Logarithmic function: $\ln \widetilde{A} \cong (\ln A_{u1}, \ln A_{l1}, \ln A_2, \ln A_{l3}, \ln A_{u3})$ whenever $A_{u1} \geq 0$.

3. Proposed Methodology

The proposed methodology comprises the following steps. First, the collected productivity data are analyzed to make sure that a productivity learning process exists. Subsequently, all parameters in the productivity learning model are fuzzified as IFNs to consider uncertainty. To derive the values of IFN-based fuzzy parameters, an MBQP model is proposed and optimized. Finally, the OWA method is applied to defuzzify an IFN-based fuzzy productivity forecast. IFNs, rather than general type-2 fuzzy numbers, are adopted in the proposed methodology because the mathematics needed for IFNs, primarily interval arithmetic, is much simpler than that needed for general type-2 fuzzy numbers [34].

3.1. Data Preanalysis

In a factory, many performance measures exhibit learning phenomena [35–37]. However, the fuzzy learning model of productivity is different from that of other performance measures, such as yield or unit cost, because the asymptotic or final value of productivity is unbounded, whereas that of yield or unit cost is bounded.

Productivity $\to \infty$; yield $\to 100\%$; the unit cost $\to 0$

Therefore, before applying the proposed methodology, it should be ensured that the collected productivity data follow a learning process:

$$P_t = P_0 e^{-\frac{b}{t} + r(t)} \tag{9}$$

where P_t is the productivity forecast at time period t ($t = 1 - T$); P_0 is the asymptotic or final productivity; $b > 0$ is the learning constant; and $r(t)$ is a homoscedastical and serially uncorrelated error term that is often ignored. Taking the logarithmic values of both sides gives the following Equation:

$$\ln P_t = \ln P_0 - \frac{b}{t} + r(t) \tag{10}$$

A linear regression model is presented in the aforementioned Equation, whose validity can be measured in terms of the coefficient of determination R^2, which is given as follows:

$$R^2 = \frac{S_{xy}^2}{S_{xx}S_{yy}} \tag{11}$$

where

$$S_{xx} = \sum_{t=1}^{T}(-\frac{1}{t})^2 - T(\frac{\sum_{t=1}^{T}(-\frac{1}{t})}{T})^2 \tag{12}$$

$$S_{yy} = \sum_{t=1}^{T}(\ln P_t)^2 - T(\frac{\sum_{t=1}^{T}(\ln P_t)}{T})^2 \tag{13}$$

$$S_{xy} = \sum_{t=1}^{T}(-\frac{\ln P_t}{t}) - T(\frac{\sum_{t=1}^{T}(-\frac{1}{t})}{T})(\frac{\sum_{t=1}^{T}\ln P_t}{T}) \tag{14}$$

R^2 is expected to approach a value of 1 if the collected productivity data follow a learning process.

3.2. IFN-Based Fuzzy Productivity Learning Model

The IFN-based fuzzy productivity learning model is proposed by defining the parameters in (8) with ITFNs.

$$\widetilde{P}_t = \widetilde{P}_0(x)e^{-\frac{\widetilde{b}}{t}+r(t)} \tag{15}$$

where

$$\widetilde{P}_t = (P_{tu1}, P_{tl1}, P_{t2}, P_{tl3}, P_{tu3}) \tag{16}$$

$$\widetilde{P}_0 = (P_{0u1}, P_{0l1}, P_{02}, P_{0l3}, P_{0u3}) \tag{17}$$

$$\widetilde{b} = (b_{u1}, b_{l1}, b_2, b_{l3}, b_{u3}) \tag{18}$$

An IFN-based fuzzy productivity forecast is meaningful in practice. The interpretation of (16) is that, according to a historical experience, the productivity within the t-th period would be within P_{0u1} and P_{0u3}. If this range is very wide, then a narrower range (from P_{0l1} to P_{0u3}) is very likely to contain actual value.

Because $t \neq 0$, according to the formula of fuzzy division, dividing $\widetilde{b}$ by $-t$ gives the following Equation:

$$-\frac{\widetilde{b}}{t} = (-\frac{b_{u3}}{t}, -\frac{b_{l3}}{t}, -\frac{b_2}{t}, -\frac{b_{l1}}{t}, -\frac{b_{u1}}{t}) \tag{19}$$

By taking the exponential of (19), we obtain the following Equation:

$$e^{-\frac{\widetilde{b}}{t}} \cong (e^{-\frac{b_{u3}}{t}}, e^{-\frac{b_{l3}}{t}}, e^{-\frac{b_2}{t}}, e^{-\frac{b_{l1}}{t}}, e^{-\frac{b_{u1}}{t}}) \tag{20}$$

$\widetilde{P}_t$ can be derived by multiplying $\widetilde{P}_0$ to both sides of (20) by using the formula of fuzzy multiplication:

$$\widetilde{P}_t = \widetilde{P}_0(x)e^{-\frac{\widetilde{b}}{t}} \cong (P_{0u1}e^{-\frac{b_{u3}}{t}}, P_{0l1}e^{-\frac{b_{l3}}{t}}, P_{02}e^{-\frac{b_2}{t}}, P_{0l3}e^{-\frac{b_{l1}}{t}}, P_{0u3}e^{-\frac{b_{u1}}{t}}) \tag{21}$$

3.3. MBQP Model for Deriving the Values of Fuzzy Parameters

Mathematical programming models involving type-2 or other types of fuzzy numbers have been extensively applied in the literature [38–40]. By taking the logarithm of (15), we obtain the following Equation:

$$\ln \widetilde{P}_t \cong (\ln P_{0u1} - \frac{b_{u3}}{t}, \ln P_{0l1} - \frac{b_{l3}}{t}, \ln P_{02} - \frac{b_2}{t}, \ln P_{0l3} - \frac{b_{l1}}{t}, \ln P_{0u3} - \frac{b_{u1}}{t}) \tag{22}$$

The following MBQP model is optimized to derive the values of fuzzy parameters.
Model MBQP:

$$\text{Min } Z = \sum_{t=1}^{T} (\ln P_{0u3} - \frac{b_{u1}}{t} - \ln P_{0u1} + \frac{b_{u3}}{t} + \ln P_{0l3} - \frac{b_{l1}}{t} - \ln P_{0l1} + \frac{b_{l3}}{t}) \tag{23}$$

subject to

$$\ln P_t \geq (1-s)(\ln P_{0u1} - \frac{b_{u3}}{t}) + s(\ln P_{0u2} - \frac{b_{u2}}{t});\ t = 1 \sim T \tag{24}$$

$$\ln P_t \leq (1-s)(\ln P_{0u3} - \frac{b_{u1}}{t}) + s(\ln P_{0u2} - \frac{b_{u2}}{t});\ t = 1 \sim T \tag{25}$$

$$\frac{\sum_{t=1}^{T} X_{t1} X_{t2}}{T} \geq (1-\alpha) \tag{26}$$

$$\ln P_t \geq X_{t1}(\ln P_{0l1} - \frac{b_{l3}}{t});\ t = 1 \sim T \tag{27}$$

$$\ln P_t \leq X_{t2}(\ln P_{0l3} - \frac{b_{l1}}{t});\ t = 1 \sim T \tag{28}$$

$$X_{t1}, X_{t2} \in \{0,1\};\ t = 1 \sim T \tag{29}$$

$$\ln P_{0u1} \leq \ln P_{0l1} \leq \ln P_{02} \leq \ln P_{0l3} \leq \ln P_{0u3} \tag{30}$$

$$0 \leq b_{u1} \leq b_{l1} \leq b_2 \leq b_{l3} \leq b_{u3} \tag{31}$$

The objective function minimizes the sum of the widths of fuzzy productivity forecasts by considering both LMF and UMF, thereby narrowing both the ranges of LMF and UMF (Figure 4) to maximize the forecasting precision [41]. Constraints (24) and (25) suggest that the membership of an actual value in the corresponding fuzzy forecast should be higher than the satisfaction level (s) based on UMF. X_{t1} and X_{t2} are binary variables, as defined in (29). When both X_{t1} and X_{t2} are equal to 1, an actual value lies within the range of LMF, as suggested by Constraints (27) and (28). Otherwise, the actual value lies outside the LMF range. In this manner, the inclusion level [42] is higher than $100(1 - \alpha)\%$ (Figure 5), as required by Constraint (26). Constraints (26)–(29) are quadratic constraints or can be converted into quadratic constraints. Constraints (30) and (31) define the sequences of endpoints in the ITFNs. The MBQP model has one linear objective function, $2T + 6$ variables, $4T + 9$ linear constraints, and $2T + 1$ quadratic constraints.

By moving variables independent of t out of the summation function, the objective function changes as follows:

$$\text{Min } Z = T \ln P_{0u3} - T \ln P_{0u1} + T \ln P_{0l3} - T \ln P_{0l1} + \sum_{t=1}^{T}(-\frac{b_{u1}}{t} + \frac{b_{u3}}{t} - \frac{b_{l1}}{t} + \frac{b_{l3}}{t}) \tag{32}$$

Let

$$\sum_{t=1}^{T} \frac{1}{t} = K \tag{33}$$

Then,
$$Z = T\ln P_{0u3} - T\ln P_{0u1} + T\ln P_{0l3} - T\ln P_{0l1} - Kb_{u1} + Kb_{u3} - Kb_{l1} + Kb_{l3} \quad (34)$$

Note that (33) is a divergent harmonic series [43].

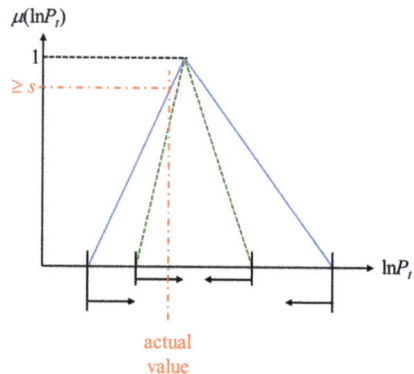

Figure 4. Effects of the objective function.

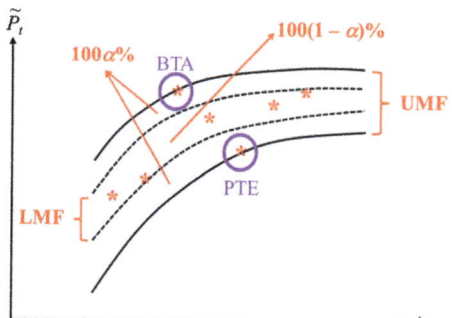

Figure 5. Inclusion interval constructed by solving the MBQP problem.

3.4. OWA for Defuzzifying a Fuzzy Productivity Forecast

In the literature, various formulas have been proposed to defuzzify an ITFN. For example, according to Dahooie et al. [44], an ITFN $\tilde{A}$ can be defuzzified as follows:

$$D_1(\tilde{A}) = \frac{A_{u1} + A_{l1} + A_2 + A_{l3} + A_{u3}}{5} \quad (35)$$

which is an extension of the center-of-gravity (COG) formula or

$$D_2(\tilde{A}) = \frac{(1-\lambda)A_{u1} + \lambda A_{l1} + A_2 + \lambda A_{l3} + (1-\lambda)A_{u3}}{3}; \lambda \in [0,1] \quad (36)$$

Lee et al. [31] proposed the following formula:

$$D_3(\tilde{A}) = \frac{A_{u1} + A_{l1} + 4A_2 + A_{l3} + A_{u3}}{8} \quad (37)$$

However, existing defuzzification formulas consider PTE and BTA cases likely, which is questionable because they have distinct meanings in practice.

Definition 4. *A PTE case is a case that lies outside the LMF on the left-hand side, that is, $P_t \le P_{tl1}$.*

Definition 5. *A BTA case is a case that lies outside the LMF on the right-hand side, that is, $P_t \geq P_{tl3}$.*

To address the aforementioned problem, the concept of OWA is applied in the proposed methodology. The rationale for applying OWA to defuzzify an IFN-based fuzzy productivity forecast is explained as follows:

(1) Using existing defuzzification methods, the defuzzification result of an IFN-based fuzzy productivity forecast is usually the weighted sum of its endpoints. OWA also calculates the weighted sum of data.
(2) OWA aggregates data that have been sorted. The endpoints of an IFN-based fuzzy productivity forecast, from the leftmost to the rightmost, also form a sorted series.

There exist five decision strategies in OWA that assign unequal weights to different attributes according to their performances. The five strategies are optimistic, moderately optimistic, neutral, moderately pessimistic, and pessimistic strategies [44,45]. Most formulas for defuzzifying an ITFN also assign weights to its endpoints. Therefore, assigning weights to the endpoints of $\tilde{P}_t$ according to their possibilities is reasonable. In the training data, if the number of PTE cases is considerably higher than that of BTA cases, then the "pessimistic" strategy appears to be suitable. By contrast, if the number of BTA cases is considerably higher than that of PTE cases, then the "pessimistic" strategy can be selected. On the basis of these beliefs, a fuzzy productivity forecast is defuzzified according to the selected forecasting strategy, as presented in Table 1. These strategies are subjective selections based on objective historical statistics [46].

Table 1. Defuzzification method based on the forecasting strategy.

Strategy	$D_4(\tilde{P}_t)$
Optimistic	$0P_{tu1} + 0P_{tl1} + 0P_{t2} + 0P_{tl3} + 1P_{tu3}$
Moderately Optimistic	$0.06P_{tu1} + 0.08P_{tl1} + 0.10P_{t2} + 0.14P_{tl3} + 0.62P_{tu3}$
Neutral	$0.2P_{tu1} + 0.2P_{tl1} + 0.2P_{t2} + 0.2P_{tl3} + 0.2P_{tu3}$
Moderately Pessimistic	$0.49P_{tu1} + 0.30P_{tl1} + 0.15P_{t2} + 0.06P_{tl3} + 0.01P_{tu3}$
Pessimistic	$0.89P_{tu1} + 0.10P_{tl1} + 0.01P_{t2} + 0P_{tl3} + 0P_{tu3}$

Property 2. *The "neutral" forecasting strategy is equivalent to the COG defuzzification method.*

4. Application of the Proposed Methodology to a Real Case

The effectiveness of the proposed methodology was evaluated by applying it for forecasting the productivity of a real dynamic random access memory (DRAM) factory. This case was first investigated by Wang and Chen [19]. In this case, the multi-item productivity of the DRAM factory, which was derived by dividing the monetary value of outputs by that of inputs, was recorded for 14 periods. The recorded data are displayed in Figure 6. Wang and Chen [19] proposed a fuzzy collaborative forecasting approach to forecast the future productivity. For the same purpose, Chen et al. [21] proposed a fuzzy polynomial fitting and mathematical programming approach. The differences between the two approaches and the proposed methodology are summarized in Table 2. The most obvious difference is that only the proposed methodology forecasts productivity with an IFN, thereby differentiating between extreme cases and normal cases to construct a narrow interval of productivity.

The productivity data were divided into two parts, the training data (including the data of the first 10 periods) and test data (including the remaining data). First, to ensure that the collected data followed a learning process, the coefficient of determination (R^2) was calculated. R^2 was found to be 0.87, which was sufficiently high to ensure that the collected data followed a learning process. Subsequently, the training data were used to build the MBQP model, which was solved using a branch-and-bound algorithm [47–50] on a personal computer with Intel core i7-7700 CPU @ 3.60 GHz and 8 GB RAM in 10 s. Moreover, α was set to 0.2 so that an 80% inclusion interval was constructed. The satisfaction level s was set to 0.3. The optimal solution was

$$\widetilde{P_0^*} = (1.267, 1.343, 1.343, 1.569, 1.683)$$
$$\widetilde{b^*} = (0.990, 0.990, 0.990, 1.260, 1.260)$$

The optimal objective function value Z^* was 5.972. The forecasting results are displayed in Figure 7. The average width of the ranges of LMFs was 0.234. As expected, the ranges of LMFs were too narrow to include all actual values. Nevertheless, most actual values could be contained in such narrow ranges, which is very advantageous for practical applications. The productivity at the eighth period was a PTE case (the purple circle in Figure 7) because the actual value was below the LMF curve, as illustrated in Figure 8. By contrast, no BTA case was observed, which implied that the pessimistic or moderately pessimistic strategy may be suitable.

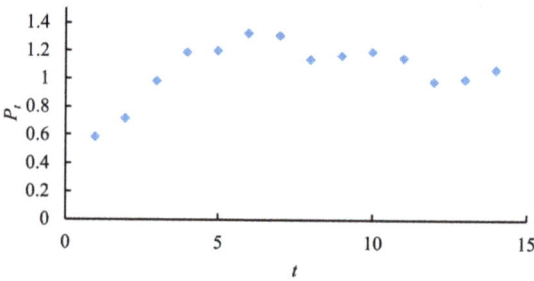

Figure 6. Real case.

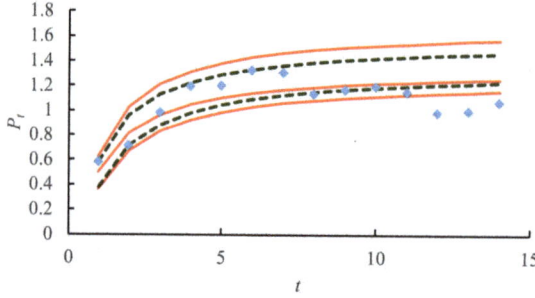

Figure 7. Forecasting results using the proposed methodology.

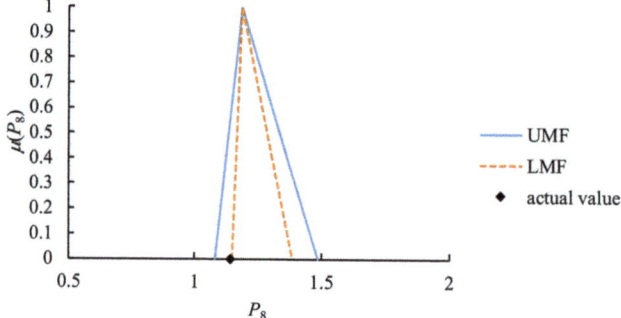

Figure 8. IFN-based fuzzy productivity forecast for $t = 8$.

Table 2. Differences between the two approaches and the proposed methodology.

Method	Type of Productivity Forecast	Optimization Models	Discriminating Extreme Cases	Number of Experts Required
Wang and Chen [19]	Fuzzy number	NLP, QP	No	Multiple
Chen et al. [21]	Fuzzy number	PP	No	One
The proposed methodology	IFN	MBQP	Yes	One

After applying the proposed methodology to test data, the hit rate was 25%. Subsequently, various formulas were applied to defuzzify interval-valued fuzzy productivity forecasts for test data to evaluate the forecasting accuracy of the proposed methodology in terms of mean absolute error (MAE), mean absolute percentage error (MAPE), and root mean square error (RMSE). The results are summarized in Table 3. The defuzzification formula D4 (the moderately pessimistic strategy) exhibited the best performance.

Table 3. Forecasting accuracy achieved using the proposed methodology (for test data).

Defuzzification Formula	MAE	MAPE	RMSE
D_1	0.270	26.2%	0.279
D_2 (λ = 0.4)	0.255	24.8%	0.265
D_3	0.240	23.3%	0.250
D_4 (Moderately Optimistic)	0.402	38.9%	0.409
D_4 (Moderately Pessimistic)	0.150	14.7%	0.166

The linear programming (LP) method of Tanaka and Watada [41], quadratic programing (QP) method of Peters [51], QP method of Donoso et al. [52], two NLP models of Chen and Lin [53], artificial neural network (ANN) method of Chen [54], and the PP method of Chen et al. [21] were applied to the real case for comparison. Similar to the proposed methodology, all the aforementioned methods are based on a single expert's forecast.

Tanaka and Watada's LP method minimized the sum of the ranges of fuzzy productivity forecasts. The satisfaction level (s) was set to 0.3 for a fair comparison. By contrast, Peters' QP method maximized the forecasting accuracy in terms of the average satisfaction level by requesting the average range of fuzzy productivity forecasts to be less than $d = 1$. To simultaneously optimize the forecasting accuracy and precision, the QP method of Donoso et al. minimized the weighted sum of the squared deviations from the core as well as the squared deviations from the estimated spreads. In this case, the two weights w_1 and w_2 were set to 0.45 and 0.55, respectively. Chen and Lin's two NLP models were extensions of Tanaka and Watada's LP model and Peters's QP model, respectively. The two NLP methods adopted the following high-order objectives and/or constraints: $o = 2$, $s = 0.15$, $m = 2$, and $d = 1.2$, where o and m are the orders of the two objective functions, respectively. In Chen's ANN method, the initial values of the network parameters were set as follows: the connection weight ($\widetilde{w}$) = (0.10, 0.77, 1.15); the threshold ($\widetilde{\theta}$) = (−0.18, −0.12, 0.26); and the learning rate (η) = 0.25. The training of the ANN was completed in 10 epochs. The PP method of Chen et al. overcame the global optimality problem of Chen and Lin's NLP method by converting the NLP models into PP models, for which the Karush–Kuhn–Tucker conditions were easy to solve. The performance of existing methods is summarized in Table 4. A comparison of the performances of existing methods and the proposed methodology is displayed in Figure 9. The "moderately pessimistic" strategy was adopted in the proposed methodology.

Table 4. Forecasting performances of existing methods for test data.

Method	MAE	MAPE	RMSE	Hit Rate	Average Range
Tanaka and Watada's LP method	0.283	27.4%	0.292	25%	0.346
Peters's QP method	0.487	47.0%	0.492	25%	1.233
Donoso et al.'s QP method	0.269	26.1%	0.278	0%	0.273
Chen and Lin's NLP I model	0.276	26.8%	0.285	0%	0.288
Chen and Lin's NLP II model	0.282	27.4%	0.290	100%	1.006
Chen's ANN method	0.185	18.1%	0.198	100%	0.803
Chen et al.'s PP method	0.168	16.4%	0.181	0%	0.249

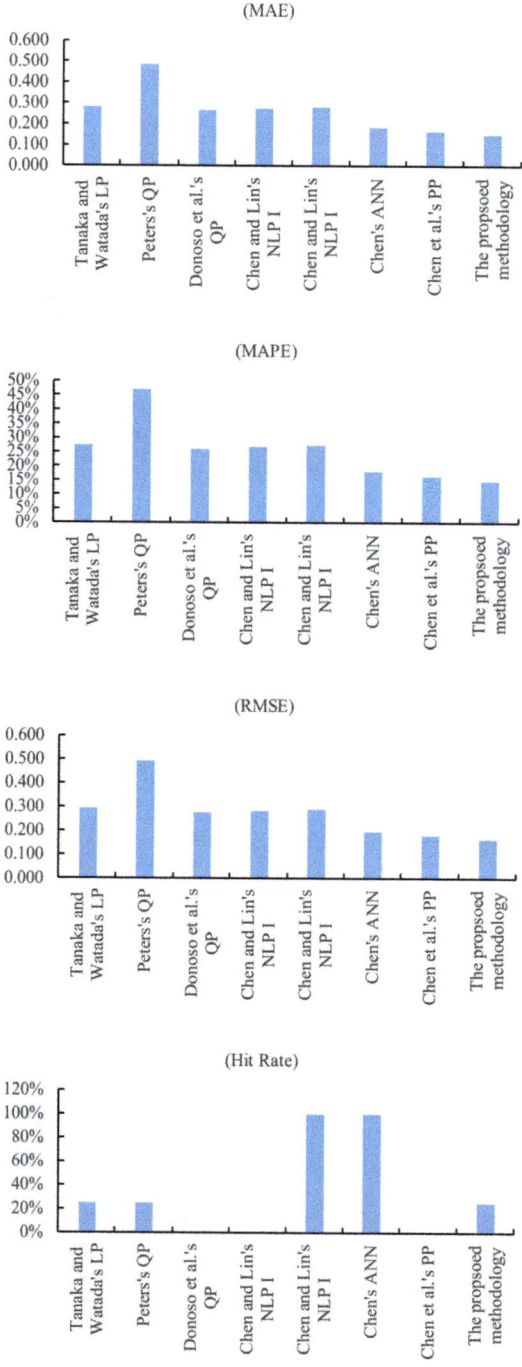

Figure 9. *Cont.*

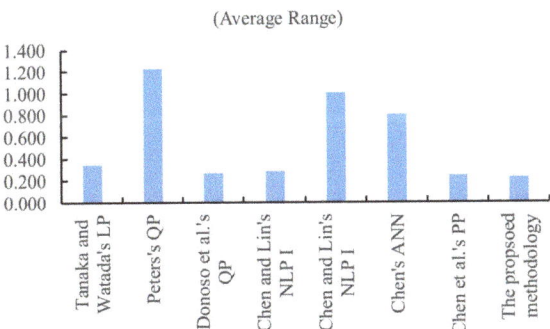

Figure 9. Comparison between the performances of various methods.

According to the experimental results, the following inferences are obtained:

(1) By excluding extreme (PTE and BTA) cases, the average range of fuzzy productivity forecasts was narrowed by 35%. In other words, the average range was widened by 35% when including a single extreme case.

(2) The proposed methodology outperformed existing methods in terms of MAE, MAPE, and RMSE in evaluating the forecasting accuracy. The detection of PTE and BTA cases enabled the selection of a suitable forecasting strategy, which contributed to the superiority of the proposed methodology over existing methods. The most significant advantage was over the QP method of Peters. The proposed method was up to 69% more effective than the QP method in minimizing MAPE.

(3) Conversely, the proposed methodology optimized the forecasting precision measured in terms of the average range. Despite such a narrow average range, the hit rate achieved using the proposed methodology was also satisfactory.

(4) To ascertain whether the differences between the performances of various methods were statistically significant, the sums of ranks of all methods were compared [55–57]. The results are presented in Table 5. For example, the proposed methodology ranked the first among the compared methods in reducing MAE, MAPE, RMSE, and the average range, and ranked the fifth in elevating the hit rate. As a result, the sum of ranks was 9 for the proposed methodology. The ranks of methods that performed equally well were averaged. For example, Donoso et al.'s QP method and Chen and Li's NLP I method performed equally well in elevating the hit rate and outperformed the other methods. Therefore, both of their ranks were (1 + 2)/2 = 1.5. According to the sums of ranks achieved by these methods, the proposed methodology ranked first, followed by the PP method of Chen et al., the QP method of Donoso et al., and the ANN method of Chen.

(5) To further elaborate the effectiveness of the proposed methodology, it has been applied to another case of forecasting the productivity of a factory. This case was first investigated by Akano and Asaolu [58], in which four factors (preventive maintenance time, off-duty time, machine downtime, and power failure time) were considered to be influential to the productivity of a factory. To forecast the productivity, Akano and Asaolu constructed an adaptive network-based fuzzy inference system (ANFIS), which resulted in a MAPE of up to 34%. In this study, an expert applied the IFN-based MBQP–OWA approach to forecast productivity, for which the neutral strategy was adopted. The forecasting results are shown in Figure 10. The forecasting accuracy, in terms of MAPE, was elevated by 19%.

Table 5. Comparing the sums of ranks of various methods.

Method	Rank (MAE)	Rank (MAPE)	Rank (RMSE)	Rank (Hit Rate)	Rank (Average Range)	Sum of Ranks
Tanaka and Watada's LP	7	7	7	5	5	31
Peters's QP	8	8	8	5	8	37
Donoso et al.'s QP	4	4	4	1.5	3	16.5
Chen and Lin's NLP I	5	5	5	1.5	4	20.5
Chen and Lin's NLP I	6	7	6	7.5	7	33.5
Chen's ANN	3	3	3	7.5	6	22.5
Chen et al.'s PP	2	2	2	3	2	11
The proposed methodology	1	1	1	5	1	9

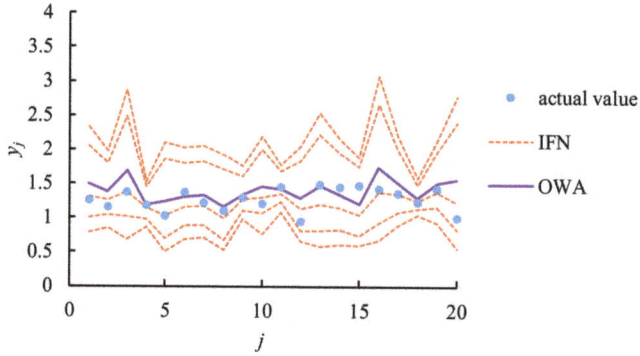

Figure 10. Forecasting results using the IFN-based MBQP–OWA approach.

5. Conclusions

An IFN-based MBQP–OWA approach is proposed in this study to model an uncertain productivity learning process. This study aims to resolve a problem of existing methods, that is, a few extreme (PTE and BTA) cases determine the lower and upper bounds on productivity. This problem causes the range of productivity to be unacceptably wide. To solve this problem, the range of productivity is divided into inner and outer sections that correspond to the LMF and UMF of an IFN-based fuzzy productivity forecast, respectively. In this manner, all actual values are included in the outer section, whereas most of the values lie within the inner section. Moreover, a suitable forecasting strategy can be determined according to the percentages of PTE and BTA cases. To derive the values of parameters in the IFN-based fuzzy productivity learning model, an MBQP model is proposed and optimized. Subsequently, the OWA method based on the selected forecasting strategy is applied to defuzzify the fuzzy productivity forecast. The contribution of this study resides in the following:

(1) Using the characteristics of IFNs, a systematic mechanism was established to avoid extreme cases from widening the ranges of fuzzy productivity forecasts.
(2) An innovative idea was proposed to defuzzify an IFN-based fuzzy productivity forecast using OWA.

The IFN-based MBQP–OWA approach has been applied to a real case of a DRAM factory to evaluate its effectiveness. According to the experiment results, the following findings are obtained:

(1) In terms of MAE, MAPE, and RMSE, the accuracy of the forecasted productivity obtained using the proposed methodology was superior to those obtained using several existing methods.
(2) The forecasting precision achieved using the proposed methodology was also satisfactory, especially for minimizing the average range of fuzzy productivity forecasts.

(3) By identifying PTE and BTA cases, an expert was able to select a suitable forecasting strategy, which further enhanced the forecasting precision and accuracy.

The proposed methodology has several advantages, but there are also some drawbacks. For example, extreme cases may affect the range of productivity in different ways in the future. Nevertheless, in future studies, other types of fuzzy numbers, such as interval-valued intuitionistic fuzzy numbers [59], hesitant IFNs [60,61], Pythagorean fuzzy numbers [62], and interval-valued Pythagorean fuzzy numbers [63,64] can be adopted to model uncertain productivity instead. The proposed methodology can also be applied to other learning processes in various fields that are subject to uncertainty, such as unit cost learning [65] and energy efficiency learning [66]. Another interesting topic is how to build the IFN-based fuzzy productivity learning model if the collected productivity data are incomplete [67]. The proposed methodology can also be extended to fulfill a multiple-expert collaborative forecasting task [68–72].

Author Contributions: Data curation, methodology and writing original draft: T.-C.T.C. and M.-C.C.; writing—review and editing: T.-C.T.C., M.-C.C., and K.-W.H. All authors contributed equally to the writing of this paper. All authors read and approved the final manuscript.

Funding: This research received no external funding.

Conflicts of Interest: The authors declare no conflicts of interest.

References

1. Stevenson, W.J. *Operations Management*; McGraw-Hill: New York, NY, USA, 2005.
2. Chen, T. New fuzzy method for improving the precision of productivity pre-dictions for a factory. *Neural Comput. Appl.* **2017**, *28*, 3507–3520. [CrossRef]
3. Geylani, P.C.; Kapelko, M.; Stefanou, S.E. Dynamic productivity change differences between global and non-global firms: A firm-level application to the US food and beverage industries. *Oper. Res.* **2019**, 1–23. [CrossRef]
4. Mitropoulos, P. Production and quality performance of healthcare services in EU countries during the economic crisis. *Oper. Res.* **2019**, 1–17. [CrossRef]
5. Lapré, M.A.; Van Wassenhove, L.N. Creating and transferring knowledge for productivity improvement in factories. *Manag. Sci.* **2001**, *47*, 1311–1325. [CrossRef]
6. Chen, T. A collaborative and artificial intelligence approach for semiconductor cost forecasting. *Comput. Ind. Eng.* **2013**, *66*, 476–484. [CrossRef]
7. Klein, P.; Bergmann, R. Generation of complex data for AI-based predictive maintenance research with a physical factory model. In Proceedings of the 16th International Conference on Informatics in Control Automation and Robotics, Prague, Czech Republic, 29–31 July 2019; pp. 40–50.
8. Asemi, A.; Safari, A.; Zavareh, A.A. The role of management information system (MIS) and Decision support system (DSS) for manager's decision making process. *Int. J. Bus. Manag.* **2011**, *6*, 164–173. [CrossRef]
9. Al-Mamary, Y.; Shamsuddin, A.; Hamid, A.; Aziati, N. The role of different types of information systems in business organizations: A review. *Int. J. Res.* **2014**, *1*, 1279–1286.
10. Gerogiannis, V.C.; Fitsilis, P.; Voulgaridou, D.; Kirytopoulos, K.A.; Sachini, E. A case study for project and portfolio management information system selection: A group AHP-scoring model approach. *Int. J. Proj. Organ. Manag.* **2010**, *2*, 361–381. [CrossRef]
11. Gerogiannis, V.C.; Fitsilis, P.; Kameas, A.D. Using a combined intuitionistic fuzzy set-TOPSIS method for evaluating project and portfolio management information systems. In *Artificial Intelligence Applications and Innovations*; Springer: Berlin/Heidelberg, Germany, 2011; pp. 67–81.
12. Hashemian, H.M.; Bean, W.C. State-of-the-art predictive maintenance techniques. *IEEE Trans. Instrum. Meas.* **2011**, *60*, 3480–3492. [CrossRef]
13. Brynjolfsson, E.; Rock, D.; Syverson, C. Artificial intelligence and the modern productivity paradox: A clash of expectations and statistics. In *The Economics of Artificial Intelligence: An Agenda*; University of Chicago Press: Chicago, IL, USA, 2018.
14. Appelbaum, E. Uncertainty and the measurement of productivity. *J. Product. Anal.* **1991**, *2*, 157–170. [CrossRef]

15. Chen, T.; Romanowski, R. Forecasting the productivity of a virtual enterprise by agent-based fuzzy collaborative intelligence—With Facebook as an example. *Appl. Soft Comput.* **2014**, *24*, 511–521. [CrossRef]
16. Zadeh, L.A. The concept of a linguistic variable and its application to approximate reasoning—II. *Inf. Sci.* **1975**, *8*, 301–357. [CrossRef]
17. Hougaard, J.L. A simple approximation of productivity scores of fuzzy production plans. *Fuzzy Sets Syst.* **2005**, *152*, 455–465. [CrossRef]
18. Emrouznejad, A.; Rostamy-Malkhalifeh, M.; Hatami-Marbini, A.; Tavana, M.; Aghayi, N. An overall profit Malmquist productivity index with fuzzy and interval data. *Math. Comput. Model.* **2011**, *54*, 2827–2838. [CrossRef]
19. Wang, Y.C.; Chen, T. A fuzzy collaborative forecasting approach for forecasting the productivity of a factory. *Adv. Mech. Eng.* **2013**, *5*, 234571. [CrossRef]
20. Chen, T.; Wang, Y.C. Evaluating sustainable advantages in productivity with a systematic procedure. *Int. J. Adv. Manuf. Technol.* **2016**, *87*, 1435–1442. [CrossRef]
21. Chen, T.; Ou, C.; Lin, Y.C. A fuzzy polynomial fitting and mathematical programming approach for enhancing the accuracy and precision of productivity forecasting. *Comput. Math. Organ. Theory* **2019**, *25*, 85–107. [CrossRef]
22. Guijun, W.; Xiaoping, L. The applications of interval-valued fuzzy numbers and interval-distribution numbers. *Fuzzy Sets Syst.* **1998**, *98*, 331–335. [CrossRef]
23. Broumi, S.; Talea, M.; Bakali, A.; Smarandache, F.; Nagarajan, D.; Lathamaheswari, M.; Parimala, M. Shortest path problem in fuzzy, intuitionistic fuzzy and neutrosophic environment: An overview. *Complex Intell. Syst.* **2019**, *5*, 371–378. [CrossRef]
24. Mohamadghasemi, A.; Hadi-Vencheh, A.; Lotfi, F.H.; Khalilzadeh, M. An integrated group FWA-ELECTRE III approach based on interval type-2 fuzzy sets for solving the MCDM problems using limit distance mean. *Complex Intell. Syst.* **2020**, 1–35. [CrossRef]
25. Muhuri, P.K.; Ashraf, Z.; Lohani, Q.D. Multiobjective reliability redun-dancy allocation problem with interval type-2 fuzzy uncertainty. *IEEE Trans. Fuzzy Syst.* **2017**, *26*, 1339–1355.
26. Wang, Y.J. Combining quality function deployment with simple additive weighting for interval-valued fuzzy multi-criteria decision-making with depend-ent evaluation criteria. *Soft Comput.* **2019**, 1–11. [CrossRef]
27. Blanco-Mesa, F.; León-Castro, E.; Merigó, J.M.; Xu, Z. Bonferroni means with induced ordered weighted average operators. *Int. J. Intell. Syst.* **2019**, *34*, 3–23. [CrossRef]
28. Hu, J.; Zhang, Y.; Chen, X.; Liu, Y. Multi-criteria decision making method based on possibility degree of interval type-2 fuzzy number. *Knowl.-Based Syst.* **2013**, *43*, 21–29. [CrossRef]
29. Dimuro, G.P. On interval fuzzy numbers. IEEE Workshop-School on Theoretical Computer Science, Pelotas, Brazil, 24–26 August 2011; pp. 3–8.
30. Baležentis, T.; Zeng, S. Group multi-criteria decision making based upon interval-valued fuzzy numbers: An extension of the MULTIMOORA method. *Expert Syst. Appl.* **2013**, *40*, 543–550. [CrossRef]
31. Lee, C.S.; Chung, C.C.; Lee, H.S.; Gan, G.Y.; Chou, M.T. An intervalvalued fuzzy number approach for supplier selection. *J. Mar. Sci. Technol.* **2016**, *24*, 384–389.
32. Chen, T.; Wang, Y.C. Interval fuzzy number-based approach for modeling an uncertain fuzzy yield learning process. *J. Ambient Intell. Humaniz. Comput.* **2020**, *11*, 1213–1223. [CrossRef]
33. Javanmard, M.; Nehi, H.M. Rankings and operations for interval type-2 fuzzy numbers: A review and some new methods. *J. Appl. Math. Comput.* **2019**, *59*, 597–630. [CrossRef]
34. Mendel, J.M. Type-2 fuzzy sets and systems: An overview. *IEEE Comput. Intell. Mag.* **2007**, *2*, 20–29. [CrossRef]
35. Chen, T.; Lin, C.-W. An innovative yield learning model considering multiple learning sources and learning source interactions. *Comput. Ind. Eng.* **2019**, *131*, 455–463. [CrossRef]
36. Baena, F.; Guarin, A.; Mora, J.; Sauza, J.; Retat, S. Learning factory: The path to industry 4.0. *Procedia Manuf.* **2017**, *9*, 73–80. [CrossRef]
37. Chen, T. An innovative fuzzy and artificial neural network approach for forecasting yield under an uncertain learning environment. *J. Ambient Intell. Humaniz. Comput.* **2018**, *9*, 1013–1025. [CrossRef]
38. Khalilpourazari, S.; Pasandideh, S.H.R.; Ghodratnama, A. Robust possibilistic programming for multi-item EOQ model with defective supply batches: Whale Optimization and Water Cycle Algorithms. *Neural Comput. Appl.* **2018**, in press. [CrossRef]
39. Das, A.; Bera, U.K.; Maiti, M. A solid transportation problem in uncertain environment involving type-2 fuzzy variable. *Neural Comput. Appl.* **2019**, in press. [CrossRef]

40. Samanta, S.; Jana, D.K. A multi-item transportation problem with mode of transportation preference by MCDM method in interval type-2 fuzzy environment. *Neural Comput. Appl.* **2019**, *31*, 605–617. [CrossRef]
41. Tanaka, H.; Watada, J. Possibilistic linear systems and their application to the linear regression model. *Fuzzy Sets Syst.* **1988**, *272*, 275–289. [CrossRef]
42. Chen, T. A collaborative fuzzy-neural system for global CO_2 concentration forecasting. *Int. J. Innov. Comput. Inf. Control* **2012**, *8*, 7679–7696.
43. Dunham, W. *Journey Through Genius: The Great Theorems of Mathematics*; Wiley: New York, NY, USA, 1990.
44. Dahooie, J.H.; Zavadskas, E.K.; Abolhasani, M.; Vanaki, A.; Turskis, Z. A novel approach for evaluation of projects using an intervalvalued fuzzy additive ratio assessment (ARAS) method: A case study of oil and gas well drilling projects. *Symmetry* **2018**, *10*, 45. [CrossRef]
45. Yager, R.R.; Kacprzyk, J. *The Ordered Weighted Averaging Operators: Theory and Applications*; Springer: New York, NY, USA, 2012.
46. Blanco-Mesa, F.; Gil-Lafuente, A.M.; Merigó, J.M. Subjective stakeholder dynamics relationships treatment: A methodological approach using fuzzy decision-making. *Comput. Math. Organ. Theory* **2018**, *24*, 441–472. [CrossRef]
47. Lin, Y.C.; Chen, T. A multibelief analytic hierarchy process and nonlinear programming approach for diversifying product designs: Smart backpack design as an example. *Proc. Inst. Mech. Eng. Part B J. Eng. Manuf.* **2020**, *234*, 1044–1056. [CrossRef]
48. Chen, T.; Wang, Y.C. An advanced IoT system for assisting ubiquitous manufacturing with 3D printing. *Int. J. Adv. Manuf. Technol.* **2019**, *103*, 1721–1733. [CrossRef]
49. Tsai, H.R.; Chen, T. Enhancing the sustainability of a location-aware service through optimization. *Sustainability* **2014**, *6*, 9441–9455. [CrossRef]
50. Lin, C.W.; Chen, T. 3D printing technologies for enhancing the sustainability of an aircraft manufacturing or MRO company—A multi-expert partial consensus-FAHP analysis. *Int. J. Adv. Manuf. Technol.* **2019**, *105*, 4171–4180. [CrossRef]
51. Peters, G. Fuzzy linear regression with fuzzy intervals. *Fuzzy Sets Syst.* **1994**, *63*, 45–55. [CrossRef]
52. Donoso, S.; Marin, N.; Vila, M.A. Quadratic programming models for fuzzy regression. In Proceedings of the International Conference on Mathematical and Statistical Modeling in Honor of Enrique Castillo, Ciudad Real, Spain, 28–30 June 2006.
53. Chen, T.; Lin, Y.C. A fuzzy-neural system incorporating unequally important expert opinions for semiconductor yield forecasting. *Int. J. Uncertain. Fuzziness Knowl.-Based Syst.* **2008**, *16*, 35–58. [CrossRef]
54. Chen, T Fitting an uncertain productivity learning process using an artificial neural network approach. *Comput. Math. Organ. Theory* **2018**, *24*, 422–439. [CrossRef]
55. Chen, T.; Wang, Y.C. An agent-based fuzzy collaborative intelligence approach for precise and accurate semiconductor yield forecasting. *IEEE Trans. Fuzzy Syst.* **2013**, *22*, 201–211. [CrossRef]
56. de Barros, R.S.M.; Hidalgo, J.I.G.; de Lima Cabral, D.R. Wilcoxon rank sum test drift detector. *Neurocomputing* **2018**, *275*, 1954–1963. [CrossRef]
57. Chen, T.; Wu, H.C.; Wang, Y.C. Fuzzy-neural approaches with example post-classification for estimating job cycle time in a wafer fab. *Appl. Soft Comput.* **2009**, *9*, 1225–1231. [CrossRef]
58. Akano, T.T.; Asaolu, O.S. Productivity forecast of a manufacturing sys-tem through intelligent modelling. *Futo J. Ser.* **2017**, *3*, 102–113.
59. Atanassov, K.; Gargov, G. Interval valued intuitionistic fuzzy sets. *Fuzzy Sets Syst.* **1989**, *31*, 343–349. [CrossRef]
60. Wei, G.; Zhao, X.; Lin, R. Some hesitant interval-valued fuzzy aggregation operators and their applications to multiple attribute decision making. *Knowl.-Based Syst.* **2013**, *46*, 43–53. [CrossRef]
61. Zhang, C.; Wang, C.; Zhang, Z.; Tian, D. A novel technique for multiple attribute group decision making in interval-valued hesitant fuzzy environments with incomplete weight information. *J. Ambient Intell. Humaniz. Comput.* **2018**, in press. [CrossRef]
62. Garg, H. Confidence levels based Pythagorean fuzzy aggregation operators and its application to decision-making process. *Comput. Math. Organ. Theory* **2017**, *23*, 546–571. [CrossRef]
63. Blancett, R.S. Learning from productivity learning curves. *Res. Technol. Manag* **2002**, *45*, 54–58. [CrossRef]
64. Rahman, K.; Abdullah, S.; Ali, A.; Amin, F. Interval-valued Pythagorean fuzzy Einstein hybrid weighted averaging aggregation operator and their application to group decision making. *Complex Intell. Syst.* **2019**, *5*, 41–52. [CrossRef]

65. Lin, Y.C.; Chen, T. An advanced fuzzy collaborative intelligence approach for fitting the uncertain unit cost learning process. *Complex Intell. Syst.* **2019**, *5*, 303–313. [CrossRef]
66. Jaeger, H.; Haas, H. Harnessing nonlinearity: Predicting chaotic systems and saving energy in wireless communication. *Science* **2004**, *304*, 78–80. [CrossRef]
67. Zeng, J.; Li, Z.; Liu, M.; Liao, S. Information structures in an incomplete interval-valued information system. *Int. J. Comput. Intell. Syst.* **2019**, *12*, 809–821. [CrossRef]
68. Chen, T.; Wang, Y.-C.; Lin, C.-W. A fuzzy collaborative forecasting approach considering experts' unequal levels of authority. *Appl. Soft Comput.* **2020**, *94*, 106455. [CrossRef]
69. Zhang, X.; Song, H. An integrative framework for collaborative forecasting in tourism supply chains. *Int. J. Tour. Res.* **2018**, *20*, 158–171. [CrossRef]
70. Wang, Y.C.; Chen, T.C.T. A direct-solution fuzzy collaborative intelligence approach for yield forecasting in semiconductor manufacturing. *Procedia Manuf.* **2018**, *17*, 110–117. [CrossRef]
71. Chen, T. Incorporating fuzzy c-means and a back-propagation network ensemble to job completion time prediction in a semiconductor fabrication factory. *Fuzzy Sets Syst.* **2007**, *158*, 2153–2168. [CrossRef]
72. Chen, T.; Lin, Y.C. Feasibility evaluation and optimization of a smart manufacturing system based on 3D printing: A review. *Int. J. Intell. Syst.* **2017**, *32*, 394–413. [CrossRef]

© 2020 by the authors. Licensee MDPI, Basel, Switzerland. This article is an open access article distributed under the terms and conditions of the Creative Commons Attribution (CC BY) license (http://creativecommons.org/licenses/by/4.0/).

Article

Using a Fuzzy Inference System to Obtain Technological Tables for Electrical Discharge Machining Processes

C. J. Luis Pérez

Materials and Manufacturing Engineering Research Group, Engineering Department, Public University of Navarre, Campus de Arrosadía s/n, Pamplona, 31006 Navarra, Spain; cluis.perez@unavarra.es

Received: 12 May 2020; Accepted: 3 June 2020; Published: 5 June 2020

Abstract: Technological tables are very important in electrical discharge machining to determine optimal operating conditions for process variables, such as material removal rate or electrode wear. Their determination is of great industrial importance and their experimental determination is very important because they allow the most appropriate operating conditions to be selected beforehand. These technological tables are usually employed for electrical discharge machining of steel, but their number is significantly less in the case of other materials. In this present research study, a methodology based on using a fuzzy inference system to obtain these technological tables is shown with the aim of being able to select the most appropriate manufacturing conditions in advance. In addition, a study of the results obtained using a fuzzy inference system for modeling the behavior of electrical discharge machining parameters is shown. These results are compared to those obtained from response surface methodology. Furthermore, it is demonstrated that the fuzzy system can provide a high degree of precision and, therefore, it can be used to determine the influence of these machining parameters on technological variables, such as roughness, electrode wear, or material removal rate, more efficiently than other techniques.

Keywords: fuzzy; manufacturing; modeling; electrical discharge machining (EDM); technological tables

1. Introduction

Electrical discharge machining (EDM) is a manufacturing process which is typically classified as a non-traditional manufacturing process. EDM has several advantages over traditional manufacturing processes such as turning or milling, because there is no direct contact between the part and the tool, and the hardness of the so-processed materials does not affect the result. In the field of EDM, technological tables are of great interest since, by using them, it is possible to determine in advance the optimal machining conditions for a certain strategy that either maximizes material removal or reduces electrode wear, among other objectives. These technological tables are usually employed for electrical discharge machining of steel, but their number is significantly less in the case of other materials. In the research study of Torres et al. [1], technological tables were obtained for the case of TiB_2, which is a low-machinability material, by using response surface methodology (RSM) that fitted a second-order polynomial regression model along with nonlinear programming. However, when regression models are not adequate to predict the behavior of response variables, because the values of the coefficients of determination are low, it is necessary to use other alternative methodologies. Therefore, in this present study, a methodology is proposed to obtain the technological tables using a Sugeno type fuzzy inference system (FIS). As shown, the results obtained with this FIS significantly improve those obtained using response surface methodology and, therefore, the results obtained are more reliable than those obtained by RSM. In the research study of Torres et al. [2], a new energy density model was proposed and a 4^3 factorial design was employed for modeling the behavior of the arithmetical mean roughness (Ra), the electrode wear (EW), and the material removal rate (MRR) in the EDM machining of an Inconel® 600 alloy using Cu–C electrodes (Inconel is a registered trademark of Special Metals Family of Companies). However, in this study, the technological tables for this alloy were not developed. Furthermore, as shown in this study [2], the regression models obtained using RSM were able to adequately predict Ra and MRR values with R-squared values greater than 0.95; however, in the case of EW, response surface methodology was not able to adequately predict the EW behavior. Therefore, to fill these gaps, a Takagi–Sugeno [3,4] fuzzy inference system (FIS) is proposed in this present study to model the behavior of Ra, MRR, and EW and to obtain the technological tables for this Inconel® 600 alloy, within the range of the considered variation levels of the parameters under study. In addition, a comparative study is performed between the results provided by RSM and the results provided by the FIS system. In [5] a methodology was developed to obtain the values of technological tables for the case of B_4C, SiSiC and WC-Co conductive ceramic materials. However, as in the technological tables developed in [1], when regression models are not adequate to predict the behaviour of response variables, it is necessary to use other alternative methodologies. As shown below, the FIS can predict the output values more efficiently than by using regression. Data shown in Tables 1 and 2 that were taken from the above-mentioned study [2] are used in this present work in order to analyze a case study and to develop a fuzzy inference system for modeling the behavior of these technological variables (Ra, EW, and MRR), as well as show the application of the proposed methodology in order to obtain the technological tables. These technological tables are widely used for steel, while their number is significantly less in the case of other materials. In any case, it is considered that the proposed methodology could be generally applied to any other material and for other manufacturing processes. Hence, it is considered that the present methodology for obtaining the technological tables may be of interest in the event that the input variables can be continuously varied and, thus, in this way, it could be possible to select the most appropriate operating conditions in advance.

Table 1. Design factors and levels. These values were taken from Reference [2] Torres Salcedo, A.; Puertas Arbizu I.; Luis Pérez, C. J. Analytical Modeling of Energy Density and Optimization of the EDM Machining Parameters of Inconel 600. Metals 2017, 7, 166. (Open access article distributed under the terms and conditions of the Creative Commons Attribution (CC BY) license: http://creativecommons.org/licenses/by/4.0/).

Design Factors	Levels and Values							
	Positive Polarity				Negative Polarity			
	1	2	3	4	1	2	3	4
Current intensity (A)	2	4	6	8	2	4	6	8
Pulse time (µs)	25	50	75	100	25	50	75	100
Duty cycle (%)	0.3	0.4	0.5	0.6	0.3	0.4	0.5	0.6

Table 2. Mean values of arithmetical mean roughness (Ra), material removal rate (MRR), and electrode wear (EW), obtained with positive and negative polarity. These values were taken from Reference [2] Torres Salcedo, A.; Puertas Arbizu I.; Luis Pérez, C. J. Analytical Modeling of Energy Density and Optimization of the EDM Machining Parameters of Inconel 600. Metals 2017, 7, 166. (Open access article distributed under the terms and conditions of the Creative Commons Attribution (CC BY) license: http://creativecommons.org/licenses/by/4.0/). (See Reference [2] or Appendix A for all data).

E	Positive Polarity (+)			E	Negative Polarity (−)		
	Ra (µm)	MRR (mm³/min)	EW (%)		Ra (µm)	MRR (mm³/min)	EW (%)
1	1.39	0.1778	35.81	1	1.57	0.4961	96.67
2	3.34	3.0897	10.66	2	3.59	4.7944	28.23
63	6.33	8.4132	1.30	63	7.52	23.2371	171.94
64	7.08	15.3894	0.37	64	7.83	30.4894	17.49

2. State of the Art

Over the past few years, the number of applications of fuzzy systems increased significantly [6]. Takagi–Sugeno [3,4] and Mamdani [7,8] fuzzy inference systems are commonly used, and there exist a large number of research studies in different scientific fields, dealing with control, pattern recognition, modeling, etc. Among the studies that can be found in the literature, it is worth mentioning the study of Mouralova et al. [9] which proposed a Mamdani FIS, based on 18 rules provided by an expert in the field, for modeling the cutting speed in wire electrical discharge machining (WEDM) from five inputs (gap voltage, pulse on time, pulse off time, discharge current, and wire feed). These authors employed a maximum of results for aggregation and the centroid in order to de-fuzzify the aggregated output. Among the conclusions, these authors found that the FIS may be employed in order to determine the optimum machine parameters to maximize the cutting speed for the WEDM of Creusabro steel [9]. In another study, Aamir et al. [10] employed a Mamdani FIS to predict surface roughness and hole size as a function of feed rate and cutting speed in multi-hole drilling. These authors calculated the outputs based on the centroid method. They found that the FIS was able to predict hole quality at different levels of process parameters [10]. On the other hand, Alarifi et al. [11] employed genetic algorithms and particle swarm optimization to determine the parameters of an adaptive neuro-fuzzy inference system (ANFIS) model to predict the thermo-physical properties of Al_2O_3–multi-walled carbon nanotube (MWCNT)/thermal oil hybrid nanofluid. In order to evaluate and compare the performance of the models analyzed, root-mean-square error (RMSE) and the R-squared coefficient (R^2) were employed. These authors found that the models were able to appropriately predict the thermo-physical properties [11]. In the research study of Wang et al. [12], a fuzzy multicriteria decision-making model (MCDM) for raw material supplier selection in the plastic industry was employed. Likewise, in the research study of Kang et al. [13], a heating temperature estimation method using an ANFIS algorithm was proposed for diagnosis and assessment of fire-damaged concrete structures. These authors employed as input variables ultrasonic pulse velocity, reflectance of the concrete surface, and design compressive strength of the concrete. Moreover, these authors estimated the heating temperatures of the specimens using the proposed ANFIS algorithm. They found that their model estimated the heating temperatures of the specimens with a high degree of accuracy [13]. On the other hand, Tayyab et al. [14] applied fuzzy theory to consider uncertainty in demand information in a multi-stage lean manufacturing system. These authors employed the centroid to de-fuzzify the objective function. Other studies such as that of Faisal et al. [15] used particle swarm optimization (PSO) and biogeography-based optimization (BBO) algorithms for a multiple-objective optimization of the MRR and Ra for the EDM process, and they validated their models with experimental results. Lin et al. [16] applied a fuzzy collaborative intelligence approach for fall detection in four existing smart technology applications, while Cavallaro employed a Takagi–Sugeno FIS to assess the sustainability of biomass of production [17].

Regarding fuzzy modeling for industrial applications, there exist several studies which were applied to different industrial sectors. Among these research studies, it is worth mentioning the application of soft computing techniques for both detection and classification of defects [18,19], fault diagnosis of rolling bearing in industrial robots [20], airport classification [21], control of piezoelectric actuators [22], monitoring of fuel system of an industrial gas turbine [23], control of brushless direct current (DC) motors [24], and fault detection in wind turbines [25]. In addition, fuzzy systems are able to handle uncertainties in an efficient way, as shown in Reference [26], where a Takagi–Sugeno–Kang (TSK) type-2 fuzzy neural network was proposed for system modeling and noise cancellation, or in Reference [27], where a design methodology based on interval type-2 TSK fuzzy logic controllers for modular and reconfigurable robots manipulators with uncertain dynamic parameters was shown, among many others [28,29].

Some other studies such as that of Shabgard et al. [30] employed a Mamdani inference system to predict material removal rate, electrode wear, and surface roughness in the EDM and ultrasonic-assisted EDM (US/EDM) processes of tungsten carbide. An analysis of the particle swarm optimization (PSO) implementation in designing parameters of manufacturing processes, as well as a benchmark with other optimization techniques can be found in the review study of Sibalija [31]. EDM process variables were modeled by using artificial neural networks (ANNs) and ANFIS, as shown in studies such as that of Rahul et al. [32], where the authors employed a Taguchy design of experiments, as well as the concept of satisfaction function, to improve machining performances responses in EDM of Inconel 718. Babu et al. [33] employed a Taguchy design of experiments and an ANN in order to determine optimal parameters in the wire electrical discharge machining (WEDM) of Inconel 750. Likewise, Al-Ghamdi et al. employed an adaptive neuro-fuzzy inference system (ANFIS) and polynomial modeling approaches to model the material removal rate in EDM of a Ti–6Al–4V alloy [34]. These authors employed five ANFIS models and a first-order Sugeno, along with a back-propagation neural network training algorithm. Among the results, these authors found that ANFIS models perform more efficiently than convectional polynomial models [34]. Devarasiddappa et al. [35] employed an artificial neural network (ANN) to predict surface roughness in the wire-cut electrical discharge machining (WEDM) of Inconel 825. These authors found that this methodology is effective for modeling surface roughness in this Inconel alloy [35]. Maher et al. [36] employed an adaptive neuro-fuzzy inference system (ANFIS) to predict cutting speed, surface roughness, and heat-affected zone in WEDM. Another example is the study of Joshi et al. [37] which investigated the management and quantification of surface roughness and MRR of Inconel 800 HT when machined with a copper electrode on EDM, whereas Torres et al. [38] studied an Inconel® 718 alloy during electrical discharge machining.

From previous studies, it is possible to see that EDM is commonly used for manufacturing materials such as tungsten carbide [39], titanium diboride [1], and Inconel® alloys [2], boron carbide and silicon carbide [5], among many others. In this present research study, the main aim is to use a FIS to obtain technological tables from EDM experimental data. As previously mentioned, these tables are very usual for steel; however, in other materials, the number of technological tables is significantly less. Hence, this study may have interest because these tables allow machining strategies to be selected in advance to obtain either maximum material removal rate or minimum electrode wear, among other manufacturing strategies.

3. Methodology

This study presents a methodology in order to obtain technological tables that can be used in electrical discharge machining (EDM) processes. This methodology is based, first of all, on experimentation, which can be carried out through design of experiments (DOE) or another type of experimental study. Technological tables are of great interest in the field of EDM since, by using them, it is possible to determine in advance the optimal machining conditions for a certain strategy that either maximizes material removal or reduces electrode wear. The methodology presented in this present study could be used generally for other manufacturing processes; however, in this present case, it is focused on EDM in order to analyze a case study. Most current EDM devices have (Computer Numerical Control) CNCs; thus, it is possible to enter these technological tables in the memory of their CNCs. Currently, most EDM equipment is programmed based on the existence of these technological tables. The usual practice is to obtain the technological tables both from experimental tests and from the experience of the users [1,5].

Technological tables could be developed from previous experience on EDM in order to determine the most appropriate operating conditions. Moreover, it would be possible to train and then adjust an ANFIS by using experiments, that is to say, inputs and measured outputs. However, these techniques are not used in this present study because it is possible to get more precision by using a FIS from the experimental data. In a future study, a FIS will be adjusted from inputs and outputs which may have a lower number of rules compared to that proposed in this present study. However, the precision of this so-adjusted FIS would be lower than that obtained with the proposed model. Therefore, the FIS employed in this present study starts from the knowledge of the experimental tests. As previously mentioned, the knowledge of these technological tables is very important since it makes it possible to select a machining strategy to obtain certain values of roughness, as well as to specify a certain strategy for the material removal rate or electrode wear. For this reason, these technological tables are widely used for steel, with their number being significantly lower in the case of other materials, as in the case analyzed in this present study. In any case, it is considered that the proposed methodology could be generally applied for any other material. These technological tables are generated in a bottom-up approach, since they start from experimental tests because of the fact that more precise results can be obtained. Therefore, the proposed methodology is as described below.

Firstly, a FIS is developed from the inputs $(x_1 \ldots x_n)$ and outputs $(y_1 \ldots y_n)$. A zero-order Sugeno fuzzy model is employed in this study. Triangular membership functions are used for modeling the inputs and constant values are used for the outputs. Figure 1 shows the membership function selected for fuzzification of the inputs. The membership functions for the independent variables are triangular, as shown in Figure 1. The membership function is obtained from Equation (1).

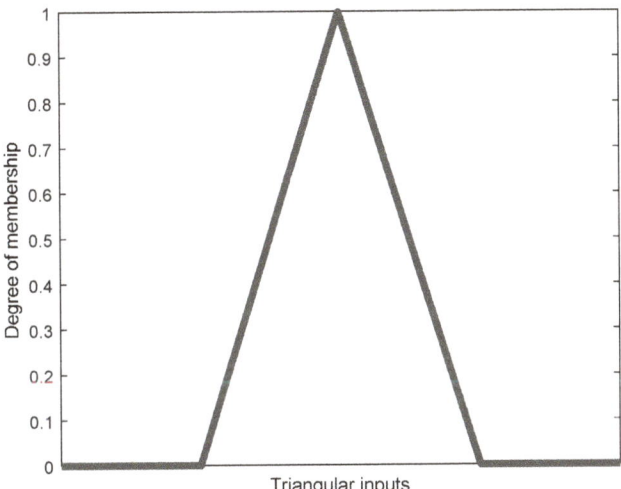

Figure 1. Degree of membership of the independent variables.

It should be mentioned that the membership functions may have different shapes such as triangular, trapezoidal, Gaussian, and bell-shape, among many others [40]. In this case, triangular functions are used for their simplicity and because using these types of functions with overlap between them produces acceptable values to model the response.

$$\mu_x = \left\{ \begin{array}{l} \frac{x-a}{b-a}, \; if \; a \leq x \leq b \\ \frac{c-x}{c-b}, \; if \; b \leq x \leq c \\ 0, \; otherwise \end{array} \right\}. \quad (1)$$

Therefore, the procedure for obtaining the technological tables starts from obtaining a Sugeno FIS [3,4,40], which can be developed from the experimental data. The aggregation method is the sum of fuzzy sets, and the aggregated output is obtained from the weighted average of all output rules. For the i-th rule, the implication method is obtained from Equation (2), where the product implication method is used in Sugeno systems [40].

$$\lambda_i(x) = AndMethod\{\mu_{i1}(x_1), \ldots, \mu_{in}(x_n)\}. \quad (2)$$

Once the FIS is developed, it is then possible to evaluate the outputs and to obtain the response values for each of the inputs using the FIS, that is, $for \; x_i = \min\{x_i\} : inc_i : \max\{x_i\}$. The increment "$inc_i$" defines the number of points to be evaluated in order to generate the response with the fuzzy inference system (FIS). In general, it is possible to have several inputs and outputs. The general procedure to define the technological tables is shown in Algorithm 1.

Algorithm 1. Methodology for obtaining the technological tables. FIS—fuzzy inference system.

(1) Develop a FIS from the inputs $(x_1 \ldots x_n)$ and outputs $(y_1 \ldots y_n)$. A zero-order Sugeno fuzzy model is employed in this study.

(2) Transform each of the inputs into a vector as follows: $x_i = \min\{x_{i,j}\} : inc_i : \max\{x_{i,j}\}$, where inc_i values are selected so that the length of each vector "x_i" is the same for all inputs.

(3) Evaluate the output to be classified, using the fuzzy inference system. That is, evaluate $output_{1,j}$ using the FIS.

(4) Select a pitch = $output_{sup_{1,1}} - output_{inf_{1,1}}$ = constant for the output to be classified, so that $output_{inf_{1,1}} \leq output_{1,j} \leq output_{sup_{1,1}}$. This defines the number of levels "l" used to classify the output.

(5) Classify $output_1$ using these "l" levels. Each of these levels has "m_l" values.

(6) The strategy for obtaining each value of the technological table is as follows:
If the optimal value of one output "k" is given by the maximum, for example, material removal rate, then the value of the technological table which corresponds to the level "l" of $output_1$ is obtained from the following function:

$$table\_output_{k,l} = \max\{output_{k,m}\}_{FIS, classifed}.$$

Otherwise, if the manufacturing strategy is given by the minimum, for example, tool wear, then the values of the technological tables are obtained from the following function:

$$table\_output_{k,l} = \min\{output_{k,m}\}_{FIS, classifed}.$$

That is, for each level of $output_1$, select the value that either maximises or minimises $output_k$, where the values are obtained using the FIS.

(7) Then, obtain inputs $(x_1 \ldots x_n)$ which correspond to $table\_output_{k,l}$ and, using the FIS, evaluate other outputs ($output_m$, for $m \neq 1$ and k).

As shown in Algorithm 1, from the experimental results, a fuzzy inference system is generated from all the independent variables and the dependent variables under study. For this reason, the FIS is capable of predicting the values of the dependent variables within the range defined by the minimum and maximum values of the experiments with greater precision than that obtained by using RSM, as shown later. The intervals used to classify the $output_1$ values are established based on a pitch which could be whatever. The selection of $output_1$ as the output to be classified can be done without loss of generality since, in the methodology presented, a single output is selected as classifiable to establish the ranges of variation, and the remaining outputs vary either at their maximum levels or at their minimum levels, depending on the manufacturing strategy.

The proposed methodology has the advantage that several manufacturing conditions can be determined from a reduced number of experimental tests, within the range defined by experimentation (minimum and maximum values of the input variables). Once the outputs are classified, it is a matter of selecting the conditions that maximize a variable.

In order to show the application of the above-mentioned methodology, the technological tables for the case of Inconel® 600 are obtained, within the range of values defined by the DOE shown in Table 1. The surface quality is characterized from the arithmetic mean roughness parameter (Ra). This roughness parameter is commonly employed in industry to characterize the surface finish of manufactured parts because most roughness measurement equipment is able to provide this parameter. However, the proposed methodology could be generally applied for other roughness parameters. In order to develop the technological tables, roughness classes with a certain value should be established beforehand and, thus, the roughness values are then classified according to the specified roughness classes. With this objective in mind, it is necessary to start from the experimental values which can be obtained from a DOE or from any other experimental methodology. Therefore, the method to be used is to establish roughness classes and, from these classes, to determine the values of the input variables that allow either to minimize the electrode wear or to maximize the material removal rate.

4. Results and Discussion

This section presents the results obtained by applying the methodology described in the previous section. In order to develop the present study, experimental values obtained by Torres et al. [2] are employed. As previously mentioned, this material is a nickel–chromium alloy (Inconel® 600). The ranges of variation of the inputs and outputs are shown in Tables 1 and 2.

Table 2 shows the results obtained after EDM of Inconel® 600 alloy, where the material removal rate (MRR) and the electrode wear (EW) are defined from Equations (2) and (3), respectively.

$$\text{Material Removal Rate (MRR)} = \frac{\text{Volume of material removed from the part}}{\text{Machining time}} (\text{mm}^3/\text{min}). \quad (3)$$

$$\text{Electrode Wear (EW)} = \frac{\text{Volume of material removed from the electrode}}{\text{Volume of material removed from the part}} \times 100(\%). \quad (4)$$

As is well known, (Ra) is defined from the UNE-EN-ISO 4287:1999 norm [41] as the arithmetic average roughness of the absolute values of the roughness profile ordinates $Z(x)$ (where $Z(x)$ is the height of the profile evaluated in any position "x") that are included in a sampling length (lr) of the roughness profile, which can be obtained from Equation (5). This value is one of the most commonly employed parameters in industry. Therefore, it is used in order to classify the roughness values in order to develop the technological tables.

$$\text{Ra} = \frac{1}{lr} \int_0^{lr} |Z(x)| dx. \quad (5)$$

Figure 2 shows the profile for the determination of the Ra parameter, where $Z(x)$ is the profile measured from the mean line, and lr is the sampling length, while Figure 3 shows the EDM equipment.

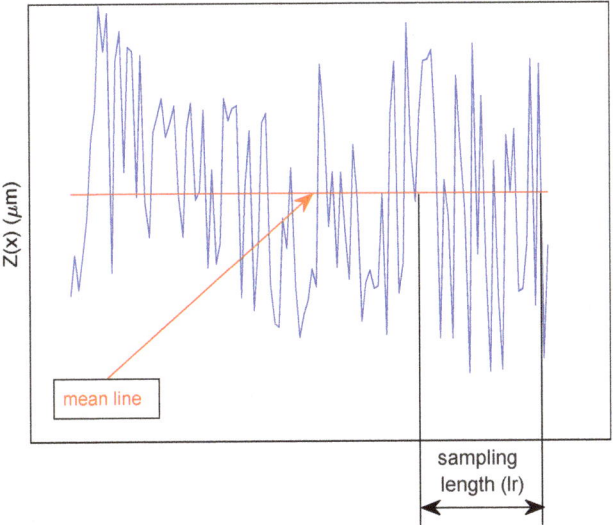

Figure 2. Roughness profile for determination of Ra parameter.

Figure 3. Electrical discharge machining (EDM) machine ONA Datic D-2030-S.

4.1. Analysis of Experimentation Using the FIS

This section is included in order to demonstrate that the FIS is able to model the behavior of the response variables more efficiently than by using RSM. Data shown in Tables 1 and 2 are employed in order to develop a FIS which can be then employed to obtain the technological tables following the procedure previously mentioned in Section 3. As can be seen in Reference [1], a method for obtaining the technological tables from a conventional design of experiments along with multiple linear regression techniques was proposed, where technological tables were obtained for TiB_2, which is a sintered ceramic material and in Reference [5] technological tables were obtained for B_4C, SiSiC and WC-Co. However, as was previously mentioned, if the regression is not able to adequately predict the behavior of a response variable, the technological tables obtained from these models will not be accurate. In this section, the proposed methodology in this present study is applied for the case of the EDM of Inconel® 600. However, it should be mentioned that this methodology could be applied for other kinds of materials. Figure 1 shows the membership functions that were used to fuzzify the inputs. As can be observed, triangular functions were selected for the inputs. On the other hand, the present study assumes that it is possible to linearly vary the parameters in the EDM equipment in order to be able to select the values obtained from the technological tables which are determined to be optimal ones. If this is not possible, the FIS would have to be used on the possible values of these independent variables. As Table 2 shows, the design of experiments does not continuously vary the values of the independent variables; thus, it is possible that the optimal values are not selected if only these values are considered. In addition, it may be that there are levels vacant when establishing the levels of roughness, which is the dependent variable that was selected as $output_1$ since, as explained above, it is one of the most widely used parameters for characterizing surface quality and, therefore, its determination is of great importance and interest in industry.

In this present study, the FIS was obtained using Matlab™2019b. Therefore, from Table 2, it is possible to directly obtain the set of rules that make up the FIS. As previously mentioned, a Sugeno FIS was employed by using the Fuzzy Logic Toolbox™ of Matlab™2019b [40]. Mamdani systems are more intuitive and the rules are easier to understand, making them more suitable for expert systems, developed from human knowledge [40,42,43]. On the other hand, the defuzzification process for a

Sugeno system is more computationally efficient compared to that of a Mamdani system [40,42,43]. Figure 4 shows the employed FIS which was developed from the rules shown in Table 3. This table shows the rules implemented in the fuzzy system, in symbolic format, codified from the outputs. For each output value, a FIS was developed. In this way, it is possible to model the behavior of Ra, MRR, and EW for each of the manufacturing strategies.

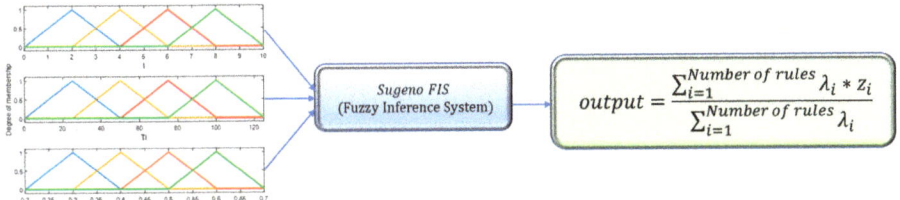

Figure 4. Fuzzy inference system employed.

Table 3. Codification of the rules.

1 1 1, 1 (1) : 1	1 1 2, 17 (1) : 1	1 1 3, 33 (1) : 1	1 1 4, 49 (1) : 1
2 1 1, 2 (1) : 1	2 1 2, 18 (1) : 1	2 1 3, 34 (1) : 1	2 1 4, 50 (1) : 1
3 1 1, 3 (1) : 1	3 1 2, 19 (1) : 1	3 1 3, 35 (1) : 1	3 1 4, 51 (1) : 1
4 1 1, 4 (1) : 1	4 1 2, 20 (1) : 1	4 1 3, 36 (1) : 1	4 1 4, 52 (1) : 1
1 2 1, 5 (1) : 1	1 2 2, 21 (1) : 1	1 2 3, 37 (1) : 1	1 2 4, 53 (1) : 1
2 2 1, 6 (1) : 1	2 2 2, 22 (1) : 1	2 2 3, 38 (1) : 1	2 2 4, 54 (1) : 1
3 2 1, 7 (1) : 1	3 2 2, 23 (1) : 1	3 2 3, 39 (1) : 1	3 2 4, 55 (1) : 1
4 2 1, 8 (1) : 1	4 2 2, 24 (1) : 1	4 2 3, 40 (1) : 1	4 2 4, 56 (1) : 1
1 3 1, 9 (1) : 1	1 3 2, 25 (1) : 1	1 3 3, 41 (1) : 1	1 3 4, 57 (1) : 1
2 3 1, 10 (1) : 1	2 3 2, 26 (1) : 1	2 3 3, 42 (1) : 1	2 3 4, 58 (1) : 1
3 3 1, 11 (1) : 1	3 3 2, 27 (1) : 1	3 3 3, 43 (1) : 1	3 3 4, 59 (1) : 1
4 3 1, 12 (1) : 1	4 3 2, 28 (1) : 1	4 3 3, 44 (1) : 1	4 3 4, 60 (1) : 1
1 4 1, 13 (1) : 1	1 4 2, 29 (1) : 1	1 4 3, 45 (1) : 1	1 4 4, 61 (1) : 1
2 4 1, 14 (1) : 1	2 4 2, 30 (1) : 1	2 4 3, 46 (1) : 1	2 4 4, 62 (1) : 1
3 4 1, 15 (1) : 1	3 4 2, 31 (1) : 1	3 4 3, 47 (1) : 1	3 4 4, 63 (1) : 1
4 4 1, 16 (1) : 1	4 4 2, 32 (1) : 1	4 4 3, 48 (1) : 1	4 4 4, 64 (1) : 1

The codification shown in Table 3, which was obtained from Table 2, is "current intensity, pulse time, and duty cycle": "$I(i)\ Ti(j)\ dc(k)$, output ($1 =$ and, $2 =$ or) : weight". In this case, weight = 1, so that each rule has the same effect relative to others [40], where the numbering 1, 2, 3, and 4 is employed for the inputs in order to select the levels of the variables. As can be observed in Table 1, these variables have four levels. For example, the levels for the intensity are given by {2 A, 4 A, 6 A, and 8 A}. Therefore, these values are coded as {1, 2, 3, and 4} in Table 3. The same procedure is applied for both pulse time and duty cycle. In the case of the output, there are 64 values which are obtained from the DOE with the different input conditions. That is, for the case of Ra, for instance, 1 1 1,1 (1) : 1 corresponds to the following:

1. If (Intensity is 2 A) AND (Pulse Time is 25 µs) AND (duty cycle is 0.3 %) THEN (Ra is 1.39 µm).

That is,

1. If $(I == I2)$ & $(Ti == Ti25)$ & $(dc == dc0.3)$ Then (Output $= mf1$),

2. If $(I == I4)$ & $(Ti == Ti25)$ & $(dc == dc0.3)$ Then (Output $= mf2$),

63. If $(I == I6)$ & $(Ti == Ti100)$ & $(dc == dc0.6)$ Then (Output $= mf63$),

64. If $(I == I8)$ & $(Ti == Ti100)$ & $(dc == dc0.6)$ Then (Output $= mf64$),

where the input values "$I(i),\ Ti(j),\ dc(k)$" and the outputs $mf_1 \ldots mf_n$ are selected from Table 1.

RSM model:

$$y \sim (b_0 + b_1 \times x_1 + b_2 \times x_2 + b_3 \times x_3 + b_4 \times x_1 \times x_2 + b_5 \times x_1 \times x_3 + b_6 \times x_2 \times x_3 + b_7 \times x_1^2 + b_8 \times x_2^2 + b_9 \times x_3^2). \quad (6)$$

The FIS was generated directly from experimental data. Therefore, as shown later, the precision of the obtained results is much higher than that obtained using RSM. Figures 5–8 are included to compare the response surfaces obtained with the proposed methodology using the FIS and those obtained from the RSM, as done in Reference [2], where the experimental data were fitted by using a second degree polynomial, which is shown by Equation (6).

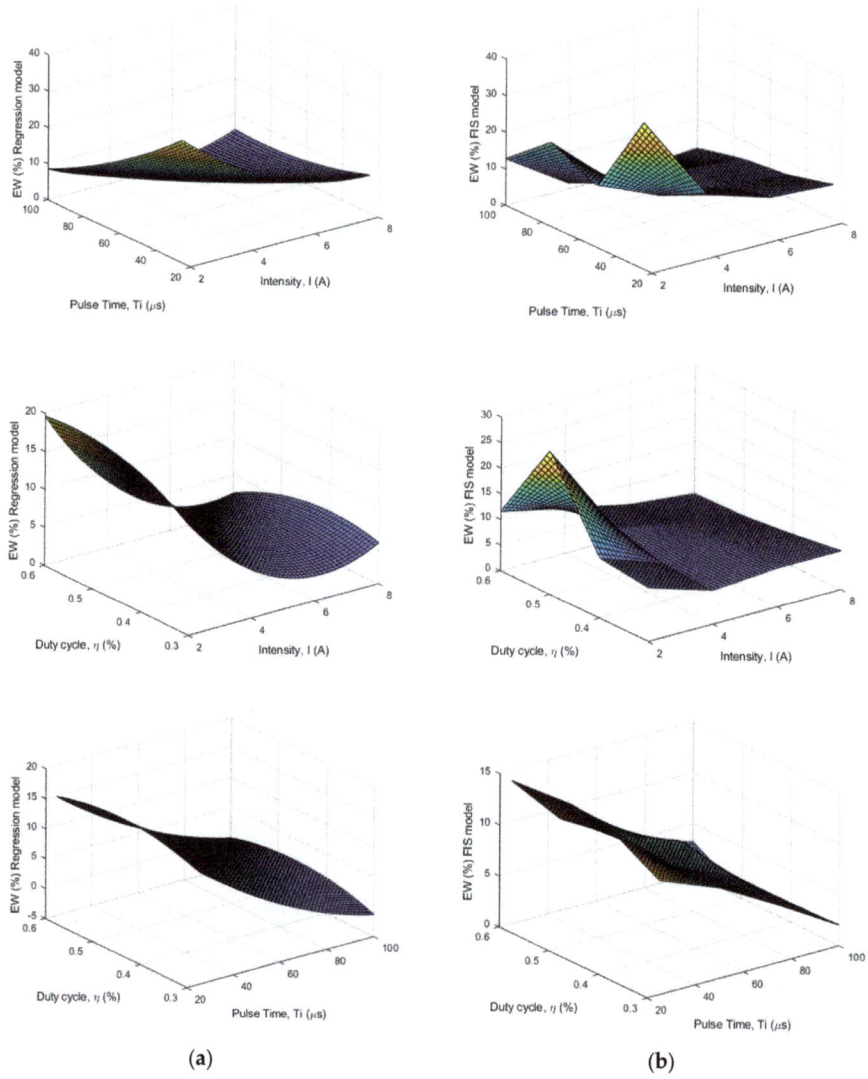

Figure 5. Response surfaces for EW in the case of positive polarity: (**a**) obtained from the regression [2]; (**b**) obtained with the proposed methodology using the FIS.

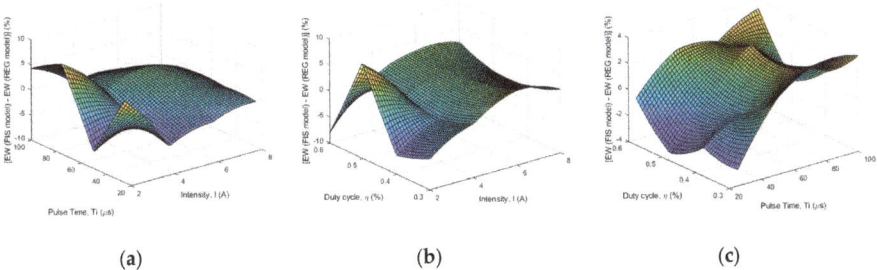

Figure 6. Difference between EW (FIS model) and EW (regression [2]) vs.: (**a**) Pulse Time and Intensity; (**b**) Duty cycle and Intensity; (**c**) Duty cycle and Pulse Time.

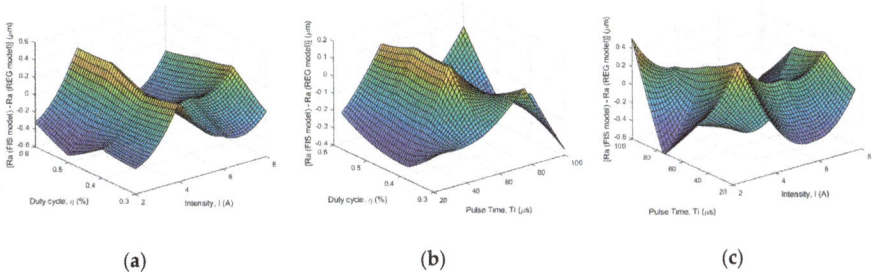

Figure 7. Difference between Ra (FIS model) and Ra (regression [2]) vs.: (**a**) Pulse Time and Intensity; (**b**) Duty cycle and Intensity; (**c**) Duty cycle and Pulse Time.

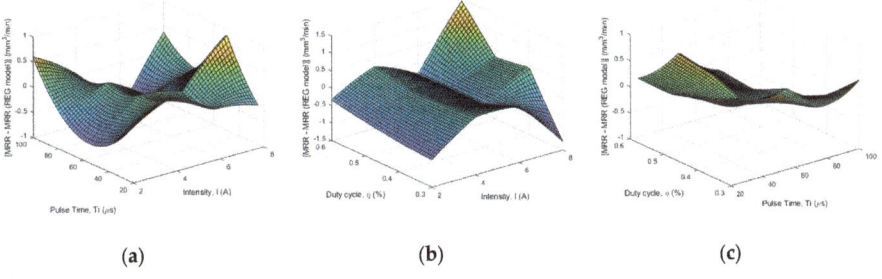

Figure 8. Difference between MRR (FIS model) and MRR (regression [2]) vs.: (**a**) Pulse Time and Intensity; (**b**) Duty cycle and Intensity; (**c**) Duty cycle and Pulse Time.

As can be observed in Figures 7 and 8, the results obtained with the FIS are close to those obtained with the regression as a consequence of Ra and MRR being fitted adequately by a quadratic polynomial, as can be seen from the coefficients of determination of the fit and from the RMSE and mean absolute error (MAE) statistics, which are shown in Equation (7) and in Table 4. However, as Table 4 shows, this is not the case for the electrode wear (EW), which is shown in Figure 5; hence, it is possible to conclude that the FIS is more accurate than RSM. Therefore, it is able to predict more adequately the values of the response, within the range of study, than the RSM.

Figures 6–8 show a comparison between the EW, Ra, and MRR results obtained with the RSM and with the FIS. As can be observed in Figures 7 and 8, differences are not significant as a consequence of the fact that experimental Ra and MRR results are well fitted by a second-order polynomial, such as that shown in Equation (6). However, this is not the case for electrode wear, as shown in Figures 5 and 6. As Table 4 shows, the polynomial model is not accurate and, in this case, the differences between the FIS and the regression model are significant. Therefore, data provided by the FIS are more accurate than those obtained by using the RSM, and the technological tables are more accurate if the FIS is used instead of the regression model.

Table 4. Accuracy for predicted values of Ra, MRR, and EW using the regression model [2] and the FIS.

Positive Polarity (+)		Negative Polarity (−)	
Ra (using the FIS)	Ra (Regression)	Ra (using the FIS)	Ra (Regression)
RMSE = 0 MAE = 0 $R^2 = 1$	RMSE = 0.3286 MAE = 0.2693 $R^2 = 0.9639$	RMSE = 0 MAE = 0 $R^2 = 1$	RMSE = 0.4461 MAE = 0.3705 $R^2 = 0.9606$
MRR (using the FIS)	MRR (Regression)	MRR (using the FIS)	MRR (Regression)
RMSE = 0 MAE = 0 $R^2 = 1$	RMSE = 0.7184 MAE = 0.4879 $R^2 = 0.9778$	RMSE = 0 MAE = 0 $R^2 = 1$	RMSE = 1.4713 MAE = 1.0625 $R^2 = 0.9712$
EW (using the FIS)	EW (Regression)	EW (using the FIS)	EW (Regression)
RMSE = 0 MAE = 0 $R^2 = 1$	RMSE = 5.5290 MAE = 3.5873 $R^2 = 0.6958$	RMSE = 0 MAE = 0 $R^2 = 1$	RMSE = 49.7581 MAE = 33.3053 $R^2 = 0.6783$

Figure 9 shows the response surfaces for both Ra and MRR obtained with the proposed methodology using the FIS for the case of positive polarity. Equation (7) shows the statistical parameters that were used to determine the precision of the models used for modeling the dependent variables, that is, Ra, MRR, and EW. As can be observed in Table 4, the FIS accuracy is higher than that provided by the RSM. Data shown in Table 4 were obtained by using Matlab™2019b.

$$\text{RMSE} = \sqrt{\frac{1}{n}\sum_{j=1}^{n}(y_j - \hat{y}_j)^2} \text{ and } \text{MAE} = \frac{1}{n}\sum_{j=1}^{n}|y_j - \hat{y}_j|. \tag{7}$$

As can be observed in Table 4, the fuzzy inference system fits all the data perfectly, which is logical since the FIS was built according to the procedure shown in the previous section. However, this is not the case with the RSM which, despite using all the DOE points for the determination of the models, is not able to adequately adjust the electrode wear surface response. Therefore, the values predicted by the regression have lower accuracy than those predicted by the FIS. In this case, the polynomial models for the case of both roughness and material removal rate are acceptable. Nevertheless, the precision is lower than that of the FIS. In any case, in other types of experimentation in which there is less precision in the least squares adjustments, the employment of the FIS becomes more important since it adjusts to all the points of the model.

In Torres et al. [2], the model with the highest value of *adjusted* R^2 was selected. However, in this present study, the model with all the regression coefficients is used because these models have higher R^2 values than those shown in Reference [2] and, with the aim of considering all the effects in the models such as the models shown in Reference [2], some of the independent variables could be eliminated.

Figure 10b shows that it is possible to analyze the experimental results in a similar way to that done with regression models. It is shown that the most important effects are the current intensity and the pulse time, followed to a lesser extent by the duty cycle. In addition, by using the FIS, the values obtained are more precise, as can be seen in Table 4. As can be observed, the differences between the values predicted by the regression model and those predicted by the FIS are significant. Specifically, in the case of positive polarity, the regression model does not adequately predict the behavior of electrode wear, as can be seen in Table 4. Therefore, the results provided by the regression model when predicting electrode wear are not accurate. In this case, the FIS is shown to have significant advantages over the regression model. Specifically, it is shown that, with increasing intensity, there is less wear on the electrode, which is logical because, as seen in Figure 11a,b, if the intensity decreases, so does the removal of material, while the surface roughness assumes smaller values, with the wear of the electrode in these cases being greater, which is in good agreement with experimental values. Finally, Figure 12 shows the interaction effects plot. As can be observed, the most significant interactions are those related to the current intensity and the pulse time. On the other hand, it is observed that the differences between both the FIS and the regression are significant, as a consequence of the fact that the regression model is not able to adequately predict the behavior of the electrode wear. In addition, Table 4 shows that the FIS is able to predict the behavior of the response variables more adequately than the regression, which is logical as a consequence of the methodology employed for defining the FIS. Hence, the fit is perfect in the case of the FIS, and this is not so in the case of the regression model. Therefore, the technological tables with values provided by the FIS are more accurate than those provided by conventional methods.

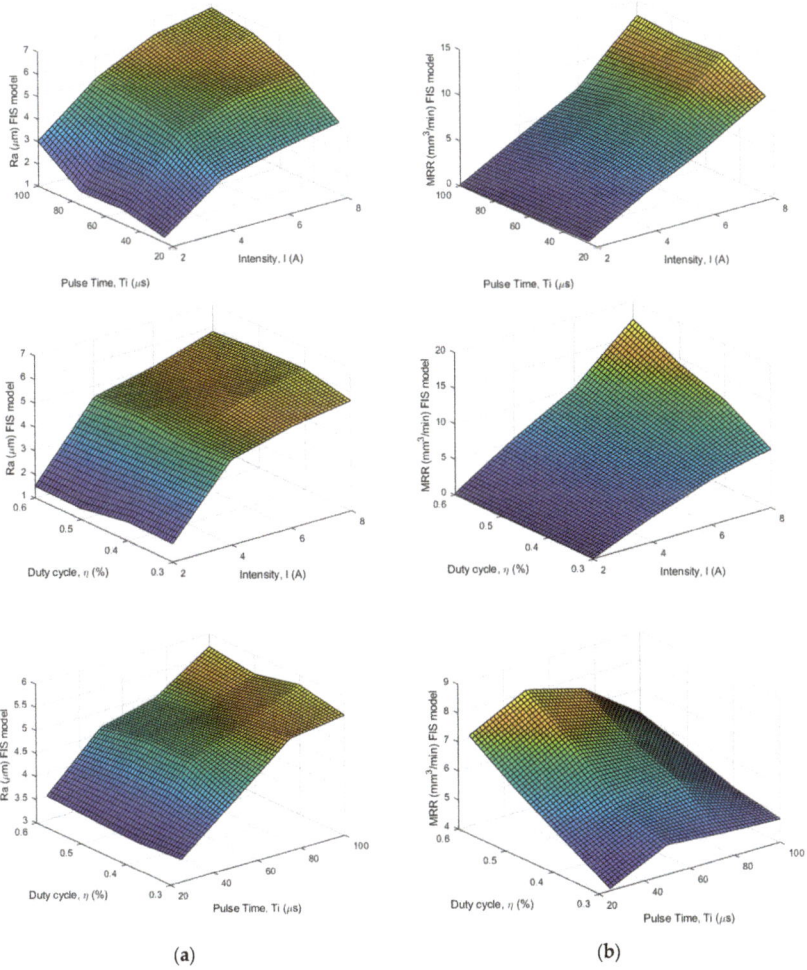

Figure 9. Response surfaces obtained with the FIS for the case of positive polarity: (**a**) Ra; (**b**) MRR.

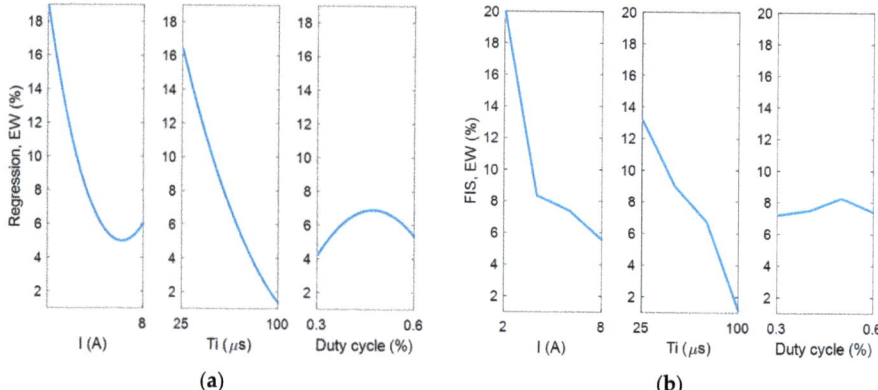

Figure 10. Main effects plot for EW in the case of positive polarity: (**a**) obtained from the regression [2]; (**b**) obtained by using the FIS.

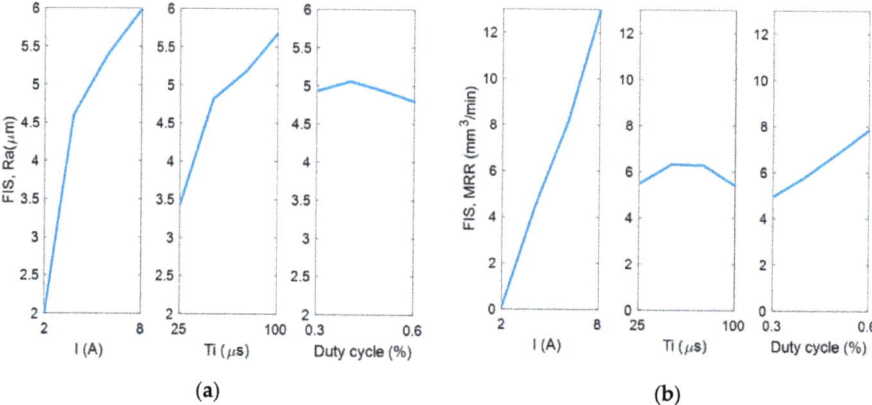

Figure 11. Main effects plot for (**a**) Ra and (**b**) MRR in the case of positive polarity, obtained using the FIS.

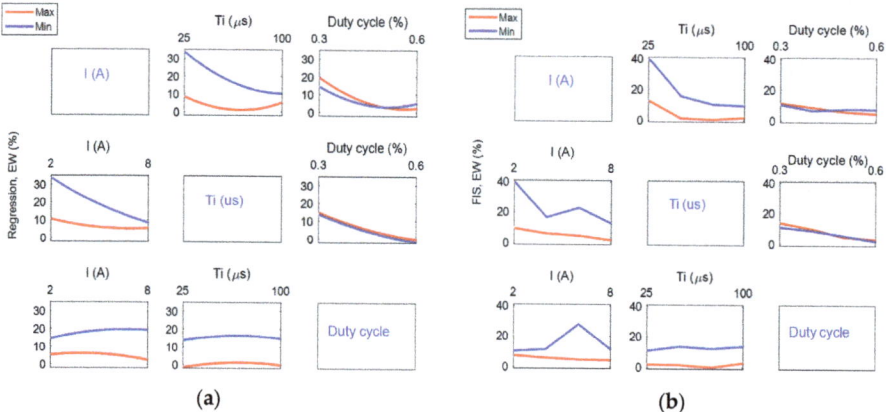

Figure 12. Interaction effects plot for EW in the case of positive polarity: (**a**) obtained from the regression [2]; (**b**) obtained with the proposed methodology using the FIS.

Figure 11 shows that the current intensity is the variable that has the greatest impact on both Ra and MRR, which is logical since, within the values considered in the present study, a higher intensity reflects higher material removal and worse surface roughness. On the other hand, it can be observed in Figure 11b that the pulse time affects the material removal rate to only a slight extent and that, approximately for values of the pulse time within the range 50 µs $< Ti$ (µs) < 75 µs, the material removal rate stands at its maximum value, being constant when the current intensity and the duty cycle are at their average values.

Figure 12 $b_{(3x3)}$ shows that it is possible to analyze the interaction effects between factors by using the FIS in a similar way to conventional analysis of factorial 2^k experiments along with regression models. These factors are represented in an array (3 $files \times 3\ columns$). The results were generated by analyzing the variation of one factor between its maximum and minimum levels, when all the other factors were held at their average level. For example, in Figure 12 $b_{(1,2)}$, it is shown that, when the current intensity is held at its lowest level, the electrode wear values are lower with increasing pulse time, when the duty cycle is at its average level of 0.45%. Moreover, if the current intensity is held at its highest level, the electrode wear values are lower than those obtained when the current intensity is held at its lower level. On the other hand, in the case of duty cycle, which is represented in Figure 12 $b_{(1,3)}$, it is shown that the electrode wear remains approximately constant versus the duty cycle when the pulse time is held at a constant value of 62.5 µs, showing that the electrode wear values are independent of either higher or lower values of intensity. A similar analysis could be done with all the interaction effects. Figure 13 shows the interaction plots effect, using the FIS, for the three independent variables under study in the case of positive polarity when Ra and MRR are considered as response variables.

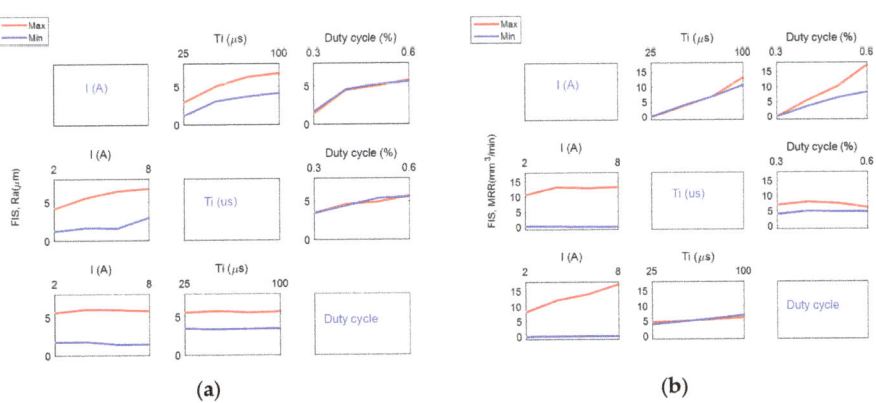

Figure 13. Interaction effects plot for (**a**) Ra and (**b**) MRR in the case of positive polarity, obtained using the FIS.

Figures 14 and 15 show the main effects plot and the interaction effects plot for the case of negative polarity, using the FIS. As can be observed, a similar behavior to that of positive polarity is obtained. The same comments regarding the precision of the models are applicable in the negative polarity case.

As demonstrated in this section, the response surfaces generated with the FIS have greater precision than those obtained with the RSM; thus, the technological tables are determined according to the methodology described in the previous Section. It should be mentioned that it was considered necessary to develop the previous analysis in order to show the higher accuracy of the FIS model to predict the surface roughness, the material removal rate, and the wear of the electrode.

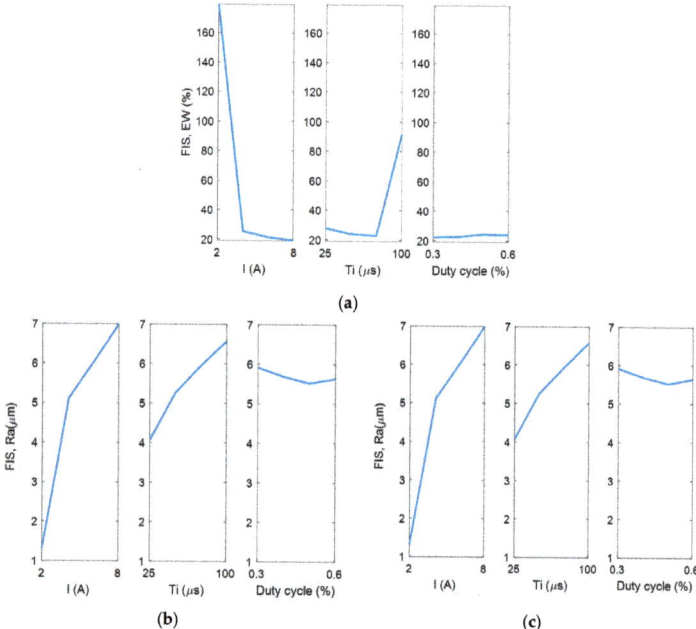

Figure 14. Main effects plot for (**a**) EW, (**b**) Ra, and (**c**) MRR in the case of negative polarity, obtained using the FIS.

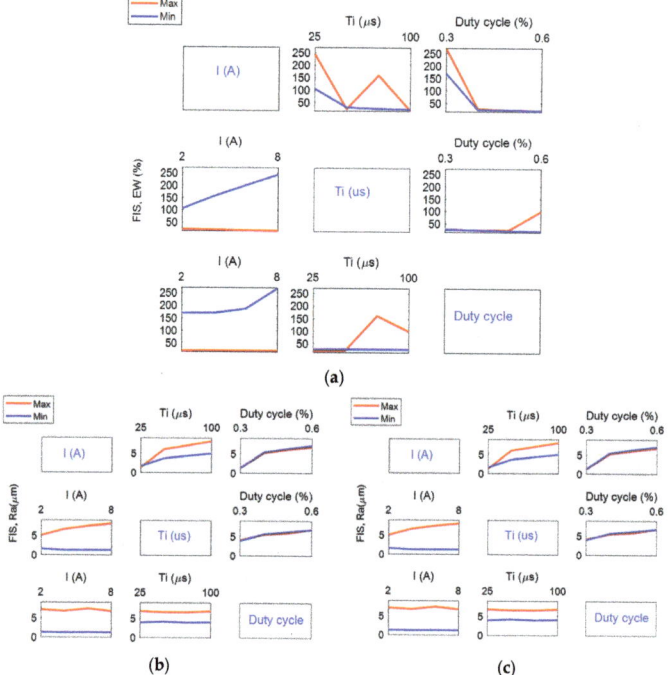

Figure 15. Interaction effects plot for (**a**) EW, (**b**) Ra, and (**c**) MRR in the case of negative polarity, obtained using the FIS.

4.2. Development of the Technological Tables

In this section, the technological tables for the Inconel® 600 alloy are obtained from the methodology previously described in Section 3. As can be observed in Tables 5–8, Ra is classified with a pitch of 0.20 µm. Although it would be possible to generate the technological tables only using the experimental data, it could be that there exist roughness classes in which there are no input variables to obtain them, since the dependent variables are obtained afterward and, therefore, their value is not known in advance. Moreover, it could happen that MRR and EW values were not optimized as a consequence of the fact that the inputs are not linearly varied in the DOE.

Table 5 shows the technological table for the case of positive polarity that was obtained by selecting a specific class of roughness values with the maximum values of the material removal rate. The electrode wear is given by the FIS after selecting the input variables that lead to a specific roughness value, and Table 6 shows the technological table for the case of minimum electrode wear. In this case, the material removal rate is obtained from the FIS once the input variables are defined.

In previous research studies, in which the author participated, technological tables were obtained using regression models [1,5]. However, as shown in the previous section, the FIS is capable of providing more precise values than those obtained by means of a conventional regression. Therefore, the methodology described in Section 3 was used in this present study to generate the technological tables. It should be mentioned that a pitch of 0.20 µm was selected for classifying Ra. However, this value could be whatever without loss of generality. From the values shown in Tables 1 and 2, an interval that encompasses both the minimum and the maximum values was selected. In this interval, the roughness classes are established from the selected pitch and, thus, the technological tables can then be obtained.

Figures 16 and 17 show the values obtained from the technological table with the fuzzy inference system for the strategy of maximum material removal rate using positive and negative polarities, respectively. These figures were obtained from Tables 5 and 7, respectively.

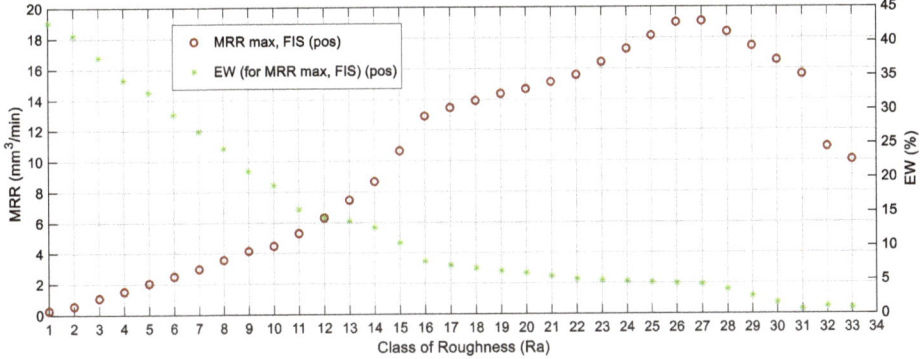

Figure 16. Values obtained from the technological table with the fuzzy inference system for the strategy of maximum removal rate using positive polarity.

Figures 18 and 19 show the values obtained from the technological table with the fuzzy inference system for the strategy of minimum electrode wear using positive and negative polarities, respectively. These figures were obtained from Tables 6 and 8, respectively.

Table 5. Strategy of maximum material removal rate. Technological table obtained from the FIS, for the case of maximum removal rate strategy (positive polarity).

Class of Roughness	Lower Value (μm)	Ra Value (μm)	Upper Value (μm)	Intensity (A)	Pulse Time (μs)	Duty Cycle (%)	MRR Max ($\frac{mm^3}{min}$)	EW (%)
Ra1	1.00	1.19	1.20	2.00	25.00	0.51	0.27	42.80
Ra2	1.20	1.40	1.40	2.12	25.00	0.57	0.56	40.97
Ra3	1.40	1.59	1.60	2.37	25.00	0.54	1.08	37.71
Ra4	1.60	1.79	1.80	2.61	25.00	0.51	1.52	34.43
Ra5	1.80	2.00	2.00	2.73	25.00	0.59	2.05	32.62
Ra6	2.00	2.20	2.20	2.98	25.00	0.56	2.50	29.35
Ra7	2.20	2.39	2.40	3.10	26.53	0.60	2.98	26.84
Ra8	2.40	2.57	2.60	3.35	25.00	0.60	3.56	24.34
Ra9	2.60	2.79	2.80	3.59	25.00	0.60	4.15	21.03
Ra10	2.80	2.97	3.00	3.71	26.53	0.60	4.48	18.96
Ra11	3.00	3.20	3.20	4.08	25.00	0.60	5.30	15.39
Ra12	3.20	3.40	3.40	4.69	25.00	0.58	6.31	14.26
Ra13	3.40	3.57	3.60	5.18	25.00	0.60	7.46	13.70
Ra14	3.60	3.78	3.80	5.80	25.00	0.60	8.65	12.75
Ra15	3.80	3.99	4.00	6.78	25.00	0.60	10.65	10.50
Ra16	4.00	4.19	4.20	7.88	25.00	0.60	12.91	7.75
Ra17	4.20	4.36	4.40	8.00	28.06	0.60	13.46	7.15
Ra18	4.40	4.58	4.60	8.00	32.65	0.60	13.92	6.71
Ra19	4.60	4.80	4.80	8.00	37.24	0.60	14.37	6.26
Ra20	4.80	4.94	5.00	8.00	40.31	0.60	14.67	5.97
Ra21	5.00	5.17	5.20	8.00	44.90	0.60	15.13	5.53
Ra22	5.20	5.39	5.40	8.00	49.49	0.60	15.58	5.09
Ra23	5.40	5.59	5.60	8.00	55.61	0.60	16.42	4.89
Ra24	5.60	5.79	5.80	8.00	61.73	0.60	17.28	4.73
Ra25	5.80	6.00	6.00	8.00	67.86	0.60	18.13	4.58
Ra26	6.00	6.20	6.20	8.00	73.98	0.60	18.99	4.42
Ra27	6.20	6.25	6.40	8.00	75.51	0.60	19.06	4.31
Ra28	6.40	6.40	6.60	8.00	80.10	0.60	18.37	3.57
Ra29	6.60	6.61	6.80	8.00	86.22	0.60	17.45	2.59
Ra30	6.80	6.82	7.00	8.00	92.35	0.60	16.54	1.60
Ra31	7.00	7.03	7.20	8.00	98.47	0.60	15.62	0.62
Ra32	7.20	7.22	7.40	8.00	100.00	0.33	10.88	1.06
Ra33	7.40	7.41	7.60	8.00	100.00	0.30	10.04	0.81

Table 6. Strategy of minimum electrode wear. Technological table obtained from the FIS, for the case of minimum electrode wear strategy (positive polarity).

Class of Roughness	Lower Value (μm)	Ra Value (μm)	Upper Value (μm)	Intensity (A)	Pulse Time (μs)	Duty Cycle (%)	EW Min (%)	MRR ($\frac{mm^3}{min}$)
Ra1	1.00	1.20	1.20	2.00	26.53	0.50	40.93	0.26
Ra2	1.20	1.40	1.40	2.00	52.55	0.60	16.57	0.18
Ra3	1.40	1.59	1.60	2.00	72.45	0.60	6.48	0.14
Ra4	1.60	1.80	1.80	2.00	90.82	0.60	3.20	0.11
Ra5	1.80	1.99	2.00	2.00	75.51	0.31	1.03	0.09
Ra6	2.00	2.02	2.20	2.00	75.51	0.30	0.49	0.08
Ra7	2.20	2.21	2.40	2.12	75.51	0.30	0.73	0.28
Ra8	2.40	2.43	2.60	2.24	77.04	0.30	1.09	0.48
Ra9	2.60	2.61	2.80	2.37	77.04	0.30	1.31	0.68
Ra10	2.80	2.82	3.00	2.49	78.57	0.30	1.63	0.87
Ra11	3.00	3.12	3.20	2.73	75.51	0.30	1.89	1.28
Ra12	3.20	3.21	3.40	2.73	80.10	0.30	2.12	1.25
Ra13	3.40	3.49	3.60	2.98	75.51	0.30	2.36	1.68
Ra14	3.60	3.67	3.80	3.10	75.51	0.30	2.59	1.88
Ra15	3.80	3.85	4.00	3.22	75.51	0.30	2.82	2.08
Ra16	4.00	4.01	4.20	3.22	89.29	0.30	3.00	1.90
Ra17	4.20	4.21	4.40	3.35	93.88	0.30	3.12	2.02
Ra18	4.40	4.41	4.60	3.47	100.00	0.30	3.16	2.10
Ra19	4.60	4.79	4.80	3.84	100.00	0.40	3.02	3.11
Ra20	4.80	5.00	5.00	3.84	100.00	0.49	1.86	3.61
Ra21	5.00	5.19	5.20	4.08	100.00	0.48	0.76	4.02
Ra22	5.20	5.36	5.40	4.45	100.00	0.50	0.47	4.72
Ra23	5.40	5.55	5.60	4.94	100.00	0.50	0.43	5.59
Ra24	5.60	5.79	5.80	5.55	100.00	0.50	0.37	6.63
Ra25	5.80	5.94	6.00	5.92	100.00	0.50	0.33	7.26
Ra26	6.00	6.00	6.20	6.04	100.00	0.50	0.37	7.49
Ra27	6.20	6.21	6.40	6.04	100.00	0.47	0.62	7.34
Ra28	6.40	6.58	6.60	6.65	100.00	0.30	0.83	7.84
Ra29	6.60	6.79	6.80	7.27	100.00	0.59	0.76	12.74
Ra30	6.80	6.99	7.00	7.76	100.00	0.60	0.48	14.54
Ra31	7.00	7.08	7.20	8.00	100.00	0.60	0.37	15.39
Ra32	7.20	7.33	7.40	7.88	100.00	0.30	0.81	9.84
Ra33	7.40	7.41	7.60	8.00	100.00	0.30	0.81	10.04

Table 7. Strategy of maximum material removal rate. Technological table obtained from the FIS, for the case of maximum removal rate strategy (negative polarity).

Class of Roughness	Lower Value (µm)	Ra Value (µm)	Upper Value (µm)	Intensity (A)	Pulse Time (µs)	Duty Cycle (%)	MRR Max ($\frac{mm^3}{min}$)	EW (%)
Ra2	1.20	1.39	1.40	2.00	44.90	0.50	0.51	145.31
Ra3	1.40	1.60	1.60	2.24	25.00	0.60	1.76	219.37
Ra4	1.60	1.80	1.80	2.37	29.59	0.60	2.48	212.79
Ra5	1.80	1.99	2.00	2.49	31.12	0.60	3.21	201.03
Ra6	2.00	2.18	2.20	2.61	32.65	0.60	3.94	188.91
Ra7	2.20	2.37	2.40	2.86	25.00	0.60	5.26	153.08
Ra8	2.40	2.60	2.60	2.98	28.06	0.60	6.02	142.45
Ra9	2.60	2.76	2.80	3.10	28.06	0.60	6.73	128.83
Ra10	2.80	2.98	3.00	3.35	25.00	0.60	8.07	100.04
Ra11	3.00	3.19	3.20	3.47	26.53	0.60	8.81	87.37
Ra12	3.20	3.35	3.40	3.59	26.53	0.60.	9.51	73.93
Ra13	3.40	3.60	3.60	3.84	25.00	0.60	10.87	47.01
Ra14	3.60	3.75	3.80	3.96	25.00	0.60	11.57	33.75
Ra15	3.80	3.98	4.00	4.69	25.00	0.60	14.20	27.80
Ra16	4.00	4.18	4.20	5.43	25.00	0.60	16.73	26.18
Ra17	4.20	4.35	4.40	6.04	25.00	0.60	18.94	24.86
Ra18	4.40	4.57	4.60	6.53	25.00	0.60	21.78	24.13
Ra19	4.60	4.79	4.80	7.02	25.00	0.60	24.63	23.39
Ra20	4.80	4.96	5.00	7.39	25.00	0.60	26.76	22.85
Ra21	5.00	5.18	5.20	7.88	25.00	0.60	29.60	22.11
Ra22	5.20	5.39	5.40	8.00	28.06	0.60	30.33	21.62
Ra23	5.40	5.55	5.60	8.00	31.12	0.60	30.35	21.31
Ra24	5.60	5.78	5.80	8.00	35.71	0.60	30.38	20.84
Ra25	5.80	5.93	6.00	8.00	38.78	0.60	30.40	20.52
Ra26	6.00	6.17	6.20	8.00	43.37	0.60	30.43	20.06
Ra27	6.20	6.40	6.40	8.00	47.96	0.60	30.46	19.59
Ra28	6.40	6.47	6.60	8.00	49.49	0.60	30.47	19.43
Ra29	6.60	6.61	6.80	8.00	55.61	0.60	29.23	19.40
Ra30	6.80	6.80	7.00	8.00	63.27	0.59	27.19	19.41
Ra31	7.00	7.19	7.20	7.76	83.16	0.60	26.19	25.20
Ra32	7.20	7.39	7.40	7.88	87.76	0.60	27.44	23.36
Ra33	7.40	7.57	7.60	8.00	92.35	0.60	28.78	18.10
Ra34	7.60	7.78	7.80	8.00	98.47	0.60	30.15	17.61
Ra35	7.80	7.83	8.00	8.00	100.00	0.60	30.49	17.49
Ra36	8.00	8.01	8.20	8.00	100.00	0.56	28.07	16.96
Ra37	8.20	8.23	8.40.	8.00	100.00	0.52	25.24	16.34

Table 8. Strategy of minimum electrode wear. Technological table obtained from the FIS, for the case of minimum electrode wear strategy (negative polarity).

Class of Roughness	Lower Value (μm)	Ra Value (μm)	Upper Value (μm)	Intensity (A)	Pulse Time (μs)	Duty Cycle (%)	EW Min (%)	MRR ($\frac{mm^3}{min}$)
Ra2	1.20	1.39	1.40	2.00	41.84	0.30	138.16	0.37
Ra3	1.40	1.57	1.60	2.00	25.00	0.30	96.67	0.50
Ra4	1.60	1.69	1.80	2.12	25.00	0.30	92.48	0.76
Ra5	1.80	1.94	2.00	2.37	25.00	0.30	84.10	1.29
Ra6	2.00	2.19	2.20	2.61	25.00	0.30	75.72	1.81
Ra7	2.20	2.31	2.40	2.73	25.00	0.30	71.53	2.08
Ra8	2.40	2.56	2.60	2.98	25.00	0.30	63.15	2.60
Ra9	2.60	2.68	2.80	3.10	25.00	0.30	58.96	2.86
Ra10	2.80	2.93	3.00	3.35	25.00	0.30	50.58	3.39
Ra11	3.00	3.18	3.20	3.59	25.00	0.30	42.20	3.92
Ra12	3.20	3.30	3.40	3.71	25.00	0.30	38.01	4.18
Ra13	3.40	3.55	3.60	3.96	25.00	0.30	29.63	4.71
Ra14	3.60	3.79	3.80	4.57	25.00	0.30	27.56	5.31
Ra15	3.80	3.96	4.00	5.06	25.00	0.30	26.99	5.75
Ra16	4.00	4.20	4.20	5.55	25.00	0.58	26.05	16.12
Ra17	4.20	4.40	4.40	6.16	25.00	0.59	24.77	18.85
Ra18	4.40	4.59	4.60	7.27	25.00	0.30	22.86	9.02
Ra19	4.60	4.76	3.40	4.80	8.00	0.30	21.09	10.42
Ra20	4.80	4.88	5.00	8.00	26.53	0.30	20.97	10.66
Ra21	5.00	5.13	5.20	8.00	29.59	0.30	20.72	11.14
Ra22	5.20	5.38	5.40	8.00	32.65	0.30	20.47	11.62
Ra23	5.40	5.54	5.60	4.08	75.51	0.30	20.02	7.91
Ra24	5.60	5.64	5.80	4.08	78.57	0.30	20.05	8.20
Ra25	5.80	5.99	6.00	8.00	40.31	0.30	19.84	12.82
Ra26	6.00	6.11	6.20	8.00	41.84	0.30	19.72	13.06
Ra27	6.20	6.36	6.40	8.00	44.90	0.30	19.47	13.54
Ra28	6.40	6.48	6.60	8.00	46.43	0.30	19.34	13.78
Ra29	6.60	6.80	6.80	7.02	75.51	0.40	18.82	17.61
Ra30	6.80	7.00	7.00	7.51	73.98	0.40	18.37	19.49
Ra31	7.00	7.16	7.20	7.76	75.51	0.40	17.93	20.47
Ra32	7.20	7.36	7.40	8.00	78.57	0.40	17.53	21.59
Ra33	7.40	7.59	7.60	8.00	87.76	0.40	17.23	22.07
Ra34	7.60	7.79	7.80	8.00	95.41	0.40	16.98	22.47
Ra35	7.80	8.00	8.00	8.00	100.00	0.42	16.65	23.02
Ra36	8.00	8.18	8.20	8.00	100.00	0.47	16.31	23.50
Ra37	8.20	8.32	8.40	8.00	100.00	0.50	16.07	24.03

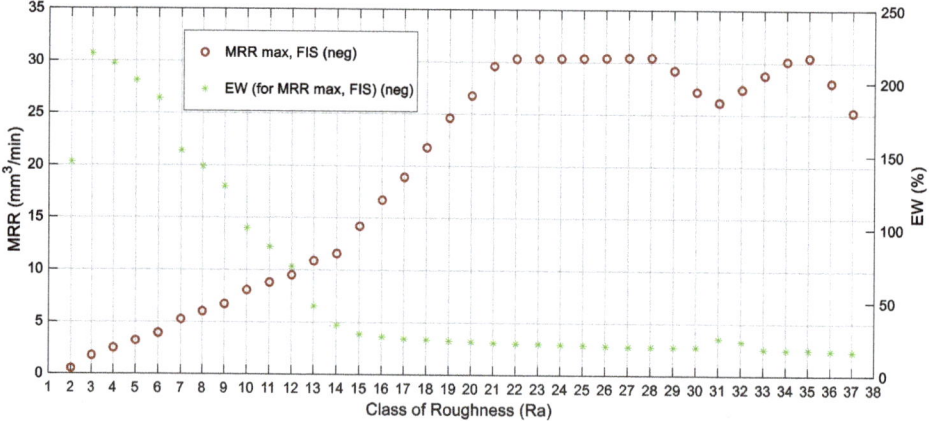

Figure 17. Values obtained from the technological table with the fuzzy inference system for the strategy of maximum removal rate using negative polarity.

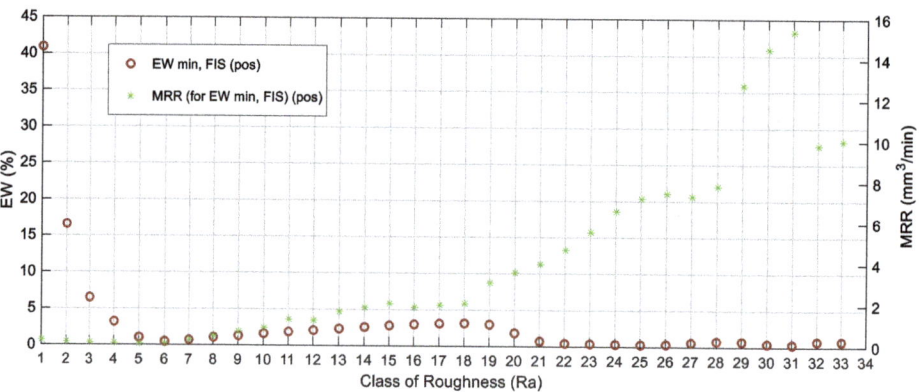

Figure 18. Values obtained from the technological table with the fuzzy inference system for the strategy of minimum electrode wear using positive polarity.

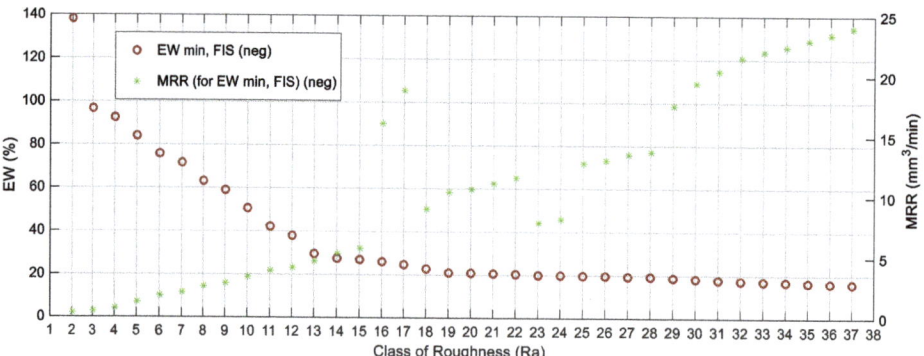

Figure 19. Values obtained from the technological table with the fuzzy inference system for the strategy of minimum electrode wear using negative polarity.

5. Conclusions

In this present study, a methodology that combines an experimental design with fuzzy modeling was used in order to obtain the technological tables that make it possible to select in advance the most suitable machining conditions in order to either maximize or minimize a certain objective function (in this case the material removal rate and wear of the electrode) in a process of EDM. In addition, a case study was analyzed for an Inconel® alloy.

Knowledge of the technological tables is very important since it makes it possible to select a certain machining strategy, so that it is possible to obtain certain values of roughness along with maximum material removal or minimum electrode wear. It was shown that the fuzzy model is capable of generating the results in a more efficient way than that obtained by conventional regression techniques. Moreover, the fuzzy model has the advantage that it is easy to incorporate new rules into the model, in the event that there are additional experimental tests.

In this present study, it was shown that the FIS allows the behavior of the technological variables used in the EDM processes to be adequately modeled and that the statistical values provided by this methodology, which were quantified by RMSE, MAE, and R-squared, are much better than those obtained by conventional methods. Therefore, the use of a FIS to obtain the EDM technology tables may be an interesting alternative, due to the fact that higher precision can be obtained compared to that obtained by traditional RSM-based methodologies.

It is felt that the present methodology for obtaining the technological tables may be of interest in the event that the input variables to the EDM equipment can be varied continuously and, thus, it could be possible to select the most appropriate operating conditions in advance. Likewise, it is felt that the proposed methodology could be generally applied for any other material and for other manufacturing processes.

Finally, it should be mentioned that it would have been possible to perform a reverse approach, that is, to train the model from the experimental data in order to obtain an adaptive neuro-fuzzy inference system; then, the technological tables could have been obtained. This will be done in a future study.

Funding: This research received no external funding.

Conflicts of Interest: The author declares no conflict of interest.

Appendix A

Table A1. Mean values of Ra, MRR, and EW, obtained with positive polarity. These values were taken from Reference [2] Torres Salcedo, A.; Puertas Arbizu I.; Luis Pérez, C. J. Analytical Modeling of Energy Density and Optimization of the EDM Machining Parameters of Inconel 600. Metals 2017, 7, 166. (Open access article distributed under the terms and conditions of the Creative Commons Attribution (CC BY) license: http://creativecommons.org/licenses/by/4.0/).

			Positive Polarity (+)				
E	Ra (μm)	MRR (mm³/min)	EW (%)	E	Ra (μm)	MRR (mm³/min)	EW (%)
1	1.39	0.1778	35.81	33	1.17	0.2650	42.84
2	3.34	3.0897	10.66	34	3.15	4.2338	15.45
3	3.66	5.0825	11.69	35	3.78	7.7099	9.61
4	4.22	7.4984	11.68	36	4.18	11.5649	9.31
5	1.57	0.1331	20.74	37	1.46	0.1792	14.94
6	4.20	3.7383	9.14	38	4.52	4.8556	10.68
7	4.70	6.3535	8.58	39	5.12	9.1444	7.93
8	4.71	6.6319	11.26	40	5.62	14.5645	6.77
9	2.01	0.0846	0.44	41	1.47	0.1332	41.45
10	5.01	3.3606	4.32	42	4.83	4.6985	8.08
11	5.84	6.4197	6.76	43	5.31	8.5279	6.41
12	6.57	9.8827	3.92	44	6.35	13.6608	3.21
13	2.73	0.0884	3.02	45	3.11	0.0852	16.31
14	5.01	2.8219	3.21	46	5.19	3.9846	0.43
15	6.18	6.7786	0.84	47	5.96	7.3741	0.30

Table A1. *Cont.*

			Positive Polarity (+)				
E	Ra (µm)	MRR (mm³/min)	EW (%)	E	Ra (µm)	MRR (mm³/min)	EW (%)
16	7.41	10.0405	0.81	48	6.80	13.8606	2.32
17	1.34	0.2297	37.33	49	1.33	0.2907	42.54
18	3.12	3.6482	16.26	50	3.17	5.1434	15.52
19	3.72	6.3632	11.44	51	3.85	9.0528	12.44
20	4.24	9.9951	9.80	52	4.21	13.1599	7.44
21	1.88	0.1520	18.76	53	1.37	0.1808	17.86
22	4.28	4.0843	8.58	54	4.36	5.7782	11.63
23	5.37	7.2087	8.92	55	4.94	10.4558	8.42
24	5.57	11.9972	5.72	56	5.41	15.6323	5.04
25	1.75	0.1169	4.80	57	1.62	0.1328	5.19
26	4.79	4.2463	6.15	58	4.69	5.3637	5.90
27	5.81	7.6840	6.31	59	5.21	9.8216	3.60
28	6.56	12.2552	6.47	60	6.23	19.1347	4.39
29	2.91	0.1056	9.32	61	1.90	0.1031	2.05
30	4.95	3.3520	2.52	62	5.10	3.9857	5.15
31	6.65	6.9094	1.13	63	6.33	8.4132	1.30
32	6.78	12.7827	1.63	64	7.08	15.3894	0.37

Table A2. Mean values of Ra, MRR, and EW, obtained with negative polarity. These values were taken from Reference [2] Torres Salcedo, A.; Puertas Arbizu I.; Luis Pérez, C. J. Analytical Modeling of Energy Density and Optimization of the EDM Machining Parameters of Inconel 600. Metals 2017, 7, 166. (Open access article distributed under the terms and conditions of the Creative Commons Attribution (CC BY) license: http://creativecommons.org/licenses/by/4.0/).

			Negative Polarity (−)				
E	Ra (µm)	MRR (mm³/min)	EW (%)	E	Ra (µm)	MRR (mm³/min)	EW (%)
1	1.57	0.4961	96.67	33	1.70	0.6719	107.46
2	3.59	4.7944	28.23	34	3.66	7.9205	29.72
3	4.29	6.6012	25.90	35	4.26	12.5716	25.79
4	4.76	10.4203	21.09	36	5.23	18.9419	21.67
5	1.31	0.3048	158.27	37	1.31	0.4777	154.88
6	5.43	7.4086	25.33	38	4.56	9.5215	27.75
7	5.84	10.3921	22.60	39	5.52	15.1031	21.94
8	6.77	14.3346	19.05	40	7.10	19.9893	19.59
9	1.39	0.3060	181.88	41	1.36	0.3882	221.58
10	5.47	7.7107	19.97	42	5.49	11.3645	26.01
11	6.90	11.5521	20.97	43	6.49	16.7606	21.72
12	7.44	17.7658	18.06	44	7.76	23.8823	18.76
13	1.58	0.3257	197.44	45	1.33	0.2949	263.67
14	6.24	9.9400	20.35	46	5.90	12.3596	24.44
15	7.36	16.1073	19.36	47	7.23	19.5421	297.77
16	8.04	20.0082	16.99	48	8.33	23.8906	16.04
17	1.62	0.5149	104.63	49	1.29	0.3546	245.89
18	3.82	6.2876	30.88	50	3.80	11.8064	29.33
19	4.53	10.5888	25.27	51	4.33	18.7034	24.92
20	4.83	13.1696	22.11	52	5.24	30.3120	21.93
21	1.28	0.4136	158.90	53	1.33	0.3144	291.16
22	4.90	9.7806	24.26	54	5.06	12.7525	26.09
23	6.06	12.7843	22.21	55	5.86	19.7280	21.70
24	6.30	22.1590	21.45	56	6.50	30.4760	19.38
25	1.28	0.3693	181.61	57	1.30	0.3561	248.44
26	5.51	9.2448	23.96	58	5.35	12.7624	26.15
27	6.26	13.5873	20.01	59	6.27	21.7225	21.94
28	7.27	21.4791	17.64	60	6.99	24.9210	19.47
29	1.36	0.3159	224.40	61	1.39	0.2823	320.70
30	6.24	11.3532	23.00	62	6.16	13.5013	25.88
31	6.93	17.2709	21.05	63	7.52	23.2371	171.94
32	7.90	22.7672	16.83	64	7.83	30.4894	17.49

References

1. Torres, A.; Luis, C.J.; Puertas, I. EDM machinability and surface roughness analysis of TiB_2 using copper electrodes. *J. Alloys Compd.* **2017**, *690*, 337–347. [CrossRef]
2. Salcedo, A.T.; Puertas, I.; Luis Pérez, C.J. Analytical Modelling of Energy Density and Optimization of the EDM Machining Parameters of Inconel 600. *Metals* **2017**, *7*, 166. [CrossRef]
3. Nguyen, H.T.; Sugeno, M. *Fuzzy Systems, Modeling and Control*; Springer-Science+Businees Media: New York, NY, USA, 1998.
4. Takagi, T.; Sugeno, M. Fuzzy Identification of Systems and Its Applications to Modeling and Control. *IEEE Trans. Syst. ManCybern.* **1985**, *SMC-15*, 116–132. [CrossRef]
5. Luis, C.J.; Puertas, I. Methodology for developing technological tables used in EDM processes of conductive ceramics. *J. Mater. Process. Technol.* **2007**, *189*, 301–309. [CrossRef]
6. Nguyen, A.T.; Taniguchi, T.; Eciolaza, L.; Campos, V.; Palhares, R.; Sugeno, R.M. Fuzzy Control Systems: Past, Present and Future. *IEEE Comput. Intell. Mag.* **2019**, *14*, 56–68. [CrossRef]
7. Mamdani, E.H. Application of fuzzy algorithms for control of simple dynamic plant. In *Proceedings of the Institution of Electrical Engineers*; Institution of Engineering and Technology (IET): Stevenage, UK, 1974; Volume 121, pp. 1585–1588.
8. Mamdani, E.H. Application of Fuzzy Logic to Approximate Reasoning Using Linguistic Synthesis. *IEEE Trans. Comput.* **1976**, *C-26*, 1182–1191. [CrossRef]
9. Mouralova, K.; Hrabec, P.; Benes, L.; Otoupalik, J.; Bednar, J.; Prokes, T.; Matousek, R. Verification of Fuzzy Inference System for Cutting Speed while WEDM for the Abrasion-Resistant Steel Creusabro by Conventional Statistical Methods. *Metals* **2020**, *10*, 92. [CrossRef]
10. Aamir, M.; Tu, S.; Tolouei-Rad, M.; Giasin, K.; Vafadar, A. Optimization and Modeling of Process Parameters in Multi-Hole Simultaneous Drilling Using Taguchi Method and Fuzzy Logic Approach. *Materials* **2020**, *13*, 680. [CrossRef]
11. Alarifi, I.M.; Nguyen, H.M.; Naderi Bakhtiyari, A.; Asadi, A. Feasibility of ANFIS-PSO and ANFIS-GA Models in Predicting Thermophysical Properties of Al2O3-MWCNT/Oil Hybrid Nanofluid. *Materials* **2019**, *12*, 3628. [CrossRef]
12. Wang, C.-N.; Nguyen, V.T.; Chyou, J.-T.; Lin, T.-F.; Nguyen, T.N. Fuzzy Multicriteria Decision-Making Model (MCDM) for Raw Materials Supplier Selection in Plastics Industry. *Mathematics* **2019**, *7*, 981. [CrossRef]
13. Kang, H.; Cho, H.-C.; Choi, S.-H.; Heo, I.; Kim, H.-Y.; Kim, K.S. Estimation of Heating Temperature for Fire-Damaged Concrete Structures Using Adaptive Neuro-Fuzzy Inference System. *Materials* **2019**, *12*, 3964. [CrossRef] [PubMed]
14. Tayyab, M.; Sarkar, B.; Yahya, B.N. Imperfect Multi-Stage Lean Manufacturing System with Rework under Fuzzy Demand. *Mathematics* **2019**, *7*, 13. [CrossRef]
15. Faisal, N.; Kumar, K. Optimization of Machine Process Parameters in EDM for EN 31 Using Evolutionary Optimization Techniques. *Technologies* **2018**, *6*, 54. [CrossRef]
16. Lin, Y.-C.; Wang, Y.-C.; Chen, T.-C.T.; Lin, H.-F. Evaluating the Suitability of a Smart Technology Application for Fall Detection Using a Fuzzy Collaborative Intelligence Approach. *Mathematics* **2019**, *7*, 1097. [CrossRef]
17. Cavallaro, F. A Takagi-Sugeno Fuzzy Inference System for Developing a Sustainability Index of Biomass. *Sustainability* **2015**, *7*, 12359–12371. [CrossRef]
18. Versaci, M. Fuzzy approach and Eddy currents NDT/NDE devices in industrial applications. *Electron. Lett.* **2016**, *52*, 943–945. [CrossRef]
19. Versaci, M.; Calcagno, S.; Cacciola, M.; Morabito, F.C.; Palamara, I.; Pellicanò, D. Chapter 7: Innovative Fuzzy Techniques for Characterizing Defects in Ultrasonic Nondestructive Evaluation. In *Ultrasonic Nondestructive Evaluation Systems, Industrial Application Issues*; Burrascano, P., Callegari, S., Montisci, A., Ricci, M., Versaci, M., Eds.; Springer International Publishing: Cham, Switzerland, 2015; pp. 200–232.
20. Sun, X.; Jia, X. A Fault Diagnosis Method of Industrial Robot Rolling Bearing Based on Data Driven and Random Intuitive Fuzzy Decision. *IEEE Access* **2019**, *7*, 148764–148770. [CrossRef]
21. Postorino, M.N.; Versaci, M. A Geometric Fuzzy-Based Approach for Airport Clustering. *Adv. Fuzzy Syst.* **2014**, *2014*, 201243. [CrossRef]
22. Cheng, L.; Liu, W.; Hou, Z.G.; Huang, T.; Yu, J.; Tan, M. An Adaptive Takagi–Sugeno Fuzzy Model-Based Predictive Controller for Piezoelectric Actuators. *IEEE Trans. Ind. Electron.* **2017**, *64*, 3048–3058. [CrossRef]

23. Bagua, H.; Guemana, M.; Hafaifa, A. Gas Turbine Monitoring using Fuzzy Control approaches: Comparison between Fuzzy Type 1 and 2. In Proceedings of the 2018 International Conference on Applied Smart Systems (ICASS'2018), Médéa, Algeria, 24–25 November 2018.
24. Goswamia, R.; Joshib, D. Performance Review of Fuzzy Logic Based Controllers Employed in Brushless DC Motor. *Procedia Comput. Sci.* **2018**, *132*, 623–631. [CrossRef]
25. Liu, X.; Gao, Z.; Chen, M.Z. Takagi–Sugeno Fuzzy Model Based Fault Estimation and Signal Compensation with Application to Wind Turbines. *IEEE Trans. Ind. Electron.* **2017**, *64*, 5678–5689.
26. Lin, Y.Y.; Chang, J.Y.; Lin, C.T. A TSK-Type-Based Self-Evolving Compensatory Interval Type-2 Fuzzy Neural Network (TSCIT2FNN) and Its Applications. *IEEE Trans. Ind. Electron.* **2014**, *61*, 447–459. [CrossRef]
27. Biglarbegian, M.; Melek, W.W.; Mendel, J.M. Design of Novel Interval Type-2 Fuzzy Controllers for Modular and Reconfigurable Robots: Theory and Experiments. *IEEE Trans. Ind. Electron.* **2011**, *58*, 1371–1384. [CrossRef]
28. Dereli, T.; Baykasoglu, A.; Altun, K.; Durmusoglu, A.; Burhan, T. Industrial applications of type-2 fuzzy sets and systems—A concise review. *Comput. Ind.* **2011**, *62*, 125–137. [CrossRef]
29. Lei, Y.; Yang, B.; Jiang, X.; Jia, F.; Li, N.; Nandi, A.K. Applications of machine learning to machine fault diagnosis: A review and roadmap. *Mech. Syst. Signal Process.* **2020**, *138*, 106587. [CrossRef]
30. Shabgard, M.R.; Badamchizadeh, M.A.; Ranjbary, G.; Amini, K. Fuzzy approach to select machining parameters in electrical discharge machining (EDM) and ultrasonic-assisted EDM processes. *J. Manuf. Syst.* **2013**, *32*, 32–39. [CrossRef]
31. Sibalija, T.V. Particle swarm optimisation in designing parameters of manufacturing processes: A review (2008–2018). *Appl. Soft Comput.* **2019**, *84*, 105743. [CrossRef]
32. Datta, S.; Biswal, B.B.; Mahapatra, S.S. Optimization of Electro-Discharge Machining Responses of Super Alloy Inconel 718: Use of Satisfaction Function Approach Combined with Taguchi Philosophy. *Mater. Today Proc.* **2018**, *5 Pt 1*, 4376–4383. [CrossRef]
33. Babu, K.N.; Karthikeyan, R.; Punitha, A. An integrated ANN—PSO approach to optimize the material removal rate and surface roughness of wire cut EDM on INCONEL 750. *Mater. Today Proc.* **2019**, *19 Pt 2*, 501–505. [CrossRef]
34. Al-Ghamdi, K.; Taylan, O. A comparative study on modelling material removal rate by ANFIS and polynomial methods in electrical discharge machining process. *Comput. Ind. Eng.* **2015**, *79*, 27–41. [CrossRef]
35. Devarasiddappa, D.; George, J.; Chandrasekaran, M.; Teyi, N. Application of Artificial Intelligence Approach in Modeling Surface Quality of Aerospace Alloys in WEDM Process. *Procedia Technol.* **2016**, *25*, 1199–1208. [CrossRef]
36. Maher, I.; Ling, L.H.; Ahmed, A.D.S.; Hamdi, M. Improve wire EDM performance at different machining parameters—ANFIS modelling. *IFAC-PapersOnLine* **2015**, *48*, 105–110. [CrossRef]
37. Joshi, K.K.; Behera, R.K.; Kumar, R.; Mohapatra, S.K.; Patro, S.S. Machinability Assessment of Inconel 800HT and its prediction using a hybrid fuzzy controller in EDM. *Mater. Today Proc.* **2019**, *18 Pt 7*, 5270–5275. [CrossRef]
38. Torres, A.; Puertas, I.; Luis, C.J. Modelling of surface finish, electrode wear and material removal rate in electrical discharge machining of hard-to-machine alloys. *Precis. Eng.* **2015**, *40*, 33–45. [CrossRef]
39. Bhadauria, G.; Jha, S.K.; Roy, B.N.; Dhakry, N.S. Electrical-Discharge Machining of Tungsten Carbide (WC) and its composites (WC-Co)—A Review. *Mater. Today Proc.* **2018**, *5 Pt 3*, 24760–24769. [CrossRef]
40. The MathWorks, Inc. *Fuzzy Logic Toolbox™User's Guide*; The MathWorks, Inc.: Natick, MA, USA, 1999.
41. UNE-EN ISO 4287:1999, *Geometrical Product Specifications (GPS)-Surface Texture: Profile Method—Terms, Definitions and Surface Texture Parameters*; AENOR: Madrid, Spain, 1999.
42. Versaci, M.; Calcagno, S.; Cacciola, M.; Morabito, F.C.; Palamara, I.; Pellicanò, D. Chapter 6: Standard Soft Computing Techniques for Characterization of Defects in Nondestructive Evaluation. In *Ultrasonic Nondestructive Evaluation Systems, Industrial Application Issues*; Burrascano, P., Callegari, S., Montisci, A., Ricci, M., Versaci, M., Eds.; Springer International Publishing: Cham, Switzerland, 2015; pp. 175–199.
43. Egaji, O.A.; Griffiths, A.; Hasan, M.S.; Yu, H.N. A comparison of Mamdani and Sugeno fuzzy based packet scheduler for MANET with a realistic wireless propagation model. *Int. J. Autom. Comput.* **2015**, *12*, 1–13. [CrossRef]

© 2020 by the author. Licensee MDPI, Basel, Switzerland. This article is an open access article distributed under the terms and conditions of the Creative Commons Attribution (CC BY) license (http://creativecommons.org/licenses/by/4.0/).

Article

EA/AE-Eigenvectors of Interval Max-Min Matrices

Martin Gavalec [1,*] and Ján Plavka [2] and Daniela Ponce [1]

1. Faculty of Informatics and Management, University of Hradec Králové,
   50003 Hradec Králové, Czech Republic; daniela.ponce@uhk.cz
2. Faculty of Electrical Engineering and Informatics, Technical University of Košice, 04200 Košice, Slovakia; jan.plavka@tuke.sk
* Correspondence: martin.gavalec@uhk.cz

Received: 13 April 2020; Accepted: 25 May 2020; Published: 1 June 2020

Abstract: Systems working in discrete time (discrete event systems, in short: DES)—based on binary operations: the maximum and the minimum—are studied in so-called max–min (fuzzy) algebra. The steady states of a DES correspond to eigenvectors of its transition matrix. In reality, the matrix (vector) entries are usually not exact numbers and they can instead be considered as values in some intervals. The aim of this paper is to investigate the eigenvectors for max–min matrices (vectors) with interval coefficients. This topic is closely related to the research of fuzzy DES in which the entries of state vectors and transition matrices are kept between 0 and 1, in order to describe uncertain and vague values. Such approach has many various applications, especially for decision-making support in biomedical research. On the other side, the interval data obtained as a result of impreciseness, or data errors, play important role in practise, and allow to model similar concepts. The interval approach in this paper is applied in combination with forall–exists quantification of the values. It is assumed that the set of indices is divided into two disjoint subsets: the E-indices correspond to those components of a DES, in which the existence of one entry in the assigned interval is only required, while the A-indices correspond to the universal quantifier, where all entries in the corresponding interval must be considered. In this paper, the properties of EA/AE-interval eigenvectors have been studied and characterized by equivalent conditions. Furthermore, numerical recognition algorithms working in polynomial time have been described. Finally, the results are illustrated by numerical examples.

Keywords: discrete events system; max–min (fuzzy) algebra; interval matrix; interval eigenvector

MSC: Primary: 08A72; 90B35; Secondary: 90C47

---

1. Introduction

Matrices in max–min algebra (fuzzy matrices), in which the binary operations of addition and multiplication are replaced by binary operations of maximum and minimum, are useful when modeling fuzzy discrete dynamic systems. They are also useful for graph theory, scheduling, knowledge engineering, cluster analysis, fuzzy systems and when describing the diagnosis of technical devices [1,2] or medical diagnosis [3]. The problem studied in [3] leads to the problem of finding the greatest invariant of the fuzzy system.

Fuzzy DES combine fuzzy set theory with discrete events systems and are represented by vectors and matrices having entries between 0 and 1 and describing uncertain and vague values. The papers [4,5] are devoted to a generalization of DES into fuzzy DES and spreading optimal control of discrete event systems to fuzzy discrete event systems. The authors of [6] deal with predictability in fuzzy DES. In particular, these papers are motivated by an ambition to clear a difficulty with vagueness and subjectivity in real medical applications. The other possibility how to treat the possible inaccuracy of DES entries is to use interval data in combination with forall–exists quantification of values. Namely, some elements of the interval vector and the interval matrix are taken into account for each value of the interval, and some of them are only considered for at least one value. This approach allows to obtain alternative solutions.

The research of fuzzy algebra is also motivated by max-plus interaction discrete-events systems (DESs) whereby applications on the system of processors and multi-machine interactive production process were presented in [7,8], respectively. In these systems, we have n entities (e.g., processors, servers, machines, etc.) which that work in stages. In the algebraic model of their interactive work, the entry $x_i(k)$ of the state vector $x(k)$ represents the start-time of the kth stage on entity i, $i = 1, \ldots, n$, and the entry a_{ij} of the transition matrix encodes the influence of the work of entity j in the previous stage on the work of entity i in the current stage. The system is assumed to be homogeneous, in the sense that A does not change from stage to stage.

Summing up all the influence effects multiplied by the results of previous stages, we have $x_i(k+1) = \bigoplus_j a_{ij} \otimes x_j(k)$, where $\oplus = \max$ and $\otimes = +$. In max-plus algebra, the maximum is often interpreted as waiting until all works of the system are finished and all of the necessary influence constraints are satisfied. The problem of finding the vectors for which the DES reaches the steady state leads to the eigenproblem $A \otimes x = \lambda \otimes x$, and is one of the most intensively studied questions (see max–min case study in Section 3.2.

Analogously, $\otimes = \min$ in max–min algebra. The summing is then interpreted as computing the maximal capacity of the path leading to the next state of the system. Because the operations max and min do not create new values, a DES in max–min algebra necessarily comes to periodic repetition of the state vector (i.e., to a steady state) if the period is 1. The eigenproblem then has the form $A \otimes x = x$. In comparison with the max–plus algebra, the eigenvalue λ is omitted (in other words, we assume that λ is equal to the maximal value I).

In practice, the values of the matrix entries obtained as a result of roundoff, truncation, or data errors are not exact numbers and they are usually contained in some intervals. Interval arithmetic is an efficient way to represent matrices in a guaranteed way on a computer. Meanwhile, fuzzy algebra is a convenient algebraic setting for some types of optimization problems, see [9]. Matrices and vectors with interval entries play important role in practice. They can be applied in several branches of applied mathematics, as for instance, a solvability of systems of linear interval equations in classical linear algebra [10] and in max-plus algebra [11] or the stability of the matrix orbit in max–min algebra [12,13].

The motivation for the basic questions studied in this paper comes from an investigation of the steady states of max–min systems with interval coefficients. Suppose that $\mathbf{X}$ is an interval vector and $\mathbf{A}$ is an interval matrix, then $\mathbf{X}$ is called a strong eigenvector of $\mathbf{A}$ if $A \otimes x = x$ holds for every $x \in \mathbf{X}$ and for every $A \in \mathbf{A}$. The eigenvectors correspond to steady states, and it may happen in reality that this interpretation—with the universal quantifier for every index $i \in N$ and for every pair $(i, j) \in N \times N$—is too strong for all of the entries.

In other words, in some model situations only the existence of some x_i (some a_{ij}) is required for $i \in N^{\exists}$ (for $(i, j) \in \tilde{N}^{\exists}$), while all possible values of x_i (of a_{ij}) must be considered for $i \in N^{\forall} = N \setminus N^{\exists}$ (for $(i, j) \in \tilde{N}^{\forall} = N \times N \setminus \tilde{N}^{\exists}$).

Hence, we assume that $\mathbf{X}$ and $\mathbf{A}$ can be split into two subsets according to the exists/forall quantification of its interval entries; that is, $\mathbf{X} = \mathbf{X}^{\exists} \oplus \mathbf{X}^{\forall}$ or $\mathbf{A} = \mathbf{A}^{\exists} \oplus \mathbf{A}^{\forall}$ (or both splittings simultaneously) take place.

According to the first two cases, the properties of various types of the strong EA/AE-eigenvectors, or the EA/AE-strong eigenvectors, are studied in this paper. In addition, their characterizations by equivalent conditions are given. Moreover, polynomial recognition algorithms for the described conditions are presented. The mixed case (the EA/AE-strong EA/AE-eigenvectors) is briefly considered without recognition algorithms.

Related concepts of robustness (when an eigenvector of A is reached with any starting vector) and strong robustness (when the greatest eigenvector of A is reached with any starting vector) in fuzzy algebra were introduced and studied in [14,15]. Equivalent conditions for the robustness of interval matrix were presented in [11] and efficient algorithms for checking of strong robustness were described in [16]. The papers by [12,13] deal with AE/EA robustness of interval circulant matrices and X^{AE}/X^{EA} robustness of max–min matrices. Polynomial procedures for the recognition of weak robustness were described in [15].

The rest of this paper is organized as follows. The next section contains the basic definitions and notation. Sections 3 and 4 deal with the definitions and equivalent conditions for the EA/AE-eigenvectors. In particular, Section 3 is divided into two subsections, where Section 3.1 contains the methodology and Section 3.2 presents a study case application based on a numerical example. Section 5 describes the strong EA/AE-eigenvectors. Meanwhile, Section 6 is devoted to characterization of the necessary and sufficient conditions for the EA/AE-strong eigenvectors. Finally, the generalization to the mixed case of EA/AE-strong EA/AE-eigenvectors is briefly sketched in Appendix A.

2. Preliminaries and Basic Definitions

Let $(\mathcal{B}, \leq)$ be a bounded linearly ordered set with the least element in $\mathcal{B}$ denoted by O and the greatest element denoted by I. For given natural numbers m, n, we use the notation $M = \{1, 2, \ldots, m\}$ and $N = \{1, 2, \ldots, n\}$, respectively. The set of $m \times n$ matrices over $\mathcal{B}$ is denoted by $\mathcal{B}(m,n)$, the set of $n \times 1$ vectors over $\mathcal{B}$ is denoted by $\mathcal{B}(n)$ and, for $\alpha \in \mathcal{B}$, the constant vector $(\alpha, \ldots, \alpha)^T$ is denoted by α^*.

The max–min algebra is defined as a triple $(\mathcal{B}, \oplus, \otimes)$, where $a \oplus b = \max(a, b)$ and $a \otimes b = \min(a, b)$. The operations $\oplus, \otimes$ are extended to the matrix-vector algebra over $\mathcal{B}$ by the direct analogy to the conventional linear algebra. If each entry of a matrix $A \in \mathcal{B}(m,n)$ (a vector $x \in \mathcal{B}(n)$) is equal to O, then we write $A = O$ ($x = O$).

The ordering from $\mathcal{B}$ is naturally extended to vectors and matrices. For example, for $x = (x_1, \ldots, x_n)^T \in \mathcal{B}(n)$ and $y = (y_1, \ldots, y_n)^T \in \mathcal{B}(n)$ we write $x \leq y$, if $x_i \leq y_i$ holds for each $i \in N$.

For $\underline{A}, \overline{A} \in \mathcal{B}(n,n)$, $\underline{A} \leq \overline{A}$ and $\underline{x}, \overline{x} \in \mathcal{B}(n)$, $\underline{x} \leq \overline{x}$, the interval matrix $\mathbf{A}$ with bounds $\underline{A}, \overline{A}$ and the interval vector $\mathbf{X}$ with bounds $\underline{x}, \overline{x}$ are defined as follows

$$\mathbf{A} = [\underline{A}, \overline{A}] = \{A \in \mathcal{B}(n,n); \underline{A} \leq A \leq \overline{A}\},$$

$$\mathbf{X} = [\underline{x}, \overline{x}] = \{x \in \mathcal{B}(n); \underline{x} \leq x \leq \overline{x}\}.$$

In the rest of this paper we assume that subsets $N^\exists, N^\forall \subseteq N$ are given with $N = N^\exists \cup N^\forall$ and $N = N^\exists \cap N^\forall = \emptyset$. In other words, we consider a partition $N = \{N^\exists, N^\forall\}$. If $i \in N^\exists$ ($i \in N^\forall$), then we say that the index i is *associated* with the existential (universal) quantifier.

Using the given partition $N = \{N^\exists, N^\forall\}$, we can split the interval vector $\mathbf{X}$ as $\mathbf{X}^\forall \oplus \mathbf{X}^\exists$, where $\mathbf{X}^\forall = [\underline{x}^\forall, \overline{x}^\forall]$ is the interval vector comprising the universally quantified entries and $\mathbf{X}^\exists = [\underline{x}^\exists, \overline{x}^\exists]$ concerns the existentially quantified entries. In the other words, every vector $x \in \mathbf{X}$ can be written in the form $x = x^\forall \oplus x^\exists$, with $x^\forall \in \mathbf{X}^\forall$, $x^\exists \in \mathbf{X}^\exists$.

More precisely, $x_i^\forall = x_i$ for $i \in N^\forall$, $x_i^\forall = O$ for $i \in N^\exists$; and similarly, $x_i^\exists = x_i$ for $i \in N^\exists$, $x_i^\exists = O$ for $i \in N^\forall$.

Definition 1. *Let interval vector $\mathbf{X} \subseteq \mathcal{B}(n)$ and partition $N = \{N^\exists, N^\forall\}$ be given. Interval vector $\mathbf{X}^\exists = [\underline{x}^\exists, \overline{x}^\exists]$ is called*

- *E-subvector of $\mathbf{X}$, if $\underline{x}_i^\exists = \overline{x}_i^\exists = O$ for each $i \in N^\forall$ and $[\underline{x}_i^\exists, \overline{x}_i^\exists] = [\underline{x}_i, \overline{x}_i]$ for each $i \in N^\exists$,*

and interval vector $\mathbf{X}^\forall = [\underline{x}^\forall, \overline{x}^\forall]$ is called

- *A-subvector of $\mathbf{X}$, if $\underline{x}_i^\forall = \overline{x}_i^\forall = O$ for each $i \in N^\exists$ and $[\underline{x}_i^\forall, \overline{x}_i^\forall] = [\underline{x}_i, \overline{x}_i]$ for each $i \in N^\forall$,*

Example 1. *Suppose that* $\mathcal{B} = [0, 10]$, $N = \{N^\exists, N^\forall\}$. *Consider interval vector* X *which has the form*

$$X = \begin{pmatrix} [1,2] \\ [1,3] \\ [3,4] \\ [1,2] \\ [0,1] \end{pmatrix} \quad \text{with } N^\exists = \{1,2,3\} \text{ and } N^\forall = \{4,5\}.$$

Then subvectors $X^\exists$ *and* $X^\forall$ *have the form*

$$X^\exists = \begin{pmatrix} [1,2] \\ [1,3] \\ [3,4] \\ [0,0] \\ [0,0] \end{pmatrix}, \text{ and } X^\forall = \begin{pmatrix} [0,0] \\ [0,0] \\ [0,0] \\ [1,2] \\ [0,1] \end{pmatrix}.$$

For given $A \in \mathcal{B}(n,n)$, $x \in \mathcal{B}(n)$ we say that x is eigenvector of A, if

$$A \otimes x = x.$$

In the rest of this paper, we assume that a partition $N = \{N^\exists, N^\forall\}$ is given. The corresponding subvectors $X^\exists$, $X^\forall$ and entries will always be related to this fixed N, without explicit formulation. The same is true for the EA/AE-eigenvectors that are defined as follows.

Definition 2. *Let matrix* $A \in \mathcal{B}(n,n)$ *and interval vector* $X = [\underline{x}, \overline{x}] \subseteq \mathcal{B}(n)$ *be given. We say that* X *is*

- *EA-eigenvector of* A *if*

$$(\exists x^\exists \in X^\exists)(\forall x^\forall \in X^\forall) \, A \otimes (x^\exists \oplus x^\forall) = (x^\exists \oplus x^\forall),$$

- *AE-eigenvector of* A *if*

$$(\forall x^\forall \in X^\forall)(\exists x^\exists \in X^\exists) \, A \otimes (x^\exists \oplus x^\forall) = (x^\exists \oplus x^\forall).$$

All matrices belonging to A and vectors belonging to X can be represented as max–min linear combinations of so-called *generators*, which are defined as follows. For every $i, j \in N$, $A^{(ij)} \in \mathcal{B}(n,n)$ and $x^{(i)}$, $x^{[i]}$, $\in \mathcal{B}(n)$ are defined by putting, for every $k, l \in N$,

$$a_{kl}^{(ij)} = \begin{cases} \overline{a}_{ij}, & \text{for } k=i, l=j \\ \underline{a}_{kl}, & \text{otherwise} \end{cases},$$

$$x_k^{(i)} = \begin{cases} \overline{x}_i, & \text{for } k=i \\ \underline{x}_k, & \text{otherwise} \end{cases} \quad x_k^{[i]} = \begin{cases} \underline{x}_i, & \text{for } k=i \\ \overline{x}_k, & \text{otherwise} \end{cases}$$

Furthermore, we denote $x^{(n+1)} := \underline{x}^\forall$, $x^{[n+1]} := \overline{x}^\forall$ and $X_G^\forall = \{x^{(i)}, x^{[i]}; i \in N \cup \{n+1\}\}$. Notice that $|X_G^\forall| = 2n + 2$.

Lemma 1. *Let* $x \in \mathcal{B}(n)$ *and* $A \in \mathcal{B}(n,n)$. *Then,*

(i) $x \in X$ *if and only if* $x = \bigoplus_{i \in N} \beta_i \otimes x^{(i)}$ *for some* $\beta_i \in \mathcal{B}$ *with* $\underline{x}_i \leq \beta_i \leq \overline{x}_i$,

(ii) $A \in \mathcal{A}$ *if and only if* $A = \bigoplus_{i,j \in N} \alpha_{ij} \otimes A^{(ij)}$ *for some* $\alpha_{ij} \in \mathcal{B}$ *with* $\underline{a}_{ij} \leq \alpha_{ij} \leq \overline{a}_{ij}$.

Proof. For the proof of statement (i), let us suppose that $x \in X$; that is, the inequalities $\underline{x}_i \leq x_i \leq \overline{x}_i$ hold for every $i \in N$. Denoting $\beta_i = x_i$ we get $\beta_i \otimes \overline{x}_i = x_i \otimes \overline{x}_i = x_i$ and $\beta_i \otimes \underline{x}_i = x_i \otimes \underline{x}_i = \underline{x}_i \leq x_i$ for every $i \in N$. It can be easily verified that $\bigoplus_{i \in N} \beta_i \otimes x^{(i)} = x$. The proof of statement (ii) is analogous. □

3. EA-Eigenvector

3.1. Description of the Methodology

The first result is the characterization of an interval EA-eigenvector of a given (non-interval) matrix A, with the help of generators.

Theorem 1. *Let $A \in \mathcal{B}(n,n)$ and $X = [\underline{x}, \overline{x}]$ be given. Then, X is EA-eigenvector of A if and only if*

$$(\exists x^\exists \in X^\exists)(\forall i \in N^\forall \cup \{n+1\}) \, A \otimes (x^\exists \oplus x^{(i)}) = x^\exists \oplus x^{(i)}.$$

Proof. Suppose that there is $x^\exists \in X^\exists$ such that $A \otimes (x^\exists \oplus x^{(i)}) = x^\exists \oplus x^{(i)}$ holds for all $i \in N^\forall \cup \{n+1\}$. For fixed $x^\exists$ define the auxiliary interval vector $\hat{X} = (\hat{x}_1, \ldots, \hat{x}_n)^T$ as follows:

$$\hat{x}_i = \begin{cases} [x_i^\exists, x_i^\exists], & \text{for } i \in N^\exists \\ [\underline{x}_i, \overline{x}_i], & \text{for } i \in N^\forall \end{cases} \quad . \tag{1}$$

Notice that vectors $\hat{x}^{(i)}$ of $\hat{X}$ have the form

$$\hat{x}_k^{(i)} = \begin{cases} \overline{x}_i, & \text{for } k = i \wedge i \in N^\forall \\ \underline{x}_i, & \text{for } k \neq i \wedge k \in N^\forall \\ x_k^\exists, & \text{for } k \in N^\exists, \end{cases} \tag{2}$$

or equivalently, $\hat{x}^{(i)} = x^\exists \oplus x^{(i)}$ for each $i \in N^\forall$ and $\hat{x}^{(i)} = \hat{\underline{x}} = x^\exists \oplus x^{(n+1)}$ for each $i \in N^\exists$. It is easy to see that X is EA-eigenvector if and only if $A \otimes \hat{x} = \hat{x}$ holds for each $\hat{x} \in \hat{X}$. By Lemma 1, an arbitrary vector $\hat{x} \in \hat{X}$ is defined as the max–min linear combination $\hat{x} = \bigoplus_{i \in N^\forall} \beta_i \otimes \hat{x}^{(i)}$. We will then prove that the equality $A \otimes \hat{x} = \hat{x}$ holds for each $\hat{x} \in \hat{X}$. Thus, we get

$$A \otimes \hat{x} = A \otimes \bigoplus_{i \in N} \beta_i \otimes \hat{x}^{(i)} = A \otimes \left(\bigoplus_{i \in N^\exists} \beta_i \otimes \hat{x}^{(i)} \oplus \bigoplus_{i \in N^\forall} \beta_i \otimes \hat{x}^{(i)} \right) =$$

$$A \otimes \left(\bigoplus_{i \in N^\exists} \beta_i \otimes \hat{\underline{x}} \oplus \bigoplus_{i \in N^\forall} \beta_i \otimes \hat{x}^{(i)} \right) = \left(\bigoplus_{i \in N^\exists} \beta_i \otimes A \otimes \hat{\underline{x}} \right) \oplus \left(\bigoplus_{i \in N^\forall} \beta_i \otimes A \otimes \hat{x}^{(i)} \right) =$$

$$\left(\bigoplus_{i \in N^\exists} \beta_i \otimes A \otimes (x^\exists \oplus x^{(n+1)}) \right) \oplus \left(\bigoplus_{i \in N^\forall} \beta_i \otimes A \otimes (x^\exists \oplus x^{(i)}) \right) =$$

$$\left(\bigoplus_{i \in N^\exists} \beta_i \otimes (x^\exists \oplus x^{(n+1)}) \right) \oplus \left(\bigoplus_{i \in N^\forall} \beta_i \otimes (x^\exists \oplus x^{(i)}) \right) =$$

$$\left(\bigoplus_{i \in N^\exists} \beta_i \otimes \hat{x}^{(i)} \oplus \bigoplus_{i \in N^\forall} \beta_i \otimes \hat{x}^{(i)} \right) = \hat{x}.$$

The reverse implication is trivial. □

The next result shows that the conditions in Theorem 1 can be equivalently formulated as the solvability condition of a system of two-sided max–min linear equations. Hence, the interval EA-eigenvectors of a given non-interval matrix can be recognized in polynomial time.

Without loss of generality, suppose that $N^\exists = \{1, 2, \ldots, k\}$ and $N^\forall = \{k+1, k+2, \ldots, n\}$; that is,

$$X^\exists = ([\underline{x}_1, \overline{x}_1], \ldots, [\underline{x}_k, \overline{x}_k], [O, O] \ldots, [O, O])^T$$

and

$$X^\forall = ([O, O] \ldots, [O, O], [\underline{x}_{k+1}, \overline{x}_{k+1}], \ldots, [\underline{x}_n, \overline{x}_n])^T.$$

Define the matrices $C, D \in \mathcal{B}(n(n-k+1), n+1)$ as follows

$$C = \begin{pmatrix} A \otimes x^{(1)} & \ldots & A \otimes x^{(k)} & A \otimes x^{(k+1)} & O & O & \ldots & O \\ A \otimes x^{(1)} & \ldots & A \otimes x^{(k)} & O & A \otimes x^{(k+2)} & O & \ldots & O \\ \vdots & & & & & & & \\ A \otimes x^{(1)} & \ldots & A \otimes x^{(k)} & O & O & O & \ldots & A \otimes x^{(n+1)} \end{pmatrix}$$

and

$$D = \begin{pmatrix} x^{(1)} & \ldots & x^{(k)} & x^{(k+1)} & O & O & \ldots & O \\ x^{(1)} & \ldots & x^{(k)} & O & x^{(k+2)} & O & \ldots & O \\ \vdots & & & & & & & \\ x^{(1)} & \ldots & x^{(k)} & O & O & O & \ldots & x^{(n+1)} \end{pmatrix}.$$

Theorem 2. *Let A and $X = [\underline{x}, \overline{x}]$ be given. Then, X is EA-eigenvector of A if and only if the system $C \otimes \beta = D \otimes \beta$ is solvable with $\underline{x}_i \leq \beta_i \leq \overline{x}_i$ for $i \in N^\exists$ and $\beta_j = I$ for $j \in N^\forall \cup \{n+1\}$.*

Proof. By Lemma 1, if $\underline{x}_i \leq \beta_i \leq \overline{x}_i$ for $i \in N^\exists$, then $x^\exists = \bigoplus_{i=1}^{k} \beta_i \otimes x^{(i)}$ belongs to $X^\exists$; and if $x^\exists \in X^\exists$, then we can find $\underline{x}_i \leq \beta_i \leq \overline{x}_i$ for $i \in N^\exists$ such that $x^\exists = \bigoplus_{i=1}^{k} \beta_i \otimes x^{(i)}$.

We also have that the system $C \otimes \beta = D \otimes \beta$ is solvable with $\underline{x}_i \leq \beta_i \leq \overline{x}_i$ for $i \in N^\exists$ and $\beta_j = I$ for $j \in N^\forall \cup \{n+1\}$ if and only if the following equivalences hold true:

$$C \otimes \beta = D \otimes \beta \Leftrightarrow$$

$$(\forall j \in N^\forall \cup \{n+1\}) \bigoplus_{i \in N^\exists} (A \otimes x^{(i)} \otimes \beta_i) \oplus (A \otimes x^{(j)} \otimes \beta_j) =$$

$$\bigoplus_{i \in N^\exists} (x^{(i)} \otimes \beta_i) \oplus (x^{(j)} \otimes \beta_j) \Leftrightarrow$$

$$(\forall j \in N^\forall \cup \{n+1\}) A \otimes (\bigoplus_{i \in N^\exists} (x^{(i)} \otimes \beta_i) \oplus x^{(j)}) = \bigoplus_{i \in N^\exists} (x^{(i)} \otimes \beta_i) \oplus x^{(j)} \Leftrightarrow$$

$$(\exists x^\exists \in X^\exists)(\forall j \in N^\forall \cup \{n+1\}) A \otimes (x^\exists \oplus x^{(j)}) = x^\exists \oplus x^{(j)}$$

because of $\beta_j = I$ for $j \in N^\forall \cup \{n+1\}$. Thus by Theorem 1, the assertion follows. □

A polynomial algorithm for solving a general two-sided system $C \otimes \beta = D \otimes \beta$ of max–min linear equations with $C, D \in \mathcal{B}(r, s)$, is presented in [17]. This method finds the maximum possible solution, $\beta^{\max}$, of the system. If this possible solution does not satisfy all of the conditions of the system, then the system is not solvable. In our case, the insolvability means that the considered X is not an EA-eigenvector of A. The computational complexity of the proposed algorithm is $O(rs \cdot \min(r, s))$.

Theorem 3. *Suppose that we are given a matrix A and an interval vector $X = [\underline{x}, \overline{x}]$. The recognition problem of whether a given interval vector X of A is EA-eigenvector is then solvable in $O(n^4)$ time.*

Proof. According to Theorem 2, the recognition problem of EA-eigenvector of A is equivalent to recognizing whether the system $C \otimes \beta = D \otimes \beta$ is solvable with $\underline{x}_j \leq \beta_j \leq \overline{x}_j$ for $j \in N^{\exists}$ and $\beta_j = I$ for $j \in N^{\forall}$. In the general case, the computation of the needs $O(rs \cdot \min(r,s))$ time (see [17]). In our case, we have $r = n(n - k + 1)$, $s = n + 1$; therefore, the computation of $C \otimes \beta = D \otimes \beta$ is done in $O(n^2 \cdot n \cdot n) = O(n^4)$ time. □

3.2. Case Study Application of the Methodology Based on Numerical Example

Consider a data transfer system consisting of n computers and one server S. The computed data from computer c_i, $i \in N$ are sent to S whereby the corrected data have to return to c_i. We assume that the connection between c_i and S is only possible via one of n security processors p_j, the connections between c_i and p_j are one-way connections, and the capacity of the connection between $c_i \in N$ and $p_j \in N$ is equal to a_{ij}. Moreover, suppose that security processors $p_j \in N$ are connected with S by two-way connections with capacities x_j in both directions. The data are transmitted in data packets, and every data packet is transmitted over just one connection as an inseparable unit. Therefore, the total capacity of the connection between i and S is equal to $\max_{j \in N}\{\min\{a_{ij}, x_j\}\}$, that is, different used connections are comprised as the maximum of capacities (not as their sum).

The transfer from S to i is carried out via other one-way connections between security processors $j \in N$ and $i \in N$ with capacities between j and i equal to the constant I (the greatest element) if $i = j$, and equal to O (the least element), otherwise. Since the connections between S and j are two-way connections, the total capacity of the connection between S and i is equal to $\min\{I, x_i\} = x_i$ for every $i \in N$. The goal is to find optimal capacities x_j, $j \in N$ such that the maximal capacity of all connections between i and S via j is equal to the maximal capacity of connections between S and i on the way back, that is, we have to choose x_j, $j \in N$ in such a way that $\max_{j \in N}\{\min\{a_{ij}, x_j\}\} = x_i$ for all $i \in N$.

Consider a data transfer system which consists of 4 computers, 4 security processors and one server (see Figure 1). To find optimal capacities x_j, $j \in M = \{1, 2, 3, 4\}$ means to solve an eigenproblem for a matrix A. Then for $B = [0, 10]$ and the matrix A we look for a solution of the equality $A \otimes x = x$, or in matrix-vector form, we have

$$A \otimes x = \begin{pmatrix} 0 & 2 & 2 & 1 \\ 1 & 0 & 2 & 2 \\ 2 & 1 & 4 & 1 \\ 1 & 2 & 1 & 5 \end{pmatrix} \otimes \begin{pmatrix} x_1 \\ x_2 \\ x_3 \\ x_4 \end{pmatrix} = \begin{pmatrix} x_1 \\ x_2 \\ x_3 \\ x_4 \end{pmatrix}$$

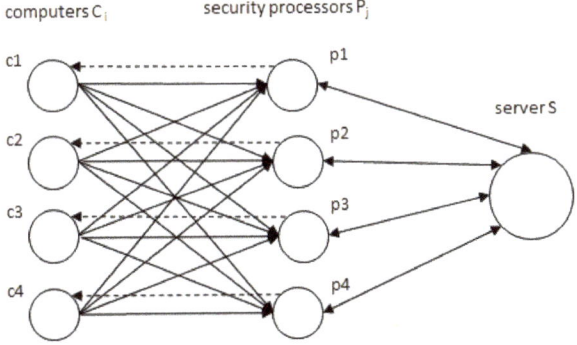

Figure 1. Data transfer system (application).

One solution of the set of all solutions describing optimal capacities $x_j, j \in N$ of the data transfer system is vector $x = (2, 2, 4, 5)^T$.

Assume now that the capacities $x_j, j \in N$ are limited by the lower bound $\underline{x}_j$ and upper bound $\overline{x}_j$. Furthermore, we assume that not all of the processed data have the same importance: whereby, for some more important types of data, all values of the interval must be taken into account (all capacities of the data transfer system have to be involved in optimal solutions), and for some—less important data types—it is sufficient to be considered for at least one value (some value of these capacities of the data transfer system are optimal). In the above defined terminology, the optimal solution has to satisfy the definition of the EA-eigenvector of A.

For numerical illustration of this situation suppose that interval vector X has the form

$$\underline{x} = \begin{pmatrix} 2 \\ 2 \\ 3 \\ 2 \end{pmatrix}, \overline{x} = \begin{pmatrix} 4 \\ 5 \\ 4 \\ 3 \end{pmatrix}$$

with $N^\exists = \{1, 2\}$, $N^\forall = \{3, 4\}$ and $N^\forall \cup \{n+1\} = \{3, 4, 5\}$.

Then generators of X and its matrix-vector products can be computed as follows:

$$x^{(1)} = \begin{pmatrix} 4 \\ 2 \\ 0 \\ 0 \end{pmatrix}, x^{(2)} = \begin{pmatrix} 2 \\ 5 \\ 0 \\ 0 \end{pmatrix}, x^{(3)} = \begin{pmatrix} 0 \\ 0 \\ 4 \\ 2 \end{pmatrix}, x^{(4)} = \begin{pmatrix} 0 \\ 0 \\ 3 \\ 3 \end{pmatrix}, x^{(5)} = \begin{pmatrix} 0 \\ 0 \\ 3 \\ 2 \end{pmatrix}.$$

and

$$A \otimes x^{(1)} = \begin{pmatrix} 2 \\ 1 \\ 2 \\ 2 \end{pmatrix}, A \otimes x^{(2)} = \begin{pmatrix} 2 \\ 1 \\ 2 \\ 2 \end{pmatrix}, A \otimes x^{(3)} = \begin{pmatrix} 2 \\ 2 \\ 4 \\ 2 \end{pmatrix},$$

$$A \otimes x^{(4)} = \begin{pmatrix} 2 \\ 2 \\ 3 \\ 3 \end{pmatrix}, A \otimes x^{(5)} = \begin{pmatrix} 2 \\ 2 \\ 3 \\ 2 \end{pmatrix},$$

By Theorem 2 we will show that X is EA-eigenvector. At first we shall construct matrices C and D and after that we shall solve the system $C \otimes \beta = D \otimes \beta$ with $\underline{x}_j \leq \beta_j \leq \overline{x}_j$ for $j \in N^\exists$ and $\beta_i = I$ for $i \in N^\forall \cup \{n+1\}$, i.e.,

$$\begin{pmatrix} 2 & 2 & 2 & 0 & 0 \\ 1 & 1 & 2 & 0 & 0 \\ 2 & 2 & 4 & 0 & 0 \\ 2 & 2 & 2 & 0 & 0 \\ 2 & 2 & 0 & 2 & 0 \\ 1 & 1 & 0 & 2 & 0 \\ 2 & 2 & 0 & 3 & 0 \\ 2 & 2 & 0 & 3 & 0 \\ 2 & 2 & 0 & 0 & 2 \\ 1 & 1 & 0 & 0 & 2 \\ 2 & 2 & 0 & 0 & 3 \\ 2 & 2 & 0 & 0 & 2 \end{pmatrix} \otimes \begin{pmatrix} \beta_1 \\ \beta_2 \\ \beta_3 \\ \beta_4 \\ \beta_5 \end{pmatrix} = \begin{pmatrix} 4 & 2 & 0 & 0 & 0 \\ 2 & 5 & 0 & 0 & 0 \\ 0 & 0 & 4 & 0 & 0 \\ 0 & 0 & 2 & 0 & 0 \\ 4 & 2 & 0 & 0 & 0 \\ 2 & 5 & 0 & 0 & 0 \\ 0 & 0 & 0 & 3 & 0 \\ 0 & 0 & 0 & 3 & 0 \\ 4 & 2 & 0 & 0 & 0 \\ 2 & 5 & 0 & 0 & 0 \\ 0 & 0 & 0 & 0 & 3 \\ 0 & 0 & 0 & 0 & 2 \end{pmatrix} \otimes \begin{pmatrix} \beta_1 \\ \beta_2 \\ \beta_3 \\ \beta_4 \\ \beta_5 \end{pmatrix} \quad (3)$$

with $2 \leq \beta_1 \leq 4$; $2 \leq \beta_2 \leq 5$; $10 \leq \beta_3 \leq 10$; $10 \leq \beta_4 \leq 10$; $10 \leq \beta_5 \leq 10$.

To obtain a solution of the system (3), we use the Algorithm 1 presented in [17]. For the convenience of the reader, the algorithm is described in the original notation.

Let $A, B \in \mathcal{B}(m, n)$ be given matrices. Denote

$$\hat{M} = \{x \in \mathcal{B}(n); A \otimes x = B \otimes x\},$$
$$I = \{1, \ldots, m\}, J = \{1, \ldots, n\},$$
$$a_i(x) = \max_{j \in J}(a_{ij} \otimes x_j), \quad b_i(x) = \max_{j \in J}(b_{ij} \otimes x_j),$$
$$M(\bar{x}) = \{x; x \in \hat{M} \wedge x \leq \bar{x}\},$$
$$I^<(\bar{x}) = \{i \in I; a_i(\bar{x}) < b_i(\bar{x})\},$$
$$I^=(\bar{x}) = \{i \in I; a_i(\bar{x}) = b_i(\bar{x})\},$$
$$\alpha(\bar{x}) = \min\{a_i(\bar{x}); i \in I^<(\bar{x})\},$$
$$I^<(\alpha(\bar{x})) = \{i \in I^<(\bar{x}); a_i(\bar{x}) = \alpha(\bar{x})\},$$
$$I^=(\alpha(\bar{x})) = \{i \in I^=(\bar{x}); a_i(\bar{x}) \leq \alpha(\bar{x})\},$$
$$J(\alpha(\bar{x})) = \{j \in J; (\exists i \in I^<(\alpha(\bar{x}))[b_{ij} \otimes \bar{x}_j > \alpha(\bar{x})]\}.$$

Algorithm 1: Solving a general two-sided system.

Input: $m, n, \bar{x}$.
Output: $x^{\max}$.
begin
1 If $\bar{x} \in M(\bar{x})$, then $x^{\max} := \bar{x}$, STOP;
2 Change notation so that $a_i(\bar{x}) \leq b_i(\bar{x})$ for all $i \in I$;
3 Compute $\alpha(\bar{x}), I^<(\alpha(\bar{x})), I^=(\alpha(\bar{x}))$;
4 Set $\tilde{x}_j := \alpha(\bar{x})$ if $j \in J(\alpha(\bar{x}))$, $\tilde{x}_j := \bar{x}_j$ otherwise;
5 If $\tilde{x} \in M(\bar{x})$, then $x^{\max} := \tilde{x}$, STOP;
6 Put $\bar{x} := \tilde{x}$ go to 2;
end

We will now apply the items of the Algorithm 2 to obtain the greatest solution of the system (3) whereby $\bar{x}, a_i(\bar{x}), b_i(\bar{x})$ will be substituted by $\bar{\beta}, c_i(\bar{\beta}), d_i(\bar{\beta})$, respectively:

Algorithm 2: Solving a general two-sided system - example.

Input: $m = 12, n = 5, I = \{1, \ldots, 12\}, J = \{1, \ldots, 5\}, \bar{x} = (4, 5, 10, 10, 10)^T$.
Output: $\beta^{\max}$.
1 $\bar{\beta} = (4, 5, 10, 10, 10) \notin M(\bar{\beta})$;
2 $(c_1(\bar{\beta}), \ldots, c_{12}(\bar{\beta})) = (2, 2, 4, 2, 2, 2, 3, 3, 2, 2, 3, 2) \leq$
   $(d_1(\bar{\beta}), \ldots, d_{12}(\bar{\beta})) = (4, 5, 4, 2, 4, 5, 3, 3, 4, 5, 3, 2)$;
3 $\alpha(\bar{\beta}) = 2, I^<(\alpha(\bar{\beta})) = I^<(2) = \{1, 2, 5, 6, 9, 10\}, I^=(\alpha(\bar{\beta})) = I^=(2) =$
   $\{4, 12\}, J(\alpha(\bar{\beta})) = J(2) = \{1, 2\}$;
4 $\tilde{\beta} = (2, 2, 10, 10, 10)$;
5 $\tilde{\beta} = (2, 2, 10, 10, 10) \in M(\bar{\beta}), \beta^{\max} = \tilde{\beta}$, STOP.

The output of the Algorithm 2 is vector $\beta^{\max} = (2, 2, 10, 10, 10) \in M(\bar{\beta})$, which is the greatest possible solution of the system (3). It is easy to verify that the possible solution $\beta^{\max}$ satisfies all conditions of (3). In other words, $\beta^{\max}$ is the solution, and we can conclude that X is an EA-eigenvector of A.

4. AE-Eigenvector

As in the previous section, we characterize an interval AE-eigenvector of a given non-interval matrix A with the help of generators. We recall that $X_G^\forall = \{x^{(i)}, x^{[i]}; i \in N \cup \{n+1\}\} \subseteq X^\forall$, where

$$x_k^{(i)} = \begin{cases} \underline{x}_i, & \text{for } k = i \\ \overline{x}_k, & \text{otherwise,} \end{cases} \qquad x_k^{[i]} = \begin{cases} \overline{x}_i, & \text{for } k = i \\ \underline{x}_k, & \text{otherwise,} \end{cases}$$

for $i \in N$, and $x^{(n+1)} := \underline{x}^\forall$, $x^{[n+1]} := \overline{x}^\forall$.

Theorem 4. *Let $A \in \mathcal{B}(n,n)$ and $X = [\underline{x}, \overline{x}]$ be given. Then, X is an AE-eigenvector of A if and only if*

$$(\forall x^\forall \in X_G^\forall)(\exists x^\exists \in X^\exists)\, A \otimes (x^\exists \oplus x^\forall) = x^\exists \oplus x^\forall.$$

Proof. Suppose that X is not an AE-eigenvector of A; that is,

$$(\exists x^\forall \in X^\forall)(\forall x^\exists \in X^\exists)\, A \otimes (x^\exists \oplus x^\forall) \neq (x^\exists \oplus x^\forall)$$

or equivalently

$$(\exists x^\forall \in X^\forall)(\forall x^\exists \in X^\exists)(\exists i \in N)\,(A \otimes (x^\exists \oplus x^\forall))_i \neq (x^\exists \oplus x^\forall)_i.$$

We shall prove that either there is $k \in N \cup \{n+1\}$ such that for each $x^\exists \in X^\exists$ the inequality $A \otimes (x^\exists \oplus x^{(k)}) \neq (x^\exists \oplus x^{(k)})$ holds true or there is $k \in N \cup \{n+1\}$ such that for each $x^\exists \in X^\exists$ the inequality $A \otimes (x^\exists \oplus x^{[k]}) \neq (x^\exists \oplus x^{[k]})$ is fulfilled.

We will next analyze four cases:

Case (i).

Suppose that $i \in N^\exists$ and $(A \otimes (x^\exists \oplus x^\forall))_i < (x^\exists \oplus x^\forall)_i$. We then have

$$\bigoplus_{j \in N} a_{ij} \otimes (x^\exists \oplus x^\forall)_j < (x^\exists \oplus x^\forall)_i$$

and for $\underline{x}^\forall = x^{(n+1)}$ we obtain

$$\bigoplus_{j \in N} a_{ij} \otimes (x^\exists \oplus \underline{x}^\forall)_j \leq \bigoplus_{j \in N} a_{ij} \otimes (x^\exists \oplus x^\forall)_j < (x^\exists \oplus x^\forall)_i = x_i^\exists = (x^\exists \oplus \underline{x}^\forall)_i.$$

Case (ii).

Suppose that $i \in N^\exists$ and $(A \otimes (x^\exists \oplus x^\forall))_i > (x^\exists \oplus x^\forall)_i$. We then have

$$\bigoplus_{j \in N} a_{ij} \otimes (x^\exists \oplus x^\forall)_j = a_{ii} \otimes (x^\exists \oplus x^\forall)_i \oplus \bigoplus_{j \neq i} a_{ij} \otimes (x^\exists \oplus x^\forall)_j > (x^\exists \oplus x^\forall)_i$$

and hence

$$\bigoplus_{j \neq i} a_{ij} \otimes (x^\exists \oplus x^\forall)_j > (x^\exists \oplus x^\forall)_i$$

because $a_{ii} \otimes (x^\exists \oplus x^\forall)_i \leq (x^\exists \oplus x^\forall)_i$. Moreover, there exists $k \in N$, $k \neq i$ such that

$$\bigoplus_{j \neq i} a_{ij} \otimes (x^\exists \oplus x^\forall)_j = a_{ik} \otimes (x^\exists \oplus x^\forall)_k > (x^\exists \oplus x^\forall)_i.$$

We will consider two subcases:

Subcase 1: $k \in N^\forall$. Then, for $x^{(k)}$, we obtain

$$\bigoplus_{j \in N} a_{ij} \otimes (x^\exists \oplus x^{(k)})_j \geq a_{ik} \otimes (x^\exists \oplus x^{(k)})_k = a_{ik} \otimes (x^\exists \oplus \overline{x}^\forall)_k \geq$$

$$a_{ik} \otimes (x^\exists \oplus x^\forall)_k > (x^\exists \oplus x^\forall)_i = x_i^\exists = (x^\exists \oplus x^{(k)})_i.$$

Subcase 2: $k \in N^\exists$. Then, for $x^{[n+1]} = \overline{x}^\forall$, we obtain

$$\bigoplus_{j \in N} a_{ij} \otimes (x^\exists \oplus \overline{x}^\forall)_j \geq a_{ik} \otimes (x^\exists \oplus \overline{x}^\forall)_k \geq$$

$$a_{ik} \otimes (x^\exists \oplus x^\forall)_k > (x^\exists \oplus x^\forall)_i = x_i^\exists = (x^\exists \oplus \overline{x}^\forall)_i.$$

Case (iii).
Suppose that $i \in N^\forall$ and $(A \otimes (x^\exists \oplus x^\forall))_i < (x^\exists \oplus x^\forall)_i$. We then have

$$\bigoplus_{j \in N} a_{ij} \otimes (x^\exists \oplus x^\forall)_j < (x^\exists \oplus x^\forall)_i \Leftrightarrow$$

$$a_{ii} \otimes (x^\exists \oplus x^\forall)_i \oplus \bigoplus_{j \in N} a_{ij} \otimes (x^\exists \oplus x^\forall)_j < (x^\exists \oplus x^\forall)_i$$

and hence it follows that

$$a_{ii} \otimes (x^\exists \oplus x^\forall)_i < (x^\exists \oplus x^\forall)_i \Rightarrow a_{ii} < (x^\exists \oplus x^\forall)_i.$$

Thus, for $x^{(i)}$ we obtain

$$\bigoplus_{j \in N} a_{ij} \otimes (x^\exists \oplus x^{(i)})_j = a_{ii} \otimes (x^\exists \oplus \overline{x}^\forall)_i \oplus \bigoplus_{j \neq i} a_{ij} \otimes (x^\exists \oplus \underline{x}^\forall)_j \leq$$

$$a_{ii} \otimes (x^\exists \oplus \overline{x}^\forall)_i \oplus \bigoplus_{j \neq i} a_{ij} \otimes (x^\exists \oplus x^\forall)_j < (x^\exists \oplus x^\forall)_i = x_i^\forall \leq \overline{x}_i^\forall = x_i^{(i)} = (x^\exists \oplus x^{(i)})_i.$$

Case (iv).
Suppose that $i \in N^\forall$ and $(A \otimes (x^\exists \oplus x^\forall))_i > (x^\exists \oplus x^\forall)_i$. We then have

$$\bigoplus_{j \in N} a_{ij} \otimes (x^\exists \oplus x^\forall)_j > (x^\exists \oplus x^\forall)_i,$$

hence there is $k \in N$, $k \neq i$ such that $a_{ik} \otimes (x^\exists \oplus x^\forall)_k > (x^\exists \oplus x^\forall)_i$ because $a_{ii} \otimes (x^\exists \oplus x^\forall)_i \leq (x^\exists \oplus x^\forall)_i$.

We will consider two subcases:
Subcase 1: $k \in N^\forall$. Then, for $x^{(k)}$, we obtain

$$\bigoplus_{j \in N} a_{ij} \otimes (x^\exists \oplus x^{(k)})_j \geq a_{ik} \otimes (x^\exists \oplus x^{(k)})_k = a_{ik} \otimes (x^\exists \oplus \overline{x}^\forall)_k \geq$$

$$a_{ik} \otimes (x^\exists \oplus x^\forall)_k > (x^\exists \oplus x^\forall)_i = x_i^\forall \geq \underline{x}_i^\forall = x_i^{(k)} = (x^\exists \oplus x^{(k)})_i.$$

Subcase 2: $k \in N^\exists$. Then, for $x^{[i]}$, we obtain

$$\bigoplus_{j \in N} a_{ij} \otimes (x^\exists \oplus x^{[i]})_j \geq a_{ik} \otimes (x^\exists \oplus x^{[i]})_k = a_{ik} \otimes (x^\exists \oplus \overline{x}^\forall)_k \geq$$

$$a_{ik} \otimes (x^{\exists} \oplus x^{\forall})_k > (x^{\exists} \oplus x^{\forall})_i = x_i^{\forall} \geq \underline{x}_i^{\forall} = x_i^{[i]} = (x^{\exists} \oplus x^{[i]})_i.$$

The reverse implication is trivial. □

The last theorem can be rewritten in the following form:

Corollary 1. *Let $A \in \mathcal{B}(n,n)$ and $X = [\underline{x}, \overline{x}]$ be given. Then, X is AE-eigenvector of A if and only if*

$$(\forall i \in N \cup \{n+1\})(\exists x(i)^{\exists} \in X^{\exists}) A \otimes (x(i)^{\exists} \oplus x^{(i)}) = x(i)^{\exists} \oplus x^{(i)},$$

$$(\forall i \in N \cup \{n+1\})(\exists x[i])^{\exists} \in X^{\exists}) A \otimes (x[i])^{\exists} \oplus x^{[i]}) = x[i]^{\exists} \oplus x^{[i]}.$$

The next two theorems show that the conditions in Corollary 1 can be equivalently formulated as the solvability conditions of a finite set of two-sided max–min linear systems. Consequently, the interval AE-eigenvectors of a given non-interval matrix can be recognized in polynomial time.

Without loss of generality suppose that $N = N^{\exists} \cup N^{\forall}$, where $N^{\exists} = \{1, 2, \ldots, k\}$ and $N^{\forall} = \{k+1, k+2, \ldots, n\}$; that is,

$$X^{\exists} = ([\underline{x}_1, \overline{x}_1], \ldots, [\underline{x}_k, \overline{x}_k], [O, O] \ldots, [O, O])^T$$

and

$$X^{\forall} = ([O, O] \ldots, [O, O], \underline{x}_{k+1}, \overline{x}_{k+1}], \ldots, [\underline{x}_n, \overline{x}_n])^T.$$

Define matrices $C(i), D(i), E(i), F(i) \in \mathcal{B}(n, k+1)$, for $i \in N^{\forall} \cup \{n+1\}$, as follows

$$C(i) = \begin{pmatrix} A \otimes x^{(1)} & \ldots & A \otimes x^{(k)} & A \otimes x^{(i)} \end{pmatrix}, \quad D(i) = \begin{pmatrix} x^{(1)} & \ldots & x^{(k)} & x^{(i)} \end{pmatrix}$$

$$E[i] = \begin{pmatrix} A \otimes x^{(1)} & \ldots & A \otimes x^{(k)} & A \otimes x^{[i]} \end{pmatrix}, \quad F[i] = \begin{pmatrix} x^{(1)} & \ldots & x^{(k)} & x^{[i]} \end{pmatrix}$$

Also, denote $\beta = (\beta_1, \ldots, \beta_k, \beta_{k+1})^T$, $\gamma = (\gamma_1, \ldots, \gamma_k, \gamma_{k+1})^T \in \mathcal{B}(k+1)$.

Theorem 5. *Let $A \in \mathcal{B}(n, n)$, X and $i \in N^{\forall} \cup \{n+1\}$ be given. Then*

- *$(\exists x^{\exists} \in X^{\exists}) A \otimes (x^{\exists} \oplus x^{(i)}) = (x^{\exists} \oplus x^{(i)})$ if and only if the system $C(i) \otimes \beta = D(i) \otimes \beta$ with $\underline{x}_j \leq \beta_j \leq \overline{x}_j$ for $j \in N^{\exists}$ and $\beta_{k+1} = I$ is solvable,*
- *$(\exists x^{\exists} \in X^{\exists}) A \otimes (x^{\exists} \oplus x^{[i]}) = (x^{\exists} \oplus x^{[i]})$ if and only if the system $E[i] \otimes \gamma = F[i] \otimes \gamma$ with $\underline{x}_j \leq \gamma_j \leq \overline{x}_j$ for $j \in N^{\exists}$ and $\gamma_{k+1} = I$ is solvable.*

Proof. By Lemma 1, if $\underline{x}_j \leq \beta_j \leq \overline{x}_j$ for $j \in N^{\exists}$, then $x^{\exists} = \bigoplus_{j=1}^{k} \beta_j \otimes x^{(j)}$ belongs to $X^{\exists}$, and if $x^{\exists} \in X^{\exists}$ then we can find $\underline{x}_j \leq \beta_j \leq \overline{x}_j$ for $j \in N^{\exists}$ such that $x^{\exists} = \bigoplus_{j=1}^{k} \beta_j \otimes x^{(j)}$.

We also have the following equivalences for an arbitrary $i \in N^{\forall} \cup \{n+1\}$

$$C(i) \otimes \beta = D(i) \otimes \beta \Leftrightarrow$$

$$\bigoplus_{j \in N^{\exists}} A \otimes x^{(j)} \otimes \beta_j \oplus A \otimes x^{(i)} \otimes \beta_{k+1} = \bigoplus_{j \in N^{\exists}} x^{(j)} \otimes \beta_j \oplus x^{(i)} \otimes \beta_{k+1} \Leftrightarrow$$

$$A \otimes \left(\bigoplus_{j \in N^{\exists}} x^{(j)} \otimes \beta_j \oplus x^{(i)} \right) = \bigoplus_{j \in N^{\exists}} x^{(j)} \otimes \beta_j \oplus x^{(i)} \Leftrightarrow$$

$$(\exists x^{\exists} \in X^{\exists}) A \otimes (x^{\exists} \oplus x^{(i)}) = x^{\exists} \oplus x^{(i)}$$

because $\beta_{k+1} = I$.

Similarly, we can prove the second part of the theorem. □

Theorem 6. *Suppose that we are given a matrix $A \in \mathcal{B}(n,n)$ and an interval vector $X = [\underline{x}, \overline{x}]$. Then, X is an AE-eigenvector of A if and only if for each $i \in N^\forall \cup \{n+1\}$ the systems $C(i) \otimes \beta = D(i) \otimes \beta$ and $C[i] \otimes \beta = D[i] \otimes \beta$ are solvable with $\underline{x}_j \leq \beta_j \leq \overline{x}_j$ for $j \in N^\exists$, $\beta_{k+1} = I$ and $\underline{x}_j \leq \gamma_j \leq \overline{x}_j$ for $j \in N^\exists$, $\gamma_{k+1} = I$, respectively.*

Proof. The assertion follows from Theorems 4 and 5. □

Theorem 7. *Suppose that we are given a matrix $A \in \mathcal{B}(n,n)$ and an interval vector $X = [\underline{x}, \overline{x}]$. The recognition problem of whether a given interval vector X is an AE-eigenvector of A is then solvable in $O(n^4)$ time.*

Proof. According to Theorem 6, the recognition problem of whether a given interval vector X is an AE-eigenvector of A is equivalent to recognizing if the system $C(x^\forall) \otimes \beta = D(x^\forall) \otimes \beta$ is solvable for each $x^\forall \in X_G^\forall$ with $\underline{x}_j \leq \beta_j \leq \overline{x}_j$ for $j \in N^\exists$ and $\beta_{k+1} = I$. The computation of a system $A \otimes y = B \otimes y$ needs $O(rs \cdot \min(r,s))$ time (see [17]), where $A, B \in \mathcal{B}(r,s)$. Therefore, the computation of at most n such systems is done in $n \cdot O(n^3) = O(n^4)$ time. □

5. Strong Eigenvectors

In this section, we study various eigenvector types for the interval matrix $A = [\underline{A}, \overline{A}]$ and the interval vector $X = [\underline{x}, \overline{x}]$. The basic type, which is called a strong eigenvector, is related to all matrices in A and all vectors in X. Further types, which are called strong EA-eigenvectors (strong AE-eigenvectors), are related to all matrices $A \in A$ and to EA-eigenvectors (AE-eigenvectors) derived from X.

Definition 3. *Let A, X be given. The interval vector X is called strong eigenvector of A if $(\forall A \in A)(\forall x \in X) \, A \otimes x = x$.*

Theorem 8. *Let A, X be given. Then, X is a strong eigenvector of A if and only if $\underline{A} \otimes x^{(k)} = x^{(k)}$ and $\overline{A} \otimes x^{(k)} = x^{(k)}$ for all $k \in N$.*

Proof. Let us assume that $x \in X$, $\underline{A} \otimes x^{(k)} = x^{(k)}$ and $\overline{A} \otimes x^{(k)} = x^{(k)}$ for all $k \in N$. Then, for arbitrary $x \in X$ we get

$$\underline{A} \otimes x = \underline{A} \otimes \bigoplus_{i=1}^{n} \beta_i \otimes x^{(i)} = \bigoplus_{i=1}^{n} \beta_i \otimes (\underline{A} \otimes x^{(i)}) = \bigoplus_{i=1}^{n} \beta_i \otimes x^{(i)} = x$$

and

$$\overline{A} \otimes x = \overline{A} \otimes \bigoplus_{i=1}^{n} \beta_i \otimes x^{(i)} = \bigoplus_{i=1}^{n} \beta_i \otimes (\overline{A} \otimes x^{(i)}) = \bigoplus_{i=1}^{n} \beta_i \otimes x^{(i)} = x.$$

The assertion follows from the monotonicity of operations; that is, $x = \underline{A} \otimes x \leq A \otimes x \leq \overline{A} \otimes x = x$ for each $A \in A$. The converse implication is trivial. □

Remark 1. *It is easy to see that the conditions in Theorem 8 can be verified in $O(n^3)$ time.*

Definition 4. *Let A, X be given. Then interval vector X is called*

- *a strong EA-eigenvector of A if*

$$(\forall A \in A)(\exists x^\exists \in X^\exists)(\forall x^\forall \in X^\forall) \, A \otimes (x^\exists \oplus x^\forall) = x^\exists \oplus x^\forall,$$

- and a strong AE-eigenvector *of A if*

$$(\forall A \in \mathcal{A})(\forall x^\forall \in X^\forall)(\exists x^\exists \in X^\exists) \, A \otimes (x^\exists \oplus x^\forall) = x^\exists \oplus x^\forall.$$

Theorem 9. *Let $\mathcal{A}$, X be given. The following conditions are equivalent*
(i) X *is a strong EA-eigenvector of $\mathcal{A}$*,
(ii) $(\exists x^\exists \in X^\exists)(\forall x^\forall \in X^\forall) \left[\underline{A} \otimes (x^\exists \oplus x^\forall) = x^\exists \oplus x^\forall \wedge \overline{A} \otimes (x^\exists \oplus x^\forall) = x^\exists \oplus x^\forall \right]$,
(iii) $(\exists x^\exists \in X^\exists)(\forall x^{(k)} \in X^\forall) \left[\underline{A} \otimes (x^\exists \oplus x^{(k)}) = x^\exists \oplus x^{(k)} \wedge \overline{A} \otimes (x^\exists \oplus x^{(k)}) = x^\exists \oplus x^{(k)} \right]$.

Proof. These assertions follow from Theorems 1 and 8. □

Theorem 10. *Let $\mathcal{A}$, X be given. The following conditions are equivalent*
(i) X *is a strong AE-eigenvector of $\mathcal{A}$*,
(ii) $(\forall x^\forall \in X^\forall)(\exists x^\exists \in X^\exists) \left[\underline{A} \otimes (x^\exists \oplus x^\forall) = x^\exists \oplus x^\forall \wedge \overline{A} \otimes (x^\exists \oplus x^\forall) = x^\exists \oplus x^\forall \right]$,
(iii) $(\forall x^\forall \in X^\forall_G)(\exists x^\exists \in X^\exists) \left[\underline{A} \otimes (x^\exists \oplus x^\forall) = x^\exists \oplus x^\forall \wedge \overline{A} \otimes (x^\exists \oplus x^\forall) = x^\exists \oplus x^\forall \right]$.

Proof. These assertions follow from Theorems 4 and 8. □

Remark 2. *By Theorems 9 and 10, the verification of whether*
(i) X *is a strong EA-eigenvector,*
(ii) X *is a strong AE-eigenvector,*

reduces to finding a vector $x^\exists \in X^\exists$ satisfying some linear max–min equations, similar to Theorems 2 and 6. Hence, the recognition problem for these types of strong eigenvectors is polynomially solvable.

6. EA/AE-Strong Eigenvectors

In the previous sections, we worked with a fixed partition $N = \{N^\exists, N^\forall\}$, with $N = N^\exists \cup N^\forall$ and $N = N^\exists \cap N^\forall = \emptyset$. In other words, every index $i \in N$ is associated either with the existential, or with the universal quantifier. According to partition N, the interval vector X is presented as a sum of subintervals $X^\exists \oplus X^\forall$. The interpretation of this partition is such that, for technical reasons, the vector entries in subinterval $X^\exists$ only require the existence of one possible value $x_i \in [\underline{x}_i, \overline{x}_i]$, while the entries in subinterval $X^\forall$ require all possible values $x_i \in [\underline{x}_i, \overline{x}_i]$.

A similar interpretation can be applied to the matrix entries. Suppose that each interval of $\mathcal{A}$ is associated either with the universal or with the existential quantifier. We can then split the interval matrix as $\mathcal{A} = \mathcal{A}^\forall \oplus \mathcal{A}^\exists$, where $\mathcal{A}^\forall$ is the interval matrix comprising universally quantified coefficients and $\mathcal{A}^\exists$ concerns existentially quantified coefficients.

Hence, we work with partition $\tilde{N} = \{\tilde{N}^\exists, \tilde{N}^\forall\}$, where $\tilde{N}^\exists \cup \tilde{N}^\forall = N \times N$ and $\tilde{N}^\exists \cap \tilde{N}^\forall = \emptyset$. In other words, $\underline{a}^\exists_{ij} = \overline{a}^\exists_{ij} = O$ for each pair $(i,j) \in \tilde{N}^\forall$ and $\underline{a}^\forall_{ij} = \overline{a}^\forall_{ij} = O$ for each $(i,j) \in \tilde{N}^\exists$.

Definition 5. *Let $\mathcal{A}$, X be given. Interval vector X is called*
- *EA-strong eigenvector of $\mathcal{A}$ if there is $A^\exists \in \mathcal{A}^\exists$ such that for any $A^\forall \in \mathcal{A}^\forall$ the vector X is a strong eigenvector of $A^\exists \oplus A^\forall$,*
- *AE-strong eigenvector of $\mathcal{A}$ if for any $A^\forall \in \mathcal{A}^\forall$ there is $A^\exists \in \mathcal{A}^\exists$ such that X is a strong eigenvector of $A^\exists \oplus A^\forall$.*

6.1. EA-Strong Eigenvector

Theorem 11. *Let A, X be given. Then, X is an EA-strong eigenvector of A if and only if*

$$(\exists A^{\exists} \in \mathcal{A}^{\exists})(\forall x \in X)\, (A^{\exists} \oplus \underline{A}^{\forall}) \otimes x = x \wedge (A^{\exists} \oplus \overline{A}^{\forall}) \otimes x = x.$$

Proof. Suppose that there is $A^{\exists} \in \mathcal{A}^{\exists}$ such that $(A^{\exists} \oplus \underline{A}^{\forall}) \otimes x = x$ and $(A^{\exists} \oplus \overline{A}^{\forall}) \otimes x = x$ hold for each $x \in X$. By monotonicity of the operations $\oplus$ and $\otimes$ for an arbitrary matrix $A^{\forall} \in \mathcal{A}^{\forall}$, we get

$$x = (A^{\exists} \oplus \underline{A}^{\forall}) \otimes x \leq (A^{\exists} \oplus A^{\forall}) \otimes x \leq (A^{\exists} \oplus \overline{A}^{\forall}) \otimes x = x.$$

The reverse implication trivially holds. □

Theorem 12. *Let A, X be given. Then, X is an EA-strong eigenvector of A if and only if*

$$(\exists A^{\exists} \in \mathcal{A}^{\exists})(\forall i \in N\, [(A^{\exists} \oplus \underline{A}^{\forall}) \otimes x^{(i)} = x^{(i)} \wedge (A^{\exists} \oplus \overline{A}^{\forall}) \otimes x^{(i)} = x^{(i)}].$$

Proof. By Lemma 1, if $\underline{x}_j \leq \beta_j \leq \overline{x}_j$ for $j \in N$ then $x = \bigoplus_{j=1}^{n} \beta_j \otimes x^{(j)}$ belongs to X; and if $x \in X$, then we can find $\underline{x}_j \leq \beta_j \leq \overline{x}_j$ for $j \in N$ such that $x = \bigoplus_{j=1}^{n} \beta_j \otimes x^{(j)}$. Then, we have

$$(A^{\exists} \oplus \underline{A}^{\forall}) \otimes x = (A^{\exists} \oplus \underline{A}^{\forall}) \otimes \bigoplus_{i \in N} \beta_i \otimes x^{(i)} =$$

$$\bigoplus_{i \in N} (A^{\exists} \oplus \underline{A}^{\forall}) \otimes x^{(i)} \otimes \beta_i = \bigoplus_{i \in N} \beta_i \otimes x^{(i)} = x.$$

Similarly, we can prove the second equality and by Theorem 11 the assertion follows. The reverse implication trivially holds. □

The last theorem enables us to check the equivalent conditions of Theorem 12 in practice, whereby $(A^{\exists} \oplus \underline{A}^{\forall}) \otimes x^{(i)} = x^{(i)}$ and $(A^{\exists} \oplus \overline{A}^{\forall}) \otimes x^{(i)} = x^{(i)}$ are joined into one system of equalities.

Let A and X be given and $\tilde{N}^{\exists} = \{(i_1, j_1), \ldots, (i_k, j_k)\}$. We denote the block matrix $\tilde{A} \in \mathcal{B}(2n^2, k+1)$ and vectors $\tilde{x} \in \mathcal{B}(2n^2)$, $\alpha \in \mathcal{B}(k+1)$ as follows

$$\tilde{A} = \begin{pmatrix} A^{(i_1 j_1)} \otimes x^{(1)} & \ldots & A^{(i_1 j_k)} \otimes x^{(1)} & A^{(i_2 j_1)} \otimes x^{(1)} & \ldots & A^{(i_k j_k)} \otimes x^{(1)} & \underline{A} \otimes x^{(1)} \\ A^{(i_1 j_1)} \otimes x^{(2)} & \ldots & A^{(i_1 j_k)} \otimes x^{(2)} & A^{(i_2 j_1)} \otimes x^{(2)} & \ldots & A^{(i_k j_k)} \otimes x^{(2)} & \underline{A} \otimes x^{(2)} \\ \vdots & & & & & & \\ A^{(i_1 j_1)} \otimes x^{(n)} & \ldots & A^{(i_1 j_k)} \otimes x^{(n)} & A^{(i_2 j_1)} \otimes x^{(n)} & \ldots & A^{(i_k j_k)} \otimes x^{(n)} & \underline{A} \otimes x^{(n)} \\ A^{(i_1 j_1)} \otimes x^{(1)} & \ldots & A^{(i_1 j_k)} \otimes x^{(1)} & A^{(i_2 j_1)} \otimes x^{(1)} & \ldots & A^{(i_k j_k)} \otimes x^{(1)} & \overline{A} \otimes x^{(1)} \\ A^{(i_1 j_1)} \otimes x^{(2)} & \ldots & A^{(i_1 j_k)} \otimes x^{(2)} & A^{(i_2 j_1)} \otimes x^{(2)} & \ldots & A^{(i_k j_k)} \otimes x^{(2)} & \overline{A} \otimes x^{(2)} \\ \vdots & & & & & & \\ A^{(i_1 j_1)} \otimes x^{(n)} & \ldots & A^{(i_1 j_k)} \otimes x^{(n)} & A^{(i_2 j_1)} \otimes x^{(n)} & \ldots & A^{(i_k j_k)} \otimes x^{(n)} & \overline{A} \otimes x^{(n)} \end{pmatrix},$$

$$\tilde{x} = \left(x_1^{(1)}, \ldots, x_n^{(1)}, \ldots, x_1^{(n)}, \ldots, x_n^{(n)}, x_1^{(1)}, \ldots, x_n^{(1)}, \ldots, x_1^{(n)}, \ldots, x_n^{(n)} \right)^T,$$

and

$$\alpha = \left(\alpha_{11}, \ldots, \alpha_{1k}, \alpha_{21}, \ldots, \alpha_{2k}, \ldots, \alpha_{k1}, \ldots, \alpha_{kk}, \alpha_{k+1} \right)^T,$$

where α_{k+1} is a variable corresponding to the last column of $\tilde{A}$.

Theorem 13. *Let A, X be given. Then X is EA-strong eigenvector of A if and only if the system $\tilde{A} \otimes \alpha = \tilde{x}$ has a solution α such that $\underline{a}_{ij} \leq \alpha_{ij} \leq \overline{a}_{ij}$ and $\alpha_{k+1} = I$.*

Proof. The system $\tilde{A} \otimes \alpha = \tilde{x}$ is solvable if and only if there is a vector α such that

$$\bigoplus_{i,j=1}^{k} \alpha_{ij} \otimes A^{(ij)} \otimes x^{(k)} \oplus \underline{A} \otimes x^{k} = x^{(k)},$$

$$\bigoplus_{i,j=1}^{k} \alpha_{ij} \otimes A^{(ij)} \otimes x^{(k)} \oplus \overline{A} \otimes x^{k} = x^{(k)}$$

for all $k \in N$ with $\underline{a}_{ij} \leq \alpha_{ij} \leq \overline{a}_{ij}$ and $\alpha_{k+1} = I$. Put $A^{\exists} = \bigoplus_{i,j=1}^{k} \alpha_{ij} \otimes A^{(ij)}$ and by Theorem 12 the assertion holds true. □

Theorem 14. *Suppose that we are given a matrix A and interval vector $X = [\underline{x}, \overline{x}]$. The recognition problem of whether a given interval vector X is EA-strong eigenvector of A is solvable in $O(n^5)$ time.*

Proof. According to Theorem 13, the recognition problem of whether a given interval vector X is EA-strong eigenvector of A is equivalent to recognizing if the system $\tilde{A} \otimes \alpha = \tilde{x}$ has a solution α with $\underline{a}_{ij} \leq \alpha_{ij} \leq \overline{a}_{ij}$ and $\alpha_{k+1} = I$. The computation of a system $A \otimes y = b$ needs $O(rs \cdot \min(r,s))$ time (see [18]), where $A \in \mathcal{B}(r,s), b \in \mathcal{B}(r)$. Therefore, the computation of such systems is done in $O(n^2 \cdot n^2 \cdot n) = O(n^5)$ time. □

6.2. AE-Strong Eigenvector

Denote $A_G^\forall = \{\underline{A}^\forall, \overline{A}^\forall\}$.

Theorem 15. *Let A, X be given. Then, X is an AE-strong eigenvector of A if and only if*

$$(\forall A^\forall \in A_G^\forall)(\exists A^\exists \in A^\exists)(\forall x \in X)\,(A^\exists \oplus A^\forall) \otimes x = x.$$

Proof. Suppose that for $\underline{A}^\forall$ there is $B^\exists \in A^\exists$ such that for all $x \in X$ the equality $(B^\exists \oplus A^\forall) \otimes x = x$ holds true and for $\overline{A}^\forall$ there is $C^\exists \in A^\exists$ such that for all $x \in X$ the equality $(C^\exists \oplus A^\forall) \otimes x = x$ is fulfilled. Moreover, assume that $x \in X$ is arbitrary but fixed. Then, for any $i \in N$ there is $k, l \in N$ such that the following

$$((A^\forall \oplus B^\exists) \otimes x)_i = \bigoplus_{j \in N}(\underline{a}_{ij}^\forall \oplus b_{ij}^\exists) \otimes x_j = (\underline{a}_{ik}^\forall \oplus b_{ik}^\exists) \otimes x_k \geq (\overline{a}_{iv}^\forall \oplus c_{iv}^\exists) \otimes x_v,$$

$$(\underline{a}_{iv}^\forall \oplus b_{iv}^\exists) \otimes x_v \leq (\overline{a}_{il}^\forall \oplus c_{il}^\exists) \otimes x_l = \bigoplus_{j \in N}(\overline{a}_{ij}^\forall \oplus c_{ij}^\exists) \otimes x_j = ((A^\forall \oplus C^\exists) \otimes x)_i$$

holds for any $v \in N$.

We will prove that for an arbitrary but fixed matrix $A^\forall \in A^\forall$, there is $A^\exists \in A^\exists$ such that $(A^\exists \oplus A^\forall) \otimes x = x$.

Put $A^\exists := B^\exists$. Then, there is $r \in N$ such that

$$((B^\exists \oplus A^\forall) \otimes x)_i = (a_{ir}^\forall \oplus b_{ir}^\exists) \otimes x_r.$$

Consider two cases.

Case 1. For $(i,r) \in \tilde{N}^\forall$, we get

$$(a_{ir}^\forall \oplus b_{ir}^\exists) \otimes x_r = a_{ir}^\forall \otimes x_r \leq \overline{a}_{ir}^\forall \otimes x_r = (\overline{a}_{ir}^\forall \oplus c_{ir}^\exists) \otimes x_r \leq (\underline{a}_{ik}^\forall \oplus b_{ik}^\exists) \otimes x_k = x_i.$$

Thus, we have

$$((A^\forall \oplus B^\exists) \otimes x)_i = (a_{ir}^\forall \oplus b_{ir}^\exists) \otimes x_r \leq x_i.$$

The reverse inequality follows from the monotonicity of operations

$$(A^\forall \oplus B^\exists) \otimes x \geq (\underline{A}^\forall \oplus B^\exists) \otimes x = x. \tag{4}$$

Case 2. For $(i,r) \in \tilde{N}^\exists$, we get

$$(a_{ir}^\forall \oplus b_{ir}^\exists) \otimes x_r = b_{ir}^\exists \otimes x_r = (\underline{a}_{ir}^\forall \oplus b_{ir}^\exists) \otimes x_r \leq (\overline{a}_{il}^\forall \oplus c_{il}^\exists) \otimes x_l = x_i.$$

Because the reverse inequality trivially follows from (4), the equality $((B^\exists \oplus A^\forall) \otimes x)_i = x_i$ is proven.

The reverse implication is trivial. □

Theorem 16. *Let A, X be given. Then, X is AE-strong eigenvector of A if and only if*

$$(\forall A^\forall \in A_G^\forall)(\exists A^\exists \in A^\exists)(\forall k \in N)\, (A^\exists \oplus A^\forall) \otimes x^{(k)} = x^{(k)}.$$

Proof. By Lemma 1, if $\underline{x}_k \leq \beta_k \leq \overline{x}_k$ for $k \in N$, then $x = \bigoplus_{k=1}^{n} \beta_k \otimes x^{(k)}$ belongs to X; and if $x \in X$, then we can find $\underline{x}_k \leq \beta_k \leq \overline{x}_k$ for $k \in N$ such that $x = \bigoplus_{k=1}^{n} \beta_k \otimes x^{(k)}$. Then, for any $A^\forall \in A_G^\forall$ there is $A^\exists \in A^\exists$ such that for and fixed $x \in X$ we have

$$(A^\exists \oplus A^\forall) \otimes x = (A^\exists \oplus A^\forall) \otimes \bigoplus_{k \in N} \beta_k \otimes x^{(k)} =$$

$$\bigoplus_{i \in N}(A^\exists \oplus A^\forall) \otimes x^{(k)} \otimes \beta_k = \bigoplus_{k \in N} x^{(k)} \otimes \beta_k = \bigoplus_{k \in N} \beta_k \otimes x^{(k)} = x$$

and by Theorem 15 the implication follows. The reverse implication trivially holds true. □

Let A and X be given and $\tilde{N}^\exists = \{(i_1, j_1), \ldots, (i_k, j_k)\}$. For each $A^\forall \in A_G^\forall$ and $v \in N$, we denote the block matrix $C(A^\forall, v) \in \mathcal{B}(n, k+1)$ and $\alpha \in \mathcal{B}(k+1)$ as follows

$$C(A^\forall, v) = \begin{pmatrix} A^{(i_1 j_1)} \otimes x^{(v)} & \cdots & A^{(i_1 j_k)} \otimes x^{(v)} & A^{(i_2 j_1)} \otimes x^{(v)} & \cdots & A^{(i_k j_k)} \otimes x^{(v)} & A^\forall \otimes x^{(v)} \end{pmatrix},$$

and

$$\alpha = \begin{pmatrix} \alpha_{11}, \ldots, \alpha_{1k}, \alpha_{21}, \ldots, \alpha_{2k}, \ldots, \alpha_{k1}, \ldots, \alpha_{kk}, \alpha_{k+1} \end{pmatrix}^T,$$

where α_{k+1} is a variable corresponding to the last column of $C(A^\forall, v)$.

Theorem 17. *Let A, X be given. Then, X is an AE-strong eigenvector of A if and only if each $A^\forall \in A_G^\forall$ and for each $v \in N$ the system $C(A^\forall, v) \otimes \alpha = x^{(v)}$ has a solution α such that $\underline{a}_{ij} \leq \alpha_{ij} \leq \overline{a}_{ij}$ and $\alpha_{k+1} = I$.*

Proof. Suppose that $v \in N$ and $A^\forall \in A_G^\forall$ are fixed. The system $C(A^\forall, v) \otimes \alpha = x^{(v)}$ is solvable if and only if there is a vector α such that

$$\bigoplus_{i,j=1}^{k} \alpha_{ij} \otimes A^{(ij)} \otimes x^{(v)} \oplus A^{(rs)} \otimes x^v = x^{(v)}$$

with $\underline{a}_{ij} \leq \alpha_{ij} \leq \overline{a}_{ij}$ and $\alpha_{k+1} = I$. Put $A^{\exists} = \bigoplus_{i,j=1}^{k} \alpha_{ij} \otimes A^{(ij)}$ and by Theorem 16 the assertion holds true. □

Theorem 18. *Let A, X be given. The recognition problem of whether a given interval vector X is an AE-strong eigenvector of A is solvable in $O(n^5)$ time.*

Proof. According to Theorem 17, the recognition problem of whether a given interval vector X is an AE-strong eigenvector of A is equivalent to recognizing if the system $C(A^{\forall}, v) \otimes \alpha = x^{(v)}$ has a solution α with $\underline{a}_{ij} \leq \alpha_{ij} \leq \overline{a}_{ij}$ and $\alpha_{k+1} = I$. The computation of a system $A \otimes y = b$ needs $O(rs \cdot \min(r,s))$ time (see [18]), where $A \in \mathcal{B}(r,s), b \in \mathcal{B}(r)$. Therefore, the computation of such systems is done in $n \cdot O(n \cdot n^2 \cdot n) = O(n^6)$ time. □

7. Conclusions

In this paper, we have presented the properties of steady states in max–min discrete event systems. This concept, in connection with inexact entries and its exists/forall quantification, represents an alternating version to fuzzy discrete events systems which are using vectors and matrices with entries between 0 and 1, and are describing uncertain and vague values. The practical significance of this approach is that some elements of the vector X and the matrix A are taken into account for all values of the interval (corresponding to A-index), and some of them are only considered for at least one value (corresponding to E-index).

The concept of various types of the strong EA/AE-eigenvectors and the EA/AE-strong eigenvectors have been studied. In addition, their characterizations by equivalent conditions are given. All findings have been formally analyzed with a target to estimate the computational complexity of checking the obtained equivalent conditions. The results have been illustrated by an application of the obtained methodology on a numerical example.

The investigation of AE/EA concepts for steady state of discrete events systems with interval data has brought new efficient equivalent conditions. There is a good reason to continue the study of exists/forall quantification method for tolerable, universal and weak eigenvectors which are still unexplored and stay open for future research.

Author Contributions: All authors contributed equally to this work. All authors have read and agreed to the published version of the manuscript.

Funding: This research was funded by Czech Science Foundation (GAČR), grant number 18-01246S.

Conflicts of Interest: The authors declare no conflict of interest. The funders had no role in the design of the study, or in the decision to publish the results.

Appendix A

The idea of EA/AE-splitting the interval vector (matrix) X (A) in the form $X^{\exists} \oplus X^{\forall}$ ($A^{\exists} \oplus A^{\forall}$), can be considered simultaneously using partitions $N = \{N^{\exists}, N^{\forall}\}$ and $\tilde{N} = \{\tilde{N}^{\exists}, \tilde{N}^{\forall}\}$. By combining both approaches, the following four notions can be defined.

Definition A1. *Let A, X be given. Then X is called*

- *an EA-strong EA-eigenvector of A if there is $A^{\exists} \in \mathbf{A}^{\exists}$ such that for each $A^{\forall} \in \mathbf{A}^{\forall}$ interval vector X is an EA-eigenvector of $A^{\exists} \oplus A^{\forall}$,*
- *an EA-strong AE-eigenvector of A if there is $A^{\exists} \in \mathbf{A}^{\exists}$ such that for each $A^{\forall} \in \mathbf{A}^{\forall}$ interval vector X is an AE-eigenvector of $A^{\exists} \oplus A^{\forall}$,*
- *an AE-strong EA-eigenvector of A if for each $A^{\forall} \in \mathbf{A}^{\forall}$ there is $A^{\exists} \in \mathbf{A}^{\exists}$ such that interval vector X is an EA-eigenvector of $A^{\exists} \oplus A^{\forall}$,*

- an AE-strong AE-eigenvector of A if for each $A^\forall \in A^\forall$ there is $A^\exists \in A^\exists$ such that interval vector X is an AE-eigenvector of $A^\exists \oplus A^\forall$.

Every of these notions can be characterized in a similar way as that used in the previous two sections: Theorems 11 and 12, or Theorems 15 and 16.

For the sake of brevity, only the first notion will be discussed here. The remaining cases are analogous.

Theorem A1. *Let A, X be given. Then, interval vector X is an EA strong EA-eigenvector of A if and only if*

$$(\exists A^\exists \in A^\exists)(\exists x^\exists \in X^\exists)(\forall x^\forall \in X^\forall)\,[(A^\exists \oplus \underline{A}) \otimes (x^\exists \oplus x^\forall) = (x^\exists \oplus x^\forall) \wedge$$

$$(A^\exists \oplus \overline{A}) \otimes (x^\exists \oplus x^\forall) = (x^\exists \oplus x^\forall)].$$

Proof. ($\Leftarrow$) The assertion follows from the monotonicity of the operations; that is,

$$x^\exists \oplus x^\forall = (A^\exists \oplus \underline{A}) \otimes (x^\exists \oplus x^\forall) \leq (A^\exists \oplus A^\forall) \otimes (x^\exists \oplus x^\forall) \leq$$

$$(A^\exists \oplus \overline{A}) \otimes (x^\exists \oplus x^\forall) = x^\exists \oplus x^\forall.$$

The converse implication is trivial. □

Theorem A2. *Let A, X be given. Then, interval vector X is an EA strong EA-eigenvector of A if and only if*

$$(\exists A^\exists \in A^\exists)(\exists x^\exists \in X^\exists)(\forall x^{(k)} \in X^\forall)\,[(A^\exists \oplus \underline{A}) \otimes (x^\exists \oplus x^{(k)}) =$$

$$(x^\exists \oplus x^{(k)}) \wedge (A^\exists \oplus \overline{A}) \otimes (x^\exists \oplus x^{(k)}) = (x^\exists \oplus x^{(k)})].$$

Proof. This assertion follows from Theorem 1 and Theorem A1. □

Remark A1. *In view of Theorem A2, the verification of whether or not X is an EA-strong EA-eigenvector of A requires us to find a vector $x^\exists \in X^\exists$ and a matrix $A^\exists \in A^\exists$ satisfying some two-sided max–min quadratic systems. This recognition problem and the analogous problems for remaining cases in Definition A1 have not been studied in this paper.*

References

1. Terano, T.; Tsukamoto, Y. Failure diagnosis by using fuzzy logic. In Proceedings of the IEEE Conference on Decision Control, New Orleans, LA, USA, 7–9 December 1977; pp. 1390–1395.
2. Zadeh, L.A. Toward a theory of fuzzy systems. In *Aspects of Network and Systems Theory*; Kalman, R.E., Claris, N.D., Eds.; Hold, Rinehart and Winston: New York, NY, USA, 1971; pp. 209–245.
3. Sanchez, E. Resolution of eigen fuzzy sets equations. *Fuzzy Sets And Syst.* **1978**, *1*, 69–74. [CrossRef]
4. Lin, F.; Ying, H. Fuzzy discrete event systems and their observability. In Proceedings of the Joint 9th IFSA World Congress and 20th NAFIPS International Conference, Vancouver, BC, Canada, 25–28 July 2011; pp. 271–1277.
5. Lin, F.; Ying, H. Modeling and control of fuzzy discrete event systems. *IEEE Trans. Cybern.* **2002**, *32*, 408–415.
6. Benmessahel, B.; Touahria, M.; Nouioua, F. Predictability of fuzzy discrete event systems. *Discret. Event Dyn. Syst.* **2017**, *27*, 641–673. [CrossRef]
7. Butkovič, P.; Schneider, H.; Sergeev, S. Recognizing weakly stable matrices. *SIAM J. Control Optim.* **2012**, *50*, 3029–3051. [CrossRef]
8. Butkovič, P. *Max-linear Systems: Theory and Algorithms*; Springer Monographs in Mathematics; Springer: Berlin, Germany, 2010.
9. Fiedler, M.; Nedoma, J.; Ramík, J.; Rohn, J.; Zimmermann, K. *Linear Optimization Problems with Inexact Data*; Springer: Berlin, Germany, 2006.

10. Rohn, J. Systems of Linear Interval Equations. *Lin. Algebra Appl.* **1989**, *126*, 39–78. [CrossRef]
11. Molnárová, M.; sková, H.M.; Plavka, J. The robustness of interval fuzzy matrices. *Lin. Algebra Appl.* **2013**, *438*, 3350–3364. [CrossRef]
12. Mysková, H.M.; Plavka, J. X^{AE} and X^{EA} robustness of max–min matrices. *Discret. Appl. Math.* **2019**, *267*, 142–150. [CrossRef]
13. Myšková, H.; Plavka, J. AE and EA robustness of interval circulant matrices in max–min algebra. *Fuzzy Sets Syst.* **2020**, *384*, 91–104. [CrossRef]
14. Plavka, J.; Szabó, P. On the λ-robustness of matrices over fuzzy algebra. *Discret. Appl. Math.* **2011**, *159*, 381–388. [CrossRef]
15. Plavka, J. On the weak robustness of fuzzy matrices. *Kybernetika* **2013**, *49*, 128–140.
16. Plavka, J. On the $O(n^3)$ algorithm for checking the strong robustness of interval fuzzy matrices. *Discret. Appl. Math.* **2012**, *160*, 640–647. [CrossRef]
17. Gavalec, M.; Zimmermann, K. Solving systems of two–sided (max,min)–linear equations. *Kybernetika* **2010**, *46*, 405–414.
18. Zimmermann, K. *Extremální Algebra*; Ekonomicko-matematická laboratoř Ekonomického ústavu ČSAV: Praha, Czech Republic, 1976.

© 2020 by the authors. Licensee MDPI, Basel, Switzerland. This article is an open access article distributed under the terms and conditions of the Creative Commons Attribution (CC BY) license (http://creativecommons.org/licenses/by/4.0/).

Article

M-CFIS-R: Mamdani Complex Fuzzy Inference System with Rule Reduction Using Complex Fuzzy Measures in Granular Computing

Tran Manh Tuan [1,2,3], Luong Thi Hong Lan [1,2], Shuo-Yan Chou [4,5], Tran Thi Ngan [2,*], Le Hoang Son [6], Nguyen Long Giang [3] and Mumtaz Ali [7]

[1] Vietnam Academy of Science and Technology, Graduate University of Science and Technology, Hanoi 010000, Vietnam; tmtuan@tlu.edu.vn (T.M.T.); lanlhbk@tlu.edu.vn (L.T.H.L.)
[2] Faculty of Computer Science and Engineering, Thuyloi University, 175 Tay Son, Dong Da, Hanoi 010000, Vietnam
[3] Institute of Information Technology, Vietnam Academy of Science and Technology, Hanoi 010000, Vietnam; nlgiang@ioit.ac.vn
[4] Department of Industrial Management, National Taiwan University of Science and Technology, No. 43, Section 4, Keelung Road, Taipei 10607, Taiwan; sychou@mail.ntust.edu.tw
[5] Taiwan Building Technology Center, National Taiwan University of Science and Technology, No. 43, Section 4, Keelung Road, Taipei 10607, Taiwan
[6] VNU Information Technology Institute, Vietnam National University, Hanoi 010000, Vietnam; sonlh@vnu.edu.vn
[7] School of Information Technology, Deakin University, 221 Burwood Highway, Burwood Victoria 3125, Australia; mumtaz.ali@deakin.edu.au
* Correspondence: ngantt@tlu.edu.vn; Tel.: +(84)-989-040454

Received: 10 April 2020; Accepted: 22 April 2020; Published: 3 May 2020

Abstract: Complex fuzzy theory has strong practical background in many important applications, especially in decision-making support systems. Recently, the Mamdani Complex Fuzzy Inference System (M-CFIS) has been introduced as an effective tool for handling events that are not restricted to only values of a given time point but also include all values within certain time intervals (i.e., the phase term). In such decision-making problems, the complex fuzzy theory allows us to observe both the amplitude and phase values of an event, thus resulting in better performance. However, one of the limitations of the existing M-CFIS is the rule base that may be redundant to a specific dataset. In order to handle the problem, we propose a new Mamdani Complex Fuzzy Inference System with Rule Reduction Using Complex Fuzzy Measures in Granular Computing called M-CFIS-R. Several fuzzy similarity measures such as Complex Fuzzy Cosine Similarity Measure (CFCSM), Complex Fuzzy Dice Similarity Measure (CFDSM), and Complex Fuzzy Jaccard Similarity Measure (CFJSM) together with their weighted versions are proposed. Those measures are integrated into the M-CFIS-R system by the idea of granular computing such that only important and dominant rules are being kept in the system. The difference and advantage of M-CFIS-R against M-CFIS is the usage of the training process in which the rule base is repeatedly changed toward the original base set until the performance is better. By doing so, the new rule base in M-CFIS-R would improve the performance of the whole system. Experiments on various decision-making datasets demonstrate that the proposed M-CFIS-R performs better than M-CFIS.

Keywords: complex fuzzy set; similarity measure; complex fuzzy measure; Mamdani Complex Fuzzy Inference System (M-CFIS); rule reduction; granular computing

1. Introduction

Zadeh [1] proposed fuzzy set (FS) as an approach for representing and processing vagueness found abundantly in the real world. Fuzzy inference systems (FIS) are used to generate fuzzy rule sets, which are applied in solving problems in various applications such as detection [2,3], prediction [4,5], classification [6–8], and other tasks [9–14]. A Complex Fuzzy Set (CFS) [15] is an extension of the fuzzy set, where the membership function consists of both the amplitude term and the phase term. Building upon this, Ramot et al. [16] proposed a novel framework for logical reasoning, termed Complex Fuzzy Logic (CFL), using the CFS theory. Although the CFS and the extensions of the CFS were not applied directly in applications, CFSs were considered as a basic concept to make intelligent systems capable of handling different issues [17–24].

Recently, the Mamdani Complex Fuzzy Inference System (M-CFIS) was proposed in [23]. Some other FISs in the CFS were also developed such as the Adaptive Neuro-complex Fuzzy Inferential System (ANCFIS) with higher-order TSK models [25], Randomized Adaptive Neuro-complex Fuzzy Inference System (RANCFIS) [26], and Fast Adaptive Neuro-complex Fuzzy Inference System (FANCFIS) [27]. However, a potential impairment of the existing M-CFIS is that the rule base may be redundant to a specific dataset. In order to remedy the problem, fuzzy similarity measures should be utilized.

The measures of the CFS were presented in [28], including complex fuzzy distances and distance measures between two CFSs. The distance measures of the CFS were introduced in [29,30]. Setnes et al. [31] proposed a similarity measure in fuzzy rule base to evaluate the equality between two fuzzy sets and to simplify the rule base. Similarity measures in complex neutrosophic sets were presented in [32], including Cosine, Dice, and Jaccard similarity measures. The candidates of multi-attribute decision-making were assessed by these measures. Apart from that, the measures based on FS, CFS, or FIS were also used to calculate weights of criteria in a decision-making system [33]. In the CFS, the complex fuzzy measure was defined as the cardinality of fuzzy rule set [29]. The complex fuzzy measures (t-norm and t-conorm) in Mamdani CFIS (M-CFIS) were introduced in [23], where the obtained rule set in M-CFIS directly affects to the results of decision-making. In most cases, there is redundancy in the rule base obtained from M-CFIS.

This paper proposes a new Mamdani Complex Fuzzy Inference System with Rule Reduction Using Complex Fuzzy Measures in Granular Computing called M-CFIS-R. Several fuzzy similarity measures, including Complex Fuzzy Cosine Similarity Measure (CFCSM), Complex Fuzzy Dice Similarity Measure (CFDSM), and Complex Fuzzy Jaccard Similarity Measure (CFJSM) together with their weighted versions are proposed. Those measures are integrated into the M-CFIS-R system by the idea of Granular Computing where only important and dominant rules will be kept in the system. These complex fuzzy measures are used to evaluate the similarity among complex fuzzy rules in the rule set of M-CFIS. Based on the values of these measures, the rules with high similarity will be reduced to guarantee high performance. The advantage of M-CFIS-R over M-CFIS is the usage of the training process in which the rule base is repeatedly changed toward the original base set until the performance is better. By doing so, the new rule base in M-CFIS-R would improve the performance of the whole system. The performance of proposed method is experimentally validated on various decision-making datasets.

2. Related Works

2.1. Complex Fuzzy Measures

Most research on complex fuzzy measure has mainly focused on certain aspects [34,35] such as the fuzzy measure and classical theory of complex fuzzy numbers, similarity, and distance with the CFS [29,30].

In a fuzzy rule base, the concept of similarity measure was mentioned by Setnes et al. [31]. Based on this, the similarity of two fuzzy sets was defined. Then, similar fuzzy sets were removed and the common presentations were kept in the rule base. Ma and Li [36] extended the classical measure to fuzzy complex number valued measure and defined some important properties on complex fuzzy set valued complex fuzzy measures. These properties generalized the corresponding results in measure theory and on the related integral theory. In another study [37], Ma et al. proposed a new concept of complex fuzzy measure, which is distinguished between the real and imaginary. Based on the complex fuzzy measure, Ma and Li [38] focused on the convergence problem of the complex fuzzy integral. Alkouri and Salleh [28] introduced the definitions of linguistic variables and linguistic hedges on the CFS. In this research, they also presented several distance measures in the CFS, which might be used as a suggestion in decision-making, prediction, and pattern recognition to find optimal solutions. Other measures and operations on other types of the complex fuzzy set were also presented in [23,29].

The information measure in Complex Intuitionistic Fuzzy Set (CIFS) was given by Garg and Rani [39] in a multiple-criteria decision-making for uncertain and vague data. The quaternion representation and distance on CIFS were proposed in [40] with an application in medical diagnosis. These formulas of quaternion representation and distance measure were used in a diagnosis model by calculating patient–disease relations. The threshold obtained via learning process was used to decide the output of model. In the Interval-Valued Complex Fuzzy Set (IvCFS), distance measures were defined on Euclidean metric and Hamming metric [37]. The authors presented an example to illustrate the use of these measures in decision-making. In the case of Complex Neutrosophic Set (CNS), similarity measures with the weighted versions were introduced in [32]. Using these measures, the decision-making model could rank the priority of candidates. The best one was selected to make a decision. These measures lead to good decisions because they considered the interaction among attributes in the dataset and the indeterminacy of data.

2.2. Fuzzy Inference System in Complex Fuzzy Set

Many intelligent systems with different applications were based on FIS [2–4,6,7]. Sagir et al. [4] proposed two extended models of ANFIS to apply to the heart disease prediction problem. The limitations of these extended models are that the accuracy of classification is not very high and the number of rules is great. A combination of multiple kernel learning and ANFIS was introduced by Manogaran and Varatharajan [7]. This method resulted in higher performance than other compared models. However, the application of this model focused on diagnosing heart disease with only two input features. ANFIS was also used in detecting lung cancer [3] by cancerous and non-cancerous segmentation on computed tomography images.

ANCFIS in time series forecasting has higher quality than other related models, including ANFIS [25]. Using the experimental results on five real datasets, the values of MSE and NDEI from applying ANCFIS are less than those of the compared models. ANCFIS was improved as FANCFIS to deal with multivariate time series problem [27,41]. This model was designed to maintain the accuracy and decrease time computing of ANCFIS. Many applications of these systems were also presented in [24,26,42]. The combination of the CFS and machine learning or other state-of-the-art tools was one of the popular approaches to carry out practical problems. In [43], a CFS with multiswarm learning was proposed for multiclass prediction problems. Granular computing was utilized for complex fuzzy sets in [44]. The granulation was used to interpret complex fuzzy contexts provided by users.

3. Preliminaries

3.1. Complex Fuzzy Set

Definition 1 [1]. *A fuzzy set F over X is defined by*

$$F = \{(x, \mu_F(x)) : x \in X\} \tag{1}$$

where the membership function of F, $\mu_F(x)$, is $\mu_F : X \to [0,1]$. For each $x \in X$, the value $\mu_F(x)$ represents the degree of membership of x in the fuzzy set F.

Definition 2 [15]. *A complex fuzzy set (CFS) S on X, is characterized by a membership function $\eta_S(x)$ that lies within the unit circle in the complex plane and has the form $p_S(x).e^{i \cdot \mu_S(x)}$ where the amplitude $p_S(x)$ and phase $\mu_S(x)$ are both real-valued, $p_S(x) \in [0,1]$, and $i = \sqrt{-1}$.*

$$S = \{x, \eta_S(x) | x \in X\} \tag{2}$$

Definition 3 [45]. *Some basic operations of CFS:*

Consider two CFSs, A and B, in a universe of discourse X with membership degrees of $\eta_A(x) = p_A(x)e^{j\mu_A(x)}$, $\eta_B(x) = p_B(x)e^{j\mu_B(x)}$, respectively. The operations of these two CFSs are defined as follows:

$$\eta_{A \cup B}(x) = [p_A(x) \oplus p_B(x)]e^{j(\mu_{A \cup B})} = \max(p_A(x), p_B(x)).e^{j(\max(\mu_A(x), \mu_B(x)))} \tag{3}$$

$$\eta_{A \cap B}(x) = [p_A(x) * p_B(x)]e^{j(\mu_{A \cap B})} = \min(p_A(x), p_B(x)).e^{j(\min(\mu_A(x), \mu_B(x)))} \tag{4}$$

where $\eta_{A \cup B}(x)$ is the *union* and $\eta_{A \cap B}(x)$ is the *intersection* operation of the CFSs A and B, $*$ is t-norm, and $\oplus$ is t-conorm.

Definition 4 [45]. *Let A be a complex fuzzy set on X. The complement of S is*

$$\eta_{c(A)}(x) = p_{c(A)}(x)e^{j\mu_{c(A)}(x)} = \left(1 - p_{c(A)}\right)(x).e^{j(2\pi - \mu_{c(A)}(x))} \tag{5}$$

Definition 5 [45]. *Let A and B be two CFSs on X with $\eta_A(x) = p_A(x)e^{j\mu_A(x)}$, $\eta_B(x) = p_B(x)e^{j\mu_B(x)}$. The complex fuzzy product of A and B is*

$$\eta_{A \circ B}(x) = p_{A \circ B}(x)e^{j\mu_{A \circ B}(x)} = (p_A(x).p_B(x)).e^{j\frac{\mu_A(x).\mu_B(x)}{2\pi}} \tag{6}$$

Definition 6 [45]. *A distance of complex fuzzy sets is $\rho : (F^*(U) \times F^*(U)) \to [0,1]$, for any A, B, and $C \in F^*(U)$*

i. $\rho(A, B) \geq 0$, $\rho(A, B) = 0$ IFF $A = B$,
ii. $\rho(A, B) = \rho(B, A)$,
iii. $\rho(A, B) \leq \rho(A, C) + \rho(C, B)$,

where $F^*(U)$ is the set of all complex fuzzy sets in U.

Definition 7 [45]. *Assume A and B, with $\eta_A(x) = p_A(x)e^{j\mu_A(x)}$, $\eta_B(x) = p_B(x)e^{j\mu_B(x)}$. A and B are δ-equal IFF $(A, B) \leq 1 - \delta$, $0 \leq \delta \leq 1$.*

Definition 8 [45]. *Assume A and B, with $\eta_A(x) = p_A(x)e^{j\mu_A(x)}$, $\eta_B(x) = p_B(x)e^{j\mu_B(x)}$. The distance of two CFSs defined on the same product space is defined as follows:*

$$d(A,B) = \max\left(\sup_{(x,y)\in U\times V} |p_A(x,y) - p_B(x,y)|, \frac{1}{2\pi} \sup_{(x,y)\in U\times V} |\mu_A(x,y) - \mu_B(x,y)|\right) \quad (7)$$

3.2. Mamdani Complex Fuzzy Inference System (M-CFIS)

In this section, we introduce the Mamdani Complex Fuzzy Inference System (M-CFIS) [23]. The general structure of Mamdani CFIS consists of six stages [23]:

Let $x_1, x_2, \ldots, x_n \in \mathbb{C}$ be the inputs of this model.

Stage 1: Establish a set of complex fuzzy rules

Based on practical application, we will determine the set of complex fuzzy rules in the form:

CFR_1 : If $x_{1,1}$ is $A_{1,1}$ $O_{1,1}x_{1,2}$ is $A_{1,2}$ $O_{1,2} \ldots O_{1,n_1-1}$ x_{1,n_1} is A_{1,n_1}, is Z_1
CFR_2 : If $x_{2,1}$ is $A_{2,1}$ $O_{2,1}x_{2,2}$ is $A_{2,2}$ $O_{2,2} \ldots O_{2,n_2-1}$ x_{2,n_2} is A_{2,n_2}, is Z_2
$\ldots$
CFR_k : If $x_{k,1}$ is $A_{k,1}$ $O_{k,1}$ $x_{k,2}$ is $A_{k,2}$ $O_{k,2} \ldots O_{k,n_k-1}$ x_{k,n_k} is A_{k,n_k}, is Z_k

With all u, v:

(i) $(u,v) \in \{1,2,\ldots,n\}$, with $1 \le u, 1 < u, 2 < \ldots < u, n_u \le n$;
(ii) $\eta_{A_{u,v}}(x_{u,v}) = p_{A_{u,v}}(x_{u,v}) e^{j\mu_{A_{u,v}}(x_{u,v})}$, with $p_{A_{u,v}} : \mathbb{C} \to [0,1]$ and $\mu_{A_{u,n}} : \mathbb{C} \to (0, 2\pi]$;
(iii) $\eta_{Z_u}(y) = p_{Z_u}(y) e^{j\mu_{Z_u}(y)}$, with $p_{Z_u} : \mathbb{C} \to [0,1]$ and $\mu_{Z_u} : \mathbb{C} \to (0, 2\pi]$;
(iv) T_0 is a T-norm, and S_0 is the S-norm (i.e., the T-conorm) that corresponds to T_0;
(v) $O_{u,v}$ = and IFF $N_{u,v} = T_0$;
(vi) $O_{u,v}$ = or IFF $N_{u,v} = S_0$.

Stage 2: Fuzzification of the inputs

Inputs are fuzzified using complex membership function $\eta(x) = p(x).e^{j\mu(x)}$, where $\mu(x) \in (0, 2\pi]$, $p(x) \in [0,1]$, and $p(x)$ and $\mu(x)$ represent the amplitude and phase terms of the elements, respectively.

Stage 3: Establish the firing strength of rule

This stage computes the firing strength ω_u for each complex fuzzy rule as: $\omega_u = \tau_u e^{j\psi_u}$.

Stage 4: Calculate the consequence of the complex fuzzy rules

In Mamdani CFIS, the value of the consequence of the complex fuzzy rules is obtained by using the Mamdani implication rule.

$$\eta_{A\to B}(x,y) = (p_A(x).p_B(y)).e^{j\,2\pi\left(\frac{\mu_A(x)}{2\pi} \cdot \frac{\mu_B(y)}{2\pi}\right)} \quad (8)$$

Choose a function $U_0 : [0,1]^2 \to [0,1]$, with $U_0(1,1) = 1$, and a function $g_0 : (0, 2\pi]^2 \to (0, 2\pi]$, with $g_0(2\pi, 2\pi) = 2\pi$. We form the consequent of CFR_u for each u:

$$\Gamma_u(y) = U_0(\tau_u, r_{C_u}(y)) e^{j\,g_0(\psi_u, \mu_{C_u}(y))} = \omega_u . \eta_{C_u}(y)$$

where "." denotes the complex dot product.

Stage 5: Aggregation

In this stage, the output distribution is calculated as follows:

$$D(y) = \Gamma_1(y) + \Gamma_2(y) + \ldots + \Gamma_k(y).$$

Stage 6: Defuzzification.

Choose a function $\Phi: \mathcal{F}(\mathbb{C}, \mathbb{C}) \to \mathbb{C}$. Determine the value of the output $y_{op} = \Phi(D)$. For example, we can choose the trapezoidal approximation such as $\Phi(D) = \frac{\int_{-\infty}^{\infty} y |D(y)| dy}{\int_{-\infty}^{\infty} |D(y)| dy}$.

3.3. Granular Computing

Granular computing [46,47] generally refers information granulation that includes probabilistic set, fuzzy set, and rough set. In the context of fuzzy sets, each element can be viewed as a granule of a certain degree of membership to the set. It is used to simplify complex problems by decomposing strategy in term of information granulation. Studying rule learning with granular computing has an important role in improving the model accuracy. Thus, the relationship between granular computing and rule-based systems is argued.

4. Proposed M-CFIS-R System

4.1. Main Ideas

It has been observed from Section 2 that changing the number of rules in a rule base for better performance of classification is still a challenge when designing a FIS model. Hence, it is necessary to have an effective measure to evaluate the importance of each rule in the rule base. This section will propose three similarity measures in the Training stage. In our decision-making model, granular computing is used in the last stage of Training. The purpose of using granular computing is to reduce the rules with high similarity or to add more rules in order to get higher coverage. The result of this stage is a new rule set with suitable number of rules with high classification accuracy compared to the original rule set. Comparing with the architecture of M-CFIS [23], we add the Training process in order to create the original complex fuzzy rule base and improve it by the Granular Computing with Complex Fuzzy Measure (i.e., Granular Complex Fuzzy Measure). The Testing phase follows the inference process in the M-CFIS discussed in Section 3.2 but with the reduced complex fuzzy base. The model is divided into two parts: (i) Training used to train the generation of fuzzy rules is discussed in detail in Section 4.2; (ii) Testing used to test the performance of the rule system is discussed in Section 4.3.

4.2. Training

In this model, we divide the dataset into the Training–Validation–Testing parts by K-Folds (where K is often small, e.g., 3). From the Training data, we build the real and imaginary data (presented in Section 4.2.1). Then, fuzzy clustering (i.e., Fuzzy C-Means [48]) is performed for each attribute of those data to obtain the set of fuzzy rules, which is considered as the original complex fuzzy rule base (see Section 4.2.2). This rule base is evaluated on the Validation data to get the performance, namely A (see Section 4.2.3). Next, we try to improve the original complex fuzzy rule base by calculating the correlations between complex fuzzy rules based on different new complex fuzzy measures (see Section 4.2.4). The similarities of complex fuzzy rules are finally determined by granular computing according to each label of Validation data (see Section 4.2.5). We then evaluate performance of the new complex fuzzy rule base called A' on the Validation data by the same inference module (similar to Section 4.2.3). If A' is better than A, we end the Training and proceed to Testing; otherwise, we repeat the process of using Granular Complex Fuzzy Measure to retrain. The Training process can be seen in Figure 1.

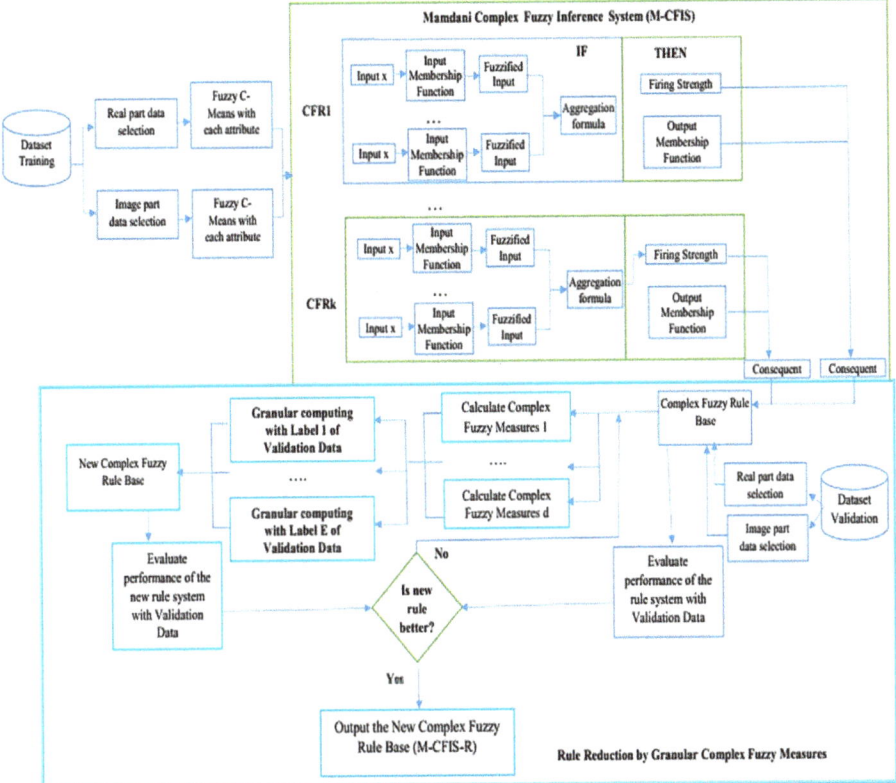

Figure 1. Training diagram for the proposed model.

4.2.1. Real and Imaginary Data Selection

From the Training data, we build the real and imaginary data as follows: The real data are defined as the original data values. The imaginary data at record P of attribute Q is determined as var.P (row) + var.Q (column), where var.P (row) is the variance in row at row P and var.Q (column) is the variance according to the column in column Q.

4.2.2. Fuzzy C-Means (FCM)

In this study, we use the Fuzzy C-Means clustering method (Algorithm 1) for dividing the data according to each attribute into several groups. The number of clusters specified for each attribute is different based on the semantic value of the attribute. The number of clusters of an attribute in the real and imaginary parts is the same. Finally, we produce complex fuzzy rules from each cluster.

Algorithm 1. Fuzzy C-Means algorithm.

Input	Datasets X of N records; C: number of clusters; m: fuzzier; MaxStep
Output	Membership U and centers V
BEGIN	
1	Iteration t = 0
2	Initialize $u_{kj}^{(t)} \leftarrow random$ $(k = \overline{1,N} j = \overline{1,C})$ within [0,1] and the sum constraint
3	Repeat
4	t = t + 1
5	Compute $V_j = \frac{\sum_{k=1}^{C} u_{kj}^m X_k}{\sum_{k=1}^{C} u_{kj}^m}$ $(j = \overline{1,C})$
6	Compute $u_{kj} = \frac{1}{\sum_{i=1}^{C} \left(\frac{\|X_k - V_j\|}{\|X_k - V_i\|}\right)^{\frac{1}{m-1}}}$ $(k = \overline{1,N} j = \overline{1,C})$
7	Until $\|U^{(t)} - U^{(t-1)}\| \leq \epsilon$ or t > MaxStep

4.2.3. Evaluating Performance of the Rule-Based System

After obtaining the complex fuzzy rule base, we use the Validation data to derive the outputs and evaluate the performance through Accuracy, Precision, and Recall.

$$Accuracy = \frac{TN + TP}{TN + FN + FP + TP}$$

Recall = $\frac{|TP|}{|TP| + |FN|}$

Precision = $\frac{|TP|}{|TP| + |FP|}$

4.2.4. Complex Fuzzy Measures

In this section, we propose three complex fuzzy similarity measures with their weighted versions as below.

Complex Fuzzy Cosine Similarity Measure (CFCSM)

Definition 9. *Assume that there are two complex fuzzy sets, namely $S_1 = r_{S_1}(x)e^{j\mu_{S_1}(x)}$ and $S_2 = r_{S_2}(x)e^{j\mu_{S_2}(x)}$, $x \in X$. A Complex Fuzzy Cosine Similarity Measure (CFCSM) between S_1 and S_2 is*

$$C_{CFS} = \frac{1}{n} \sum_{j=1}^{n} \frac{(a_1 b_1)(a_2 b_2)}{\sqrt{(a_1 b_1)^2} + \sqrt{(a_2 b_2)^2}} \quad (9)$$

where

$$a_1 = Re\left(p_{S_1}(x)e^{j\mu_{S_1}(x)}\right), b_1 = Im\left(p_{S_1}(x)e^{j\mu_{S_1}(x)}\right), a_2 = Re\left(p_{S_2}(x)e^{j\mu_{S_2}(x)}\right),$$
$$b_2 = Im\left(p_{S_2}(x)e^{j\mu_{S_2}(x)}\right)$$

Proposition 1. *Let S_1 and S_2 be complex fuzzy sets. Then,*

1. $0 \leq C_{CFS}(S_1, S_2) \leq 1$;
2. $C_{CFS}(S_1, S_2) = C_{CFS}(S_2, S_1)$;
3. $C_{CFS}(S_1, S_2) = 1$ if and only if $S_1 = S_2$;
4. If $S_1 \subset S_2 \subset S$ then $C_{CFS}(S_1, S) \leq C_{CFS}(S_1, S_2)$ and $C_{CFS}(S_1, S) \leq C_{CFS}(S_2, S)$.

Proof.

1. It is correct because all positive values of cosine function are within 0 and 1.
2. Trivial.

3. When $S_1 = S_2$ then obviously $C_{CFS}(S_1, S_2) = 1$. If $C_{CFS}(S_1, S_2) = 1, a_1 = a_2, b_1 = b_2$. This implies that $S_1 = S_2$.
4. Let $S = \langle p_S(x).e^{j\mu_S(x)} \rangle$ and also assume that $L_1 = Re[p_S(x).e^{j\mu_S(x)}]$ and $L_2 = Im[p_S(x).e^{j\mu_S(x)}]$. If $S_1 \subset S_2 \subset S$, we can write that $a_1 b_1 \leq a_2 b_2 \leq L_1 L_2$. The cosine function is a decreasing function within the interval $[0, \frac{\pi}{2}]$. Then, we can write $C_{CFS}(S_1, S) \leq C_{CFS}(S_1, S_2)$ and $C_{CFS}(S_1, S) \leq C_{CFS}(S_2, S)$. □

Definition 10. *Weighted Complex Fuzzy Cosine Similarity Measure (WCNCSM).*

Assume that there are two complex fuzzy sets, namely $S_1 = p_{S_1}(x)e^{j\mu_{S_1}(x)}$ and $S_2 = p_{S_2}(x)e^{j\mu_{S_2}(x)}$, $x \in X$. A Weighted Complex Fuzzy Cosine Similarity Measure between S_1 and S_2 is

$$C_{WCFS} = \sum_{j=1}^{n} w_j \left[\frac{\sqrt{a_1 b_1 a_2 b_2}}{\sqrt{a_1 b_1} + \sqrt{a_2 b_2}} \right] \text{ where } \sum_{j=1}^{n} w_j = 1 \quad (10)$$

Complex Fuzzy Dice Similarity Measure (CFDSM)

Definition 11. *Assume that there are two complex fuzzy sets namely $S_1 = r_{S_1}(x)e^{j\mu_{S_1}(x)}$ and $S_2 = r_{S_2}(x)e^{j\mu_{S_2}(x)}$, $x \in X$. A Complex Fuzzy Dice Similarity Measure (CFDSM) between S_1 and S_2 is*

$$D_{CFS} = \frac{1}{n} \sum_{j=1}^{n} \frac{2\sqrt{a_1 b_1 a_2 b_2}}{a_1 b_1 + a_2 b_2} \quad (11)$$

where

$$a_1 = Re(p_{S_1}(x)e^{j\mu_{S_1}(x)}), b_1 = Im(p_{S_1}(x)e^{j\mu_{S_1}(x)}), a_2 = Re(p_{S_2}(x)e^{j\mu_{S_2}(x)}),$$
$$b_2 = Im(p_{S_2}(x)e^{j\mu_{S_2}(x)}).$$

Proposition 2. *Let S_1 and S_2 be complex fuzzy sets. Then,*

1. $0 \leq D_{CFS}(S_1, S_2) \leq 1$;
2. $D_{CFS}(S_1, S_2) = D_{CFS}(S_2, S_1)$;
3. $D_{CFS}(S_1, S_2) = 1$ if and only if $S_1 = S_2$;
4. If $S_1 \subset S_2 \subset S$ then $D_{CFS}(S_1, S) \leq D_{CFS}(S_1, S_2)$ and $D_{CFS}(S_1, S) \leq D_{CFS}(S_2, S)$.

Proof. The proof is similar to Proposition 1. □

Definition 12. *Weighted Complex Fuzzy Dice Similarity Measure (WCFDSM).*

Assume that there are two complex fuzzy sets, namely $S_1 = p_{S_1}(x)e^{j\mu_{S_1}(x)}$ and $S_2 = p_{S_2}(x)e^{j\mu_{S_2}(x)}$, $x \in X$. A Weighted Complex Fuzzy Dice Similarity Measure between S_1 and S_2 is

$$D_{WCNS} = \sum_{j=1}^{n} w_j \left[\frac{2(\sqrt{a_1 b_1 a_2 b_2})}{\sqrt{a_1 b_1} + \sqrt{a_2 b_2}} \right] \text{ where } \sum_{j=1}^{n} w_j = 1 \quad (12)$$

Complex Fuzzy Jaccard Similarity Measure (CFJSM)

Definition 13. *Assume that there are two complex fuzzy sets, namely $S_1 = p_{S_1}(x)e^{j\mu_{S_1}(x)}$ and $S_2 = p_{S_2}(x)e^{j\mu_{S_2}(x)}$, $x \in X$. A Complex Fuzzy Jaccard Similarity Measure (CFJSM) between S_1 and S_2 is*

$$J_{CFS} = \frac{1}{n}\sum_{j=1}^{n} \frac{\sqrt{a_1 b_1 a_2 b_2}}{(a_1 b_1 + a_2 b_2) - \left(\sqrt{a_1 b_1} + \sqrt{a_2 b_2}\right)} \tag{13}$$

where $a_1 = Re\left(p_{S_1}(x)e^{j\mu_{S_1}(x)}\right)$, $b_1 = Im\left(p_{S_1}(x)e^{j\mu_{S_1}(x)}\right)$, $a_2 = Re\left(p_{S_2}(x)e^{j\mu_{S_2}(x)}\right)$, $b_2 = Im\left(p_{S_2}(x)e^{j\mu_{S_2}(x)}\right)$.

Proposition 3. *Let S_1 and S_2 be complex fuzzy sets. Then,*

1. $0 \leq J_{CFS}(S_1, S_2) \leq 1$;
2. $J_{CFS}(S_1, S_2) = J_{CFS}(S_2, S_1)$;
3. $J_{CFS}(S_1, S_2) = 1$ if and only if $S_1 = S_2$;
4. If $S_1 \subset S_2 \subset S$ then $J_{CFS}(S_1, S) \leq J_{CFS}(S_1, S_2)$ and $J_{CFS}(S_1, S) \leq J_{CFS}(S_2, S)$.

Proof. The proof is similar to Proposition 1. □

Definition 14. *Weighted Complex Fuzzy Jaccard Similarity Measure (WCFJSM)*

Assume that there are two complex fuzzy sets namely $S_1 = p_{S_1}(x)e^{j\mu_{S_1}(x)}$ and $S_2 = p_{S_2}(x)e^{j\mu_{S_2}(x)}$, $x \in X$. A Weighted Complex Fuzzy Dice Similarity Measure between S_1 and S_2 is

$$J_{WCNS} = \sum_{j=1}^{n} w_j \left[\frac{\sqrt{a_1 b_1 a_2 b_2}}{\sqrt{a_1 b_1} - \sqrt{a_2 b_2}}\right] \text{ where } \sum_{j=1}^{n} w_j = 1 \tag{14}$$

4.2.5. Granular Complex Fuzzy Measures

In this section, we describe how to determine the final similarity between complex fuzzy rules from the correlations of rules described in Section 4.2.4. To accomplish this, we introduce an idea of granular computing to conceptualize relationships for a combination of fuzzy correlation measures. Assume that the outputs of three similarity measures in Section 4.2.4 are three corresponding squared matrices whose elements are the correlations between pairs of complex fuzzy rules: D^1, D^2, D^3. We determine the final degree of similarity between complex fuzzy rules based on the aggregation:

$$F_{ij} = a_1 D_{ij}^1 + a_2 D_{ij}^2 + a_3 D_{ij}^3 \tag{15}$$

For each set of labels, e.g., label l, we obtain $F_{ij}(l)$ to be determined $a_1(l), a_2(l), \ldots a_e(l)$.

$$a_t(l) = \sum_{i=1}^{|D^t/l|} \sum_{j=i+1}^{|D^t/l|} \frac{\left(D_{ij}^t / t\right)}{|D^t/l|} \tag{16}$$

For rules other than labels, then $F_{ij} = 0$. From these, we obtain the matrix F.

A new complex fuzzy rule base is found from F by removing rules having a high or maximal degree of similarity within a group. Then, we proceed to the next steps to evaluate the performance of the new rule system. In cases that the performance of the new complex fuzzy rule base is worse than that of the current rule, we return to the steps of computing the complex fuzzy measures (Section 4.2.4) and granular computing (Section 4.2.5) for the new complex fuzzy rule base. The iteration stops either when the performance of the new complex fuzzy rule base is better than that of the current base or the cardinality of rules according to any label is equal to 1. The following example demonstrates the main activities of granular computing in M-CFIS-R.

Example 1. *Suppose we have a set of 6 complex fuzzy rules in which 3 rules R_1, R_3, R_4 have label 1 ($k = 1$), and 3 rules R_2, R_5, R_6 have label 2:*

R_1: If x_1 is Medium and x_2 is High and x_3 is High then k is 1
R_2: If x_1 is High and x_2 is Low and x_3 is Low then k is 2
R_3: If x_1 is Low and x_2 is Medium and x_3 is High then k is 1
R_4: If x_1 is Low and x_2 is High and x_3 is Medium then k is 1
R_5: If x_1 is High and x_2 is Low and x_3 is Medium then k is 2
R_6: If x_1 is Medium and x_2 is Low and x_3 is Low then k is 2

Using the complex fuzzy measures (Section 4.2.4), we obtain three matrices as follows:

$$D^1 = \begin{bmatrix} 0 & 0.5 & 0.8 & 0.7 & 0.4 & 0.3 \\ 0.5 & 0 & 0.5 & 0.4 & 0.8 & 0.9 \\ 0.8 & 0.5 & 0 & 0.9 & 0.4 & 0.5 \\ 0.7 & 0.4 & 0.9 & 0 & 0.5 & 0.3 \\ 0.4 & 0.8 & 0.4 & 0.5 & 0 & 0.7 \\ 0.3 & 0.9 & 0.5 & 0.3 & 0.7 & 0 \end{bmatrix}$$

$$D^2 = \begin{bmatrix} 0 & 0.2 & 0.5 & 0.4 & 0.2 & 0.1 \\ 0.2 & 0 & 0.2 & 0.3 & 0.5 & 0.6 \\ 0.5 & 0.2 & 0 & 0.5 & 0.2 & 0.1 \\ 0.4 & 0.3 & 0.5 & 0 & 0.2 & 0.3 \\ 0.2 & 0.5 & 0.2 & 0.2 & 0 & 0.5 \\ 0.1 & 0.6 & 0.1 & 0.3 & 0.5 & 0 \end{bmatrix}$$

$$D^3 = \begin{bmatrix} 0 & 0.1 & 0.4 & 0.4 & 0.2 & 0.1 \\ 0.1 & 0 & 0.1 & 0.2 & 0.4 & 0.3 \\ 0.4 & 0.1 & 0 & 0.4 & 0.1 & 0.2 \\ 0.4 & 0.2 & 0.4 & 0 & 0.2 & 0.1 \\ 0.2 & 0.4 & 0.1 & 0.2 & 0 & 0.3 \\ 0.1 & 0.3 & 0.2 & 0.1 & 0.3 & 0 \end{bmatrix}$$

We calculate the coefficients of each matrix according to the labels 1, 2:

$$a_1^1 = \frac{0.8 + 0.7 + 0.9}{3} = 0.8 \quad a_2^1 = \frac{0.5 + 0.4 + 0.5}{3} = 0.467 \quad a_3^1 = \frac{0.4 + 0.4 + 0.4}{3} = 0.4$$

$$a_1^2 = \frac{0.8 + 0.9 + 0.7}{3} = 0.8 \quad a_2^2 = \frac{0.5 + 0.6 + 0.5}{3} = 0.533 \quad a_3^2 = \frac{0.4 + 0.3 + 0.3}{3} = 0.333$$

We calculate the matrix F as follows:

$$F = \begin{bmatrix} 0 & 0 & 1.034 & 0.907 & 0 & 0 \\ 0 & 0 & 0 & 0 & 1.04 & 1.14 \\ 0.397 & 0 & 0 & 1.114 & 0 & 0 \\ 0.563 & 0 & 0.51 & 0 & 0 & 0 \\ 0 & 0.29 & 0 & 0 & 0 & 0.926 \\ 0 & 0.657 & 0 & 0 & 0.926 & 0 \end{bmatrix}$$

It is obvious that the rules with highest similarity within label 1 are R_3 and R_4, and the rules with the highest similarity within label 2 are and R_2 and R_6. Then, the new complex fuzzy rule base is: R_1, R_3 with label 1; R_2, R_5 with label 2.

We calculate performance of the new rule base. If it is worse, we return to compute the complex fuzzy measures with the current rule base including R_1, R_3 with label 1 and R_2, R_5 with label 2. Here, we demonstrate Iteration 2.

The second iteration: The second set of fuzzy rules R' is: R'_1, R'_3 have label 1, R'_2, R'_4 have label 2. For clarity, we assign a mark (') to differentiate between iterations. The corresponding measure values are:

$$D^{1'} = \begin{bmatrix} 0 & 0.5 & 0.8 & 0.3 \\ 0.5 & 0 & 0.4 & 0.7 \\ 0.8 & 0.4 & 0 & 0.3 \\ 0.3 & 0.7 & 0.3 & 0 \end{bmatrix}$$

$$D^{2'} = \begin{bmatrix} 0 & 0.2 & 0.5 & 0.1 \\ 0.2 & 0 & 0.2 & 0.4 \\ 0.5 & 0.2 & 0 & 0.1 \\ 0.1 & 0.4 & 0.1 & 0 \end{bmatrix}$$

$$D^{3'} = \begin{bmatrix} 0 & 0.1 & 0.3 & 0.1 \\ 0.1 & 0 & 0.1 & 0.4 \\ 0.3 & 0.1 & 0 & 0.2 \\ 0.1 & 0.4 & 0.2 & 0 \end{bmatrix}$$

We calculate the coefficients of each matrix according to the labels 1 and 2:

$$a'^1_1 = \frac{0.8}{1} = 0.8 \; a'^1_2 = \frac{0.5}{1} = 0.5 \; a'^1_3 = \frac{0.3}{1} = 0.3$$

$$a'^2_1 = \frac{0.7}{1} = 0.7 \; a'^2_2 = \frac{0.4}{1} = 0.4 \; a'^1_3 = \frac{0.4}{1} = 0.4$$

We calculate the matrix F as follows:

$$F' = \begin{bmatrix} 0 & 0 & 0.98 & 0 \\ 0 & 0 & 0 & 0.81 \\ 0.98 & 0 & 0 & 0 \\ 0 & 0.81 & 0 & 0 \end{bmatrix}$$

We define the similarity with the same label and determine the highest similarity. The following rules are similar: R'_1 and R'_3, R'_2, and R'_4. Then, the new rule base is: R'_1 with label 1; R'_2 with label 2. We continue to compute performance of the new rule base. Even if the performance is not better than that of the current rule base, we still stop the algorithm because the cardinality of rules in both labels 1 and 2 is 1. In order to obtain the best performance, we may use the original complex fuzzy rule base generated from Training as the final results. As a result, the proposed M-CFIS-R at least has performance equal to M-CFIS in the worst case.

4.3. Testing

We perform a similar procedure with M-CFIS [23] for testing the performance of the system with the reduced complex fuzzy rule base found in the Training phase (Figure 2).

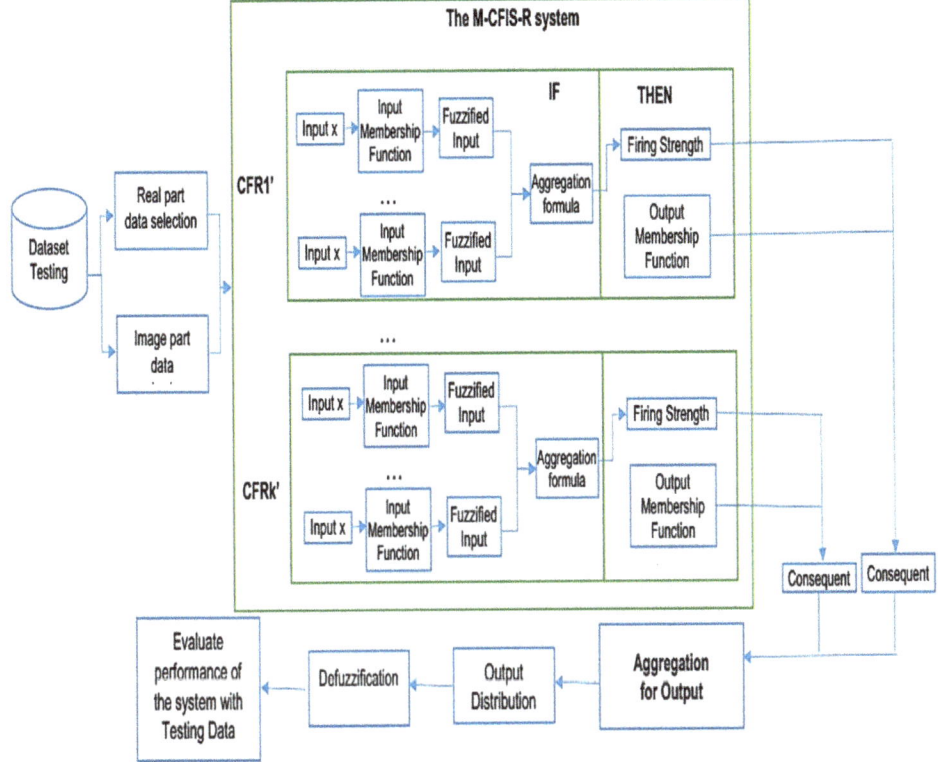

Figure 2. Testing diagram for the proposed model.

Specifically, from Testing data, we build data for the real and imaginary parts. Then, we use the reduced complex fuzzy rule base generated from the Training model to obtain the consequences. By using the Aggregation operator and Defuzzification, we obtain the output. Finally, we evaluate the performance of the outputs based on the evaluation measures (see Section 4.2.3).

4.4. Some Notes on M-CFIS-R

Advantages: The M-CFIS-R model combines M-CFIS, complex fuzzy measures and granular computing within the Training phase. The result is a new fuzzy rule system with better performance than M-CFIS. The novelty of this research lies on the complex fuzzy measures within granular computing. In M-CFIS [23], the Training phase was not described, so it is an advantage for this research to demonstrate the improvements in this phase. By doing so, we obtain the new M-CFIS with better complex fuzzy rule base, which results in better performance than M-CFIS [23].

Disadvantages: The new model only stopped at local optimization and did not yet obtain a global optimal solution because when evaluating the performance of a new fuzzy rule base in the Training, if it is better than that of M-CFIS, the algorithm stops. This should be enhanced further. Besides, implementation time of the proposed model is also longer than that of M-CFIS.

5. Experiments

5.1. Experimental Environment

We implemented the proposed M-CFIS-R against M-CFIS [23] in MATLAB 2014 and executed them on a PC VAIO laptop with Core i5 processor. The experimental data include two types:

(a) Benchmark Medical UCI Machine Learning Repository Data [49]:

   i. The first dataset is the Wisconsin Breast Cancer Diagnosis (WBCD) from UCI [50] with 699 examples (458 benign and 241 malignant) in nine integer inputs and one binary output (Table 1).

   Table 1. Wisconsin Breast Cancer Diagnosis (WBCD) data summary.

No.	Feature Name	Value Range
1	Clump Thickness	1–10
2	Uniformity of Cell Size	1–10
3	Uniformity of Cell Shape	1–10
4	Marginal Adhesion	1–10
5	Single Epithelial Cell Size	1–10
6	Bare Nuclei	1–10
7	Bland Chromatin	1–10
8	Normal Nucleoli	1–10
9	Mitoses	1–10
10	Class	(2: benign, 4: malignant)

   ii. The second dataset, named Diabetes Databases [51], is from the Department of Medicine of the University of Virginia School of Medicine. The data have 391 examples with two classes to test whether the patient is positive or negative for diabetes. This dataset consists of five attributes (Table 2).

   Table 2. Diabetes data summary.

No	Feature Names	Value Range
1	Total Cholesterol	78–443
2	Stabilized Glucose	48–385
3	High Density Lipoprotein	12–120
4	Cholesterol/HDL Ratio	1.5–19.3
5	Glycosylated Hemoglobin	2.68–16.11
6	Class	(0: negative, 1: positive)

(b) Real Medical Datasets:

   i. The third dataset is from Gangthep Hospital and Thai Nguyen National Hospital, Vietnam [52], including 4156 patients divided into two groups: 2954 examples of non-diseased patients and 1202 examples of diseased patients (Table 3).

   Table 3. Gangthep Hospital and Thai Nguyen National Hospital data summary.

No.	Feature Name	Value Range
1	Age: at the exam time	5–86
2	Gender	(0: male; 1: female)
3	AST: aspartate transaminase	11.4–659.76
4	ALT: alanine aminotransferase	78.52–647.7
5	AST/ALT index	0–8.5
6	GGT: gamma glutamyl transferase	0–3352.6
7	Albumin	0–58.2
8	TB: Total bilirubin	3–669.03
9	DB: Direct bilirubin	0–287.52
10	DB/TB (%)	0–224.8
11	Class	(0: nondisease, 1: disease)

ii. The fourth dataset is the real dental dataset from Hanoi Medical University Hospital, Vietnam [53], in which dentists provide a properly labeled dataset that consists of 447 X-ray images with the disease of wisdom teeth deviate and 200 X-ray images without wisdom teeth deviate. The dental experts are from Hanoi Medical University and are currently working as professional dentists (Figure 3).

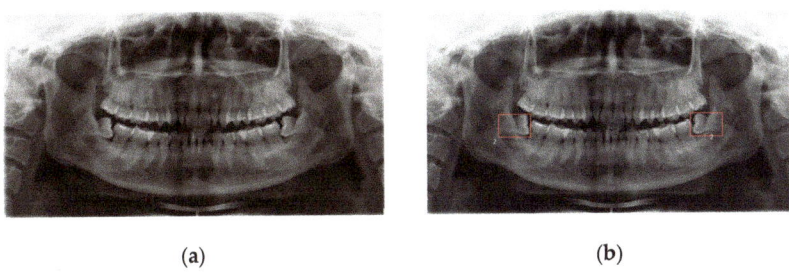

(a)   (b)

Figure 3. (a) A dental image. (b) The patient's cavity area image.

From this, we extract the following features: Gradient (GRA) [54]; Local Binary Patterns (LBP) [55]; Patch [56]; and Entropy, Edge-Value, and Intensity (EEI) [57] (Table 4). The input is an image, and the output is the label of disease or not.

Table 4. Value ranges of the dental dataset.

ID	Features	Value Range
1	LBP	27.04–55.89
2	EEI	145.65–161.76
3	GRA	85.02–125.07
4	Patch	30.54×10^{-3}–208.56×10^{-3}
5	Label	0 or 1

The evaluation criteria are Accuracy, Precision, and Recall, as defined in Section 4.2.3.

5.2. Experimental Results on the Benchmark UCI Datasets

Using 3-fold cross-validation method, the values of criteria obtained by applying M-CFIS and M-CFIS-R on the UCI datasets are visually presented in Figures 4 and 5, respectively. The average values of validity indices and time consumed are calculated separately on the training and the testing data. The number of rules is defined after applying granular computing with complex fuzzy measures. Results are taken as the average of 3-fold cross-validation.

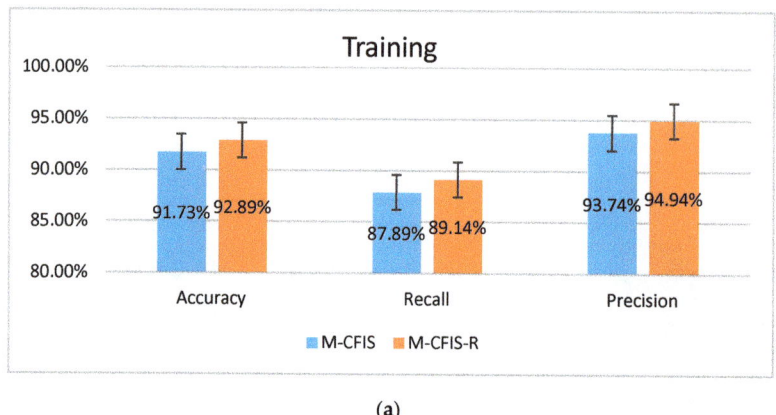

(a)

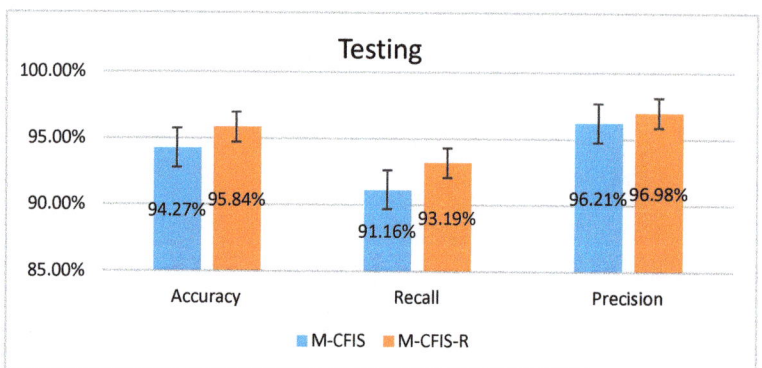

(b)

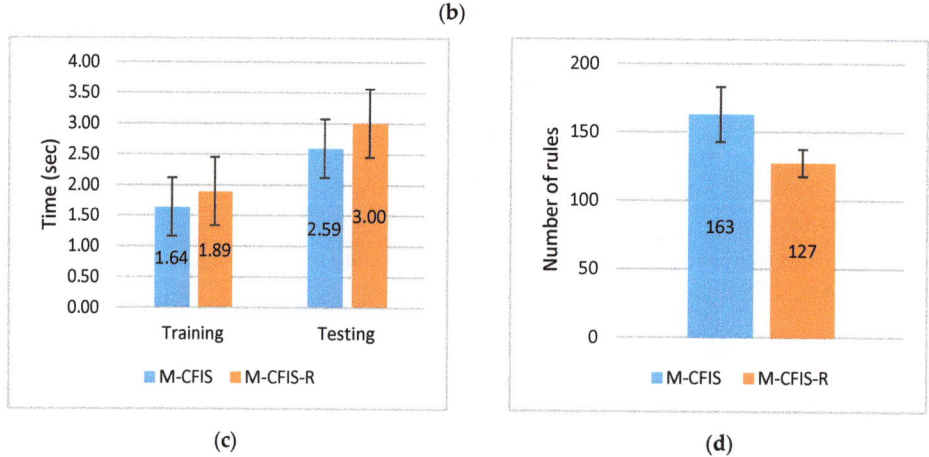

(c) (d)

Figure 4. Performance on the WBCD dataset: (**a**) Accuracy, Recall, and Precision on training set; (**b**) Accuracy, Recall, and Precision on testing set; (**c**) Time consumed; (**d**) Number of rules.

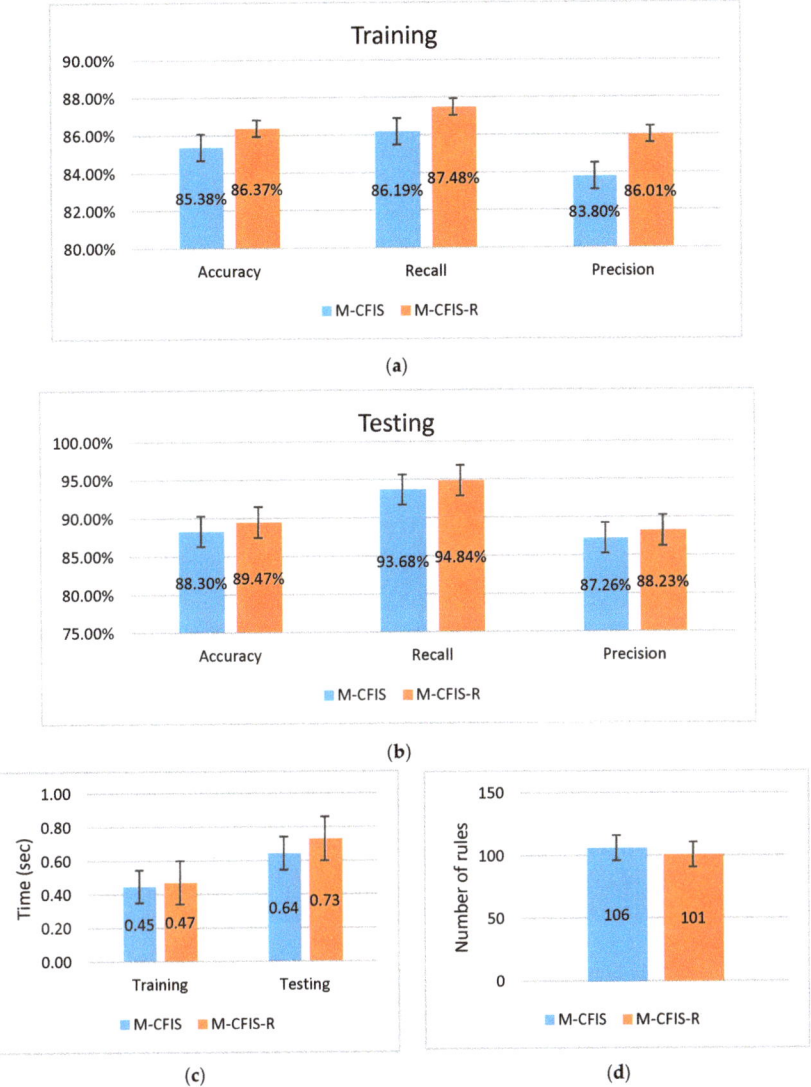

Figure 5. Performance on the Diabetes dataset: (**a**) Accuracy, Recall, Precision on training set; (**b**) Accuracy, Recall, Precision on testing set; (**c**) Time consumed; (**d**) Number of rules.

Figure 4 shows the results of applying M-CFIS and M-CFIS-R on the first dataset—WBCD. The accuracy of M-CFIS-R in the training data (Figure 4a) is higher than that of M-CFIS by 1.2% with small standard derivation (SD) (about 0.02). This value on the testing data is 1.6% higher with 0.01 of SD. Similarly, the Recall values in Figure 4b of M-CFIS-R in both the training and testing data are also higher than those of CFIS with the SD being less than 0.02. The Precision values in Figure 4a,b of M-CFIS-R are a bit higher than those of M-CFIS, with very small SD (SD is even zero in the testing data).

The computation time in Figure 4c of M-CFIS-R is a bit higher than that of M-CFIS, with only 0.25 s on the training data and 0.41 s on the testing data. Thus, the computation time of these methods can be considered as equal. The average number of rules in Figure 4d of M-CFIS-R is 127 with SD of

3.4, which is 35 rules less than the result of M-CFIS (163 rules on average with 2.06 SD). Thus, the rule base of M-CFIS-R has a lower number of rules than M-CFIS.

The performance comparison between M-CFIS and M-CFIS-R on the Diabetes dataset is presented in Figure 5. The values of validity indices (Figure 5a,b) obtained from M-CFIS-R are higher than those of M-CFIS by more than 1% and with small SD.

The running time (Figure 5c) of M-CFIS-R is higher than that of M-CFIS by only 0.02 s on the training data and 0.086 s on the testing data. The standard derivations are very small as well. The computation time of M-CFIS-F is equivalent to that of M-CFIS. The average number of rules in Figure 5d of M-CFIS-R is 5 rules less than that of M-CFIS, with SD of 0.94.

5.3. Experimental Results on the Real Datasets

On the real datasets, the classification quality evaluation between our proposed method M-CFIS-R and M-CFIS is shown in Figures 6 and 7.

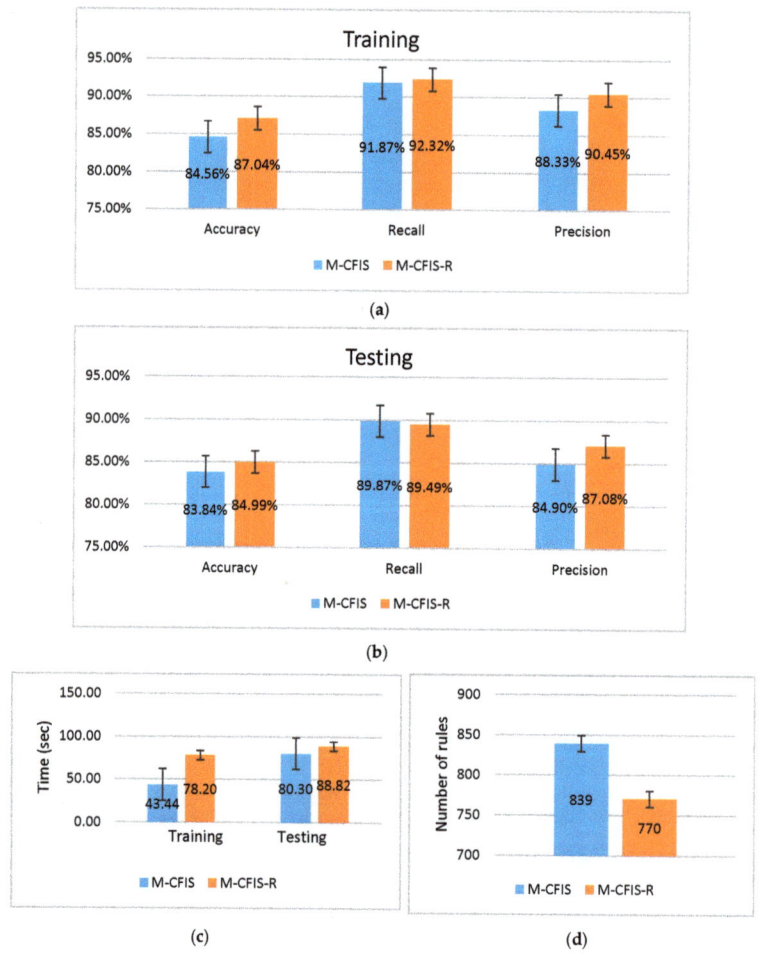

Figure 6. Performance on the Liver dataset: (**a**) Accuracy, Recall, Precision on training set; (**b**) Accuracy, Recall, Precision on testing set; (**c**) Time consumed; (**d**) Number of rules.

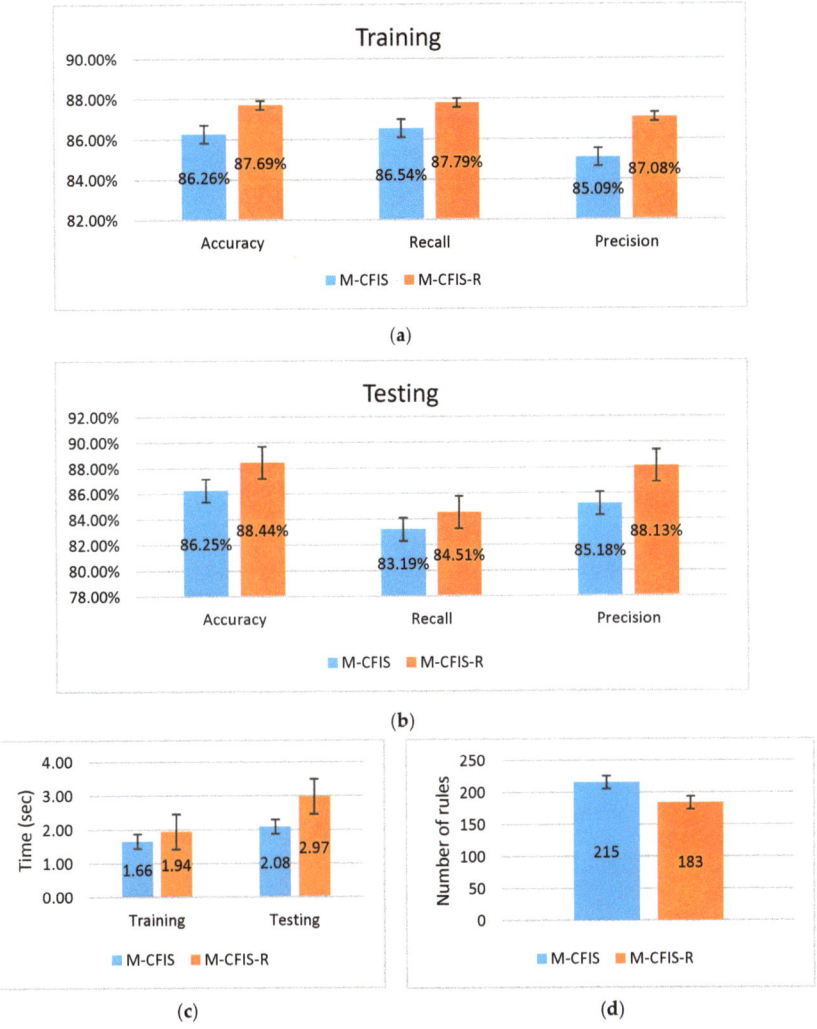

Figure 7. Performance on the Dental dataset: (**a**) Accuracy, Recall, Precision on training set; (**b**) Accuracy, Recall, Precision on testing set; (**c**) Time consumed; (**d**) Number of rules.

Figure 6 shows the performance of M-CFIS-R and M-CFIS on the Liver dataset. From Figure 6a, it is clear that the accuracy of M-CFIS-R on the training data is 2.5% higher than that of M-CFIS. Moreover, as shown in Figure 6a,b, the recall and precision values of M-CFIS-R on the training and testing data are about 2.2% higher than those of M-CFIS. Although the recall of M-CFIS-R on the testing data is 0.4% smaller than that of M-CFIS, the SD is very small (only 0.03). This is caused by the decreasing in number of rules, as shown in Figure 6d. On the Liver dataset, the number of rules in M-CFIS-R is 69 less than that of M-CFIS. This is the reason for M-CFIS-R being more time-consuming than M-CFIS (i.e., 34.5 s higher on the training data and 8.5 s higher on the testing data, as shown in Figure 6c). The standard derivations of all these results are very low.

The performance evaluation of M-CFIS-R compared to M-CFIS on Dental dataset is presented in Figure 7. All the results in this table are mostly similar to those of three datasets mentioned above. The number of rules in M-CFIS-R is 183 rules with SD of 2.5, while the number of rules in M-CFIS is 215 with 3.4 SD, as shown in Figure 7d. This explains why the accuracy, precision, and recall of M-CFIS-R are higher than those of M-CFIS, as seen in Figure 7a,b.

Apart from experimental evaluation above, the qualitative comparisons between the proposed model and others are provided in Table 5.

Table 5. Theoretical comparison between the proposed work and others.

Authors	Model	Brief Description	Results and Limitations
Selvachandran et al. [23]	Mamdani CFIS	- Extended Mamdani FIS on complex fuzzy sets (Mamdani CFIS) together with operations on this system. - Output of Mamdani CFIS is a set of complex fuzzy rules used to solve diagnosis problems.	- Applying proposed model on six real datasets with higher accuracy than Mamdani FIS and ANFIS. - Limitation: There is redundancy in the rule base.
Turabieh et al. [58]	Dynamic ANFIS	- An ANFIS based model to predict missing values of incomplete samples based on complete samples. - Optimized each rule in the rule base using MSE.	- The model was validated on two medical datasets with good results in handling missing value datasets. - Limitation: Unable to deal with data that have phase or periodic interval.
Ahmad et al. [59]	Multilayer Mamdani FIS	- Proposed two-stage model in which Mamdani FIS is used to diagnose hepatitis B. - First layer determines hepatitis and second layer diagnoses hepatitis B.	- Experiments were done on a real dataset. The correct classification rate is high. - Limitation: This method is restricted to medical dataset of hepatitis. Does not concern periodic data.
This paper	M-CFIS-R	- Proposed a new rule reduction for M-CFIS [23] by using granular computing with complex similarity measures. - Theoretical proofs and theorems were provided.	- Achieved high accuracy of prediction in both the benchmark and real datasets. - Achieved the optimal number of rules. - Able to handle the limitations of rule redundancy and periodic data. - Limitation: Time-consuming.

6. Conclusions

This paper proposed a new M-CFIS-R system that incorporated fuzzy similarity measures such as Complex Fuzzy Cosine Similarity Measure (CFCSM), Complex Fuzzy Dice Similarity Measure (CFDSM), and Complex Fuzzy Jaccard Similarity Measure (CFJSM) in the granular computing mechanism. The aim is to achieve a better rule base than that in the original M-CFIS system. The rule base is improved by calculating the correlations between complex fuzzy rules based on different complex fuzzy measures. The similarities of complex fuzzy rules are finally determined by granular computing according to each label of Validation data. We then evaluate performance of the new complex fuzzy rule base on the Validation data by the same inference module. If the performance is better, we end the Training and proceed to Testing; otherwise, we repeat the process of using Granular Complex Fuzzy Measure to retrain. In the Testing phase, we perform a similar procedure with M-CFIS for testing the performance of the system with the reduced complex fuzzy rule base found in the Training phase. The M-CFIS-R model combines M-CFIS, complex fuzzy measures, and granular computing within the Training phase. By doing so, we obtain the new M-CFIS with better complex fuzzy rule base, which results in better performance than M-CFIS.

The experiments have been performed on the benchmark datasets from UCI Machine Learning Depository and real datasets from Gangthep Hospital, Thai Nguyen National Hospital, and Hanoi Medical University Hospital, Vietnam. Obviously, the results in Sections 5.2 and 5.3 clearly affirm that the proposed M-CFIS-R is better than M-CFIS in terms of accuracy, recall and precision. In general, all these indices of M-CFIS-R are higher than those of M-CFIS on average, with very low standard derivation. In most cases, the accuracy values of M-CFIS-R in the training data are smaller than those in the testing data, e.g., 92.89% vs. 95.84% on the WBCD, 86.37% vs. 89.47% on the Diabetes, and 87.69% vs. 88.44% on the Dental data. However, M-CFIS-R takes more time to identify the labels of the input samples because of using the granular computing with complex fuzzy measures. On the other hands, the rule base obtained from M-CFIS-R has better quality with a smaller number of rules than that of M-CFIS. In summary, the accuracy of M-CFIS-R is approximately 86.3–92.9% for the Training and 85–95.8% for the Testing data. The rule reduction in M-CFIS-R compared with M-CFIS is by around 4.8–22.1%. Lastly, M-CFIS-R is slower than M-CFIS by around 1.15 times in the Testing data on average.

However, the M-CFIS-R stops at local optimization but did not yet obtain a global optimal solution, since when evaluating the performance of a new fuzzy rule base in the Training, if it is better than that of M-CFIS, the algorithm stops. This should be enhanced further. Besides, the implementation time of the proposed model is also longer than that of M-CFIS. Different concepts of complex fuzzy measures, complex fuzzy integral, and other variants (i.e., Sugeno and Tsukamoto) of M-CFIS-R should be under investigation soon.

Author Contributions: Concept: L.H.S. and S.-Y.C.; methodology: L.H.S., L.T.H.L. and T.T.N.; software: L.T.H.L., T.M.T. and M.A.; validation: T.T.N., T.M.T. and N.L.G.; data curation: L.T.H.L. and T.M.T.; writing—original draft preparation: M.A. and L.T.H.L.; writing—review and editing: T.T.N., L.H.S., N.L.G. and S.-Y.C. All authors have read and agreed to the published version of the manuscript.

Funding: This research has been funded in part by the Graduate University of Science and Technology under grant number GUST.STS.ĐT2018-TT01. This work was supported in part by the Taiwan Building Technology Center from the Featured Areas Research Center Program within the framework of the Higher Education Sprout Project by the Ministry of Education in Taiwan.

Acknowledgments: We are grateful for the support from the staff of the Institute of Information Technology, Vietnam Academy of Science and Technology.

Conflicts of Interest: The authors declare no conflict of interest.

References

1. Zadeh, L.A. Fuzzy sets. *Inf. Control* **1965**, *8*, 338–353. [CrossRef]
2. Troussas, C.; Chrysafiadi, K.; Virvou, M. An intelligent adaptive fuzzy-based inference system for computer-assisted language learning. *Expert Syst. Appl.* **2019**, *127*, 85–96. [CrossRef]
3. Tiwari, L.; Raja, R.; Sharma, V.; Miri, R. Fuzzy Inference System for Efficient Lung Cancer Detection. In *Computer Vision and Machine Intelligence in Medical Image Analysis*; Springer: Singapore, 2020; pp. 33–41.
4. Sagir, A.M.; Sathasivam, S. A Novel Adaptive Neuro Fuzzy Inference System Based Classification Model for Heart Disease Prediction. *Pertanika J. Sci. Technol.* **2017**, *25*, 43–56.
5. Afriyie Mensah, R.; Xiao, J.; Das, O.; Jiang, L.; Xu, Q.; Alhassan, M.O. Application of Adaptive Neuro-Fuzzy Inference System in Flammability Parameter Prediction. *Polymers* **2020**, *12*, 122. [CrossRef]
6. Bakhshipour, A.; Zareiforoush, H.; Bagheri, I. Application of decision trees and fuzzy inference system for quality classification and modeling of black and green tea based on visual features. *J. Food Meas. Charact.* **2020**, 1–15. [CrossRef]
7. Manogaran, G.; Varatharajan, R.; Priyan, M.K. Hybrid recommendation system for heart disease diagnosis based on multiple kernel learning with adaptive neuro-fuzzy inference system. *Multimed. Tools Appl.* **2018**, *77*, 4379–4399. [CrossRef]
8. Handoyo, S.; Kusdarwati, H. Implementation of Fuzzy Inference System for Classification of Dengue Fever on the villages in Malang. In *IOP Conference Series: Materials Science and Engineering*; IOP Publishing: Bristol, UK, 2019; Volume 546, p. 052026.

9. Shastry, K.A.; Sanjay, H.A. Adaptive Neuro-Fuzzy Inference System in Agriculture. In *Fuzzy Expert Systems and Applications in Agricultural Diagnosis*; IGI Global: Hershey, PA, USA, 2020; pp. 130–153.
10. Abdolkarimi, E.S.; Mosavi, M.R. Wavelet-adaptive neural subtractive clustering fuzzy inference system to enhance low-cost and high-speed INS/GPS navigation system. *GPS Solut.* **2020**, *24*, 36. [CrossRef]
11. Pourjavad, E.; Shahin, A. The application of Mamdani fuzzy inference system in evaluating green supply chain management performance. *Int. J. Fuzzy Syst.* **2018**, *20*, 901–912. [CrossRef]
12. Lima-Junior, F.R.; Carpinetti, L.C.R. An adaptive network-based fuzzy inference system to supply chain performance evaluation based on SCOR® metrics. *Comput. Ind. Eng.* **2020**, *139*, 106191. [CrossRef]
13. Priyadarshi, N.; Azam, F.; Sharma, A.K.; Vardia, M. An Adaptive Neuro-Fuzzy Inference System-Based Intelligent Grid-Connected Photovoltaic Power Generation. In *Advances in Computational Intelligence*; Springer: Singapore, 2020; pp. 3–14.
14. Adoko, A.C.; Yagiz, S. Fuzzy Inference System-Based for TBM Field Penetration Index Estimation in Rock Mass. *Geotech. Geol. Eng.* **2019**, *37*, 1533–1553. [CrossRef]
15. Ramot, D.; Milo, R.; Friedman, M.; Kandel, A. Complex fuzzy sets. *IEEE Trans. Fuzzy Syst.* **2002**, *10*, 171–186. [CrossRef]
16. Ramot, D.; Friedman, M.; Langholz, G.; Kandel, A. Complex fuzzy logic. *IEEE Trans. Fuzzy Syst.* **2003**, *11*, 450–461. [CrossRef]
17. Ngan, T.T.; Lan, L.T.H.; Ali, M.; Tamir, D.; Son, L.H.; Tuan, T.M.; Rishe, N.; Kandel, A. Logic connectives of complex fuzzy sets. *Rom. J. Inf. Sci. Technol.* **2018**, *21*, 344–358.
18. Ali, M.; Smarandache, F. Complex neutrosophic set. *Neural Comput. Appl.* **2017**, *28*, 1817–1834. [CrossRef]
19. Ali, M.; Dat, L.Q.; Smarandache, F. Interval complex neutrosophic set: Formulation and applications in decision-making. *Int. J. Fuzzy Syst.* **2018**, *20*, 986–999. [CrossRef]
20. Greenfield, S.; Chiclana, F.; Dick, S. Interval-valued complex fuzzy logic. In Proceedings of the 2016 IEEE International Conference on Fuzzy Systems (FUZZ-IEEE), Vancouver, BC, Canada, 24–29 July 2016; pp. 2014–2019.
21. Garg, H.; Rani, D. Some generalized complex intuitionistic fuzzy aggregation operators and their application to multicriteria decision-making process. *Arabian J. Sci. Eng.* **2019**, *44*, 2679–2698. [CrossRef]
22. Man, J.Y.; Chen, Z.; Dick, S. Towards inductive learning of complex fuzzy inference systems. In Proceedings of the NAFIPS 2007-2007 Annual Meeting of the North American Fuzzy Information Processing Society, San Diego, CA, USA, 24–27 June 2007; pp. 415–420.
23. Selvachandran, G.; Quek, S.G.; Lan, L.T.H.; Giang, N.L.; Ding, W.; Abdel-Basset, M.; Albuquerque, V.H.C. A New Design of Mamdani Complex Fuzzy Inference System for Multi-attribute Decision Making Problems. *IEEE Trans. Fuzzy Syst.* **2019**. [CrossRef]
24. Tu, C.H.; Li, C. Multiple Function Approximation-A New Approach Using Complex Fuzzy Inference System. In *Asian Conference on Intelligent Information and Database Systems*; Springer: Cham, Switzerland, 2018; pp. 243–254.
25. Chen, Z.; Aghakhani, S.; Man, J.; Dick, S. ANCFIS: A neurofuzzy architecture employing complex fuzzy sets. *IEEE Trans. Fuzzy Syst.* **2010**, *19*, 305–322. [CrossRef]
26. Liu, Y.; Liu, F. An adaptive neuro-complex-fuzzy-inferential modeling mechanism for generating higher-order TSK models. *Neurocomputing* **2019**, *365*, 94–101. [CrossRef]
27. Yazdanbakhsh, O.; Dick, S. FANCFIS: Fast adaptive neuro-complex fuzzy inference system. *Int. J. Approx. Reason.* **2019**, *105*, 417–430. [CrossRef]
28. Alkouri, A.U.M.; Salleh, A.R. Linguistic variable, hedges and several distances on complex fuzzy sets. *J. Intell. Fuzzy Syst.* **2014**, *26*, 2527–2535. [CrossRef]
29. Hu, B.; Bi, L.; Dai, S.; Li, S. Distances of complex fuzzy sets and continuity of complex fuzzy operations. *J. Intell. Fuzzy Syst.* **2018**, *35*, 2247–2255. [CrossRef]
30. Dai, S.; Bi, L.; Hu, B. Distance measures between the interval-valued complex fuzzy sets. *Mathematics* **2019**, *7*, 549. [CrossRef]
31. Setnes, M.; Babuska, R.; Kaymak, U.; van Nauta Lemke, H.R. Similarity measures in fuzzy rule base simplification. *IEEE Trans. Syst. Man Cybern. Part B Cybern.* **1998**, *28*, 376–386. [CrossRef] [PubMed]
32. Mondal, K.; Pramanik, S.; Giri, B.C. Some similarity measures for MADM under a complex neutrosophic set environment. In *Optimization Theory Based on Neutrosophic and Plithogenic Sets*; Academic Press: Cambridge, MA, USA, 2020; pp. 87–116.

33. Rani, P.; Mishra, A.R.; Rezaei, G.; Liao, H.; Mardani, A. Extended Pythagorean fuzzy TOPSIS method based on similarity measure for sustainable recycling partner selection. *Int. J. Fuzzy Syst.* **2020**, *22*, 735–747. [CrossRef]
34. Jang, L.C.; Kim, H.M. On Choquet integrals with respect to a fuzzy complex valued fuzzy measure of fuzzy complex valued functions. *Int. J. Fuzzy Log. Intell. Syst.* **2018**, *10*, 224–229. [CrossRef]
35. Jang, L.C.; Kim, H.M. Some Properties of Choquet Integrals with Respect to a Fuzzy Complex Valued Fuzzy Measure. *Int. J. Fuzzy Log. Intell. Syst.* **2011**, *11*, 113–117. [CrossRef]
36. Ma, S.; Li, S. Complex fuzzy set-valued Complex fuzzy Measures and their properties. *Sci. World J.* **2014**. [CrossRef]
37. Ma, S.Q.; Chen, M.Q.; Zhao, Z.Q. The Complex Fuzzy Measure. In *Fuzzy Information Engineering and Operations Research Management*; Springer: Berlin/Heidelberg, Germany, 2014; pp. 137–145.
38. Ma, S.Q.; Li, S.G. Complex Fuzzy Set-Valued Complex Fuzzy Integral and Its Convergence Theorem. In *Fuzzy Systems Operations Research and Management*; Springer: Cham, Switzerland, 2016; pp. 143–155.
39. Garg, H.; Rani, D. Some results on information measures for complex intuitionistic fuzzy sets. *Int. J. Intell. Syst.* **2019**, *34*, 2319–2363. [CrossRef]
40. Ngan, R.T.; Ali, M.; Tamir, D.E.; Rishe, N.D.; Kandel, A. Representing complex intuitionistic fuzzy set by quaternion numbers and applications to decision making. *Appl. Soft Comput.* **2020**, *87*, 105961. [CrossRef]
41. Yazdanbakhsh, O.; Dick, S. Forecasting of multivariate time series via complex fuzzy logic. *IEEE Trans. Syst. Man Cybern. Syst.* **2017**, *47*, 2160–2171. [CrossRef]
42. Tu, C.H.; Li, C. Multitarget prediction—A new approach using sphere complex fuzzy sets. *Eng. Appl. Artif. Intell.* **2019**, *79*, 45–57. [CrossRef]
43. Li, C.; Tu, C.H. Complex neural fuzzy system and its application on multi-class prediction—A novel approach using complex fuzzy sets, IIM and multi-swarm learning. *Appl. Soft Comput.* **2019**, *84*, 105735. [CrossRef]
44. Singh, P.K. Granular-based decomposition of complex fuzzy context and its analysis. *Prog. Artif. Intell.* **2019**, *8*, 181–193. [CrossRef]
45. Zhang, G.; Dillon, T.S.; Cai, K.Y.; Ma, J.; Lu, J. Operation properties and δ-equalities of complex fuzzy sets. *Int. J. Approx. Reason.* **2009**, *50*, 1227–1249. [CrossRef]
46. Bargiela, A.; Pedrycz, W. Granular computing. In *Handbook on Computational Intelligence: Volume 1: Fuzzy Logic, Systems, Artificial Neural Networks, and Learning Systems*; World Scientific publishing: Singapore, 2016; pp. 43–66.
47. Liu, H.; Cocea, M. Granular computing-based approach of rule learning for binary classification. *Granul. Comput.* **2019**, *4*, 275–283. [CrossRef]
48. Bezdek, J.C. *Pattern Recognition with Ffuzzy Objective Function Algorithms*; Plenum Press: New York, NY, USA, 1981.
49. The UCI Machine Learning Repository. Available online: http://archive.ics.uci.edu/ml/datasets.html (accessed on 9 April 2020).
50. Breast Cancer. Available online: http://archive.ics.uci.edu/ml/datasets/breast+cancer+wisconsin+%28original%29 (accessed on 9 April 2020).
51. Diabetes Databases. Available online: http://biostat.mc.vanderbilt.edu/wiki/Main/DataSets (accessed on 9 April 2020).
52. Gangthep Hospital. Available online: http://benhviengangthep.gov.vn/ (accessed on 9 April 2020).
53. Hanoi Medical University Hospital. Available online: http://benhviendaihocyhanoi.com/ (accessed on 9 April 2020).
54. Ghazali, K.H.; Mustafa, M.M.; Hussain, A.; Bandar, M.E.C.; Kuantan, G. Feature Extraction technique using SIFT keypoints descriptors. In Proceedings of the The International Conference on Electrical and Engineering and Informatics Institut Technology, Institut Teknologi Bandung, Bandung, Indonesia, 17–19 June 2007; pp. 17–19.
55. Ahonen, T.; Hadid, A.; Pietikainen, M. Face description with local binary patterns: Application to face recognition. *IEEE Trans. Pattern Anal. Mach. Intell.* **2006**, *28*, 2037–2041. [CrossRef]
56. Oad, K.K.; DeZhi, X.; Butt, P.K. A Fuzzy Rule Based Approach to Predict Risk Level of Heart Disease. *Glob. J. Comput. Sci. Technol.* **2014**, *14*, 16–22.

57. Lai, Y.H.; Lin, P.L. Effective segmentation for dental X-ray images using texture-based fuzzy inference system. In *International Conference on Advanced Concepts for Intelligent Vision Systems*; Springer: Berlin/Heidelberg, Germany, 2008; pp. 936–947.
58. Turabieh, H.; Mafarja, M.; Mirjalili, S. Dynamic Adaptive Network-Based Fuzzy Inference System (D-ANFIS) for the Imputation of Missing Data for Internet of Medical Things Applications. *IEEE Internet Things J.* **2019**, *6*, 9316–9325. [CrossRef]
59. Ahmad, G.; Khan, M.A.; Abbas, S.; Athar, A.; Khan, B.S.; Aslam, M.S. Automated diagnosis of hepatitis b using multilayer mamdani fuzzy inference system. *J. Healthc. Eng.* **2019**. [CrossRef]

© 2020 by the authors. Licensee MDPI, Basel, Switzerland. This article is an open access article distributed under the terms and conditions of the Creative Commons Attribution (CC BY) license (http://creativecommons.org/licenses/by/4.0/).

Article

An Integrated Approach of Best-Worst Method (BWM) and Triangular Fuzzy Sets for Evaluating Driver Behavior Factors Related to Road Safety

Sarbast Moslem [1], Muhammet Gul [2], Danish Farooq [1], Erkan Celik [2], Omid Ghorbanzadeh [3],* and Thomas Blaschke [3]

1. Department of Transport Technology and Economics, Budapest University of Technology and Economics Stoczek u. 2, H-1111 Budapest, Hungary; moslem.sarbast@mail.bme.hu (S.M.); farooq.danish@mail.bme.hu (D.F.)
2. Department of Industrial Engineering, Munzur University, 62000 Tunceli, Turkey; muhammetgul@munzur.edu.tr (M.G.); erkancelik@munzur.edu.tr (E.C.)
3. Department of Geoinformatics, University of Salzburg, 5020 Salzburg, Austria; Thomas.Blaschke@sbg.ac.at
* Correspondence: omid.ghorbanzadeh@stud.sbg.ac.at

Received: 6 February 2020; Accepted: 9 March 2020; Published: 13 March 2020

Abstract: Driver behavior plays a major role in road safety because it is considered as a significant argument in traffic accident avoidance. Drivers mostly face various risky driving factors which lead to fatal accidents or serious injury. This study aims to evaluate and prioritize the significant driver behavior factors related to road safety. In this regard, we integrated a decision-making model of the Best-Worst Method (BWM) with the triangular fuzzy sets as a solution for optimizing our complex decision-making problem, which is associated with uncertainty and ambiguity. Driving characteristics are different in different driving situations which indicate the ambiguous and complex attitude of individuals, and decision-makers (DMs) need to improve the reliability of the decision. Since the crisp values of factors may be inadequate to model the real-world problem considering the vagueness and the ambiguity, and providing the pairwise comparisons with the requirement of less compared data, the BWM integrated with triangular fuzzy sets is used in the study to evaluate risky driver behavior factors for a designed three-level hierarchical structure. The model results provide the most significant driver behavior factors that influence road safety for each level based on evaluator responses on the Driver Behavior Questionnaire (DBQ). Moreover, the model generates a more consistent decision process by the new consistency ratio of F-BWM. An adaptable application process from the model is also generated for future attempts.

Keywords: fuzzy best worst method; driver behavior factors; road safety; DBQ; Budapest city

1. Introduction

According to data from the worldwide road safety status report, annual traffic deaths are reported to reach 1.35 million [1]. According to this report, it was stated that the road safety performance for Hungary is below the EU average. In 2018, the proportion of people died on the roads in Hungary was set at 64 per million, and this statistic increased by 1% compared to the previous year [2]. However, the Road Safety Action Program (2014–2016) was integrated with the Hungarian Transport Strategy in line with the goal of reducing the number of road deaths by 50% between 2010 and 2020. According to the Road Safety Action Program situation analysis, most accidents stemmed from human-induced factors. Therefore, addressing them becomes a dynamic target of road safety actions [3]. According to the estimates of some previous studies, approximately 90% of road traffic accidents have been found to be the sole or major causative factor of human factors [4–6].

Many driver behavior factors emerge as dynamic, deliberate violations of the rules and mistakes resulting from less driving experience, while others appear as a result of carelessness, momentary errors, or failure to perform an action, the latter being generally age-related [7,8]. In order to alleviate the driver's workload and increase the basic services of active vehicle safety systems, identification of risky driver behavior factors has been handled. However, these systems based on the average driver performance on the road and individual driver's attitudes were seldom taken into consideration [9].

To analyze the risky driving behavior for road safety, the Driver Behavior Questionnaire (DBQ) was first introduced as a tool in the studies in the 1990s [10,11]. Reason et al., (1990) detected three kinds of driving behaviors, i.e., errors, lapses, and violations, and analyzed the association between driving behavior and accident involvement. Accordingly, human error is an unintended act or decision. Slips and lapses happen in very familiar tasks that we can execute without very much conscious consideration. Violations are intended failures—intentionally doing the wrong act [12–14]. In addition, the Driver Behavior Questionnaire (DBQ), with an extended version, was used to evaluate aberrant driver behaviors [12]. While the extended version of the DBQ consists of aggressive and ordinary violations, lapses and errors [14]. An aggressive violation behavior was identified as contradictory behavior towards other road users [13].

The previous study observed that the analytic hierarchy process (AHP) method was an effective approach in terms of prioritizing suburban road safety indicator to access the factors which reduce the number and severity of accidents in Iran [15]. However, the prioritizing of the AHP method is rather imprecise; and the subjective assessment by perception, evaluation, development, and assortment based on the preference of decision-makers (DMs) have a significant impact on AHP outcomes [16]. To deal with such tricky problems, many researchers integrate fuzzy theory with AHP to incorporate its results [17–21]. The fuzzy AHP, compared to AHP and the statistical methods of prioritization, has greater precision and certainty. Although in AHP, the experts compare the alternatives using their competencies and intellectual skills, but it may not completely reflect the human thinking style. However, the use of fuzzy numbers is more consistent in human linguistic representations. Therefore, the decisions can be made more reliable and more precise in the real world using fuzzy numbers [22].

However, it is not possible to ignore the inconsistency in AHP-based pairwise comparison matrices (PCMs) because inconsistency often occurs in practice [23,24]. The inconsistency in PCMs is the main drawback of AHP and can lead to uncertain results. In general, it is obvious that if the PCM is 5×5 or larger in the decision structure, the relatively consistent filling of this size of matrix by non-expert evaluators requires significant effort [16].

In order to solve this consistency problem in traditional AHP and to minimize PC surveys, Rezaei introduced the BWM method [25] to reduce the number of pairwise comparisons in the traditional AHP process. As a new technique, there are still gaps in both the theoretical structure and application areas of BWM. Thus, some questions remained open in terms of conditions and limitations on traditional AHP usage. For the BWM itself, the appropriate consistency ratio value and the inconsistency improving procedures can be addressed. Additionally, the BWM within other contexts could investigate the uncertainty. The model's multiple optimality solution in BWM can be determined from other angles [26].

Due to the statistic that BWM is sensitive to preferences of DMs, it is very complicated to calculate the accurate weights when the DM utilizes natural language, such as "very high", "medium", or "very low", to express a type of overall preferences [27]. Therefore, in this study, the crisp preferences in BMW are stretched with triangular fuzzy numbers to overcome the inherent ambiguity of the DM's decision in real decision-making problems. Furthermore, this F-BWM model gives fewer PCs with high consistency of the pairwise comparison matrix. Saaty explains that consistency will not be good when the number of factors exceeds 7 ± 2 [28]. This is also a theoretical justification of Miller's psychological investigation [29]. Therefore, the proposed model produces more consistent and reliable results with fewer PCs. In summary, BWM with triangular fuzzy sets merely considers reference pairwise comparisons and handles inconsistency in an effective manner versus conventional AHP with triangular fuzzy sets. Therefore, it presents an easy and accurate decision framework.

2. Literature Review

In the literature, BWM and its fuzzy extended versions are frequently applied to various areas, from manufacturing to supply chain management and transportation [30]. Although plenty of papers have been published in these areas, there are very few contributions applied to the evaluation of driving behaviors for road safety. Most of the recent BWM/F-BWM contributions focus on supply chain design, supplier or green supplier evaluation, and occupational or environmental safety risk analysis [31].

Regarding supply chain performance and supplier assessment, Badi and Ballem [31] studied supplier selection problems in the pharmaceutical industry using an integrated rough BWM method. While the Z-number BWM is proposed by Aboutorab et al. [32] for supplier development problem, intuitionistic F-BWM is applied for the green supplier selection problem by Tian et al. [33]. Wu et al. [34] integrated the interval type-2 fuzzy sets and BWM for green supplier selection problems.

In the risk assessment literature, AHP or F-AHP is mostly used as a weighted factor scoring method for risk parameters. After BWM is introduced, researchers have begun to use it instead of AHP due to its superiorities. BWM/F-BWM is used to assign weights to risk parameters like AHP. In many studies, it is frequently integrated with FMEA [35–40]. In some other studies, it is integrated with MCDM such as interval triangular fuzzy Delphi method under 5 × 5 matrix [41], F-TOPSIS [42], and artificial intelligence-based methods such as Bayesian networks [43,44] and business impact analysis [45].

In the light of this brief review of the previous studies related to BWM and F-BWM applied to diverse selection and ranking problems, it is observed that BWM has not integrated yet with fuzzy sets for the addressed problem "driving behavior evaluation". Therefore, in the proposed approach, F-BWM is utilized to determine the importance weight of driver behavior factors related to road safety. As fuzzy extensions, triangular fuzzy numbers are used in the existed study since they reflect uncertainty in the decision-making process well. Additionally, the DBQ is attached to the F-BWM to strengthen the methodology of the study. The benefits of the applied F-BWM methodology are as follows: (1) From the theoretical viewpoint, it has designed a solid decision-making framework with the aid of triangular fuzzy numbers and, modeled uncertainty well. Although the literature covers methods like AHP and BWM in determining the importance weights of factors, the F-BWM methodology fits well with the structure of the problem handled in this study. The full consistency method (FUCOM) is the simplest example. It is proposed by Pamučar et al. [46] and applied by many scholars [47–49] to various MCDM problems. (2) From an application viewpoint, the study considers a DBQ and priorities the driving behavior factors relating to road safety. Previous studies regarding driving behavior factor evaluation are mostly based on statistical inference logic either cross-sectional or cross-cultural. However, this study handles the problem in an MCDM manner. Additionally, as a case study, the Budapest city of Hungary is studied to demonstrate applicability. Of course, the approach can be adapted to other cities.

3. Materials and Methods

3.1. Driver Behavior Questionnaire (DBQ) Survey

The study utilized the driver behavior questionnaire (DBQ) as a tool to collect driver behavior data on perceived road safety issues from Budapest city. To do so, the car drivers having at least fifteen-year driving experience were asked to fill the DBQ by face-to-face method, which increased its reliability. The drivers who participated in this study were the faculty members of the Department of Transport Technology and Economics and the Department of Control for Transportation and Vehicle Systems at Budapest University of Technology and Economics who also have transportation engineering research experience. In addition, the participants were asked to indicate how often they likely to involve in each of the observed driver behaviors in the recent year using Saaty's traditional ratio scale (1–9). The questionnaire survey was designed in two parts: The first part intended to measure demographic data about the participants and results are tabulated in Table 1. The results stated the mean and standard deviation (SD) values of observed data such as age, gender, and driving experience based on drivers' responses. In addition, we used digits (1, 0) for assessment purposes to explain simply the characteristics of gender.

Table 1. Sample characteristics.

Variables	Data Analysis Results
N	100
Age: Mean (SD)	32.341 (3.421)
Gender (1 = male, 0 = female): Mean (SD)	0.845 (0.125)
Duration of driving license: Mean (SD)	15.312 (1.589)

The second part of DBQ designed on Saaty scale (1977) to analyze the significant driver behavior factors related to road safety. For evaluation purposes, the driver behavior factors were designed in a three-level hierarchical structure and symbolized each factor with alphabet 'F' as shown in Figure 1. These driver behavior factors have a significant influence on road safety. Some recent studies considered the specified driver behavior factors for evaluation of road safety performance by different evaluator groups [50–52].

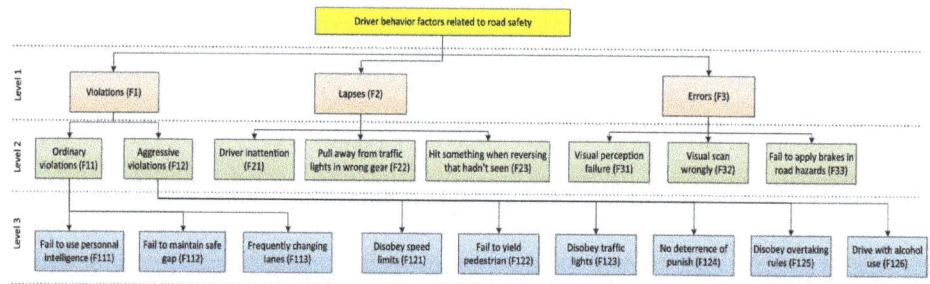

Figure 1. The hierarchical structure of the problem [50].

3.2. Overview on Best Worst Method (BWM)

The general BWM method was created by Rezaei (2015) to derive the weights of the criteria with the smaller number of comparisons and more consistent comparisons. The most important factor is the one which has the most vital role in making the decision, while the less important has the opposite role in the decision process. Furthermore, the BMW does not only derive the weights independently but it can also be combined with other multi-criteria-decision-making methods [53–55].

- The procedure of the BWM can be highlighted as follows:
- Identification of the decision-making problem and its factors
- Determination of the most crucial and least crucial factor
- Determination of the preference of the most crucial factor over all the other factors
- Determination of the preference of the least crucial factor over all the other factors
- Make the consistency check
- Determination of the importance weight of the factors

We consider a set of elements $(e_1, e_2, \ldots, e_n)$ and then select the most important element and compare it to others using Saaty's scale (1–9). Accordingly, this provides the most important element to other vectors would be: $E_a = (e_{a1}, e_{a2}, \ldots, e_{an})$, and obviously $e_{aa} = 1$. However, the least important element to other vectors would be: $E_b = (e_{1b}, e_{2b}, \ldots, e_{nb})^T$ by using the same scale.

After deriving the optimal weight scores, the consistency has been checked through computing the consistency ratio from the following formula:

$$\xi^2 - (1 + 2u_{BW})\xi + (u_{BW}^2 - u_{BW}) = 0 \quad Consistency\ Ratio = \frac{\xi^*}{Consistency\ Index} \tag{1}$$

where Table 2 provides us the consistency index values:

Table 2. Consistency index (CI) values.

e_{ab}	1	2	3	4	5	6	7	8	9
Consistency Index (max ξ)	0.0	0.44	1.0	1.63	2.3	3.0	3.73	4.47	5.23

To obtain an optimal weight for all elements, the maximum definite differences are $\left|\frac{w_a}{w_j} - e_{aj}\right|$ and $\left|\frac{w_j}{w_b} - e_{jb}\right|$, and for all j is minimized. If we assumed a positive-sum for the weights, the following problem would be solved:

$$\min \max_j \left\{ \left|\frac{w_a}{w_j} - e_{aj}\right|, \left|\frac{w_j}{w_b} - e_{jb}\right| \right\}$$

s.t.

$$\sum_j b_j = 1 \tag{2}$$

$$b_j \geq 0, \text{for all } j$$

The problem could be transferred into the following problem:

$$\min \xi$$

s.t.

$$\left|\frac{w_a}{w_j} - e_{aj}\right| \leq \xi, \text{for all } j$$

$$\left|\frac{w_j}{w_b} - e_{jb}\right| \leq \xi \text{ for all } j \tag{3}$$

$$\sum_j b_j = 1$$

$$b_j \geq 0, \text{for all } j$$

By solving this problem, we obtain the optimal weights and ξ^*. For further reading on priority criteria, one may refer to [56,57]. While w_B presents the importance weights of best criterion, w_W shows the e importance weights of the worst criterion. e_{Bj} denotes the evaluation of the best to others, e_{Wj} denotes the evaluation of the others to worst.

3.3. The Proposed F-BWM Model

3.3.1. General Information on Fuzzy Sets

Prior to explaining F-BWM, some fundamental notations regarding fuzzy sets can be useful. Zadeh [58] introduced fuzzy sets for better reflecting of the human judgments and assessment in the decision making process. It is considered as a more robust tool to deal with vagueness, ambiguity, and uncertainty. Many decision-making problems consist of goals, constraints, and possible actions that are not known precisely [58]. The usage of fuzzy sets is better for transforming the linguistic decision of human judgment. Hence, many real-world decision-making problems have used fuzzy sets [59,60]. A triangular fuzzy number consists of lower, medium and upper numbers of the fuzzy as $\tilde{A} = (l, m, u)$

where l, m and u which is crisp and real numbers ($x \leq y \leq z$). The membership function of a triangular fuzzy number can be defined as follows:

$$\mu_{\widetilde{A}} = \begin{cases} 0, & x < l \\ (x-l)/(m-l), & l \leq x \leq m \\ (u-x)/(u-m), & m \leq x \leq u \\ 0 & x \geq u \end{cases} \quad (4)$$

A triangular fuzzy number is presented in Figure 2. The linguistic terms and triangular fuzzy numbers are also given in Table 3.

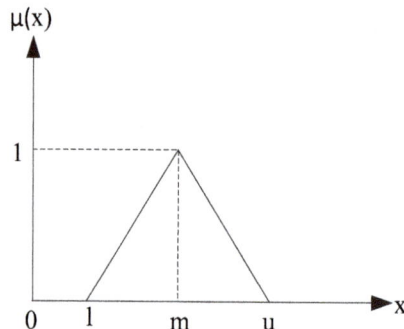

Figure 2. Triangular fuzzy number.

Table 3. The linguistic terms and fuzzy numbers.

Linguistic Term	Triangular Fuzzy Number
Equally Importance (EI)	(1, 1, 1)
Weakly Important (WI)	(2/3, 1, 1.5)
Fairly Important (FI)	(1.5, 2, 2.5)
Very Important (VI)	(2.5, 3, 3.5)
Absolutely Important (AI)	(3.5, 4, 4.5)

$\widetilde{A}_1 = (l_1, m_1, u_1)$ and $\widetilde{A}_2 = (l_2, m_2, u_2)$ are any two triangular fuzzy numbers, and the mathematical calculation of the two triangular fuzzy numbers is defined as follows:

The addition operation:

$$\widetilde{A}_1 + \widetilde{A}_2 = (l_1 + l_2, m_1 + m_2, u_1 + u_2) \quad (5)$$

The subtraction operation:

$$\widetilde{A}_1 - \widetilde{A}_2 = (l_1 - u_2, m_1 - m_2, u_1 - l_2) \quad (6)$$

The multiplication operation:

$$\widetilde{A}_1 \times \widetilde{A}_2 = (l_1 x l_2, m_1 x m_2, u_1 x u_2) \quad (7)$$

The arithmetic operation:

$$k x \widetilde{A}_1 = (kxl_1, kxm_1, kxu_1), (k > 0) \quad (8)$$

$$\frac{\widetilde{A_1}}{k} = \left(\frac{l_1}{k}, \frac{m_1}{k}, \frac{u_1}{k}\right), (k > 0) \tag{9}$$

The graded mean integration representation (GMIR) $R(\widetilde{A_i})$ of a triangular fuzzy number for the ranking of triangular fuzzy number is calculate as follows:

$$R(\widetilde{A_i}) = \frac{l_i + 4m_i + u_i}{6} \tag{10}$$

3.3.2. Fuzzy Best-Worst Method (F-BWM)

The BWM was proposed by Rezai (2015) for multi-criteria decision-making problems considering pairwise comparison manner. The best and worst criteria are determined in BWM [33]. Different fuzzy sets-based versions have been proposed as intuitionistic fuzzy sets [32,61], triangular fuzzy numbers [27,62], Z-numbers [34], dominance degree [63], and interval type-2 fuzzy number [64,65]. Mi et al. [66] presented a survey of BWM applications and extensions. The interested readers and researchers may refer to this study in detail.

In BWM, there are n criteria, and the fuzzy pairwise comparisons are applied based on the linguistic terms of decision-makers as presented in Table 3. Then, the linguistic evaluations are transformed into triangular fuzzy numbers. The fuzzy comparison matrix is getting as follows:

$$\widetilde{A} = \begin{array}{c} \\ c_1 \\ c_2 \\ \vdots \\ c_n \end{array} \begin{bmatrix} c_1 & c_2 & \cdots & c_n \\ \widetilde{a}_{11} & \widetilde{a}_{12} & \cdots & \widetilde{a}_{1n} \\ \widetilde{a}_{21} & \widetilde{a}_{22} & \cdots & \widetilde{a}_{2n} \\ \vdots & \vdots & \ddots & \vdots \\ \widetilde{a}_{n1} & \widetilde{a}_{n2} & \cdots & \widetilde{a}_{nn} \end{bmatrix}$$

where $\widetilde{a}_{ij}$ denotes the relative fuzzy preference of criterion i to criterion j, which is a triangular fuzzy number; $\widetilde{a}_{ij} = (1,1,1)$ when $i = j$.

In this paper, we will present the detailed steps of fuzzy BWM. The detailed steps of fuzzy BWM are used for obtaining the fuzzy weights [62].

Step 1. Construct the criteria system. A set of criteria reflects the performances of different criteria. Suppose there are n decision criteria $\{c_1, c_2, \ldots, c_n\}$.

Step 2. Determine the best criterion and the worst criterion. In this step, the best criterion and the worst criterion is determined by experts based on the constructed decision criteria system. The best criterion is denoted as c_B, and the worst criterion is also denoted as c_W.

Step 3. Perform the fuzzy reference comparisons for the best criterion. According to the pairwise comparison $\widetilde{a}_{ij}$, c_B is the best criterion; c_W is the worst criterion. The fuzzy preferences of the best criterion over all the criteria can be determined. Then, the fuzzy comparisons are converted to triangular fuzzy numbers. The fuzzy Best-to-Others vector is obtained as follows:

$$\widetilde{A}_B = \{\widetilde{a}_{B1}, \widetilde{a}_{B2}, \ldots, \widetilde{a}_{Bn}\}$$

where $\widetilde{A}_B$ denotes the fuzzy best-to-others vector; $\widetilde{a}_{Bj}$ denotes the fuzzy comparison of the best criterion c_B over criterion j, $j = 1, 2, \ldots, n$. It is known that $\widetilde{a}_{BB} = (1, 1, 1)$.

Step 4. Perform the fuzzy reference comparisons for the worst criterion. In this step, the fuzzy preferences of all the criteria over the worst criterion can be determined. They are transformed into triangular fuzzy numbers. The fuzzy others-to-worst vector can be obtained as:

$$\widetilde{A}_W = \{\widetilde{a}_{1W}, \widetilde{a}_{2W}, \ldots, \widetilde{a}_{nW}\}$$

where $\widetilde{A}_W$ denotes the fuzzy others-to-worst vector; $\widetilde{a}_{iW}$ denotes the fuzzy comparison of the worst criterion c_W, $i = 1, 2, \ldots, n$. It is known that $\widetilde{a}_{WW} = (1, 1, 1)$.

Step 5. Determine the optimal fuzzy weights $(\tilde{w}_1^*, \tilde{w}_2^*, \ldots, \tilde{w}_n^*)$. In this step, the optimal fuzzy weight for each criterion is determined for each fuzzy pair $\tilde{w}_B/\tilde{w}_j$ and $\tilde{w}_j/\tilde{w}_W$. It should have $\tilde{w}_B/\tilde{w}_j = \tilde{a}_{Bj}$ and $\tilde{w}_j/\tilde{w}_W = \tilde{a}_{jW}$. A solution is obtained that the maximum absolute gaps $\left|\frac{\tilde{w}_B}{\tilde{w}_j} - \tilde{a}_{Bj}\right|$ and $\left|\frac{\tilde{w}_j}{\tilde{w}_W} - \tilde{a}_{jW}\right|$ for all j are minimized to satisfy these conditions for all j. $\tilde{w}_B, \tilde{w}_j$ and $\tilde{w}_W$ in fuzzy BWM are triangular fuzzy numbers. In some cases, we prefer to use $\tilde{w}_j = \left(l_j^w, m_j^w, u_j^w\right)$ for optimal criteria selection. The triangular fuzzy weight of the criterion $\tilde{w}_j = \left(l_j^w, m_j^w, u_j^w\right)$ is transformed to a crisp value using Equation (11). Consequently, the constrained optimization problem is constructed for obtaining the optimal fuzzy weights $(\tilde{w}_1^*, \tilde{w}_2^*, \ldots, \tilde{w}_n^*)$ as follows:

$$\min \max_j \left\{ \left|\frac{\tilde{w}_B}{\tilde{w}_j} - \tilde{a}_{Bj}\right|, \left|\frac{\tilde{w}_j}{\tilde{w}_W} - \tilde{a}_{jW}\right| \right\}$$

$$\text{s.t.} \begin{cases} \sum_{j=1}^n R(\tilde{w}_i) = 1 \\ l_j^w \leq m_j^w \leq u_j^w \\ l_j^w \geq 0 \\ j = 1, 2, \ldots, n \end{cases} \tag{11}$$

where $\tilde{w}_B = \left(l_B^w, m_B^w, u_B^w\right)$, $\tilde{w}_j = \left(l_j^w, m_j^w, u_j^w\right)$, $\tilde{w}_W = \left(l_W^w, m_W^w, u_W^w\right)$, $\tilde{a}_{Bj} = \left(l_{Bj}^w, m_{Bj}^w, u_{Bj}^w\right)$ and $\tilde{a}_{jW} = \left(l_{jW}^w, m_{jW}^w, u_{jW}^w\right)$. Equation (12) is transformed to the nonlinearly constrained optimization problem:

$$\min \xi$$

$$\text{s.t.} \begin{cases} \left|\frac{\tilde{w}_B}{\tilde{w}_j} - \tilde{a}_{Bj}\right| \leq \xi \\ \left|\frac{\tilde{w}_j}{\tilde{w}_W} - \tilde{a}_{jW}\right| \leq \xi \\ \sum_{j=1}^n R(\tilde{w}_i) = 1 \\ l_j^w \leq m_j^w \leq u_j^w \\ l_j^w \geq 0 \\ j = 1, 2, \ldots, n \end{cases} \tag{12}$$

where $\xi = \left(l^\xi, m^\xi, u^\xi\right)$.

Considering $l^\xi \leq m^\xi \leq u^\xi$, it is supposed that $\xi^* = (k^*, k^*, k^*)$, $k^* \leq l^\xi$ then Equation (13) can be transferred as:

$$\min \xi^*$$

$$\text{s.t.} \begin{cases} \left|\frac{\left(l_B^w, m_B^w, u_B^w\right)}{\left(l_j^w, m_j^w, u_j^w\right)} - \left(l_{Bj}, m_{Bj}, u_{Bj}\right)\right| \leq (k^*, k^*, k^*) \\ \left|\frac{\left(l_j^w, m_j^w, u_j^w\right)}{\left(l_W^w, m_W^w, u_W^w\right)} - \left(l_{jW}, m_{jW}, u_{jW}\right)\right| \leq (k^*, k^*, k^*) \\ \sum_{j=1}^n R(\tilde{w}_i) = 1 \\ l_j^w \leq m_j^w \leq u_j^w \\ l_j^w \geq 0 \\ j = 1, 2, \ldots, n \end{cases} \tag{13}$$

Step 6. Determine the consistency ratio. The consistency ratio is determined in the same way as BWM. In this step, the consistency index for fuzzy BWM is calculated.

The main steps of the proposed F-BWM model are discussed in Figure 3.

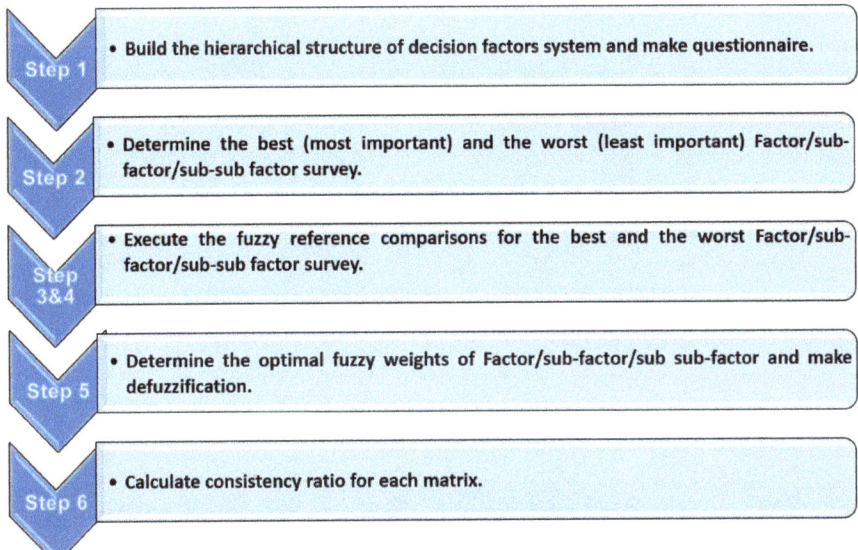

Figure 3. The main steps of the proposed F-BWM model.

4. Results

The F-BWM model was applied to evaluate driver behavior factors related to road safety and to compute weight scores. Furthermore, the reliability of the PCs consistency in F-BWM was checked, and it was acceptable for each matrix. In the following, step by step application of F-BWM to the problem is provided. In this application, three main factors, eight sub-factors, and nine sub-sub-factors are evaluated. We will first present the F-BWM model for main factors as violations (F_1), lapses (F_2), and errors (F_3). The violations (F_1) and lapses (F_2) are determined as the most significant and the less significant factor, respectively (Step 2). The fuzzy reference comparisons are applied, and the linguistic terms for fuzzy preferences of the most significant factor and the less significant factor are given in Tables 4 and 5, respectively.

Table 4. The linguistic terms for fuzzy preferences of the most important factor.

Factor	F1	F2	F3
Best factor (F1)	EI	FI	WI

Table 5. The linguistic terms for fuzzy preferences of the less important factor.

Factor	Worst Factor (F2)
F1	FI
F2	EI
F3	WI

Then, the fuzzy most significant-to-others vector and the fuzzy others-to-less significant can be obtained with respect to Table 3 as follows (Step 3).

$$\tilde{a}_B = [(1, 1, 1), (3/2, 2, 5/2), (2/3, 1, 3/2)] \tilde{a}_W = [(3/2, 2, 5/2), (1, 1, 1), (2/3, 1, 3/2)]$$

Then, for obtaining the optimal fuzzy weights of all the main factors, the nonlinearly constrained model is constructed as follows in Equation (14):

$$\min \xi^*$$

$$\text{s.t.} \begin{cases} \left| \frac{(l_{f1}^w, m_{f1}^w, u_{f1}^w)}{(l_{f1}^w, m_{f1}^w, u_{f1}^w)} - (l_{f11}, m_{f11}, u_{f11}) \right| \le (e^*, e^*, e^*) \\ \left| \frac{(l_{f1}^w, m_{f1}^w, u_{f1}^w)}{(l_{f2}^w, m_{f2}^w, u_{f2}^w)} - (l_{f12}, m_{f12}, u_{f1\|2}) \right| \le (e^*, e^*, e^*) \\ \left| \frac{(l_{f1}^w, m_{f1}^w, u_{f1}^w)}{(l_{f3}^w, m_{f3}^w, u_{f3}^w)} - (l_{f13}, m_{f13}, u_{f13}) \right| \le (e^*, e^*, e^*) \\ \left| \frac{(l_{f1}^w, m_{f1}^w, u_{f1}^w)}{(l_{f2}^w, m_{f2}^w, u_{f2}^w)} - (l_{f12}, m_{f12}, u_{f12}) \right| \le (e^*, e^*, e^*) \\ \left| \frac{(l_{f2}^w, m_{f2}^w, u_{f2}^w)}{(l_{f2}^w, m_{f2}^w, u_{f2}^w)} - (l_{f22}, m_{f22}, u_{f22}) \right| \le (e^*, e^*, e^*) \\ \left| \frac{(l_{f3}^w, m_{f3}^w, u_{f3}^w)}{(l_{f2}^w, m_{f2}^w, u_{f2}^w)} - (l_{f32}, m_{f32}, u_{f32}) \right| \le (e^*, e^*, e^*) \\ \sum_{j=1}^{3} R(\widetilde{w}_j) = 1 \\ l_{fj}^w \le m_{fj}^w \le u_{fj}^w \\ l_{fj}^w \ge 0 \\ j = 1, 2, 3 \end{cases} \quad (14)$$

Then, the following nonlinearly constrained optimization problem is obtained using represented by crisp numbers as in Equation (15).

$$\min e$$

$$\text{s.t.} \begin{cases} l_{f1} - 1.5 * u_{f2} - u_{f2} * e \le 0; l_{f1} - 1.5 * u_{f2} + u_{f2} * e \ge 0; m_{f1} - 2 * m_{f2} - m_{f2} * e \le 0; \\ m_{f1} - 2 * m_{f2} + m_{f2} * e \ge 0; u_{f1} - 2.5 * l_{f2} - l_{f2} * e \le 0; u_{f1} - 2.5 * l_{f2} + l_{f2} * e \ge 0; \\ l_{f1} - \frac{2}{3} * u_{f3} - u_{f3} * e \le 0; l_{f1} - \frac{2}{3} * u_{f3} + u_{f3} * e \ge 0; m_{f1} - 1 * m_{f3} - m_{f3} * e \le 0; \\ m_{f1} - 1 * m_{f3} + m_{f3} * e \ge 0; u_{f1} - 1.5 * l_{f3} - l_{f3} * e \le 0; u_{f1} - 1.5 * l_{f3} + l_{f3} * e \ge 0; \\ l_{f3} - \frac{2}{3} * u_{f2} - u_{f2} * e \le 0; l_{f3} - \frac{2}{3} * u_{f2} + u_{f2} * e \ge 0; m_{f3} - 1 * m_{f2} - m_{f2} * e \le 0; \\ m_{f3} - 1 * m_{f2} + m_{f2} * e \ge 0; u_{f3} - 1.5 * l_{f2} - l_{f2} * e \le 0; u_{f3} - 1.5 * l_{f2} + l_{f2} * e \ge 0; \\ l_{f1} \le m_{f1} \le u_{f1}; l_{f2} \le m_{f2} \le u_{f2}; l_{f3} \le m_{f3} \le u_{f3}; \\ \frac{1}{6} * (l_{f1} + 4 * m_{f1} + u_{f1}) + \frac{1}{6} * (l_{f2} + 4 * m_{f2} + u_{f2}) + \frac{1}{6} * (l_{f3} + 4 * m_{f3} + u_{f3}) = 1; \\ l_{f1} > 0; l_{f2} > 0; l_{f3} > 0 \\ e \ge 0 \end{cases} \quad (15)$$

The optimal fuzzy weights of three factors ('violations', 'lapses', and 'errors') are calculated as follows:

$w_{F1}^* = (0.365, 0.418, 0.500)$, $w_{F2}^* = (0.223, 0.246, 0.296)$, $w_{F3}^* = (0.283, 0.321, 0.393)$ and $\xi^* = (0.303, 0.303, 0.303)$.

Then, the crisp weights of three factors 'violations', 'lapses', and 'errors', are determined as follows: $w_{F1}^* = 0.423$, $w_{F2}^* = 0.251$, $w_{F3}^* = 0.327$. In this process, the consistency ratio is calculated. $\widetilde{a}_{Bw} = a_{12} = (1.5, 2, 2.5)$ is the largest in the interval, hence, CI is considered as 5.29 using Table 6. The consistency ratio is $CR = 0.303/5.29 = 0.0573$ which shows a very high consistency because the consistency ratio 0.0573 is very close to zero.

Table 6. Consistency index (CI) for fuzzy BWM.

Linguistic Terms.	Equally Importance (EI)	Weakly Important (WI)	Fairly Important (FI)	Very Important (VI)	Absolutely Important (AI)
$\tilde{a}_{Bw}$	(1, 1, 1)	(2/3, 1, 3/2)	(3/2, 2, 5/2)	(5/2, 3, 7/2)	(7/2, 4, 9/2)
CI	3	3.8	5.29	6.69	8.04

According to the results of the F-BWM model, among the main factors at the first level, "violations" (F1) were found to be the most crucial driver behavior factor related to road safety based on the responses given by the assessors in DBQ. One of the previous studies [67] stated that Road Traffic Violations (RTVs) are the most important factor causing certain risks for other road users. Subsequently, "errors" (F3) followed by "lapses" (F2) as shown in Table 7, as the second-ranking factor.

Table 7. The importance weights of the first-level factors.

Factor	Weight	Rank
F1	0.423	1
F2	0.251	3
F3	0.327	2

Among the second level factors, "aggressive violation" (F12) has emerged as the most crucial driver behavior factor related to road safety. According to the results of a previous study carried for Finland and Iran [68], it is found a significant relationship between aggressive violations and the number of accidents. Additionally, the results demonstrated that "fail to apply brakes in road hazards" (F33) was determined as the second most crucial factor as compared to other related factors. The previous study noticed that more fatalities can occur if the driver does not apply the brakes and has higher impact-speed crashes [69,70]. While "pull away from traffic lights in wrong gear" (F22) is observed as the lowest ranked driver behavior factor related to road safety as shown in Table 8.

Table 8. The global importance weights of the second-level factors.

Factor	Weight	Rank
F11	0.106	4
F12	0.317	1
F21	0.076	6
F22	0.042	8
F23	0.133	3
F31	0.094	5
F32	0.047	7
F33	0.186	2

According to the evaluation results of the third level factors, the most important driver behavior factor related to road safety was identified as "driving with alcohol" (F126). This result is directly proportional to the zero-tolerance policy in practice in drinking and driving according to Hungarian driving laws and can be verified in this context [71]. Subsequently, the model results observed, "failing to yield pedestrian" (F122) as second rank factor followed by "disobey traffic lights" (F123). The previous study revealed that one of the possible causes for the high number of crashes and injuries is due to beating traffic lights [72]. While the results showed "no deterrence of punishing" (F124) as the least rank driver behavior factor as compared to other related factors as shown in Table 9.

Table 9. The global importance weights of the third-level factors.

Factor	Weight	Rank
F111	0.068	7
F112	0.112	4
F113	0.071	5
F121	0.114	3
F122	0.177	2
F123	0.114	3
F124	0.057	8
F125	0.070	6
F126	0.216	1

Due to space limitations, open forms of mathematical models for the remaining two levels (levels 2 and level 3) are provided in the Appendix A. All mathematical models for the F-BWM are solved in GAMS version 23.5.1 as minimization problems by mixed-integer non-linear programming (MINLP).

5. Comparative Study

In this section, we make a comparative study between the results of the existed approach (F-BWM model) and a recent hybrid study covering AHP and BWM models [51]. Moslem et al. [51] handled evaluation of the driver behavior factors related to road safety using both AHP and BWM. They used AHP in PCMs that have a 4 × 4 or smaller structure. On the other side, they used BWM in 5 × 5 matrices or larger ones. We then observe the variations in factor rankings of both approaches. The results are shown in Table 10.

Table 10. Comparative study results of factor ranks.

Factor/Sub-Factor/Sub-sub-Factor	Rank	
	AHP-BWM Model (Moslem et al. [51])	F-BWM Model (Existed Study)
F1	1	1
F2	3	3
F3	2	2
F11	7	4
F12	1	1
F21	4	6
F22	6	8
F23	3	3
F31	5	5
F32	8	7
F33	2	2
F111	9	7
F112	6	4
F113	8	5
F121	7	3
F122	3	2
F123	2	3
F124	5	8
F125	4	6
F126	1	1

It is observed from Table 10 that, by both approaches, the ranks of main factors have remained the same. By using the AHP-BWM model of Moslem et al. [51], we notice that the ranks of sub-factors F11, F21, and F22 are changed. Regarding sub-sub-factors, F126 is the most important one by both approaches. When we compare the results obtained by both approaches, we observe that there are very small rank variations between them. The highest difference is observed in sub-sub-factor ranking results. Although we do not observe drastic rank variations between the benchmarking model that have been previously proved in the literature and our current approach, it can be claimed that the application of this approach is new in the application domain. It is also noted that, according to a correlation analysis, which measures the association between the rank of factors, there is a significant and strong positive correlation between both approaches. The Spearman rank correlation coefficient (RHO) values for every three groups are obtained as 1.00, 0.79, and 0.62.

From the methodological perspective, there exist some similar contributions in the literature [73–76]. Gerogiannis et al. [73] studied a group-AHP scoring model. The method used in [73] is differentiated from our current approach considering that the decision is based on the aggregation of both experts' and users' judgements. Similar to our approach, [73] seeks a solution in facing a very large number of PCs. However, in BWM/FBWM-based approaches, decreased PCMs are designed according to the best and the worst criterion. The two studies of [74] and [75] have focused on the improvement of the traditional BWM approach. While the first one proposes a mixed-integer linear programming model approximation, the other deals with a robust solution to BWM. In [76], the same problem which we handle in the current study is aimed to solve by using the analytic network process (ANP). A primitive version of the criteria set which we used in the current study is used to prioritize. It has also taken into account the interrelationships between the decision criteria. In light of the above critics, the integrated BWM approach with triangular fuzzy sets enables decision-makers more freedom in making the final decision and face with a decreased number of PCMs.

6. Conclusions

The significance of driver behavior factors for road safety is critical and difficult to analyze due to uncertain driver behavior. The novelty of this study is the combined use of the best-worst method (BWM) and triangular fuzzy sets as a supporting tool for ranking and prioritizing the critical driver behavior criteria. For the first level of hierarchical structure, the study evaluation results observed the 'violations' as the most significant factor related to road safety followed by 'errors'. Subsequently, for the second level, the study results observed the 'aggressive violations' as the most significant driver behavior factor related to road safety followed by 'fail to apply brakes in road hazards'. While the study results revealed the 'visual scan wrongly' as the least important driver behavior factor related to road safety. Furthermore, for the third level, the F-BWM model results evaluated the 'drive alcohol use' as the most important factor followed by 'disobey traffic lights' as compared to other specified factors. While 'failing to use personal intelligence' was observed as the least important driver behavior factor related to road safety.

Driver behavior recognition has been noticed as a significant and complex concern to obviate road issues due to the huge amount of driver behavior data and its variation [47–49]. In the current study, we explained some AHP drawbacks and then utilized an advanced F-BWM model for estimating the driver behavior factors related to road safety. To collect driver behavior data, the study utilized the driver behavior questionnaire from experienced drivers with fifteen years of driving experience or more. This causes less evaluation time and better understandability for evaluators due to fewer comparisons as compared to conventional methods, like AHP. The acquired model results are more coherent due to more consistent PCs which increase the efficiency of the proposed model.

Considering further research, more applications of the F-BWM model are essential to obtain familiar to analyze different real-world features. The objective advantages are evident: it gives quicker and cheaper survey processes, and undoubtedly the survey pattern can more easily be expanded by this method than employing the classical AHP with complex PC questionnaires. However, this paper only provided one example, but many other applications can ultimately validate the technique. The F-BWM model will help the researchers to enhance their future studies by developing consistency with fewer PCs and save time for analyzing the collected data.

For future directions, BWM can be applied to the same problem under recently released fuzzy extensions such as Pythagorean fuzzy sets [77–79], spherical fuzzy sets [80], and hexagonal fuzzy sets [81]. By doing this, a comparative framework may be developed and used to test the solidity of the integration of BWM and fuzzy set extensions.

Author Contributions: Conceptualization: S.M., D.F., M.G., and E.C.; methodology: M.G. and E.C.; software: M.G. and E.C.; analysis: M.G. and E.C.; resources: D.F. and S.M.; data curation: D.F. and S.M; writing—original draft preparation: S.M., D.F., M.G., E.C., and O.G.; editing, S.M., D.F., M.G., E.C., O.G., and T.B; funding: T.B. All authors have read and agreed to the published version of the manuscript.

Funding: This research is partly funded by the Austrian Science Fund (FWF) through the GIScience Doctoral College (DK W 1237-N23).

Acknowledgments: We would like to thank four anonymous reviewers for their valuable comments. Open Access Funding by the Austrian Science Fund (FWF).

Conflicts of Interest: The authors declare no conflict of interest.

Appendix A

Nonlinear constrained optimization problem represented by crisp numbers for F11 and F12:

$$\min e$$

$$s.t. \begin{cases} l_{f11} - 2.5*u_{f12} - u_{f12}*e \le 0; l_{f11} - 2.5*u_{f12} + u_{f12}*e \ge 0; m_{f11} - 3*m_{f12} - m_{f12}*e \le 0; \\ m_{f11} - 3*m_{f12} + m_{f12}*e \ge 0; u_{f11} - 3.5*l_{f12} - l_{f12}*e \le 0; u_{f11} - 3.5*l_{f12} + l_{f12}*e \ge 0; \\ l_{f11} \le m_{f11} \le u_{f11}; l_{f12} \le m_{f12} \le u_{f12}; \\ \frac{1}{6}*(l_{f11} + 4*m_{f11} + u_{f11}) + \frac{1}{6}*(l_{f12} + 4*m_{f12} + u_{f12}) = 1; \\ l_{f11} > 0; l_{f12} > 0; \\ e \ge 0 \end{cases}$$

Solving this model, the optimal fuzzy weights of the F11 and F12:
$W^*_{f11} = (0.232, 0.250, 0.275)$
$W^*_{f12} = (0.687, 0.749, 0.812)$
$e = (0.000, 0.000, 0.000)$

Nonlinear constrained optimization problem represented by crisp numbers for F21, F22, and F23:

$$\min e$$

$$s.t. \begin{cases} l_{f23} - 1.5*u_{f21} - u_{f21}*e \le 0; l_{f23} - 1.5*u_{f21} + u_{f21}*e \ge 0; m_{f23} - 2*m_{f21} - m_{f21}*e \le 0; \\ m_{f23} - 2*m_{f21} + m_{f21}*e \ge 0; u_{f23} - 2.5*l_{f21} - l_{f21}*e \le 0; u_{f23} - 2.5*l_{f21} + l_{f21}*e \ge 0; \\ l_{f23} - 2.5*u_{f22} - u_{f22}*e \le 0; l_{f23} - 2.5*u_{f22} + u_{f22}*e \ge 0; m_{f23} - 3*m_{f22} - m_{f22}*e \le 0; \\ m_{f23} - 3*m_{f22} + m_{f22}*e \ge 0; u_{f23} - 3.5*l_{f22} - l_{f22}*e \le 0; u_{f23} - 3.5*l_{f22} + l_{f22}*e \ge 0; \\ l_{f21} - 1.5*u_{f22} - u_{f22}*e \le 0; l_{f21} - 1.5*u_{f22} + u_{f22}*e \ge 0; m_{f21} - 2*m_{f22} - m_{f22}*e \le 0; \\ m_{f21} - 2*m_{f22} + m_{f22}*e \ge 0; u_{f21} - 2.5*l_{f22} - l_{f22}*e \le 0; u_{f21} - 2.5*l_{f22} + l_{f22}*e \ge 0; \\ l_{f21} \le m_{f21} \le u_{f21}; l_{f22} \le m_{f22} \le u_{f22}; l_{f23} \le m_{f23} \le u_{f23}; \\ \frac{1}{6}*(l_{f21} + 4*m_{f21} + u_{f21}) + \frac{1}{6}*(l_{f22} + 4*m_{f22} + u_{f22}) + \frac{1}{6}*(l_{f23} + 4*m_{f23} + u_{f23}) = 1; \\ l_{f21} > 0; l_{f22} > 0; l_{f23} > 0 \\ e \ge 0 \end{cases}$$

Solving this model, the optimal fuzzy weights of the F21, F22 and F23:
$W^*_{f21} = (0.248, 0.295, 0.374)$
$W^*_{f22} = (0.159, 0.165, 0.188)$
$W^*_{f23} = (0.495, 0.529, 0.581)$
$e = (0.209, 0.209, 0.209)$

Nonlinear constrained optimization problem represented by crisp numbers for F31, F32, and F33:

min e

s.t.
$$\begin{cases} l_{f33} - 1.5 * u_{f31} - u_{f31} * e \leq 0; l_{f33} - 1.5 * u_{f31} + u_{f31} * e \geq 0; m_{f33} - 2 * m_{f31} - m_{f31} * e \leq 0; \\ m_{f33} - 2 * m_{f31} + m_{f31} * e \geq 0; u_{f33} - 2.5 * l_{f31} - l_{f31} * e \leq 0; u_{f33} - 2.5 * l_{f31} + l_{f31} * e \geq 0; \\ l_{f33} - 3.5 * u_{f32} - u_{f32} * e \leq 0; l_{f33} - 3.5 * u_{f32} + u_{f32} * e \geq 0; m_{f33} - 4 * m_{f32} - m_{f32} * e \leq 0; \\ m_{f33} - 4 * m_{f32} + m_{f32} * e \geq 0; u_{f33} - 4.5 * l_{f32} - l_{f32} * e \leq 0; u_{f33} - 4.5 * l_{f32} + l_{f32} * e \geq 0; \\ l_{f31} - 1.5 * u_{f32} - u_{f32} * e \leq 0; l_{f31} - 1.5 * u_{f32} + u_{f32} * e \geq 0; m_{f31} - 2 * m_{f32} - m_{f32} * e \leq 0; \\ m_{f31} - 2 * m_{f32} + m_{f32} * e \geq 0; u_{f31} - 2.5 * l_{f32} - l_{f32} * e \leq 0; u_{f31} - 2.5 * l_{f32} + l_{f32} * e \geq 0; \\ l_{f31} \leq m_{f31} \leq u_{f31}; l_{f32} \leq m_{f32} \leq u_{f32}; l_{f33} \leq m_{f33} \leq u_{f33}; \\ \frac{1}{6} * (l_{f31} + 4 * m_{f31} + u_{f31}) + \frac{1}{6} * (l_{f32} + 4 * m_{f32} + u_{f32}) + \frac{1}{6} * (l_{f33} + 4 * m_{f33} + u_{f33}) = 1; \\ l_{f31} > 0; l_{f32} > 0; l_{f33} > 0 \\ e \geq 0 \end{cases}$$

Solving this model, the optimal fuzzy weights of the F31, F32 and F33 :

$W^*_{f31} = (0.234, 0.288, 0.339)$
$W^*_{f32} = (0.133, 0.144, 0.151)$
$W^*_{f33} = (0.523, 0.575, 0.594)$
$e = (0.043, 0.043, 0.043)$

Nonlinear constrained optimization problem represented by crisp numbers for level F111, F112, and F113:

min e

s.t.
$$\begin{cases} l_{f112} - 1.5 * u_{f111} - u_{f111} * e \leq 0; l_{f112} - 1.5 * u_{f111} + u_{f111} * e \geq 0; m_{f112} - 2 * m_{f111} - m_{f111} * e \leq 0; \\ m_{f112} - 2 * m_{f111} + m_{f111} * e \geq 0; u_{f112} - 2.5 * l_{f111} - l_{f111} * e \leq 0; u_{f112} - 2.5 * l_{f111} + l_{f111} * e \geq 0; \\ l_{f112} - 1.5 * u_{f113} - u_{f113} * e \leq 0; l_{f112} - 1.5 * u_{f113} + u_{f113} * e \geq 0; m_{f112} - 2 * m_{f113} - m_{f113} * e \leq 0; \\ m_{f112} - 2 * m_{f113} + m_{f113} * e \geq 0; u_{f112} - 2.5 * l_{f113} - l_{f113} * e \leq 0; u_{f112} - 2.5 * l_{f113} + l_{f113} * e \geq 0; \\ l_{f111} - 1.5 * u_{f112} - u_{f112} * e \leq 0; l_{f111} - 1.5 * u_{f112} + u_{f112} * e \geq 0; m_{f111} - 2 * m_{f112} - m_{f112} * e \leq 0; \\ m_{f111} - 2 * m_{f112} + m_{f112} * e \geq 0; u_{f111} - 2.5 * l_{f112} - l_{f112} * e \leq 0; u_{f111} - 2.5 * l_{f112} + l_{f112} * e \geq 0; \\ l_{f111} \leq m_{f111} \leq u_{f111}; l_{f112} \leq m_{f112} \leq u_{f112}; l_{f113} \leq m_{f113} \leq u_{f113}; \\ \frac{1}{6} * (l_{f111} + 4 * m_{f111} + u_{f111}) + \frac{1}{6} * (l_{f112} + 4 * m_{f112} + u_{f112}) + \frac{1}{6} * (l_{f113} + 4 * m_{f113} + u_{f113}) = 1; \\ l_{f111} > 0; l_{f112} > 0; l_{f113} > 0 \\ e \geq 0 \end{cases}$$

Solving this model, the optimal fuzzy weights of the F111, F112 and F113 :

$W^*_{f111} = (0.233, 0.266, 0.334)$
$W^*_{f112} = (0.334, 0.431, 0.614)$
$W^*_{f113} = (0.237, 0.287, 0.313)$
$e = (0.500, 0.500, 0.500)$

Nonlinear constrained optimization problem represented by crisp numbers for F121, F122, F123, F124, F125, and F126:

$$\text{min } e$$

$$s.t. \begin{cases} l_{f126} - 1.5*u_{f121} - u_{f121}*e \leq 0; l_{f126} - 1.5*u_{f121} + u_{f121}*e \geq 0; m_{f126} - 2*m_{f121} - m_{f121}*e \leq 0; m_{f126} - 2*m_{f121} + m_{f121}*e \geq 0; \\ u_{f126} - 2.5*l_{f121} - l_{f121}*e \leq 0; u_{f126} - 2.5*l_{f121} + l_{f121}*e \geq 0; l_{f126} - \frac{2}{3}*u_{f122} - u_{f122}*e \leq 0; l_{f126} - \frac{2}{3}*u_{f122} + u_{f122}*e \geq 0; \\ m_{f126} - 1*m_{f122} - m_{f122}*e \leq 0; m_{f126} - 1*m_{f122} + m_{f122}*e \geq 0; u_{f126} - 1.5*l_{f122} - l_{f122}*e \leq 0; u_{f126} - 1.5*l_{f122} + l_{f122}*e \geq 0; \\ l_{f126} - 1.5*u_{f123} - u_{f123}*e \leq 0; l_{f126} - 1.5*u_{f123} + u_{f123}*e \geq 0; m_{f126} - 2*m_{f123} - m_{f123}*e \leq 0; m_{f126} - 2*m_{f123} + m_{f123}*e \geq 0; \\ u_{f126} - 2.5*l_{f123} - l_{f123}*e \leq 0; u_{f126} - 2.5*l_{f123} + l_{f123}*e \geq 0; l_{f126} - 3.5*u_{f124} - u_{f124}*e \leq 0; l_{f126} - 3.5*u_{f124} + u_{f124}*e \geq 0; \\ m_{f126} - 4*m_{f124} - m_{f124}*e \leq 0; m_{f126} - 4*m_{f124} + m_{f124}*e \geq 0; u_{f126} - 4.5*l_{f124} - l_{f124}*e \leq 0; u_{f126} - 4.5*l_{f124} + l_{f124}*e \geq 0; \\ l_{f126} - 2.5*u_{f125} - u_{f125}*e \leq 0; l_{f126} - 2.5*u_{f125} + u_{f125}*e \geq 0; m_{f126} - 3*m_{f125} - m_{f125}*e \leq 0; m_{f126} - 3*m_{f125} + m_{f125}*e \geq 0; \\ u_{f126} - 3.5*l_{f125} - l_{f125}*e \leq 0; u_{f126} - 3.5*l_{f125} + l_{f125}*e \geq 0; l_{f121} - 1.5*u_{f124} - u_{f124}*e \leq 0; l_{f121} - 1.5*u_{f124} + u_{f124}*e \geq 0; \\ m_{f121} - 2*m_{f124} - m_{f124}*e \leq 0; m_{f121} - 2*m_{f124} + m_{f124}*e \geq 0; u_{f121} - 2.5*l_{f124} - l_{f124}*e \leq 0; u_{f121} - 2.5*l_{f124} + l_{f124}*e \geq 0; \\ l_{f122} - 2.5*u_{f124} - u_{f124}*e \leq 0; l_{f122} - 2.5*u_{f124} + u_{f124}*e \geq 0; m_{f122} - 3*m_{f124} - m_{f124}*e \leq 0; m_{f122} - 3*m_{f124} + m_{f124}*e \geq 0; \\ u_{f122} - 3.5*l_{f124} - l_{f124}*e \leq 0; u_{f122} - 3.5*l_{f124} + l_{f124}*e \geq 0; l_{f123} - 1.5*u_{f124} - u_{f124}*e \leq 0; l_{f123} - 1.5*u_{f124} + u_{f124}*e \geq 0; \\ m_{f123} - 2*m_{f124} - m_{f124}*e \leq 0; m_{f123} - 2*m_{f124} + m_{f124}*e \geq 0; u_{f123} - 2.5*l_{f124} - l_{f124}*e \leq 0; u_{f123} - 2.5*l_{f124} + l_{f124}*e \geq 0; \\ l_{f125} - \frac{2}{3}*u_{f124} - u_{f124}*e \leq 0; l_{f125} - \frac{2}{3}*u_{f124} + u_{f124}*e \geq 0; m_{f125} - 1*m_{f124} - m_{f124}*e \leq 0; m_{f125} - 1*m_{f124} + m_{f124}*e \geq 0; \\ u_{f125} - 1.5*l_{f124} - l_{f124}*e \leq 0; u_{f125} - 1.5*l_{f124} + l_{f124}*e \geq 0; l_{f121} \leq m_{f121} \leq u_{f121}; l_{f122} \leq m_{f122} \leq u_{f122}; l_{f123} \leq m_{f123} \leq u_{f123}; \\ l_{f124} \leq m_{f124} \leq u_{f124}; l_{f125} \leq m_{f125} \leq u_{f125}; l_{f126} \leq m_{f126} \leq u_{f126}; \\ \left(\frac{1}{6}*(l_{f121} + 4*m_{f121} + u_{f121}) + \frac{1}{6}*(l_{f122} + 4*m_{f122} + u_{f122}) + \frac{1}{6}*(l_{f123} + 4*m_{f123} + u_{f123}) + \atop \frac{1}{6}*(l_{f124} + 4*m_{f124} + u_{f124}) + \frac{1}{6}*(l_{f125} + 4*m_{f125} + u_{f125}) + \frac{1}{6}*(l_{f126} + 4*m_{f126} + u_{f126}) \right) = 1; \\ l_{f121} > 0; l_{f122} > 0; l_{f123} > 0; l_{f124} > 0; l_{f125} > 0; l_{f126} > 0 \\ e \geq 0 \end{cases}$$

Solving this model, the optimal fuzzy weights of the F121, F122, F123, F124, F125 and F126:

$W^*_{f121} = (0.118, 0.151, 0.192)$

$W^*_{f122} = (0.199, 0.235, 0.254)$

$W^*_{f123} = (0.118, 0.151, 0.192)$

$W^*_{f124} = (0.072, 0.076, 0.083)$

$W^*_{f125} = (0.080, 0.093, 0.112)$

$W^*_{f126} = (0.265, 0.291, 0.303)$

$e = (0.299, 0.299, 0.299)$

The consistency of the relative expert's responses regarding the weights of the factors, sub-factors, and sub-sub-factors have been checked. For each level, it is obtained a consistency ratio value lower than 0.1 as given in Table A1 below:

Table A1. The consistency ratio of all factors.

Factor/Sub-Factor/Sub-sub-Factor	Epsilon Value	Consistency Ratio
F1, F2, and F3	0.3030	0.0573
F11 and F12:	0.0000	0.0000
F21, F22 and F23:	0.2090	0.0312
F31, F32 and F33:	0.0430	0.0053
F111, F112 and F113:	0.5000	0.0945
F121, F122, F123, F124, F125, and F126	0.2990	0.0372

References

1. World Health Organization. *The Global Status Report on Road Safety*; WHO: Geneva, Switzerland, 2018.
2. EU Commission. *Road Safety Facts & Figures*; EU Commission: Brussels, Belgium, 2019.
3. OECD/ITF. *Road Safety Annual Report*; OECD: Paris, France; ITF: London, UK, 2016.

4. Choi, E.H. *Crash Factors in Intersection-Related Crashes: An On-Scene Perspective*; Technical Report No. DOT HS 811 366; U.S. Department of Transportation, National Highway Traffic Safety Administration (NHTSA): Washington, DC, USA, 2010.
5. Evans, L. *Traffic Safety*; Science Serving Society, Inc.: Bloomfield Hills, MI, USA, 2004.
6. Papaioannou, P. Driver behavior, dilemma zone and safety effects at urban signalised intersections in Greece. *Accid. Anal. Prev.* **2007**, *39*, 147–158. [CrossRef] [PubMed]
7. Stanton, N.A.; Salmon, P.M. Human error taxonomies applied to driving: Generic driver error taxonomy and its implications for intelligent transport systems. *Saf. Sci.* **2009**, *47*, 227–237. [CrossRef]
8. Wang, J.; Li, M.; Liu, Y.; Zhang, H.; Zou, W.; Cheng, L. Safety assessment of shipping routes in the South China Sea based on the fuzzy analytic hierarchy process. *Saf. Sci.* **2014**, *62*, 46–57. [CrossRef]
9. Wierwille, W.W.; Hanowski, R.J.; Hankey, J.M.; Kieliszewski, C.A.; Lee, S.E.; Medina, A.; Keisler, A.S.; Dingus, T.A. *Identification and Evaluation of Driver Errors: Overview and Recommendations*; Technical Report No. FHWA-RD-02-003; U.S. Department of Transportation, Federal Highway Administration: Washington, DC, USA, 2002.
10. Parker, D.; Reason, J.T.; Manstead, A.S.R.; Stradling, S. Driving errors, driving violations and accident involvement. *Ergonomics* **1995**, *38*, 1036–1048. [CrossRef]
11. Reason, R.T.; Manstead, A.S.R.; Stradling, S.; Baxter, J.; Campbell, K. Errors and violations on the roads. *Ergonomics* **1990**, *33*, 1315–1332. [CrossRef]
12. Lajunen, T.; Parker, D.; Summala, H. The Manchester Driver Behaviour Questionnaire: A cross-cultural study. *Accid. Anal. Prev.* **2004**, *36*, 231–238. [CrossRef]
13. Lawton, R.; Parker, D.; Stradling, S.G.; Manstead, A.S.R. Predicting road traffic accidents: The role of social deviance and violations. *Br. J. Psychol.* **1997**, *88*, 249–262. [CrossRef]
14. Bener, A.; Özkan, T.; Lajunen, T. The driver behaviour questionnaire in Arab gulf countries: Qatar and United Arab Emirates. *Accid. Anal. Prev.* **2008**, *40*, 1411–1417. [CrossRef] [PubMed]
15. Mirmohammadi, F.; Khorasani, G.; Tatari, A.; Yadollahi, A.; Taherian, H.; Motamed, H.; Fazelpour, S.; Khorasani, M.; Maleki Verki, M. Investigation of road accidents and casualties' factors with MCDM methods in Iran. *J. Am. Sci.* **2013**, *9*, 11–20.
16. Duleba, S.; Moslem, S. Examining Pareto optimality in analytic hierarchy process on real Data: An application in public transport service development. *Exp. Syst. Appl.* **2019**, *116*, 21–30. [CrossRef]
17. Moslem, S.; Ghorbanzadeh, O.; Blaschke, T.; Duleba, S. Analysing Stakeholder Consensus for a Sustainable Transport Development Decision by the Fuzzy AHP and Interval AHP. *Sustainability* **2019**, *11*, 3271. [CrossRef]
18. Moslem, S.; Duleba, S. Sustainable Urban Transport Development by Applying a Fuzzy-AHP Model: A Case Study from Mersin, Turkey. *Urban Sci.* **2019**, *3*, 55. [CrossRef]
19. Fan, G.; Zhong, D.; Yan, F.; Yue, P. A hybrid fuzzy evaluation method for curtain grouting efficiency assessment based on an AHP method extended by D numbers. *Exp. Syst. Appl.* **2016**, *44*, 289–303. [CrossRef]
20. Pourghasemi, H.R.; Pradhan, B.; Gokceoglu, C. Application of fuzzy logic and analytical hierarchy process (AHP) to landslide susceptibility mapping at Haraz watershed, Iran. *Nat. Hazards* **2012**, *63*, 965–996. [CrossRef]
21. Gumus, A.T. Evaluation of hazardous waste transportation firms by using a twostep fuzzy-AHP and TOPSIS methodology. *Exp. Syst. Appl.* **2009**, *36*, 4067–4074. [CrossRef]
22. Kwong, C.K.; Bai, H. A fuzzy AHP approach to the determination of importance weights of customer requirements in quality function deployment. *J. Intell. Manuf.* **2002**, *13*, 367–377. [CrossRef]
23. Pourghasemi, H.; Moradi, H.; Aghda, S.F.; Gokceoglu, C.; Pradhan, B. GIS-based landslide susceptibility mapping with probabilistic likelihood ratio and spatial multi-criteria evaluation models (North of Tehran, Iran). *Arab. J. Geosci.* **2014**, *7*, 1857–1878. [CrossRef]
24. Ghorbanzadeh, O.; Feizizadeh, B.; Blaschke, T. An interval matrix method used to optimize the decision matrix in AHP technique for land subsidence susceptibility mapping. *Environ. Earth Sci.* **2018**, *77*, 584. [CrossRef]
25. Rezaei, J. Best-worst multi-criteria decision-making method. *Omega* **2015**, *53*, 49–57. [CrossRef]
26. Rezaei, J. Best-worst multi-criteria decision-making method: Some properties and a linear model. *Omega* **2016**, *64*, 126–130. [CrossRef]
27. Hafezalkotob, A.; Hafezalkotob, A. A novel approach for combination of individual and group decisions based on fuzzy best-worst method. *Appl. Soft Comput.* **2017**, *59*, 316–325. [CrossRef]

28. Saaty, T.L. A scaling method for priorities in hierarchical structures. *J. Math. Psychol.* **1977**, *15*, 234–281. [CrossRef]
29. Miller, G.A. The magical number seven, plus or minus two: Some limits on our capacity for processing information. *Psychol. Rev.* **1956**, *63*, 81. [CrossRef] [PubMed]
30. Yucesan, M.; Gul, M. Failure prioritization and control using the neutrosophic best and worst method. *Granul. Comput.* **2019**, 1–15. [CrossRef]
31. Badi, I.; Ballem, M. Supplier selection using the rough BWM-MAIRCA model: A case study in pharmaceutical supplying in Libya. *Decis. Mak. Appl. Manag. Eng.* **2018**, *1*, 16–33. [CrossRef]
32. Tian, Z.P.; Zhang, H.Y.; Wang, J.Q.; Wang, T.L. Green supplier selection using improved TOPSIS and best-worst method under intuitionistic fuzzy environment. *Informatica* **2018**, *29*, 773–800. [CrossRef]
33. Yucesan, M.; Mete, S.; Serin, F.; Celik, E.; Gul, M. An integrated best-worst and interval type-2 fuzzy topsis methodology for green supplier selection. *Mathematics* **2019**, *7*, 182. [CrossRef]
34. Aboutorab, H.; Saberi, M.; Asadabadi, M.R.; Hussain, O.; Chang, E. ZBWM. The Z-number extension of Best Worst Method and its application for supplier development. *Exp. Syst. Appl.* **2018**, *107*, 115–125. [CrossRef]
35. Ghoushchi, S.J.; Yousefi, S.; Khazaeili, M. An extended FMEA approach based on the Z-MOORA and fuzzy BWM for prioritization of failures. *Appl. Soft Comput.* **2019**, *81*, 105505. [CrossRef]
36. Chang, T.W.; Lo, H.W.; Chen, K.Y.; Liou, J.J. A novel FMEA model based on rough BWM and rough TOPSIS-AL for risk assessment. *Mathematics* **2019**, *7*, 874. [CrossRef]
37. Lo, H.W.; Liou, J.J.; Huang, C.N.; Chuang, Y.C. A novel failure mode and effect analysis model for machine tool risk analysis. *Reliab. Eng. Syst. Saf.* **2019**, *183*, 173–183. [CrossRef]
38. Lo, H.W.; Liou, J.J. A novel multiple-criteria decision-making-based FMEA model for risk assessment. *Appl. Soft Comput.* **2018**, *73*, 684–696. [CrossRef]
39. Tian, Z.P.; Wang, J.Q.; Zhang, H.Y. An integrated approach for failure mode and effects analysis based on fuzzy best-worst, relative entropy, and VIKOR methods. *Appl. Soft Comput.* **2018**, *72*, 636–646. [CrossRef]
40. Ru-Xin, N.; Tian, Z.P.; Wang, X.K.; Wang, J.Q.; Wang, T.L. Risk evaluation by FMEA of supercritical water gasification system using multi-granular linguistic distribution assessment. *Knowl.-Based Syst.* **2018**, *162*, 185–201.
41. Mohandes, S.R.; Zhang, X. Towards the development of a comprehensive hybrid fuzzy-based occupational risk assessment model for construction workers. *Saf. Sci.* **2019**, *115*, 294–309. [CrossRef]
42. Norouzi, A.; Namin, H.G. A Hybrid Fuzzy TOPSIS–Best Worst Method for Risk Prioritization in Megaprojects. *Civil Eng. J.* **2019**, *5*, 1257–1272. [CrossRef]
43. Rostamabadi, A.; Jahangiri, M.; Zarei, E.; Kamalinia, M.; Alimohammadlou, M. A novel Fuzzy Bayesian Network approach for safety analysis of process systems; An application of HFACS and SHIPP methodology. *J. Clean. Prod.* **2020**, *244*, 118761. [CrossRef]
44. Rostamabadi, A.; Jahangiri, M.; Zarei, E.; Kamalinia, M.; Banaee, S.; Samaei, M.R. Model for A Novel Fuzzy Bayesian Network-HFACS (FBN-HFACS) model for analyzing Human and Organizational Factors (HOFs) in process accidents. *Process Saf. Environ. Prot.* **2019**, *132*, 59–72. [CrossRef]
45. Torabi, S.A.; Giahi, R.; Sahebjamnia, N. An enhanced risk assessment framework for business continuity management systems. *Saf. Sci.* **2016**, *89*, 201–218. [CrossRef]
46. Pamučar, D.; Stević, Ž.; Sremac, S. A new model for determining weight coefficients of criteria in mcdm models: Full consistency method (fucom). *Symmetry* **2018**, *10*, 393. [CrossRef]
47. Stević, Ž.; Brković, N. A Novel Integrated FUCOM-MARCOS Model for Evaluation of Human Resources in a Transport Company. *Logistics* **2020**, *4*, 4. [CrossRef]
48. Pamucar, D.; Deveci, M.; Canıtez, F.; Bozanic, D. A fuzzy Full Consistency Method-Dombi-Bonferroni model for prioritizing transportation demand management measures. *Appl. Soft Comput.* **2020**, *87*, 105952. [CrossRef]
49. Badi, I.; Abdulshahed, A. Ranking the Libyan airlines by using full consistency method (FUCOM) and analytical hierarchy process (AHP). *Oper. Res. Eng. Sci. Theory Appl.* **2019**, *2*, 1–14. [CrossRef]
50. Farooq, D.; Moslem, S.; Duleba, S. Evaluation of driver behavior criteria for evolution of sustainable traffic safety. *Sustainability* **2019**, *11*, 3142. [CrossRef]
51. Moslem, S.; Farooq, D.; Ghorbanzadeh, O.; Blaschke, T. Application of AHP-BWM Model for Evaluating Driver Behaviour Factors Related to Road Safety: A Case Study for Budapest City. *Symmetry* **2020**, *12*, 243. [CrossRef]

52. Farooq, D.; Moslem, S. A Fuzzy Dynamical Approach for Examining Driver Behavior Criteria Related to Road Safety. In Proceedings of the IEEE 2019 Smart City Symposium Prague (SCSP), Prague, Czech Republic, 23–24 May 2019.
53. Mahdiraji, A.H.; Arzaghi, S.; Stauskis, G.; Zavadskas, E. A hybrid fuzzy BWM-COPRAS method for analyzing key factors of sustainable architecture. *Sustainability* **2018**, *10*, 1626. [CrossRef]
54. Kolagar, M. Adherence to Urban Agriculture in Order to Reach Sustainable Cities; a BWM–WASPAS Approach. *Smart Cities* **2019**, *2*, 31–45. [CrossRef]
55. Kumar, A.; Aswin, A.; Gupta, H. Evaluating green performance of the airports using hybrid BWM and VIKOR methodology. *Tour. Manag.* **2019**, *76*, 103941. [CrossRef]
56. Mashunin, K.Y.; Mashunin, Y.K. Vector optimization with equivalent and priority criteria. *J. Comput. Syst. Sci. Int.* **2017**, *56*, 975–996. [CrossRef]
57. Mashunin, Y.K. Mathematical Apparatus of Optimal Decision-Making Based on Vector Optimization. *Appl. Syst. Innov.* **2019**, *2*, 32. [CrossRef]
58. Zadeh, L.A. Fuzzy sets. *Inf. Control* **1965**, *8*, 338–353. [CrossRef]
59. Celik, E.; Gul, M.; Aydin, N.; Gumus, A.T.; Guneri, A.F. A comprehensive review of multi criteria decision making approaches based on interval type-2 fuzzy sets. *Knowl.-Based Syst.* **2015**, *85*, 329–341. [CrossRef]
60. Gul, M.; Celik, E.; Aydin, N.; Gumus, A.T.; Guneri, A.F. A state of the art literature review of VIKOR and its fuzzy extensions on applications. *Appl. Soft Comput.* **2016**, *46*, 60–89. [CrossRef]
61. Qiong, M.; Zeshui, X.; Huchang, L. An intuitionistic fuzzy multiplicative best-worst method for multi-criteria group decision making. *Inf. Sci.* **2016**, *374*, 224–239.
62. Guo, S.; Zhao, H. Fuzzy best-worst multi-criteria decision-making method and its applications. *Knowl.-Based Syst.* **2017**, *121*, 23–31. [CrossRef]
63. Li, J.; Wang, J.Q.; Hu, J.H. Multi-criteria decision-making method based on dominance degree and BWM with probabilistic hesitant fuzzy information. *Int. J. Mach. Learn. Cybern.* **2019**, *10*, 1671–1685. [CrossRef]
64. Wu, Q.; Zhou, L.; Chen, Y.; Chen, H. An integrated approach to green supplier selection based on the interval type-2 fuzzy best-worst and extended VIKOR methods. *Inf. Sci.* **2019**, *502*, 394–417. [CrossRef]
65. Qin, J.; Liu, X. Interval Type-2 Fuzzy Group Decision Making by Integrating Improved Best Worst Method with COPRAS for Emergency Material Supplier Selection. In *Type-2 Fuzzy Decision-Making Theories, Methodologies and Applications*; Springer: Singapore, 2019; pp. 249–271.
66. Mi, X.; Tang, M.; Liao, H.; Shen, W.; Lev, B. The state-of-the-art survey on integrations and applications of the best worst method in decision making: Why, what, what for and what's next? *Omega* **2019**, *87*, 205–225. [CrossRef]
67. Stradling, S.G.; Meadows, M.L.; Beatty, S. Driving as part of your work may damage your health. *Behav. Res. Road Saf.* **2000**, *IX*, 1–9.
68. Ozkan, T.; Lajunen, T.; Chliaoutakis, J.E.I.; Parker, D.; Summala, H. Cross-cultural differences in driving behaviors: A comparison of six countries. *Transp. Res. Part F* **2006**, *9*, 227–242. [CrossRef]
69. Yanagisawa, M.; Swanson, E.; Najm, W.G. *Target Crashes and Safety Benefits Estimation Methodology for Pedestrian Crash Avoidance/Mitigation Systems*; Technical Report No. DOT HS 811 998; National Highway Traffic Safety Administration: Washington, DC, USA, 2014.
70. Zeng, W.; Chen, P.; Nakamura, H.; Asano, M. Modeling Pedestrian Trajectory for Safety Assessment at Signalized Crosswalks. In Proceedings of the 10th International Conference of the Eastern Asia Society for Transportation Studies, Taipei, Taiwan, 9–12 September 2013.
71. World Health Organization (WHO). *Legal BAC Limits by Country*; WHO: Geneva, Switzerland, 2015.
72. Subramaniam, K.; Phang, W.K.; Hayati, K.S. Traffic light violation among motorists in Malaysia. *IATSS Res.* **2007**, *31*, 67–73.
73. Gerogiannis, V.C.; Fitsilis, P.; Voulgaridou, D.; Kirytopoulos, K.A.; Sachini, E. A case study for project and portfolio management information system selection: A group AHP-scoring model approach. *Int. J. Proj. Organ. Manag.* **2010**, *2*, 361–381. [CrossRef]
74. Beemsterboer, D.J.C.; Hendrix, E.M.T.; Claassen, G.D.H. On solving the best-worst method in multi-criteria decision-making. *IFAC-PapersOnLine* **2018**, *51*, 1660–1665. [CrossRef]
75. Sadjadi, S.; Karimi, M. Best-worst multi-criteria decision-making method: A robust approach. *Decis. Sci. Lett.* **2018**, *7*, 323–340. [CrossRef]

76. Farooq, D.; Moslem, S. Evaluation and Ranking of Driver Behavior Factors Related to Road Safety by Applying Analytic Network Process. *Periodica Polytech. Transp. Eng.* **2020**, *48*, 189–195. [CrossRef]
77. Gul, M.; Guneri, A.F.; Nasirli, S.M. A fuzzy-based model for risk assessment of routes in oil transportation. *Int. J. Environ. Sci. Technol.* **2019**, *16*, 4671–4686. [CrossRef]
78. Gul, M.; Ak, M.F.; Guneri, A.F. Pythagorean fuzzy VIKOR-based approach for safety risk assessment in mine industry. *J. Saf. Res.* **2019**, *69*, 135–153. [CrossRef]
79. Ak, M.F.; Gul, M. AHP–TOPSIS integration extended with Pythagorean fuzzy sets for information security risk analysis. *Complex Intell. Syst.* **2019**, *5*, 113–126. [CrossRef]
80. Gündoğdu, F.K.; Kahraman, C. A novel fuzzy TOPSIS method using emerging interval-valued spherical fuzzy sets. *Eng. Appl. Artif. Intell.* **2019**, *85*, 307–323. [CrossRef]
81. Parveen, N.; Kamble, P.N. Decision-Making Problem Using Fuzzy TOPSIS Method with Hexagonal Fuzzy Number. In *Computing in Engineering and Technology*; Springer: Singapore, 2020; pp. 421–430.

© 2020 by the authors. Licensee MDPI, Basel, Switzerland. This article is an open access article distributed under the terms and conditions of the Creative Commons Attribution (CC BY) license (http://creativecommons.org/licenses/by/4.0/).

MDPI
St. Alban-Anlage 66
4052 Basel
Switzerland
Tel. +41 61 683 77 34
Fax +41 61 302 89 18
www.mdpi.com

Mathematics Editorial Office
E-mail: mathematics@mdpi.com
www.mdpi.com/journal/mathematics

www.ingramcontent.com/pod-product-compliance
Lightning Source LLC
LaVergne TN
LVHW070251100526
838202LV00015B/2208